## PENITENTIAL ACT

**A** I confess to almighty God
and to you, my brothers and sisters,
that I have greatly sinned,
in my thoughts and in my words,
in what I have done
    and in what I have failed to do,
*(Strike breast)*
through my fault, through my fault,
through my most grievous fault;
therefore I ask blessed Mary ever-Virgin,
all the Angels and Saints,
and you, my brothers and sisters,
to pray for me to the Lord our God.

**B** Have mercy on us, O Lord.
**For we have sinned against you.**
Show us, O Lord, your mercy.
**And grant us your salvation.**

## GLORIA

Glory to God in the highest,
and on earth peace to people of good will.

We praise you,
we bless you,
we adore you,
we glorify you,
we give you thanks for your great glory,
Lord God, heavenly King,
O God, almighty Father.

Lord Jesus Christ, Only Begotten Son,
Lord God, Lamb of God, Son of the Father,
you take away the sins of the world,
    have mercy on us;
you take away the sins of the world,
    receive our prayer;
you are seated at the right hand of
    the Father,
    have mercy on us.

For you alone are the Holy One,
you alone are the Lord,
you alone are the Most High,
Jesus Christ,
with the Holy Spirit,
in the glory of God the Father.
Amen.

## NICENE CREED

I believe in one God,
the Father almighty,
maker of heaven and earth,
of all things visible and invisible.

I believe in one Lord Jesus Christ,
the Only Begotten Son of God,
born of the Father before all ages.
God from God, Light from Light,
true God from true God,
begotten, not made, consubstantial
    with the Father;
through him all things were made.
For us men and for our salvation
he came down from heaven,

*At the words that follow, up to and
including "and became man," all bow.*

and by the Holy Spirit was incarnate of
    the Virgin Mary,
and became man.

For our sake he was crucified under
    Pontius Pilate,
he suffered death and was buried,
and rose again on the third day
in accordance with the Scriptures.
He ascended into heaven
and is seated at the right hand of
    the Father.
He will come again in glory
to judge the living and the dead
and his kingdom will have no end.

I believe in the Holy Spirit, the Lord,
    the giver of life,
who proceeds from the Father and the Son,
who with the Father and the Son is
    adored and glorified,
who has spoken through the prophets.

I believe in one, holy, catholic and
    apostolic Church.
I confess one Baptism for the forgiveness
    of sins
and I look forward to the resurrection
    of the dead
and the life of the world to come. Amen.

## INVITATION TO COMMUNION

Behold...to the supper of the Lamb.
**Lord, I am not worthy
that you should enter under my roof,
but only say the word
and my soul shall be healed.**

# JOURNEYSONGS

## THIRD EDITION

*Concordat cum originali:* ✝ John G. Vlazny, Archbishop of Portland in Oregon

Published with the approval of the Committee on Divine Worship, United States Catholic Conference of Bishops (USCCB).

Publisher: John J. Limb

Editorial Director: Eric Schumock

Executive Editor: Randall DeBruyn, DMA

Editorial Portfolio Manager: Joanne Osborn

Managing Editors: Amanda Weller, Angela Westhoff-Johnson

Managing Arranger: Rick Modlin

Editorial Assistance: Scot Crandal, Estela García-López, C. Angelyn Jáuregui, Craig Kingsbury, Travis Powers, William Schuster, Alan Tarpinian

Typesetting and Layout: Melissa Schmidt

Engraving Manager: Tia Regan

Senior Engravers: Mónica Germano, Scott Hall, William Straub, Jon Taubman

Engravers: Lars Campbell, Dan Cosley, Laura Kantor, R. Michael Sanchez

Art Direction: Judy Urben

Cover Design and Graphic Icons: Le Vu

© 2012, OCP
5536 NE Hassalo, Portland, OR 97213
Phone: (503) 281-1191
liturgy@ocp.org
ocp.org

Seventh Printing: May 2018

| | |
|---|---|
| Assembly | edition 21001 |
| Assembly with Readings | edition 21002 |
| Choir/Cantor | edition 21003 |
| Keyboard Accompaniment | edition 21004 |
| Guitar Accompaniment | edition 21005 |
| Solo Instrument | edition 21006 |
| CD Recording Library | edition 21007 |

ISBN 978-1-57992-151-4
LC:0518

Edition 21001
Printed in U.S.A.

# PREFACE

Ten years after the publication of the second edition of *Journeysongs*, it became evident that a new edition of this popular and well-received hymnal was necessary. The most compelling reason for a third edition was the introduction of the new English translation of *The Roman Missal* in November 2011. With the new text for the Order of Mass, along with the need for new musical settings of the Mass, plus the growing number of new songs published in these last ten years, the older edition of *Journeysongs* clearly needed a thorough revision.

As a result, we are proud to offer *Journeysongs: 3rd Edition* as our response to this need, especially for those parishes that have come to expect and rely upon OCP's long-established tradition of a perfect balance between new music and a well-known, stable repertoire. The Order of Mass is shown, as required, with the newly-translated chants from *The Roman Missal*. In addition, OCP offers nine Mass settings in a variety of musical styles and designed to meet various parish needs: Latin and English chant, traditional, multicultural and bilingual, and contemporary. Following these, a section of additional service music provides more possibilities for various moments during Mass.

Similar to the second edition, the Rites of Christian Initiation, the Order of Christian Funerals, Eucharistic Exposition and Benediction, as well as Morning and Evening Prayer are given here. The Psalms and Canticles section was also thoroughly analyzed and updated to give a good selection of psalms for all the most important Sundays and feasts. Bilingual English/Spanish psalmody was chosen for those occasions when the entire parish community might gather to worship, such as during Holy Week, or for weddings, funerals, and the RCIA.

In deciding which hymns and songs to carry over from OCP's current hymnals, the hymnal committee looked at both previous editions of *Journeysongs* and *Glory & Praise: 2nd Edition* to make sure that important repertoire from these hymnals was not omitted. Therefore, the best-known music of the St. Louis Jesuits, the Dameans, Michael Joncas, Carey Landry, Bernadette Farrell, Christopher Walker, Bob Hurd, and many others, which has formed the basis for numerous parish music programs over the last thirty years, has been retained. To supplement this, a large number of hymns and songs new to *Journeysongs* was drawn from music that has become known and loved in OCP's missal programs over the last ten years, including a substantial number of songs from the popular *Spirit & Song* repertoire.

As in past editions of *Journeysongs*, a sturdy plastic pocket is attached to the inside back cover of the third edition to allow for custom-made parish music supplements, if desired, or for a variety of music supplements published by OCP for several specialized genres: Latin-language chants, Mass settings and hymns, Spanish-language songs and service music, and youth-oriented contemporary songs. The usual accompaniment editions are also provided: keyboard/vocal, guitar/vocal, assorted C and B-flat instrument parts for those hymns and songs that have them, a CD and digital recording library, and a hardbound Choir/Cantor book. For liturgy preparation, in addition to the complete set of indexes provided in the back and in the accompaniments, OCP now provides song suggestions for this edition in its popular *Today's Liturgy* magazine as well as on liturgy.com.

*Journeysongs: 3rd Edition* is also available in an edition with the complete three-year cycle of *Lectionary* readings. Music for the responsorial psalms and gospel acclamations in that edition is taken from OCP's popular resource *Respond & Acclaim*, which may be purchased each year as needed or may be ordered as a standing subscription.

We must express our gratitude to the music advisory committee for *Journeysongs: 3rd Edition*, whose recommendations were essential to the final content of this book: Mr. Frank Brownstead, Sr. Jeremy Gallet, SP, Dr. Jennifer Pascual, Sr. Mary Jo Quinn, SCL, and Dr. Elaine Rendler-McQueeney. Additional recognition is once again given to Amanda Weller and her editorial team, without whose assistance and hard work this hymnal would not have been possible.

*Journeysongs: 3rd Edition* Hymnal Committee:

Randall DeBruyn, D.M.A., Chair
Barbara Bridge, B. Mus.
Rick Modlin, B. Mus.
Joanne Osborn, B. Mus.
Thomas N. Tomaszek, M.A., M.T.S.
Angela Westhoff-Johnson, M. Mus.

# CONTENTS

## LITURGY OF THE HOURS

## RITES OF THE CHURCH

## MASS

# Hymns & Songs

## Seasons and Solemnities of the Lord

274 Advent
300 Christmas
325 Holy Family
328 Epiphany
337 Baptism of the Lord
339 Ash Wednesday
343 Ash Wednesday/Lent
345 Lent
365 Palm Sunday
370 Holy Thursday
379 Good Friday
394 Easter Vigil
396 Easter
425 Easter/Ascension/Pentecost
429 Ascension
432 Pentecost
445 Holy Trinity
453 Body and Blood of Christ
455 Sacred Heart
458 Christ the King

## Solemnities and Feasts

471 Blessed Virgin Mary
488 Presentation of the Lord
489 St. Joseph
492 Annunciation of the Lord
494 Nativity of St. John the Baptist
495 Ss. Peter and Paul, Apostles
496 Transfiguration of the Lord
498 Assumption of the
     Blessed Virgin Mary
500 Holy Cross
503 All Saints
507 All Souls
508 Dedication of a Church
511 Immaculate Conception

## Ritual Music

513 Christian Initiation
526 Penance & Reconciliation
536 Marriage
545 Pastoral Care of the Sick
550 Funeral
563 Benediction

## General Music for Worship

566 Praise
602 Thanksgiving
614 Creation
621 Providence
629 Light
636 Jesus Christ
642 Word
646 Petition & Prayer
663 Faith
671 Trust
688 Comfort
700 Peace
709 Love
724 Discipleship
735 Christian Life
744 Church
748 Saints & Martyrs
752 Second Coming
756 Eternal Life & Heaven
760 Gathering
774 Communion
804 Eucharistic Hymns
809 Blessing
812 Ministry & Mission
822 Social Concern & Justice
830 Unity
836 Devotional
842 Nation & Patriotic
849 Morning
852 Evening
857 Night

# Indexes

*These indexes are available in the accompaniment editions.

# MORNING PRAYER
## (LAUDS)

*The Liturgy of the Hours is the Church's public worship of Christ, the communal celebration of praise and thanksgiving of the Church at prayer. The Hours, along with the Eucharist, take their meaning solely from the Paschal Mystery of salvation in Christ. Morning Prayer proclaims the themes of Christ as light of the world and sun of justice. It is the praise of God in creation that unites us with the prayer of Christ.*

## OPENING VERSE: INVITATORY

### 1

*All make the sign of the cross on their lips as the Cantor/Presiding Minister sings:*

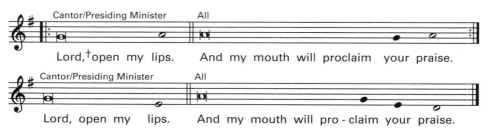

Text: *The Liturgy of the Hours,* © 1970, 1973, 1975, ICEL. All rights reserved. Used with permission.
Music: Camaldolese Monks, OSB, © 1994, Camaldolese Monks, OSB. Published by OCP. All rights reserved.

## MORNING HYMN

### 2

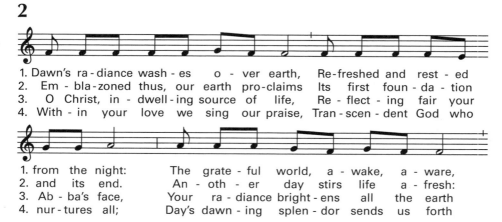

1. Dawn's ra-diance wash-es o-ver earth, Re-freshed and rest-ed
2. Em-bla-zoned thus, our earth pro-claims Its first foun-da-tion
3. O Christ, in-dwell-ing source of life, Re-flect-ing fair your
4. With-in your love we sing our praise, Tran-scen-dent God who

1. from the night: The grate-ful world, a-wake, a-ware,
2. and its end. An-oth-er day stirs life a-fresh:
3. Ab-ba's face, Your ra-diance bright-ens all the earth
4. nur-tures all; Day's dawn-ing splen-dor sends us forth

1. Is bathed in Christ's bap - tis - mal light.
2. Its gifts from God to God all tend.
3. As we a - wake in your em - brace.
4. To an - swer with our lives your call. A - men.

Text: 88 88; Aelred-Seton Shanley, d. 1999, © 1999, Aelred-Seton Shanley, from *Hymns for Morning and Evening Prayer*,
   Archdiocese of Chicago: Liturgy Training Publications. All rights reserved. Used with permission.
Music: Chant, Mode VI.

## PSALMODY*                                                    3

*(Water may be used as a baptismal remembrance during the singing of Psalm 63)*

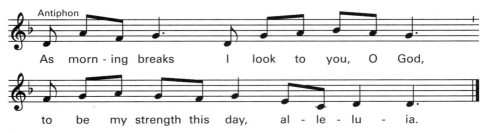

As morn - ing breaks I look to you, O God,

to be my strength this day, al - le - lu - ia.

Verses 1-4: Cantor

1. O God, you are my God, for you I long;
   for you my soul is thirsting.
   My body pines for you
   like a dry, weary land without water.

2. So I gaze on you in the temple
   to see your strength and your glory.
   For your love is better than life,
   my lips will speak your praise.

3. So I will bless you all my life,
   in your name I will lift up my hands.
   My soul shall be filled as with a banquet,
   my mouth shall praise you with joy.

4. On my bed I remember you.
   On you I muse through the night
   for you have been my help;
   in the shadow of your wings I rejoice.
   My soul clings to you;
   your right hand holds me fast.

Verse 5: All

5. Glory to the Father and to the Son,
   and to the Holy Spirit:
   as it was in the beginning, is now,
   and will be for ever. Amen.

Text: Psalm 63:2, 3–4, 5–6, 7–9. Antiphon © 1974, ICEL. All rights reserved. Used with permission.
   Verses 1–4 © 1963, The Grail (England). All rights reserved. Used with permission of A.P. Watt, Ltd.
   Music: Camaldolese Monks, OSB, © 1994, 2001, 2010, Camaldolese Monks, OSB. Published by OCP. All rights reserved.

*Other psalms, canticles and their antiphons may be taken from the proper of the
day (see No. 52–54). On Wednesday, Friday and other penitential days, Psalm 51
may be used (see No. 48–51).*

## PSALM-PRAYER

## READING

## HOMILY/PREACHING

## GOSPEL CANTICLE

*All make the sign of the cross.*

**4**

1. Blest be the Lord, the God of Is - ra - el,
2. The proph-ets tell a sto - ry just be - gun
3. This is the oath once sworn to A - bra - ham:
4. And you, my child, this day you shall be called
5. The ten - der love God prom-ised from our birth
6. All glo - ry be to God, Cre - a - tor blest,

1. Who brings the dawn and dark - est night dis - pels,
2. Of van-quished foe and glo - rious vic - t'ry won,
3. All shall be free to dwell up - on the land,
4. The prom - ised one, the proph - et of our God,
5. Is soon to dawn up - on this shad - owed earth,
6. To Je - sus Christ, God's love made man - i - fest,

1. Who rais - es up a might - y Sav - ior from the earth,
2. Of prom-ise made to all who keep the law as guide:
3. Free now to praise, un-harmed by the op - pres-sor's rod,
4. For you will go be - fore the Lord to clear the way,
5. To shine on those whose sor - rows seem to nev - er cease,
6. And to the Ho - ly Spir - it, gen - tle Com-fort - er,

1. Of Da - vid's line, a son of roy - al birth.
2. God's faith - ful love and mer-cy will a - bide.
3. Ho - ly and righ - teous in the sight of God.
4. And shep-herd all in - to the light of day.
5. To guide our feet in - to the path of peace.
6. All glo - ry be, both now and ev - er - more.

## INTERCESSIONS

**5**

Intercession/Response

Cantor: ...We pray to the Lord: Lord, have mercy.

Lord, have mer - cy. Lord, have mer - cy; hear our prayer.

## THE LORD'S PRAYER 6

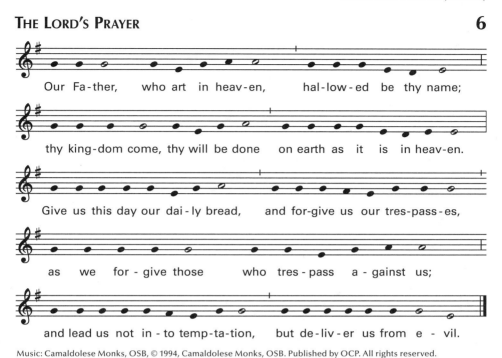

Our Fa-ther, who art in heav-en, hal-low-ed be thy name;

thy king-dom come, thy will be done on earth as it is in heav-en.

Give us this day our dai-ly bread, and for-give us our tres-pass-es,

as we for - give those who tres - pass a - gainst us;

and lead us not in - to temp-ta-tion, but de-liv-er us from e - vil.

## CONCLUDING PRAYER

*The presiding minister says the concluding prayer.*

## BLESSING 7

Presiding Minister

May the Lord bless us, protect us from all evil

All

and bring us to ever-last-ing life. A - men.

## SIGN OF PEACE

*All share a sign of Christ's peace as a conclusion.*

# EVENING PRAYER
## (VESPERS)

*Evening Prayer is an occasion to give thanks for the blessings of the day and for redemption in Christ. Prayer rises "like incense in the Lord's sight," and "upraised hands" become "an evening sacrifice" (Psalm 141:2). It is appropriate to begin Evening Prayer with the lighting of candles, stemming from the ancient practice known as the* Lucernarium, *"the lighting of the lamps." In doing so, we call to mind the light of Jesus Christ in our hearts as we offer our thanks.*

## OPENING VERSE/LUCERNARIUM

### 8

*All make the sign of the cross as the Cantor/Presiding Minister sings:*

## EVENING HYMN 9

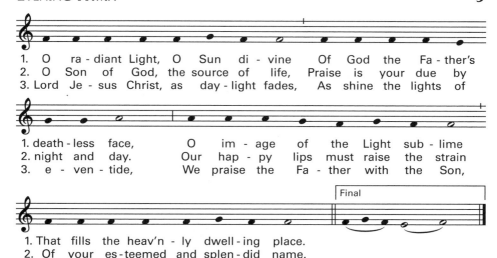

1. O ra - diant Light, O Sun di - vine Of God the Fa - ther's
2. O Son of God, the source of life, Praise is your due by
3. Lord Je - sus Christ, as day - light fades, As shine the lights of

1. death - less face, O im - age of the Light sub - lime
2. night and day. Our hap - py lips must raise the strain
3. e - ven - tide, We praise the Fa - ther with the Son,

**Final**

1. That fills the heav'n - ly dwell - ing place.
2. Of your es - teemed and splen - did name.
3. The Spir - it blest, and with them one. A - men.

Text: *Phos Hilaron*, Greek, ca. 200; tr. by William G. Storey, b. 1923, © William G. Storey.
All rights reserved. Used with permission.
Music: Chant, Mode VI.

## PSALMODY* 10

*(Incense may be used during the singing of Psalm 141)*

Antiphon

Like burn - ing in - cense, O Lord, let my prayer rise up to you.

Verses 1-4: Cantor

1. I have called to you, Lord;
hasten to help me!
Hear my voice when I cry to you.
Let my prayer arise before you like incense,
the raising of my hands
like an evening oblation.

2. Set, O Lord, a guard over my mouth;
keep watch, O Lord, at the door of my lips!
Do not turn my heart
to things that are wrong,
to evil deeds with those who are sinners.

3. Never allow me to share in their feasting.
If the righteous strike or reprove me
it is kindness;

but let the oil of the wicked
not anoint my head.
Let my prayer be ever against their malice.

4. To you, Lord God, my eyes are turned;
in you I take refuge; spare my soul!
From the trap they have laid for me
keep me safe;
keep me from the snares
of those who do evil.

Verse 5: All

5. Glory to the Father and to the Son,
and to the Holy Spirit:
as it was in the beginning, is now,
and will be for ever. Amen.

Text: Psalm 141:1–5, 8–9. Antiphon and verses 1–4, © 1963, The Grail (England).
All rights reserved. Used with permission of A.P. Watt, Ltd.
Music: Camaldolese Monks, OSB, © 1994, 2001, 2010, Camaldolese Monks, OSB. Published by OCP. All rights reserved.

*See also No. 111. Other psalms, canticles and their antiphons may be taken from the proper of the day.*

## PSALM-PRAYER

## READING

## HOMILY/PREACHING

## GOSPEL CANTICLE

*All make the sign of the cross.*

**11**

1. My soul pro - claims the great-ness of the Lord.
2. Through me great deeds will God make man - i - fest,
3. God's might-y arm, pro - tec - tor of the just,
4. Soon will the poor and hun - gry of the earth
5. All glo - ry be to God, Cre - a - tor blest,

1. My spir - it sings to God, my sav - ing God,
2. And all the earth will come to call me blest.
3. Will guard the weak and raise them from the dust.
4. Be rich - ly blest, be giv - en great - er worth.
5. To Je - sus Christ, God's love made man - i - fest,

1. Who on this day a - bove all oth - ers fa - vored me
2. Un - bound-ed love and mer - cy sure will I pro - claim
3. But might-y kings will swift - ly fall from thrones cor - rupt.
4. And Is - ra - el, as once fore-told to A - bra - ham,
5. And to the Ho - ly Spir - it, gen - tle Com - fort - er,

1. And raised me up, a light for all to see.
2. For all who know and praise God's ho - ly name.
3. The strong brought low, the low - ly lift - ed up.
4. Will live in peace through-out the prom-ised land.
5. All glo - ry be, both now and ev - er - more.

Text: Based on Luke 1:46–55; Owen Alstott, b. 1947, © 1993, Owen Alstott. Published by OCP. All rights reserved.
Music: Bernadette Farrell, b. 1957, © 1993, Bernadette Farrell. Published by OCP. All rights reserved.

## INTERCESSIONS

**12**

Intercession/Response

Cantor: ...We pray to the Lord: Lord, have mercy.

Lord, have mer - cy. Lord, have mer - cy; hear our prayer.

Text and music: Cyprian Consiglio, OSB Cam., b. 1958, © 1995, Cyprian Consiglio, OSB Cam. Published by OCP.
    All rights reserved.

## THE LORD'S PRAYER 13

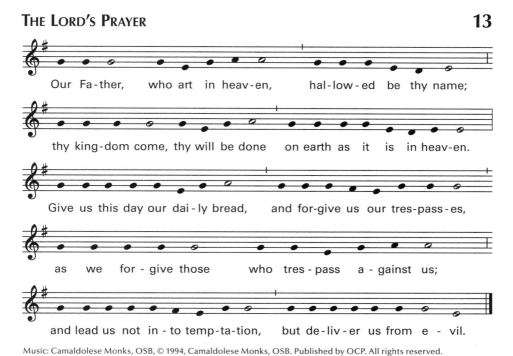

Our Fa-ther, who art in heav-en, hal-low-ed be thy name; thy king-dom come, thy will be done on earth as it is in heav-en. Give us this day our dai-ly bread, and for-give us our tres-pass-es, as we for-give those who tres-pass a-gainst us; and lead us not in-to temp-ta-tion, but de-liv-er us from e-vil.

## CONCLUDING PRAYER

*The presiding minister says the concluding prayer.*

## BLESSING 14

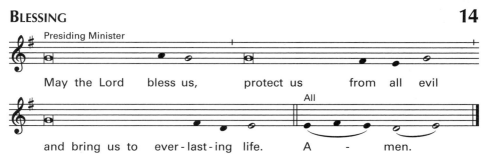

Presiding Minister

May the Lord bless us, protect us from all evil

All

and bring us to ever-last-ing life. A - men.

## SIGN OF PEACE

*All share a sign of Christ's peace as a conclusion.*

# PSALMS & CANTICLES

*Biblical psalms and canticles form the heart of the Church's song. Several kinds of religious lyrics, poems and prayers comprise the psalter. The canticles are poems, other than the psalms, found in the Jewish and Christian scriptures. Usually psalms and canticles are sung responsorially at eucharistic celebrations and antiphonally in the Liturgy of the Hours. These musical settings can help us remember key words and phrases and carry them in our hearts as we walk in the world.*

## PSALMS

**15**   ### PSALM 16: THE PATH OF LIFE

You will show me the path of life, the de-lights that a-
wait me in your pres - ence. With-out you there is noth-ing; no
joy can be com-plete un - til at last I sit by your side.

1. O God, you are my refuge,
   do not turn me away;
   I say "You are my God."
   Without you there can be no good.

2. I bless the Lord who guides me
   even in my sleep;

my face is turned to God.
With the Lord at my side I shall stand firm.

3. My heart exults, my spirit sings,
   even my body trusts in you;
   for you will not abandon my soul to death,
   nor let me sink into the grave.

Text: Based on Psalm 16:11, 1–2, 7–10; Scott Soper, b. 1961.
Music: Scott Soper.
Text and music © 1991, OCP. All rights reserved.

## PSALM 16: YOU ARE MY INHERITANCE

**16**

You are my in-her-i-tance, O Lord, my in-her-i-tance, O Lord.

1. O LORD, my allotted portion and my cup,
you it is who hold fast my lot.
I set the LORD ever before me;
with him at my right hand
I shall not be disturbed.

2. Keep me, O God, for in you I take refuge;
I say to the LORD, "My Lord are you.
O LORD, my allotted portion and my cup,
you it is who hold fast my lot."

3. I bless the LORD who counsels me;
even in the night my heart exhorts me.
I set the LORD ever before me;
with him at my right hand
I shall not be disturbed.

4. Therefore my heart is glad
and my soul rejoices,
my body, too, abides in confidence;
because you will not abandon my soul
to the netherworld,
nor will you suffer your faithful one
to undergo corruption.

5. You will show me the path to life,
fullness of joys in your presence,
the delights at your right hand,
at your right hand forever.

Text: Psalm 16:5, 8, 9–10, 11; 1–2, 5, 7–8, 9–10, 11. Refrain © 1969, 1981, 1997, ICEL.
All rights reserved. Used with permission. Verses © 1970, 1997, 1998, CCD. All rights reserved. Used with permission.
Music: Barbara Bridge, b. 1950, © 2005, 2010, Barbara Bridge. Published by OCP. All rights reserved.

## PSALM 16: KEEP ME SAFE, O GOD

**17**

Keep me safe, O God, I take ref-uge in you.

Keep me safe, O God, I take ref-uge in you.

1. O Lord, it is you who are my portion and cup;
it is you yourself who are my prize.
I keep the Lord ever in my sight:
since he is at my right hand
I shall stand firm.

2. And so my heart rejoices, my soul is glad;
even my body shall rest in safety.

For you will not leave my soul among
the dead,
nor let your beloved know decay.

3. You will show me the path of life,
the fullness of joy in your presence,
at your right hand, at your right hand
happiness for ever.

Text: Based on Psalm 16:1, 5, 8, 9–10, 11. Refrain, Paul Inwood, b. 1947, © 1985, 1992, Paul Inwood. Published by OCP.
All rights reserved. Verses © 1963, The Grail (England). All rights reserved. Used with permission of A.P. Watt, Ltd.
Music: Paul Inwood, © 1985, 1992, Paul Inwood. Published by OCP. All rights reserved.

## 18    PSALM 18: I LOVE YOU, LORD, MY STRENGTH

I love you, Lord,      I love you, Lord, my strength.

1. I love you, O Lord, my strength,
   O Lord, my rock,
   my fortress, and my Savior.

2. My God, my rock of refuge,
   my shield, my help, my stronghold!

The Lord is worthy of all praise.
When I call I am saved from my foes.

3. Long life to the Lord, my rock!
   Praised be the God who saves me.
   You who gave great victories to your king,
   and love shown to your anointed.

## 19    PSALM 19: LORD, YOU HAVE THE WORDS

Lord, you have the words of ev-er-last - ing life.

1. The law of the LORD is perfect,
   refreshing the soul;
   the decree of the LORD is trustworthy,
   giving wisdom to the simple.

2. The precepts of the LORD are right,
   rejoicing the heart;
   the command of the LORD is clear,
   enlightening the eye.

3. The fear of the LORD is pure,
   enduring forever;
   the ordinances of the LORD are true,
   all of them just.

4. They are more precious than gold,
   than a heap of purest gold;
   sweeter also than syrup
   or honey from the comb.

## 20    PSALM 19: YOUR WORDS, LORD, ARE SPIRIT AND LIFE

Your words, Lord, are Spir-it,      Spir - it and life.

1. The law of the LORD is perfect,
   refreshing the soul.
   The decree of the LORD is trustworthy,
   giving wisdom to the simple.

2. The precepts of the LORD are right,
   rejoicing the heart;
   the command of the LORD is clear,
   enlight'ning the eye.

3. The fear of the LORD is pure,
   enduring forever;

the statutes of the LORD are true,
all of them just.

4. They are more precious than gold,
   than a heap of purest gold;
   sweeter also than syrup
   or honey from the comb.

5. Let the words of my mouth
   and the thought of my heart
   find favor before you, O LORD,
   my rock and my redeemer.

## PSALM 22: MY GOD, MY GOD

**21**

My God, my God, why have you a-ban-doned me, my God, my God?

1. All who see me deride me.
They curl their lips,
they toss their heads.
"He trusted in the Lord,
let him save him;
let him release him if this is his friend."

2. Many dogs have surrounded me,
a band of the wicked beset me.
They tear holes in my hands and my feet.
I can count every one of my bones.

3. They divide my clothing among them.
They cast lots for my robe.
O Lord, do not leave me alone;
my strength,
make haste to help me!

4. I will tell of your name to my people,
and praise you where they are assembled.
"You who fear the Lord,
give him praise;
children of Jacob, give him glory."

## PSALM 22: MY GOD, MY GOD

**22**

My God, my God, why have you a - ban-doned me?

1. All who see me scoff;
they mock me with parted lips,
they wag their heads:
"He relied on the LORD; let him deliver him,
let him rescue him, if he loves him."

2. Indeed, many dogs surround me,
a pack of evildoers close upon me;
They have pierced my hands and feet.
I can number all my bones.

3. They divide my garments among them,
for my vesture they cast lots.
But you, O LORD, be not far from me;
O my help, hasten to my aid.

4. I will proclaim your name to my brethren;
amidst the assembly I will praise you:
"You who fear the LORD, praise him;
all you descendants of Jacob,
give glory to him."

## 23  PSALM 23: THE LORD IS MY SHEPHERD/
### I SHALL LIVE IN THE HOUSE OF THE LORD

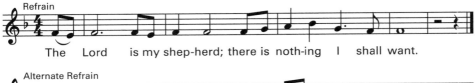

Refrain

The Lord is my shep-herd; there is noth-ing I shall want.

Alternate Refrain

I shall live in the house of the Lord all the days of my life.

1. The LORD is my shepherd; I shall not want.
In verdant pastures he gives me repose;
beside restful waters he leads me;
he refreshes my soul.

2. He guides me in right paths
for his name's sake.
Even though I walk in the dark valley
I fear no evil; for you are at my side
with your rod and your staff
that give me courage.

3. You spread the table before me
in the sight of my foes;
you anoint my head with oil;
my cup overflows.

4. Only goodness and kindness
follow me all the days of my life;
and I shall dwell in the house of the LORD
for years to come.

Text: Psalm 23:1–3a, 3b–4, 5, 6. Refrains © 1969, 1981, 1997, ICEL. All rights reserved. Used with permission.
Verses © 1970, 1997, 1998, CCD. All rights reserved. Used with permission.
Music: Scot Crandal, b. 1970, © 2001, Scot Crandal. Published by OCP. All rights reserved.

## 24  PSALM 23: I SHALL LIVE IN THE HOUSE OF THE LORD/
### THE LORD IS MY SHEPHERD

Refrain

I shall live in the house of the Lord all the days
of my life, all the days of my life.

Alternate Refrain

The Lord is my shep-herd; there is noth-ing
I shall want, there is noth-ing I shall want.

1. The LORD is my shepherd; I shall not want.
In verdant pastures he gives me repose;
beside restful waters he leads me;
he refreshes my soul.

2. He guides me in right paths
for his name's sake.
Even though I walk in the dark valley
I fear no evil; for you are at my side
with your rod and your staff
that give me courage.

3. You spread the table before me
in the sight of my foes;
you anoint my head with oil;
my cup overflows.

4. Only goodness and kindness follow me
all the days of my life;
and I shall dwell in the house of the LORD
for years to come.

## PSALM 23: THE LORD IS MY SHEPHERD/ EL SEÑOR ES MI PASTOR

**25**

El Se-ñor es mi pas-tor, na-da me fal-ta.

The Lord is my shep-herd; there is noth-ing I shall want.

1. El Señor es mi pastor, nada me falta:
en verdes praderas me hace recostar;
me conduce hacia fuentes tranquilas
y repara mis fuerzas.

2. Me guía por el sendero justo,
por el honor de su nombre.
Aunque camine por cañadas oscuras,
nada temo, porque tú vas conmigo:
tu vara y tu cayado me sosiegan.

3. Preparas una mesa ante mí,
enfrente de mis enemigos;
me unges la cabeza con perfume,
y mi copa rebosa.

4. Tu bondad y tu misericordia me acompañan
todos los días de mi vida,
y habitaré en la casa del Señor
por años sin término.

1. The LORD is my shepherd;
I shall not want.
In verdant pastures he gives me repose;
beside restful waters he leads me;
he refreshes my soul.

2. He guides me in right paths
for his name's sake.
Even though I walk in the dark valley
I fear no evil;
for you are at my side with your rod
and your staff that give me courage.

3. You spread the table before me
in the sight of my foes;
you anoint my head with oil;
my cup overflows.

4. Only goodness and kindness follow me
all the days of my life;
and I shall dwell in the house of the LORD
for years to come.

## 26 PSALM 24: LORD, THIS IS THE PEOPLE/LET THE LORD ENTER

1. All creation is the work of God.
   The earth and all creatures
   belong to the Lord.
   From mountains to valleys,
   from ocean to land,
   the Lord God made them all.

2. Who will climb the sacred mountain,
   the holy place of God?

   Those who have not done evil,
   whose hearts are pure,
   whose eyes are not blind.

3. God will send a blessing
   to honor his faithful ones.
   Lord, this is the people
   who seek the face of Jacob's God.

## 27 PSALM 25: TO YOU, O LORD

1. Your ways, O Lord,
   make known to me;
   teach me your paths.
   Guide me in your truth and teach me,
   for you are God my savior.

2. Good and upright is the Lord;
   thus he shows sinners the way.

   The humble he guides to justice;
   he teaches the humble his way.

3. Kindness and constancy
   the paths of the Lord
   for those who keep covenant with him.
   The friendship of the Lord
   with those who revere him,
   his covenant for their instruction.

## PSALM 25: TO YOU, O LORD 28

To you, O Lord, I lift up, I lift up my soul, my God.

1. Your ways, O Lord, make known to me;
   teach me your paths.
   Guide me in your truth, for you are my God,
   and for you I will wait.

2. Good and upright is the Lord;
   he shows us the way.

He guides the meek to justice,
he teaches the humble to follow his ways.

3. Your way, O Lord,
   is kindness to those who are true.
   Your friendship is
   with those who love you;
   you reveal to them your Word.

## PSALM 25: TO YOU, O LORD 29

To you, O Lord, I lift my soul, O Lord, I lift my soul.

1. Your ways, O LORD, make known to me;
   teach me your paths,
   guide me in your truth and teach me,
   for you are God my savior.

2. Good and upright is the LORD;
   thus he shows sinners the way.
   He guides the humble to justice,
   and teaches the humble his way.

3. All the paths of the LORD are kindness
   and constancy toward those
   who keep his covenant and his decrees.
   The friendship of the LORD
   is with those who fear him,
   and his covenant, for their instruction.

## PSALM 27: THE GOODNESS OF THE LORD 30

I be-lieve, I be-lieve I shall see the good-ness of the Lord in the land, in the land of the liv-ing.

1. The Lord is my light,
   the Lord is my rock, my salvation.
   The Lord is my refuge, guarding my life;
   of whom should I be afraid?

2. Only one thing I ask:
   may I live in the house of my Lord.

I shall gaze on God's goodness all of my days;
I shall live in the shelter of God.

3. I believe I shall see
   the goodness of God
   in the land of the living.
   Be strong, wait for the Lord.

**31**     ### PSALM 27: THE LORD IS MY LIGHT

The Lord is my light, the Lord is my light, the Lord is my light and my sal - va - tion.

1. The Lord is my light and my salvation;
   if God is my help, whom should I fear?
   The Lord is my refuge,
   my stronghold and my strength;
   why should I be afraid?

2. There is but one thing that I want:
   to live in the dwelling place of God;
   to look all my days on the beauty of the Lord,
   and contemplate God's holy temple.

3. I shall see for myself the grace of God,
   the dawn of that day among the living.
   Wait for the Lord,
   find strength in your hearts;
   have courage and wait for God.

**32**     ### PSALM 29: THE LORD WILL BLESS HIS PEOPLE WITH PEACE

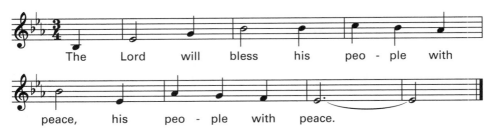

The Lord will bless his peo - ple with peace, his peo - ple with peace.

1. Give to the LORD, you sons of God,
   give to the LORD glory and praise,
   give to the LORD the glory due his name;
   adore the LORD in holy attire.

2. The voice of the LORD is over the waters,
   the LORD, over vast waters.

   The voice of the LORD is mighty;
   the voice of the LORD is majestic.

3. The God of glory thunders,
   and in his temple all say, "Glory!"
   The LORD is enthroned above the flood;
   the LORD is enthroned as king forever.

## PSALM 30: I WILL PRAISE YOU, LORD     **33**

I will praise you, Lord, you have res-cued me, I will praise you,

Lord, for your mer - cy. I will praise you, Lord,

you have res-cued me: I will praise you, Lord.

1. I will praise you, Lord,
   you have rescued me
   and have not let
   my enemies rejoice over me.
   O Lord, you have raised my soul
   from the dead,
   restored me to life
   from those who sink into the grave.

2. Sing psalms to the Lord,
   you who love him,
   give thanks to his holy name.

His anger lasts but a moment;
his favor through life.
At night there are tears,
but joy comes with dawn.

3. The Lord listened and had pity.
   The Lord came to my help.
   For me you have changed
   my mourning into dancing;
   O Lord my God,
   I will thank you for ever.

## PSALM 31: FATHER, I PUT MY LIFE IN YOUR HANDS     **34**

Fa - ther, I put my life in your hands.

1. In you, O Lord, I take refuge;
   let me never be put to shame.
   Into your hands I commend my spirit;
   you will redeem me, faithful God.

2. For all my foes reproach me,
   neighbors laugh and friends stand off.
   I am forgotten like dead unremembered;
   I am like a dish cast down.

3. But my trust is in you, O Lord;
   I say, "You are my God."
   Into your hands I place my future;
   from the clutch of foes you rescue me.

4. Let your face shine on your servant;
   O save me in your love.
   Be stouthearted, and come, take courage,
   all you who now hope in the Lord.

## 35 PSALM 31: FATHER, INTO YOUR HANDS

Ostinato Refrain

Fa - ther, in - to your hands I com-mend my Spir-it.

1. In you, O Lord, I take refuge.
   Let me never be put to shame.
   In your justice, set me free.
   It is you who will redeem me, Lord.

2. In the face of all my foes
   I am a reproach,
   an object of scorn to my neighbors
   and of fear to my friends.

3. Those who see me in the street
   run far away from me.

   I am like the dead, forgotten by all,
   a thing thrown away.

4. But as for me, I trust in you, Lord;
   I say, 'You are my God.'
   My life is in your hands,
   deliver me from those who hate me.

5. Let your face shine on your servant.
   Save me in your love.
   Be strong, let your heart take courage,
   all who hope in the Lord.

Text: Luke 23:46; Psalm 31:2 & 6b, 12a, 12b–13, 15–16, 17 & 25. Refrain © 1969, 1981, 1997, ICEL. All rights reserved.
Used with permission. Verses © 1963, The Grail (England). All rights reserved. Used with permission of A.P. Watt, Ltd.
Music: Martin Foster, b. 1966, © 1998, Martin Foster. Published by OCP. All rights reserved.

## 36 PSALM 31: FATHER, INTO YOUR HANDS/ PADRE, EN TUS MANOS

(Español) Pa - dre, _____ en tus ma - nos en - co - mien - do mi es-
(Bilingual) Pa - dre, _____ en tus ma - nos en - co - mien - do mi es-
(English) Fa - ther, ____ in - to your hands __ I com-mend ____ my

pí - ri - tu.
pí - ri - tu.
spir - it.

Pa - dre, _____ en tus
Fa - ther, ____ in - to your
Fa - ther, ____ in - to your

ma - nos en - co - mien-do mi es - pí - ri - tu.
hands __ I com-mend __ my spir - it.
hands __ I com-mend __ my spir - it.

1. A ti, Señor, me acojo:
   no quede yo nunca defraudado;
   tú que eres justo, ponme a salvo.
   En tus manos encomiendo mi espíritu:
   tú, el Dios leal, me librarás.

2. Soy la burla de todos mis enemigos,
   la irrisión de mis vecinos,
   el espanto de mis conocidos;
   me ven por la calle y escapan de mí.
   Me han olvidado como a un muerto,
   me han desechado
   como a un cacharro inútil.

1. In you, O LORD, I take refuge;
   let me not be put to shame.
   In your justice save me.
   Into your hands I commend my spirit;
   you will redeem me, faithful God.

2. I am scorned by all my enemies,
   dreaded by friends and neighbors;
   when they see me they turn away.
   I am like one dead and forgotten,
   like a vessel broken and discarded.

3. Pero yo confío en ti, Señor,
te digo: "Tú eres mi Dios".
En tu mano están mis azares;
líbrame de los enemigos,
los enemigos que me persiguen.

4. Haz brillar tu rostro sobre tu siervo,
sálvame por tu misericordia.
Sean fuertes y valientes de corazón,
los que esperan en el Señor.

3. *But Lord, I trust in you;*
*I say: "You are my God."*
*My life is in your hands;*
*save me from my enemies,*
*from the hands of those who pursue me.*

4. *Let your face shine upon your servant;*
*in your steadfast kindness save me.*
*Take courage, be strong of heart,*
*all you who wait for the Lord,*
*all you who hope in the Lord.*

## PSALM 33: BLESSED THE PEOPLE          37

Bless-ed     the     peo-ple     the     Lord     has     cho-sen     to     be     his     own.

1. Upright is the word of the LORD,
and all his works are trustworthy.
He loves justice and right;
of the kindness of the LORD the earth is full.

2. By the word of the LORD
the heavens were made;
by the breath of his mouth all their host.
For he spoke, and it was made;
he commanded, and it stood forth.

3. Exult, you just, in the LORD;
praise from the upright is fitting.
Blessed the nation whose God is the LORD,

the people he has chosen
for his own inheritance.

4. See, the eyes of the LORD
are upon those who fear him,
upon those who hope for his kindness,
to deliver them from death
and preserve them in spite of famine.

5. Our soul waits for the LORD,
who is our help and our shield.
May your kindness, O LORD, be upon us
who have put our hope in you.

Note: Holy Trinity, Year B: Verses 1, 2, 4, 5; 19th Sunday in Ordinary Time: Verses 3, 4, 5

## PSALM 33: LORD, LET YOUR MERCY          38

Lord, let your mer-cy be on us          as we place our trust in     you.

1. Exult, you just, in the Lord.
It is good to sound your praises,
giving thanks to God
with your strings and voice,
making music before the Lord.

2. The word of God ever true,
all the works of God enduring.

Every mountain peak, every ocean floor,
loving labor, loving Lord.

3. Behold, the eyes of the Lord
look with love on those who hunger,
bringing health and hope
to our days of want,
bringing mercy in every need.

## 39     Psalm 34: Taste and See/Gusten y Vean

(Español) Gus - ten   y   ve - an   qué bue - no es el   Se - ñor.
(Bilingual) Gus - ten   y   ve - an   qué bue - no es el   Se - ñor.
(English) *Taste* ___ *and see* ___ *the good - ness of the Lord.*

Gus - ten   y   ve - an ___ qué bue - no es el   Se - ñor.
*Taste and see* ___ *the* ___ *good - ness of the Lord.*
*Taste and see* ___ *the* ___ *good - ness of the Lord.*

1. Bendigo al Señor en todo momento,
   su alabanza está siempre en mi boca;
   mi alma se gloría en el Señor:
   que los humildes lo escuchen
   y se alegren.

2. Proclamen conmigo
   la grandeza del Señor,
   ensalcemos juntos su nombre.
   Yo consulté al Señor y me respondió,
   me libró de todas mis ansias.

3. Miren al Señor y quedarán radiantes,
   no asomará en sus caras la vergüenza.
   Si el afligido invoca al Señor,
   lo escuchará y lo salva
   de sus angustias.

4. El ángel del Señor protege y salva
   a los que honran y temen al Señor.
   Gusten y vean qué bueno es el Señor,
   dichoso aquel que se acoge a Dios.

1. *I will bless the LORD at all times,*
   *his praise shall be ever in my mouth.*
   *Let my soul glory in the LORD;*
   *the lowly will hear me and be glad.*

2. *Glorify the LORD with me,*
   *let us together extol his name.*
   *I sought the LORD, [who] answered me*
   *and delivered me from my fears.*

3. *Look to the Lord; be radiant with joy.*
   *And let your faces*
   *not blush with shame.*
   *The poor called out,*
   *and the Lord heard and rescued them*
   *from all their distress.*

4. *The angel of the Lord*
   *encamps around those who fear God*
   *and delivers them.*
   *O taste and see that the Lord is good;*
   *happy are those who take refuge in God.*

Text: Psalm 34 (33):2–3, 4–5, 6–7, 8–9. Spanish refrain and verses 1 and 2 © 1970, Comisión Episcopal Española de Liturgia.
All rights reserved. Used with permission. English refrain © 1969, 1981, 1997, ICEL. All rights reserved.
Used with permission. English verses 1 and 2 © 1970, 1986, CCD. All rights reserved. Used with permission.
English and Spanish verses 3 and 4, Mary Frances Reza, © 1998, Mary Frances Reza.
Published by OCP. All rights reserved.
Music: Mary Frances Reza, © 1998, Mary Frances Reza. Published by OCP. All rights reserved.

## 40     Psalm 34: Taste and See

Taste and see   the good - ness of the Lord;

taste and see   the good - ness of the Lord.

1. I will bless the Lord at all times,
   with praise always on my lips;
   in the Lord my soul shall make its boast.
   The humble shall hear and be glad.

2. Glorify the Lord with me.
   Together let us praise his name.
   I sought the Lord and was answered;
   from my terrors God set me free.

3. Look towards the Lord and shine in light;
   let your faces be not ashamed.
   This poor man called; the Lord heard him
   and rescued him from all his distress.

4. The angel of the Lord is encamped
   around those who revere him.
   Taste and see that the Lord is good.
   They are happy who seek refuge in him.

Text: Psalm 34:2–3, 4–5, 6–7, 8–9. Refrain © 1969, ICEL. All rights reserved. Used with permission.
Verses © 1963, The Grail (England). All rights reserved. Used with permission of A.P. Watt, Ltd.
Music: Christopher Willcock, b. 1947, © 1977, 1990, 1997, Christopher Willcock, SJ.
Published by OCP. All rights reserved.

## PSALM 34: TASTE AND SEE THE GOODNESS OF THE LORD/ 41
## I WILL BLESS THE LORD AT ALL TIMES

1. I will bless the LORD at all times;
   his praise shall be ever in my mouth.
   Let my soul glory in the LORD;
   the lowly will hear me and be glad.

2. Glorify the LORD with me,
   let us together extol his name.
   I sought the LORD, and he answered me
   and delivered me from all my fears.

3. Look to him that you may be
   radiant with joy,
   and your faces may not blush with shame.
   When the poor one called out,
   the LORD heard,
   and from all his distress he saved him.

4. The angel of the LORD encamps
   around those who fear him
   and delivers them.

   Taste and see how good the LORD is;
   blessed the man who takes refuge in him.

5. The LORD has eyes for the just,
   and ears for their cry.
   The LORD confronts the evildoers,
   to destroy remembrance of them
   from the earth.

6. When the just cry out, the LORD hears them,
   and from all their distress he rescues them.
   The LORD is close to the brokenhearted;
   and those who are
   crushed in spirit he saves.

7. Many are the troubles of the just one,
   but out of them all the LORD delivers him;
   he watches over all his bones;
   not one of them shall be broken.

Text: Psalm 34:2–3, 4–5, 6–7, 8–9, 16–17, 18–19, 20–21. Refrain © 1969, 1981, 1997, ICEL. All rights reserved.
Used with permission. Verses © 1970, 1997, 1998, CCD. All rights reserved. Used with permission.
Music: Kevin Keil (ASCAP), b. 1956, © 2005, Kevin Keil. Published by OCP. All rights reserved.

## 42 PSALM 34: TASTE AND SEE

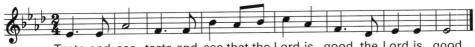

Taste and see, taste and see that the Lord is good, the Lord is good.

1. I will bless the Lord at all times,
   his praise always on my lips.
   The Lord shall be the glory of my soul;
   the humble shall hear and be glad.

2. Glorify the Lord with me,
   together let us praise his name.
   I sought the Lord: he answered me;
   he set me free from all my fear.

3. Look upon the Lord and be radiant;
   hide not your face from the Lord.
   He heard the cry of the poor;
   he rescued them from all their woes.

4. The angel of the Lord is with his people
   to rescue those who trust in him.

   Taste and see the goodness of the Lord;
   seek refuge in him and be glad.

5. Saints of the Lord, revere him;
   those who fear him lack nothing.
   Lions suffer want and go hungry,
   but those who seek him lack no blessing.

6. Children of the Lord come and hear,
   and learn the fear of the Lord.
   Who is he who longs for life,
   whose only love is for his wealth?

7. Keep evil words from your tongue,
   your lips from speaking deceit.
   Turn aside from evil and do good;
   seek and strive after peace.

Text: Based on Psalm 34:2–3, 4–5, 6–7, 8–9, 10–11, 12–13, 14–15; Stephen Dean, b. 1948.
Music: Stephen Dean.
Text and music © 1981, Stephen Dean. Published by OCP. All rights reserved.

## 43 PSALM 40: HERE I AM/GOD, MY GOD, COME TO MY AID

Refrain

Here I am, Lord, here I am. I come to do your will.

Alternate Refrain

God, my God, come to my aid, come to my aid, come to my aid; come.

1. Long was I waiting for God,
   and then he heard my cry.
   It was he who taught this song to me,
   a song of praise to God.

2. You asked me not for sacrifice,
   for slaughtered goats or lambs.
   No, my heart,
   you gave me ears to hear you,
   then I said, "Here I am."

3. You wrote it in the scrolls of law
   what you would have me do.
   Doing that is what has made me happy,
   your law is in my heart.

4. I spoke before your holy people,
   the good news that you save.
   Now you know that I will not be silent,
   I'll always sing your praise.

Text: Based on Psalm 40:8, 14, 2, 4, 7–10. Refrains © 1969, 1981, ICEL. All rights reserved. Used with permission.
  Verses, Rory Cooney, b. 1952, © 1971, 1991, OCP. All rights reserved.
Music: Rory Cooney, © 1971, 1991, OCP. All rights reserved.

## PSALM 42/43: AS THE DEER LONGS

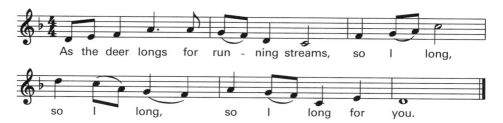

As the deer longs for run - ning streams, so I long,

so I long, so I long for you.

1. Athirst my soul for you,
   the God who is my life!
   When shall I see, when shall I see,
   see the face of God?

2. Echoes meet
   as deep is calling unto deep,
   over my head, all your mighty waters,
   sweeping over me.

3. Continually the foe delights in taunting me:

"Where is God, where is your God?"
Where, O where are you?

4. Defend me, God;
   send forth your light and your truth.
   They will lead me to your holy mountain,
   to your dwelling place.

5. Then I shall go unto the altar of my God.
   Praising you, O my joy and gladness,
   I shall praise your name.

Text: Based on Psalm 42:2, 3, 8, 4; 43:3, 4; Bob Hurd, b. 1950.
Music: Bob Hurd.
Text and music © 1988, Bob Hurd. Published by OCP. All rights reserved.

## PSALM 42/43: LIKE A DEER THAT LONGS/
## MY SOUL IS THIRSTING FOR YOU

Refrain

Like a deer that longs for run - ning streams, my

soul longs for you, my God.

Alternate Refrain

My soul is thirst-ing for you, thirst-ing for you, my God.

1. Athirst is my soul for God,
   for God, the living God.
   When shall I go
   and behold the face of God?

2. I went with the throng
   and led them in procession
   to the house of God.
   Amid loud cries of joy and thanksgiving,
   with the multitude keeping festival.

3. Send forth your light and your fidelity;
   they shall lead me on
   and bring me to your holy mountain,
   to your dwelling-place.

4. Then will I go in to the altar of God,
   the God of my gladness and joy;
   then will I give you thanks
   upon the harp,
   give you thanks, O God, my God!

Text: Psalm 42:3, 5; 43:3, 4. Refrain © 1969, 1981, 1997, ICEL. All rights reserved. Used with permission.
Verses © 1970, 1997, 1998, CCD. All rights reserved. Used with permission.
Music: Refrain based on *Sicut cervus desiderat*, Giovanni Pierluigi da Palestrina, 1525–1594; adapt. by
Barbara Bridge, b. 1950. Verses and refrain adapt. © 2010, Barbara Bridge. Published by OCP. All rights reserved.

## 46     PSALM 45: THE QUEEN STANDS

The queen stands at your right hand, ar-rayed in gold.

1. The queen takes her place
at your right hand in gold of Ophir.

2. Hear, O daughter and see; turn your ear,
forget your people and your father's house.

3. So shall the king desire your beauty;
for he is your lord.

4. They are borne in with gladness,
borne in with joy;
they enter the palace of the king.

## 47     PSALM 47: GOD MOUNTS HIS THRONE

God mounts his throne to shouts of joy: Al-le-lu-ia, al-le-lu-ia!

1. All peoples, clap your hands,
cry to God with shouts of joy!
For the Lord Most High we must fear,
great King over all the earth.

2. God goes up with shouts of joy;
the Lord goes up with trumpet blast.

Sing praise for God, sing praise for God,
sing praise to our King.

3. God is King of all the earth.
Sing praise with all your skill.
God is King over the nations;
he reigns on his holy throne.

## 48     PSALM 51: CREATE IN ME

Cre-ate in me a clean heart, O God, a
clean heart, O God, cre-ate in me.

1. O God, in your goodness have mercy
on me.
In your compassion wipe out my offense.
Thoroughly wash me from my guilt,
and cleanse me from my sins.

2. For I acknowledge my offense
and my sin is always before me;
against only you have I sinned,
and done what is evil in your eyes.

3. A clean heart create for me, O God,
a steadfast spirit renew in me.
Cast me not out from your presence,
O God.
Take not your Holy Spirit from me.

4. Give us back the joy of our salvation,
and renew in us a willing spirit.
O Lord, open my lips, Lord, open my lips.
And we will sing your praise.

## Psalm 51: Be Merciful, O Lord/
## Create a Clean Heart in Me/I Will Rise and Go to My Father

1. Have mercy on me, O God,
   in your goodness;
   in the greatness of your compassion
   wipe out my offense.
   Thoroughly wash me from my guilt
   and of my sin cleanse me.

2. For I acknowledge my offense,
   and my sin is before me always:
   "Against you only have I sinned,
   and done what is evil in your sight."

3. A clean heart create for me, O God,
   and a steadfast spirit renew within me.
   Cast me not out from your presence,
   and your Holy Spirit take not from me.

4. Give me back the joy of your salvation,
   and a willing spirit sustain in me.
   O Lord, open my lips,
   and my mouth shall proclaim your praise.

Text: Psalm 51:3–4, 5–6, 12–13, 17. Refrain © 1969, 1981, 1997, ICEL. All rights reserved. Used with permission.
Verses © 1970, 1997, 1998, CCD. All rights reserved. Used with permission.
Music: Ricky Manalo, CSP, b. 1965, © 2006, Ricky Manalo, CSP. Published by OCP. All rights reserved.

## 50      Psalm 51: Be Merciful, O Lord

Be mer-ci-ful, O Lord. Have mer-cy on us, for we have sinned. We come be-fore you; cleanse us from with-in. Have mer-cy on us, Lord.

1. Have mercy on me in your goodness, Lord.
   In your great compassion
   wipe out my offense.
   Wash me from guilt, Lord,
   cleanse me from my sin.
   Have mercy on me, Lord.

2. Create a clean heart for me, O God.
   And a steadfast spirit, renew within me.

Cast me not out from your presence, O Lord.
Take not your Spirit from me.

3. Give me the joy of your salvation, Lord,
   and a willing spirit sustain within me.
   Open my lips,
   let my mouth proclaim your praise.
   Have mercy on me, Lord.

## 51      Psalm 51: Create in Me/Oh Dios, Crea en Mí

Oh Dios, cre-a en mí, oh Dios, cre-a en mí, ____
*Cre-ate in ____ me, cre-ate in ____ me a*

cre-a un co-ra-zón, un co-ra-zón pu-ro.
*pure ____ heart, O God, a will-ing spir-it.*

1. Piedad de mí, Señor,
   por tu bondad,
   por tu inmensa compasión
   borra mi culpa;
   lava del todo mi delito,
   purifícame, tú, de mi pecado.

2. Oh Dios, crea en mí
   un corazón puro,
   pon en mí un espíritu firme;
   no me arrojes lejos de tu rostro,
   no me quites tu santo espíritu.

1. *Have mercy on me, O God,*
   *in your kindness*
   *blot out my offenses;*
   *wash me, wash away my guilt,*
   *cleanse me completely of my sin.*

2. *Create in me, God,*
   *a pure heart*
   *and give me a steadfast spirit;*
   *do not cast me out*
   *from your presence,*
   *nor remove your holy spirit.*

3. Dame la alegría de tu salvación,
   mantén en mí un alma generosa.
   Enseñaré a los malvados
   tus caminos,
   se volverán a ti los pecadores.

3. *Give me back the joy
   of your salvation,
   sustain in me a willing spirit.
   Open my lips, O Lord,
   and I shall proclaim your praise.*

Text: Psalm 51 (50):3–4, 12–13, 14–15. Spanish refrain © 1970, Comisión Episcopal Española de Liturgia.
All rights reserved. Used with permission. Spanish verses and all English, Eleazar Cortés, b. 1947,
© 1994, 1998, Eleazar Cortés. Published by OCP. All rights reserved.
Music: Eleazar Cortés, © 1994, Eleazar Cortés. Published by OCP. All rights reserved.

## PSALM 63: MY SOUL IS THIRSTING/AS MORNING BREAKS    52

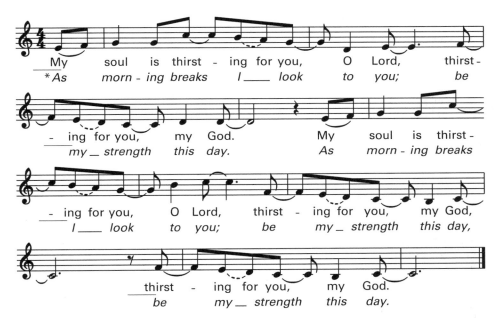

1. O God, you are my God,
   and I will always praise you.
   In the shadow of your wings
   I cling to you and you hold me high.

2. Through the day you walk with me;
   all the night your love surrounds me.

   To the glory of your name I lift my hands,
   I sing your praise.

3. I will never be afraid,
   for I will not be abandoned.
   Even when the road grows long and
   weary your love will rescue me.

*Alternate refrain.

Text: Based on Psalm 63:2, 5–9. Refrain © 1969, 1981, ICEL. Alternate refrain fr. *The Liturgy of the Hours* © 1974, ICEL.
All rights reserved. Used with permission. Verses, Steve Angrisano, b. 1965, © 1997, 1998, Steve Angrisano.
Published by OCP. All rights reserved.
Music: Steve Angrisano, © 1997, 1998, Steve Angrisano. Published by OCP. All rights reserved.

# 53     PSALM 63: AS MORNING BREAKS

As morn-ing breaks   I look to you;   I look to you, O Lord, to be my strength this day,   as morn-ing breaks,   as morn-ing breaks.

1. O God, you are my God, for you I long;
   for you my soul is thirsting.
   My body pines for you,
   like a dry, weary land without water.
   So I gaze on you in your holy place
   to see your strength and your glory.

2. For your love is better than life,
   my lips will speak your praise.
   So I will bless you all my life,
   in your name I will lift up my hands.
   My soul shall be filled as with a banquet,
   my mouth shall praise you with joy.

3. On my bed I remember you.
   On you I muse through the night,
   for you have been my help;
   in the shadow of your wings I rejoice.
   My soul clings to you;
   your right hand holds me fast.

4. Glory to the Father, and to the Son,
   and to the Holy Spirit:
   as it was in the beginning,
   is now, and will be forever. Amen.

# 54   PSALM 63: MY SOUL IS THIRSTING/AS MORNING BREAKS

My soul   is thirst-ing   for you,   O Lord my   God.
*As morn - ing breaks   I look   to you, O   God.

1. O God, you are my God whom I seek;
   for you my flesh pines and my soul thirsts
   like the earth, parched and barren,
   lifeless without water.

2. Thus have I gazed toward you in the sanctuary
   to see your power and your glory,
   for your kindness is a greater good than life;
   my lips shall glorify you.

3. Thus will I bless you while I live;
   lifting up my hands,
   I will call upon your name.
   As with the riches of a banquet
   shall my soul be satisfied,
   and with exultant lips my mouth shall praise you.

4. I will remember you upon my couch,
   and through the night-watches
   I will meditate on you:
   you are my help,
   and in the shadow of your wings
   I shout for joy.

5. You are my help, and in the
   shadow of your wings I shout for joy.
   My soul clings fast to you;
   your right hand upholds me.

6. Glory to the Father, and to the Son,
   and to the Holy Spirit;
   as it was in the beginning,
   is now, and will be forever. Amen.

*Alternate refrain.

Note: 12th Sunday in Ordinary Time, Year C and 22nd Sunday in Ordinary Time, Year A: Refrain and verses 1–3, 5–6.
32nd Sunday in Ordinary Time, Year A: Refrain and verses 1–4, 6. Morning Prayer: Alternate Refrain and verses 1–4,
the last half of verse 5, and verse 6.

# PSALM 66: LET ALL THE EARTH

**55**

Let all the earth cry out, cry out to God with joy!

Let all the earth cry out, cry out to God with joy!

1. Sing out your joy;
   praise the glory of God's holy name.
   Say to the Lord:
   "Oh, how awesome are your mighty ways."

2. Come now and hear all the things
   our God has done for me.

Blessed be the Lord who holds me close,
whose love is surrounding me.

3. All the earth shall bow before you,
   singing to your holy name.
   See the work of God,
   the wonders of his deeds from age to age.

Text: Based on Psalm 66:1–3, 16, 20, 4–5. Refrain © 1969, 1981, ICEL. All rights reserved. Used with permission.
   Verses, Steve Angrisano, b. 1965, and Tom Tomaszek, b. 1950, © 1997, Steve Angrisano and Thomas N. Tomaszek.
   Published by OCP. All rights reserved.
Music: Steve Angrisano and Tom Tomaszek, © 1997, Steve Angrisano and Thomas N. Tomaszek.
   Published by OCP. All rights reserved.

# PSALM 66: LET ALL THE EARTH CRY OUT

**56**

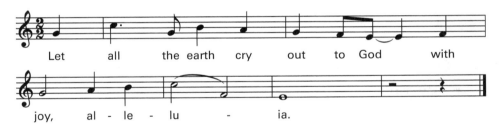

Let all the earth cry out to God with joy, al-le-lu-ia.

1. Shout joyfully to God, all the earth,
   sing praise to the glory of his name;
   proclaim his glorious praise.
   Say to God,
   "How tremendous are your deeds!"

2. "Let all on earth sing praise and worship you,
   sing praise to the holiest of names!"
   Come and see the Lord's wondrous deeds
   among the children of Adam.

3. He has changed the sea into dry land;
   through the river they passed on foot.
   Let us rejoice in him.
   He rules by his might forever.

4. Hear now, all you who fear God,
   while I declare what he has done for me.
   Blessed be God who refused me not
   my prayer or his kindness.

Text: Psalm 66:1–3, 4–5, 6–7, 16, 20. Refrain © 1969, 1981, 1997, ICEL. All rights reserved. Used with permission.
   Verses 1, 3 and 4 © 1970, 1997, 1998, CCD. All rights reserved. Used with permission.
   Verse 2, Bob Halligan Jr., b. 1953, © 2004, Bob Halligan Jr. Published by OCP. All rights reserved.
Music: Bob Halligan Jr., © 2004, Bob Halligan Jr. Published by OCP. All rights reserved.

## 57     PSALM 66: LET ALL THE EARTH CRY OUT

Let all the earth cry out to God with joy, with joy.

1. Cry out with joy to God, all the earth!
   O sing to the glory of his name!
   O render him glorious praise,
   say to God:
   "How tremendous your deeds."

2. Before you all the earth shall bow,
   shall sing to you, sing to your name!
   Come and see the works of God!
   Tremendous his deeds among men!

3. He turned the sea into dry land;
   they passed through the river dry-shod.
   Let our joy then be in him—
   he rules evermore by his might!

4. Come and hear,
   all who fear God,
   I will tell what he did for my soul:
   to him I cried aloud,
   with high praise ready on my tongue!

## 58     PSALM 67: O GOD, LET ALL THE NATIONS

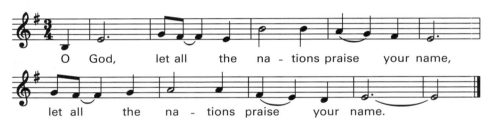

O God, let all the na - tions praise your name,

let all the na - tions praise your name.

1. Lord, look with favor on us;
   show us your face.
   Reveal to the faithful your way, Lord,
   salvation for all the world.

2. May the nations sing and be glad,
   for your word governs all the world.

   Your justice will guide all nations,
   all people on the earth.

3. Lord, may we sing your praise;
   may we sing to you all of our days.
   O God, we ask you to bless us,
   as we honor your name.

## 59   PSALM 72: JUSTICE SHALL FLOURISH/LORD, EVERY NATION

Refrain        to Verses 1-2, 4-5

Jus-tice shall flour-ish in his time, and full-ness of peace for ev - er.

Alternate Refrain        to Verses 1-4

Lord, ev-'ry na-tion on earth will a - dore you.

1. O God, with your judgment
   endow the king,
   and with your justice, the king's son;
   he shall govern your people
   with justice
   and your afflicted ones with judgment.

2. Justice shall flower in his days,
   and profound peace,
   'til the moon be no more.
   May he rule from sea to sea,
   and from the River to the ends of the earth.

3. From the islands and Tarshish
   shall kings come with gifts;
   from Arabia and Sheba they come.

All the kings of the earth pay him homage;
all the nations shall serve him.

4. For he shall rescue the poor
   when he cries out,
   and the afflicted
   when he has no one to help him.
   He shall have pity for the lowly and poor;
   the lives of the poor he shall save.

5. May his name be blessed forever,
   and while the sun lasts
   his name shall remain.
   In him shall all the tribes
   of the earth be blessed;
   all the nations
   shall proclaim his happiness.

## PSALM 80: THE VINEYARD OF THE LORD/ LORD, MAKE US TURN TO YOU 60

Ord. Time  The vine-yard of the Lord is the house of Is - ra - el. The
Advent  Lord, make us turn to you, show your face, we shall be saved. Lord,

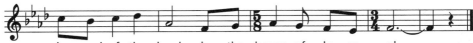

vine-yard of the Lord is the house of Is - ra - el.
make us turn to you, show your face, we shall be saved.

### Ordinary Time Verses

1. A vine from Egypt you transplanted;
   you drove away the nations and planted it.
   It put forth its foliage to the Sea,
   its shoots as far as the River.

2. Why have you broken down its walls,
   so that every passer-by plucks its fruit,
   the boar from the forest lays it waste,
   and the beasts of the field feed upon it?

3. Once again, O LORD of hosts,
   look down from heaven, and see;
   take care of this vine,

and protect what your right hand
   has planted,
   the son of man whom you yourself
   made strong.

4. Then we will no more withdraw from you;
   give us new life,
   and we will call upon your name.
   O LORD, God of hosts, restore us;
   if your face shine upon us,
   then we shall be saved.

### Advent Verses

1. O shepherd of Israel, hearken,
   from your throne upon the cherubim,
   shine forth.
   Rouse your power,
   and come to save us.

2. Once again, O LORD of hosts,
   look down from heaven, and see;
   take care of this vine,
   and protect what your right hand
   has planted,

the son of man whom you yourself
   made strong.

3. May your help be with the man
   of your right hand,
   with the son of man whom you yourself
   made strong.
   Then we will no more withdraw from you;
   give us new life,
   and we will call upon your name.

# 61    Psalm 84: How Lovely Is Your Dwelling Place

How love-ly is your dwell-ing place, O Lord God of Hosts!

1. My soul yearns and pines
for the courts of the Lord,
my heart and my flesh cry out;
Even the sparrow may find a home,
the swallow a nest for her young;
Your altars, my king and my God!

2. How happy are they
who may dwell in your courts,
how happy when you are their strength;

Though they might go through
the valley of death,
they make it a place of springs.
Your first rain will bring it to life.

3. O Lord of Hosts, hear my cry,
and hearken, O God of Jacob;
One day in your house
is worth much more to me
than ten thousand anywhere else;
The Lord is my sun and my shield!

Text: Based on Psalm 84:2–7, 9, 11–12; Michael Joncas, b. 1951.
Music: Michael Joncas.
Text and music © 1979, OCP. All rights reserved.

# 62    Psalm 85: Let Us See Your Kindness

Let us see your kind-ness, O Lord, grant us your sal-va-tion, O God.

1. God, how I long
for the peace you proclaim,
your salvation and glory
near to all who revere your name.

2. Kindness and truth shall meet,
justice and peace shall kiss;

truth shall spring forth from the earth
and justice look down from heaven.

3. You, yourself, will give these gifts;
our land shall yield its fruit.
Justice shall walk before you,
and salvation along your way.

Text: Based on Psalm 85:8, 9–10, 11–12, 13–14; Dominic MacAller, b. 1959.
Music: Dominic MacAller.
Text and music © 1988, Dominic MacAller. Published by OCP. All rights reserved.

# 63    Psalm 85: Lord, Let Us See Your Kindness

Lord, let us see your kind-ness, and grant us your sal - va - tion.

1. I will hear what God proclaims;
the Lord—for he proclaims
peace to his people.
Near indeed is his salvation
to those who fear him,
glory dwelling in our land.

2. Kindness and truth shall meet;
justice and peace shall kiss.

Truth shall spring out of the earth,
and justice shall look down from heaven.

3. The Lord himself will give his benefits;
our land shall yield its increase.
Justice shall walk before him,
and prepare the way of his steps.

Text: Psalm 85:9–10, 11–12, 13–14. Refrain © 1969, 1981, 1997, ICEL. All rights reserved. Used with permission.
Verses © 1970, 1997, 1998, CCD. All rights reserved. Used with permission.
Music: John Schiavone, b. 1947, © 2001, John Schiavone. Published by OCP. All rights reserved.

## PSALM 85: LORD, LET US SEE YOUR KINDNESS    64

Lord, let us see your kind-ness; Lord, let us see your kind-ness.

Your kind - ness and sal - va - tion grant us, O Lord.

1. I will hear what the Lord proclaims:
   peace and salvation close at hand,
   always near to those who fear him;
   glory dwelling in our land.

2. Kindness and truth shall meet at last;
   justice and peace embrace in love.

Truth shall spring up from the earth,
and justice shall look down from heaven above.

3. God will grant abundant grace;
   earth will spring up with boundless life.
   Blessings flow ever before him
   to prepare his way.

Text: Based on Psalm 85:9–10, 11–12, 13–14; Scott Soper, b. 1961.
Music: Scott Soper.
Text and music © 2003, Scott Soper. Published by OCP. All rights reserved.

## PSALM 89: FOR EVER I WILL SING    65
## THE GOODNESS OF THE LORD

For ev - er I will sing the good-ness of the Lord.

1. I have made a covenant
   with my chosen one,
   I have sworn to David my servant:
   forever will I confirm your posterity
   and establish your throne
   for all generations.

2. Blessed the people who know
   the joyful shout;
   In the light of your countenance,
   O LORD, they walk.
   At your name they rejoice all the day,
   and through your justice they are exalted.

3. He shall say of me,
   "You are my father,
   my God, the rock, my savior."

Forever I will maintain
my kindness toward him,
and my covenant with him stands firm.

4. The promises of the LORD
   I will sing forever,
   through all generations my mouth
   shall proclaim your faithfulness.
   For you have said, "My kindness
   is established forever";
   in heaven you have confirmed
   your faithfulness.

5. You are the splendor of their strength,
   and by your favor our horn is exalted.
   For to the LORD belongs our shield,
   and to the Holy One of Israel, our king.

Note: 4th Sunday in Advent, Year B: Verses 4, 1, 3; Christmas: Verses 1, 2, 3;
   13th Sunday in Ordinary Time, Year A: Verses 4, 2, 5.

Text: Psalm 89:4–5, 16–17, 27, 29, 2–3, 18–19. Refrain © 1969, 1981, 1997, ICEL. All rights reserved. Used with permission.
   Verses © 1970, 1997, 1998, CCD. All rights reserved. Used with permission.
Music: Owen Alstott, b. 1947, © 1977, 1990, OCP. All rights reserved.

**66**  ## PSALM 89: FOR EVER I WILL SING

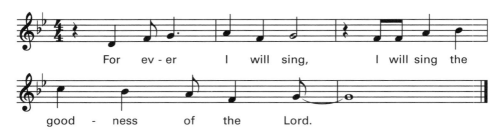

1. I have made a covenant with my chosen one,
   I have sworn to David my servant:
   forever will I confirm your posterity
   and establish your throne for all generations.

2. Blessed the people who know the joyful shout;
   in the light of your countenance, O LORD,
   they walk.

   At your name they rejoice all the day,
   and through your justice they are exalted.

3. He shall say of me, "You are my father,
   my God, the rock, my savior."
   Forever I will maintain
   my kindness toward him,
   and my covenant with him stands firm.

**67**  ## PSALM 90: IN EVERY AGE

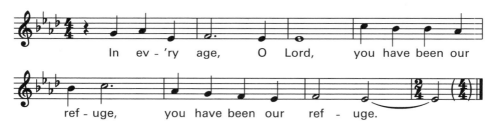

1. You return us to dust,
   saying, "Return, O children, to earth."
   For to you a thousand years
   are like yesterday passed,
   or as a watch of the night.

2. You sweep us away in a dream.
   At dawn we are like morning grass
   that rises to the morning sun,
   then withers and fades.

3. Teach us to treasure our days.
   Give wisdom to our hearts.
   Return, O Lord, how long must we wait?
   Pity your servants.

4. Fill our day-break with your love
   that we may rejoice in song.
   May your gracious eye watch over us
   and the work of our hands.

## PSALM 91: BE WITH ME, LORD

**68**

Be with me, Lord, when I am in trou-ble.

Be with me, Lord, be with me.

1. You who dwell in the shelter
of the Most High,
who abide in the shadow
of the Almighty, say to the LORD,
"My refuge and my fortress,
my God in whom I trust."

2. No evil shall befall you,
no affliction come near your tent,
for God commands the angels
to guard you in all your ways.

3. Upon their hands they shall bear you up,
lest you dash your foot against a stone.
You shall tread upon the asp and the viper;
you shall trample down the lion and the dragon.

4. Because he clings to me, I will deliver him;
I will set him on high
because he acknowledges my name.
He shall call upon me, and I will answer him;
I will be with him in distress;
I will deliver him and glorify him.

## PSALM 91: BE WITH ME, LORD

**69**

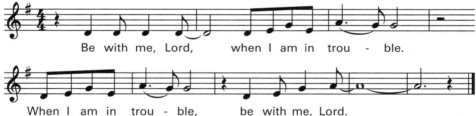

Be with me, Lord, when I am in trou - ble.

When I am in trou - ble, be with me, Lord.

1. If you seek a shelter,
then come to the Lord, our God.
Say to the Lord,
"My refuge, I place my trust in you."

2. No evil shall snare you,
no harm come upon your home.
God sends to you his angels
to guard you on your way.

3. Your feet shall not stumble;
the angels will lift you high.
You shall defy the viper
and those who cause you harm.

4. Because of your love,
because of your faithfulness,
God will indeed be with you
to save you from all fear.

**70**      PSALM 91: BE WITH ME, LORD

Be with me, Lord; be with me, Lord, when I am in trou-ble and need.

1. You who dwell in the shelter
   of God, Most High,
   who abide in Almighty's shade,
   say to the Lord: "My refuge, my
   stronghold, my God in whom I trust."

2. Evil shall never befall you,
   nor affliction come near to your tent.
   Unto his angels he's given command
   to guard you in all your ways.

3. On their hands the angels will bear you up,
   lest you dash your foot 'gainst a stone.
   Lion or viper might strike at your life,
   but you will not come to harm.

4. Cling to the Lord and
   he'll surely deliver you;
   he raises up all who call on his name.
   He will bring joy to your hearts and
   bless you with peace in all your days.

**71**      PSALM 95: IF TODAY YOU HEAR HIS VOICE

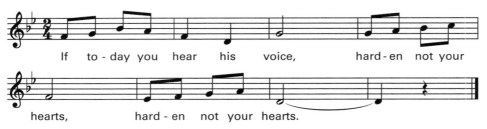

If to-day you hear his voice, hard-en not your

hearts, hard-en not your hearts.

1. Come, let us sing with joy,
   sing praise to the Rock who saves us.
   Come now with open hearts,
   singing songs of thanks,
   singing songs of praise.

2. Come, let us kneel to God,
   bow down to the Lord who made us.
   We are the flock of God;

   God who shepherds us,
   God who guides us home.

3. If you should hear God's voice,
   do not let your hearts be hardened
   as in that desert land;
   there they saw my works,
   still they tested me.

**72**      PSALM 95: IF TODAY YOU HEAR GOD'S VOICE

If to-day you hear God's voice, hard-en not your hearts.

If to-day you hear God's voice, hard-en not your hearts.

1. Come, let us sing joyfully to the LORD;
   let us acclaim the Rock of our salvation.
   Let us come into his presence with
   thanksgiving;
   let us joyfully sing psalms to him.

2. Come, let us bow down and worship;
   let us kneel before the LORD who
   made us.
   For he is our God,
   and we are the people he shepherds,
   the flock he guides.

3. O, that today you would
   hear his voice:
   "Harden not your hearts
   as at Meribah,
   as in the day of Massah in the desert."
   Where your fathers tempted me;
   they tested me though they had seen
   my works.

## PSALM 95: IF TODAY YOU HEAR HIS VOICE — 73

If to-day you hear his voice, hard-en not your hearts.

1. Come, let us sing joyfully to the LORD;
   let us acclaim the Rock of our salvation.
   Let us come into his presence
   with thanksgiving;
   let us joyfully sing psalms to him.

2. Come, let us bow down in worship;
   let us kneel before the LORD who made us.
   For he is our God,

   and we are the people he shepherds,
   the flock he guides.

3. Oh, that today you would hear his voice:
   "Harden not your hearts as at Meribah,
   as in the day of Massah in the desert,
   where your fathers tempted me;
   they tested me
   though they had seen my works."

## PSALM 96: TODAY OUR SAVIOR IS BORN — 74

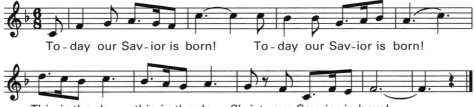

To-day our Sav-ior is born!   To-day our Sav-ior is born!

This is the day,   this is the day, Christ, our Sav-ior is born!

1. Sing to our God a joyful song!
   Everyone bless God's name.
   Tell of God's wondrous deeds;
   sing to all the world.

2. Heaven be glad and earth rejoice,
   let every ocean roar!

   Every forest, every tree
   joins the song of joy!

3. Cry out with joy for God has come,
   come to rule the earth.
   God will rule the world with love,
   righteousness and truth.

# 75 PSALM 96: TODAY IS BORN OUR SAVIOR/ALLELUIA

Refrain: 1st time: Cantor/All; thereafter: All

Resp. Psalm To - day is born our Sav-ior Je - sus Christ the

Gospel Acc. Al - le - lu - ia, al - le - lu - ia, al - le - lu

Lord. Lord. Lord. Je - sus Christ the Lord.

ia! ia! ia, al - le - lu - ia!

*Verses (Responsorial Psalm only)

1. Sing to the LORD a new song;
   sing to the LORD, all the earth.
   Sing to the LORD; bless his holy name.

2. Announce his salvation, day after day.
   Tell his glory among all the nations;
   among all peoples
   his marvelous deeds.

3. Let the heavens be glad
   and the earth rejoice;

   let the sea and what fills it resound;
   let the plains be joyful
   and all that is in them be joyful.
   Then let all the trees
   of the forest rejoice.

4. They shall rejoice before the LORD,
   who comes to govern the earth,
   to govern the world with justice
   and all the peoples with faithfulness.

*Gospel Acclamation verse is available in accompaniment books.

# 76 PSALM 96: PROCLAIM HIS MARVELOUS DEEDS

Pro-claim his mar-vel-ous deeds to all the na-tions.

1. Sing to the LORD, sing a new song;
   sing to the LORD, all you lands.
   Sing to the LORD; bless his name.

2. Announce his salvation, day after day.
   Tell his glory among all the lands;
   among all peoples, his wondrous deeds.

3. Give to the LORD, you families of nations,
   give the LORD glory and praise;
   give to the LORD the glory due his name!

4. Worship the LORD in holy attire.
   Tremble before him, all the earth;
   say among the nations: The LORD is king.
   He governs his people with equity.

## PSALM 96: TODAY A SAVIOR IS BORN

**77**

1. Sing a new song to the Lord.
   Sing to the Lord, all the earth.
   Sing to the Lord, sing to the Lord.
   Sing to the Lord, bless his name!

2. Proclaim his help day by day.
   Tell among the nations his glory.

   Tell of his works, tell of his works,
   and his wonders among all the peoples.

3. Let the heavens rejoice and earth be glad,
   let the sea and all within it thunder praise.
   All of the land, all that it bears:
   rejoice at the presence of the Lord.

## PSALM 97: THE LORD IS KING

**78**

1. Let earth rejoice, the Lord God reigns.
   Exult, you shores; be glad, you plains.
   Justice serves as God's high throne, alleluia!

2. The skies proclaim that God is just:
   God's glory plain to all of us.

   Unseen spirits, join our song, alleluia!

3. You alone bring hope to birth:
   greater you than all the earth.
   Far beyond all other gods, alleluia!

## 79     PSALM 98: ALL THE ENDS OF THE EARTH

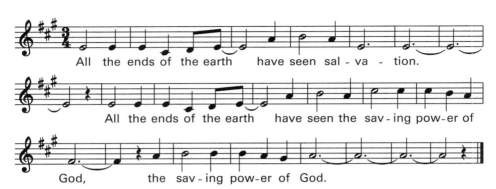

1. Let us sing a new song
   for the wondrous deeds of our God,
   whose holy arm has prevailed,
   bringing salvation and victory.

2. All the ends of the earth
   have seen the power of God.

Ring out your joy, break into song;
all you lands sing praise.

3. Sing the praises of God;
   with the harp and song give praise.
   O trumpets sound! Joyfully sing;
   sing to the ruler of all.

Text: Based on Psalm 98:3, 1, 3–6; Bob Hurd, b. 1950.
Music: Bob Hurd.
Text and music © 1988, Bob Hurd. Published by OCP. All rights reserved.

## 80     PSALM 98: THE LORD HAS REVEALED

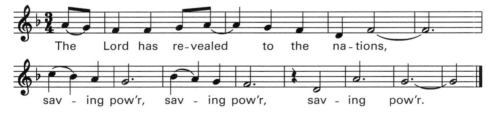

1. Sing a new song, all you lands,
   of the marvelous deeds of the Lord.
   Salvation is born of God's right hand
   and holy arm.

2. The saving power of God
   has been revealed to all the lands.
   His kindness and truth
   forever faithful to the house of Israel.

3. All of the ends of the earth
   have seen the salvation of God.
   Shout to the Lord, dance for joy,
   sing your praise.

4. Play out your song on the harp,
   create a melodious song.
   With trumpets and horn
   acclaim our King and our God.

Text: Based on Psalm 98:1, 2–3, 3–4, 5–6. Refrain © 1969, 1981, ICEL. All rights reserved. Used with permission.
Verses, Timothy R. Smith, b. 1960, © 1996, 2000, Timothy R. Smith. Published by OCP. All rights reserved.
Music: Timothy R. Smith, © 1996, 2000, Timothy R. Smith. Published by OCP. All rights reserved.

## PSALM 98: ALL THE ENDS OF THE EARTH

81

All the ends of the earth have seen the sav-ing pow-er of God.

1. Sing to the LORD a new song,
for he has done wondrous deeds;
his right hand has won vict'ry for him,
his holy arm.

2. The LORD has made
his salvation known:
in the sight of the nations
he has revealed his justice.
He has remembered his kindness
and his faithfulness
toward the house of Israel.

3. All the ends of the earth have seen
the salvation by our God.
Sing joyfully to the LORD, all you lands;
break into song; sing praise.

4. Sing praise to the LORD with the harp,
with the harp and melodious song.
With trumpets and
the sound of the horn
sing joyfully before the King, the LORD.

## PSALM 98: ALL THE ENDS OF THE EARTH

82

All the ends of the earth have

seen the sav-ing pow-er of God.

1. O sing to the Lord a new song,
for he has done wondrous deeds.
Yes, his right hand and holy arm
have won the victory.

2. The Lord has revealed salvation;
his justice prevails on earth.

And to the house of Israel
the Lord bestows his love.

3. Give praise with a soaring melody;
O sing with the strings and harp.
With trumpets and the sound of horn,
acclaim the King, the Lord.

## PSALM 100: WE ARE HIS PEOPLE

83

We are his peo-ple: the sheep of his flock.

1. Sing joyfully to the LORD, all you lands;
serve the LORD with gladness;
come before him with joyful song.

2. Know that the LORD is God,
he made us, his we are;

his people, the flock he tends.

3. The LORD is good:
his kindness endures forever,
and his faithfulness, to all generations.

## 84     PSALM 100: WE ARE GOD'S PEOPLE

We are God's peo-ple, the flock of the Lord.

1. Let all the earth shout for joy.
   Serve the Lord with gladness.
   Sing to the Lord with joyful song.

2. Know that the Lord is God.
   He made us, to him we belong,
   and we are the sheep of his flock.

3. Enter his gates with thanks,
   the courts of the Lord with praise.
   Give thanks and bless his name.

4. Forever God is good.
   His love is everlasting,
   faithful for all generations.

Text: Based on Psalm 100:3b, 1–2, 4, 5; Timothy R. Smith, b. 1960.
Music: Timothy R. Smith.
Text and music © 1996, 2000, Timothy R. Smith. Published by OCP. All rights reserved.

## 85     PSALM 103: THE LORD IS KIND AND MERCIFUL

The Lord is kind, the Lord is kind and mer - ci - ful.

The Lord is kind and mer - ci - ful, mer - ci - ful;

mer - ci - ful is the Lord.

1. O my soul,
   bless the Lord and praise his holy name.
   Bless the Lord, O my soul
   keep in mind what God has done for me.

2. God forgives,
   healing all our pain and sinfulness;
   saves us from an empty life,
   covers us with gentleness and love.

3. Full of grace,
   full of mercy and abundant love,
   slow to anger is the Lord;
   God does not repay us for our sins.

4. Far as the east from the west,
   God placed our sin from us.
   God's compassion rests on us
   like a father's mercy for his own.

Text: Based on Psalm 103:1–2, 3–4, 8–9, 12–13. Refrain © 1969, 1981, 1997, ICEL. All rights reserved. Used with permission.
  Verses, Rick Modlin, b. 1966, © 1999, Rick Modlin. Published by OCP. All rights reserved.
Music: Rick Modlin, © 1999, Rick Modlin. Published by OCP. All rights reserved.

## PSALM 103: THE LORD IS KIND AND MERCIFUL  86

The Lord is kind and mer - ci - ful.

The Lord is kind and mer - ci - ful.

1. Bless the LORD, O my soul;
   and all my being, bless his holy name.
   Bless the LORD, bless the LORD, O my soul,
   and forget not all his benefits.

2. He pardons all your iniquities,
   he heals all your ills.
   He redeems your life from destruction,
   he crowns you with kindness
   and compassion.

3. Merciful and gracious is the LORD,
   slow to anger and abounding in kindness.
   Not according to our sins
   does he deal with us,
   nor does he requite us
   according to our crimes.

4. As far as the east is from the west,
   so far has he put our transgressions from us.
   As a father has compassion on his children,
   so the LORD has compassion
   on those who fear him.

## PSALM 103: THE LORD IS KIND AND MERCIFUL  87

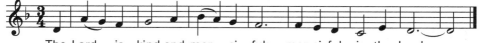

The Lord is kind and mer - ci - ful; mer-ci-ful is the Lord.

1. Bless the LORD, O my soul;
   and all my being, bless his holy name.
   Bless the LORD, O my soul,
   forget not all his benefits.

2. He pardons all your iniquities,
   he heals all your ills.
   He redeems your life from destruction,
   and crowns you with kindness
   and compassion.

3. The LORD secures justice
   and the rights of all the oppressed.
   He has made known his ways to Moses,
   and his deeds to the children of Israel.

4. Merciful and gracious is the LORD,
   slow to anger and abounding in kindness.
   For as the heavens are high above the earth,
   so surpassing is his kindness
   toward those who fear him.

## 88    PSALM 104: SEND FORTH YOUR SPIRIT, O LORD

Send forth your Spir- it, O Lord, and re - new the face of the earth.

1. Bless the Lord, O my soul,
   O Lord, how great you are!
   How many are your works, O Lord,
   the earth is full of your riches!

2. You take back your Spirit, they die,
   back to the dust from which they came;

you send forth your Spirit,
they are created, the whole earth is renewed!

3. Your glory will last forever,
   may you rejoice in all your works.
   May my thoughts be pleasing to you,
   I find my joy in you, Lord.

**Alternate Verses for the Easter Vigil**

1. Bless the Lord, O my soul,
   O Lord, how great you are!
   With glory and with majesty clothed;
   you are covered with light!

2. Foundation of earth you made sure,
   standing firm from age to age.
   You placed the ocean like a robe,
   the waters covered the hills.

3. The valleys are flowing with springs;
   rivers run between the hills;

the birds of heaven dwell on their banks,
they make their nests as they sing.

4. You send down your rain on the hills.
   All your blessings fill the earth.
   You give the cattle grass for their food,
   and plants for crops to be grown.

5. In wisdom you made all these things.
   Lord, they are numberless.
   Your riches fill the whole of the earth.
   Bless the Lord, O my soul!

## 89    PSALM 104: LORD, SEND OUT YOUR SPIRIT

Lord, send out your Spir-it, and re - new the face of the earth.

1. Bless the LORD, O my soul!
   O LORD, my God, you are great indeed!
   How manifold are your works, O LORD!
   The earth is full of your creatures.

2. If you take away their breath,
   they perish and return to their dust.
   When you send forth your spirit,

they are created,
and you renew the face of the earth.

3. May the glory of the LORD endure forever;
   may the LORD be glad in his works!
   Pleasing to him be my theme;
   I will be glad in the LORD.

## PSALM 104: LORD, SEND OUT YOUR SPIRIT    90

Lord, send out your Spir-it, and re-new the face of the earth.

1. Bless the LORD, O my soul!
O LORD, my God, you are great indeed!
How manifold are your works, O LORD!
The earth is full of your creatures;

2. May the glory of the LORD endure forever;
may the LORD be glad in his works!

Pleasing to him be my theme;
I will be glad in the LORD.

3. If you take away their breath, they perish
and return to their dust.
When you send forth your spirit,
they are created,
and you renew the face of the earth.

## PSALM 110: YOU ARE A PRIEST FOR EVER    91

You are a priest for ev-er, in the line of Mel-chiz-e-dek.

1. The LORD said to my Lord:
"Sit at my right hand
till I make your enemies your footstool."

2. The scepter of your power
the LORD will stretch forth from Zion:
"Rule in the midst of your enemies."

3. "Yours is princely power
in the day of your birth,
in holy splendor;
before the daystar,
like the dew, I have begotten you."

4. The LORD has sworn,
and he will not repent:
"You are a priest forever,
according to the order of Melchizedek."

## PSALM 113: BLESSED BE THE NAME OF THE LORD    92

Bless-ed be the name of the Lord for ev-er, for ev-er.

1. Praise, you servants of the LORD,
praise the name of the LORD.
Blessed be the name of the LORD
both now and forever.

2. From the rising to the setting of the sun
is the name of the LORD to be praised.
High above all nations is the LORD;
above the heavens is his glory.

3. Who is like the LORD, our God,
who is enthroned on high
and looks upon the heavens
and the earth below?

4. He raises up the lowly from the dust;
from the dunghill he lifts up the poor
to seat them with princes,
with the princes of his own people.

## 93    PSALM 116: OUR BLESSING-CUP/ I WILL WALK WITH THE LORD/THE CUP OF SALVATION

Refrain I

Our bless-ing-cup is a com-mu-nion with the Blood, the Blood of Christ.

Refrain II

I will walk with the Lord in the land, the land of the liv-ing.

Refrain III

The cup of sal-va-tion I will take, and call the name of the Lord.

Verses

1. How shall I make a return
   for the goodness God has done for me?
   The cup of salvation I will take
   and call God's name.

2. Precious in the eyes of the Lord
   is the dying of his faithful one.

I am the servant of the Lord
who set me free.

3. Sacrifice and thanks I will give
   in the presence of God's chosen ones.
   My vow to the Lord I shall fulfill
   and call God's name.

## 94    PSALM 116: OUR BLESSING-CUP

Our bless-ing-cup is a com-mu-nion in the Blood of Christ.

1. How shall I make a return to the LORD
   for all the good he has done for me?
   The cup of salvation I will take up,
   and I will call upon the name of the LORD.

2. Taste and see, taste and see
   the sweetness of the Lord,
   the goodness of the Lord.

3. Every time you eat of this bread,
   every time you drink of this cup
   you proclaim the death of the Lord
   until he comes.

# PSALM 116: OUR BLESSING-CUP/ EL CÁLIZ QUE BENDECIMOS

**95**

*Estribillo

El cá - liz que ben - de - ci - mos
es la co - mu - nión de la san - gre de Cris - to.

*Refrain

Our bless-ing-cup is a com-mu-nion with the Blood of Christ.

1. ¿Cómo pagaré al Señor
   todo el bien que me ha hecho?
   Alzaré la copa de la salvación,
   invocando tu nombre, Señor.

2. Tenía fe, aún cuando dije:
   "Cómo soy de desgraciado".
   Mucho le cuesta al Señor
   la muerte de sus fieles.

3. Señor, yo soy tu siervo,
   el hijo de tu esclava;
   tú rompiste mis cadenas.
   A ti ofrezco un sacrificio de alabanza,
   invocando tu nombre, Señor.

4. Mis votos al Señor cumpliré
   en presencia de todo su pueblo;
   en el atrio de la casa del Señor,
   en medio de ti, Jerusalén.

1. What shall I return to the LORD
   for all his bounty to me?
   I will lift the cup of salvation
   and call on the name of the LORD.

2. I believed, even when I said,
   "I am greatly afflicted."
   Precious in the eyes of the LORD
   the dying of his faithful ones.

3. O LORD, I am your servant,
   your servant, the son of your handmaid;
   you have brought me freedom.
   To you will I offer sacrifice of thanksgiving
   and call upon your name, O LORD.

4. My vows to the LORD I will pay
   in the presence of all his people,
   in the courts of the house of the LORD,
   in the midst of you, Jerusalem.

*The response may be sung in only one language or bilingually. It is repeated in either case.

## 96     PSALM 116: IN THE PRESENCE OF GOD

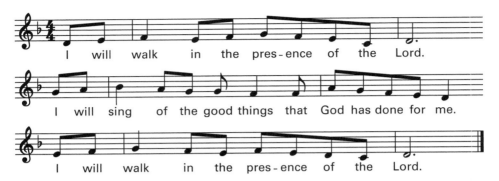

**Verses: Ordinary Time**

1. Love you, I love you;
   you have heard my voice.
   I will call your name, cry out your name,
   as long as I shall live.

2. Comfort me, you care for me,
   you have rescued me.
   You have heard my cry,
   have heard my plea.
   You save my soul from death.

3. Gracious is your hand, O God,
   merciful and just.
   God, your love protects the lowly ones;
   your kindness has no end.

4. Deliver me, deliver me.
   Deliver my soul from death,
   my eyes from tears, my feet from snares.
   In the land of the living, I shall walk.

**Verses: Lent**

1. In my grief, in my pain
   I believed in you.
   How precious is our death to you,
   how precious in your eyes.

2. Here I am, your servant, Lord,
   free to speak your name.

   Words of thanks and praise be on my lips,
   and ever in my heart.

3. I will pay my vows to you,
   here among your people.
   In the presence of your faithful ones,
   I give my life to you.

Text: Based on Psalm 116:9, 1–10, 15–18; Tom Kendzia, b. 1954.
Music: Tom Kendzia.
Text and music © 1996, Tom Kendzia. Published by OCP. All rights reserved.

## 97     PSALM 117: GO OUT TO ALL THE WORLD AND TELL THE GOOD NEWS

1. Praise the LORD, all you nations;
   glorify him, all you peoples!

2. For steadfast is his kindness toward us,
   and the fidelity of the LORD endures forever.

Text: Psalm 117:1, 2. Refrain © 1969, 1981, 1997, ICEL. All rights reserved. Used with permission.
   Verses © 1970, 1997, 1998, CCD. All rights reserved. Used with permission.
Music: Owen Alstott, b. 1947, © 1977, 1990, OCP. All rights reserved.

## PSALM 118: THIS IS THE DAY

**98**

This is the day the Lord has made; let us re-joice and be glad.

This is the day the Lord has made; let us re-joice and be glad.

1. Give thanks to the LORD, for he is good,
his mercy endures forever.
Let the house of Israel say,
"His mercy endures forever."

2. The LORD's right hand has struck with pow'r;
the LORD's right hand is exalted.

I shall not die, but live, and
declare the works of the LORD.

3. The stone which the builders rejected
has become the cornerstone.
By the LORD has this been done;
it is wonderful in our eyes.

## PSALM 118: THIS IS THE DAY

**99**

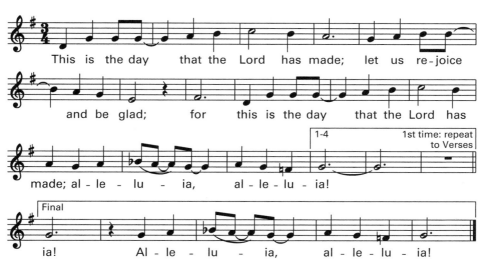

This is the day that the Lord has made; let us re-joice
and be glad; for this is the day that the Lord has
made; al - le - lu - ia, al - le - lu - ia!

1-4
1st time: repeat to Verses

Final
ia! Al - le - lu - ia, al - le - lu - ia!

1. Give thanks to God; the Lord is good.
God's mercy endures forever.
Let the house of Israel say:
"God's mercy endures forever."

2. The Lord's right hand is lifted up;
the hand of the Lord is mighty.

I shall not die, but live to tell
the marvelous works of God.

3. The stone which the builders rejected
has become the cornerstone.
This is the work of the Lord;
how wonderful, how wonderful in our eyes!

# 100 PSALM 118: GIVE THANKS TO THE LORD FOR HE IS GOOD

Give thanks to the Lord for he is good, his love is ev-er-last-ing.

1. Let the house of Israel say,
   "His mercy endures forever."
   Let the house of Aaron say,
   "His mercy endures forever."
   Let those who fear the LORD say,
   "His mercy endures forever."

2. I was hard pressed and was falling,
   but the LORD helped me.
   My strength and my courage is the LORD,

and he has been my savior.
The joyful shout of victory
in the tents of the just:

3. The stone which the builders rejected
   has become the cornerstone.
   By the LORD has this been done;
   it is wonderful in our eyes.
   This is the day the LORD has made;
   let us be glad and rejoice in it.

Text: Psalm 118:2–4, 13–15, 22–24. Refrain © 1969, 1981, 1997, ICEL. All rights reserved. Used with permission.
Verses © 1970, 1997, 1998, CCD. All rights reserved. Used with permission.
Music: John Schiavone, b. 1947, © 2001, John Schiavone. Published by OCP. All rights reserved.

# 101 PSALM 118: THE STONE WHICH THE BUILDERS REJECTED

The stone which the build-ers re-ject-ed has be-come the cor-ner-stone.

Al-le-lu - ia, al-le-lu - ia, has be-come the cor-ner-stone.

1. Let the family of Israel say:
   "God's love has no end,
   God's love has no end."
   Let the family of Aaron say:
   "God's love has no end,
   God's love has no end."
   And let all who fear God,
   and let all who fear God
   say his love is without end.
   Alleluia, alleluia,
   say his love is without end.

2. I called to the Lord in my distress,
   he answered me and set me free.
   God is at my side, God is at my side,
   God is here to help me now.
   Alleluia, alleluia,
   God is here to help me now.

3. Open to me the gates of holiness;
   I will enter and give thanks.
   This is the Lord's own gate,
   the gate where the just may enter in.
   I will thank you, Lord,
   I will thank you, Lord,
   for you hear and answer me.
   Alleluia, alleluia,
   for you hear and answer me.

4. Go forward with branches,
   go forward processing,
   go to the altar of the Lord
   and give thanks to God,
   and give thanks to God
   for his love is without end.
   Alleluia, alleluia,
   for his love is without end.

Text: Psalm 118:1, 2–4, 5–7, 19–21, 27b–29. Refrain © 1963, The Grail (England). All rights reserved. Used with permission
of A.P. Watt, Ltd. Verses, Bernadette Farrell, b. 1957, © 1990, Bernadette Farrell. Published by OCP. All rights reserved.
Music: Bernadette Farrell, © 1990, Bernadette Farrell. Published by OCP. All rights reserved.

## PSALM 122: LET US GO REJOICING 102

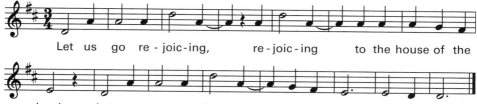

Let us go re-joic-ing, re-joic-ing to the house of the Lord. Let us go re-joic-ing to the house of the Lord.

1. How I rejoiced to hear them say,
   "Let us go to the house of the Lord."
   And now within your walls
   we are standing, O Jerusalem.

2. Jerusalem, a city firmly built,
   knit together in unity and strength.
   There the tribes go up,
   the tribes of the Lord,
   making pilgrimage.

3. There the tribes give thanks
   to the name of the Lord,
   according to the law of Israel.

There are set the thrones of judgment
for the house of David.

4. Let us pray for the good of Jerusalem,
   and for those who love you
   prosperity and peace,
   peace within your ramparts and your towers,
   peace in your dwellings.

5. For the sake of my people and my friends,
   I say peace be to you, Jerusalem.
   For love of God's house
   I pray for you and your prosperity.

## PSALM 122: LET US GO REJOICING 103

Let us go re-joic-ing to the house of the Lord.

1. I rejoiced because they said to me,
   "We will go up to the house of the LORD."
   And now we have set foot
   within your gates, O Jerusalem.

2. A city that the LORD has joined fast,
   unity is yours, O Jerusalem.
   And to it all of the tribes go up,
   the tribes of the LORD.

3. According to the decree for Israel,
   to give thanks to the name of the LORD.

In it there are set up judgment seats,
seats for the house of David.

4. Pray for peace in you, Jerusalem!
   May those who love you prosper and grow!
   And may peace prevail within your walls,
   prosperity in your buildings.

5. Because of friends and relatives I say,
   "Peace be always within you!"
   Because of this house of the LORD, our God,
   I will pray for your good.

## 104    PSALM 126: THE LORD HAS DONE GREAT THINGS

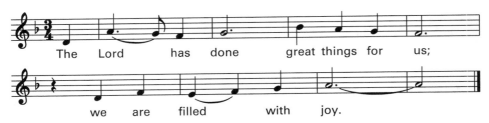

The Lord has done great things for us; we are filled with joy.

1. When the LORD brought back
   the captives of Zion,
   we were like *people dreaming.
   Then our mouth was filled with laughter,
   and our tongue with rejoicing.

2. Then they said among the nations,
   "The LORD has done great things for them."
   The LORD has done great things for us;
   we are glad indeed.

3. Restore our fortunes, O LORD,
   like the torrents in the southern desert.
   Those that sow in tears
   shall reap rejoicing.

4. Although they go forth weeping,
   carrying the seed to be sown,
   They shall come back rejoicing,
   carrying their sheaves.

*Original text "men."

## 105    PSALM 128: O BLESSED ARE THOSE

O blessed are those who fear the Lord and walk in his ways.

1. O blessed are those who fear the Lord
   and walk in his ways!
   By the labor of your hands you shall eat.
   You will be happy and prosper.

2. Your wife like a fruitful vine
   in the heart of your house;

   your children like shoots of the olive
   around your table.

3. Indeed thus shall be blest
   all those who fear the Lord.
   May the Lord bless you from Zion
   all the days of your life!

## 106    PSALM 130: WITH THE LORD THERE IS MERCY

With the Lord there is mer-cy and full-ness of re-

1-5    1st time: repeat to Verses    Final

demp-tion.    demp-tion,    re-demp-tion.

1. Out of the depths I cry to you, O Lord.
   Hear my voice.
   Turn not your ears from the sound
   of my voice pleading.

2. Lord, who could stand
   if you recalled our sins?
   But because of your mercy
   we bow to your name.

3. I hold fast to God, I cling to his word.
   Like watching for dawn I wait for the Lord.
   My soul longs for the Lord.

4. With the Lord is mercy and redemption.
   For the Lord's great kindness
   and the Lord's compassion
   will set Israel free.

## PSALM 130: WITH THE LORD THERE IS MERCY 107

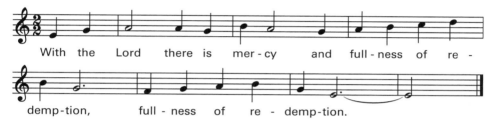

With the Lord there is mer-cy and full-ness of re-demp-tion, full-ness of re-demp-tion.

1. Out of the depths I cry to you, O LORD;
   LORD, hear my voice!
   Let your ears be attentive
   to my voice in supplication.

2. If you, O LORD, mark iniquities,
   LORD, who can stand?
   But with you is forgiveness,
   that you may be revered.

3. I trust in the LORD;
   my soul trusts in his word.
   More than sentinels wait for the dawn,
   let Israel wait for the LORD.

4. For with the LORD is kindness
   and with him is plenteous redemption;
   and he will redeem Israel
   from all their iniquities.

## PSALM 130: WITH THE LORD THERE IS MERCY 108

With the Lord there is mer-cy, and full-ness of re-demp-tion.

1. Out of the depths I cry to you, O LORD;
   LORD, hear my voice!
   Let your ears be attentive
   to my voice in supplication.

2. If you, LORD, mark our iniquities,
   LORD, who can stand?
   But with you is forgiveness,
   and so you may be revered.

3. I trust in the LORD;
   my soul trusts in his word.
   My soul waits for the LORD
   more than sent'nels wait for the dawn.

4. For with the LORD is kindness
   and with him is plenteous redemption;
   and he will redeem Israel
   from all their iniquities.

## 109    PSALM 130: OUT OF THE DEPTHS

Out of the depths, I cry to you, O Lord.

1. From out of the depths,
   I cry to you, Lord;
   O hear the sound of my voice.
   Lord, open your ears and listen to me;
   I plead for your kindness, O God.

2. If you, O Lord, should number our sins,
   then Lord, who would survive?
   But you are forgiveness for our sins;
   for this we adore you, O God.

3. I trust in you, Lord, my soul looks to you
   as watchmen wait for the dawn.
   And more than the watchmen
   wait for the dawn,
   let Israel wait for the Lord.

4. For with you is found forgiveness of sin;
   you show your mercy to all.
   And you will deliver your chosen ones;
   deliver your people, O God.

## 110    PSALM 138: ON THE DAY I CALLED

Lord, on the day I called for help, you an-swered me, you an-swered me.

1. I shall thank you, God of my heart,
   you have heard my troubled word.
   While angels watch, your name I praise;
   I dance before your holy place.

2. For your love and your faithfulness,
   I thank your name,
   your promise surpasses your fame.
   I called for your help
   all night and day long:
   you heard me, and made me strong.

3. From on high,
   from the heavens the poor you see,
   you drive the proud to their knees.
   Though I live
   in the midst of trouble and woe,
   you save me, and foil my foe.

4. Your strong hand shall come to my aid:
   you shall be all good to me.
   Forever shall your love abide;
   do not cast your child aside.

## 111    PSALM 141: O LORD, LET MY PRAYER RISE

Refrain

O Lord, let my prayer rise be-fore you like in-cense,

my hands like an eve - ning of - fer - ing.

Verses

1. Lord, I am calling: hasten to help me.
   Listen to me as I cry to you.
   Let my prayer rise before you like incense,
   my hands like an evening offering.

2. Lord, set a guard at my mouth,
   keep watch at the gate of my lips.
   Let my heart not turn to things that
   are wrong,
   to sharing the evil deeds done by the sinful.
   No, I will never taste their delights.

3. The good may reprove me,
   in kindness chastise me,
   but the wicked shall never anoint my head.
   Every day I counter their malice with prayer.

4. To you, Lord my God, my eyes are turned:
   in you I take refuge; do not forsake me.
   Keep me safe from
   the traps they have set for me,
   from the snares of those who do evil.

Doxology

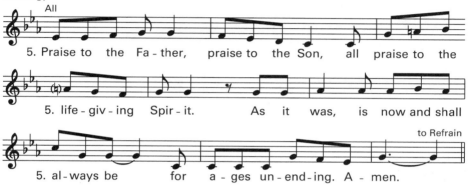

5. Praise to the Fa-ther, praise to the Son, all praise to the

5. life-giv-ing Spir-it. As it was, is now and shall

to Refrain

5. al-ways be for a-ges un-end-ing. A-men.

Text: Based on Psalm 141:1–5, 8–9, Doxology; Paul Inwood, b. 1947.
Music: Paul Inwood.
Text and music © 1984, 1985, Paul Inwood. Published by OCP. All rights reserved.

## Psalm 145: I Will Praise Your Name    112

I will praise your name for ev-er, my king and my God.

1. I will give you glory, O God my king,
   I will bless your name for ever.
   I will bless you day after day
   and praise your name for ever.

2. The Lord is kind and full of compassion,
   slow to anger, abounding in love.
   How good is the Lord to all,
   compassionate to all creation.

3. All your creatures
   shall give you thanks, O Lord,
   and your friends shall repeat their blessing.
   They shall speak of the glory of your reign
   and declare your might, O God.

4. The Lord is faithful in all his words
   and loving in all his deeds.
   The Lord supports all who fall
   and raises up all who are bowed down.

Text: Psalm 145:1–2, 8–9, 10–11, 13–14. Refrain © 1969, ICEL. All rights reserved. Used with permission.
Verses © 1963, The Grail (England). All rights reserved. Used with permission of A.P. Watt, Ltd.
Music: Christopher Willcock, b. 1947, © 1977, 1990, Christopher Willcock, SJ. Published by OCP. All rights reserved.

## 113    PSALM 145: I WILL PRAISE YOUR NAME/ THE HAND OF THE LORD

Refrain          to Verses 1, 3, 4

I will praise your name for ev-er, my king and my God.

Alternate Refrain          to Verses 1, 2, 4

The hand of the Lord feeds us, and an-swers all our needs.

1. God is merciful and gracious,
   slow to anger, full of kindness.
   The Lord is faithful to all his people,
   compassionate to all creation.

2. Lord, we lift our eyes to the heavens,
   and you feed us in due season.
   The treasures, Lord, that you impart
   fulfill every desire.

3. All of your people bless your name
   in a holy song of thanksgiving,
   singing of your eternal reign,
   declaring your holy power.

4. Lord, your justice lasts forever,
   your loving deeds from age to age.
   You are near to all who call,
   never far from faithful hearts.

## 114    PSALM 145: THE LORD IS NEAR/ I WILL PRAISE YOUR NAME

The Lord is near to all who call him.
(Alternate Refrain) I will praise your name for ev - er,

The Lord is near to all who call in truth. truth.
I will praise my king and my God. God.

1. Ev'ry day will I bless you,
   I will praise your name forever and ever.
   Great is the LORD
   and highly to be praised.

2. His greatness is unsearchable.
   The LORD is gracious and merciful,

   slow to anger
   and of great kindness.

3. The LORD is good to all
   and compassionate toward all his works.
   The LORD is just in all his ways
   and holy in all his works.

## PSALM 145: I WILL PRAISE YOUR NAME/ THE HAND OF THE LORD FEEDS US

**115**

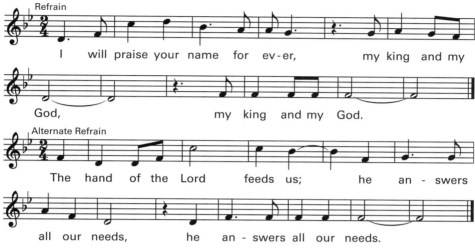

1. I will praise you, God and king;
   I will bless your name forever.
   Every day I will bless you,
   praise your name forever.

2. You are grace and mercy, Lord,
   slow to anger, filled with kindness.
   You are good to all your children,
   loving all creation.

3. Let your works give thanks to you;
   let your faithful ever bless you;
   let them praise your strength, your glory,
   and proclaim your kingdom.

4. Every word you speak in faith,
   every work you do is holy.
   You lift up all who stumble,
   you raise up the lowly.

## PSALM 146: PRAISE THE LORD, MY SOUL

**116**

1. The God of Jacob keeps faith forever,
   secures justice for the oppressed,
   gives food to the hungry.
   The LORD sets captives free.

2. The LORD gives sight to the blind;
   the LORD raises up
   those who were bowed down.

   The LORD loves the just;
   the LORD protects strangers.

3. The fatherless and the widow the LORD sustains,
   but the way of the wicked he thwarts.
   The LORD shall reign forever;
   your God, O Zion, through all generations.
   Alleluia.

**117**  **EXODUS 15: TO GOD BE PRAISE AND GLORY**

Verses
Cantor/Choir                                                                    All

1. I sing ___ to ___ God,  tri-um-phant is  he.
2. O Pha-roah, your ___  ar-my, they sink  like  a  stone. ) To
3. By wa-ter and the  Spir-it,  all blest with new  birth,  }
4. ɤ In sav-ing ___  wa-ters we sink  like  a  stone. )

Cantor/Choir

1-4. God  be praise and glo-ry!  The  horse ___  and  char-iot he
                                  My  God, ___  he plunged them in the
                                  we  work to re-new ___  the
                                  From death in-to  liv-ing we

All

1. cast  in-to  the sea.
2. Red  Sea  all  a-lone.   To  God  be praise  and
3. face  of  the  earth.
4. each  must go  a-lone.

Cantor/Choir

1-4. glo  -  ry!  My  strength ___  and  cour  -  age
                 We  come  to  this  land,  the
                 As  Je-sus  was  raised,  now
                 But  stand  in  the  light  of  this

All                                                    Cantor/Choir

1. comes from  the  Lord.          All
2. moun-tain of  the  free.  To God  be praise and  glo - ry!  The
3. all  death must  die.                                         Come
4. great fam-i-ly;                                               God's

All

1. clothed ___  in  glo-ry,  for  ev-er be  a-dored.
2. peo-ple give thanks in  your sanc-tu-ar  -  y.  } To
3. lift  up  your voice ___  in  one  joy-ful  cry:
4. love will  u-nite  us  and make  us  all  free.

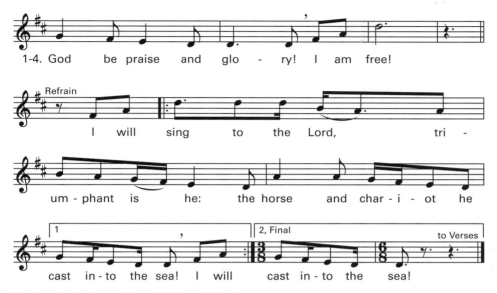

1-4. God be praise and glo - ry! I am free!

Refrain

I will sing to the Lord, tri -

um - phant is he: the horse and char - i - ot he

1. cast in - to the sea! I will | 2, Final cast in - to the sea!

to Verses

Text: Based on Exodus 15:19–21; Janèt Sullivan Whitaker, b. 1958.
Music: Janèt Sullivan Whitaker.

## ISAIAH 12: WE SHALL DRAW WATER                118

We shall draw wa - ter joy - ful-ly, sing-ing joy - ful-ly,

sing-ing joy - ful-ly; we shall draw wa - ter

joy - ful-ly from the well - springs of sal - va - tion.

1. Truly God is our salvation;
   we trust, we shall not fear.
   For the Lord is our strength,
   the Lord is our song;
   he became our Savior.

2. Give thanks, O give thanks to the Lord;
   give praise to his holy name!
   Make his mighty deeds known to
   all of the nations; proclaim his greatness.

3. Sing a psalm, sing a psalm to the Lord
   for he has done glorious deeds.
   Make known his works to all of the earth;
   people of Zion, sing for joy,
   for great in your midst, great in your midst
   is the Holy One of Israel.

Text: Based on Isaiah 12:3, 2, 4–6; Paul Inwood, b. 1947.
Music: Paul Inwood.

# 119     Daniel 3: Glory and Praise for Ever

Glo-ry and praise, glo-ry and praise, glo-ry and praise for ev-er!

1. Blessed are you, O Lord, the God of our fathers,
   praiseworthy and exalted above all forever;
   and blessed is your holy and glorious name, **(to Response I)**

Resp. I: praise-wor-thy and ex - alt-ed a-bove all for all    a - ges.
Resp. II: praise-wor-thy and ex - alt-ed a-bove__ all for - ev - er.

2. Blessed are you in the temple of your holy glory, **(to Response II)**

3. Blessed are you on the throne of your kingdom, **(to Response II)**

4. Blessed are you who look into the depths
   from your throne upon the cherubim, **(to Response II)**

# 120     Luke 1: My Soul Rejoices

My soul re-joic-es    in God, my Sav-ior.    My spir-it finds its

joy in God, the liv-ing God.

1. My soul pro-claims your
2. Your mer-cy flows through-
3. You cast the might - y
4. You fill the hun - gry
5. Just as you prom - ised

1. might-y   deeds. My spir-it sings the great-ness of   your name.
2. out the   land and ev-'ry gen-er-a-tion knows your love.
3. from their thrones and raise the poor and low-ly   to   new life.
4. with good things. With emp-ty hands you send the   rich   a - way.
5. A-bra-ham, you come to free your peo-ple, Is - ra - el.

# LUKE 1: MAGNIFICAT

1. Sing out, my soul, for God has raised and
2. The proud of heart he shall make low and
3. Glo - ry to you, the God of all cre -

1. blessed me And looked on me with kind - ly, lov - ing
2. hum - ble. The gen - tle, poor and hun - gry shall be
3. a - tion. Glo - ry to you, O Christ, the prom - ised

1. eyes. A ser - vant low - ly, yet am I be - lov - ed.
2. filled. O Is - ra - el! God shall up - hold the prom - ise
3. one. Glo - ry to you, O Spir - it of Com - pas - sion.

1. This won - drous God has done great things for me.
2. Made long a - go to you and A - bra - ham.
3. In - spire our hearts to sing our moth - er's song.

1-3. For - ev - er - more, O might - y God of mer - cy,

1-3. I will sing praise, for ho - ly is your name!

Text: 11 10 11 10 11 10; based on Luke 1:46–55; Janèt Sullivan Whitaker, b. 1958, © 2006, Janèt Sullivan Whitaker. Published by OCP. All rights reserved.
Music: FINLANDIA; Jean Sibelius, 1865–1957.

# 122     LUKE 1: CANTICLE OF ZACHARY

Verses 1, 3, 5

1. Blest be the God of  Is - ra - el, The  ev - er - liv - ing Lord, Who
3. Of  old he gave his  sol - emn oath To  Fa - ther A - bra-ham; His
5. The  ris-ing sun shall shine  on  us To  bring the light of  day  To

1. comes in pow'r to save  his own, His  peo-ple Is - ra - el.  For
3. seed  a  might-y race  should be  And  blest for-ev - er-more. He
5. all  who dwell in dark - est night And  shad-ow of  the grave.  Our

1. Is - ra - el  he  rais-es  up  Sal - va-tion's tow'r  on high  In
3. vowed to  set  his  peo-ple free From  fear of  ev - 'ry foe,  That
5. foot-steps God shall  safe-ly guide To  walk the  ways  of peace;  His

1. Da-vid's house who reigned  as king And  ser - vant of  the Lord.
3. we might serve him  all  our days In  good-ness, love, and peace.
5. name for - ev - er - more  be blest, Who  lives and loves and saves.

Verses 2, 4

2. Through  ho - ly proph-ets  did  he  speak His  Word in days of  old,
4. O  ti - ny child, your name shall  be The  proph-et  of  the Lord;

2. That  he would save us from  our  foes And  all who bear us  ill.
4. The  way  of  God you shall  pre - pare To  make his com-ing known.

2. To  our  an - ces-tors did  he give His  cov - e - nant of  love,
4. You shall pro-claim to  Is - ra - el Sal - va-tion's dawn-ing  day,

to Verses 3, 5

2. So  with  us  all he keeps  his  Word In  love that knows no end.
4. When  God shall wipe a - way  all  sins In  his re - deem-ing love.

# LUKE 1: BENEDICTUS

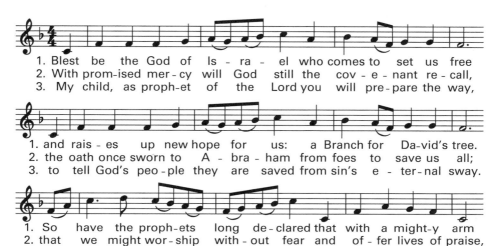

1. Blest be the God of Is - ra - el who comes to set us free
2. With prom-ised mer - cy will God still the cov - e - nant re - call,
3. My child, as proph-et of the Lord you will pre - pare the way,

1. and rais - es up new hope for us: a Branch for Da-vid's tree.
2. the oath once sworn to A - bra - ham from foes to save us all;
3. to tell God's peo - ple they are saved from sin's e - ter - nal sway.

1. So have the proph-ets long de - clared that with a might-y arm
2. that we might wor - ship with - out fear and of - fer lives of praise,
3. Then shall God's mer - cy from on high shine forth and nev - er cease

1. God would turn back our en - e - mies and all who wish us harm.
2. in ho - li - ness and righ-teous-ness to serve God all our days.
3. to drive a - way the gloom of death and lead us in - to peace.

Text: CMD; based on Luke 1:68–79; adapt. by Carl P. Daw, Jr., b. 1944, © 1989, Hope Publishing Co.
  All rights reserved. Used with permission.
Music: FOREST GREEN; trad. English Melody; collected and adapt. by Ralph Vaughan Williams, 1872–1958.

# 124     LUKE 2: SONG OF SIMEON

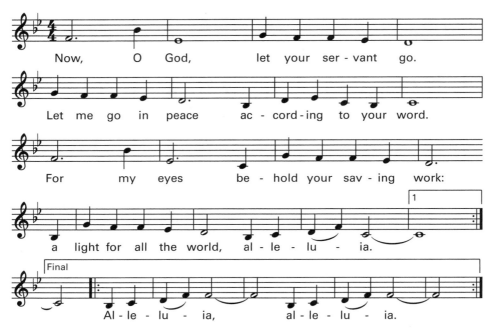

Now,    O    God,     let   your   ser - vant    go.

Let   me   go   in   peace    ac - cord - ing   to   your   word.

For     my    eyes    be - hold   your   sav - ing   work:

a   light   for   all   the   world,   al - le - lu - ia.

Al - le - lu - ia,    al - le - lu - ia.

Text: Based on Luke 2:29–32; *Nunc dimittis*; Janèt Sullivan Whitaker, b. 1958.
Music: Janèt Sullivan Whitaker.

# LUKE 2: CANTICLE OF SIMEON

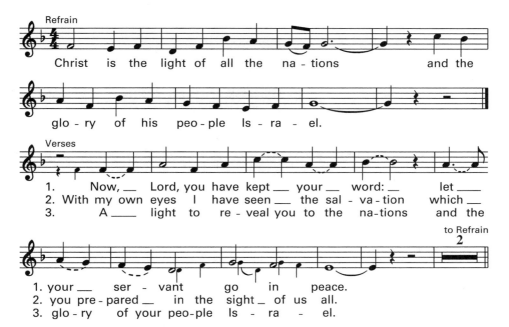

**Refrain**

Christ is the light of all the na - tions and the glo - ry of his peo - ple Is - ra - el.

**Verses**

1. Now, __ Lord, you have kept __ your __ word: __ let __
2. With my own eyes I have seen __ the sal - va - tion which __
3. A __ light to re - veal you to the na - tions and the

to Refrain
2

1. your __ ser - vant go in peace.
2. you pre - pared __ in the sight __ of us all.
3. glo - ry of your peo-ple Is - ra - el.

# RITES OF CHRISTIAN INITIATION

---

## DISMISSAL OF THE CATECHUMENS/ELECT

---

*When the catechumens and the elect are present at liturgy, they are usually dismissed after the homily or preaching. After the dismissal, the catechumens and elect gather with their catechists to pray and break open the scriptures of the day. The following acclamation may be sung during the dismissal to accompany those who are preparing for the sacraments of initiation.*

**126**

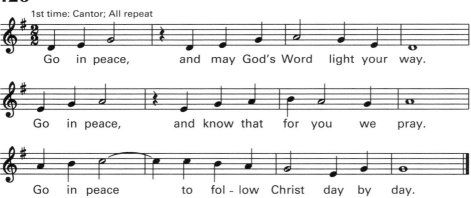

1st time: Cantor; All repeat

Go in peace, and may God's Word light your way.

Go in peace, and know that for you we pray.

Go in peace to fol-low Christ day by day.

Text and music: John Schiavone, b. 1947, © 1997, John Schiavone. Published by OCP. All rights reserved.

*Or*

**127**

May you jour-ney in faith by the light of Christ. May you

live by his gos-pel in spir-it and truth.

Text and music: Dan Schutte, b. 1947, © 2000, Daniel L. Schutte. Published by OCP. All rights reserved.

# SCRUTINIES

*The scrutinies occur on the third, fourth and fifth Sundays of Lent and are accompanied by the readings from Year A. The elect are called before the community to pray for the spirit of repentance. The following song may be sung as the elect are dismissed to continue their reflection on the word of God.*

**128**

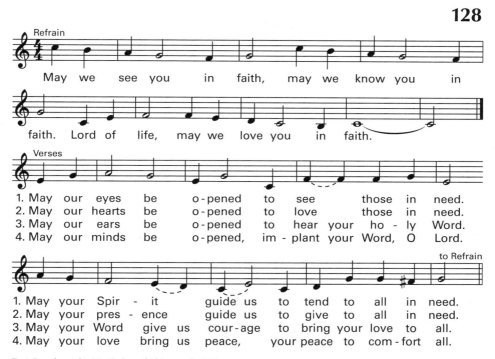

May we see you in faith, may we know you in faith. Lord of life, may we love you in faith.

Verses

1. May our eyes be o-pened to see those in need.
2. May our hearts be o-pened to love those in need.
3. May our ears be o-pened to hear your ho - ly Word.
4. May our minds be o-pened, im - plant your Word, O Lord.

to Refrain

1. May your Spir - it guide us to tend to all in need.
2. May your pres - ence guide us to give to all in need.
3. May your Word give us cour-age to bring your love to all.
4. May your love bring us peace, your peace to com - fort all.

Text: Based on John 9:1–12; Gerard Chiusano, b. 1965.
Music: Gerard Chiusano.

# ORDER OF CHRISTIAN FUNERALS

---

## VIGIL FOR THE DECEASED

---

### INTRODUCTORY RITES

**GREETING**

**OPENING SONG**

**129**

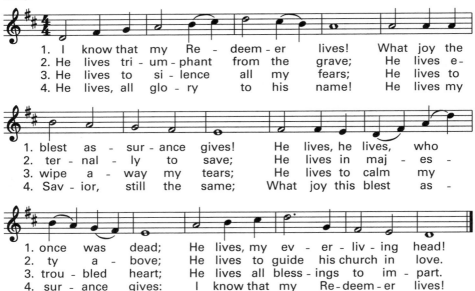

1. I know that my Re - deem - er lives! What joy the
2. He lives tri - um - phant from the grave; He lives e -
3. He lives to si - lence all my fears; He lives to
4. He lives, all glo - ry to his name! He lives my

1. blest as - sur - ance gives! He lives, he lives, who
2. ter - nal - ly to save; He lives in maj - es -
3. wipe a - way my tears; He lives to calm my
4. Sav - ior, still the same; What joy this blest as -

1. once was dead; He lives, my ev - er - liv - ing head!
2. ty a - bove; He lives to guide his church in love.
3. trou - bled heart; He lives all bless - ings to im - part.
4. sur - ance gives: I know that my Re - deem - er lives!

Text: LM; based on Job 19:25; Samuel Medley, 1738–1799, alt.
Music: DUKE STREET; John Hatton, ca. 1710–1793.

**INVITATION TO PRAYER**

**OPENING PRAYER**

# LITURGY OF THE WORD

## FIRST READING

## RESPONSORIAL PSALM     130

Note: Verses available in the accompaniment books.
Text: Psalm 27:1, 4, 7 and 8b and 9a, 13–14. Refrains © 1969, 1981, 1997, ICEL. All rights reserved. Used with permission.
Music: John Schiavone, b. 1947, © 2001, John Schiavone. Published by OCP. All rights reserved.

## GOSPEL

## HOMILY/PREACHING

# PRAYER OF INTERCESSION

## LITANY     131

Response: 1st time: Cantor, All repeat; thereafter: All

Text: *Order of Christian Funerals*, © 1985, ICEL. All rights reserved. Used with permission.
Music: Based on *Dies Irae*; Chant, Mode I; Michael R. Prendergast, b. 1955, © 2002, Michael R. Prendergast.
   Published by OCP. All rights reserved.

## THE LORD'S PRAYER

## CONCLUDING PRAYER

*A member or friend of the family may speak in remembrance of the deceased.*

# CONCLUDING RITE

## BLESSING

*The vigil may conclude with a song or a few moments of silent prayer or both.*

# FUNERAL MASS

## RITE OF RECEPTION AT THE CHURCH

*The presiding minister greets the mourners at the entrance of the church. As a baptismal remembrance the coffin is sprinkled with holy water and the pall may be placed on the coffin. The funeral procession then moves into the church accompanied by the following or another appropriate song.*

### PROCESSIONAL SONG
### 132

Grant them e-ter-nal rest, O Lord, and let per-pet-u-al light shine up-on them.

Note: Verses available in the accompaniment books.
Text and music: Owen Alstott, b. 1947, © 1983, OCP. All rights reserved.

*A symbol of Christian life may be carried in procession, then placed on the coffin.*

*If the introductory rites have not taken place at the church door, the liturgy begins in the usual manner with a song, the greeting, and the penitential rite.*

### OPENING PRAYER

## LITURGY OF THE WORD

*Appropriate readings should be chosen from those provided in the Order of Christian Funerals or the Lectionary.*

### READINGS

*Either one or two readings from scripture may be read before the Gospel reading.*

### RESPONSORIAL PSALM
### 133

The Lord is my shep-herd; there is noth-ing I shall want.

Note: Verses available in the accompaniment books.
Text: Psalm 23:1–3a, 3b–4, 5, 6. Refrain © 1969, 1981, 1997, ICEL. All rights reserved. Used with permission.
Music: John Schiavone, b. 1947, © 2001, John Schiavone. Published by OCP. All rights reserved.

### GOSPEL ACCLAMATION

### GOSPEL

## HOMILY

## GENERAL INTERCESSIONS

# LITURGY OF THE EUCHARIST
# FINAL COMMENDATION

*If the Final Commendation takes place in church, the ministers go to a place near the coffin. After a silent prayer, the coffin may be sprinkled with holy water and honored with incense. Meanwhile, the following or another appropriate hymn (see Funeral section, No. 550–562) may be sung.*

## SONG OF FAREWELL 134

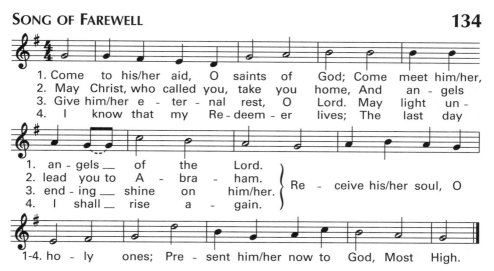

1. Come to his/her aid, O saints of God; Come meet him/her,
2. May Christ, who called you, take you home, And an - gels
3. Give him/her e - ter - nal rest, O Lord. May light un -
4. I know that my Re - deem - er lives; The last day

1. an - gels __ of the Lord.
2. lead you to A - bra - ham.
3. end - ing __ shine on him/her.   Re - ceive his/her soul, O
4. I shall __ rise a - gain.

1-4. ho - ly ones; Pre - sent him/her now to God, Most High.

Text: LM; *Subvenite sancti Dei; Requiem aeternam; Credo quod Redemptor;* tr. by Dennis C. Smolarski, SJ, b. 1947,
© 1981, Dennis C. Smolarski, SJ. All rights reserved. Used with permission.
Music: OLD HUNDREDTH; *Genevan Psalter,* 1551; attr. to Louis Bourgeois, ca. 1510–1561, alt.

## PRAYER OF COMMENDATION

## PROCESSION TO THE PLACE OF COMMITTAL

*After the prayer, the following or another appropriate psalm or hymn is sung while the coffin is being carried to the place of committal.*

135

Response: 1st time: Cantor, All repeat; thereafter: All

Lord, have mer - cy. Lord, have mer - cy.

Note: Intercessions available in the accompaniment books.
Text: *Order of Christian Funerals,* © 1985, ICEL. All rights reserved. Used with permission.
Music: Based on *Dies Irae;* Chant, Mode I; Michael R. Prendergast, b. 1955, © 2002, 2006, Michael R. Prendergast.
Published by OCP. All rights reserved.

*Or*

**136**

In pa - ra - dí - sum de - dú - cant te án - ge - li:
*May an - gels guide you and bring you in - to par - a - dise:*

in tu - o ad - vén - tu su - scí - pi - ant te már - ty - res,
*and may all the mar - tyrs come forth to wel - come you home;*

et per - dú - cant te in ci - vi - tá - tem san - ctam
*and may they lead you in - to the ho - ly cit - y,*

Je - rú - sa - lem. Cho - rus an - ge - ló - rum te___
*Je - ru - sa - lem. May the an - gel cho - rus sing___*

su - scí - pi - at, et cum Lá - za - ro quon - dam
*to wel - come you, and like Laz - a - rus, for - got -*

páu - pe - re ae - tér - nam há - be - as ré - qui - em.
*ten and poor, you shall have ev - er - last - ing rest.*

Text: *In paradisum* and *Chorus angelorum*; Latin, 11th cent.; English tr. by Owen Alstott, b. 1947, © 1987, OCP.
  All rights reserved.
Music: Chant, Mode VII and Mode VIII.

# EUCHARISTIC EXPOSITION & BENEDICTION

*During the celebration of this rite there should be prayers, songs, readings, silent prayer and a homily or preaching to direct the attention of the faithful to the worship of Christ the Lord.*

## EXPOSITION

*The following or another suitable eucharistic song or seasonal psalm is sung.*

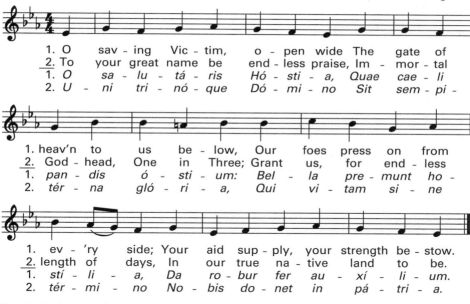

1. O sav - ing Vic - tim, o - pen wide The gate of
2. To your great name be end - less praise, Im - mor - tal
1. *O sa - lu - tá - ris Hó - sti - a, Quae cae - li*
2. *U - ni tri - nó - que Dó - mi - no Sit sem - pi -*

1. heav'n to us be - low, Our foes press on from
2. God - head, One in Three; Grant us, for end - less
1. *pan - dis ó - sti - um: Bel - la pre - munt ho -*
2. *tér - na gló - ri - a, Qui vi - tam si - ne*

1. ev - 'ry side; Your aid sup - ply, your strength be - stow.
2. length of days, In our true na - tive land to be.
1. *stí - li - a, Da ro - bur fer au - xí - li - um.*
2. *tér - mi - no No - bis do - net in pá - tri - a.*

Text: LM; *O Salutaris*; St. Thomas Aquinas, 1227–1274; tr. by Edward Caswall, 1814–1878, alt.
Music: DUGUET; attr. to Abbé Dieudonne Duguet, 1794–1849.

## ADORATION

*The Liturgy of the Hours may be celebrated during the period of exposition, or there may be prayers, songs, readings from the Word of God and a brief homily or preaching along with time for silent prayer.*

*Psalms 23, 34, 72, 84, 85, 122 or 128 may be sung during the period of adoration (see Psalms section, No. 15–116).*

## BENEDICTION

℣. You have given them Bread from heaven. (Easter: alleluia)
℟. **Having within it all Sweetness. (Easter: alleluia)**

*The minister incenses the Blessed Sacrament while the following or another appropriate song is sung.*

## 138

1. Tan - tum er - go Sac - ra - mén - tum Ve - ne - ré - mur
2. Ge - ni - tó - ri, Ge - ni - tó - que Laus et ju - bi -
1. *Ho - ly sac - ra - ment, most ho - ly, Let us bow on*
2. *God Be - get - ter and Be - got - ten, Yours be praise and*

1. cér - nu - i: Et an - tí - quum do - cu - mén - tum
2. lá - ti - o, Sa - lus, ho - nor, vir - tus quo - que
1. *bend - ed knee: Vi - sions of the an - cient prom - ise*
2. *maj - es - ty, Hon - or, glo - ry and sal - va - tion,*

1. No - vo ce - dat rí - tu - i: Prae - stet fi - des
2. Sit et be - ne - dí - cti - o: Pro - ce - dén - ti
1. *Now ful - filled in mys - te - ry. Faith de - clares what*
2. *Bless - ing for e - ter - ni - ty, With the One pro -*

1. sup - ple - mén - tum Sén - su - um de - fé - ctu - i.
2. ab u - tró - que Com - par sit lau - dá - ti - o.
1. *none dare fath - om; Faith re - veals what none may see.*
2. *ceed - ing al - ways, E - qual - ly in u - ni - ty.*

Text: 87 87 87; *Tantum ergo*; St. Thomas Aquinas, 1227–1274; tr. by Harry Hagan, OSB, b. 1947,
© 1990, St. Meinrad Archabbey. Published by OCP. All rights reserved.
Music: ST. THOMAS (TANTUM ERGO); John F. Wade, 1711–1786.

*After a prayer, the priest or deacon blesses those present with the Blessed Sacrament.*

## REPOSITION

*While a minister places the Blessed Sacrament in the tabernacle the people may sing or recite the following or other appropriate acclamations or hymns.*

## 139

Cantor sings each invocation first; assembly repeats

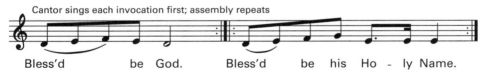

Bless'd be God. Bless'd be his Ho - ly Name.

Bless'd be Je - sus Christ, true God and true Man.

Bless'd be the Name of Je - sus. Bless'd be his most Sa - cred Heart.

Bless'd be his most Pre - cious Blood. Bless'd be Je - sus in the most Ho - ly

Sac - ra - ment of the Al - tar. Bless'd be the Ho - ly

Spir - it, the Par - a - clete. Bless'd be the great Moth - er of God,

Ma - ry most ho - ly. Bless'd be her ho - ly and Im -

ma - cu - late Con - cep - tion. Bless'd be her glo - ri - ous As - sump - tion.

Bless'd be the name of Ma - ry, Vir - gin and Moth - er.

Bless'd be Saint Jo - seph, her most chaste spouse.

*(Fine)*

Bless'd be God in his an - gels. Bless'd be God in his saints.

Text: The Divine Praises.
Music: John Schiavone, b. 1947, © 1990, John Schiavone. Published by OCP. All rights reserved.

# THE ORDER OF MASS

*At the Eucharist, the Church comes together to hear the Word of the Lord, to pray for the world's needs, to offer the sacrifice of the Cross in praise and thanks to God, to receive Christ Jesus in Communion, and then to be sent forth in the Spirit as disciples of the Gospel. Through the experience of these sacred mysteries in the liturgy, the "summit toward which the activity of the Church is directed," the people of God are renewed and given new strength to live out the Christian faith daily (Sacrosanctum Concilium, No. 10).*

## 140      THE INTRODUCTORY RITES

*As the Church gathers, "the faithful, who come together as one, establish communion and dispose themselves properly to listen to the Word of God and to celebrate the Eucharist worthily" (GIRM, No. 46).*

### ENTRANCE CHANT         *STAND*

*A processional chant or hymn may be sung.*

### GREETING

*After the Entrance Chant, all make the Sign of the Cross.*

> In the name of the Father, and of the Son, and of the Holy Spirit.

**A - men.**

*Any of the three forms of Greeting may be used.*

> The grace of our Lord Jesus Christ,…be with you all.

*Or*     Grace to you and peace from God our Father and the Lord Jesus Christ.

*Or*     The Lord be with you.

*Or*     *(A Bishop says, "Peace be with you.")*

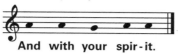

And with your spir-it.

## RITE FOR THE BLESSING AND SPRINKLING OF WATER

*From time to time on Sundays, especially in Easter Time, there may be a blessing and sprinkling of holy water to recall Baptism. This replaces the Penitential Act below. For music during the sprinkling, see No. 166, 167, 242, 254–256. Continue with the "Gloria," No. 146, except on Sundays of Advent, Ash Wednesday and Sundays of Lent.*

## PENITENTIAL ACT *(Omit on Ash Wednesday)*

*The celebration of God's mercy takes one of the following forms:*

**141**

**I confess to almighty God
and to you, my brothers and sisters,
that I have greatly sinned,
in my thoughts and in my words,
in what I have done and in what I have failed to do,**
*(Strike breast)* **through my fault, through my fault,
through my most grievous fault;
therefore I ask blessed Mary ever-Virgin,
all the Angels and Saints,
and you, my brothers and sisters,
to pray for me to the Lord our God.**

May almighty God have mercy on us,
forgive us our sins,
and bring us to everlasting life.

A - men.

*Continue with the "Lord, Have Mercy/Kyrie," No. 144 or No. 145.*

## 142

*Or* Have mercy on us, O Lord.

**For we have sinned a - gainst you.**

Show us, O Lord, your mercy.

**And grant us your sal - va - tion.**

May almighty God have mercy on us,
forgive us our sins,
and bring us to everlasting life.

**A - men.**

*Continue with the "Lord, Have Mercy/Kyrie," No. 144 or No. 145.*

## 143

*Or  Invocation…*

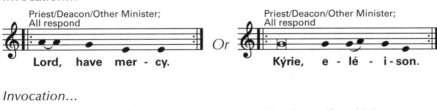

Priest/Deacon/Other Minister;
All respond

**Lord, have mer - cy.**  *Or*  **Kýrie, e - lé - i - son.**

*Invocation…*

Priest/Deacon/Other Minister;
All respond

**Christ, have mer - cy.**  *Or*  **Christe, e - lé - i - son.**

*Invocation…*

Priest/Deacon/Other Minister;
All respond

**Lord, have mer - cy.**  *Or*  **Kýrie, e - lé - i - son.**

May almighty God have mercy on us,
forgive us our sins,
and bring us to everlasting life.

A - men.

*Continue with the "Gloria," No. 146, except on Sundays of Advent,
Ash Wednesday and Sundays of Lent.*

## LORD, HAVE MERCY/KYRIE     144

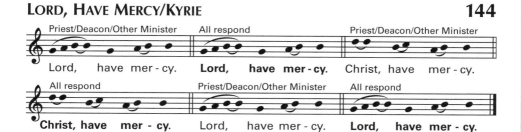

Lord, have mer - cy. **Lord, have mer - cy.** Christ, have mer - cy.

**Christ, have mer - cy.** Lord, have mer - cy. **Lord, have mer - cy.**

*Or*     145

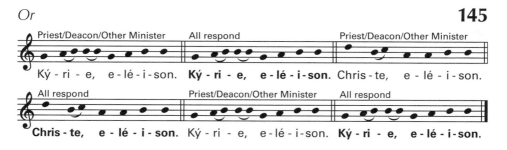

Ký - ri - e, e - lé - i - son. **Ký - ri - e, e - lé - i - son.** Chris - te, e - lé - i - son.

**Chris - te, e - lé - i - son.** Ký - ri - e, e - lé - i - son. **Ký - ri - e, e - lé - i - son.**

*Or*

**Ký - ri - e, e - lé - i - son.**

## GLORIA

*Except on Sundays of Advent, Ash Wednesday and Sundays of Lent, all sing or say:*

## 146

Glo-ry to God in the high-est, and on earth peace to peo-ple of good will.

We praise you, we bless you, we a-dore you, we glo-ri-fy you,

we give you thanks for your great glo-ry, Lord God, heav-en-ly King,

O God, al-might-y Fa-ther. Lord Je-sus Christ, On-ly Be-got-ten Son,

Lord God, Lamb of God, Son of the Fa-ther, you take a-way the sins of the world,

have mer-cy on us; you take a-way the sins of the world,

re-ceive our prayer; you are seat-ed at the right hand of the Fa-ther,

have mer-cy on us. For you a-lone are the Ho-ly One, you a-lone are the Lord,

you a-lone are the Most High, Je-sus Christ, with the Ho-ly Spir-it,

in the glo-ry of God the Fa - ther. A - men.

*Or*   **Glory to God in the highest,**
**and on earth peace to people of good will.**

**We praise you,**
**we bless you,**
**we adore you,**
**we glorify you,**
**we give you thanks for your great glory,**
**Lord God, heavenly King,**
**O God, almighty Father.**

**Lord Jesus Christ, Only Begotten Son,**
**Lord God, Lamb of God, Son of the Father,**
**you take away the sins of the world,**
    **have mercy on us;**
**you take away the sins of the world,**
    **receive our prayer;**
**you are seated at the right hand of the Father,**
    **have mercy on us.**

**For you alone are the Holy One,**
**you alone are the Lord,**
**you alone are the Most High,**
**Jesus Christ,**
**with the Holy Spirit,**
**in the glory of God the Father.**
**Amen.**

## COLLECT

*After a period of silence, the Priest says the Collect, and all respond:*

   **Amen.**

---

# THE LITURGY OF THE WORD          147

---

*The Lectionary (book of readings) and the Book of Gospels open the rich trea-sure of God's word from the Jewish and Christian Scriptures. Sunday readings follow a three-year cycle: Year A emphasizes the Gospel of Matthew, Year B the Gospel of Mark, Year C the Gospel of Luke. The Church proclaims the Gospel of John especially during the seasons of Lent and Easter.*

## FIRST READING

*After the reading, the reader says, "The word of the Lord," and all respond:*

**Thanks be to God.**

## RESPONSORIAL PSALM

*For music for the responsorial psalm see No. 15–125.*

## SECOND READING

*After the reading, the reader says, "The word of the Lord," and all respond:*

**Thanks be to God.**

## GOSPEL ACCLAMATION

*The assembly welcomes the proclamation of the Gospel by singing an acclamation. If it cannot be sung, it is to be omitted. For music, see Mass Settings and No. 259–264 . During Lent, see Mass Settings and No. 265–266.*

## GOSPEL

*Before the Gospel, the Deacon/Priest says, "The Lord be with you," and all respond:*

**And with your spirit.**

*The Deacon/Priest says, "A reading from the holy Gospel according to N.," and all respond:*

**Glory to you, O Lord.**

*After the Gospel reading, the Deacon/Priest says, "The Gospel of the Lord," and all respond:*

**Praise to you, Lord Jesus Christ.**

## HOMILY

*The Priest or Deacon preaches the good news of Christ's saving mystery.*

## DISMISSAL OF THE CATECHUMENS AND THE ELECT

*In Masses at which catechumens or elect are present for the Liturgy of the Word, the Priest may use these or similar words:*

My dear friends, this community now sends you forth to reflect more deeply upon the word of God which you have shared with us today. Be assured of our loving support and prayers for you. We look forward to the day when you will share fully in the Lord's Table.

*A song may be sung while the catechumens/elect are dismissed (see No. 126, 127, 520).*

## PROFESSION OF FAITH

*On Sundays and solemnities, all sing or say the Nicene Creed (for music, see No. 267):*

I believe in one God,
the Father almighty,
maker of heaven and earth,
of all things visible and invisible.

I believe in one Lord Jesus Christ,
the Only Begotten Son of God,
born of the Father before all ages.
God from God, Light from Light,
true God from true God,
begotten, not made, consubstantial with the Father;
through him all things were made.
For us men and for our salvation
he came down from heaven,

*At the words that follow, up to and including "and became man," all bow.*

and by the Holy Spirit was incarnate of the Virgin Mary,
and became man.

For our sake he was crucified under Pontius Pilate,
he suffered death and was buried,
and rose again on the third day
in accordance with the Scriptures.
He ascended into heaven
and is seated at the right hand of the Father.
He will come again in glory
to judge the living and the dead
and his kingdom will have no end.

I believe in the Holy Spirit, the Lord, the giver of life,
who proceeds from the Father and the Son,
who with the Father and the Son is adored and glorified,
who has spoken through the prophets.

I believe in one, holy, catholic and apostolic Church.
I confess one Baptism for the forgiveness of sins
and I look forward to the resurrection of the dead
and the life of the world to come. Amen.

*Instead of the Nicene (Niceno-Constantinopolitan) Creed, especially during Lent and Easter Time, the baptismal Symbol of the Roman Church, known as the Apostles' Creed, may be used.*

*STAND*

**I believe in God,**
**the Father almighty,**
**Creator of heaven and earth,**
**and in Jesus Christ, his only Son, our Lord,**

*At the words that follow, up to and including "the Virgin Mary," all bow.*

**who was conceived by the Holy Spirit,**
**born of the Virgin Mary,**
**suffered under Pontius Pilate,**
**was crucified, died and was buried;**
**he descended into hell;**
**on the third day he rose again from the dead;**
**he ascended into heaven,**
**and is seated at the right hand of God the Father almighty;**
**from there he will come to judge the living and the dead.**

**I believe in the Holy Spirit,**
**the holy catholic Church,**
**the communion of saints,**
**the forgiveness of sins,**
**the resurrection of the body,**
**and life everlasting. Amen.**

## UNIVERSAL PRAYER *(Prayer of the Faithful)*

*As a priestly people, we unite with one another to pray for today's needs in the Church and the world. The Deacon, cantor or other minister offers the petitions and then says or sings:*

We pray to the Lord.
**Lord, hear our prayer.**

**149**

Deacon/Cantor/Other Minister      All

*(Intercessions)*   Let us pray   to the Lord.   **Lord, hear our prayer.**

Music: Byzantine chant.

*Christians are baptized into the paschal mystery of Christ's death and resurrection for the forgiveness of sin and fullness of salvation. This mystery is celebrated at every Mass, remembering Christ's loving deed and giving thanks and praise to God. By this action the "Sacrifice of the Cross is continuously made present in the Church" (GIRM, No. 72).*

## PRESENTATION AND PREPARATION OF THE GIFTS                    *SIT*

*The gifts are brought forward. If no chant is sung, the Priest may pray aloud, and all may respond:*

**Blessed be God for ever.**

*The Priest prays "…that my sacrifice and yours may be acceptable to God, the almighty Father," and all respond:*

*STAND*

**151**

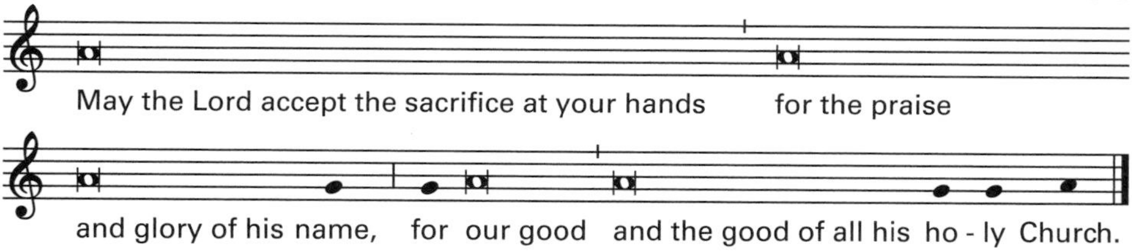

May the Lord accept the sacrifice at your hands for the praise and glory of his name, for our good and the good of all his ho - ly Church.

*Or* **May the Lord accept the sacrifice at your hands
for the praise and glory of his name,
for our good
and the good of all his holy Church.**

## PRAYER OVER THE OFFERINGS

*The Priest says the Prayer over the Offerings; following this, the people respond:*

**Amen.**

# THE EUCHARISTIC PRAYER

## PREFACE

*The Eucharistic Prayer begins with a dialogue between the Priest and the assembly.*

## 152

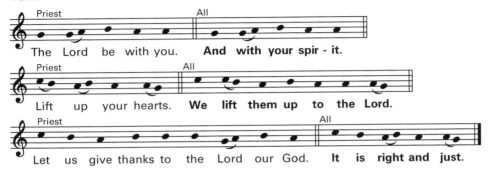

Priest — The Lord be with you. **And with your spir - it.**

Priest — Lift up your hearts. **We lift them up to the Lord.**

Priest — Let us give thanks to the Lord our God. **It is right and just.**

*At the conclusion of the Preface, the following acclamation is sung or said by all:*

## HOLY

## 153

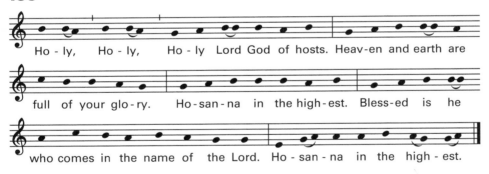

Ho - ly, Ho - ly, Ho - ly Lord God of hosts. Heav-en and earth are full of your glo - ry. Ho-san-na in the high-est. Bless-ed is he who comes in the name of the Lord. Ho - san - na in the high - est.

*KNEEL*

*After the words of institution of the Eucharist, the Priest sings or says:*

The mystery of faith.

*All respond:*

**154**

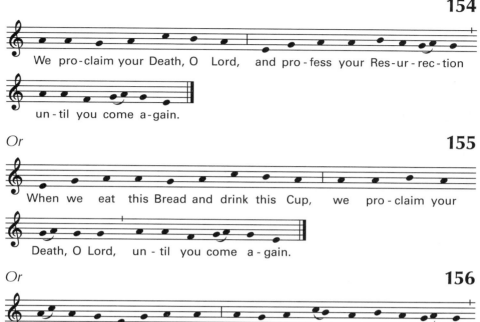

We pro-claim your Death, O Lord, and pro-fess your Res-ur-rec-tion

un-til you come a-gain.

*Or* **155**

When we eat this Bread and drink this Cup, we pro-claim your

Death, O Lord, un-til you come a-gain.

*Or* **156**

Save us, Sav-ior of the world, for by your Cross and Res-ur-rec-tion

you have set us free.

*The Eucharistic Prayer culminates and concludes when the Priest sings or says:*

Through him, and with him, and in him,
O God, almighty Father,
in the unity of the Holy Spirit,
all glory and honor is yours,
for ever and ever.

A - men.

# THE COMMUNION RITE

## THE LORD'S PRAYER

*STAND*

*The Priest invites all to join in the Lord's Prayer:*

**157**

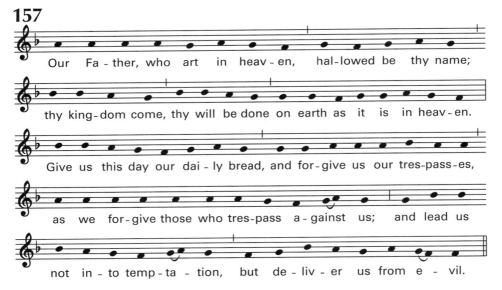

Our Fa-ther, who art in heav-en, hal-lowed be thy name; thy king-dom come, thy will be done on earth as it is in heav-en. Give us this day our dai-ly bread, and for-give us our tres-pass-es, as we for-give those who tres-pass a-gainst us; and lead us not in-to temp-ta-tion, but de-liv-er us from e-vil.

> Deliver us, Lord, we pray, from every evil,
> graciously grant peace in our days,
> that, by the help of your mercy,
> we may be always free from sin
> and safe from all distress,
> as we await the blessed hope
> and the coming of our Savior, Jesus Christ.

For the king-dom, the power and the glo-ry are yours now and for ev-er.

Music: Chant; adapt. by Robert J. Snow, 1926–1998.

## SIGN OF PEACE

> Lord Jesus Christ,
> who said to your Apostles:
> Peace I leave you, my peace I give you,
> look not on our sins,
> but on the faith of your Church,
> and graciously grant her peace and unity
> in accordance with your will.
> Who live and reign for ever and ever.

**A - men.**

The peace of the Lord be with you always.

**And with your spir-it.**

Let us offer each other the sign of peace.

*The people exchange a sign of peace, according to local custom.*

## LAMB OF GOD

*During the breaking of the bread and the commingling, the following litany is sung and may be repeated several times until the fraction rite is completed, ending only the final time with "grant us peace."*

**158**

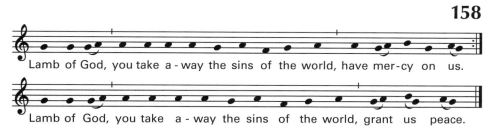

Lamb of God, you take a - way the sins of the world, have mer-cy on us.

Lamb of God, you take a - way the sins of the world, grant us peace.

*The faithful kneel after the "Agnus Dei" ("Lamb of God") unless the Diocesan Bishop determines otherwise.*

## COMMUNION

*KNEEL*

Behold the Lamb of God,
behold him who takes away the sins of the world.
Blessed are those called to the supper of the Lamb.

*All respond:*

**159**

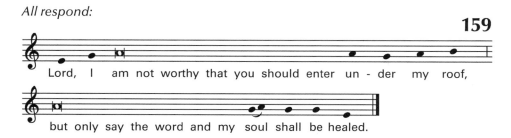

Lord, I am not worthy that you should enter un - der my roof,

but only say the word and my soul shall be healed.

*Or* **Lord, I am not worthy
that you should enter under my roof,
but only say the word
and my soul shall be healed.**

## COMMUNION CHANT

*While the Priest is receiving the Sacrament, the Communion Chant or song is begun.*

*The minister of Communion says,* STAND

"*The Body of Christ" or "The Blood of Christ"*

*and the communicant answers:*

**Amen.**

## PERIOD OF SILENCE OR SONG OF PRAISE SIT (OR KNEEL)

*A period of silence may now be observed, or a psalm or song of praise may be sung.*

## PRAYER AFTER COMMUNION STAND

*The Communion Rite concludes with a prayer to which all respond:*

**Amen.**

*On Thursday of the Lord's Supper, the Evening Mass concludes at this point with the Transfer of the Most Blessed Sacrament.*

---

# 160 THE CONCLUDING RITES

---

## GREETING

The Lord be with you.

**And with your spir-it.**

## FINAL BLESSING

May almighty God bless you,
the Father, and the Son, † and the Holy Spirit.

**A - men.**

*A Solemn Blessing or Prayer over the People may be chosen by the Priest, in place of the above blessing.*

## Dismissal

*The Deacon/Priest invites all to go in the peace of Christ:*

**161**

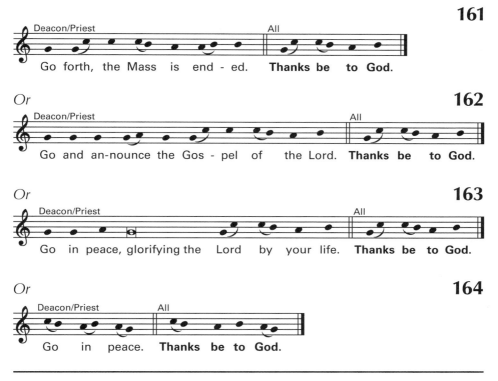

Deacon/Priest   All

Go forth, the Mass is end-ed. **Thanks be to God.**

*Or* **162**

Deacon/Priest   All

Go and an-nounce the Gos-pel of the Lord. **Thanks be to God.**

*Or* **163**

Deacon/Priest   All

Go in peace, glorifying the Lord by your life. **Thanks be to God.**

*Or* **164**

Deacon/Priest   All

Go in peace. **Thanks be to God.**

---

*At the Easter Vigil in the Holy Night, Easter Sunday during the Day, the Octave of Easter, and the Vigil Mass and Mass during the Day on Pentecost Sunday:*

**165**

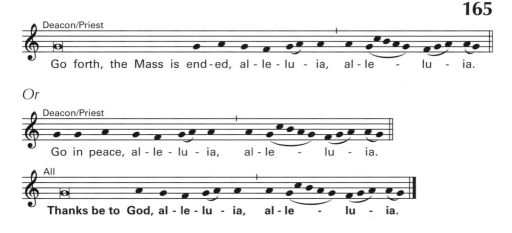

Deacon/Priest

Go forth, the Mass is end-ed, al-le-lu-ia, al-le - lu - ia.

*Or*

Deacon/Priest

Go in peace, al-le-lu-ia, al-le - lu - ia.

All

**Thanks be to God, al-le-lu-ia, al-le - lu - ia.**

---

*A final psalm or hymn may be sung.*

# MASS SETTINGS

The music with which the Church celebrates the Eucharist has developed over the centuries, clothing ancient ritual elements in idioms expressive of the assembly's faith. A broad range of settings — contemporary, gospel, and traditional — invigorates the assembly's celebration and expands its vocabulary of praise. Each of these offers a unified musical approach to the Order of Mass.

## CHANT MASS

**166**     **ASPERGES ME**

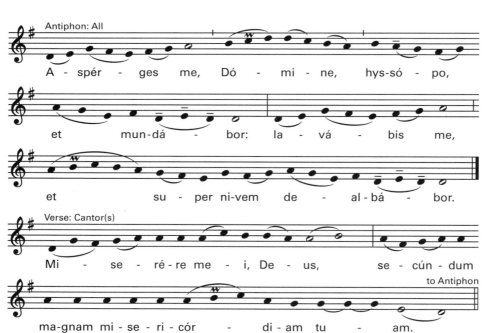

Note: For use in all seasons but Eastertide.
English translation of antiphon: *Sprinkle me with hyssop, O Lord, and I shall be cleansed; wash me and I shall be whiter than snow.*
Translation of the verse (Psalm 51:1): *Have mercy on me, O God, according to your great compassion.*
English translation of the antiphon © 2010, ICEL. All rights reserved. Used with permission.

Text and music: *Chant Mass*; Chant, Mode VII; *Graduale Romanum*, 1974.

# VIDI AQUAM

**Antiphon: All**

Vi - di a - quam e - gre - di - én - tem de tem - plo, a lá - te - re dex - tro, al - le - lú - ia; et o - mnes, ad quos per - vé - nit a - qua i - sta, sal - vi fa - cti sunt et di - cent: Al - le-lú - ia, al - le - lú - ia.

Verse (Cantor): Confitémini Dómino...misericórdia eius. **(to Antiphon)**

Note: For use during Eastertide
English translation of antiphon: *I saw water flowing from the Temple, from its right-hand side, alleluia;*
  *and all to whom this water came were saved and shall say: Alleluia, alleluia.*
The verse appears in the Choir/Cantor edition and accompaniment editions.
English translation of the verse (Psalm 118:1): *Give thanks to the Lord, for he is good, for his mercy endures forever.*
English translation of the antiphon © 2010, ICEL. All rights reserved. Used with permission.
  English translation of the verse © 1969, 1981, 1997, ICEL. All rights reserved. Used with permission.

Text and music: *Chant Mass;* Chant, Mode VIII; *Graduale Romanum,* 1974.

**168**  **KYRIE**

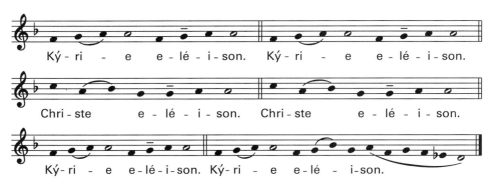

Kýri - e e - lé - i - son. Kýri - e e - lé - i - son.

Chri - ste e - lé - i - son. Chri - ste e - lé - i - son.

Kýri - e e - lé - i - son. Kýri - e e - lé - i - son.

Text and music: *Chant Mass; Mass XVI*; Chant, Mode III; *Graduale Romanum*, 1974.

**169**  **GLORIA**

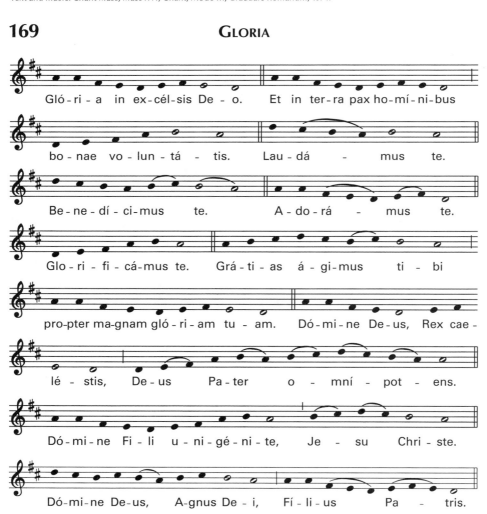

Gló - ri - a in ex - cél - sis De - o. Et in ter - ra pax ho - mí - ni - bus

bo - nae vo - lun - tá - tis. Lau - dá - mus te.

Be - ne - dí - ci - mus te. A - do - rá - mus te.

Glo - ri - fi - cá - mus te. Grá - ti - as á - gi - mus ti - bi

pro - pter ma - gnam gló - ri - am tu - am. Dó - mi - ne De - us, Rex cae -

lé - stis, De - us Pa - ter o - mní - pot - ens.

Dó - mi - ne Fi - li u - ni - gé - ni - te, Je - su Chri - ste.

Dó - mi - ne De - us, A - gnus De - i, Fí - li - us Pa - tris.

Qui tol-lis pec-cá-ta mun – di, mi-se-ré – re no-bis.

Qui tol-lis pec-cá-ta mun-di, sú-sci-pe de-pre-ca-ti-ó-

nem no – stram. Qui se-des ad déx-te-ram Pa – tris,

mi-se-ré-re no-bis. Quó-ni-am tu so-lus San-ctus.

Tu so-lus Dó – mi – nus. Tu so-lus Al – tís – si-mus,

Je – su Chri-ste. Cum San-cto Spí – ri-tu,

in gló-ri-a De-i Pa – tris. A – men.

Text and music: *Chant Mass; Mass VIII; Chant, Mode V; Graduale Romanum,* 1974.

## SANCTUS 170

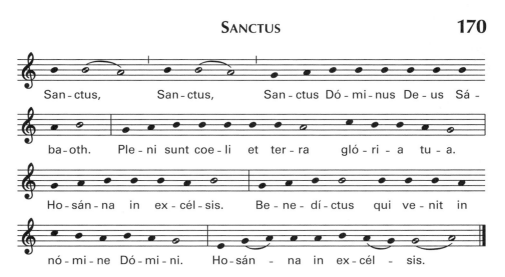

San-ctus, San-ctus, San-ctus Dó-mi-nus De-us Sá-

ba-oth. Ple-ni sunt coe-li et ter-ra gló-ri-a tu-a.

Ho-sán-na in ex-cél-sis. Be-ne-dí-ctus qui ve-nit in

nó-mi-ne Dó-mi-ni. Ho-sán – na in ex-cél – sis.

Text and music: *Chant Mass; Mass XVIII; Graduale Romanum,* 1974.

## 171     POST CONSECRATIONEM

Priest        or

My-sté - ri - um fí-de - i.    My-sté - ri-um   fí    -    de - i.

All

Mor-tem tu - am an-nun-ti - á-mus, Dó   -   mi-ne,   et tu - am

re-sur-re-cti - ó-nem con-fi - té - mur,   do - nec   vé-ni - as.

Text and music: *Chant Mass; Graduale Romanum*, 1974.

## 172     AMEN

Priest                                              All

...per ó - mni - a sáe-cu - la sae-cu-ló - rum. A-men.

Text and music: *Chant Mass; Graduale Romanum*, 1974.

## 173     PATER NOSTER

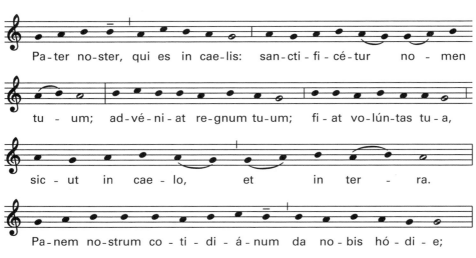

Pa-ter no-ster, qui es in cae-lis: san-cti - fi - cé-tur   no - men

tu - um; ad-vé-ni - at re-gnum tu-um; fi - at vo-lún-tas tu - a,

sic - ut   in   cae - lo,     et     in   ter - ra.

Pa-nem no-strum co - ti - di - á - num da no - bis hó - di - e;

et di - mít - te no - bis dé - bi - ta no-stra,   sic - ut et nos

di - mít - ti - mus de - bi - tó - ri - bus no - stris; et ne nos

in - dú - cas in ten - ta - ti - ó - nem; sed lí - be - ra nos a ma - lo.

Priest: Libera nos, quaesumus, Domine...
et adventum Salvatoris nostri Jesu Christi.

All

Qui - a tu - um est re - gnum, et po - té -

stas, et gló - ri - a in sáe - cu - la.

Priest                                        All

Pax Dó - mi-ni sit sem-per vo-bís - cum.   Et cum spí - ri - tu tu - o.

Text and music: *Chant Mass; Graduale Romanum*, 1974.

## AGNUS DEI                                     **174**

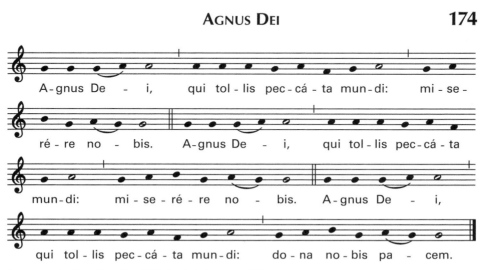

A-gnus De - i, qui tol - lis pec - cá - ta mun-di: mi - se -

ré - re no - bis. A-gnus De - i, qui tol - lis pec - cá - ta

mun-di: mi - se - ré - re no - bis. A-gnus De - i,

qui tol - lis pec - cá - ta mun-di: do - na no - bis pa - cem.

Text and music: *Chant Mass; Mass XVIII; Graduale Romanum*, 1974.

## 175     KYRIE, ELEISON/LORD, HAVE MERCY

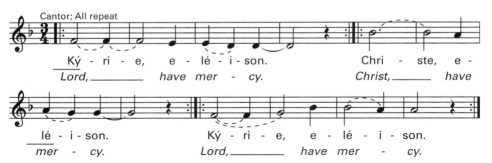

Ký - ri - e, e - lé - i - son.     Chri - ste, e -
Lord, _____ have mer - cy.     Christ, _____ have

lé - i - son.     Ký - ri - e, e - lé - i - son.
mer - cy.     Lord, _____ have mer - cy.

## 176     GLORY TO GOD

Glo-ry to God in the high - est,     and on earth peace to peo-ple

of good will.     We praise you, we bless you, we a -

dore you,     we glo-ri-fy you,     we give you

thanks for your great glo - ry, Lord God, heav-en - ly

King, O God, al-might-y Fa - ther.

Lord Je - sus Christ, On-ly Be-got-ten Son, Lord God,

Lamb of God, Son of the Fa - ther, you take a-

way the sins of the world, have mer - cy on us; you take a -

way the sins of the world, re - ceive our prayer; you are seat - ed

at the right hand of the Fa - ther, have mer -

cy, have mer - cy on us. For you a - lone are the

Ho - ly One, you a - lone are the Lord, you a - lone are the

Most High, Je - sus Christ, with the Ho - ly Spir - it,

in the glo - ry of God the Fa - ther. A - men, a - men.

Music: *Mass of Renewal*; Curtis Stephan, b. 1973, © 2009, Curtis Stephan. Published by OCP. All rights reserved.

## ALLELUIA 177

Al - le - lu - ia, al - le - lu - ia, al - le - lu - ia.

Al - le - lu - ia, al - le - lu - ia, al - le - lu - ia.

Note: Verses available in accompaniment books.

Music: *Mass of Renewal*; Curtis Stephan, b. 1973, © 2009, Curtis Stephan. Published by OCP. All rights reserved.

## 178 LENTEN GOSPEL ACCLAMATION

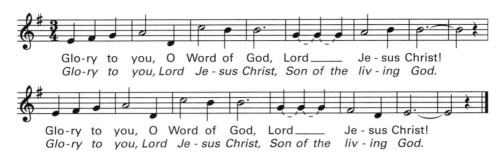

Glo-ry to you, O Word of God, Lord_____ Je-sus Christ!
*Glo-ry to you, Lord Je-sus Christ, Son of the liv-ing God.*

Glo-ry to you, O Word of God, Lord_____ Je-sus Christ!
*Glo-ry to you, Lord Je-sus Christ, Son of the liv-ing God.*

Note: Verses available in accompaniment books.

## 179 HOLY

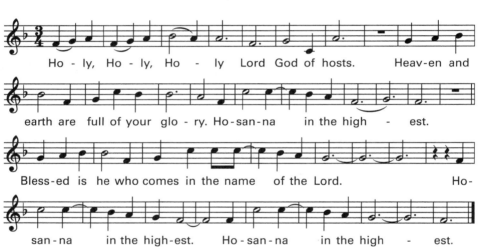

Ho-ly, Ho-ly, Ho-ly Lord God of hosts. Heav-en and

earth are full of your glo-ry. Ho-san-na in the high - est.

Bless-ed is he who comes in the name of the Lord. Ho-

san-na in the high-est. Ho-san-na in the high - est.

## 180 WE PROCLAIM YOUR DEATH

We pro-claim your Death, O Lord, and pro-fess your

Res-ur-rec-tion un-til you come a-gain.

## When We Eat This Bread 181

When we eat this Bread and drink this Cup, we pro-

claim your Death, O Lord, un - til you come a - gain.

## Save Us, Savior 182

Save us, Sav - ior of the world, for by your Cross and Res - ur -

rec - tion you have set us free, you have set us free.

## Amen 183

A - men, a - men, a - men.

## Lamb of God 184

Lamb of God, you take a-way the sins of the world, have mer - cy,

have mer - cy on us. world, grant us, grant us peace.

## 185    LORD, HAVE MERCY/KYRIE, ELEISON

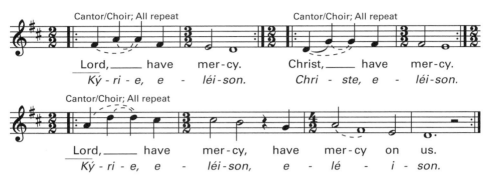

Music: *Mass of Christ the Savior*; Dan Schutte, b. 1947, © 2007, 2009, Daniel L. Schutte.
Published by OCP. All rights reserved.

## 186    GLORY TO GOD

2. Lord Jesus Christ, On - ly Be - got - ten Son, Lord God,

2. Lamb of God, Son of the Fa - ther, you take a - way the sins of the world,

2. have mer - cy on us; you take a - way the sins of the world,

2. re - ceive our prayer; you are seat - ed at the right hand,

to Verse 3 or Refrain

2. the right hand of the Fa - ther, have mer - cy on us.

Verse 3

3. For you a - lone are the Ho - ly One, you a - lone are the Lord,

3. you a - lone are the Most High, Je - sus Christ, with the Ho - ly

to Coda or Refrain

3. Spir - it, in the glo - ry of God the Fa - ther.

## ALLELUIA

**187**

Al - le - lu - ia. Al - le - lu - ia. Al - le - lu - ia.

Note: Verses available in accompaniment books.

## 188     Lenten Gospel Acclamation

Glo-ry to you, Word of God, Lord Je-sus Christ!

Note: Verses available in accompaniment books.

Text © 1969, 1981, 1997, ICEL. All rights reserved. Used with permission.
Music: *Mass of Christ the Savior*; Dan Schutte, b. 1947, © 2007, 2009, Daniel L. Schutte.
    Published by OCP. All rights reserved.

## 189     Holy

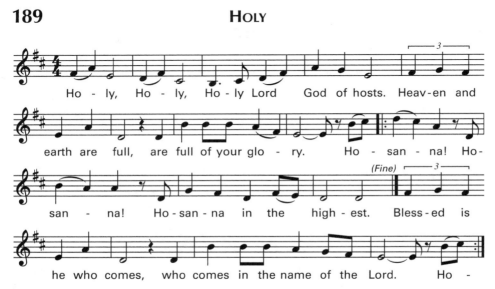

Ho - ly, Ho - ly, Ho - ly Lord God of hosts. Heav-en and

earth are full, are full of your glo - ry. Ho - san - na! Ho-

san - na! Ho-san-na in the high - est. Bless-ed is

he who comes, who comes in the name of the Lord. Ho -

Text © 2010, ICEL. All rights reserved. Used with permission.
Music: *Mass of Christ the Savior*; Dan Schutte, b. 1947, © 2007, 2009, Daniel L. Schutte.
    Published by OCP. All rights reserved.

## 190     We Proclaim Your Death

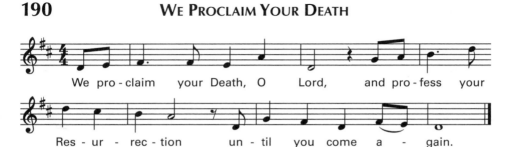

We pro-claim your Death, O Lord, and pro-fess your

Res - ur - rec - tion un - til you come a - gain.

Text © 2010, ICEL. All rights reserved. Used with permission.
Music: *Mass of Christ the Savior*; Dan Schutte, b. 1947, © 2007, 2009, Daniel L. Schutte.
    Published by OCP. All rights reserved.

## WHEN WE EAT THIS BREAD 191

When we eat this Bread and drink this Cup, we pro-
claim your Death, O Lord, un - til you come a - gain.

Text © 2010, ICEL. All rights reserved. Used with permission.
Music: *Mass of Christ the Savior*; Dan Schutte, b. 1947, © 2007, 2009, Daniel L. Schutte.
Published by OCP. All rights reserved.

## SAVE US, SAVIOR 192

Save us, save us, Sav - ior of the world, for by your
Cross and Res - ur - rec - tion you have set us free.

Text © 2010, ICEL. All rights reserved. Used with permission.
Music: *Mass of Christ the Savior*; Dan Schutte, b. 1947, © 2007, 2009, Daniel L. Schutte.
Published by OCP. All rights reserved.

## AMEN 193

A - men. A - men. A - men.

Music: *Mass of Christ the Savior*; Dan Schutte, b. 1947, © 2007, 2009, 2010, Daniel L. Schutte.
Published by OCP. All rights reserved.

## LAMB OF GOD 194

*Lamb of God, you take a - way the sins of the
world, have mer-cy on us. world, grant us peace.

*Other Invocations available in accompaniment books.

Music: *Mass of Christ the Savior*; Dan Schutte, b. 1947, © 2007, 2009, Daniel L. Schutte.
Published by OCP. All rights reserved.

# MASS OF SPIRIT AND GRACE

## 195    PENITENTIAL ACT WITH INVOCATIONS

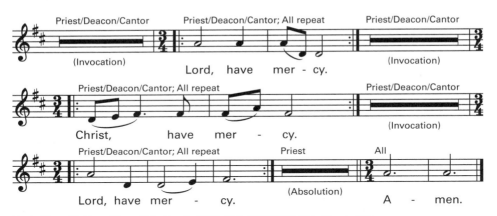

Lord, have mer - cy.

Christ, have mer - cy.

Lord, have mer - cy.

A - men.

Music: *Mass of Spirit and Grace*; Ricky Manalo, CSP, b. 1965, © 2007, 2009, Ricky Manalo, CSP.
Published by OCP. All rights reserved.

## 196    GLORY TO GOD

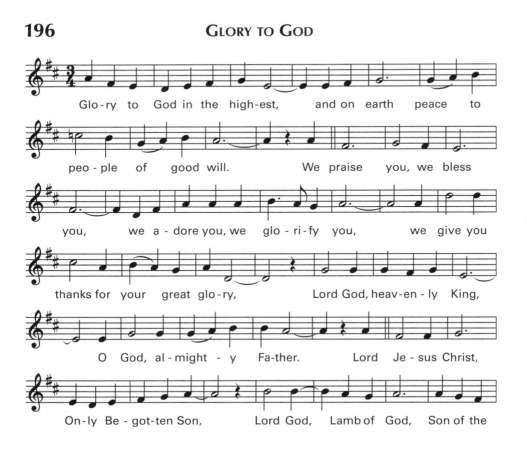

Glo-ry to God in the high-est, and on earth peace to

peo - ple of good will. We praise you, we bless

you, we a - dore you, we glo - ri-fy you, we give you

thanks for your great glo-ry, Lord God, heav-en - ly King,

O God, al-might - y Fa-ther. Lord Je - sus Christ,

On-ly Be - got-ten Son, Lord God, Lamb of God, Son of the

Fa-ther, you take a-way the sins of the world, have mer-cy on us; re-ceive our prayer; you are seat-ed at the right hand of the Fa - ther, have mer-cy on us. For you a-lone are the Ho - ly One, you a-lone are the Lord, you a-lone are the Most High, Je - sus Christ, with the Ho - ly Spir-it, in the glo-ry of God the Fa-ther. A - men.

Music: *Mass of Spirit and Grace*; Ricky Manalo, CSP, b. 1965, © 2007, 2009, Ricky Manalo, CSP.

## ALLELUIA

**197**

Al - le - lu - ia! Al - le-lu - ia! Al - le-lu - ia!

Note: Verses available in accompaniment books.

Music: *Mass of Spirit and Grace*; Ricky Manalo, CSP, b. 1965, © 2007, 2009, Ricky Manalo, CSP.

## 198      LENTEN GOSPEL ACCLAMATION

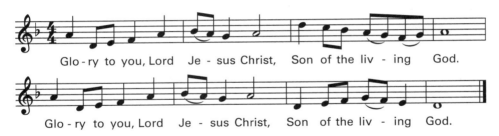

Glo - ry to you, Lord Je - sus Christ, Son of the liv - ing God.

Glo - ry to you, Lord Je - sus Christ, Son of the liv - ing God.

Note: Verses available in accompaniment books.

## 199      HOLY

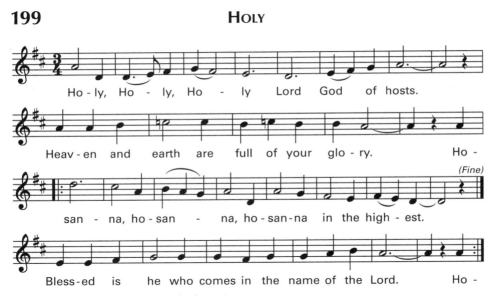

Ho - ly, Ho - ly, Ho - ly Lord God of hosts.

Heav - en and earth are full of your glo - ry. Ho -

*(Fine)*

san - na, ho - san - na, ho - san - na in the high - est.

Bless - ed is he who comes in the name of the Lord. Ho -

## 200      WE PROCLAIM YOUR DEATH

We pro - claim your Death, O Lord, and pro -

fess your Res - ur - rec - tion un - til you come a -

gain,        un - til   you   come  a - gain.

### WHEN WE EAT THIS BREAD     201

When  we   eat   this  Bread  and  drink   this   Cup,

we pro - claim your Death,   O   Lord,    un - til   you

come   a - gain,   un - til  you  come a - gain.

### SAVE US, SAVIOR     202

Save us, Sav - ior  of the world,   for by your Cross and Res - ur -

rec - tion   you have set  us free,    you have set  us free.

### AMEN     203

A - men!  A - men!  A - men!   A - men!

**204**          LAMB OF GOD

Lamb of God, you take a - way the sins of the

**1, 2**                      **4**

world, have mer - cy on us.

**Final**

world, grant us peace, grant us peace.

Music: *Mass of Spirit and Grace*; Ricky Manalo, CSP, b. 1965, © 2007, 2009, Ricky Manalo, CSP.
Published by OCP. All rights reserved.

## BELMONT MASS

**205**          PENITENTIAL ACT WITH INVOCATIONS

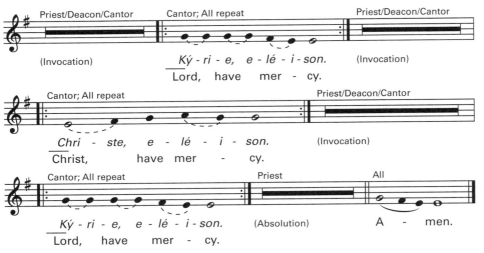

Priest/Deacon/Cantor      Cantor; All repeat          Priest/Deacon/Cantor

(Invocation)     *Ký - ri - e, e - lé - i - son.*     (Invocation)
            Lord, have mer - cy.

Cantor; All repeat                  Priest/Deacon/Cantor

*Chri - ste, e - lé - i - son.*     (Invocation)
Christ, have mer - cy.

Cantor; All repeat         Priest         All

*Ký - ri - e, e - lé - i - son.*     (Absolution)     A - men.
Lord, have mer - cy.

Music: *Belmont Mass*; Christopher Walker, b. 1947, © 2007, 2010, Christopher Walker.
Published by OCP. All rights reserved.

**206**          GLORY TO GOD

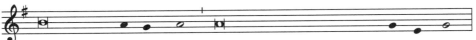

Glory to God in the highest, and on earth peace to people of good will.

We praise you, we bless you, we a - dore you, we glorify you,

we give you thanks for your great glory, Lord God, heav-en-ly King,

O God, al-might-y Father. Lord Jesus Christ, Only Be-got-ten Son,

Lord God, Lamb of God, Son of the Father, you take away the sins of the

world, have mer-cy on us; you take away the sins of the world,

re-ceive our prayer; you are seated at the right hand of the Father,

have mer-cy on us. For you a-lone are the Holy One, you a-lone

are the Lord, you alone are the Most High, Je - sus Christ, with the

Ho-ly Spirit, in the glory of God the Father. A-men, a - men.

## ALLELUIA 207

Al - le - lu - ia, al - le - lu - ia, al - le - lu - ia.

Note: Verses available in accompaniment books.

## 208      LENTEN GOSPEL ACCLAMATION

Praise and hon-or to you, Lord Je - sus Christ!

Note: Verses available in accompaniment books.

## 209      HOLY

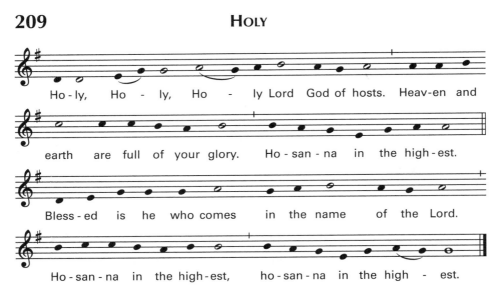

Ho-ly, Ho - ly, Ho - ly Lord God of hosts. Heav-en and

earth are full of your glory. Ho - san - na in the high-est.

Bless - ed is he who comes in the name of the Lord.

Ho - san - na in the high-est, ho-san-na in the high - est.

## 210      WE PROCLAIM YOUR DEATH

We pro-claim your Death, O Lord, and pro-fess your

Res - ur - rec - tion un - til you come a - gain.

## WHEN WE EAT THIS BREAD

**211**

When we eat this Bread and drink this Cup, we pro-
claim your Death, O Lord, un - til you come a - gain.

Text © 2010, ICEL. All rights reserved. Used with permission.
Music: *Belmont Mass*; Christopher Walker, b. 1947, © 2007, 2010, Christopher Walker.
    Published by OCP. All rights reserved.

## SAVE US, SAVIOR

**212**

Save us, Sav - ior of the world, for by your
Cross and Res - ur - rec - tion you have set us free.

Text © 2010, ICEL. All rights reserved. Used with permission.
Music: *Belmont Mass*; Christopher Walker, b. 1947, © 2007, 2010, Christopher Walker.
    Published by OCP. All rights reserved.

## AMEN

**213**

Priest    All
...for ev - er and ev - er. A - men, a - men.

Music: *Belmont Mass*; Christopher Walker, b. 1947, © 2007, 2010, Christopher Walker.
    Published by OCP. All rights reserved.

## LAMB OF GOD

**214**

Cantor or All    (All)
*Lamb of God, you take a - way the sins of the world,

1...    Repeat as needed    Final
have mer - cy on us.    grant us peace, grant us peace.

*Other Invocations available in accompaniment books.

Music: *Belmont Mass*; Christopher Walker, b. 1947, © 2007, 2010, Christopher Walker.
    Published by OCP. All rights reserved.

# MASS OF THE RESURRECTION

**215**   PENITENTIAL ACT WITH INVOCATIONS

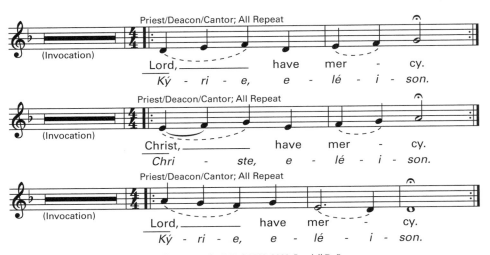

Priest/Deacon/Cantor; All Repeat

(Invocation)

Lord, _____ have mer - cy.
*Ký - ri - e, e - lé - i - son.*

Priest/Deacon/Cantor; All Repeat

(Invocation)

Christ, _____ have mer - cy.
*Chri - ste, e - lé - i - son.*

Priest/Deacon/Cantor; All Repeat

(Invocation)

Lord, _____ have mer - cy.
*Ký - ri - e, e - lé - i - son.*

Music: *Mass of the Resurrection*; Randall DeBruyn, b. 1947, © 2002, 2009, Randall DeBruyn.
Published by OCP. All rights reserved.

**216**   GLORY TO GOD

Glo-ry to God in the high-est, and on earth peace, peace to peo-ple of good

will. We praise you, we bless you, we a - dore you, we glo-ri-fy you, we

give you thanks for your great glo - ry, Lord God, heav-en-ly King, O

God, al-might-y Fa - ther. Lord Je-sus Christ, On-ly Be-got-ten Son,

Lord God, Lamb of God, Son of the Fa-ther, you take a-way the sins of the

world, have mer-cy on us; you take a-way the sins of the world, re-

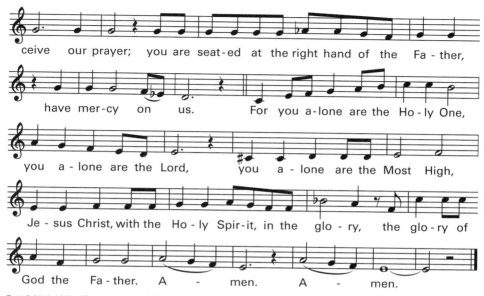

ceive our prayer; you are seat-ed at the right hand of the Fa-ther, have mer-cy on us. For you a-lone are the Ho-ly One, you a-lone are the Lord, you a-lone are the Most High, Je-sus Christ, with the Ho-ly Spir-it, in the glo-ry, the glo-ry of God the Fa-ther. A - men. A - men.

## ALLELUIA  217

Al-le-lu - ia, al - le-lu-ia, al-le-lu - ia, al-le-lu - ia, al-le - lu-ia, al - le - lu-ia, al-le - lu-ia, al-le-lu - ia!

Note: Verses available in accompaniment books.

## LENTEN GOSPEL ACCLAMATION  218

Praise to you, Lord Je - sus Christ, King of end - less glo - ry.

Praise to you, Lord Je - sus Christ, King of end - less glo - ry.

Note: Verses available in accompaniment books.

**219**  **HOLY**

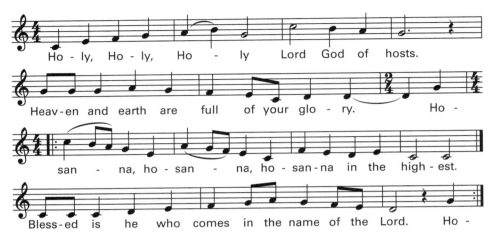

Ho-ly, Ho-ly, Ho-ly Lord God of hosts.

Heav-en and earth are full of your glo-ry. Ho-

san-na, ho-san-na, ho-san-na in the high-est.

Bless-ed is he who comes in the name of the Lord. Ho-

**220**  **WE PROCLAIM YOUR DEATH**

We pro-claim your Death, O Lord, and pro-fess your Res-ur-

rec-tion un-til you come a-gain, un-til you come a-gain.

**221**  **WHEN WE EAT THIS BREAD**

When we eat this Bread and drink this Cup, we pro-

claim your Death, O Lord, un-til you come a-gain.

## SAVE US, SAVIOR

**222**

Save us, Sav-ior of the world, for by your Cross and Res-ur-rec-tion you have set us free, you have set us free.

## AMEN

**223**

A - men, a - men, a - men, a - men.

## LAMB OF GOD

**224**

Lamb of God, you take a - way the sins of the world, have mer - cy on us. world, grant us peace.

1, 2     Final

# HERITAGE MASS

## LORD, HAVE MERCY

**225**

Lord, have mer - cy. Christ, have mer - cy. Lord, have mer - cy.

**226**     GLORY TO GOD

## HOLY

Ho-ly, Ho-ly, Ho - ly Lord God of hosts. Heav'n and earth are full of your glo - ry. Ho-san-na! Ho-san-na in the high - est. Blessed is he who comes in the name of the Lord.

## WE PROCLAIM YOUR DEATH

We pro - claim your Death, O Lord, and pro - fess your Res-ur-rec-tion un - til you come, un - til you come a - gain.

## WHEN WE EAT THIS BREAD

When we eat this Bread and drink this Cup, we pro-claim your Death, O Lord, un - til you come a - gain.

**230**    SAVE US, SAVIOR

Save us, Sav-ior of the world, for by your
Cross and Res-ur-rec-tion you have set us free.

**231**    AMEN

A - men, a - men, a - men.

**232**    LAMB OF GOD

Lamb of God, you take a - way the sins of the

**1, 2**

**3**

world, have mer-cy on us. world, grant us peace.

# MISA SANTA FE

**233**    ACTO PENITENCIAL, FORMULARIO 3/
PENITENTIAL ACT WITH INVOCATIONS

Sacerdote/Diácono/Cantor
Priest/Deacon/Cantor

Cantor/All

(Invocación/
Invocation)

Se - ñor, ten pie-dad.    Se - ñor, ten pie-dad.
Lord, have mer-cy.    Lord, have mer-cy.

Sacerdote/Diácono/Cantor
Priest/Deacon/Cantor

Cantor/All

(Invocación/
Invocation)

Cris-to, ten pie-dad.
*Christ, have mer-cy.*
Cris-to, ten pie-dad.
*Christ, have mer-cy.*

Sacerdote/Diácono/Cantor
Priest/Deacon/Cantor

Cantor/All

(Invocación/
Invocation)

Se-ñor, ten pie-dad.
*Lord, have mer-cy.*
Se-ñor, ten pie-dad.
*Lord, have mer-cy.*

## GLORIA/GLORY TO GOD

**234**

Estribillo/Refrain

Glo - ria a Dios en el cie - lo, y en la tie - rra
*Glo - ry to God in the high - est, and on earth*

paz a los hom - bres que a - ma el Se - ñor.
*peace to peo - ple, to peo - ple of good will.*

**Estrofas**

1. Por tu inmensa gloria te alabamos,
   te bendecimos, te adoramos,
   te glorificamos, te damos gracias,
   Señor Dios, Rey celestial,
   Dios Padre todopoderoso.

2. Señor, Hijo único, Jesucristo,
   Señor Dios, Cordero de Dios,
   Hijo del Padre,
   tú que quitas el pecado del mundo,
   ten piedad de nosotros,
   tú que quitas el pecado del mundo,
   atiende nuestra súplica;
   tú que estás sentado
   a la derecha del Padre,
   ten piedad de nosotros.

3. Porque sólo tú eres Santo,
   sólo tú Señor,
   sólo tú Altísimo, Jesucristo,
   con el Espíritu Santo
   en la gloria de Dios Padre. Amén.

**Verses**

1. *We praise you, we bless you,*
   *we adore you, we glorify you,*
   *we give you thanks for your great glory,*
   *Lord God, heavenly King,*
   *O God, almighty Father.*

2. *Lord Jesus Christ, Only Begotten Son,*
   *Lord God, Lamb of God,*
   *Son of the Father,*
   *you take away the sins of the world,*
   *have mercy on us;*
   *you take away the sins of the world,*
   *receive our prayer;*
   *you are seated at the right hand*
   *of the Father,*
   *have mercy on us.*

3. *For you alone are the Holy One,*
   *you alone are the Lord,*
   *you alone are the Most High, Jesus Christ,*
   *with the Holy Spirit,*
   *in the glory of God the Father. Amen.*

## 235 ACLAMACIÓN AL EVANGELIO/GOSPEL ACCLAMATION

¡A - le - lu - ya, a - le - lu - ya,    a - le - lu - ya!

Cuaresma   A - la - ban - za a ti, oh Cris-to,   Rey de e-ter - na glo-ria.

Al - le - lu - ia, al-le - lu - ia,   al - le - lu - ia!

Lent   Praise to you, Lord Je - sus Christ,   King of end-less glo-ry!

## 236 SANTO/HOLY

Español   San-to, San-to, San-to es el Se - ñor, Dios del U - ni - ver - so.

English   *Ho - ly, Ho - ly, Ho - ly Lord God of hosts.*

Biling.   San-to, San-to, San-to es el Se - ñor, Dios del U - ni - ver - so.

Lle - nos es-tán el cie - lo y la tie - rra de tu glo - ria. Ho -

*Heav - en and earth are full of your glo - ry. Ho -*

*Heav - en and earth are full of your glo - ry. Ho -*

san - na en el cie - lo. Ho - san - na en el cie - lo. Ben -

*san - na in the high-est. Ho - san - na in the high - est.*

san - na en el cie - lo. Ho - san - na en el cie - lo.

di - to el que vie - ne en nom - bre del Se - ñor. Ho -

*Bless - ed is he who comes in the name of the Lord. Ho -*

*Bless - ed is he who comes in the name of the Lord. Ho -*

san - na en el cie - lo. Ho - san - na en el cie - lo.

*san - na in the high-est. Ho - san - na in the high-est.*

san - na en el cie - lo. Ho - san - na en el cie - lo.

## Anunciamos Tu Muerte/We Proclaim Your Death  **237**

## Cada Vez que Comemos/When We Eat This Bread  **238**

## 239     POR TU CRUZ/SAVE US, SAVIOR

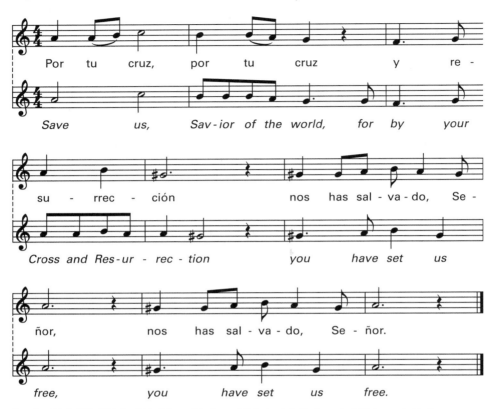

Por tu cruz, por tu cruz y re -

Save us, Sav-ior of the world, for by your

su - rrec - ción nos has sal - va - do, Se -

Cross and Res-ur - rec - tion you have set us

ñor, nos has sal - va - do, Se - ñor.

free, you have set us free.

## 240     AMÉN/AMEN

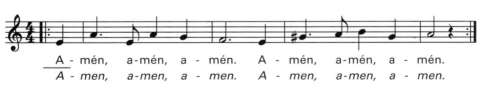

A - mén, a-mén, a - mén. A - mén, a-mén, a - mén.

A - men, a-men, a - men. A - men, a-men, a - men.

## 241     CORDERO DE DIOS/LAMB OF GOD

1-3. Cor - de - ro de Dios, que qui-tas el pe - ca - do del mun-do,

1-3. Lamb of God, you take a-way the sins of the world,

1, 2. ten pie-dad de no-so-tros, ⅟ ten pie-dad de no-so-tros.
3. ⅟ da-nos la paz, ⅟ da-nos la paz.
1, 2. *have mer-cy on us,* ⅟ *have mer-cy on us.*
3. ⅟ *grant us peace,* ⅟ *grant us peace.*

# MASS OF GLORY

## COME TO THE RIVER

**242**

**Refrain**

Come, O come, come to the riv-er

flow-ing from the bod-y of Christ.

We'll go down, deep in the wa-ter,

but in the Lord we shall a-rise.

**Verses**

| | | | | | |
|---|---|---|---|---|---|
| 1. | Washed in | wa-ters | of | re-birth, | |
| 2. | Priest-ly | peo-ple | are | we, | |
| 3. | Blest are | those | who | thirst | |
| 4. | Let us | walk | in | the light | |
| 5. | Those who | sow | in | tears | |

*to Refrain*

1. we have put on Christ Je-sus.
2. sealed and sent by the Spir-it.
3. for the reign of God's jus-tice.
4. of God's ho-ly prom-ise.
5. reap the har-vest re-joic-ing.

*Repeat last phrase final time.

## 243    PENITENTIAL ACT WITH INVOCATIONS

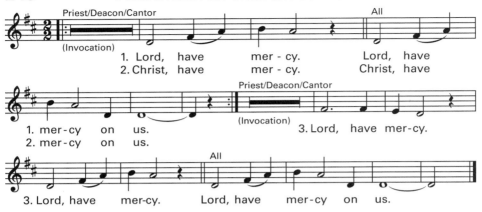

Priest/Deacon/Cantor      All

(Invocation)
1. Lord, have mer - cy.    Lord, have
2. Christ, have mer - cy.    Christ, have

Priest/Deacon/Cantor

1. mer - cy on us.    (Invocation)   3. Lord, have mer - cy.
2. mer - cy on us.

All

3. Lord, have mer-cy.    Lord, have mer - cy on us.

Note: Invocations from *The Roman Missal*, 3rd Edition are in the accompaniment books.
Music: *Mass of Glory*; Bob Hurd, b. 1950, © 1991, 2009, Bob Hurd. Published by OCP. All rights reserved.

## 244    GLORY TO GOD

Refrain: 1st time: Cantor, All repeat; thereafter: All

Glo-ry to God, glo-ry to God, glo-ry to God in the high - est,

2 to Vss.

and on earth peace to peo-ple of good will.

Last time

Glo - ry to God, glo - ry to God, glo - ry to God in the

high - est, and on earth peace to peo-ple of good will.

A - men, a - men, a - men.

Verses

1. We praise you, we bless you,
we adore you, we glorify you,
we give you thanks for your great glory,
Lord God, heavenly King,
O God, almighty Father.

2. Lord Jesus Christ, Only Begotten Son,
Lord God, Lamb of God,
Son of the Father,
you take away the sins of the world,
have mercy on us;

you take away the sins of the world,
receive our prayer;
you are seated at the right hand
of the Father,
have mercy on us.

3. For you alone are the Holy One,
you alone are the Lord,
you alone are the Most High, Jesus Christ,
with the Holy Spirit,
in the glory of God the Father.

Text © 2010, ICEL. All rights reserved. Used with permission.
Music: *Mass of Glory*; Ken Canedo, b. 1953, and Bob Hurd, b. 1950, © 1998, 2009, Ken Canedo and Bob Hurd.
Published by OCP. All rights reserved.

## Alleluia! Give the Glory 245

Al - le - lu - ia! Al - le - lu - ia!

Al - le - lu - ia! Give the glo - ry

1. and the hon - or to the Lord!

2. and the hon - or to the Lord!

Note: Gathering, Gospel Acclamation and Easter Vigil Psalm 118 verses are available in the accompaniment books.

## Lenten Gospel Acclamation 246

Praise and hon-or to you, O Lord Je - sus Christ.

Note: Verses available in accompaniment books.

## Universal Prayer/Prayer of the Faithful 247

Refrain: 1st time: Cantor, All repeat; thereafter: All

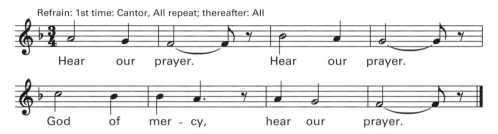

Hear our prayer. Hear our prayer.

God of mer - cy, hear our prayer.

Note: Verses available in accompaniment books.

**248** HOLY

Ho - ly, Ho - ly, Ho - ly Lord God of

hosts. Heav - en and earth are full of your

glo - ry. Ho - san - na, ho - san - na, ho - san - na

in the high-est. Bless-ed is he who comes

in the name of the Lord. Ho -

**249** WE PROCLAIM YOUR DEATH

We pro - claim your Death, O Lord, and pro - fess your

Res - ur - rec - tion un - til you come a - gain.

**250** WHEN WE EAT THIS BREAD

When we eat this Bread and drink this Cup,

we pro - claim your Death, O Lord, un - til you

come a - gain, un - til you come a - gain.

## SAVE US, SAVIOR                                                                  251

Save us, Sav - ior of the world, for by your Cross and

Res - ur - rec - tion you have set us free.

## AMEN                                                                             252

A - men.    A - men.    Al - le - lu - ia, a - men.    men.
**During Lent:** Praise and glo - ry,

## LAMB OF GOD                                                                      253

Cantor or Choir                All
*Lamb of God, you take a - way the sins of the world,

1, etc.                                           (repeat as needed)
have mer - cy on us; have mer - cy on us.

Final
grant us peace; grant us peace.

*Other Invocations available in accompaniment books.

# GUIDELINES FOR THE RECEPTION OF COMMUNION

*For Catholics:* As Catholics, we fully participate in the celebration of the Eucharist when we receive Holy Communion. We are encouraged to receive Communion devoutly and frequently. In order to be properly disposed to receive Communion, participants should not be conscious of grave sin and normally should have fasted for one hour. A person who is conscious of grave sin is not to receive the Body and Blood of the Lord without prior sacramental confession except for a grave reason where there is no opportunity for confession. In this case, the person is to be mindful of the obligation to make an act of perfect contrition, including the intention of confessing as soon as possible *(Code of Canon Law, canon 916)*. A frequent reception of the Sacrament of Penance is encouraged for all.

*For our fellow Christians:* We welcome our fellow Christians to this celebration of the Eucharist as our brothers and sisters. We pray that our common baptism and the action of the Holy Spirit in this Eucharist will draw us closer to one another and begin to dispel the sad divisions which separate us. We pray that these will lessen and finally disappear, in keeping with Christ's prayer for us "that they may all be one" *(Jn 17:21)*.

Because Catholics believe that the celebration of the Eucharist is a sign of the reality of the oneness of faith, life, and worship, members of those churches with whom we are not yet fully united are ordinarily not admitted to Holy Communion. Eucharistic sharing in exceptional circumstances by other Christians requires permission according to the directives of the diocesan bishop and the provisions of canon law *(canon 844 ¶ 4)*. Members of the Orthodox Churches, the Assyrian Church of the East, and the Polish National Catholic Church are urged to respect the discipline of their own Churches. According to Roman Catholic discipline, the Code of Canon Law does not object to the reception of communion by Christians of these Churches *(canon 844 ¶ 3)*.

*For those not receiving Holy Communion:* All who are not receiving Holy Communion are encouraged to express in their hearts a prayerful desire for unity with the Lord Jesus and with one another.

*For non-Christians:* We also welcome to this celebration those who do not share our faith in Jesus Christ. While we cannot admit them to Holy Communion, we ask them to offer their prayers for the peace and the unity of the human family.

# ADDITIONAL SERVICE MUSIC

To foster the assembly's sung participation in the ritual moments of the Eucharistic Celebration, the following selection of acclamations, litanies and other music allows additional choices to suit the community and the occasion. *"Authentic sacred music supports the Church's prayer by enriching its elements."* (Sing to the Lord, No. 15)

## SPRINKLING RITE

### AGUA DE VIDA/WATER OF LIFE                254

Estribillo/Refrain: Todos/All

A-gua de vi - da, _____ san-to re - cuer - do;
*Wa-ter of life, _____ ho-ly re-mind - er;*

u - ne y re - nue - va _____ al cuer-po de Cris - to. _____
*touch-ing, re-new-ing _____ the bod-y of Christ. _____*

al cuer-po de Cris - to. _____
*the bod-y of Christ. _____*

Note: Verses available in accompaniment books.

Text and music: *Misa del Pueblo Inmigrante*; Jaime Cortez, b. 1963, © 1994, Jaime Cortez. Published by OCP. All rights reserved.

## 255  WATER OF LIFE

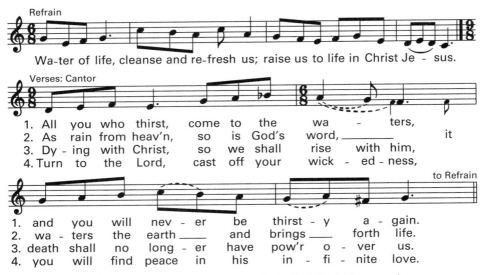

Refrain

Wa-ter of life, cleanse and re-fresh us; raise us to life in Christ Je - sus.

Verses: Cantor

1. All you who thirst, come to the wa - ters,
2. As rain from heav'n, so is God's word, _____ it
3. Dy - ing with Christ, so we shall rise with him,
4. Turn to the Lord, cast off your wick - ed - ness,

to Refrain

1. and you will nev - er be thirst - y a - gain.
2. wa - ters the earth ____ and brings ____ forth life.
3. death shall no long - er have pow'r o - ver us.
4. you will find peace in his in - fi - nite love.

Text and music: Stephen Dean, b. 1948, © 1981, Stephen Dean. Published by OCP. All rights reserved.

## 256  I SAW WATER FLOWING

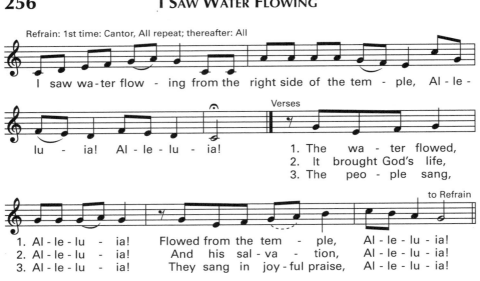

Refrain: 1st time: Cantor, All repeat; thereafter: All

I saw wa-ter flow - ing from the right side of the tem - ple, Al - le -

lu - ia! Al - le - lu - ia!

Verses

1. The wa - ter flowed,
2. It brought God's life,
3. The peo - ple sang,

to Refrain

1. Al - le - lu - ia! Flowed from the tem - ple, Al - le - lu - ia!
2. Al - le - lu - ia! And his sal - va - tion, Al - le - lu - ia!
3. Al - le - lu - ia! They sang in joy - ful praise, Al - le - lu - ia!

Text: Based on Ezekiel 47:1–2, 9; © 1973, ICEL. All rights reserved. Used with permission.
Music: Randall DeBruyn, b. 1947, © 1987, OCP. All rights reserved.

# LORD, HAVE MERCY

## LORD, HAVE MERCY

**257**

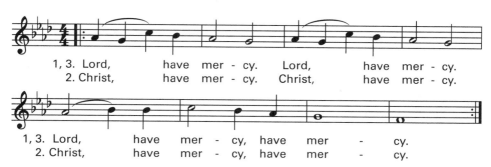

1, 3. Lord, have mer - cy. Lord, have mer - cy.
2. Christ, have mer - cy. Christ, have mer - cy.

1, 3. Lord, have mer - cy, have mer - cy.
2. Christ, have mer - cy, have mer - cy.

# GLORY TO GOD

## A CHRISTMAS GLORIA

**258**

*Refrain: All

Glo - ri - a

in ex - cel - sis De - o, De - o.

*Verses available in accompaniment books.

# ALLELUIA

## ADVENT GOSPEL ACCLAMATION

**259**

Al - le - lu - ia, al - le - lu - ia, al - le - lu - ia, al - le - lu - ia,

al - le - lu - ia, al - le - lu - ia, al - le - lu - ia, al - le - lu - ia.

Note: Verses for each Sunday of Advent are available in the accompaniment books.

## 260 ADVENT/CHRISTMAS GOSPEL ACCLAMATION

Refrain: 1st time: Cantor, All repeat; thereafter: All

Al-le-lu - ia, al-le-lu - ia. Al-le-lu - ia, al-le-lu - ia.

*Verses 1-4
Cantor

All    to Refrain

1. You are the joy of ev'ry human heart,    Lord Je-sus, come!
   king of all the nations.
2. You are Lord, our justice and our mercy.
   Show us how to live:
3. Eternal light, and sun of justice,
   shine in all our darkness:
4. Emmanuel, the joy of all nations,
   come to us and save us:

*Verses 5-7
Cantor

All    to Refrain

5. Born today, our justice and our mercy,    Lord, Je-sus Christ!
   God in flesh among us:
6. You are light that shines in the darkness,
   star to guide the nations:
7. You are born of water and the Spirit,
   fountain of our dreams:

*Verses 1–4, Advent; verse 5, Christmas; verse 6, Epiphany; verse 7, Baptism of the Lord.

Text and music: David Haas, b. 1957, © 1986, David Haas. Published by OCP. All rights reserved.

## 261 CHRISTMAS SEASON GOSPEL ACCLAMATION

Al - le - lu - ia, al - le - lu - ia!    Al - le - lu - ia, al - le - lu - ia!

Note: Verses available in accompaniment books.

Music: Adapt. fr. *Sussex Carol*; Barbara Bridge, b. 1950, © 2005, Barbara Bridge. Published by OCP. All rights reserved.

## 262 ALLELUIA FOR THE EASTER SEASON/ALELUYA PARA PASCUA

Al - le - lu - ia!    Al - le - lu - ia!    Al - le - lu - ia!
*A - le - lu - ya!    A - le - lu - ya!    A - le - lu - ya!*

Note: Verses available in accompaniment books.

Music: O FILII ET FILIAE; Chant, Mode II; *Airs sur les hymnes sacrez, odes et noëls*, 1623.

## Eastertide Alleluia 263

Al - le - lu - ia, al - le - lu - ia, al - le - lu - ia.

Note: Verses available in accompaniment books.

Music: Chant, Mode VI.

## Celtic Alleluia 264

Al - le - lu - ia, al - le - lu - ia.

Al - le - lu - ia, al - le - lu - ia.

Note: Verses available in accompaniment books.

Music: *Celtic Mass*; Fintan O'Carroll, d. 1977, and Christopher Walker, b. 1947, © 1985, Fintan O'Carroll and Christopher Walker. Published by OCP. All rights reserved.

# Lenten Gospel Acclamation

## Glory and Praise 265

Glo - ry and praise to you, Word of Life! Je - sus!

Je - sus Christ! Glo - ry and praise to you,

Word of Life! Je - sus! Je - sus Christ!

Note: Verses available in accompaniment books.

Text and music: Jesse Manibusan, b. 1958, © 1993, Jesse Manibusan. Published by OCP. All rights reserved.

## 266      LENTEN GOSPEL ACCLAMATION

Praise to you, Lord__ Je-sus Christ,     King of end-less glo-ry!
Alt. Ref.: *Praise and glo-ry to you, O   Christ, to-day__ and for-ev-er!*

Note: Verses available in accompaniment books.

Text: Refrain © 1969, 1981, 1997, ICEL. All rights reserved. Used with permission. Alternate refrain,
    Michael R. Prendergast, b. 1955, © 1999, Michael R. Prendergast. Published by OCP. All rights reserved.
Music: Michael R. Prendergast and Joseph B. Sullivan, b. 1956, © 1999, Michael R. Prendergast and Joseph B. Sullivan.
    Published by OCP. All rights reserved.

# PROFESSION OF FAITH

## 267      CREDO III

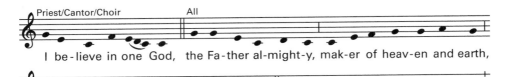

Priest/Cantor/Choir      All

I be-lieve in one God, the Fa-ther al-might-y, mak-er of heav-en and earth,

of all things vis-i-ble and in-vis - i-ble. I be-lieve in one Lord Je - sus Christ,

the On-ly Be-got-ten Son of God, born of the Fa - ther be-fore all a - ges.

God from God, Light from Light, true God from true God,   be-got-ten, not made,

con - sub - stan - tial with the   Fa - ther; through him all things were made.

For us men and for our sal - va - tion   he came down from   heav - en,

*At the words that follow, up to and including "and became man," all bow.*

and by the Ho - ly Spir - it was in-car-nate of the Vir-gin Mar - y,

and be-came man. For our sake he was cru - ci-fied un-der Pon-tius Pi - late,

he suf-fered death and was bur - ied, and rose a-gain on the third day

in ac-cord-ance with the Scrip-tures. He as-cend-ed in-to heav - en

and is seat-ed at the right hand of the Fa - ther. He will come a-gain in glo-ry

to judge the liv-ing and the dead and his king-dom will have no end.

I be-lieve in the Ho - ly Spir-it, the Lord, the giv - er of life, who pro -

ceeds from the Fa - ther and the Son, who with the Fa - ther and the Son

is a-dored and glo - ri-fied, who has spo-ken through the proph - ets.

I be-lieve in one, ho-ly, ca-tho-lic and a-pos-tol-ic Church. I con-fess one Bap-tism

for the for-give-ness of sins and I look for-ward to the res-ur-rec-tion of

the dead and the life of the world to come. A - men.

# UNIVERSAL PRAYER (PRAYER OF THE FAITHFUL)

## 268      O GOD, HEAR US

O God, hear us; hear our prayer.

Note: Verses available in accompaniment books.
Text and music: Bob Hurd, b. 1950, © 1984, Bob Hurd. Published by OCP. All rights reserved.

## 269      ÓYENOS, SEÑOR/LISTEN TO YOUR PEOPLE

Estribillo Ostinato/Ostinato Refrain

Ó - ye - nos, Se - ñor.    Ó - ye - nos, Se - ñor.
*Ding - gin mo ka - mi.*
(Filipino)

Lis - ten to your peo - ple.    Ó - ye - nos, Se - ñor.
*Chúng con cầu xin Ngài.*
(Vietnamese)

Note: Verses available in accompaniment books.
Text and music: *Misa de las Américas*; Bob Hurd, b. 1950, © 1988, 2002, Bob Hurd. Published by OCP. All rights reserved.

# EUCHARISTIC ACCLAMATION: AMEN

## 270      DANISH AMEN

A - men, a - men, a - men.

Music: Traditional Danish.

# LAMB OF GOD

## 271      ADVENT LAMB OF GOD

Cantor      1-5   All

1. Lamb of God,
2. Lord of Light,
3. Morn - ing Star,
4. God With Us,
5. Prince of Peace,
6. Lamb of God,

you take a - way the sins of the world, have

1-5. mer - cy on us, have mer - cy on us.

**Final** **All**
6. world, grant us your peace, O grant us your peace.

## LAMB OF GOD     272

Lamb of God, you take a - way the sins of the

**1, 2** **Final**
world, have mer - cy on us. world, grant us peace.

## AGNUS DEI     273

| | | | | | | |
|---|---|---|---|---|---|---|
| Latin | 1. A | - | gnus | De | - | i, |
| Vietnamese | 2. Chi | - | en Thi - en | Chu | - | a, |
| Hmong | 3. Yaj | Txiv | Tswr | Ntuj, | | |
| | (Yah | dzee | jer | ndu,) | | |
| Laotian | 4. O | pra sum pa noy | kog pra | jau, | | |
| Spanish | 5. Pan | | de | Vi | - | da, |
| English | 6. Cup | of Sal | - | va | - | tion, |
| Latin | 7. A | gnus | De | - | i, | |

qui

tol - lis pec-ca-ta mun - di: mi-se-re-re no - bis.
**(Final)** do-na no-bis pa - cem.

# HYMNS & SONGS

*"Thankfully sing to God psalms, hymns and holy songs" (Colossians 3:16). From the earliest centuries of Christianity, hymns and songs have played a major role in the liturgies and devotions of the faithful. A hymn is a song of praise or thanksgiving to God. All hymns are songs; but in contemporary liturgy the term "song" includes a wide variety of other musical forms: verse-refrain, litany, ostinato, chant, acclamation, spiritual and call-response. Often, but not always, liturgical song is based on scripture. Songs bring to expression and realize externally the inner attitudes of adoration, joy, sadness or petition, and they draw together in unity the diverse dispositions of community members. "A liturgical celebration can have no more solemn or pleasing feature than the whole assembly's expressing its faith and devotion in song." (Musicam Sacram, No. 16) St. Augustine said simply, "They who love, sing."*

## SEASONS AND SOLEMNITIES OF THE LORD

### 274     O COME, O COME, EMMANUEL

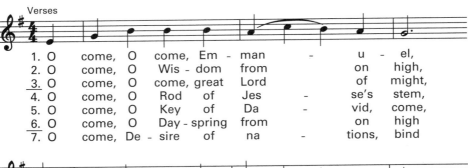

1. That mourns in lone - ly ex - ile here
2. To us the path of knowl - edge show,
3. In an - cient times did give the law,
4. That trust your might - y pow'r to save,
5. Make safe the way that leads on high,
6. Dis - perse the gloom - y clouds of night,
7. Make all our sad di - vi - sions cease,

1. Un - til the Son of God ap - pear.
2. And teach us in her ways to go.
3. In cloud, and maj - es - ty, and awe.
4. And give them vic - t'ry o'er the grave.
5. And close the path to mis - er - y.
6. And death's dark shad - ow put to flight.
7. And be for us our King of Peace.

Refrain
Re - joice! Re - joice! Em - man - u - el

Shall come to you, O Is - ra - el!

Text: LM with refrain; Latin, 9th cent.; verses 1, 3–6, para. in *Psalteriolum Cantionum Catholicarum*, Cologne, 1710;
tr. by John Mason Neale, 1818–1866; verses 2, 7 tr. fr. *The Hymnal 1940*, alt.
Music: VENI, VENI, EMMANUEL; Chant, Mode I; *Processionale*, French, 15th cent.;
adapt. by Thomas Helmore, 1811–1890.

## Maranatha! Come, Lord Jesus     275

*Refrain: 1st time: Cantor, All repeat; thereafter: All

Ma-ra - na - tha! Come, Lord Je - sus. Al-le - lu-ia! Al-le - lu-ia!

Ma-ra - na - tha! Come, Lord Je - sus. Al-le - lu-ia! A - men!

*Verses available in accompaniment books.

Text and music: Janèt Sullivan Whitaker, b. 1958, © 2002, Janèt Sullivan Whitaker. Published by OCP. All rights reserved.

# 276     A VOICE CRIES OUT

**Verse 1**

1. Con - sole my peo - ple, the ones dear to me; speak to the
1. heart of Je - ru - sa - lem: the time of your mourn - ing is
1. end - ed now, the Lord of life will come.

**Refrain**

A voice cries out in the wil - der - ness: "Pre - pare a
way for the Lord!" A voice cries out in the wil - der -
ness: "Make straight a high - way for God!"

**Verses 2, 4**

2. Ev - 'ry val - ley is made a plain, ev - 'ry moun - tain is
4. Zi - on, shout from the moun - tain top, lift up your voice, O Je -

2. lev - eled; the glo - ry of God __ shall then be re -
4. ru - sa - lem, and say to the peo - ple of God's __ own

*to Refrain*

2. vealed, and the na - tions will sing in praise.
4. land, "Be - hold, be - hold your God!"

**Verse 3**

3. A voice shouts: "Cry!" O what shall I cry? All flesh is like
3. grass and its flow - ers: the grass may with - er, the

3. flow-ers may fade, but the Word of the Lord is for - ev - er.

Verse 5

5. The Lord will ap - pear as a shep - herd, hold-ing his

5. lambs in his arms, keep-ing his flock so

to Refrain

5. close to his heart, lead-ing them all, old and young.

Text: Based on Isaiah 40:1–11; Michael Joncas, b. 1951.
Music: Michael Joncas.

## PATIENCE, PEOPLE 277

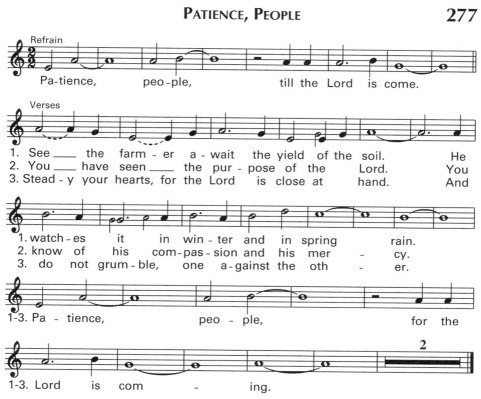

Refrain

Pa-tience, peo-ple, till the Lord is come.

Verses

1. See ___ the farm - er a - wait the yield of the soil. He
2. You ___ have seen ___ the pur - pose of the Lord. You
3. Stead - y your hearts, for the Lord is close at hand. And

1. watch - es it in win - ter and in spring rain.
2. know of his com-pas - sion and his mer - cy.
3. do not grum - ble, one a - gainst the oth - er.

1-3. Pa - tience, peo - ple, for the

1-3. Lord is com - ing.

Text: Based on James 5:7–9, 11; John Foley, S.J., b. 1939.
Music: John Foley, S.J.

## 278     On Jordan's Bank

1. On Jor-dan's bank the Bap-tist's cry An-
2. Then cleansed be ev-'ry soul from sin; Make
3. We hail you as our Sav-ior, Lord, Our
4. To heal the sick stretch out your hand, And
5. To God the Son all glo-ry be, Whose

1. nounc-es that the Lord is nigh; A-wake and heark-en,
2. straight the way of God with-in, And let each heart pre-
3. ref-uge, and our great re-ward; With-out your grace we
4. bid the fall-en sin-ner stand; Shine forth, and let your
5. ad-vent set your peo-ple free; Whom with the Fa-ther

1. for he brings Glad tid-ings of the King of kings.
2. pare a home, Where such a might-y guest may come.
3. waste a-way Like flow'rs that with-er and de-cay.
4. light re-store Earth's own true love-li-ness once more.
5. we a-dore, And Ho-ly Spir-it, ev-er-more.

Text: LM; Charles Coffin, 1676–1749; tr. by John Chandler, 1806–1876, alt.
Music: WINCHESTER NEW; Georg Wittwe's *Musicalishes Hand-Buch*, Hamburg, 1690;
   adapt. by William H. Havergal, 1793–1870.

## 279     O Come, Divine Messiah

Verses

1. O come, di-vine Mes-si-ah; The world in
2. O Christ, whom na-tions sigh for, Whom priest and
3. You come in peace and meek-ness And low-ly

1. si-lence waits the day When hope shall sing its
2. proph-et long fore-told, Come, break the cap-tive's
3. will your cra-dle be; All clothed in hu-man

1. tri-umph And sad-ness flee a-way.
2. fet-ters, Re-deem the long-lost fold.
3. weak-ness Shall we your God-head see.

Dear Sav-ior, haste! Come, come to earth. Dis-pel the
night and show your face, and bid us hail the dawn of grace. O
come, di-vine Mes-si - ah; the world in si-lence waits the day when
hope shall sing its tri - umph and sad-ness flee a - way.

Text: 78 76 with refrain; Abbé Simon-Joseph Pellegrin, 1663–1745; tr. by Sr. Mary of St. Philip, 1825–1904.
Music: VENEZ, DIVIN MESSIE; trad. French Carol, 16th cent.

## THE ANGEL GABRIEL FROM HEAVEN CAME 280

1. The an - gel Ga - bri - el from heav - en came, His
2. "For know a bless - ed Moth - er you shall be, All
3. Then gen - tle Ma - ry meek - ly bowed her head; "To
4. Of her, Em - man - u - el, the Christ, was born In

1. wings as drift - ed snow, his eyes as flame; "All
2. gen - er - a - tions praise con - tin - ual - ly, Your
3. me be as it pleas - es God!" she said. "My
4. Beth - le - hem, all on a Christ - mas morn; And

1. hail," said he, "O low - ly maid - en Ma - ry,"
2. Son shall be Em - man - u - el, by seers fore-told."
3. soul shall laud and mag - ni - fy his ho - ly name." } "Most
4. Chris - tian folk through-out the world will ev - er say:

1-4. high-ly fa-vored la - dy!" Glo - ri - a!

Text: 10 10 12 10; *Birjina gaztettobat zegoen*; trad. Basque Carol; tr. by Sabine Baring-Gould, 1834–1924.
Music: GABRIEL'S MESSAGE; trad. Basque Carol Melody.

## 281    WHEN THE KING SHALL COME AGAIN

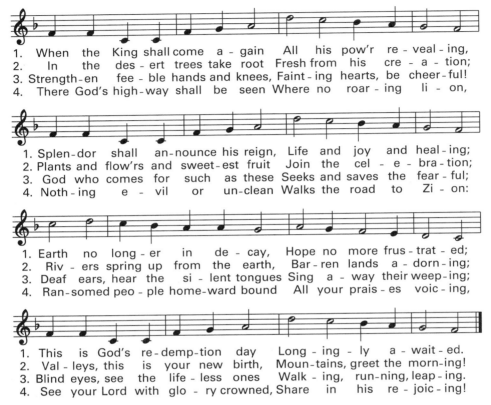

1. When the King shall come a - gain All his pow'r re - veal - ing,
2. In the des - ert trees take root Fresh from his cre - a - tion;
3. Strength-en fee - ble hands and knees, Faint - ing hearts, be cheer - ful!
4. There God's high-way shall be seen Where no roar - ing li - on,

1. Splen-dor shall an-nounce his reign, Life and joy and heal - ing;
2. Plants and flow'rs and sweet-est fruit Join the cel - e - bra - tion;
3. God who comes for such as these Seeks and saves the fear - ful:
4. Noth - ing e - vil or un-clean Walks the road to Zi - on:

1. Earth no long - er in de - cay, Hope no more frus - trat - ed;
2. Riv - ers spring up from the earth, Bar - ren lands a - dorn - ing;
3. Deaf ears, hear the si - lent tongues Sing a - way their weep - ing;
4. Ran-somed peo - ple home-ward bound All your prais - es voic - ing,

1. This is God's re - demp - tion day Long - ing - ly a - wait - ed.
2. Val - leys, this is your new birth, Moun-tains, greet the morn - ing!
3. Blind eyes, see the life - less ones Walk - ing, run-ning, leap - ing.
4. See your Lord with glo - ry crowned, Share in his re - joic - ing!

Text: 76 76 D; Isaiah 35; Christopher Idle, b. 1938, © 1982, The Jubilate Group. All rights reserved.
    Administered by Hope Publishing Co. Used with permission.
Music: GAUDEAMUS PARITER; Johann Horn, ca. 1495–1547.

## 282    THE KING SHALL COME WHEN MORNING DAWNS

1. The King shall come when morn - ing dawns And
2. Not, as of old, a lit - tle child, To
3. O bright - er than the ris - ing morn When
4. O bright - er than that glo - rious morn Shall
5. The King shall come when morn - ing dawns And

1. light tri - um - phant breaks, When beau - ty gilds the
2. bear, and fight, and die, But crowned with glo - ry
3. he, vic - to - rious, rose And left the lone-some
4. this fair morn - ing be, When Christ, our King, in
5. light and beau - ty brings. Hail, Christ, the Lord! Thy

1. east - ern hills And life to joy a - wakes.
2. like the sun That lights the morn - ing sky.
3. place of death, De - spite the rage of foes.
4. beau - ty comes, And we his face shall see!
5. peo - ple pray: Come quick - ly King of kings.

Text: CM; Greek; tr. by John Brownlie, 1859–1925, alt.
Music: MORNING SONG; *Sixteen Tune Settings*, Philadelphia, 1812; *Kentucky Harmony*, 1816.

## MARANATHA

**283**

Refrain

Ma - ra - na - tha, we long for your peace.

Ma - ra - na - tha, we long for your mer - cy. Ma - ra - na -

tha, we long for your com - ing, O God.

Verses

1. In your im - age you have fash - ioned us, in the
2. In our weak - ness we have turned from you, turned from
3. In your love ____ you have sent your Son, your sal -
4. We a - wait your day of glo - ry, Christ ____

1. gar - den you made ____ us; you have giv - en us your
2. light to the dark - ness, ev - er long - ing for sal -
3. va - tion for ev - 'ry - one; Word in - car - nate, God's com -
4. Je - sus, re - turn for us. Gen - tle King, ____ Just De -

to Refrain

1. breath of life, voice to praise your name, voice to praise your name.
2. va - tion, O ____ Lord of light, O ____ Lord of light.
3. pas - sion, hope for hu - man - kind, hope for hu - man - kind.
4. liv - er - er, you will bring us home, you will bring us home.

Text and music: Gerard Chiusano, b. 1965, © 2000, Gerard Chiusano. Published by OCP.

## 284 CHRIST, CIRCLE ROUND US

**Verses**

1. Come, O Ra - diant Dawn, splen-dor of the morn-ing
2. Come, O Flow'r of Love, ho - ly branch of Jes - se's
3. Come, O Word of Truth, font of know-ledge from on
4. Come, O Gate of Hope, ho - ly door of heav-en's
5. Come, O Might - y Lord, mas - ter of the stars of
6. Come, Em - man - u - el, cher-ished hope of Is - ra -
7. Come, Lord Je - sus Christ, long a - wait - ed Prince of

1. light. Come, Sun of Jus - tice,
2. tree. Come, Bough of Bless - ing,
3. high. Come, Ho - ly Wis - dom,
4. throne. Come, Key of Da - vid,
5. night. Come, Strength of Pil - grims,
6. el. Come, live a - mong us,
7. Peace. Come, Hope of Na - tions,

1. turn a - way the pow'r of night.
2. bloom for all the world to see.
3. be our faith - ful friend and guide.
4. o - pen wide the path - way home.
5. keep us in your lov - ing sight.
6. ev - er in our hearts to dwell.
7. ev - er make our love in - crease.

**Refrain**

Christ, cir - cle round us. Christ, may your light sur -

round us. Shine in our liv - ing. Fill our hearts

with great thanks - giv - ing.

Text: Based on Advent 'O' Antiphons; Dan Schutte, b. 1947.
Music: Based on *Salve Regina* (Chant, Mode V); Dan Schutte.

# LET THE KING OF GLORY COME

**Refrain**

Lift up, you gates, lift up your arch - es: let the King of glo - ry come! Lift up your hearts and sing, you peo - ple: let the King of glo - ry come!

*Last time to Coda ⊕*

**Verses**

1. Who is the King of glo - ry? Our God,
2. Come, O___ come, Em - man - u - el: come and
3. Come, O___ come, bright Wis - dom: come and
4. Come, you___ Key of Da - vid, come: o - pen our

1. ho - ly and strong! Who is the Lord of
2. dwell__ with us! Come, O___ come, you
3. make__ us wise! Come, O___ come, you
4. heav - en - ly home! Come, De - sire of

*to Refrain*

1. ma - jes - ty? Our God, might - y and strong!
2. Lord of might: ban - ish death__ and fear!
3. Day - spring: love, un - close__ our eyes!
4. na - tions, come: bring us in - to your peace!

**⊕ Coda**

Let the King of glo - ry come!

## 286     LIFT UP YOUR HEADS, YE MIGHTY GATES

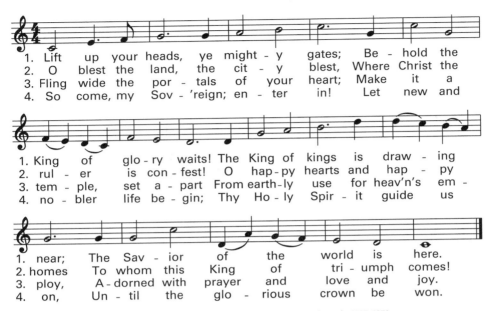

1. Lift up your heads, ye might-y gates; Be-hold the
2. O blest the land, the cit-y blest, Where Christ the
3. Fling wide the por-tals of your heart; Make it a
4. So come, my Sov-'reign; en-ter in! Let new and

1. King of glo-ry waits! The King of kings is draw-ing
2. rul-er is con-fest! O hap-py hearts and hap-py
3. tem-ple, set a-part From earth-ly use for heav'n's em-
4. no-bler life be-gin; Thy Ho-ly Spir-it guide us

1. near; The Sav-ior of the world is here.
2. homes To whom this King of tri-umph comes!
3. ploy, A-dorned with prayer and love and joy.
4. on, Un-til the glo-rious crown be won.

Text: LM; based on Psalm 24; George Weissel, 1590–1635; tr. by Catherine Winkworth, 1827–1878.
Music: TRURO; Williams' *Psalmodia Evangelica, Part II*, 1789.

## 287     THE ADVENT OF OUR KING

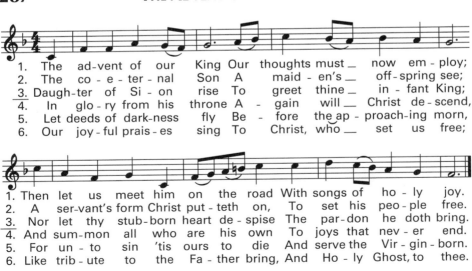

1. The ad-vent of our King Our thoughts must _ now em-ploy;
2. The co-e-ter-nal Son A maid-en's _ off-spring see;
3. Daugh-ter of Si-on rise To greet thine _ in-fant King;
4. In glo-ry from his throne A-gain will _ Christ de-scend,
5. Let deeds of dark-ness fly Be-fore the ap-proach-ing morn,
6. Our joy-ful prais-es sing To Christ, who _ set us free;

1. Then let us meet him on the road With songs of ho-ly joy.
2. A ser-vant's form Christ put-teth on, To set his peo-ple free.
3. Nor let thy stub-born heart de-spise The par-don he doth bring.
4. And sum-mon all who are his own To joys that nev-er end.
5. For un-to sin 'tis ours to die And serve the Vir-gin-born.
6. Like trib-ute to the Fa-ther bring, And Ho-ly Ghost, to thee.

Text: SM; Charles Coffin, fr. *Paris Breviary*, 1736; tr. by Robert Campbell, 1814–1868, alt.
Music: ST. THOMAS (WILLIAMS); *New Universal Psalmodist*, 1770; Aaron Williams, 1731–1776.

# READY THE WAY

1. "Read - y the way of the Lord!
2. "Let ev - 'ry val - ley be filled.
3. Des - ert and waste-land will bloom.
4. Those who are blind will then see.
5. Strength-en the ones who are weak.

Read - y the
Let ev - 'ry
Des - ert and
Those who are
Strength-en the

1. way of the Lord!" A voice ___ cries out in the wil - der-
2. val - ley be filled. Let ev - 'ry moun-tain be hum -
3. waste-land will bloom. Glo - ry and splen - dor will fill the
4. deaf will then hear. Those who are lame will then leap for
5. ones who are weak. Say to the fright-ened: "Have cour -

1. ness: "Read - y the way of the Lord!" (to Verse 2)
2. bled; let ev - 'ry val - ley be filled." (to Refrain)
3. land. Des - ert and waste-land will bloom. (to Verse 4)
4. joy. Those who are mute will then sing. (to Refrain)
5. age." Strength-en the ones who are weak. (to Refrain)

**Refrain**

Here is your God, com-ing with your vin-di-ca - tion.

Look and be-hold the sav - ing pow - er of God.

1, 2 to Verses 3, 5 | Final

The sav - ing pow - er of God.

Text: Based on Isaiah 35:1–6; 40:1–5, 9–11; Ezekiel 11:19–20; Bob Hurd, b. 1950.
Music: Bob Hurd.

**289**     EVERY VALLEY

Refrain

Ev-'ry val-ley shall be ex-alt-ed and ev-'ry hill made low. And all God's peo-ple shall see to-geth-er the glo-ry of the Lord.

Verses 1, 3

1. A voice cries out in the wil-der-ness, "Pre-pare the way
3. Stand up-on the __ moun-tain-top. O lift your voice

1. of the Lord. Make straight in the des-ert a
3. to the world. Sing joy - ful-ly, Je -

1. high - way, a high-way __ for our God."
3. ru - sa - lem: "Be-hold, __ be-hold your God."

Verse 2

2. Com-fort all my peo - ple. The time for war is gone. The

2. blind shall see, the deaf shall hear, the lame shall leap for joy.

Text: Based on Isaiah 40:1, 3, 4, 9; Bob Dufford, SJ, b. 1943.
Music: Bob Dufford, SJ.
Text and music © 1970, Robert J. Dufford, SJ. Published by OCP. All rights reserved.

**290**     CREATOR OF THE STARS OF NIGHT

1. Cre - a - tor of the stars of night, Your peo - ple's
2. In sor - row that the an - cient curse Should doom to
3. When this old world drew on toward night, You came; but
4. At your great Name, O Je - sus, now All knees must
5. Come in your ho - ly might, we pray, Re - deem us
6. To God Cre - a - tor, God the Son, And God the

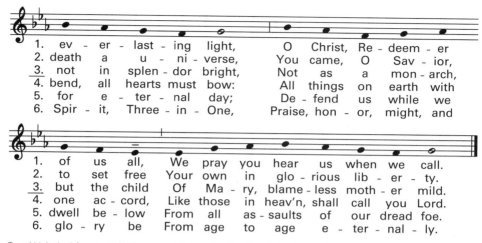

1. ev - er - last - ing light, O Christ, Re - deem - er
2. death a u - ni - verse, You came, O Sav - ior,
3. not in splen - dor bright, Not as a mon - arch,
4. bend, all hearts must bow: All things on earth with
5. for e - ter - nal day; De - fend us while we
6. Spir - it, Three - in - One, Praise, hon - or, might, and

1. of us all, We pray you hear us when we call.
2. to set free Your own in glo - rious lib - er - ty.
3. but the child Of Ma - ry, blame - less moth - er mild.
4. one ac - cord, Like those in heav'n, shall call you Lord.
5. dwell be - low From all as - saults of our dread foe.
6. glo - ry be From age to age e - ter - nal - ly.

Text: LM; Latin, 9th cent.; tr. fr. *The Hymnal 1982* © 1985, The Church Pension Fund. All rights reserved.
Used with permission of Church Publishing, Inc., New York, NY.
Music: CONDITOR ALME SIDERUM; Chant, Mode IV.

## ADVENT LITANY/LETANÍA DE ADVIENTO     291

O come, O come.
*Oh ven, oh ven.*
O come, O come.
*Oh ven, oh ven.*

1. True light of the world.
   Promised one from God.
   Wonder Counselor.
   Holy Prince of Peace.

2a. Shoot from Jesse's tree.
   King from David's throne.
   Heaven's brightest star.
   Light amidst the darkness.

2b. Fullness of God's glory.
   Son of the Most High.
   Eternal Word made flesh.
   Recompense divine.

3a. Lover of the just.
   Protector of the stranger.
   Sustainer of the widow.
   Justice for the world.

3b. Food for those who hunger.
   Freedom for the captives.
   Day of vindication.
   Anointed One, Emmanuel.

1. *Luz verdadera.*
   *Prometido de Dios.*
   *Consejero admirable.*
   *Príncipe de paz.*

2a. *Linaje de Jesé.*
   *Hijo de David.*
   *La estrella más brillante.*
   *Luz en las tinieblas.*

2b. *Gloria de los cielos.*
   *Hijo del Altísimo.*
   *Verbo encarnado.*
   *Divina recompensa.*

3a. *Amor para el que es justo.*
   *Protector del forastero.*
   *Aliento para la viuda.*
   *Justicia para el mundo.*

3b. *Sustento de los pobres.*
   *Liberación para los cautivos.*
   *Día de venganza.*
   *El Ungido, Emmanuel.*

*Verses available in accompaniment books.

Text: Based on Isaiah 11; 12; 35 and 'O' Antiphons; Jaime Cortez, b. 1963.
Music: Jaime Cortez.
Text and music © 2005, Jaime Cortez. Published by OCP. All rights reserved.

## 292      LET THE VALLEYS BE RAISED

**Refrain**

Let the val - leys be raised and the moun - tains made low. Ev-'ry mead-
- ow and field o-ver-turn. Make the path - way straight
and the high-way run smooth for the com - ing of God in our day.

**Verses**

1. God, _____ you come to your peo - ple      as you prom-
2. You, lit-tle _ child, go be - fore him      like the proph-
3. God, _____ you come like the morn - ing      on the dark-

1. - ised of old.      You have raised    up a Sav-
2. - ets of old,      bring-ing news    of his com-
3. - ness of night,      as a light    to the peo-

*to Refrain*

1. - ior      in the sight   of us   all.
2. - ing      by the mer - cy of God.
3. - ple,      like the break - ing of day.

Text: Based on Isaiah 40:3–5; Luke 1:68–79; Dan Schutte, b. 1947.
Music: Dan Schutte.

## 293      LITANY OF THE WORD

Cantor      All      Cantor      All

1. Word of jus - tice,    Al-le-lu - ia,    Come to dwell here.    Ma-ra-na-tha!
2. Word of mer - cy,    Al-le-lu - ia,    Live a-mong us.    Ma-ra-na-tha!
3. Word of pow - er,    Al-le-lu - ia,    Live with - in us.    Ma-ra-na-tha!
*4. Word of free-dom,    Al-le-lu - ia,    Save your peo - ple.    Ma-ra-na-tha!

*Additional verses available in accompaniment books.

# READY THE WAY

Text: Based on Isaiah 40:3, 4a; Curtis Stephan, b. 1973.
Music: Curtis Stephan.

## 295     COMFORT, COMFORT, O MY PEOPLE

1. Com - fort, com - fort, O my peo - ple, Speak of peace, now
2. Hark, the voice of one who's cry - ing In the des - ert
3. O make straight what long was crook - ed, Make the rough - er

1. says our God; Com - fort those who sit in dark - ness,
2. far and near, Bid - ding all to full re - pent - ance
3. plac - es plain; Let your hearts be true and hum - ble,

1. Mourn-ing 'neath their sor-rows' load. Speak un - to Je - ru - sa -
2. Since the king-dom now is here. O that warn - ing cry o -
3. As be - fits his ho - ly reign. For the glo - ry of the

1. lem Of the peace that waits for them; Tell of all the
2. bey! Now pre - pare for God a way; Let the val - leys
3. Lord Now o'er earth is shed a - broad; And all flesh shall

1. sins I cov - er, And that war - fare now is o - ver.
2. rise to meet him And the hills bow down to greet him.
3. see the to - ken That his word is nev - er bro - ken.

Text: 87 87 77 88; based on Isaiah 40:1–8; Johann G. Olearius, 1611–1684; tr. by Catherine Winkworth, 1827–1878, alt.
Music: GENEVA 42; Claude Goudimel, ca. 1514–1572; *Genevan Psalter*, 1551.

## 296     COME, O LONG-EXPECTED JESUS

1. Come, O long - ex - pect - ed Je - sus, Born to
2. Is - rael's strength and con - so - la - tion, Hope to
3. Born your peo - ple to de - liv - er, Born a
4. By your own e - ter - nal Spir - it Rule in

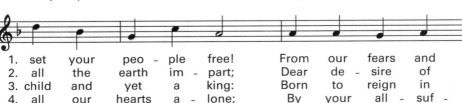

1. set your peo - ple free! From our fears and
2. all the earth im - part; Dear de - sire of
3. child and yet a king: Born to reign in
4. all our hearts a - lone; By your all - suf -

1. sins re - lease us, You in whom our rest shall be.
2. ev - 'ry na - tion, Joy of ev - 'ry long - ing heart.
3. us for - ev - er, Now your gra - cious king - dom bring.
4. fi - cient mer - it Raise us to your glo - rious throne.

Text: 87 87; Charles Wesley, 1707–1788, alt.
Music: STUTTGART; Christian F. Witt's *Psalmodia Sacra*, Gotha, 1715; adapt. by Henry J. Gauntlett, 1805–1876.

## PEOPLE, LOOK EAST 297

1. Peo - ple, look East. The time is near Of the
2. Fur - rows, be glad, though earth is bare. One more
3. Birds, though you long have ceased to build, Guard the
4. Stars, keep the watch when night is dim. One more
5. An - gels, an - nounce on this great feast: Him who

1. crown - ing of the year. Make your house fair as you are
2. seed is plant - ed there; Give up your strength the seed to
3. nest that must be filled. E - ven the hour when wings are
4. light the bowl shall brim. Shin - ing be - yond the frost - y
5. com - eth from the East. Set ev - 'ry peak and val - ley

1. a - ble. Trim the hearth and set the ta - ble. Peo - ple, look
2. nour - ish, That in course the flow'r may flour - ish. Peo - ple, look
3. fro - zen He for fledg - ing time has cho - sen. Peo - ple, look
4. weath - er, Bright as sun and moon to - geth - er. Peo - ple, look
5. hum - ming With the word, the Lord is com - ing. Peo - ple, look

1. East, and sing to - day: Love, the Guest, is on the way.
2. East, and sing to - day: Love, the Rose, is on the way.
3. East, and sing to - day: Love, the Bird, is on the way.
4. East, and sing to - day: Love, the Star, is on the way.
5. East, and sing to - day: Love, the Lord, is on the way.

Text: 87 98 87; *Oxford Book of Carols*, 1928; Eleanor Farjeon, 1881–1965, © 1957, Eleanor Farjeon. All rights reserved.
Reprinted by permission of Harold Ober Assoc., Inc.
Music: BESANÇON; Trad. French Carol.

## 298     WAKE, O WAKE, AND SLEEP NO LONGER

1. Wake, O wake, and sleep no long - er, For he who calls you
2. Zi - on hears the sound of sing - ing; Our hearts are thrilled with
3. Glo - ry, glo - ry, sing the an - gels, While mu - sic sounds from

1. is no strang - er: A - wake, God's own Je - ru - sa - lem!
2. sud - den long - ing: She stirs, and wakes, and stands pre - pared.
3. strings and cym - bals; All hu - man - kind, with songs a - rise!

1. Hear, the mid-night bells are chim - ing The sig - nal for his
2. Christ, her friend, and lord, and lov - er, Her star and sun and
3. Twelve the gates in - to the cit - y, Each one a pearl of

1. roy - al com - ing: Let voice to voice an-nounce his name!
2. strong re - deem - er— At last his might - y voice is heard.
3. shin - ing beau - ty; The streets of gold ring out with praise.

1. We feel his foot-steps near, The Bride-groom at the
2. The Son of God has come To make with us his
3. All crea - tures round the throne A - dore the ho - ly

1. door— Al - le - lu - ia! The lamps will shine with
2. home: Sing ho - san - na! The fight is won, the
3. One With re - joic - ing: A - men be sung by

1. light di - vine As Christ the Sav - ior comes to reign.
2. feast be - gun; We fix our eyes on Christ a - lone.
3. ev - 'ry tongue To crown their wel - come to the King.

Text: 898 898 664 88; based on Matthew 25:1–13; tr. and adapt. by Christopher Idle, b. 1938, © 1982, The Jubilate Group.
   All rights reserved. Administered by Hope Publishing Co. Used with permission.
Music: WACHET AUF; Philipp Nicolai, 1556–1608; adapt. by Johann Sebastian Bach, 1685–1750.

# EMMANUEL

Come, come, Em-man-u-el! Son of God, ap-pear. Heav-en and
earth, re-joice! Sal - va-tion is draw-ing near.

**Verses**

1. O come, O come, Em - man - u - el,
___ That mourns in lone - ly ex - ile here
2. O come, O Wis - dom from on high,
___ To us the path of knowl-edge show,
3. O come, O Rod of Jes - se's stem;
___ That trust your might - y pow'r to save,
4. O come, De - sire of na - tions, bind
___ Make all our sad di - vi - sions cease,
5. Re - joice! Em - man - u - el
   Re - joice! Em - man - u - el

*(to Refrain)*

1. And ran - som cap - tive Is - ra - el,
___ Un - til the Son of God ap - pear.
2. Who or - dered all things might - i - ly;
___ And teach us in her ways to go.
3. From ev - 'ry foe de - liv - er them
___ And give them vic - t'ry o'er the grave.
4. In one the hearts of hu - man - kind;
___ And be for us the King of Peace.
5. shall come to thee, O Is - ra - el.
   shall come to thee, O Is - ra - el. *(Fine)*

Text: Refrain, Steve Angrisano, b. 1965, © 2004, Steve Angrisano. Published by OCP. All rights reserved.
   Verses based on Advent 'O' Antiphons.
Music: Steve Angrisano, © 2004, Steve Angrisano. Published by OCP. All rights reserved.

# 300      O COME, ALL YE FAITHFUL

Text: Irregular with refrain; John F. Wade, ca. 1711–1786; tr. by Frederick Oakeley, 1802–1880, alt.
Music: ADESTE FIDELES; John F. Wade.

## WAKE FROM YOUR SLEEP 301

1. Wake from your sleep, a Sav-ior is born. God's ho-ly
2. Come from your fields as shep-herds of old. Wel-come this
3. Stay with us now, O Lord of the earth. Make of our
4. Now shall the earth take joy in her tears. Now shall our

1. child gives light to this morn, all our dark-ness
2. child whom proph-ets fore-told. God has made the
3. hearts a place for your birth. Though our cares be
4. hearts be turned from their fears. All the earth shall

1. to dis-pel. Praise to our God whose glo-ry we tell.
2. earth his home. Praise to our God, the Sav-ior has come.
3. great or small, Je-sus the Lord, be born in us all.
4. sing God's praise. Je-sus the Lord, be born on this day.

Text and music: Dan Schutte, b. 1947, © 1977, 1978, Daniel L. Schutte and OCP. All rights reserved.

## LO, HOW A ROSE E'ER BLOOMING 302

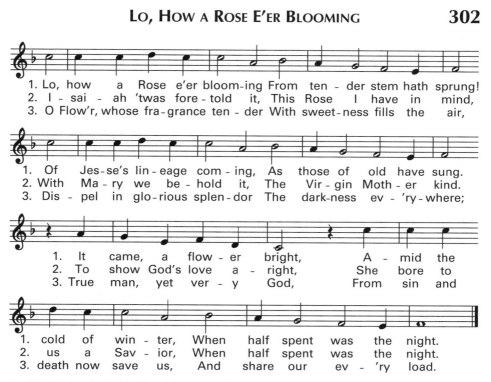

1. Lo, how a Rose e'er bloom-ing From ten-der stem hath sprung!
2. I-sai-ah 'twas fore-told it, This Rose I have in mind,
3. O Flow'r, whose fra-grance ten-der With sweet-ness fills the air,

1. Of Jes-se's lin-eage com-ing, As those of old have sung.
2. With Ma-ry we be-hold it, The Vir-gin Moth-er kind.
3. Dis-pel in glo-rious splen-dor The dark-ness ev-'ry-where;

1. It came, a flow-er bright, A-mid the
2. To show God's love a-right, She bore to
3. True man, yet ver-y God, From sin and

1. cold of win-ter, When half spent was the night.
2. us a Sav-ior, When half spent was the night.
3. death now save us, And share our ev-'ry load.

Text: 76 76 6 76; based on Isaiah 11:1; trad. German Carol, 15th cent.; tr. by Theodore Baker, 1851–1934, alt.
Music: ES IST EIN' ROS' ENTSPRUNGEN; *Alte Catholische Geistliche Kirchengesänge*, Cologne, 1599.

**303**       JOY TO THE WORLD

1. Joy to the world! the Lord is come; Let earth re-
2. Joy to the world! the Sav-ior reigns; Let us our
3. No more let sins and sor-rows grow, Nor thorns in-
4. He rules the world with truth and grace, And makes the

1. ceive her King; Let ev-'ry heart pre-pare him
2. songs em-ploy; While fields and floods, rocks, hills and
3. fest the ground; He comes to make his bless-ings
4. na-tions prove The glo-ries of his righ-teous-

1. room, And heav'n and na-ture sing, And heav'n and na-ture
2. plains Re-peat the sound-ing joy, Re-peat the sound-ing
3. flow Far as the curse is found, Far as the curse is
4. ness, And won-ders of his love, And won-ders of his

1. sing, And heav'n, and heav'n and na-ture sing.
2. joy, Re-peat, re-peat the sound-ing joy.
3. found, Far as, far as the curse is found.
4. love, And won-ders, won-ders of his love.

Text: CM with repeats: based on Psalm 98; Isaac Watts, 1764–1748, alt.
Music: ANTIOCH; T. Hawkes' *Collection of Tunes*, 1833; George Frideric Handel, 1685–1759;
     adapt. by Lowell Mason, 1792–1872, alt.

**304**       GOD REST YOU MERRY, GENTLEMEN

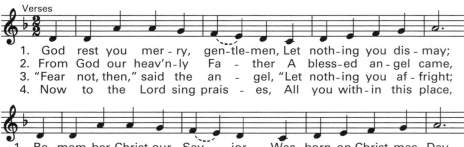

Verses

1. God rest you mer-ry, gen-tle-men, Let noth-ing you dis-may;
2. From God our heav'n-ly Fa-ther A bless-ed an-gel came,
3. "Fear not, then," said the an-gel, "Let noth-ing you af-fright;
4. Now to the Lord sing prais-es, All you with-in this place,

1. Re-mem-ber Christ our Sav-ior Was born on Christ-mas Day
2. And un-to cer-tain shep-herds Brought tid-ings of the same,
3. This day is born a Sav-ior Of Vir-gin pure and bright,
4. And with true love and char-i-ty Each oth-er now em-brace;

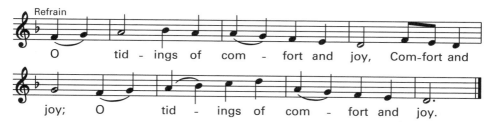

1. To save us all from Sa-tan's pow'r When we were gone a-stray.
2. How that in Beth-le-hem was born The Son of God by name.
3. To free all those who trust in him From Sa-tan's pow'r and might."
4. This ho-ly tide of Christ-mas Is filled with heav'n-ly grace.

**Refrain**

O tid-ings of com-fort and joy, Com-fort and joy; O tid-ings of com-fort and joy.

Text: 86 86 86 with refrain; trad. English Carol, 18th cent.
Music: GOD REST YOU MERRY; trad. English Carol; melody fr. *Little Book of Christmas Carols*, ca. 1846.

## WHILE SHEPHERDS WATCHED THEIR FLOCKS    305

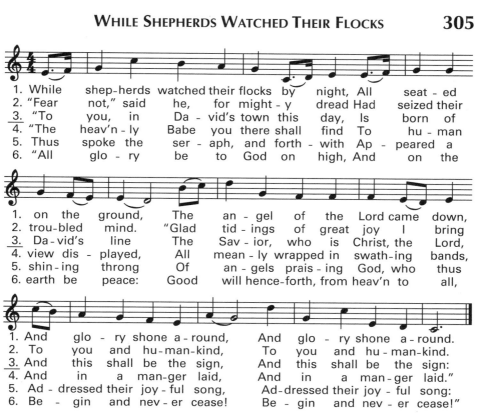

1. While shep-herds watched their flocks by night, All seat-ed
2. "Fear not," said he, for might-y dread Had seized their
3. "To you, in Da-vid's town this day, Is born of
4. "The heav'n-ly Babe you there shall find To hu-man
5. Thus spoke the ser-aph, and forth-with Ap-peared a
6. "All glo-ry be to God on high, And on the

1. on the ground, The an-gel of the Lord came down,
2. trou-bled mind. "Glad tid-ings of great joy I bring
3. Da-vid's line The Sav-ior, who is Christ, the Lord,
4. view dis-played, All mean-ly wrapped in swath-ing bands,
5. shin-ing throng Of an-gels prais-ing God, who thus
6. earth be peace: Good will hence-forth, from heav'n to all,

1. And glo-ry shone a-round, And glo-ry shone a-round.
2. To you and hu-man-kind, To you and hu-man-kind.
3. And this shall be the sign, And this shall be the sign:
4. And in a man-ger laid, And in a man-ger laid."
5. Ad-dressed their joy-ful song, Ad-dressed their joy-ful song:
6. Be-gin and nev-er cease! Be-gin and nev-er cease!"

Text 86 86 6; based on Luke 2:8–14; Nahum Tate, 1652–1715, alt.
Music: CHRISTMAS; George Frideric Handel, 1685–1759; adapt. in *Harmonia Sacra*, 1812.

## 306 It Came upon the Midnight Clear

1. It came up-on the mid-night clear, That glo - rious
2. Still through the clo - ven skies they come, With peace - ful
3. And ye, be-neath life's crush-ing load, Whose forms are
4. For, lo, the days are has-tening on, By proph - et

1. song of old, From an - gels bend - ing near the
2. wings un-furled, And still their heav'n - ly mu - sic
3. bend - ing low, Who toil a - long the climb - ing
4. bards fore-told, When with the ev - er - cir - cling

1. earth To touch their harps of gold: "Peace on the earth, good
2. floats O'er all the wea - ry world: A - bove its sad and
3. way With pain-ful steps and slow, Look now! for glad and
4. years Comes 'round the age of gold; When peace shall o - ver

1. will to all From heav'n's all gra - cious King;" The
2. low - ly plains They bend on hov - 'ring wing, And
3. gold - en hours Come swift - ly on the wing: O
4. all the earth Its an - cient splen - dors fling, And

1. world in sol - emn still-ness lay, To hear the an - gels sing.
2. ev - er o'er its Ba - bel sounds The bless-ed an - gels sing.
3. rest be - side the wea - ry road And hear the an - gels sing.
4. all the world give back the song Which now the an - gels sing.

Text: CMD; Edmund H. Sears, 1810–1876, alt.
Music: CAROL; Richard S. Willis, 1819–1900, alt.

## 307 A Child Is Born in Bethlehem

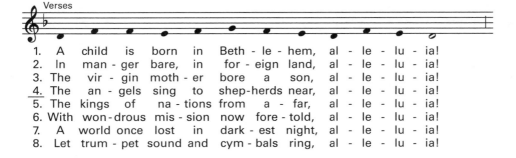

Verses

1. A child is born in Beth - le - hem, al - le - lu - ia!
2. In man - ger bare, in for - eign land, al - le - lu - ia!
3. The vir - gin moth - er bore a son, al - le - lu - ia!
4. The an - gels sing to shep-herds near, al - le - lu - ia!
5. The kings of na - tions from a - far, al - le - lu - ia!
6. With won-drous mis - sion now fore-told, al - le - lu - ia!
7. A world once lost in dark - est night, al - le - lu - ia!
8. Let trum - pet sound and cym - bals ring, al - le - lu - ia!

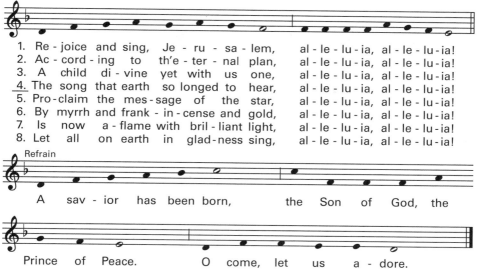

1. Re - joice and sing, Je - ru - sa - lem, al - le - lu - ia, al - le - lu - ia!
2. Ac - cord - ing to th'e - ter - nal plan, al - le - lu - ia, al - le - lu - ia!
3. A child di - vine yet with us one, al - le - lu - ia, al - le - lu - ia!
4. The song that earth so longed to hear, al - le - lu - ia, al - le - lu - ia!
5. Pro - claim the mes - sage of the star, al - le - lu - ia, al - le - lu - ia!
6. By myrrh and frank - in - cense and gold, al - le - lu - ia, al - le - lu - ia!
7. Is now a - flame with bril - liant light, al - le - lu - ia, al - le - lu - ia!
8. Let all on earth in glad - ness sing, al - le - lu - ia, al - le - lu - ia!

**Refrain**

A sav - ior has been born, the Son of God, the

Prince of Peace. O come, let us a - dore.

Text: 88 with alleluias and refrain; *Puer natus in Bethlehem*; Latin, 14th cent.;
tr. by Owen Alstott, b. 1947, © 2002, OCP. All rights reserved.
Music: PUER NATUS; Chant, Mode I.

## ANGELS WE HAVE HEARD ON HIGH 308

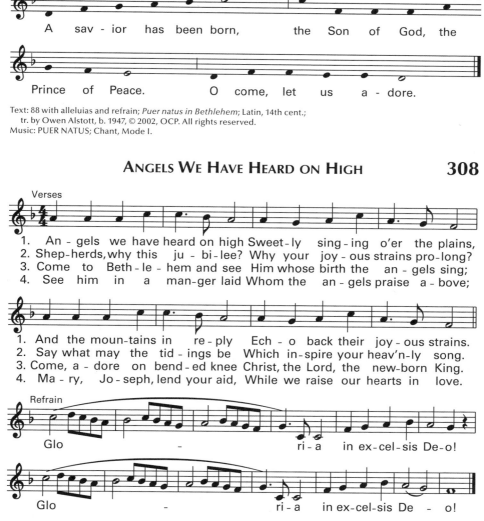

**Verses**

1. An - gels we have heard on high Sweet - ly sing - ing o'er the plains,
2. Shep - herds, why this ju - bi - lee? Why your joy - ous strains pro - long?
3. Come to Beth - le - hem and see Him whose birth the an - gels sing;
4. See him in a man - ger laid Whom the an - gels praise a - bove;

1. And the moun - tains in re - ply Ech - o back their joy - ous strains.
2. Say what may the tid - ings be Which in - spire your heav'n - ly song.
3. Come, a - dore on bend - ed knee Christ, the Lord, the new - born King.
4. Ma - ry, Jo - seph, lend your aid, While we raise our hearts in love.

**Refrain**

Glo - ri - a in ex - cel - sis De - o!

Glo - ri - a in ex - cel - sis De - o!

Text: 77 77 with refrain; Trad. French Carol, ca. 18th cent.; tr. fr. *Crown of Jesus Music, II*, London, 1862;
tr. by James Chadwick, 1813–1882, and others, alt.
Music: GLORIA; Trad. French Carol.

## 309     SILENT NIGHT

1. Si - lent night! Ho - ly night! All is calm, all is bright Round yon
2. Si - lent night! Ho - ly night! Shep-herds quake at the sight; Glo - ries
3. Si - lent night! Ho - ly night! Son of God, love's pure light Ra - diant

1. Vir - gin Moth-er and child! Ho - ly in-fant so ten-der and mild,
2. stream from heav-en a - far; Heav'n-ly hosts__ sing "Al - le - lu - ia!
3. beams from thy ho-ly face, With the dawn of re-deem - ing grace,

1. Sleep in heav-en-ly peace, Sleep in heav-en-ly peace.
2. Christ the Sav-ior is born, Christ the Sav-ior is born."
3. Je - sus, Lord, at thy birth, Je - sus, Lord, at thy birth.

Text: Irregular; Joseph Mohr, 1792–1849; English tr. by John F. Young, 1820–1885.
Music: STILLE NACHT; Franz X. Gruber, 1787–1863.

## 310     AWAY IN A MANGER

1. A - way in a man-ger, no crib for a bed, The
2. The cat - tle are low - ing, the ba - by a - wakes, But
3. Be near me, Lord Je - sus! I ask thee to stay Close

1. lit - tle Lord Je - sus laid down his sweet head. The
2. lit - tle Lord Je - sus, no cry - ing he makes. I
3. by me for - ev - er, and love me, I pray. Bless

1. stars in the bright sky looked down where he lay, The
2. love thee, Lord Je - sus! Look down from the sky, And
3. all the dear chil - dren in thy ten - der care, And

1. lit - tle Lord Je - sus, a - sleep on the hay.
2. stay by my side un - til morn - ing is nigh.
3. fit us for heav - en, to live with thee there.

Text: 11 11 11 11; verses 1–2, *Little Children's Book for Schools and Families*, ca. 1885;
verse 3, John T. McFarland, 1851–1913; Gabriel's *Vineyard Songs*, 1892, alt.
Music: CRADLE SONG; William J. Kirkpatrick, 1838–1921.

# GO, TELL IT ON THE MOUNTAIN

**311**

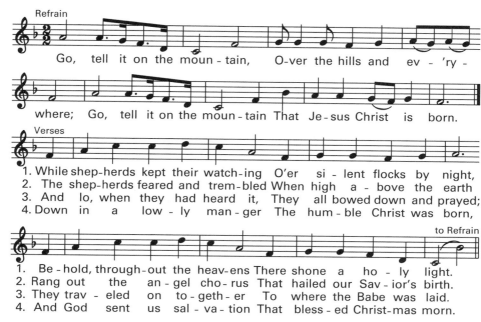

Refrain

Go, tell it on the moun-tain, O-ver the hills and ev-'ry-where; Go, tell it on the moun-tain That Je-sus Christ is born.

Verses

1. While shep-herds kept their watch-ing O'er si-lent flocks by night,
2. The shep-herds feared and trem-bled When high a-bove the earth
3. And lo, when they had heard it, They all bowed down and prayed;
4. Down in a low-ly man-ger The hum-ble Christ was born,

to Refrain

1. Be-hold, through-out the heav-ens There shone a ho-ly light.
2. Rang out the an-gel cho-rus That hailed our Sav-ior's birth.
3. They trav-eled on to-geth-er To where the Babe was laid.
4. And God sent us sal-va-tion That bless-ed Christ-mas morn.

Text: 76 76 with refrain; fr. *American Negro Songs and Spirituals*, 1940; John W. Work, Jr., 1872–1925, alt.
Music: GO TELL IT; Spiritual.

# INFANT HOLY, INFANT LOWLY

**312**

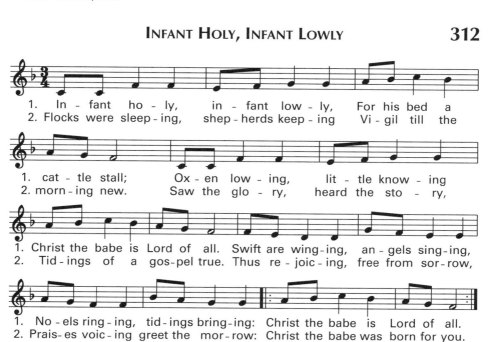

1. In-fant ho-ly, in-fant low-ly, For his bed a
2. Flocks were sleep-ing, shep-herds keep-ing Vi-gil till the

1. cat-tle stall; Ox-en low-ing, lit-tle know-ing
2. morn-ing new. Saw the glo-ry, heard the sto-ry,

1. Christ the babe is Lord of all. Swift are wing-ing, an-gels sing-ing,
2. Tid-ings of a gos-pel true. Thus re-joic-ing, free from sor-row,

1. No-els ring-ing, tid-ings bring-ing: Christ the babe is Lord of all.
2. Prais-es voic-ing greet the mor-row: Christ the babe was born for you.

Text: 87 87 88 77; Polish Carol; tr. by Edith Margaret Gellibrand Reed, 1885–1933.
Music: W ZLOBIE LEZY; Polish Carol.

**313**    HARK! THE HERALD ANGELS SING

1. Hark! the her-ald an-gels sing: "Glo-ry to the
2. Christ, by high-est heav'n a-dored, Christ, the ev-er-
3. Hail the heav'n-born Prince of Peace! Hail the Sun of

1. new-born King; Peace on earth, and mer-cy mild,
2. last-ing Lord; Late in time, be-hold him come,
3. Righ-teous-ness! Light and life to all he brings,

1. God and sin-ners rec-on-ciled!" Joy-ful, all ye
2. Off-spring of a vir-gin's womb. Veiled in flesh the
3. Ris'n with heal-ing in his wings. Mild he lays his

1. na-tions, rise, Join the tri-umph of the skies; With an-
2. God-head see! Hail th'in-car-nate De-i-ty! Pleased as
3. glo-ry by, Born that we no more may die, Born to

1. gel-ic hosts pro-claim: "Christ is born in Beth-le-hem!"
2. man with us to dwell; Je-sus, our Em-man-u-el!
3. raise us from the earth, Born to give us sec-ond birth.

**Refrain**

Hark! the her-ald an-gels sing, "Glo-ry to the new-born King."

Text: 77 77 D with refrain; Charles Wesley, 1707–1788, alt.
Music: MENDELSSOHN; Felix Mendelssohn, 1809–1847; adapt. by William H. Cummings, 1831–1915.

**314**    GOOD CHRISTIAN FRIENDS, REJOICE

1-3. Good Chris-tian friends, re-joice, With heart and soul and voice;

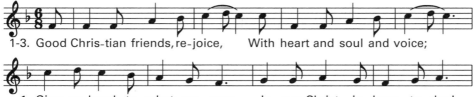

1. Give ye heed to what we say: Je-sus Christ is born to-day!
2. Now ye hear of end-less bliss; Je-sus Christ was born for this!
3. Now ye need not fear the grave; Je-sus Christ was born to save!

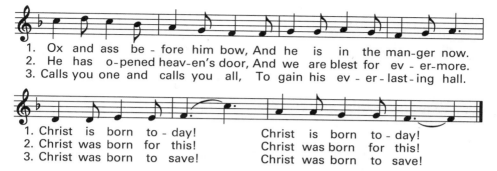

1. Ox and ass be-fore him bow, And he is in the man-ger now.
2. He has o-pened heav-en's door, And we are blest for ev-er-more.
3. Calls you one and calls you all, To gain his ev-er-last-ing hall.

1. Christ is born to-day! Christ is born to-day!
2. Christ was born for this! Christ was born for this!
3. Christ was born to save! Christ was born to save!

Text: 66 77 78 55; Latin and German, 14th cent.; tr. by John M. Neale, 1818–1866, alt.
Music: IN DULCI JUBILO; J. Klug's *Geistliche Lieder*, Wittenberg, 1535.

## RISE UP, SHEPHERD, AND FOLLOW  315

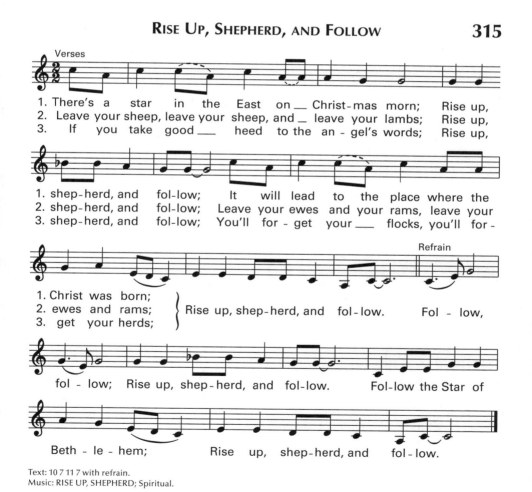

Verses

1. There's a star in the East on __ Christ-mas morn; Rise up,
2. Leave your sheep, leave your sheep, and __ leave your lambs; Rise up,
3. If you take good __ heed to the an - gel's words; Rise up,

1. shep-herd, and fol-low; It will lead to the place where the
2. shep-herd, and fol-low; Leave your ewes and your rams, leave your
3. shep-herd, and fol-low; You'll for - get your __ flocks, you'll for -

Refrain

1. Christ was born;
2. ewes and rams;   Rise up, shep-herd, and fol-low. Fol - low,
3. get your herds;

fol - low; Rise up, shep-herd, and fol-low. Fol-low the Star of

Beth - le - hem; Rise up, shep-herd, and fol-low.

Text: 10 7 11 7 with refrain.
Music: RISE UP, SHEPHERD; Spiritual.

## 316      O LITTLE TOWN OF BETHLEHEM

1. O lit - tle town of Beth - le - hem, How still we see thee lie!
2. For Christ is born of Ma - ry, And gath - ered all a - bove,
3. How si - lent - ly, how si - lent - ly, The won - drous gift is giv'n!
4. O ho - ly Child of Beth - le - hem! De - scend to us, we pray;

1. A - bove thy deep and dream - less sleep The si - lent stars go by;
2. While mor - tals sleep, the an - gels keep Their watch of won - d'ring love.
3. So God im - parts to hu - man hearts The bless - ings of his heav'n.
4. Cast out our sin and en - ter in; Be born in us to - day.

1. Yet in thy dark streets shin - eth The ev - er - last - ing Light:
2. O morn - ing stars, to - geth - er Pro - claim the ho - ly birth!
3. No ear may hear his com - ing, But in this world of sin,
4. We hear the Christ - mas an - gels The great glad tid - ings tell;

1. The hopes and fears of all the years Are met in thee to - night.
2. And prais - es sing to God the King, And peace to all on earth.
3. Where meek souls will re - ceive him, still The dear Christ en - ters in.
4. O come to us, a - bide with us, Our Lord Em - man - u - el!

Text: 86 86 76 86; Phillips Brooks, 1835–1893, alt.
Music: ST. LOUIS; Lewis H. Redner, 1831–1908.

## 317      OF THE FATHER'S LOVE BEGOTTEN

1. Of the Fa - ther's love be - got - ten, Ere the worlds be -
2. Bless - ed was the day for ev - er When the Vir - gin,
3. This is he whom seers in old time Chant - ed of with
4. O ye heights of heav'n, a - dore him; An - gel hosts, his
5. Glo - ry be to God the Fa - ther, Glo - ry be to

1. gan to be, He is Al - pha and O - me - ga,
2. full of grace, By the Ho - ly Ghost con - ceiv - ing,
3. one ac - cord, Whom the voic - es of the proph - ets
4. prais - es sing; All do - min - ions, bow be - fore him,
5. God the Son, Glo - ry to the Ho - ly Spir - it,

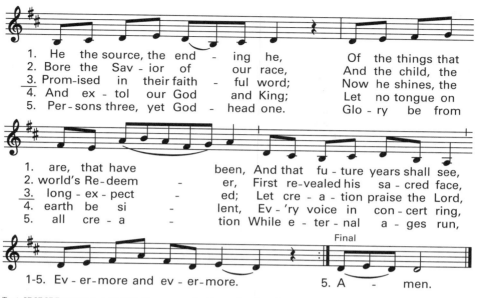

1. He the source, the end - ing he, Of the things that
2. Bore the Sav - ior of our race, And the child, the
3. Prom-ised in their faith - ful word; Now he shines, the
4. And ex - tol our God and King; Let no tongue on
5. Per - sons three, yet God - head one. Glo - ry be from

1. are, that have been, And that fu - ture years shall see,
2. world's Re - deem - er, First re-vealed his sa - cred face,
3. long - ex - pect - ed; Let cre - a - tion praise the Lord,
4. earth be si - lent, Ev - 'ry voice in con - cert ring,
5. all cre - a - tion While e - ter - nal a - ges run,

1-5. Ev - er-more and ev - er-more.   5. A - men.

Text: 87 87 87 7; verses 1–4, *Corde natus ex parentis*; Marcus Aurelius Clemens Prudentius, 348–413;
   tr. by John M. Neale, 1818–1866, and Henry W. Baker, 1827–1877, alt.; verse 5, Horatius Bonar, 1808–1889.
Music: DIVINUM MYSTERIUM; *Sanctus* trope, 11th cent.; Chant, Mode V; adapt. fr. *Piae Cantiones*, 1582.

## CHRIST WAS BORN ON CHRISTMAS DAY   318

1. Christ was born on Christ-mas day: Wreathe the hol - ly,
2. He is born to set us free, He is born our
3. Let the bright red ber - ries glow Ev - 'ry-where in
4. Chris - tians all, re - joice and sing, 'Tis the birth - day

1. twine the bay, *Chri - stus na - tus ho - di - e:* The
2. Lord to be, *Ex Ma - ri - a Vir - gi - ne:* The
3. good - ly show: *Chri - stus na - tus ho - di - e:* The
4. of a King, *Ex Ma - ri - a Vir - gi - ne:* The

1. Babe, the Son, the Ho - ly One of Ma - ry.
2. God, the Lord, by all a - dored for ev - er.
3. Babe, the Son, the Ho - ly One of Ma - ry.
4. God, the Lord, by all a - dored for ev - er.

Text: 777 11; Traditional.
Music: RESONET IN LAUDIBUS; German Carol, 14th cent.

## 319   THE SNOW LAY ON THE GROUND

1. The snow lay on the ground, the stars shone bright, When
2. 'Twas Ma - ry, Vir - gin pure of ho - ly Anne, That
3. Saint Jo - seph, too was near to tend the child; To
4. And thus that man - ger poor be - came a throne; For

1. Christ our Lord was born on Christ - mas night. Ve - ní - te,
2. brought in - to this world the God made man. She laid him
3. guard him and pro - tect his moth - er mild: The an - gels
4. he whom Ma - ry bore was God the Son. O come, then,

1. a - do - ré - mus Dó - mi - num, Ve - ní - te, a - do-
2. in a stall at Beth - le - hem; The ass and ox - en
3. hov - er'd 'round, and sang this song: Ve - ní - te, a - do-
4. let us join the heav'n - ly host, To praise the Fa - ther,

**Refrain**

1. ré - mus Dó - mi - num. Ve - ní - te, a - do - ré - mus
2. shared the roof with them.
3. ré - mus Dó - mi - num.
4. Son, and Ho - ly Ghost.

Dó - mi - num, Ve - ní - te, a - do - ré - mus Dó - mi - num.

Text: 10 10 10 10 with refrain; based on Isaiah 7:14; 19th cent.; anon.
Music: VENITE ADOREMUS; trad. Melody; adapt. in *Catholic Hymns*, Albany, New York, 1860.

## 320   SING WE NOW OF CHRISTMAS

1. Sing we now of Christ - mas, No - el, __ sing we here!
2. An - gels called to shep - herds, "Leave your __ flocks at rest,
3. In Beth - le - hem they found him; Jo - seph and Ma - ry mild,
4. From the east - ern coun - try Came the __ kings a - far,
5. Gold and myrrh they took there, Gifts of __ great - est price;

1. Hear our grate-ful prais-es   To the   Babe so   dear.
2. Jour-ney forth to Beth-l'em,   Find the   lamb-kin blest."
3. Seat-ed by the man-ger,   Near the   ho-ly   child.
4. Bear-ing gifts to Beth-l'em,   Guid-ed   by a   star.
5. Frank-in-cense to greet the   Child of   par-a-dise.

**Refrain**

Sing   we No-el,   the   King is born, No-el!

Sing we now of Christ-mas,   Sing we   now No-el!

Text: 65 65 with refrain; Trad. Provençal Carol.
Music: NOËL NOUVELET; Trad. French Carol.

## SEE AMID THE WINTER'S SNOW       321

1. See a-mid the win-ter's snow,   born for us on earth be-low,
2. Say, you ho-ly shep-herds, say,   tell your joy-ful news to-day.

1. see, the gen-tle lamb ap-pears, prom-ised from e-ter-nal years.
2. Why have you now left your sheep   on the lone-ly moun-tain steep?

1. There with-in a man-ger lies   he who built the star-ry skies;
2. "As we watched at dead of night, there ap-peared a won-drous light;

[1]                                    to Verse 2

1. he who, throned in heights sub-lime,   sits a-mid the cher-u-bim.

[Final]

2. an-gels sing-ing 'Peace on earth' told us of   the Sav-ior's birth."

Text: 77 77 D; Edward Caswall, 1814–1878.
Music: WINTER'S SNOW; Kevin Keil, ASCAP, b. 1956, © 1992, Kevin Keil. Published by OCP. All rights reserved.

## 322     O COME, LITTLE CHILDREN

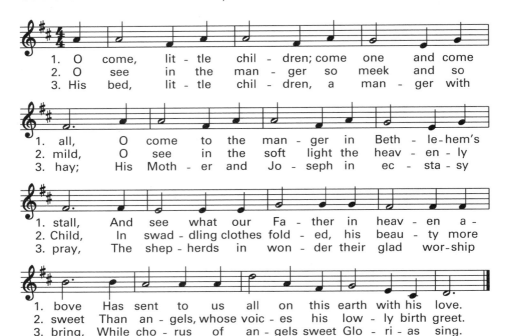

1. O come, lit-tle chil-dren; come one and come
2. O see in the man-ger so meek and so
3. His bed, lit-tle chil-dren, a man-ger with

1. all, O come to the man-ger in Beth-le-hem's
2. mild, O see in the soft light the heav-en-ly
3. hay; His Moth-er and Jo-seph in ec-sta-sy

1. stall, And see what our Fa-ther in heav-en a-
2. Child, In swad-dling clothes fold-ed, his beau-ty more
3. pray, The shep-herds in won-der their glad wor-ship

1. bove Has sent to us all on this earth with his love.
2. sweet Than an-gels, whose voic-es his low-ly birth greet.
3. bring, While cho-rus of an-gels sweet Glo-ri-as sing.

Text: 11 11 11 11; Johann C. von Schmid, 1768–1854; tr. by Melanie Schute, 1885–1922, alt.
Music: IHR KINDERLEIN, KOMMET; Johann A. Schulz, 1749–1800.

## 323     CHILDREN, RUN JOYFULLY

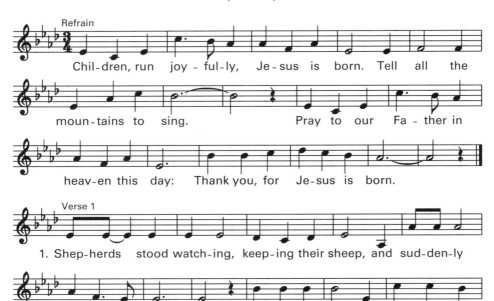

Refrain

Chil-dren, run joy-ful-ly, Je-sus is born. Tell all the

moun-tains to sing. Pray to our Fa-ther in

heav-en this day: Thank you, for Je-sus is born.

Verse 1

1. Shep-herds stood watch-ing, keep-ing their sheep, and sud-den-ly

1. an-gels ap-peared. "Don't be a-fraid. We bring you great

1. joy: Your Sav-ior is born this night."

Verse 2

2. "And this will be a sign to you: the ba-by will

2. lie in a man-ger in the cit-y of Da-vid, in

2. Beth - le - hem. Go now, vis - it your Lord."

Text: Verses based on Luke 2:8–12; Bob Dufford, SJ, b. 1943.
Music: Bob Dufford, SJ.

## AWAY IN A MANGER 324

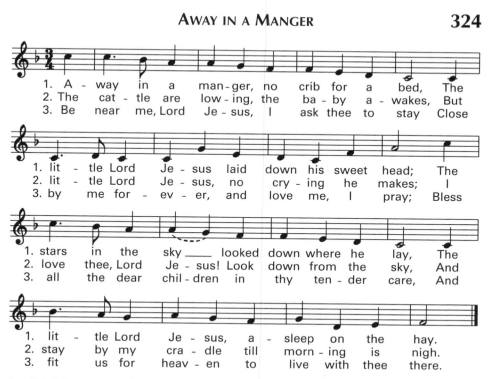

1. A - way in a man-ger, no crib for a bed, The
2. The cat - tle are low-ing, the ba - by a - wakes, But
3. Be near me, Lord Je - sus, I ask thee to stay Close

1. lit - tle Lord Je - sus laid down his sweet head; The
2. lit - tle Lord Je - sus, no cry - ing he makes; I
3. by me for - ev - er, and love me, I pray; Bless

1. stars in the sky ____ looked down where he lay, The
2. love thee, Lord Je - sus! Look down from the sky, And
3. all the dear chil - dren in thy ten - der care, And

1. lit - tle Lord Je - sus, a - sleep on the hay.
2. stay by my cra - dle till morn - ing is nigh.
3. fit us for heav - en to live with thee there.

Text: 11 11 11 11; verses 1–2, *Little Children's Book for Schools and Families*, ca. 1885;
    verse 3, John T. McFarland, 1851–1913; *Gabriel's Vineyard Songs*, 1892, alt.
Music: MUELLER; attr. to James R. Murray, 1841–1905.

## 325     GOD OF EVE AND GOD OF MARY

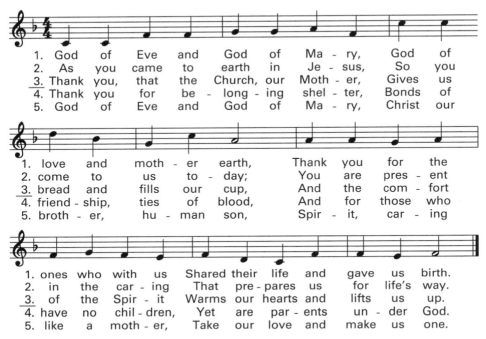

1. God of Eve and God of Ma - ry, God of
2. As you came to earth in Je - sus, So you
3. Thank you, that the Church, our Moth - er, Gives us
4. Thank you for be - long - ing shel - ter, Bonds of
5. God of Eve and God of Ma - ry, Christ our

1. love and moth - er earth, Thank you for the
2. come to us to - day; You are pres - ent
3. bread and fills our cup, And the com - fort
4. friend - ship, ties of blood, And for those who
5. broth - er, hu - man son, Spir - it, car - ing

1. ones who with us Shared their life and gave us birth.
2. in the car - ing That pre - pares us for life's way.
3. of the Spir - it Warms our hearts and lifts us up.
4. have no chil - dren, Yet are par - ents un - der God.
5. like a moth - er, Take our love and make us one.

Text: 87 87; Fred Kaan, b. 1929, © 1989, Hope Publishing Co. All rights reserved. Used with permission.
Music: STUTTGART; Christian F. Witt's *Psalmodia Sacra*, Gotha, 1715; adapt. by Henry J. Gauntlett, 1805–1876.

## 326     GOD OF ADAM, GOD OF JOSEPH

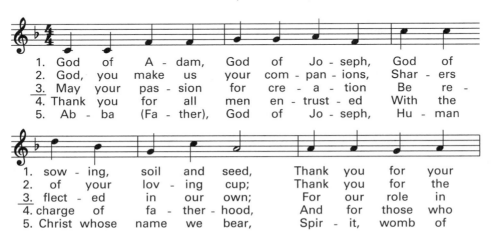

1. God of A - dam, God of Jo - seph, God of
2. God, you make us your com - pan - ions, Shar - ers
3. May your pas - sion for cre - a - tion Be re -
4. Thank you for all men en - trust - ed With the
5. Ab - ba (Fa - ther), God of Jo - seph, Hu - man

1. sow - ing, soil and seed, Thank you for your
2. of your lov - ing cup; Thank you for the
3. flect - ed in our own; For our role in
4. charge of fa - ther - hood, And for those who
5. Christ whose name we bear, Spir - it, womb of

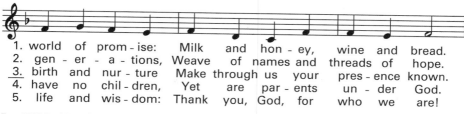

1. world of prom-ise: Milk and hon-ey, wine and bread.
2. gen-er-a-tions, Weave of names and threads of hope.
3. birth and nur-ture Make through us your pres-ence known.
4. have no chil-dren, Yet are par-ents un-der God.
5. life and wis-dom: Thank you, God, for who we are!

Text: 87 87; Fred Kaan, b. 1929, © 1989, Hope Publishing Co. All rights reserved. Used with permission.
Music: STUTTGART; Christian F. Witt's *Psalmodia Sacra*, Gotha, 1715; adapt. by Henry J. Gauntlett, 1805–1876.

## ONCE IN ROYAL DAVID'S CITY 327

1. Once in roy-al Da-vid's cit-y
2. He came down to earth from heav-en
3. And through all his won-drous child-hood
4. For he is our child-hood's pat-tern,
5. And our eyes at last shall see him,

1. Stood a low-ly cat-tle shed, Where a
2. Who is God and Lord of all, And his
3. He would hon-or and o-bey, Love and
4. Day by day like us he grew; He was
5. Through his own re-deem-ing love; For that

1. moth-er laid her ba-by In a man-ger
2. shel-ter was a sta-ble, And his cra-dle
3. watch the low-ly maid-en In whose gen-tle
4. lit-tle, weak, and help-less, Tears and smiles like
5. child so dear and gen-tle Is our Lord in

1. for his bed. Mar-y was that moth-er
2. was a stall. With the poor and mean and
3. arms he lay. Chris-tian chil-dren all should
4. us he knew: And he feels for all our
5. heav'n a-bove: And he leads his chil-dren

1. mild, ___ Je-sus Christ her lit-tle Child. ___
2. low-ly Lived on earth our Sav-ior ho-ly.
3. be ___ Kind, o-be-dient, good as he. ___
4. sad-ness, And he shares in all our glad-ness.
5. on ___ To the place where he has gone. ___

Text: 87 87 77; Cecil Frances Alexander, 1818–1895, alt.
Music: IRBY; Henry J. Gauntlett, 1805–1876.

## 328 THE FIRST NOWELL

**Verses**

1. The first No - well, the an - gel did say,
2. They look - ed up and saw __ a star
3. And by the light of that __ same star
4. This star drew nigh to the __ north - west,
5. Then en - tered in those wise __ men three,
6. Then let us all with one __ ac - cord

1. Was to cer - tain poor shep-herds in fields as they lay;
2. Shin-ing in __ the east, __ be - yond __ them far;
3. Three __ wise __ men came __ from coun - try far;
4. O'er __ Beth - le - hem __ it took __ its rest,
5. Full __ rev - 'rent - ly __ up - on __ the knee,
6. Sing __ prais - es to __ our heav - 'nly Lord;

1. In fields where __ they lay keep - ing their sheep,
2. And to the __ earth it gave __ great light,
3. To seek for a king was their __ in - tent,
4. And there it __ did both stop __ and stay,
5. And of - fered __ there, in his __ pres - ence,
6. Who with the __ Fa - ther we __ a - dore

1. On a cold win - ter's night __ that was __ so deep.
2. And __ so it con - tin - ued both day __ and night.
3. And to fol - low the star __ wher - ev - er it went.
4. Right __ o - ver the place __ where Je - sus lay.
5. Their __ gold __ and myrrh __ and frank - in - cense.
6. And __ Spir - it blest __ for ev - er - more.

**Refrain**

No - well, No - well, No - well, No - well,

Born is the King of Is - ra - el.

Text: Irregular with refrain; trad. English Carol, 17th cent.; verse 6, alt.
Music: THE FIRST NOWELL; trad. English Carol, 17th cent.

# WE THREE KINGS

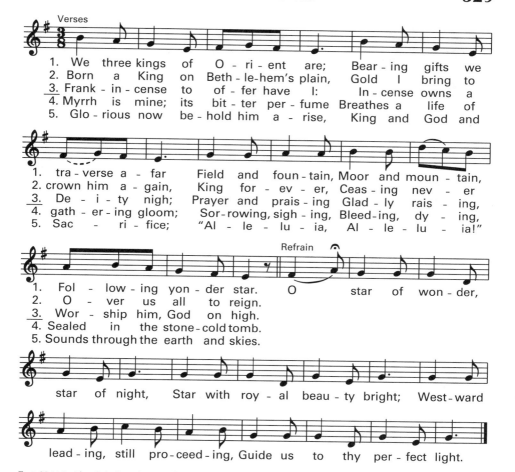

**Verses**

1. We three kings of O - ri - ent are; Bear - ing gifts we
2. Born a King on Beth - le-hem's plain, Gold I bring to
3. Frank - in - cense to of - fer have I: In - cense owns a
4. Myrrh is mine; its bit - ter per - fume Breathes a life of
5. Glo - rious now be - hold him a - rise, King and God and

1. tra - verse a - far Field and foun - tain, Moor and moun - tain,
2. crown him a - gain, King for - ev - er, Ceas - ing nev - er
3. De - i - ty nigh; Prayer and prais - ing Glad - ly rais - ing,
4. gath - er - ing gloom; Sor - rowing, sigh - ing, Bleed - ing, dy - ing,
5. Sac - ri - fice; "Al - le - lu - ia, Al - le - lu - ia!"

**Refrain**

1. Fol - low - ing yon - der star. O star of won - der,
2. O - ver us all to reign.
3. Wor - ship him, God on high.
4. Sealed in the stone - cold tomb.
5. Sounds through the earth and skies.

star of night, Star with roy - al beau - ty bright; West - ward

lead - ing, still pro - ceed - ing, Guide us to thy per - fect light.

Text: 88 44 6 with refrain; based on Matthew 2:1–11; John H. Hopkins, Jr., 1820–1891, alt.
Music: KINGS OF ORIENT; *Carols, Hymns and Songs*, 1863; John H. Hopkins, Jr.

## 330     WHAT CHILD IS THIS

**Verses**

1. What child is this, who, laid to rest, On Ma-ry's lap is
2. Why lies he in such mean es-tate Where ox and ass are
3. So bring him in-cense, gold, and myrrh, Come peas-ant, king, to

1. sleep-ing? Whom an-gels greet with an-thems sweet, While
2. feed-ing? Good Chris-tian, fear: for sin-ners here The
3. own him; The King of kings sal-va-tion brings, Let

**Refrain**

1. shep-herds watch are keep-ing? This, this is Christ the
2. si-lent Word is plead-ing.
3. lov-ing hearts en-throne him.

King, Whom shep-herds guard and an-gels sing; Haste,

haste to bring him laud, the babe, the son of Ma-ry.

Text: 87 87 with refrain; Bramley and Stainer's *Christmas Carols New and Old*, 1871; William C. Dix, 1837–1898.
Music: GREENSLEEVES; trad. English Melody, 16th cent.; Bramley and Stainer's *Christmas Carols New and Old*, 1871.

## 331     CHILD OF THE POOR

**Verses**

1. Help-less and hun-gry, low-ly he lies, wrapped in the
2. Who is the strang-er here in our midst, look-ing for
3. Bring all the thirst-y, all who seek peace; bring those with

1. chill of mid-win-ter; comes now a-mong us, born in-to
2. shel-ter a-mong us? Who is the out-cast? Who do we
3. noth-ing to of-fer. Strength-en the fee-ble, say to the

1. pov-er-ty's em-brace, new life for the world.
2. see a-mid the poor, the chil-dren of God?
3. fright-ened heart: "Fear not: here is your God!"

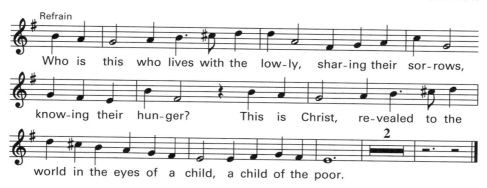

Refrain

Who is this who lives with the low-ly, shar-ing their sor-rows,
know-ing their hun-ger? This is Christ, re-vealed to the
world in the eyes of a child, a child of the poor.

Note: *Child of the Poor* may be sung with *What Child Is This* (No. 330) in the following manner:
*Child of the Poor*, verse 1, followed by *What Child Is This*, verse 1; *Child of the Poor*, verse 2, followed by
*What Child Is This*, verse 2; both songs sung simultaneously on verse 3.

Text and music: Scott Soper, b. 1961, © 1994, OCP. All rights reserved.

## ANGELS FROM THE REALMS OF GLORY　　332

1. An - gels, from the realms of glo - ry, Wing your flight o'er
2. Shep-herds, in the fields a - bid - ing, Watch-ing o'er your
3. Sag - es, leave your con - tem - pla-tions, Bright - er vi - sions
4. Though an in - fant now we view him, He shall fill his
5. All cre - a - tion, join in prais-ing God, the Fa - ther,

1. all the earth; Ye who sang cre - a - tion's sto - ry,
2. flocks by night, God on earth is now re - sid - ing;
3. beam a - far; Seek the great De - sire of Na - tions,
4. Fa - ther's throne, Gath - er all the na - tions to him;
5. Spir - it, Son, Ev - er - more your voic - es rais - ing,

1. Now pro - claim Mes - si - ah's birth:
2. Yon - der shines the in - fant light:
3. Ye have seen his na - tal star:    Come and wor-ship,
4. Ev - 'ry knee shall then bow down:
5. To the e - ter - nal Three - in - One:

1-5. come and wor - ship, Wor - ship Christ, the new - born King.

Text: 87 87 87; verses 1–3, James Montgomery, 1771–1854; verse 4, *Christmas Box*, 1825;
　　verse 5, *Salisbury Hymn Book*, 1857.
Music: REGENT SQUARE; Henry T. Smart, 1813–1879.

## 333    Songs of Thankfulness and Praise

1. Songs of thank-ful-ness and praise, Je-sus, Lord, to thee we raise,
2. Man-i-fest at Jor-dan's stream, Proph-et, Priest, and King su-preme;
3. Man-i-fest in mak-ing whole Pal-sied limbs and faint-ing soul;
4. Grant us grace to see thee, Lord, Mir-rored in thy ho-ly Word;

1. Man-i-fest-ed by the star To the sag-es from a-far;
2. And at Ca-na, wed-ding guest, In thy God-head man-i-fest;
3. Man-i-fest in val-iant fight, Quell-ing all the dev-il's might;
4. May we im-i-tate thee now, And be pure, as pure art thou;

1. Branch of roy-al Da-vid's stem In thy birth at Beth-le-hem;
2. Man-i-fest in pow'r di-vine, Chang-ing wa-ter in-to wine;
3. Man-i-fest in gra-cious will, Ev-er bring-ing good from ill;
4. That we like to thee may be At thy great E-piph-a-ny;

1. Prais-es be to thee ad-dressed,
2. Prais-es be to thee ad-dressed,
3. Prais-es be to thee ad-dressed,
4. And may praise thee, ev-er-blessed,
} God in flesh made man-i-fest.

Text: 77 77 D; Christopher Wordsworth, 1807–1885, alt.
Music: SALZBURG; Jakob Hintze, 1622–1702.

## 334    As with Gladness Men of Old

1. As with glad-ness men of old Did the guid-ing
2. As with joy-ful steps they sped To that low-ly
3. As they of-fered gifts most rare At that man-ger
4. Ho-ly Je-sus, ev-'ry day Keep us in the
5. In the heav'n-ly coun-try bright Need they no cre-

1. star be-hold, As with joy they hailed its light,
2. man-ger-bed, There to bend the knee be-fore
3. rude and bare; So may we with ho-ly joy,
4. nar-row way; And, when earth-ly things are past,
5. at-ed light; Thou, its light, its joy, its crown,

1. Lead - ing on - ward, beam - ing bright, So, most gra - cious
2. Him whom heav'n and earth a - dore; So may we with
3. Pure and free from sin's al - loy, All our cost - liest
4. Bring our ran - somed souls at last Where they need no
5. Thou its sun which goes not down; There for ev - er

1. Lord, may we Ev - er - more be led to thee.
2. will - ing feet Ev - er seek the mer - cy - seat.
3. trea - sures bring, Christ! to thee, our heav'n - ly King.
4. star to guide, Where no clouds thy glo - ry hide.
5. may we sing Al - le - lu - ias to our King.

Text: 77 77 77; William C. Dix, 1837–1898.
Music: DIX; Conrad Kocher, 1786–1872; adapt. by William H. Monk, 1823–1889.

## IN THE BLEAK MIDWINTER 335

1. In the bleak mid - win - ter, frost - y wind made moan,
2. Our God, heav'n can - not hold him, nor____ earth sus - tain;
3. An - gels and arch - an - gels may have gath - ered there,
4. What____ can I give him, poor____ as I am?

1. Earth stood hard as i - ron, wa - ter like a stone;
2. Heav'n and earth shall flee a - way when he comes to reign.
3. Cher - u - bim and ser - a - phim throng - ed the air;
4. If I were a shep - herd, I would bring a lamb;

1. Snow had fall - en, snow on snow, snow____ on____ snow,
2. In the bleak mid - win - ter a sta - ble place suf - ficed The
3. But his moth - er on - ly, in her maid - en bliss,
4. If I were a Wise____ Man, I would do my part; Yet

1. In the bleak mid - win - ter, long a - go.
2. Lord____ God Al - might - y, Je - sus Christ.
3. Wor - shiped the be - lov - ed with a kiss.
4. what I can I give him: give my heart.

Text: Irregular; Christina G. Rosetti, 1830–1894.
Music: CRANHAM; Gustav T. Holst, 1874–1934.

## 336     WHAT STAR IS THIS

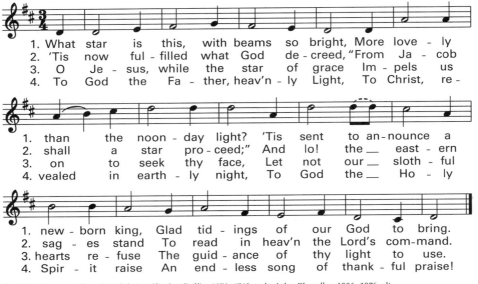

1. What star is this, with beams so bright, More love - ly
2. 'Tis now ful - filled what God de - creed, "From Ja - cob
3. O Je - sus, while the star of grace Im - pels us
4. To God the Fa - ther, heav'n - ly Light, To Christ, re -

1. than the noon - day light? 'Tis sent to an - nounce a
2. shall a star pro - ceed;" And lo! the __ east - ern
3. on to seek thy face, Let not our __ sloth - ful
4. vealed in earth - ly night, To God the __ Ho - ly

1. new - born king, Glad tid - ings of our God to bring.
2. sag - es stand To read in heav'n the Lord's com - mand.
3. hearts re - fuse The guid - ance of thy light to use.
4. Spir - it raise An end - less song of thank - ful praise!

Text: LM; *Quem stella sole pulchrior*; Charles Coffin, 1676–1749; tr. by John Chandler, 1806–1876, alt.
Music: PUER NOBIS; *Trier MS*, 15th cent.; adapt. by Michael Praetorius, 1571–1621.

## 337     WHEN JESUS COMES TO BE BAPTIZED

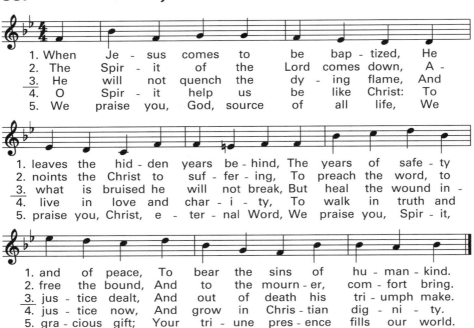

1. When Je - sus comes to be bap - tized, He
2. The Spir - it of the Lord comes down, A -
3. He will not quench the dy - ing flame, And
4. O Spir - it help us be like Christ: To
5. We praise you, God, source of all life, We

1. leaves the hid - den years be - hind, The years of safe - ty
2. noints the Christ to suf - fer - ing, To preach the word, to
3. what is bruised he will not break, But heal the wound in -
4. live in love and char - i - ty, To walk in truth and
5. praise you, Christ, e - ter - nal Word, We praise you, Spir - it,

1. and of peace, To bear the sins of hu - man - kind.
2. free the bound, And to the mourn - er, com - fort bring.
3. jus - tice dealt, And out of death his tri - umph make.
4. jus - tice now, And grow in Chris - tian dig - ni - ty.
5. gra - cious gift; Your tri - une pres - ence fills our world.

Text: LM. Verses 1–3, alt., © 1974, Stanbrook Abbey. All rights reserved. Used with permission.
Verses 4–5, © 1989, Concacan Inc. All rights reserved. Used with permission.
Music: WINCHESTER NEW; Georg Wittwe's *Musikalisches Hand-Buch*, Hamburg, 1690;
adapt. by William H. Havergal, 1793–1870.

# When John Baptized by Jordan's River

**338**

1. When John bap-tized by Jor-dan's riv - er  In  faith and
2. There  as  the Lord, bap-tized and pray - ing,  Rose  from the
3. O  Son  of  Man, our  na - ture shar - ing,  In  whose o -

1. hope  the  peo - ple  came,  That  John and  Jor - dan might de -
2. stream, the  sin - less  one,  A  voice was heard from heav - en
3. be - dience all  are  blest,  Sav - ior, our  sins  and  sor - rows

1. liv - er  Their  trou - bled souls from  sin  and shame.
2. say - ing,  "This  is  my  own  be - lov - ed  Son."
3. bear - ing,  Hear  us  and grant us  this  re - quest:

1. They  came to seek  a  new be - gin - ning,  The  hu - man
2. There  as  the Fa - ther's  word was spo - ken,  Not  in  the
3. Dai - ly  to grow,  by  grace de - fend - ed,  Filled  with the

1. spir - it's  age - less  quest,  Re - pen - tance, and  an
2. pow'r of  wind  and  flame,  But  of  his love and
3. Spir - it from  a - bove;  In  Christ bap-tized, be -

1. end  of  sin - ning,  Re - nounc-ing ev - 'ry wrong con-fessed.
2. peace the  to - ken,  Seen  as  a  dove, the Spir - it  came.
3. loved, be - friend - ed,  Chil - dren  of  God  in peace and  love.

## 339 ASHES

1. We rise a-gain from ash-es, from the good we've failed to
2. We of-fer you our fail-ures, we ___ of-fer you at-
3. Then rise a-gain from ash-es, let ___ heal-ing come to
4. Thanks be to the Fa-ther, who ___ made us like him-

1. do. We rise a-gain from ash-es, to cre-ate our-selves a-
2. tempts, the gifts not ful-ly giv-en, the ___ dreams not ful-ly
3. pain, though spring has turned to win-ter, and ___ sun-shine turned to
4. self. Thanks be to his Son, ___ who ___ saved us by his

1. new. If ___ all our world is ash-es, then ___ must our lives be
2. dreamt. Give our stum-bl-ings di-rec-tion, give our vi-sions wid-er
3. rain. The ___ rain we'll use for grow-ing, and cre-ate the world a-
4. death. Thanks be to the Spir-it who cre-ates the world a-

1. true, an ___ of-fer-ing of ash-es, an of-fer-ing to you.
2. view, an ___ of-fer-ing of ash-es, an of-fer-ing to you.
3. new from an of-fer-ing of ash-es, an of-fer-ing to you.
4. new from an of-fer-ing of ash-es, an of-fer-ing to you.

## 340 SIGNED BY ASHES

Ostinato Refrain

Signed by wa-ter; signed by ash-es; se-cure in your love, O God.

**Verses**

1. Have mercy on us, God, in your compassion.
Wipe out our offenses by your might.
Wash away our guilt;
make us worthy to walk your path in justice.

2. My sinfulness is visible, ever before you.
Against you alone I've transgressed.
But in you is the mighty power of mercy;
when I forgive, I am blest.

3. Cleanse me of my sin and I'll be pure, O Lord.
Wash me so I'm cleaner than the snow.
Let me hear the sounds of joy and gladness
that only those forgiven ever know.

4. Create for me a clean heart,
God of mercy.
Renew a steadfast spirit in me.
Cast me not out
from your loving presence,
that I may worship, sacrifice and sing.

5. O God, my heart and voice
are raised to praise you.
You are not pleased with sacrifice alone.
My sacrifice: a contrite, humble spirit;
I've heard your invitation:
"Child, come home!"

# WITH THESE ASHES

Refrain

With these ash-es, we know your love, O Lord. With these ash-es, we turn our hearts to you. Daugh-ters and sons, we jour-ney as one. With these ash-es, we know your love, O Lord.

Verses

1. Join - ing to - geth - er on this jour-ney with you,
2. With prayer and ser - vice, we will an - swer your call.
3. We give of what we have to all those in need.
4. And for those man - y times we stum - ble and fall,

1. we walk these for - ty days and nights. Called by your
2. With voic - es raised, we share your word. Called by your
3. We give as you would have us do. Called by your
4. your mer - cy rains from heav'n a - bove. Called by your

to Refrain

1. grace, we an-swer in faith; O Lord, lead us to your light.
2. grace, we an-swer in faith; O Lord, let our cry be heard.
3. grace, we an-swer in faith; O Lord, lead us back to you.
4. grace, we an-swer in faith; O Lord, lead us to your love.

Text: Mary Hochman, b. 1967.
Music: Gerard Chiusano, b. 1965.
Text and music © 2006, Gerard Chiusano and Mary Hochman. Published by spiritandsong.com®, a division of OCP.
   All rights reserved.

## 342     LEAVE THE PAST IN ASHES

*Refrain

Leave the past in ash-es and turn to God, re-
turn to God with tears and fast-ing.

*Verses available in accompaniment books.

Text: Joel 2:13; fr. the *Sacramentary*, © 1973, 1985, ICEL. All rights reserved. Used with permission.
Music: Cyprian Consiglio, OSB Cam., b. 1958, © 2004, Cyprian Consiglio, OSB Cam. Published by OCP.
   All rights reserved.

## 343     NOW IS THE ACCEPTABLE TIME

Refrain

Now is the ac-cept-a-ble time. Now is the day of sal-
va-tion. We are called to be-come the ho-li-ness of God. Be
rec-on-ciled with God now! Re-ceive the grace of God.

Verses

1. Break o-pen your hearts of stone. __ Re-turn to the Lord
2. Keep se-cret your deeds of love __ and cheer-ful-ly give
3. With fast-ing and con-stant prayer, _____ strength-en your-selves

1. with your whole heart! God's mer-cy a-waits us all:
2. to the need-y. God's bless-ing is ours to share:
3. on the jour-ney. God walks with us day by day:

to Refrain

1-3. God is gra-cious, rich in kind-ness.

Text: Based on Joel 2:12–13; 2 Corinthians 5:20—6:2; Matthew 6:1–4; Barbara Bridge, b. 1950, © 2003, Barbara Bridge.
   Published by OCP. All rights reserved.
Music: Barbara Bridge, © 2003, Barbara Bridge. Published by OCP. All rights reserved.

## PARCE DOMINE/SPARE YOUR PEOPLE, LORD 344

**Refrain**

Par - ce Dó - mi - ne,   par - ce pó - pu - lo ___ tu - o: ___
*Spare your peo-ple, Lord,   spare your peo-ple in your lov-ing kind-ness!*

ne in ae - tér-num   i - ra - scá - ris no - bis.
*Show us your mer-cy;   we have sinned   a - gainst you, Lord.*

**Verses**

1. Have mercy on me, God, in   your   good - ness;
2. For I know my   of - fense; ___
3. A clean heart create   for   me, ___ God;
4. Restore my joy in your   sal - va - tion;
5. For you do not   de - sire   sac - ri - fice;

1. In your abundant compassion blot out my of - fense. ___
2. My sin is always   be - fore ___ me.
3. Renew in me a   stead - fast   spir - it.
4. Sustain in me a   will - ing   spir - it.
5. A burnt offering you would not   ac - cept. ___

1. Wash away all   my   guilt; ___
2. Against you alone have   I   sinned; ___
3. Do not drive me away from   your   pres - ence
4. Lord, open   my   lips; ___
5. My sacrifice, God, is a   bro - ken   spir - it;

*to Refrain*

1. From my   sin cleanse me. ___
2. I have done such evil in   your sight. ___
3. Nor take from me your   ho - ly   spir - it. ___
4. My mouth will proclaim   your praise. ___
5. God, do not spurn a broken,   hum - bled heart. ___

Text: Refrain based on Joel 2:17; English refrain by Owen Alstott, b. 1947, © 1973, OCP. All rights reserved.
   Verses, Psalm 51:3–6, 12–13, 17–19; fr. the *New American Bible*, © 1991, CCD.
   All rights reserved. Used with permission.
Music: Refrain, Chant, Mode I. Verses, Randall DeBruyn, b. 1947, © 1992, OCP. All rights reserved.

# 345

## TURN TO ME

**Refrain**

Turn to me, O turn, and be saved, says the Lord, for I am God; there is no oth-er, none be-side me. I call your name.

**Verse 1**

1. I am God, who com-forts you; who are you to be a-fraid of flesh that fades, is made like the grass of the field, soon to with-er. *to Refrain*

**Verses 2, 3**

2. Lis-ten __ to me, __ my peo-ple; give ear to __ me, __ and my jus-tice for a light to the peo-ple.
3. Lift __ up your eyes to the heav-ens, and look at the earth down be-low. __ The heav-ens will van-ish like smoke, and the earth __ will wear out like a gar-ment. *to Refrain*

## HAVE MERCY ON US, LORD/ATTENDE DOMINE

**346**

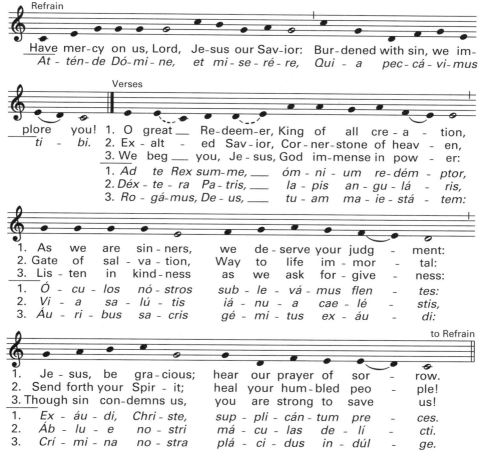

**Refrain**

Have mer-cy on us, Lord, Je-sus our Sav-ior: Bur-dened with sin, we im-
At - tén- de Dó-mi-ne, et mi-se-ré-re, Qui - a pec-cá-vi-mus

**Verses**

plore you! 1. O great __ Re-deem-er, King of all cre - a - tion,
ti - bi. 2. Ex - alt - ed Sav-ior, Cor-ner-stone of heav - en,
3. We beg __ you, Je - sus, God im-mense in pow - er:
1. Ad te Rex sum-me, __ óm-ni-um re-dém - ptor,
2. Déx - te - ra Pa - tris, __ la - pis an - gu - lá - ris,
3. Ro - gá-mus, De - us, __ tu - am ma - ie-stá - tem:

1. As we are sin - ners, we de-serve your judg - ment:
2. Gate of sal - va - tion, Way to life im - mor - tal:
3. Lis - ten in kind-ness as we ask for-give - ness:
1. Ó - cu - los nó - stros sub - le - vá - mus flen - tes:
2. Ví - a sa - lú - tis iá - nu - a cae - lé - stis,
3. Áu - ri - bus sa - cris gé - mi - tus ex - áu - di:

**to Refrain**

1. Je - sus, be gra-cious; hear our prayer of sor - row.
2. Send forth your Spir - it; heal your hum-bled peo - ple!
3. Though sin con-demns us, you are strong to save us!
1. Ex - áu - di, Chri - ste, sup - pli - cán-tum pre - ces.
2. Áb - lu - e no - stri má - cu - las de - lí - cti.
3. Crí - mi - na no - stra plá - ci - dus in - dúl - ge.

4. We stand convicted, owning our offenses;
   Guilty before you, yet we seek your pardon:
   O gentle Savior, great is your compassion!

4. *Tibi fatémur, crímina admíssa:*
   *Contríto corde pándimus occúlta:*
   *Túa redémptor, píetas ignóscat.*

5. Remember, Jesus, you gave all to save us;
   Dying for sinners, you endured the Passion:
   Savior, immortal, grant your gift of freedom!

5. *Innocens captus, nec repúgnans ductus,*
   *Téstibus falsis, pro ímpiis damnátus:*
   *Quos redemísti, tu consérva, Christe.*

Text: 11 11 11 with refrain; Latin, 10th cent.; tr. by Melvin Farrell, SS, 1930–1986, © 1977, OCP. All rights reserved.
Music: ATTENDE DOMINE; Chant, Mode V; *Paris Processionale*, 1824.

## 347     THE GLORY OF THESE FORTY DAYS

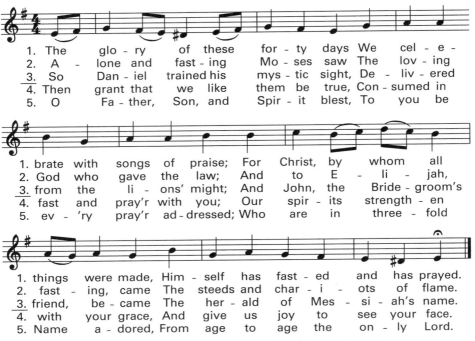

1. The glo-ry of these for-ty days We cel-e-
2. A-lone and fast-ing Mo-ses saw The lov-ing
3. So Dan-iel trained his mys-tic sight, De-liv-ered
4. Then grant that we like them be true, Con-sumed in
5. O Fa-ther, Son, and Spir-it blest, To you be

1. brate with songs of praise; For Christ, by whom all
2. God who gave the law; And to E-li-jah,
3. from the li-ons' might; And John, the Bride-groom's
4. fast and pray'r with you; Our spir-its strength-en
5. ev-'ry pray'r ad-dressed; Who are in three-fold

1. things were made, Him-self has fast-ed and has prayed.
2. fast-ing, came The steeds and char-i-ots of flame.
3. friend, be-came The her-ald of Mes-si-ah's name.
4. with your grace, And give us joy to see your face.
5. Name a-dored, From age to age the on-ly Lord.

Text: LM; *Clarum decus jejunii*; St. Gregory the Great, ca. 540–604; tr. fr. the *English Hymnal*, 1906;
    Maurice F. Bell, 1862–1947, alt.
Music: ERHALT UNS, HERR; J. Klug's *Geistliche Lieder*, Wittenberg, 1543;
    adapt. by Johann Sebastian Bach, 1685–1750, alt.

## 348     THIS SEASON CALLS US

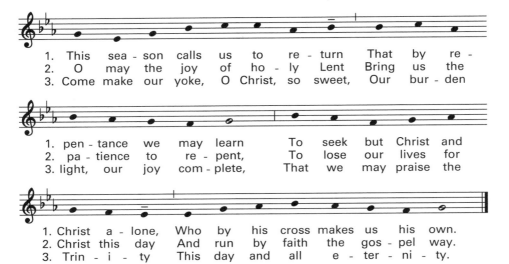

1. This sea-son calls us to re-turn That by re-
2. O may the joy of ho-ly Lent Bring us the
3. Come make our yoke, O Christ, so sweet, Our bur-den

1. pen-tance we may learn To seek but Christ and
2. pa-tience to re-pent, To lose our lives for
3. light, our joy com-plete, That we may praise the

1. Christ a-lone, Who by his cross makes us his own.
2. Christ this day And run by faith the gos-pel way.
3. Trin-i-ty This day and all e-ter-ni-ty.

Text: LM; Harry Hagan, OSB, b. 1947, © 1999, St. Meinrad Archabbey. Published by OCP. All rights reserved.
Music: CONDITOR ALME SIDERUM; Chant, Mode IV.

## BEHOLD, BEFORE OUR WONDERING EYES 349

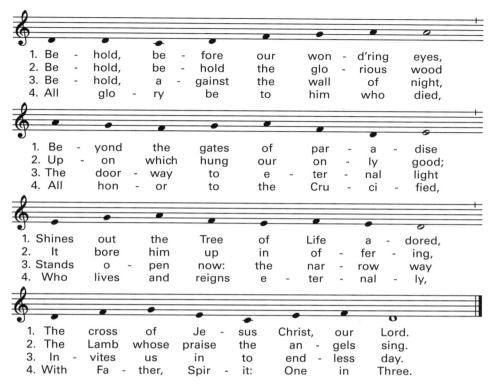

1. Be - hold, be - fore our won - d'ring eyes,
2. Be - hold, be - hold the glo - rious wood
3. Be - hold, a - gainst the wall of night,
4. All glo - ry be to him who died,

1. Be - yond the gates of par - a - dise
2. Up - on which hung our on - ly good;
3. The door - way to e - ter - nal light
4. All hon - or to the Cru - ci - fied,

1. Shines out the Tree of Life a - dored,
2. It bore him up in of - fer - ing,
3. Stands o - pen now: the nar - row way
4. Who lives and reigns e - ter - nal - ly,

1. The cross of Je - sus Christ, our Lord.
2. The Lamb whose praise the an - gels sing.
3. In - vites us in to end - less day.
4. With Fa - ther, Spir - it: One in Three.

Text: Genevieve Glen, OSB, b. 1945, © 1992, 2000, The Benedictine Nuns of the Abbey of St. Walburga.
Published by OCP. All rights reserved.
Music: Barney Walker, ASCAP, and Gael Berberick, ASCAP, © 2005, Barney Walker and Gael Berberick.
Published by OCP. All rights reserved.

## FORTY DAYS AND FORTY NIGHTS 350

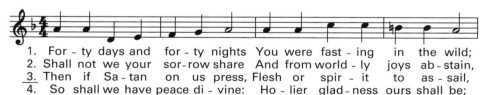

1. For - ty days and for - ty nights You were fast - ing in the wild;
2. Shall not we your sor - row share And from world - ly joys ab - stain,
3. Then if Sa - tan on us press, Flesh or spir - it to as - sail,
4. So shall we have peace di - vine: Ho - lier glad - ness ours shall be;
5. Keep, O keep us, Sav - ior dear, Ev - er con - stant by your side;

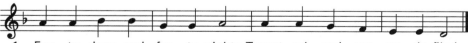

1. For - ty days and for - ty nights Tempt - ed, and yet un - de - filed.
2. Fast - ing with un - ceas - ing prayer, Strong with you to suf - fer pain?
3. Vic - tor in the wil - der - ness, Grant we may not faint nor fail!
4. Round us, too, shall an - gels shine, Such as served you faith - ful - ly.
5. That with you we may ap - pear At th'e - ter - nal Eas - ter - tide.

Text: 77 77; George H. Smyttan, 1822–1870, alt.
Music: HEINLEIN; melody attr. to Martin Herbst, 1654–1681, alt.

**351**     LED BY THE SPIRIT

1. Led by the Spir-it of our God, we go to fast and
2. Led by the Spir-it, we con-front temp-ta-tion face to
3. Led by the Spir-it, now draw near the wa-ters of re-
4. Led by the Spir-it, now sing praise to God the Trin-i-

1. pray With Christ in-to the wil-der-ness; we join his
2. face, And know full well we must re-ly on God's re-
3. birth With hearts that long to wor-ship God in spir-it
4. ty: The Source of Life, the liv-ing Word made flesh to

1. pas-chal way. "Rend not your gar-ments, rend your hearts. Turn
2. deem-ing grace. On bread a-lone we can-not live, but
3. and in truth. "Who-ev-er drinks the drink I give shall
4. set us free, The Spir-it blow-ing where it will to

1. back your lives to me." Thus says our kind and
2. nour-ished by the Word We seek the will of
3. nev-er thirst a-gain." Thus says the Lord who
4. make us friends of God: This mys-t'ry far be-

1. gra-cious God, whose reign is lib-er-ty.
2. God to do: this is our drink and food.
3. died for us, our Sav-ior, kin and friend.
4. yond our reach, yet near in heal-ing love.

Text: CMD; based on Joel 2:12–13; Matthew 4:1–4; Mark 1:12–15; John 4:5–42; Bob Hurd, b. 1950, © 1996, Bob Hurd.
Published by OCP. All rights reserved.
Music: KINGSFOLD; trad. English Melody; *English Country Songs*, 1893; adapt. by Ralph Vaughan Williams, 1872–1958.

**352**     LORD, WHO THROUGHOUT THESE FORTY DAYS

1. Lord, who through-out these for-ty days, For
2. As you with Sa-tan did con-tend, And
3. As you did hun-ger bear and thirst, So
4. And through these days of pen-i-tence, And
5. A-bide with us that when this life Of

1. us did fast and pray, Teach us with you to
2. did the vic - t'ry win, O give us strength in
3. teach us, gra - cious Lord, To die to self, and
4. through your Pas - sion - tide, For - ev - er - more, in
5. suf - fer - ing is past, An Eas - ter of un -

1. mourn our sins, And close by you to stay.
2. you to fight, In you to con - quer sin.
3. al - ways live By your most ho - ly word.
4. life and death, O Lord, with us a - bide.
5. end - ing joy We may at - tain at last!

Text: CM; Claudia F. Hernaman, 1838–1898, alt.
Music: ST. FLAVIAN; *The Whole Psalmes in Foure Partes*, 1563; adapt. by Richard Redhead, 1820–1901.

## AGAIN WE KEEP THIS SOLEMN FAST 353

1. A - gain we keep this sol - emn fast, A gift of
2. The law and proph - ets from of old In fig - ured
3. More spar - ing, there - fore, let us make The words we
4. Let us a - void each harm - ful way That lures the
5. We pray, O bless - ed Three - in - One, Our God while

1. faith from ag - es past, This Lent which binds us
2. ways this Lent fore - told, Which Christ, all ag - es'
3. speak, the food we take, Our sleep, our laugh - ter,
4. care - less mind a - stray; By watch - ful prayer our
5. end - less ag - es run, That this, our Lent of

1. lov - ing - ly To faith and hope and char - i - ty.
2. Lord and Guide, In these last days has sanc - ti - fied.
3. ev - 'ry sense; Learn peace through ho - ly pen - i - tence.
4. spir - its free From schem - ing of the e - ne - my.
5. for - ty days, May bring us growth and give you praise.

Text: LM; *Ex more docti mystico*; ascr. to St. Gregory the Great, ca. 540–604; tr. by Peter J. Scagnelli, b. 1949,
and John M. Neale, 1818–1866, alt. © Peter J. Scagnelli. All rights reserved. Used with permission.
Music: ERHALT UNS, HERR; J. Klug's *Geistliche Lieder*, Wittenberg, 1543;
adapt. by Johann Sebastian Bach, 1685–1750, alt.

## 354     SOMEBODY'S KNOCKIN' AT YOUR DOOR

1, 6. Some-bod - y's knock-in' at your door; Some-bod - y's knock-in' at your

1, 6. door;    O    sin - ner, why don't you an - swer? Some-bod - y's

*(Fine)* Cantor

1, 6. knock-in' at your door.

2. Knocks like    Je - sus,
3. Can't you    hear him?
4. Je - sus calls you,
5. Can't you    trust him?

All           Cantor

2-5. Some-bod - y's knock-in' at your door.

2. Knocks like    Je - sus,
3. Can't you    hear him?
4. Je - sus calls you,
5. Can't you    trust him?

All

2-5. Some-bod - y's knock-in' at your door.    O    sin - ner,

2-5. why don't you an - swer? Some-bod - y's knock-in' at your door.

Text and music: Spiritual.

## 355     TURN OUR HEARTS

*Ostinato Refrain

Turn our hearts to you, O God. With you there is heal-ing,

whole-ness and for-give-ness, free-dom from fear, last-ing peace.

*Verses available in accompaniment books.

Text: Verses based on Psalm 51:1, 6, 12; Barbara Bridge, b. 1950.
Music: Barbara Bridge.

## JESUS WALKED THIS LONESOME VALLEY

**356**

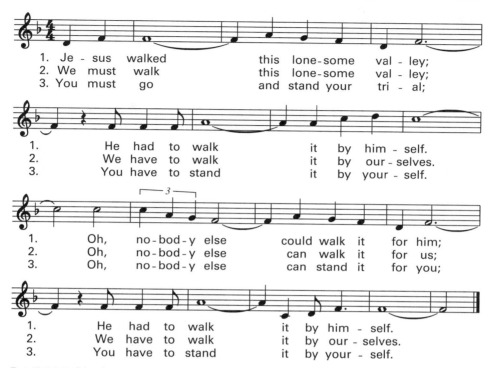

1. Je - sus walked this lone-some val - ley;
2. We must walk this lone-some val - ley;
3. You must go and stand your tri - al;

1. He had to walk it by him - self.
2. We have to walk it by our - selves.
3. You have to stand it by your - self.

1. Oh, no-bod-y else could walk it for him;
2. Oh, no-bod-y else can walk it for us;
3. Oh, no-bod-y else can stand it for you;

1. He had to walk it by him - self.
2. We have to walk it by our - selves.
3. You have to stand it by your - self.

Text: 88 10 8; Traditional.
Music: LONESOME VALLEY; Spiritual.

## FROM THE DEPTHS WE CRY TO THEE

**357**

1. From the depths we cry to thee, God of sov-'reign maj-es-ty!
2. Gra-cious God, our hearts re-new; Strength-en us thy will to do.
3. Lord, ac - cept our Len-ten fast And for-give our sin-ful past,

1. Hear our prayers and hymns of praise; Bless our Lent of for-ty days.
2. Wash us, make us pure with - in; Cleanse us from the stain of sin.
3. That we may par - take with thee In the Eas-ter mys-ter - y.

Text: 77 77; verses 1, 3, Alan G. McDougall, 1895–1964, alt. Verse 2, Owen Alstott, b. 1947, © 1977, OCP.
    All rights reserved.
Music: HEINLEIN; melody attr. to Martin Herbst, 1654–1681, alt.

**358**    **CREATE A CLEAN HEART**

**Refrain**

Cre - ate a clean heart in me, O God.

Re - new in me a stead-fast spir - it.

**Verses**

1. Have mer - cy, God, in com - pas - sion, and for-
2. You are jus - ti - fied giv - ing sen - tence, and with-
3. Make me hear re - joic - ing and glad - ness, that the
4. Give me back the joy of sal - va - tion, with a
5. When I sac - ri - fice, you re - fuse it, and my

1. get that I have de - fied you. Wash a - way all my
2. out re - proach when you judge. You see me just as I
3. bones you bruised may re - vive! Shut your eyes to my
4. fer - vent spir - it sus - tain me. I will show to oth - ers your
5. ho - lo - causts do not please you. My bro - ken spir - it I

1. sin, and cleanse me from my guilt. Ver - y
2. am, a sin - ner be - fore my birth. Be -
3. sin; make my guilt dis - ap - pear. O Cre-
4. way; those in sin will re - turn to you. O
5. of - fer; you will wel - come my hum - ble heart. In your

1. well do I know what is ev - il, and my sins are al - ways be-
2. hold, you love truth in the heart; in my se - cret heart teach me
3. a - tor, re - shape my heart; put a stur - dy spir - it with-
4. res - cue me, God, be my help - er, and my tongue shall ring out your
5. mer - cy show fa - vor to Si - on, and re - build the walls of your

1. fore me. Done to you a - lone, my of - fens - es,
2. wis - dom. With a sprig of hys - sop and wa - ter,
3. in me. De - prive me not of your spir - it;
4. good - ness. O Lord, o - pen my lips and my
5. cit - y. Then our ho - lo - causts will be pleas - ing

1. crimes com - mit - ted right be - fore your eyes.
2. wash me; make me bright - er than the snow.
3. cast me not a - way from your side.
4. mouth will de - clare your praise.
5. sac - ri - fic - es of - fered in your sight.

## REMEMBER NOT THE THINGS OF THE PAST 359

**Refrain**

Re - mem - ber not the things of the past;   now I do some - thing new,

do you not see it?   Now I do some - thing new, says the Lord.

**Verses**

1. In our dis - tress God has grasped us by the hand,
2. In our parched land of hy - poc - ri - sy and hate,
3. And who a - mong us is sin - less in God's sight?
4. Press - ing a - head, let - ting go what lies be - hind,

1. o - pened a path in the sea, and we shall pass o - ver,
2. God makes a riv - er spring forth, a riv - er of mer - cy,
3. Then who will cast the first stone, when he who was sin - less
4. may we be found in the Lord, and shar - ing his dy - ing,

to Refrain

1. we shall pass o - ver, free at last.
2. truth and com - pas - sion; come and drink.
3. car - ried our fail - ings to the cross?
4. share in his ris - ing from the dead.

## 360     BEYOND THE DAYS

Refrain

Be - yond the days of hope and mys - t'ry we
see a light of faith re - newed, and in our long - ing

*1-4 to Verses*

we thirst for guid - ance to walk with you day by day.

**Final**

day, to walk with you day by day.

**Verses**

1. For - ty days and
2. Not on bread a -
3. In your hands, O
4. On our Lent - en

1. nights, you guide the steps of our jour - ney. May your
2. lone are we to walk on this jour - ney. Speak the
3. God, we feel the touch of your guid - ance. Keep us
4. path we see the dawn of a new day. Be our

*to Refrain*

1. pres - ence be felt in the whis - per of your voice.
2. words that give life to the yearn - ings of our hearts.
3. safe in your care: may your gen - tle - ness be there.
4. vi - sion of hope; be the prom - ise of our lives.

## 361     WITH THE LORD

Verse 1

1. Out of the depths I cry to you, I cry to you, O Lord. Lord,

1. o - pen your ears and hear my voice, at - tend to the sound of my plea.

**Refrain**

With the Lord there is mer-cy and the full-ness of re-demp-tion, call to him in your tri-als, he will an-swer when-ev-er you call. *(1, 3 to Vss 2, 4)* call. *(2 to Vs 3)* call. *(Final)*

**Verses 2, 4**

2. If you ___ O Lord, ___ should mark ___ our guilt, then, Lord, who could hope to sur-vive? But with you is found for-give-ness of sin, and mer-cy that we might re - vere you.

4. More than the sen - ti-nels wait for the dawn, let Is - ra - el wait for the Lord. For kind-ness is his, re - demp-tion for all, for - give-ness of sins for his peo - ple.

**Verse 3**

3. Trust in the Lord, count on his word, wait for the Lord, my soul. I will wait for the Lord all the days of my life as sen - ti-nels wait for the dawn.

## 362     In These Days of Lenten Journey

**Refrain**

In these days of Len-ten jour-ney we have seen and we have heard

the call to sow jus-tice in the lives of those we serve.

**Verses**

1. We reach out to those who are home-less, to
2. We o - pen our eyes to the hun - gry and
3. We o - pen our ears to the wea - ry and
4. We call on the Spir - it of Jus - tice and

1. those who live with - out warmth. In the cool-ness of
2. see the fac - es of Christ. As we nour - ish all
3. hear the cry of the poor. To the voic - es that
4. pray for right-teous-ness' sake. We will sing for the

1. eve - ning we'll shel - ter their dreams; we will
2. peo - ple who hun - ger for food, may their
3. ech - o the song of de - spair, we will
4. free - dom of all the op - pressed; we will

*to Refrain*

1. clothe them in mer - cy and peace.
2. faith in our God be re - newed.
3. show our com - pas - sion and care.
4. loos - en the bonds of dis - tress.

Text and music: Ricky Manalo, CSP, b. 1965, © 1997, Ricky Manalo, CSP. Published by OCP. All rights reserved.

## 363     At the Cross Her Station Keeping

1. At the cross her sta - tion keep-ing, Stood the mourn-ful
2. Through her heart, his sor - row shar - ing, All his bit - ter
3. O how sad and sore dis-tressed, _ Was that Moth - er

1. *Sta - bat Ma - ter do - lo - ró - sa Ju - xta cru - cem*
2. *Cu - jus á - ni - mam ge - mén-tem, Con - tri - stá - tam*
3. *O quam tri - stis et af - flí - cta Fu - it il - la*

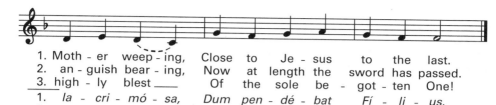

1. Moth - er weep - ing, Close to Je - sus to the last.
2. an - guish bear - ing, Now at length the sword has passed.
3. high - ly blest ____ Of the sole be - got - ten One!

1. *la - cri - mó - sa,* *Dum pen - dé - bat* *Fí - li - us.*
2. *et do - lén - tem,* *Per - tran - sí - vit* *glá - di - us.*
3. *be - ne - dí - cta* *Ma - ter U - ni - gé - ni - ti!*

4. Christ above in torment hangs,
   She beneath beholds the pangs
   Of her dying, glorious Son.

5. Is there one who would not weep,
   Whelmed in miseries so deep,
   Christ's dear Mother to behold?

6. Can the human heart refrain
   From partaking in her pain,
   In that Mother's pain untold?

7. Bruised, derided, cursed, defiled,
   She beheld her tender Child,
   All with bloody scourges rent.

8. For the sins of his own nation
   Saw him hang in desolation
   Till his spirit forth he sent.

9. O thou Mother! Font of love,
   Touch my spirit from above,
   Make my heart with thine accord.

10. Make me feel as thou hast felt;
    Make my soul to glow and melt
    With the love of Christ, my Lord.

11. Holy Mother, pierce me through,
    In my heart each wound renew
    Of my Savior crucified.

12. Let me share with thee his pain,
    Who for all my sins was slain,
    Who for me in torment died.

13. Let me mingle tears with thee,
    Mourning him who mourned for me,
    All the days that I may live.

14. By the cross with thee to stay;
    There with thee to weep and pray,
    All I ask of thee to give.

15. Virgin of all Virgins best!
    Listen to my fond request:
    Let me share thy grief divine.

4. *Quae maerébat et dolébat,*
   *Pia Mater, dum vidébat*
   *Nati poenas íncliti.*

5. *Quis non posset contristári,*
   *Piam Matrem contemplári*
   *Doléntem cum Fílio?*

6. *Quis est homo qui non fleret,*
   *Matrem Christi si vidéret*
   *In tanto supplício?*

7. *Pro peccátis suae gentis*
   *Vidit Jesum in torméntis,*
   *Et flagéllis súbditum.*

8. *Vidit suum dulcem Natum*
   *Moriéntem desolátum,*
   *Dum emísit spíritum.*

9. *Eia Mater, fons amóris,*
   *Me sentíre vim dolóris*
   *Fac, ut tecum lúgeam.*

10. *Fac ut árdeat cor meum*
    *in amándo Christum Deum,*
    *ut sibi compláceam.*

11. *Sancta Mater, istud agas,*
    *Crucifíxi fige plagas*
    *Cordi meo válide.*

12. *Tui Nati vulneráti,*
    *Tam dignáti pro me pati,*
    *Poenas mecum dívide.*

13. *Fac me vere tecum flere,*
    *Crucifíxo condolére,*
    *Donec ego víxero.*

14. *Juxta crucem tecum stare,*
    *Ac me tibi sociáre*
    *In planctu desídero.*

15. *Virgo vírginum praeclára,*
    *Mihi jam non sis amára:*
    *Fac me tecum plángere.*

Text: 88 7; *Stabat Mater dolorosa;* Jacapone da Todi, 1230–1306; tr. by Edward Caswall, 1814–1878, alt.
Music: STABAT MATER; *Maintzisch Gesangbuch,* 1661.

# 364

## SAVE YOUR PEOPLE

Save your peo-ple, O Lord. Show us the way to come home. We have been wan-der-ing far from your love. Save your peo-ple, O Lord.

**Verses**

1. One thing I ask, __ O __
2. For you will hide me in the
3. Lis - ten, O Lord, __ to the
4. Thus will I bless you all the

1. Lord, __ this I seek: to dwell for - ev - er in your
2. shel - ter of your wings and from the ar - rows of my
3. sound __ of my call, for I ac - knowl-edge my of -
4. days __ of my life. Lift - ing my hands, I call your

1. house, that I may gaze __ on your love - li - ness
2. foes. You set me high __ on a moun-tain-top,
3. fense. Wash me and I __ shall be pur - i - fied.
4. name: "O Lord, re - mem-ber your in - her - i - tance.

_to Refrain_

1. all __ the days of my life.
2. saved __ me from my dis - tress.
3. I shall be whit - er than snow.
4. Save __ your peo - ple, O Lord!"

Text: Based on Psalm 27; Jim Farrell, b. 1947.
Music: Jim Farrell.

## HOSANNA TO THE SON OF DAVID

Ho-san-na to the Son of Da-vid; bless-ed is he who comes

in the name of the Lord, the King of Is-

ra-el. Ho-san-na in the high-est.

Text: Based on Matthew 21:9. English tr. © 2010, ICEL. All rights reserved. Used with permission.
Music: Chant, Mode VII; music adapt. © 2010, ICEL. All rights reserved. Used with permission.

## ALL GLORY, LAUD, AND HONOR

**366**

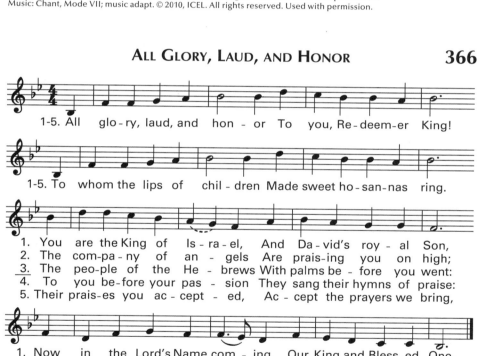

1-5. All glo-ry, laud, and hon-or To you, Re-deem-er King!

1-5. To whom the lips of chil-dren Made sweet ho-san-nas ring.

1. You are the King of Is-ra-el, And Da-vid's roy-al Son,
2. The com-pa-ny of an-gels Are prais-ing you on high;
3. The peo-ple of the He-brews With palms be-fore you went:
4. To you be-fore your pas-sion They sang their hymns of praise:
5. Their prais-es you ac-cept-ed, Ac-cept the prayers we bring,

1. Now in the Lord's Name com-ing, Our King and Bless-ed One.
2. And mor-tals, joined with all things Cre-a-ted, make re-ply.
3. Our praise and prayers and an-thems Be-fore you we pre-sent.
4. To you, now high ex-alt-ed, Our mel-o-dy we raise.
5. Great source of love and good-ness, Our Sav-ior and our King.

Text: 76 76 D; Theodulph of Orleans, ca. 760–821; tr. by John M. Neale, 1818–1866, alt.
Music: ST. THEODULPH; Melchior Teschner, 1584–1635.

**367**  HOSANNA TO THE SON OF DAVID

Refrain

Ho - san - na   to the Son of Da - vid!   O blest is he, O blest is he who comes in the name of the Lord!

Verses

1. Re - joice, daugh - ter of Zi - on,
2. Re - joice, all who are thirst - ing
3. Re - joice, all who are long - ing
4. Re - joice, all who are search - ing
5. Re - joice, all who are hop - ing
6. Re - joice, all who are wait - ing
7. Re - joice, all who are call - ing
8. Re - joice, all who are hun - gry

1. in the One who brings great joy!
2. for the streams of liv - ing joy!
3. to be - hold the face of God!
4. for the truth of ho - ly light!
5. for the reign of peace and love!
6. for the dawn of heav - en's light!
7. on the name of God on high!
8. for the taste of liv - ing bread!

Sing praise, chil - 

to Refrain

1-8. - dren of Ju - dah, for the Lord is close at hand!

Text: Refrain based on Matthew 21:9; Dan Schutte, b. 1947.
Music: Dan Schutte.

**368**  PASSION ACCLAMATION

There is no great - er love than this: To lay down your life for your friends.

Text: Based on John 15:13; Christopher Walker, b. 1947.
Music: Christopher Walker.

# AT THE NAME OF JESUS

**369**

Refrain

At the name of Je-sus ev-'ry knee shall bend,
at the name of Je-sus ev-'ry knee shall bend.

Verses

1. 'Tis our God's great plea-sure we should speak God's name,
2. Hum-bled for a sea-son, to re-ceive a name
3. Christ is tru-ly Sav-ior, Christ, the God a-dored,
4. In your hearts en-throne him, there let him sub-due
5. Sis-ters, broth-ers, Je-sus dwells with us a-gain

to Refrain

1. who from the be-gin-ning was for-e'er the same.
2. from the lips of peo-ples un-to whom he came.
3. ev-er to be wor-shiped, ev-er-more a-dored.
4. all that is not ho-ly, all that is not true.
5. now to let his vi-sion o'er our hearts to reign.

# RITE FOR RECEIVING THE HOLY OILS

**370**

1. Behold the oil of the sick, blessed by our Bishop,
   sent to us for the anointing of all who suffer illness.

Refrain

Thanks be to God! Thanks be to God!
Alt. Refrain Blessed be God for-ev-er! Blessed be God for-ev-er!

2. Behold the oil of the catechumens, blessed by our Bishop,
   sent to us for the anointing of our catechumens in preparation for their baptism.

3. Behold the sacred chrism, oil mixed with sweet perfume,
   and consecrated by our Bishop, sent to us for the anointing
   of the baptized who are to be sealed with the Holy Spirit.

**371**

## JESU, JESU

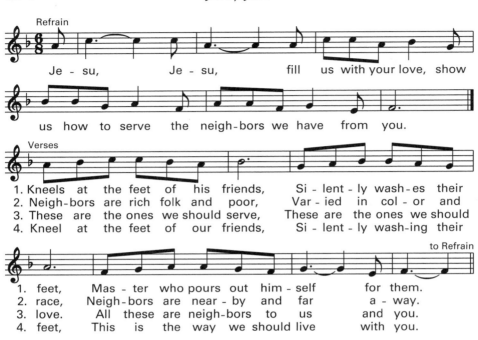

**Refrain**

Je - su, Je - su, fill us with your love, show
us how to serve the neigh - bors we have from you.

**Verses**

1. Kneels at the feet of his friends, Si - lent - ly wash - es their
2. Neigh - bors are rich folk and poor, Var - ied in col - or and
3. These are the ones we should serve, These are the ones we should
4. Kneel at the feet of our friends, Si - lent - ly wash - ing their

*to Refrain*

1. feet, Mas - ter who pours out him - self for them.
2. race, Neigh - bors are near - by and far a - way.
3. love. All these are neigh - bors to us and you.
4. feet, This is the way we should live with you.

Note: Jesu is pronounced "yay-zoo"

Text: 779 with refrain; John 13:3–5; Ghanaian Folk Song; tr. by Tom Colvin, b. 1925.
Music: CHEREPONI; Ghanaian Folk Song; adapt. by Tom Colvin.
Text and music © 1969, Hope Publishing Co. All rights reserved. Used with permission.

**372**

## AS I HAVE DONE FOR YOU

**Refrain**

I, your Lord and Mas - ter, now be - come your ser - vant.

I who made the moon and stars will kneel to wash your feet.

This is my com - mand - ment: to love as I have loved you.

Kneel to wash each oth - er's feet as I have done for you.

Verses

1. All the world will know / you are my dis - ci - ples
2. I must leave you now / on - ly for a mo - ment.
3. I am like a vine, / you are like the branch-es.
4. I have called you friends, / now no long - er ser-vants.
5. You will weep for now / while the world re - joic - es.
6. I will give you peace; / this will be my bless-ing.

1. by the love that you of - fer, the kind - ness you
2. I must go to my Fa - ther to make you a
3. If you cling to my teach - ing you sure - ly will
4. What I told you in se - cret, the world longs to
5. But the tears of your sor - row will soon turn to
6. Though the world churns a - round you, I leave you my

1. show. You have heard the voice of God in the
2. home. On the day of my re - turn, I will
3. live. If you make your home in me, I will
4. know. There can be no great - er love than to
5. joy. As a moth - er cries in child - birth and her
6. peace. I have told you all these things that my

1. words that I have spo - ken. You be - held heav-en's
2. come to take you with me to the place I have
3. come to dwell with - in you. You can count on my
4. give your life for oth - ers. As the Fa - ther has
5. pain is turned to glad - ness, you will know great re -
6. peace may dwell with - in you. Let your faith be un -

to Refrain

1. glo - ry and have seen the face of God.
2. prom - ised where your joy will have no end.
3. mer - cy when you ask for what you need.
4. loved me, so I love you as my own.
5. joic - ing on the day of my re - turn.
6. shak - en and your hope be ev - er strong.

Text: Based on John 13–16; Dan Schutte, b. 1947.
Music: Dan Schutte.

**373**       IF I, YOUR LORD AND MASTER

Refrain

If I, your Lord and Mas-ter, have washed your feet, you must do the same for one an-oth-er.

Verses

1. The Lord____ Je - sus, when he had
2. But Si - mon Pe - ter asked why the
3. "You call me Mas - ter, but here you

1. eat - en with his dis - ci - ples, took
2. Lord had____ stooped to wash him, and
3. see me____ as your ser - vant. If

1. wa - ter in a ba - sin and knelt down to wash their
2. Je - sus an-swered, "Pe - ter, if I do not wash your
3. I whom you call Mas - ter have done such a thing for

to Refrain

1. feet, say - ing: "This ex - am - ple I leave you."
2. feet for you, you have no part with me."
3. you, you must now do the same for each oth - er."

Text: Based on John 13:4–6, 8, 13–15; Stephen Dean, b. 1948.
Music: Stephen Dean.
Text and music © 2000, Stephen Dean. Published by OCP. All rights reserved.

# Ubi Caritas/Where True Charity and Love Dwell 374

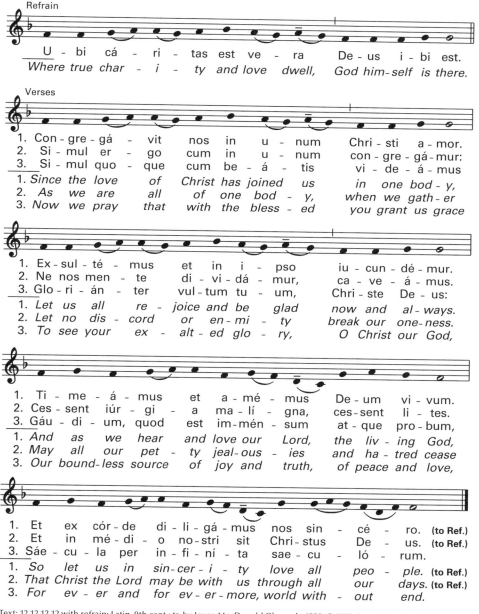

Text: 12 12 12 12 with refrain; Latin, 9th cent.; tr. by Joyce MacDonald Glover, b. 1923, © 1982, Joyce MacDonald Glover.
    All rights reserved. Used with permission.
Music: UBI CARITAS; Chant, Mode VI.

## 375 GLORY IN THE CROSS

Holy Thursday
(Vss. 1–4)

1. Let us ev-er glo-ry in the cross of Christ, our sal-
2. Let us make our jour-ney to the cross of Christ, who sur-
3. Let us tell the sto-ry of the cross of Christ as we
4. Let us stand to-geth-er at the cross of Christ where we

1. va - tion and __ our hope.
2. ren-dered glo-ry and grace
3. share this heav-en-ly feast.
4. see God's bound-less love.

Let us bow in hom-age to the
to be-come a ser-vant of the
We be-come one bod-y in the
We are saints and sin-ners who are

1. Lord of Life, who was bro-ken to make us whole.
2. great and small, that all peo-ple may know God's face.
3. blood of Christ, from the great to the ver-y least.
4. joined by faith here on earth and in heav'n a-bove.

There is
Though his
When we
Nei-ther

1. no great-er love, as bless-ed as this: to lay down one's
2. birth was di-vine, he knelt as a slave, to wash com-mon
3. eat of this bread, and drink of this cup, we hon-or the
4. wom-an nor man, not ser-vant or free, but one in the

1. life for a friend.
2. dust from our feet.
3. death of the Lord.
4. eyes of the Lord.

Let us ev-er glo-ry in the cross of Christ and the

Fine

1, 2     2          3

1-4. tri-umph of God's great love.

**Good Friday**

1. Let us ever glory in the cross of Christ
who redeems us with his blood.
Let us tell the story of the cross of Christ
and the pow'r of his saving love.
Like a lamb he was slain;
he carried our shame,
to show us the mercy of God.
Let us ever glory in the cross of Christ
and the triumph of God's great love.

2. Let us bring our burdens
to the cross of Christ
who has known our sorrow and tears.
In the great compassion of
the heart of Christ,
God has walked in our hopes and fears.
He was mocked and betrayed,
deserted by friends, and banished
to die among thieves.
Let us ever glory in the cross of Christ
and the triumph of God's great love.

3. Let us kneel in homage at
the cross of Christ
where we see God's human face.
We behold the Maker of the sun and stars
as he hangs on the throne of grace.
As we share in his pain,
his sorrow and shame,
our hearts will be tested in fire.
Let us ever glory in the cross of Christ
and the triumph of God's great love.

**Easter**

1. Let us ever glory in the cross of Christ,
our salvation and our hope.
Let us bow in homage to the Lord of Life,
who was broken to make us whole.
There is no greater love, as blessed as this:
to lay down one's life for a friend.
Let us ever glory in the cross of Christ
and the triumph of God's great love.

2. Let us ever glory in the cross of Christ
who is risen from the grave.
He will come in glory to receive our hearts
at the dawn of the lasting day.
For the trumpet will sound,
the dead shall be raised,
and death shall defeat us no more.
Let us ever glory in the cross of Christ
and the triumph of God's great love.

3. Let us raise our voices to the cross of Christ
where the earth and heaven unite.
God has wed creation on the tree of hope
where the darkness becomes our light.
Let us join in the dance of heaven and earth,
give thanks for the goodness of God.
Let us ever glory in the cross of Christ
and the triumph of God's great love.

Text and music: Dan Schutte, b. 1947, © 2000, Daniel L. Schutte. Published by OCP. All rights reserved.

## WHEN JESUS WEPT

**376**

When Jesus wept the fall - ing tear In mer - cy flow'd be - yond all bound, When Je - sus groan'd, a trem-bling fear Seiz'd all the guil - ty world a - round.

Text: LM; *The New England Psalm Singer*, 1770.
Music: WHEN JESUS WEPT; William Billings, 1746–1800.

# 377 PANGE, LINGUA, GLORIOSI/SING OF GLORY

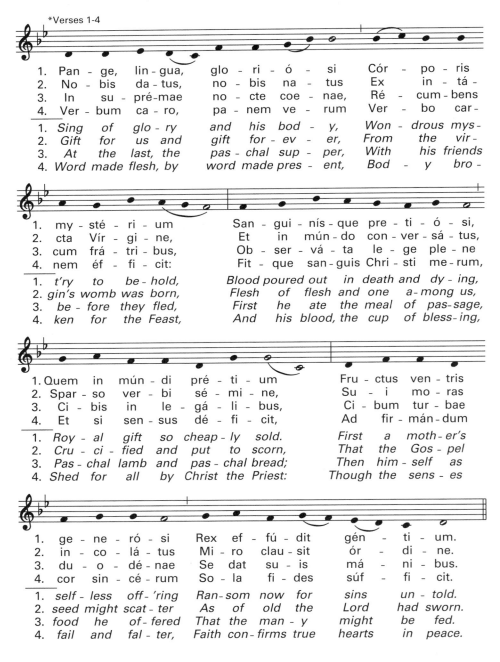

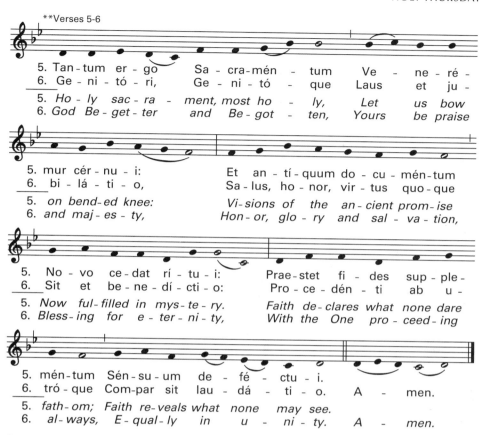

**Verses 5-6

5. Tan-tum er - go Sa - cra-mén - tum Ve - ne - ré -
6. Ge - ni - tó - ri, Ge - ni - tó - que Laus et ju -

5. *Ho - ly sac - ra - ment, most ho - ly, Let us bow*
6. *God Be - get - ter and Be - got - ten, Yours be praise*

5. mur cér - nu - i: Et an - tí - quum do - cu - mén-tum
6. bi - lá - ti - o, Sa - lus, ho - nor, vir - tus quo - que

5. *on bend-ed knee: Vi - sions of the an - cient prom-ise*
6. *and maj - es - ty, Hon - or, glo - ry and sal - va - tion,*

5. No - vo ce - dat rí - tu - i: Prae-stet fi - des sup - ple -
6. Sit et be - ne - dí - cti - o: Pro - ce - dén - ti ab u -

5. *Now ful - filled in mys - te - ry. Faith de - clares what none dare*
6. *Bless-ing for e - ter - ni - ty, With the One pro - ceed - ing*

5. mén-tum Sén - su - um de - fé - ctu - i.
6. tró - que Com-par sit lau - dá - ti - o. A - men.

5. *fath - om; Faith re - veals what none may see.*
6. *al - ways, E - qual - ly in u - ni - ty. A - men.*

*Verses 1–4 are repeated as necessary until the procession reaches the place of repose.
**Verses 5–6 are sung while the priest, kneeling, incenses the Blessed Sacrament.
  Then the Blessed Sacrament is placed in the tabernacle of repose.

Text: 87 87 87; *Pange lingua gloriosi*; St. Thomas Aquinas, 1227–1274; tr. by Harry Hagan, OSB, b. 1947,
  © 1990, St. Meinrad Archabbey. Published by OCP. All rights reserved.
Music: PANGE LINGUA GLORIOSI; Chant, Mode III.

# 378    PANGE, LINGUA, GLORIOSI/SING OF GLORY

1. Pan - ge, lin - gua, glo - ri - ó - si   Cór - po - ris   my - sté - ri - um
2. No - bis da - tus, no - bis na - tus   Ex in - tá - cta Vír - gi - ne,
3. In su - pré - mae no - cte coe - nae,   Ré - cum - bens cum frá - tri - bus,
4. Ver - bum ca - ro, pa - nem ve - rum   Ver - bo car - nem éf - fi - cit:
5. Tan - tum er - go   Sa - cra - mén - tum   Ve - ne - ré - mur cér - nu - i:
6. Ge - ni - tó - ri,   Ge - ni - tó - que Laus et ju - bi - lá - ti - o,

1. San - gui - nís - que pre - ti - ó - si, Quem in mun - di pré - ti - um
2. Et in mun - do con - ver - sá - tus, Spar - so ver - bi sé - mi - ne,
3. Ob - ser - vá - ta le - ge ple - ne   Ci - bis in le - gá - li - bus,
4. Fit - que san - guis Chri - sti me - rum, Et si sen - sus dé - fi - cit,
5. Et an - tí - quum do - cu - mén - tum   No - vo ce - dat rí - tu - i:
6. Sa - lus, ho - nor, vir - tus quo - que   Sit et be - ne - dí - cti - o:

1. Fru - ctus ven - tris ge - ne - ró - si   Rex ef - fú - dit gén - ti - um.
2. Su - i mo - ras in - co - lá - tus   Mi - ro clau - sit ór - di - ne.
3. Ci - bum tur - bae du - o - dé - nae   Se dat su - is má - ni - bus.
4. Ad fir - mán - dum cor sin - cé - rum   So - la fi - des súf - fi - cit.
5. Prae - stet fi - des sup - ple - mén - tum   Sén - su - um de - fé - ctu - i.
6. Pro - ce - dén - ti ab u - tró - que   Com - par sit lau - dá - ti - o.

* 1. Sing of glory and his body,
  Wondrous myst'ry to behold,
  Blood poured out in death and dying,
  Royal gift so cheaply sold.
  First a mother's selfless off'ring
  Ransom now for sins untold.

2. Gift for us and gift forever,
  From the virgin's womb was born,
  Flesh of flesh and one among us,
  Crucified and put to scorn,
  That the Gospel seed might scatter
  As of old the Lord had sworn.

3. At the last, the paschal supper,
  With his friends before they fled,
  First he ate the meal of passage:
  Paschal lamb and paschal bread;
  Then himself as food he offered
  That the many might be fed.

4. Word made flesh, by word made present,
  Body broken for the Feast,
  And his blood, the cup of blessing,
  Shed for all by Christ the Priest:
  Though the senses fail and falter,
  Faith confirms true hearts in peace.

** 5. Holy sacrament, most holy,
  Let us bow on bended knee:
  Visions of the ancient promise
  Now fulfilled in mystery.
  Faith declares what none dare fathom;
  Faith reveals what none may see.

6. God Begetter and Begotten,
  Yours be praise and majesty,
  Honor, glory and salvation,
  Blessing for eternity,
  With the One proceeding always,
  Equally in unity.

*Verses 1–4 are repeated as necessary until the procession reaches the place of repose.
**Verses 5–6 are sung while the priest, kneeling, incenses the Blessed Sacrament.
   Then the Blessed Sacrament is placed in the tabernacle of repose.

Text: 87 87 87; *Pange lingua gloriosi*; St. Thomas Aquinas, 1227–1274; tr. by Harry Hagan, OSB, b. 1947,
  © 1990, St. Meinrad Archabbey. Published by OCP. All rights reserved.
Music: ST. THOMAS (TANTUM ERGO); John F. Wade, 1711–1786.

## No Greater Love

**379**

There can be no great-er love than to lay down your life for a friend.

*Verses available in accompaniment books.

Text: Refrain, John 15:13; adapt. by Tim Schoenbachler, b. 1952, © 1986, OCP. All rights reserved.
Music: Tim Schoenbachler, © 1986, OCP. All rights reserved.

## Wood of the Cross

**380**

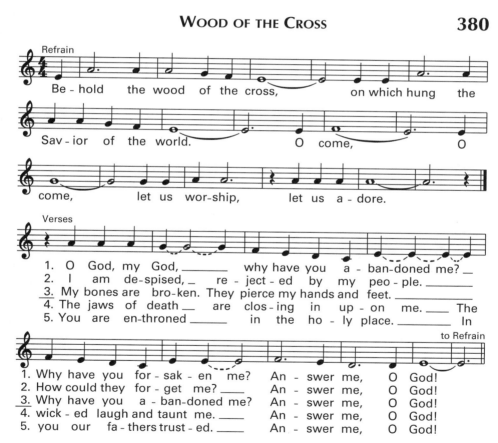

Refrain

Be-hold the wood of the cross, on which hung the Sav-ior of the world. O come, O come, let us wor-ship, let us a-dore.

Verses

1. O God, my God, _____ why have you a-ban-doned me? _
2. I am de-spised, _ re-ject-ed by my peo-ple. _____
3. My bones are bro-ken. They pierce my hands and feet. _____
4. The jaws of death _ are clos-ing in up-on me. ___ The
5. You are en-throned _____ in the ho-ly place. _____ In

to Refrain

1. Why have you for-sak-en me? An-swer me, O God!
2. How could they for-get me? ___ An-swer me, O God!
3. Why have you a-ban-doned me? An-swer me, O God!
4. wick-ed laugh and taunt me. ___ An-swer me, O God!
5. you our fa-thers trust-ed. ___ An-swer me, O God!

Text: Based on *Good Friday Liturgy*; Psalm 22; Owen Alstott, b. 1947.
Music: Owen Alstott.
Text and music © 1982, OCP. All rights reserved.

**381**     **BEHOLD THE CROSS**

Verses 1-3, 5

1, 5. Be-hold the cross on which was hung life's ver - y Lord, _____
2. Nails in his hands, nails in his feet, a trai-tor kiss __ up-
3. Eyes that won't see, ears that won't hear, lips that de - ny __ the

1, 5. God's on - ly Son; Ma - ry's own babe, so cold and so
2. on __ his cheek; and his pierced heart, now bro - ken in
3. friend once so dear; slow - ly he turns and cap - tures your

1, 5. still, help - less be - fore her on Cal - va - ry hill. (to Vs 2)
2. two, love cru - ci - fied __ for me and for you. (to Vs 3)
3. eye, then pass - es on __ to Cal - v'ry to die. (to Vs 4)

Verse 4

4. Be-hold the cross of Christ in our midst: all those who bear his

4. wounds in their flesh. Suf - f'ring for crimes of mer - cy and peace,

2 to Vs. 5

4. signs of the king - dom on Cal - va - ry street.

Text: Based on the *Liturgy for Good Friday*; Bob Hurd, b. 1950.
Music: Bob Hurd.

**382**     **LORD, WE ADORE YOU**

Ostinato Refrain

Lord, we a - dore you, kneel - ing be - fore you; bring - ing our sor - rows,

leav - ing our bur - dens for you, our Re - deem - er, here at your cross.

# O SACRED HEAD, SURROUNDED

1a. O Sa-cred Head, sur-round-ed By crown of pierc-ing thorn!
2a. In this, your bit-ter pas-sion, Good Shep-herd, think of me
3a. What lan-guage shall I bor-row To thank you, dear-est friend,
*1b. O Sa-cred Head, sur-round-ed By crown of pierc-ing thorn!
2b. O Love, all love tran-scend-ing, O Wis-dom from on high!
3b. O Je-sus, we a-dore thee, Up-on the cross our King!

1a. O bleed-ing Head, so wound-ed, Re-viled and put to scorn!
2a. With your most kind com-pas-sion, Un-worth-y though I be:
3a. For this, your dy-ing sor-row, Your mer-cy with-out end?
1b. O bleed-ing Head, so wound-ed, Re-viled and put to scorn!
2b. O Truth, un-changed, un-chang-ing, Sur-ren-dered up to die!
3b. We hum-bly bow be-fore thee, And of thy vic-t'ry sing!

1a. The pow'r of death comes o'er you, The glow of life de-cays,
2a. Be-neath your cross a-bid-ing, For-ev-er would I rest,
3a. Lord, make me yours for-ev-er, A loy-al ser-vant true,
1b. No come-li-ness or beau-ty Thy wound-ed face be-trays,
2b. Was e'er a love so won-drous! That from his heav'n-ly throne
3b. Thy cross is our sal-va-tion, Our hope from day to day,

1a. Yet an-gel hosts a-dore you, And trem-ble as they gaze.
2a. In your dear love con-fid-ing, And with your pres-ence blest.
3a. And let me nev-er, nev-er Out-live my love for you.
1b. Yet an-gel hosts a-dore thee And trem-ble as they gaze.
2b. God should de-scend a-mong us To suf-fer for his own.
3b. Our peace and con-so-la-tion When life shall fade a-way.

*Alternate verses.

Text: 76 76 D; *Salve caput cruentatum*; ascr. to Bernard of Clairvaux, 1091–1153.
 Verses 1, 2 tr. by Henry W. Baker, 1821–1877, alt.; verse 3 tr. by James W. Alexander, 1804–1859, alt.
 Alternate verses: verse 1 tr. by Henry W. Baker, alt.; verse 2, Owen Alstott, b. 1947;
 verse 3, Owen Alstott, composite. Alternate verses 2, 3 © 1977, OCP. All rights reserved.
Music: PASSION CHORALE; Hans Leo Hassler, 1564–1612; adapt. by Johann Sebastian Bach, 1685–1750.

## 384    Sing, My Tongue, the Savior's Glory

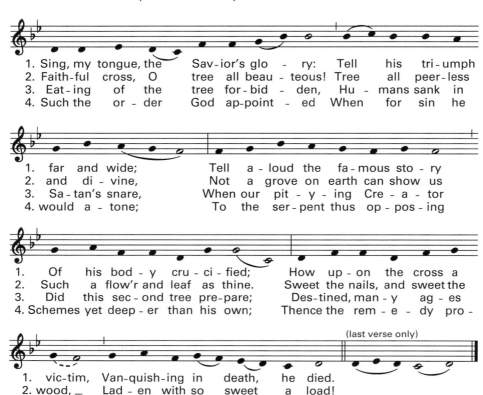

1. Sing, my tongue, the Sav-ior's glo - ry: Tell his tri - umph
2. Faith-ful cross, O tree all beau - teous! Tree all peer-less
3. Eat-ing of the tree for-bid - den, Hu - mans sank in
4. Such the or - der God ap-point - ed When for sin he

1. far and wide; Tell a - loud the fa-mous sto - ry
2. and di - vine, Not a grove on earth can show us
3. Sa - tan's snare, When our pit - y - ing Cre - a - tor
4. would a - tone; To the ser - pent thus op - pos - ing

1. Of his bod - y cru - ci - fied; How up - on the cross a
2. Such a flow'r and leaf as thine. Sweet the nails, and sweet the
3. Did this sec - ond tree pre-pare; Des-tined, man - y ag - es
4. Schemes yet deep - er than his own; Thence the rem - e - dy pro -

(last verse only)

1. vic-tim, Van-quish-ing in death, he died.
2. wood, _ Lad - en with so sweet a load!
3. lat - er, That first e - vil to re - pair.
4. cur-ing, When the fa - tal wound had come. A - men.

5. So when now at length the fullness
Of the sacred time drew nigh,
Then the Son, the world's Creator,
Left his Father's throne on high;
From a virgin's womb appearing,
Clothed in our mortality.

6. Thus did Christ to perfect manhood
In our mortal flesh attain:
Then of his free choice he goes on
To a death of bitter pain;
And as lamb upon the altar
Of the cross, for us is slain.

7. Lofty tree, bend down your branches,
To embrace your sacred load;
Oh, relax the native tension
Of that all too rigid wood;
Gently, gently bear the members
Of your dying King and God.

8. Blessing, honor everlasting,
To the immortal Deity;
To the Father, Son, and Spirit,
Equal praises ever be;
Glory through the earth and heaven,
Trinity in Unity. Amen.

Text: 87 87 87; Venantius Honorius Fortunatus, 530–609; tr. by John M. Neale, 1818–1866.
Music: PANGE LINGUA GLORIOSI; Chant, Mode III; *Liber Hymnarius*, 1983.

# WERE YOU THERE

1. Were you there when they cru - ci - fied my Lord?
2. Were you there when they nailed him to the tree?
3. Were you there when they pierced him in the side?
4. Were you there when the sun re - fused to shine?
5. Were you there when they laid him in the tomb?
6. Were you there when he rose up from the grave?

1. Were you there when they cru - ci - fied my Lord?
2. Were you there when they nailed him to the tree?
3. Were you there when they pierced him in the side?
4. Were you there when the sun re - fused to shine?
5. Were you there when they laid him in the tomb?
6. Were you there when he rose up from the grave?

1-6. Oh! Some - times it caus - es

1-6. me to trem - ble, trem - ble, trem - ble,

1. Were you there when they cru - ci - fied my Lord?
2. Were you there when they nailed him to the tree?
3. Were you there when they pierced him in the side?
4. Were you there when the sun re - fused to shine?
5. Were you there when they laid him in the tomb?
6. Were you there when he rose up from the grave?

Text: 10 10 14 10; Spiritual; *Old Plantation Hymns*, Boston, 1899.
Music: WERE YOU THERE; Spiritual; *Old Plantation Hymns*, Boston, 1899.

## 386     Behold the Lamb of God

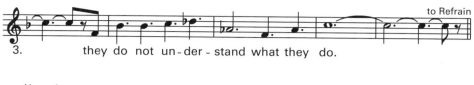

3. they do not un-der-stand what they do.

Verse 4

4. The king-dom of this world has be-come the

4. king-dom of Christ, and he shall reign for

4. end-less days. Worth-y is the Lamb.

Text: Based on John 1:29; Isaiah 53:4–5; Luke 23:34; Revelation 11:15; Bob Dufford, b. 1943.
Music: Bob Dufford.

## WHEN I SURVEY THE WONDROUS CROSS 387

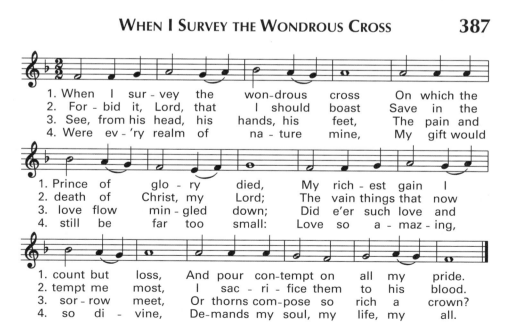

1. When I sur-vey the won-drous cross On which the
2. For-bid it, Lord, that I should boast Save in the
3. See, from his head, his hands, his feet, The pain and
4. Were ev-'ry realm of na-ture mine, My gift would

1. Prince of glo-ry died, My rich-est gain I
2. death of Christ, my Lord; The vain things that now
3. love flow min-gled down; Did e'er such love and
4. still be far too small: Love so a-maz-ing,

1. count but loss, And pour con-tempt on all my pride.
2. tempt me most, I sac-ri-fice them to his blood.
3. sor-row meet, Or thorns com-pose so rich a crown?
4. so di-vine, De-mands my soul, my life, my all.

Text: LM; Isaac Watts, 1674–1748, alt.
Music: HAMBURG; Lowell Mason, 1792–1872.

**388**     **BEHOLD THE WOOD**

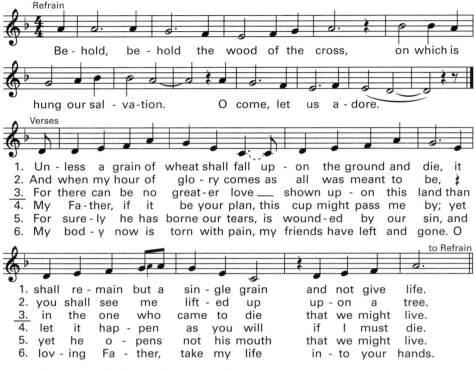

Refrain

Be - hold, be - hold the wood of the cross, on which is hung our sal - va-tion. O come, let us a - dore.

Verses

1. Un - less a grain of wheat shall fall up - on the ground and die, it
2. And when my hour of glo - ry comes as all was meant to be,
3. For there can be no great-er love ___ shown up - on this land than
4. My Fa - ther, if it be your plan, this cup might pass me by; yet
5. For sure - ly he has borne our tears, is wound-ed by our sin, and
6. My bod - y now is torn with pain, my friends have left and gone. O

to Refrain

1. shall re - main but a sin - gle grain and not give life.
2. you shall see me lift - ed up up - on a tree.
3. in the one who came to die that we might live.
4. let it hap - pen as you will if I must die.
5. yet he o - pens not his mouth that we might live.
6. lov - ing Fa - ther, take my life in - to your hands.

Text: Based on John 12:24, 32; 15:13; Good Friday Liturgy; Dan Schutte, b. 1947.
Music: Dan Schutte.

**389**     **OURS WERE THE GRIEFS HE BORE**

Ours were the griefs he bore, ours were the pains he car - ried. Ours were the sins he took on him, and by his wounds we are healed.

Text: Based on Isaiah 53:4–5; 1 Peter 2:24; Stephen Dean, b. 1948.
Music: Stephen Dean.

## My Song Is Love Unknown

1. My song is love unknown, My Savior's love to me,
   Love to the loveless shown That they might lovely be.
   O who am I That for my sake The Lord should take Frail flesh, and die?

2. He came from his blest throne Salvation to bestow,
   But all made strange, and none The longed-for Christ would know.
   But O my friend, My friend indeed, Who at my need His life did spend!

3. Sometimes they strew his way, And his sweet praises sing,
   Resounding all the day Hosannas to their King.
   Then "Crucify!" Is all their breath, And for his death They thirst and cry.

4. Why, what hath my Lord done? What makes this rage and spite?
   He made the lame to run, He gave the blind their sight.
   Sweet injuries! Yet they at these Themselves displease, And 'gainst him rise.

5. They rise and needs will have My dear Lord made away;
   A murderer they save, The Prince of Life they slay.
   Yet steadfast he To suffering goes, That he his foes From thence might free.

6. In life no house, no home My Lord on earth might have;
   In death no friendly tomb But what a stranger gave.
   What may I say? Heav'n was his home; But mine the tomb Wherein he lay.

7. Here might I stay and sing, No story so divine!
   Never was love, dear King, Never was grief like thine.
   This is my friend, In whose sweet praise I all my days Could gladly spend!

Text: 66 66 44 44; Samuel Crossman, ca. 1624–1683.
Music: LOVE UNKNOWN; John Ireland, 1879–1962, © 1924, 1995, John Ireland. All rights reserved.
   Administered by the John Ireland Trust, London. Used with permission.

**391** Your Only Son

1. Your on-ly Son, no sin to hide, but you have
2. Your gift of love they cru-ci-fied, they laughed and
3. I was so lost I should have died, but you have

1. sent him from your side to walk up-on this guilt-y
2. scorned him as he died; the hum-ble King they named a
3. brought me to your side to be led by your staff and

1. sod, and to be - come the Lamb of God.
2. fraud, and sac - ri - ficed the Lamb of God.
3. rod, and to be called a lamb of God.

Refrain

O Lamb of God, sweet Lamb of God; I love the
ho - ly Lamb of God. O wash me in his pre-cious
blood. My Je - sus Christ, the Lamb of God.

Text and music: Twila Paris, b. 1958, © 1985, Straightway Music (ASCAP)/Mountain Spring Music (ASCAP). All rights reserved. Administered by EMI CMG Publishing. Used with permission.

**392** The Seven Last Words from the Cross

*Refrain

O vos o - mnes qui tran - si - tis per vi - am at -
ten - di - te et vi-de-te si est do - lor si-cut do-lor me-us.

*Translation: O all you who pass this way, look and see is any sorrow like the sorrow that afflicts me.*

*Verses available in accompaniment books.

Text: Refrain based on Lamentations 1:12.
Music: Anne Quigley, b. 1956, © 2001, Anne Quigley. Published by OCP. All rights reserved.

## O Sacred Head

**393**

Verses 1, 2, 4

1. O  Sa - cred Head,  sur - round - ed  by
2. No  come - li - ness  or  beau - ty  your
4. Life - giv - ing  love,  em - pow'r  us  with

1. crown of pierc - ing  thorn!  O bleed - ing Head, so
2. wound - ed face  be - trays.  Yet an - gel hosts  a -
4. cour - age bold and  true  to  walk the road  of

|1|  to Verse 2
1. wound - ed,  re - viled and put  to scorn!
2. dore  you  and trem - ble  as  they
4. jus - tice,  and bear the cross with

|2|  to Verse 3 | Final
2. gaze.  4. you,  and bear the cross  with you.

Verse 3

3. My sis - ter  ren - dered voice - less,  de - meaned and

3. still  in  chains,  my broth - er  still  ex -

to Verse 4

3. ploit - ed,  im - ag - es  of  your  pain.

**394**  LITANY OF THE SAINTS

Lord, have mer - cy. **Lord, have mer - cy.**
Christ, have mer - cy. **Christ, have mer - cy.**
Lord, have mer - cy. **Lord, have mer - cy.**

Holy Mary, Mother of Gód, **pray for us.**
Saint Mích - ael,

| | |
|---|---|
| Holy Angels of Gód, | Saint Grégory, |
| Saint John the Báptist, | Saint Augústine, |
| Saint Jóseph, | Saint Athanásius, |
| Saint Peter and Saint Pául, | Saint Básil, |
| Saint Ándrew, | Saint Mártin, |
| Saint Jóhn, | Saint Bénedict, |
| Saint Mary Mágdalene, | Saint Francis and Saint Dóminic, |
| Saint Stéphen, | Saint Francis Xávier, |
| Saint Ignatius of Ántioch, | Saint John Viánney, |
| Saint Láwrence, | Saint Catherine of Siéna, |
| Saint Perpetua and Saint Felícity, | Saint Teresa of Jésus, |
| Saint Ágnes, | All holy men and women, Saints of Gód, |

Lord, be mer - ci - ful, **Lord, de - liv - er us, we pray.**

From àll é - vil, **Lord, de - liv - er us, we pray.**

From èverý sin,                           By your Death and Rèsurréction,
From everlàsting déath,              By the outpouring of the
By your Ìncarnátion,                      Hòly Spírit,

Be merciful to us sin - ners, **Lord, we ask you, hear our prayer.**

*If there are candidates to be baptized*

Bring these chosen ones to new birth through the grace of Bap - tism,

**Lord, we ask you, hear our prayer.**

*If there is no one to be baptized*

Cantors

Make this font holy by your grace for the new birth of your chil - dren,

All

**Lord, we ask you, hear our prayer.**

Cantors | All

Jesus, Son of the liv - ing God, **Lord, we ask you, hear our prayer.**

Cantors, All repeat | Cantors, All repeat

**Christ, hear us. Christ, gra-cious-ly hear us.**

## OUT OF DARKNESS

# 395

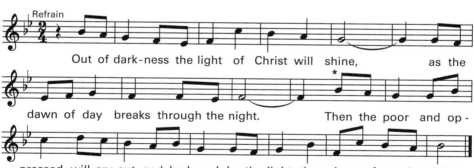

Refrain

Out of dark-ness the light of Christ will shine, as the

dawn of day breaks through the night. Then the poor and op -

pressed will cry out and be heard by the light that ris - es from the night.

Verses

1. Let the darkness flee from here.
   Put an end to sadness and fear.
   The hungry will eat, the sick will dance,
   the dead will live again.

2. This is the night, O holy of nights,
   the chains of death are destroyed.

This is the light;
the glory of God is raised to life again.

3. A single flame,
   a flicker of hope spreads like a sea of fire.
   Open the door, shout to the night:
   We will live again.

*Last time repeat final phrase.

## 396    Christians, to the Paschal Victim

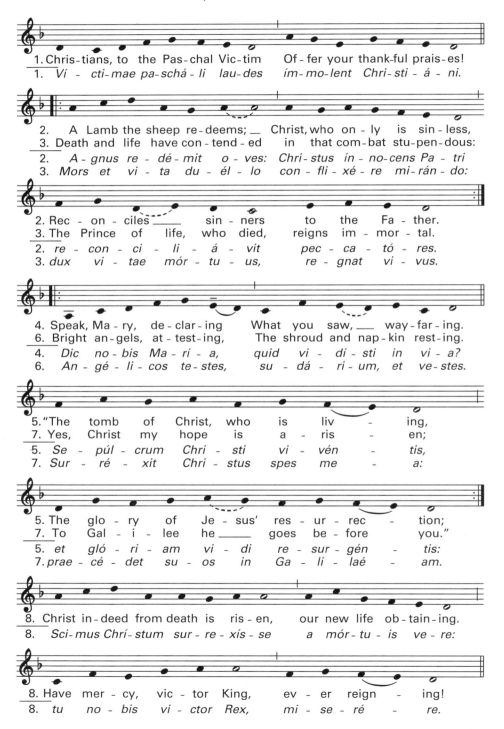

1. Chris-tians, to the Pas-chal Vic-tim    Of - fer your thank-ful prais-es!
1. *Ví - cti-mae pa-schá - li lau-des    ím - mo-lent Chri-sti - á - ni.*

2. A Lamb the sheep re-deems; — Christ, who on - ly is sin-less,
3. Death and life have con-tend-ed   in that com-bat stu-pen-dous:
2. *A - gnus re - dé-mit o - ves: Chri-stus ín - no-cens Pa - tri*
3. *Mors et vi - ta du - él - lo con - fli - xé - re mi-rán - do:*

2. Rec - on - ciles_____ sin - ners to the Fa - ther.
3. The Prince of life, who died, reigns im - mor - tal.
2. *re - con - ci - li - á - vit pec - ca - tó - res.*
3. *dux vi - tae mór - tu - us, re - gnat vi - vus.*

4. Speak, Ma - ry, de - clar-ing What you saw, — way-far-ing.
6. Bright an-gels, at - test-ing, The shroud and nap-kin rest-ing.
4. *Dic no - bis Ma - rí - a, quid vi - dí-sti in vi - a?*
6. *An - gé - li - cos te-stes, su - dá - ri - um, et ve-stes.*

5. "The tomb of Christ, who is liv - ing,
7. Yes, Christ my hope is a - ris - en;
5. *Se - púl - crum Chri - sti vi - vén - tis,*
7. *Sur - ré - xit Chri - stus spes me - a:*

5. The glo - ry of Je - sus' res - ur - rec - tion;
7. To Gal - i - lee he_____ goes be - fore you."
5. *et gló - ri - am vi - di re - sur - gén - tis:*
7. *prae - cé - det su - os in Ga - li - laé - am.*

8. Christ in-deed from death is ris - en, our new life ob - tain-ing.
8. *Sci - mus Chrí - stum sur - re - xís - se a mór - tu - is ve - re:*

8. Have mer - cy, vic - tor King, ev - er reign - ing!
8. *tu no - bis vi - ctor Rex, mi - se - ré - re.*

A - men. Al - le - lú - ia.

Text: Irregular; Poetic Sequence for Easter, *Victimae paschali laudes*; fr. *The Roman Missal*,
English text © 1964, The National Catholic Welfare Conference, Inc. (now US Conference of Catholic Bishops).
All rights reserved. Used with permission.
Music: VICTIMAE PASCHALI LAUDES; Chant, Mode I; *Graduale Romanum*, 1974.

## CHRIST, THE LORD, IS RISEN TODAY
### 397

1. Christ, the Lord, is ris'n to - day; Chris-tians, haste your
2. Christ, the Vic - tim un - de - filed, God and sin - ners
3. Say, O won-d'ring Ma - ry, say What you saw a -
4. Christ, who once for sin - ners bled, Now the first-born

1. vows to pay; Make your joy and prais - es known At the
2. re - con-ciled; When in strange and awe-some strife Met to -
3. long the way. "I be - held two an - gels bright, Emp - ty
4. from the dead, Throned in end - less might and pow'r, Lives and

1. Pas - chal Vic - tim's throne; For the sheep the Lamb has bled,
2. geth - er death and life; Chris-tians, on this hap - py day
3. tomb and wrap-pings white; I be - held the glo - ry bright
4. reigns for - ev - er - more. Hail, e - ter - nal Hope on high!

1. Sin - less in the sin - ner's stead; Christ, the Lord, is
2. Haste with joy your vows to pay; Christ, the Lord, is
3. Of the ris - en Lord of light; Christ, my hope, is
4. Hail, our King of Vic - to - ry! Hail, our Prince of

1. ris'n on high; Now he lives, no more to die!
2. ris'n on high; Now he lives, no more to die!
3. ris'n a - gain; Now he lives, and lives to reign!"
4. Life a - dored! Help and save us, gra - cious Lord!

Text: 77 77 D; *Victimae Paschali laudes*; ascr. to Wipo of Burgundy, ca. 1000–1050; tr. by Jane E. Leeson, 1808–1881, alt.
Music: VICTIMAE PASCHALI; Würth's *Katholisches Gesangbuch*, 1859.

**398**    CHRIST IS ARISEN

Verses

1. To the Pas-chal Vic-tim   Give thank-ful   praise!
2. Ma-ry, speak, con-fess-ing   What you   have   seen.
3. Chris-tians, sing his   glo-ry   With ev-'ry   breath;

1. Christ, ev-er   sin-less, his   sheep now he   saves.
2. "Christ's tomb lies   emp-ty where once he   had   been;
3. Sing of his   king-dom, vic-to-rious o'er   death!

1. Death and   life con-tend-ed   In   dread-ful   strife;
2. An-gels bright, con-firm-ing;   Shroud laid   a-side;
3. Je-sus, grant us   mer-cy:   New life   from   heav'n!

1. Death did not   hold __ him, im-mor-tal his   life.
2. He goes to   Gal-i-lee, he   lives though he   died."
3. Christ ev-er   reigns! __ Al-le-lu-ia!   A-men!

Refrain

Al-le-lu-ia,   his   tri-umph we   sing!

Christ is a-ris-en, the   Vic-tor, the   King!

Text: 64 10 D with refrain; based on the Sequence for Easter (*Victimae paschali laudes*); Randall DeBruyn, b. 1947.
Music: RISEN KING; Randall DeBruyn.
Text and music © 1993, OCP. All rights reserved.

**399**    SPRINGS OF WATER, BLESS THE LORD

*Refrain

Springs of wa-ter, bless the Lord! Give him glo-ry and praise for-ev-er.

to Verses
last time: to Coda

Springs of wa-ter, bless the Lord! Give him glo-ry and praise for-ev-er.

*Verses available in accompaniment books.

Coda

Give him glo-ry and praise for-ev-er. Give him glo-ry and praise for-ev-er.

Give him glo-ry and praise for-ev-er. Al-le-lu-ia! Al-le-lu-ia!

## The Day of Resurrection

### 400

1. The day of res-ur-rec-tion! Earth, spread the news a-broad;
2. Our hearts be free from e-vil That we may see a-right
3. His love is ev-er-last-ing; His mer-cies nev-er cease;
4. Now let the heav'ns be joy-ful, And earth her song be-gin;

1. The Pas-chal feast of glad-ness, The Pas-chal feast of God.
2. The Sav-ior res-ur-rect-ed In his e-ter-nal light,
3. The res-ur-rect-ed Sav-ior, Will all our joys in-crease.
4. The whole world keep high tri-umph And all that is there-in;

1. From death to life e-ter-nal, From earth to heav-en's height
2. And hear his mes-sage plain-ly, De-liv-ered calm and clear:
3. He'll keep us in his fa-vor, Sup-ply-ing ho-ly grace,
4. Let all things in cre-a-tion Their notes of glad-ness blend,

1. Our Sav-ior Christ has brought us, The glo-rious Lord of Light.
2. "Re-joice with me in tri-umph, Be glad and do not fear."
3. To all his pil-grim peo-ple Who seek his heav'n-ly place.
4. For Christ the Lord is ris-en, Our joy that has no end.

## 401     JESUS CHRIST IS RISEN TODAY

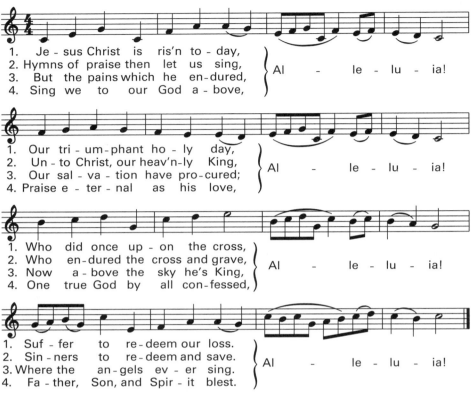

1. Je - sus Christ is ris'n to - day,
2. Hymns of praise then let us sing,
3. But the pains which he en - dured,
4. Sing we to our God a - bove,

Al - le - lu - ia!

1. Our tri - um - phant ho - ly day,
2. Un - to Christ, our heav'n-ly King,
3. Our sal - va - tion have pro-cured;
4. Praise e - ter - nal as his love,

Al - le - lu - ia!

1. Who did once up - on the cross,
2. Who en-dured the cross and grave,
3. Now a - bove the sky he's King,
4. One true God by all con-fessed,

Al - le - lu - ia!

1. Suf - fer to re-deem our loss.
2. Sin - ners to re-deem and save.
3. Where the an-gels ev - er sing.
4. Fa - ther, Son, and Spir - it blest.

Al - le - lu - ia!

Text: 77 77 with alleluias; verse 1, Latin, 14th cent., para. in *Lyra Davidica*, 1708, alt.;
    verses 2–3, *The Compleat Psalmodist*, ca. 1750, alt.; verse 4, Charles Wesley, 1707–1788, alt.
Music: EASTER HYMN; later form of melody fr. *Lyra Davidica*, 1708.

## 402     COME, YE FAITHFUL, RAISE THE STRAIN

1. Come, ye faith - ful, raise the strain Of tri - um - phant glad-ness;
2. 'Tis the spring of souls to - day; Christ has burst his pris - on,
3. Now the queen of sea-sons bright With the day of splen-dor,
4. Nei - ther could the gates of death, Nor the tomb's dark por - tal,
5. "Al - le - lu - ia!" now we cry To our King im - mor - tal,

1. God has brought his Is - ra - el In - to joy from sad-ness;
2. And from three days' sleep in death As a sun has ris - en;
3. With the roy - al feast of feasts Comes its joy to ren - der;
4. Nor the watch-ers, nor the seal Hold him as a mor - tal;
5. Who, tri - um - phant, burst the bars Of the tomb's dark por - tal;

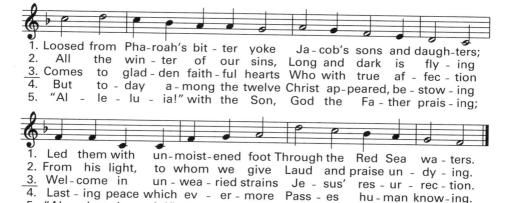

1. Loosed from Pha-roah's bit - ter yoke  Ja - cob's sons and daugh-ters;
2. All the win - ter of our sins,  Long and dark is fly - ing
3. Comes to glad - den faith - ful hearts  Who with true af - fec - tion
4. But to - day a - mong the twelve  Christ ap-peared, be - stow - ing
5. "Al - le - lu - ia!" with the Son,  God the Fa - ther prais - ing;

1. Led them with un-moist-ened foot  Through the Red Sea wa - ters.
2. From his light, to whom we give  Laud and praise un - dy - ing.
3. Wel - come in un - wea - ried strains  Je - sus' res - ur - rec - tion.
4. Last - ing peace which ev - er - more  Pass - es hu - man know-ing.
5. "Al - le - lu - ia!" yet a - gain  To the Spir - it rais - ing.

Text: 76 76 D; based on Exodus 15; St. John of Damascus, 8th cent.; tr. by John M. Neale, 1818–1866, alt.
Music: GAUDEAMUS PARITER; Johann Horn, ca. 1495–1547.

## CHRIST, THE LORD, IS RISEN TODAY　403

1. Christ, the Lord, is ris'n to - day:
2. Lives a - gain our glo - rious King;
3. Love's re - deem - ing work is done;
4. Soar we now where Christ has led,

Al - le - lu - ia!

1. All on earth with an - gels say:
2. Where, O death, is now your sting?
3. Fought the fight, the bat - tle won;
4. Fol - l'wing our ex - alt - ed Head;

Al - le - lu - ia!

1. Raise your joys and tri - umphs high:
2. Once he died our souls to save;
3. Death in vain for - bids him rise:
4. Made like him, like him we rise:

Al - le - lu - ia!

1. Sing, O heav'ns, and earth re - ply:
2. Where your vic - to - ry, O grave?
3. Christ has o - pened par - a - dise.
4. Ours the cross, the grave, the skies.

Al - le - lu - ia!

Text: 77 77 with alleluias; Charles Wesley, 1707–1788, alt.
Music: LLANFAIR; Robert Williams, 1781–1821.

# 404

## RESUCITÓ/HE IS RISEN

Text: Spanish, Kiko Argüello; English tr., OCP.
Music: Kiko Argüello.

# O Sons and Daughters

**Refrain**

Al - le - lu - ia! Al - le - lu - ia! Al - le - lu - ia!

**Verses**

1. O sons and daugh - ters, let us sing! The King of
2. That Eas - ter morn, at break of day, The faith - ful
3. An an - gel clad in white they see, Who sat, and
4. That night the a - pos - tles met in fear; A - mid them
5. When Thom - as first the tid - ings heard, How they had
6. "My wound - ed side, O Thom - as, see; Be - hold my
7. No long - er Thom - as then de - nied; He saw the
8. How blest are they who have not seen, And yet whose
9. On this most ho - ly day of days, To God your

1. heav'n, the glo - rious King, O'er death to - day rose
2. wom - en went their way To seek the tomb where
3. spoke un - to the three: "Your Lord has gone to
4. came their Lord most dear, And said, "My peace be
5. seen the ris - en Lord, He doubt - ed the dis -
6. hands, my feet," said he. "Not faith - less, but be -
7. feet, the hands, the side; "You are my Lord and
8. faith has con - stant been, For they e - ter - nal
9. hearts and voic - es raise, In laud, and ju - bi -

*to Refrain*

1. tri - um - phing. Al - le - lu - ia!
2. Je - sus lay. Al - le - lu - ia!
3. Gal - i - lee." Al - le - lu - ia!
4. on all here." Al - le - lu - ia!
5. ci - ples' word. Al - le - lu - ia!
6. liev - ing be." Al - le - lu - ia!
7. God," he cried. Al - le - lu - ia!
8. life shall win. Al - le - lu - ia!
9. lee and praise. Al - le - lu - ia!

Text: 888 with alleluias; attr. to Jean Tisserand, d. 1494; tr. by John M. Neale, 1818–1866, alt.
Music: O FILII ET FILIAE; Chant, Mode II; *Airs sur les hymnes sacrez, odes et noëls,* 1623.

# 406

**THREE DAYS**

1. Three days our world was bro - ken; the
2. Three days— and on the third day, the
3. Three days our world was bro - ken and

1. Lord of life lay dead. "Take up your cross," he
2. wom - en came at dawn. His tomb, they said, was
3. in an in - stant healed, God's cov - e - nant of

1. told us who fol - lowed where he led. Would
2. emp - ty, his bro - ken bod - y gone. Who
3. mer - cy in mys - ter - y re - vealed. Two

1. we now hang in tor - ment with thieves on ev - 'ry side,
2. could be - lieve their sto - ry? The dead do not a - rise,
3. thou - sand years are one day in God's e - ter - nal sight,

1. our Pass - o - ver shat - tered, our hope cru - ci - fied?
2. yet he walks a - mong us, and with our own eyes
3. and yes - ter - day's sor - rows are this day's de - light.

1. Three days we hid in si - lence, in
2. we've seen him at this ta - ble; we've
3. Though still Christ's bod - y suf - fers, pierced

1. bit - ter fear and grief. Three days we clung to -
2. shared his bread and wine. Hearts burn - ing bright with -
3. dai - ly by the sword, yet death has no do -

1. geth - er where he had washed our feet.
2. in us, we've seen his glo - ry shine.
3. min - ion: the ris - en Christ is Lord!

## AT THE LAMB'S HIGH FEAST 407

1. At the Lamb's high feast we sing Praise to our vic -
2. Where the Pas - chal blood is poured, Death's dark an - gel
3. Might - y vic - tim from the sky, Hell's fierce pow'rs be -
4. Eas - ter tri - umph, Eas - ter joy, This a - lone can

1. to - rious King, Who has washed us in the tide
2. sheathes his sword; Is - rael's hosts tri - um - phant go
3. neath you lie; You have con - quered in the fight,
4. sin de - stroy; From sin's pow'r, Lord, set us free,

1. Flow - ing from his wound - ed side; Praise we him, whose
2. Through the wave that drowns the foe. Praise we Christ whose
3. You have brought us life and light: Now no more can
4. New - born souls in you to be. Hymns of glo - ry,

1. love di - vine Gives his sa - cred blood for wine, Gives his
2. blood was shed, Pas - chal vic - tim, Pas - chal bread! With sin -
3. death ap - pall, Now no more the grave en - thrall; You have
4. songs of praise, Fa - ther, un - to you we raise: And to

1. bod - y for the feast, Christ the vic - tim, Christ the priest.
2. cer - i - ty and love Eat we man - na from a - bove.
3. o - pened Par - a - dise, And in you the saints shall rise.
4. you, our ris - en King, With the Spir - it, praise we sing.

# 408

## THE STRIFE IS O'ER

**Refrain**

Al - le - lu - ia! Al - le - lu - ia! Al - le - lu - ia!

**Verses**

1. The strife is o'er, the bat - tle done;
2. The pow'rs of death have done their worst,
3. On the third morn he rose a - gain,
4. He closed the yawn - ing gates of hell;
5. O Ris - en Lord, all praise to thee,

1. Now is the Vic - tor's tri - umph won; O let the
2. But Christ their le - gions has dis - persed; Let shouts of
3. Glo - rious in maj - es - ty to reign; O let us
4. The bars from heav'n's high por - tals fell; Let hymns of
5. Who from our sin has set us free, That we may

*to Refrain*

1. song of praise be sung: Al - le - lu - ia!
2. praise and joy out - burst: Al - le - lu - ia!
3. swell the joy - ful strain: Al - le - lu - ia!
4. praise his tri - umph tell: Al - le - lu - ia!
5. live e - ter - nal - ly! Al - le - lu - ia!

Text: 888 with alleluias; *Finita iam sunt praelia*; Latin, 12th cent.; tr. by Francis Pott, 1832–1909, alt.
Music: VICTORY; Giovanni Pierluigi da Palestrina, 1525–1594; adapt. by Willam H. Monk, 1823–1889.

# 409

## BE JOYFUL, MARY, HEAVENLY QUEEN

1. Be joy - ful, Ma - ry, heav'n - ly Queen, Be joy - ful, Ma -
2. The Son you bore by heav - en's grace, Be joy - ful, Ma -
3. The Lord has ris - en from the dead, Be joy - ful, Ma -
4. Now pray to God, O Vir - gin fair, Be joy - ful, Ma -

1. ry! Your Son who died was liv - ing seen,
2. ry! Did all our guilt and sin ef - face,     Al -
3. ry! He rose with might as he had said,
4. ry! That he our souls to heav - en bear,

1-4. le - lu - ia, Re - joice, re - joice, O Ma - ry!

Text: 85 84 7; *Regina Caeli, jubila*; Latin, 17th cent.; tr. anon. in *Psallite*, 1901, alt.
Music: REGINA CAELI; Johann Leisentritt's *Catholicum Hymnologium*, 1584.

## JOIN IN THE DANCE    410

**Refrain**

Join in the dance of the earth's ju - bi - la - tion! This is the feast of the
love of God. Shout from the heights to the ends of cre - a - tion:
Je - sus the Sav - ior is ris - en from the grave!

**Verses**

1. Wake, O peo - ple; sleep no long - er: greet the
2. All cre - a - tion, like a moth - er, la - bors
3. Now our shame be - comes our glo - ry on this
4. None on earth, no prince or pow - er, nei - ther
5. Love's tri - um - phant day of vic - t'ry heav - en
6. Christ for - ev - er, Lord of a - ges, Love be -

1. break - ing day! Christ, Re - deem - er,
2. to give birth. Soon the pain will
3. ho - ly tree. Now the reign of
4. death nor life, noth - ing now can
5. o - pens wide. On the tree of
6. yond our dreams: Christ, our hope of

*to Refrain*

1. Lamb and Li - on, turns the night a - way!
2. be for - got - ten, joy for all the earth!
3. death is end - ed; now we are set free!
4. ev - er part us from the love of Christ!
5. hope and glo - ry death it - self has died!
6. heav - en's glo - ry, all that yet will be!

## 411 ALLELUIA! ALLELUIA! LET THE HOLY ANTHEM RISE

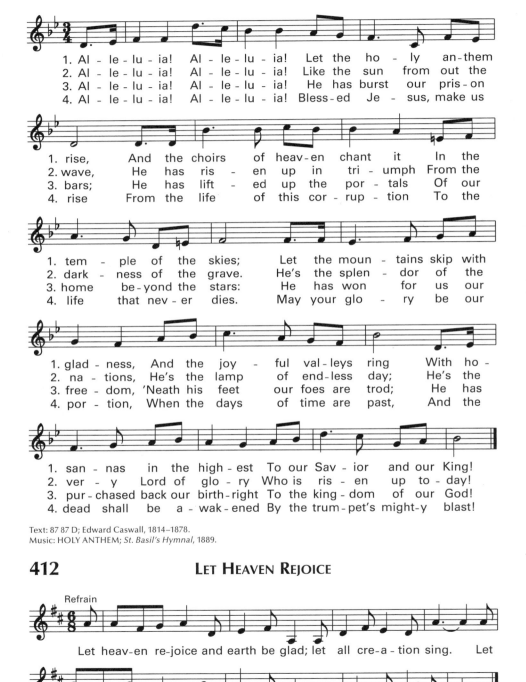

1. Al - le - lu - ia! Al - le - lu - ia! Let the ho - ly an-them
2. Al - le - lu - ia! Al - le - lu - ia! Like the sun from out the
3. Al - le - lu - ia! Al - le - lu - ia! He has burst our pris - on
4. Al - le - lu - ia! Al - le - lu - ia! Bless-ed Je - sus, make us

1. rise, And the choirs of heav-en chant it In the
2. wave, He has ris - en up in tri - umph From the
3. bars; He has lift - ed up the por - tals Of our
4. rise From the life of this cor - rup - tion To the

1. tem - ple of the skies; Let the moun - tains skip with
2. dark - ness of the grave. He's the splen - dor of the
3. home be-yond the stars: He has won for us our
4. life that nev - er dies. May your glo - ry be our

1. glad - ness, And the joy - ful val-leys ring With ho -
2. na - tions, He's the lamp of end-less day; He's the
3. free - dom, 'Neath his feet our foes are trod, He has
4. por - tion, When the days of time are past, And the

1. san - nas in the high - est To our Sav - ior and our King!
2. ver - y Lord of glo - ry Who is ris - en up to - day!
3. pur - chased back our birth-right To the king - dom of our God!
4. dead shall be a - wak-ened By the trum-pet's might-y blast!

Text: 87 87 D; Edward Caswall, 1814–1878.
Music: HOLY ANTHEM; *St. Basil's Hymnal*, 1889.

## 412 LET HEAVEN REJOICE

Refrain

Let heav-en re-joice and earth be glad; let all cre-a-tion sing. Let

chil-dren pro-claim through ev - 'ry land: "Ho - san - na to our King."

**Verses 1-3**

1. Sound the trum - pet in - to the night; the day of the Lord is
2. Rise in splen-dor; shake off your sleep; put on your robes of
3. Raise your voic - es, be not a - fraid. Pro-claim it in ev - 'ry

to Refrain

1. near. Wake your peo - ple, lift your voice, pro-claim it to the world.
2. joy. And in the morn-ing you shall see the glo - ry of the Lord.
3. land. Christ has died, but he has ris - en; he will come a - gain.

**Verse 4**

4. Sing a new song un-to the Lord, whose la-bor has led us to life. With

to Refrain

4. grate-ful hearts and joy-ful danc-ing, play be-fore the Lord.

Text and music: Bob Dufford, SJ, b. 1943, © 1972, 1997, Robert J. Dufford, SJ. Published by OCP. All rights reserved.

## ALLELUIA No. 1

**413**

**Refrain**

Al - le - lu - ia, al - le - lu - ia! Give thanks to the ris-en Lord. Al - le -

**Verses**

lu - ia, al-le-lu-ia! Give praise to his name. 1. Je - sus is Lord of
2. Spread the good news o'er
3. We have been cru - ci-
4. Come, let us praise the

to Refrain

1. all the earth; He is the king of cre - a - tion.
2. all the earth; Je - sus has died and has ris - en.
3. fied with Christ; Now we shall live ___ for - ev - er.
4. liv - ing God; Joy - ful - ly sing to our Sav - ior.

Text: 88 with refrain; Donald Fishel, b. 1950.
Music: ALLELUIA NO. 1; Donald Fishel.
Text and music © 1973, International Liturgy Publications, PO Box 50476, Nashville, TN 37205, www.ilpmusic.org
888-898-SONG. All rights reserved. Used with permission.

## 414

# THIS JOYFUL EASTERTIDE

**Verses**

1. This joy - ful Eas - ter - tide, A - way with sin and
2. Death's flood has lost its chill, Since Je - sus crossed the
3. My flesh in hope shall rest, And for a sea - son

1. sor - row! My Love, the Cru - ci -
2. riv - er: Lord of all life, from
3. slum - ber, Till trump from east to

1. fied, Has sprung to life this mor - row.
2. ill My pass - ing life de - liv - er.
3. west Shall wake the dead in num - ber.

**Refrain**

Had Christ, that once was slain, Ne'er burst his three-day pris -

on, Our faith had been in vain; But now is Christ a - ris - en, a -

ris - en, a - ris - en, a - ris - en.

Text: 67 67 with refrain; George R. Woodward, 1848–1934.
Music: VREUCHTEN; Oudaen's *David's Psalmen*, 1685, alt.

## 415

# ALLELUIA! ALLELUIA

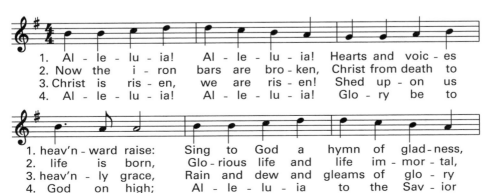

1. Al - le - lu - ia! Al - le - lu - ia! Hearts and voic - es
2. Now the i - ron bars are bro - ken, Christ from death to
3. Christ is ris - en, we are ris - en! Shed up - on us
4. Al - le - lu - ia! Al - le - lu - ia! Glo - ry be to

1. heav'n - ward raise: Sing to God a hymn of glad - ness,
2. life is born, Glo - rious life and life im - mor - tal,
3. heav'n - ly grace, Rain and dew and gleams of glo - ry
4. God on high; Al - le - lu - ia to the Sav - ior

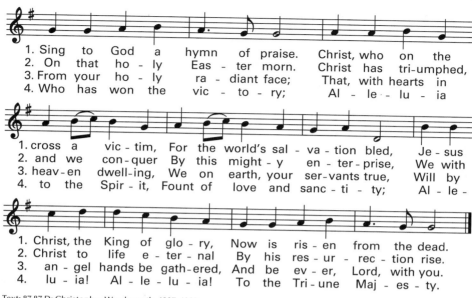

1. Sing to God a hymn of praise. Christ, who on the
2. On that ho - ly Eas - ter morn. Christ has tri-umphed,
3. From your ho - ly ra - diant face; That, with hearts in
4. Who has won the vic - to - ry; Al - le - lu - ia

1. cross a vic - tim, For the world's sal - va - tion bled, Je - sus
2. and we con - quer By this might - y en - ter-prise, We with
3. heav - en dwell-ing, We on earth, your ser-vants true, Will by
4. to the Spir - it, Fount of love and sanc - ti - ty; Al - le -

1. Christ, the King of glo - ry, Now is ris - en from the dead.
2. Christ to life e - ter - nal By his res - ur - rec - tion rise.
3. an - gel hands be gath-ered, And be ev - er, Lord, with you.
4. lu - ia! Al - le - lu - ia! To the Tri - une Maj - es - ty.

Text: 87 87 D; Christopher Wordsworth, 1807–1885.
Music: HYMN TO JOY; Ludwig van Beethoven, 1770–1827; adapt. by Edward Hodges, 1796–1867.

## Regina Caeli/O Queen of Heaven 416

Re - gí - na cae - li, lae - tá - re, al - le - lú - ia,
O Queen of heav - en, be joy - ful, al - le - lu - ia,

qui - a quem me - ru - í - sti por - tá - re, al - le - lú - ia,
For he whom you have hum - bly borne for us, al - le - lu - ia,

re - sur - ré - xit si - cut di - xit, al - le - lú - ia,
Has a - ris - en, as he prom-ised, al - le - lu - ia,

O - ra pro no - bis De - um, al - le - lú - ia.
Of - fer now our prayer to God, al - le - lu - ia.

Text: Irregular; Latin, 12th cent.; tr. by C. Winfred Douglas, 1867–1944, alt.
Music: REGINA CAELI LAETARE; Chant, Mode VI; *Liber Cantualis*, 1983.

## 417     TWO WERE BOUND FOR EMMAUS

1, 5. Two were bound for Em - ma - us, dis - heart - ened
2. On the Sea of Ti - ber - ius, when the night was
3. Then they knew it was Je - sus and they has - tened
4. When the road makes us wea - ry, when our la - bor

1, 5. and ___ lost; all their hope for the fu - ture had been
2. near - ly gone and their toil seemed so use - less, not one
3. in to shore; bread and fish for their break - fast from the
4. seems but loss, when the fire of faith weak - ens and too

1, 5. nailed to a cross. Love un - known then walked be - side ___ them,
2. fish had they caught, from the shore the strang - er called to them:
3. hands of their Lord. "O ___ Pe - ter, if you love ___ me
4. high seems the cost, let the Church turn to its ris - en Lord,

1, 5. come ___ back from the dead, and they knew he was
2. "Cast your net, friends, once more." And they filled it to
3. you must care for my sheep; if you fol - low your
4. who for us bore the cross, and we'll find our hearts

1, 5. ris - en in the break - ing of bread.
2. burst - ing, but the net was not torn.
3. Shep - herd, then a shep - herd you'll be."
4. burn - ing at the sound of his voice.

Text: 11 13 13 13; based on Luke 24:13–35; John 21:1–19; Bob Hurd, b. 1950.
Music: KENMARE; Bob Hurd.
Text and music © 2000, Bob Hurd. Published by OCP. All rights reserved.

## 418     CHRIST IS ALIVE

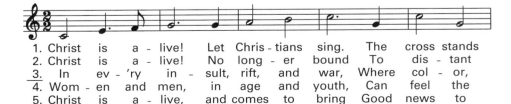

1. Christ is a - live! Let Chris - tians sing. The cross stands
2. Christ is a - live! No long - er bound To dis - tant
3. In ev - 'ry in - sult, rift, and war, Where col - or,
4. Wom - en and men, in age and youth, Can feel the
5. Christ is a - live, and comes to bring Good news to

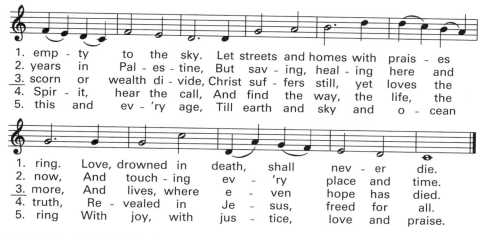

1. emp - ty    to the sky. Let streets and homes with prais - es
2. years in Pal - es - tine, But sav - ing, heal - ing here and
3. scorn or wealth di - vide, Christ suf - fers still, yet loves the
4. Spir - it, hear the call, And find the way, the life, the
5. this and ev - 'ry age, Till earth and sky and o - cean

1. ring. Love, drowned in death, shall nev - er die.
2. now, And touch - ing ev - 'ry place and time.
3. more, And lives, where e - ven hope has died.
4. truth, Re - vealed in Je - sus, freed for all.
5. ring With joy, with jus - tice, love and praise.

Text: LM; Romans 6:5–11; Brian Wren, b. 1936, © 1975, revised 1995, Hope Publishing Co.
All rights reserved. Used with permission.
Music: TRURO; Williams' *Psalmodia Evangelica, Part II,* 1789.

## THIS DAY WAS MADE BY THE LORD    419

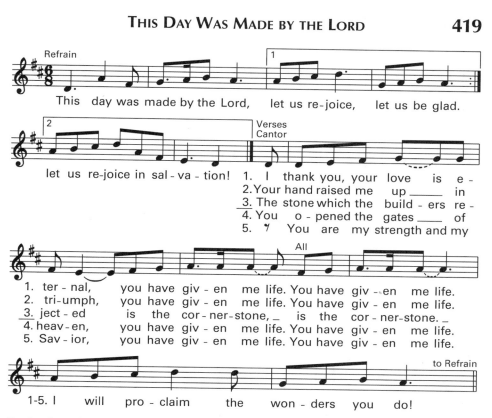

*Refrain*

This day was made by the Lord, let us re-joice, let us be glad.

let us re-joice in sal - va - tion!

*Verses
Cantor*

1. I thank you, your love is e -
2. Your hand raised me up _____ in
3. The stone which the build - ers re -
4. You o - pened the gates ____ of
5. ϒ You are my strength and my

*All*

1. ter - nal, you have giv - en me life. You have giv - en me life.
2. tri - umph, you have giv - en me life. You have giv - en me life.
3. ject - ed is the cor - ner-stone, _ is the cor - ner-stone. _
4. heav - en, you have giv - en me life. You have giv - en me life.
5. Sav - ior, you have giv - en me life. You have giv - en me life.

*to Refrain*

1-5. I will pro - claim the won - ders you do!

Text: Based on Psalm 118; Christopher Walker, b. 1947.
Music: Christopher Walker.
Text and music © 1988, 1989, Christopher Walker. Published by OCP. All rights reserved.

## 420    CHRIST, THE LORD, IS RISEN AGAIN

1. Christ, the Lord, is ris'n a - gain, Christ has
2. Christ who gave for us his life, Who for
3. Christ who bore all pain and loss Com - fort -
4. He who slum - bered in the grave Is ex -
5. Now he bids us tell a - broad How the
6. You, our Pas - chal Lamb in - deed, Christ, to -

1. bro - ken ev - 'ry chain! Hark, the an - gels
2. us en - dured the strife, Is our Pas - chal
3. less up - on the cross, Lives in glo - ry
4. alt - ed now to save; Now through - out the
5. lost may be re - stored, How the pen - i -
6. day your peo - ple feed; Take our sins and

1. shout for joy, Sing - ing ev - er - more on high:
2. Lamb to - day. We, too, sing for joy and say:
3. now on high, Pleads for us and hears our cry:
4. world it rings That the Lamb is King of kings.
5. tent for - giv'n, How we, too, may en - ter heav'n.
6. guilt a - way, That we all may sing for joy:

1-6. Al - le - lu - ia! Al - le - lu - ia!

1-6. Al - le - lu - ia! Al - le - lu - ia!

Text: 7777 with alleluias; Michael Weisse, ca. 1480–1534; tr. by Catherine Winkworth, 1827–1878, alt.
Music: CHRIST IST ERSTANDEN; German Melody, 12th cent.

## 421    THIS IS THE DAY

Refrain: 1st time: Cantor, All repeat; thereafter: All

This is the day! This is the day! This

is the day that the Lord has made! Let us re - joice!

(to Verses)

Let us re-joice! Let us re-joice and be glad!

Final time only

Let us re-joice and be glad!

**Verses: Cantor**

1. This is the day that the Lord has made.
   Let us rejoice and be glad.

2. Give thanks to the Lord!
   Our God is good.
   Whose love endures forever.
   Let all the children of Israel say:
   God's love endures forever.

3. The right hand of God has struck with power.
   The right hand of God is exalted.
   I shall not die, but I shall live
   and proclaim the works of the Lord!

4. The stone which the builders rejected
   has become the foundation of our house!
   By the Lord has this been done.
   How wonderful to behold!

## Now the Green Blade Rises 422

1. Now the green blade ris - es from the bur-ied grain,
2. In the grave they laid him, love by ha-tred slain,
3. Forth he came at Eas - ter, like the ris - en grain,
4. When our hearts are win - try, griev-ing, or in pain,

1. Wheat that in dark earth man - y days has lain;
2. Think - ing that he would nev - er wake a - gain,
3. He that for three days in the grave had lain;
4. Your touch can call us back to life a - gain,

1. Love lives a - gain, that with the dead has been:
2. Laid in the earth like grain that sleeps un - seen:
3. Raised from the dead, my liv - ing Lord is seen:
4. Fields of our hearts that dead and bare have been:

1-4. Love is come a - gain like wheat a - ris - ing green.

# 423

## HOLY, HOLY, HOLY CRY

**Verses**

1. The Lamb of God stands on the height
2. In bit - ter sac - ri - fice once slain,
3. To him now let our prayers a - rise
4. While heav - ens' prais - es hail his worth,

1. a - mong the glo - rious clouds of light,
2. he lives in tri - umph there to reign
3. in clouds of in - cense to the skies,
4. he catch - es up the prayers of earth

1. a - bove the cit - y paved in gold
2. a - mong the saints clad all in white
3. from cen - ser borne by an - gel hands,
4. in wound - ed hands, till, count - less throng,

*[1 — to Verse 2]*

1. where death and dark - ness have no hold.
2. in realms where day yields not to night.
3. bright tongues of fire from far - flung lands.
4. the sing - ers come to join the song.

*[2-4]* **Refrain**

And, "Ho - ly, ho - ly, ho - ly" cry to you,

our Lord Most High. "Ho - ly, ho - ly, ho - ly" cry

*[1, 2, Final — to Verses 3, 4 (Fine)]*
**3**

to you, our God Most High.

Text: Genevieve Glen, OSB, b. 1945, © 1998, 2001, The Benedictine Nuns of the Abbey of St. Walburga. Published by OCP. All rights reserved.
Music: Rick Modlin, b. 1966, © 2004, Rick Modlin. Published by OCP. All rights reserved.

**424**   FESTIVAL CANTICLE: WORTHY IS CHRIST

1. Wor-thy is Christ, the __ Lamb who was slain, whose
2. Pow - er, rich - es, __ wis - dom, and strength, and
3. Sing with all the __ peo - ple of God, and
4. Bless - ing, hon - or, __ glo - ry, and might be to
5. For the Lamb _____ who was slain has be -

1. blood set us free ___ to be peo - ple of God.
2. hon - or, ___ bless - ing, and glo - ry are his.
3. join in the hymn of all cre - a - tion.
4. God and the Lamb for ev - er. A - men.
5. gun his ___ reign. ___ Al - le - lu - ia.

**425**   JESUS IS RISEN

1. Je - sus is ris - en! Let us sing! Praise to the ev - er - liv - ing
2. On this most ho - ly day of days, Let us to - geth - er sing his
3. To God the Fa - ther let us sing, To God the Son, our ris - en

1. King! Al - le - lu - ia! Al - le - lu - ia! Praise him in song, ye Ser - a -
2. praise! Al - le - lu - ia! Al - le - lu - ia! Raise joy - ful voic - es to the
3. King! Al - le - lu - ia! Al - le - lu - ia! And e - qual - ly let us a -

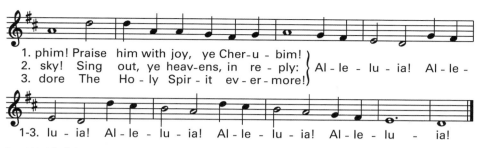

1. phim! Praise him with joy, ye Cher-u - bim!
2. sky! Sing out, ye heav-ens, in re - ply: } Al - le - lu - ia! Al - le -
3. dore The Ho - ly Spir - it ev - er - more!

1-3. lu - ia! Al - le - lu - ia! Al - le - lu - ia! Al - le - lu - ia!

Text: LM with alleluias; Compilers, 1978.
Music: LASST UNS ERFREUEN; *Auserlesene Catholische Geistliche Kirchengesänge*, Cologne, 1623.

## SING WE TRIUMPHANT HYMNS OF PRAISE  426

1. Sing we triumphant hymns of praise
To greet our Lord these festive days,
Alleluia, alleluia!
Who by a road before untrod
Ascended to the throne of God,
Alleluia, alleluia, alleluia,
alleluia, alleluia!

2. In wond'ring awe his faithful band
Upon the Mount of Olives stand.
Alleluia, alleluia!
And with the Virgin Mother see
Their Lord ascend in majesty.
Alleluia, alleluia, alleluia,
alleluia, alleluia!

3. O risen Christ, ascended Lord,
All praise to you let earth accord,
Alleluia, alleluia!
Who are, while endless ages run,
With Father and with Spirit, One.
Alleluia, alleluia, alleluia,
alleluia, alleluia!

4. To God the Father let us sing,
To God the Son, our risen King,
Alleluia, alleluia!
And equally let us adore
The Holy Spirit evermore,
Alleluia, alleluia, alleluia,
alleluia, alleluia!

Text: LM with alleluias; St. Bede the Venerable, 673–735; verses 1, 2, 4 tr. by John D. Chambers, 1805–1893;
verse 3 tr. by Benjamin Webb, 1819–1885.
Music: LASST UNS ERFREUEN; *Auserlesene Catholische Geistliche Kirchengesänge*, Cologne, 1623.

## CREATOR SPIRIT, BY WHOSE AID  427

1. Creator Spirit, by whose aid
The world's foundations first were laid!
Alleluia! Alleluia!
Give us thyself that we may see
The Father and the Son by thee.
Alleluia! Alleluia! Alleluia!
Alleluia! Alleluia!

2. O Source of uncreated light,
The Father's promised Paraclete;
Alleluia! Alleluia!

Thrice holy Font, Thrice holy Fire,
Our hearts with heav'nly love inspire.
Alleluia! Alleluia! Alleluia!
Alleluia! Alleluia!

3. All adoration ever be,
Eternal Paraclete to thee.
Alleluia! Alleluia!
From sin and sorrow set us free
That we may live eternally.
Alleluia! Alleluia! Alleluia!
Alleluia! Alleluia!

Text: LM with alleluias; *Veni, Creator Spiritus*; attr. to Rabanus Maurus, 776–856;
para. by John Dryden, 1631–1700; alt. Compilers, 1977.
Music: LASST UNS ERFREUEN; *Auserlesene Catholische Geistliche Kirchengesänge*, Cologne, 1623.

# 428

## HAIL THEE, FESTIVAL DAY

**Refrain**

Hail thee, fes-ti-val day! Blest day to be hal-lowed for ev-er;

Day when our Lord was raised, Break-ing the king-dom of death.

**Verses 1, 3, 5**

Easter 1. All the fair beau-ty of earth From
Ascension 3. He who was nailed to the cross Is
Pentecost 5. Bright in the like-ness of fire, On

1. death of the win-ter a-ris-ing! Ev-'ry good
3. Rul-er and Lord of all peo-ple. All things cre-
5. those who a-wait his ap-pear-ing, He whom the

to Refrain

1. gift of the year Now with its Mas-ter re-turns:
3. a-ted on earth Sing to the glo-ry of God:
5. Lord had fore-told, Sud-den-ly, swift-ly de-scends:

**Verses 2, 4, 6**

Easter 2. Rise from the grave now, O Lord, The Au-thor of
Ascension 4. Dai-ly the love-li-ness grows, A-dorned with the
Pentecost 6. Forth from the Fa-ther he comes With sev-en-fold

2. life and cre-a-tion. Tread-ing the path-way of
4. glo-ry of blos-som; Heav-en her gates un-
6. mys-ti-cal of-f'ring, Pour-ing on all hu-man

to Refrain

2. death, New life you give to us all:
4. bars, Fling-ing her in-crease of light:
6. souls In-fi-nite rich-es of God:

Text: 79 77 with refrain; Venantius Honorius Fortunatus, ca. 530–609; tr. composite.
Music: SALVE FESTA DIES; Ralph Vaughan Williams, 1872–1958.

# Hail the Day That Sees Him Rise

1. Hail the day that sees him rise
2. There for him high tri-umph waits:
3. See! the heav'n its Lord re-ceives,
4. See! he lifts his hands a-bove.
5. Lord, though part-ed from our sight
6. There with you we shall re-main,

Al - le - lu - ia!

1. To his throne be-yond the skies,
2. Lift your heads, e-ter-nal gates,
3. Yet he loves the earth he leaves;
4. See! he shows the wounds of love.
5. Far be-yond the star-ry height,
6. Share the glo-ry of your reign,

Al - le - lu - ia!

1. Christ, the Lamb for sin-ners giv'n,
2. He has con-quered death and sin,
3. Though re-turn-ing to his throne,
4. Hark! his gra-cious lips be-stow,
5. Lift our hearts that we may rise
6. There your face un-cloud-ed view,

Al - le - lu - ia!

1. En-ters now the high-est heav'n!
2. Take the King of glo-ry in.
3. Still he calls the world his own.
4. Bless-ings on his church be-low.
5. One with you be-yond the skies:
6. Find our heav'n of heav'ns in you.

Al - le - lu - ia!

Text: 77 77 with alleluias; Charles Wesley, 1707–1788, and Thomas Cotterill, 1779–1823, alt.
Music: LLANFAIR; Robert Williams, 1781–1821.

# 430  GO MAKE OF ALL DISCIPLES

1. "Go make of all dis - ci - ples:" We hear the
2. "Go make of all dis - ci - ples:" Bap - tiz - ing
3. "Go make of all dis - ci - ples:" We at your
4. "Go make of all dis - ci - ples:" We wel - come

1. call, O Lord, That comes from you, our Fa - ther, In
2. in the name Of Fa - ther, Son, and Spir - it— From
3. feet would stay Un - til each life's vo - ca - tion Ac -
4. your com - mand; "Lo, I am with you al - ways:" We

1. your e - ter - nal Word. In - spire our ways of
2. age to age the same. We call each new dis -
3. cents your ho - ly way. We cul - ti - vate the
4. take your guid - ing hand. The task looms large be -

1. learn - ing Through earn - est, fer - vent prayer, And let our
2. ci - ple To fol - low you, O Lord, Re - deem - ing
3. na - ture God plants in ev - 'ry heart, Re - veal - ing
4. fore us— We fol - low with - out fear. In heav'n and

1. dai - ly liv - ing Re - veal you ev - 'ry - where.
2. soul and bod - y By wa - ter and the Word.
3. in our wit - ness The Mas - ter Teach-er's art.
4. earth your pow - er Shall bring God's king - dom here.

Text: 76 76 D; Matthew 12:19–20; "Go Make of All Disciples" words by Leon M. Adkins, 1896–1986, alt.
© 1964, Abingdon Press (Administered by The Copyright Company, Nashville, TN). All rights reserved.
International copyright secured. Used with permission.
Music: ELLACOMBE; *Gesangbuch der Herzogl, Wirtembergischen Katholischen Hofkapelle*, 1784, alt.;
adapt. fr. Würth's *Katholisches Gesangbuch*, 1863.

## LORD, YOU GIVE THE GREAT COMMISSION

1. Lord, you give the great com-mis-sion: "Heal the sick and
2. Lord, you call us to your ser-vice: "In my name bap-
3. Lord, you make the com - mon ho - ly: "This my bod - y,
4. Lord, you show us love's true mea-sure: "Fa - ther, what they
5. Lord, you bless with words as - sur - ing: "I am with you

1. preach the word." Lest the church ne - glect its mis-sion
2. tize and teach." That the world may trust your prom-ise,
3. this my blood." Let us all, for earth's true glo - ry,
4. do, for - give." Yet we hoard as pri - vate trea-sure
5. to the end." Faith and hope and love re - stor-ing,

1. And the gos - pel go un-heard, Help us wit-ness to your
2. Life a - bun - dant meant for each, Give us all new fer - vor,
3. Dai - ly lift life heav - en - ward, Ask - ing that the world a -
4. All that you so free - ly give. May your care and mer - cy
5. May we serve as you in - tend And, a - mid the cares that

1. pur-pose With re-newed in - teg - ri - ty:
2. draw us Clos - er in com-mu - ni - ty:
3. round us Share your chil - dren's lib - er - ty:  } With the Spir-it's
4. lead us To a just so - ci - e - ty:
5. claim us, Hold in mind e - ter - ni - ty:

1-5. gifts em-pow'r us For the work of min - is - try.

Text: 87 87 D; Jeffery Rowthorn, b. 1934, © 1978, Hope Publishing Co. All rights reserved. Used with permission.
Music: ABBOT'S LEIGH; Cyril Vincent Taylor, 1907–1991, © 1942, renewed 1970, Hope Publishing Co.
   All rights reserved. Used with permission.

## 432 Come, O Holy Spirit, Come/Veni Sancte Spiritus

1. Come, O Ho-ly Spir-it, come! And from your ce-
2. Come, O Fa-ther of the poor! Come, ___ source of
1. *Ve-ni San-cte Spí-ri-tus, Et e-mít-te*
2. *Ve-ni pa-ter páu-pe-rum, Ve-ni da-tor*

1. les-tial home Shed a ray of light di-vine!
2. all our store! Come, with-in our bos-oms shine!
1. *caé-li-tus Lu-cis tu-ae rá-di-um.*
2. *mú-ne-rum, Ve-ni lu-men cór-di-um.*

3. You, of com-fort-ers the best; You, the soul's most
4. In our la-bor, rest most sweet; Grate-ful cool-ness
3. *Con-so-lá-tor ó-pti-me, Dul-cis ho-spes*
4. *In la-bó-re ré-qui-es, In ae-stu tem-*

3. wel-come guest; Sweet re-fresh-ment here be-low;
4. in the heat; Sol-ace in the midst of woe.
3. *á-ni-mae, Dul-ce re-fri-gé-ri-um.*
4. *pé-ri-es, In fle-tu so-lá-ti-um.*

5. O most bless-ed Light di-vine, Shine with-in
6. Where you are not, we have naught, Noth-ing good
5. *O lux be-a-tís-si-ma, Re-ple cor-*
6. *Si-ne tu-o nú-mi-ne, Ni-hil est*

5. these hearts of yours, And our in-most be-ing fill!
6. in deed or thought, Noth-ing free from taint of ill.
5. *dis ín-ti-ma Tu-ó-rum fi-dé-li-um.*
6. *in hó-mi-ne, Ni-hil est in-nó-xi-um.*

7. Heal our wounds, our strength re-new; On our dry-ness
8. Bend the stub-born heart and will; Melt the fro-zen,
7. *La-va quod est sór-di-dum, Ri-ga quod est*
8. *Fle-cte quod est rí-gi-dum, Fo-ve quod est*

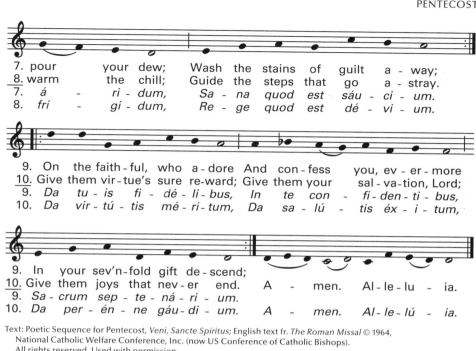

7. pour your dew; Wash the stains of guilt a - way;
8. warm the chill; Guide the steps that go a - stray.
7. *á - ri - dum,* *Sa - na quod est sáu - ci - um.*
8. *frí - gi - dum,* *Re - ge quod est dé - vi - um.*

9. On the faith - ful, who a - dore And con - fess you, ev - er - more
10. Give them vir - tue's sure re - ward; Give them your sal - va - tion, Lord;
9. *Da tu - is fi - dé - li - bus, In te con - fi - den - ti - bus,*
10. *Da vir - tú - tis mé - ri - tum, Da sa - lú - tis éx - i - tum,*

9. In your sev'n - fold gift de - scend;
10. Give them joys that nev - er end. A - men. Al - le - lu - ia.
9. *Sa - crum sep - te - ná - ri - um.*
10. *Da per - én - ne gáu - di - um.* A - men. Al - le - lú - ia.

Text: Poetic Sequence for Pentecost, *Veni, Sancte Spiritus*; English text fr. *The Roman Missal* © 1964,
  National Catholic Welfare Conference, Inc. (now US Conference of Catholic Bishops).
  All rights reserved. Used with permission.
Music: Chant, Mode I.

## SEND US YOUR SPIRIT 433

1. Send us your spir - it, O Lord. Eve - ning en - folds us and
2. Hold us with mer - cy, O Lord. Sor - row has spo - ken, has
3. Teach us your wis - dom, O Lord. Shad - ows have cloud - ed, have
4. Send us good sum - mer, O Lord. Win - ters have chilled us, and

1. holds us too near. Wake the morn - ing light. Make our liv - ing
2. bro - ken our hearts. Clothe us in your care. Be the life we
3. crowd - ed our sight. Give us hearts that see. Set our lov - ing
4. stilled us too long. Give us love's own fire. Be our true de-

1. bright. Shine on our dark - ness, O Lord.
2. bear. Feed us and fill us, O Lord.
3. free. Hear us and help us, O Lord.
4. sire. Send us your spir - it, O Lord.

Text: Inspired by *Veni, Sancte Spiritus*; Dan Schutte, b. 1947.
Music: Dan Schutte.
Text and music © 1985, OCP. All rights reserved.

# 434 COME, O HOLY SPIRIT

1. Come, O Ho - ly Spir - it, come! And from your ce -
2. You, of com - fort - ers the best; You, the soul's most
3. O most bless - ed Light di - vine, May that Light with -
4. Heal our wounds, our strength re - new; On our dry - ness
5. On the faith - ful who a - dore And con - fess you

1. les - tial home Shed a ray of light di - vine!
2. wel - come guest; Sweet re - fresh-ment here be - low;
3. in us shine, And our in - most be - ing fill!
4. pour your dew; Wash the stains of guilt a - way;
5. ev - er more, In your sev'n - fold gift de - scend;

1. Come, O Ho - ly Spir - it, come! Come, O Fa - ther of the
2. Come, O Ho - ly Spir - it, come! In our la - bor, rest most
3. Come, O Ho - ly Spir - it, come! In your ab-sence, we have
4. Come, O Ho - ly Spir - it, come! Bend the stub-born heart and
5. Come, O Ho - ly Spir - it, come! Give them vir - tue's sure re -

1. poor! Come, O Source of all our store! Come, with -
2. sweet; Grate - ful cool - ness in the heat; Sol - ace
3. naught; Noth - ing good in deed or thought, Noth - ing
4. will; Melt the fro - zen, warm the chill; Guide the
5. ward; Give them your sal - va - tion, Lord; Give them

1. in our bos-oms shine! Come, O Ho - ly Spir - it, come!
2. in the midst of woe. Come, O Ho - ly Spir - it, come!
3. free from taint of ill. Come, O Ho - ly Spir - it, come!
4. steps that go a - stray. Come, O Ho - ly Spir - it, come!
5. joys that nev - er end. Come, O Ho - ly Spir - it, come!

Text: 77 77 D; fr. the Pentecost Sequence, *Veni, Sancte Spiritus*, alt.; adapt. by Owen Alstott, b. 1947,
© 1980, OCP. All rights reserved.
Music: HYMN TO JOY; Ludwig van Beethoven, 1770–1827; adapt. by Edward Hodges, 1796–1867.

# COME, O HOLY SPIRIT, COME

Verses 1-2, 5-6, 9-10

1. Come, O Ho-ly Spir - it, come! And from your ce -
2. Come, O Fa - ther of the poor! Come, O source of
5. O most bless - ed Light di - vine, Shine with - in these
6. Where you are not, we have naught, Noth - ing good in
9. On the faith - ful, who a - dore And con - fess you,
10. Give them vir - tue's sure re - ward; Give them your sal -

1. les - tial home Shed a ray __ of light di - vine! (to Vs 2)
2. all our store! Come, with - in __ our bos-oms shine. (to Vs 3)
5. hearts of yours, And our in - most be - ing fill! (to Vs 6)
6. deed or thought, Noth - ing free __ from taint of ill. (to Vs 7)
9. ev - er - more In your sev-en-fold gift de - scend; (to Vs 10)
10. va - tion, Lord; Give them joys __ that nev - er end. (to Final)

Final

10. A - men. Al - le - lu - ia!

Verses 3-4, 7-8

3. You, of com - fort - ers the best; You, the soul's most
4. In our la - bor, rest most sweet; Grate - ful cool - ness
7. Heal our wounds, our strength re - new; On our dry - ness
8. Bend the stub - born heart and will; Melt the fro - zen,

3. wel - come guest; Sweet re - fresh - ment here be - low; (to Vs 4)
4. in the heat; So - lace in the midst of woe. (to Vs 5)
7. pour your dew; Wash the stains of guilt a - way; (to Vs 8)
8. warm the chill; Guide the steps that go a - stray. (to Vs 9)

## 436    HOLY SPIRIT, COME NOW

**Refrain**

Ho - ly Spir - it, come,    Ho - ly Spir - it, come now,

*1.*    *2. to Verses*    Verses

come now.

1. Oh, the sweet -
2. In the faith
3. With the rev -

1. - ness of your mer - cy and grace!    Bring us true wis -
2. we share, flow - ing from truth,    bring us the knowl -
3. - 'rence of the Lord, love is shown.    Serv - ing each oth -

1. - dom right here in this place.    Bring a glim -
2. - edge that brings us to you.    Through the dark -
3. - er, God's pres - ence is known.    Oh, the good -

1. - mer of the depth of God's will.    Bring un - der - stand -
2. - ness of de - spair and of fear,    give us the cour -
3. - ness and the glo - ry of God!    Hearts o - ver - flow -

*to Refrain*

1. - ing; God's plan be ful - filled.
2. - age to know you are here.
3. - ing with won - der and awe.

## 437    COME, HOLY SPIRIT

**Ostinato Refrain**

Come, Ho - ly Spir - it; come, Ho - ly Spir - it;

come, Ho - ly Spir - it; set our hearts on fire.

**Verses**

1. Come, Spirit, Lord of Light,
   come from your heav'nly height,
   come and restore our sight.
   Come, O Spirit.

2. Consoler, Spirit blest,
   the soul's most welcome guest,
   our ease in toil and stress;
   come, O Spirit.

3. Blest Spirit, guide our way;
   without your help we stray.
   Come to our hearts today;
   come, O Spirit.

4. Come set our hearts on fire,
   make goodness our desire,
   our weak'ning souls inspire;
   come, O Spirit.

5. Come to us from above
   and fill our hearts with love,
   descend, O Heav'nly Dove.
   Come, O Spirit.

6. Give comfort when we die,
   give life with you on high,
   unending joys supply;
   come, O Spirit.

Text: Based on *Veni, Sancte Spiritus*, 12th cent.; Stephen Dean, b. 1948.
Music: Stephen Dean.

## COME DOWN, O LOVE DIVINE 438

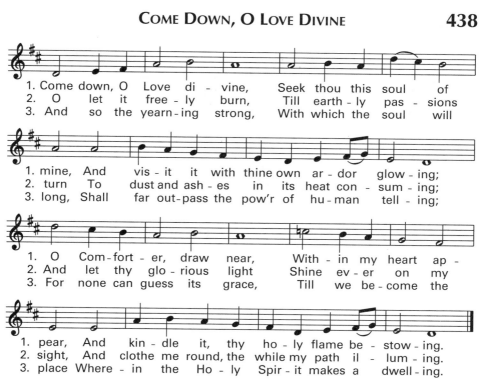

1. Come down, O Love di - vine, Seek thou this soul of
2. O let it free - ly burn, Till earth - ly pas - sions
3. And so the yearn - ing strong, With which the soul will

1. mine, And vis - it it with thine own ar - dor glow - ing;
2. turn To dust and ash - es in its heat con - sum - ing;
3. long, Shall far out-pass the pow'r of hu - man tell - ing;

1. O Com - fort - er, draw near, With - in my heart ap -
2. And let thy glo - rious light Shine ev - er on my
3. For none can guess its grace, Till we be - come the

1. pear, And kin - dle it, thy ho - ly flame be - stow - ing.
2. sight, And clothe me round, the while my path il - lum - ing.
3. place Where - in the Ho - ly Spir - it makes a dwell - ing.

Text: 66 11 D; Bianco da Siena, d. 1434; tr. by Richard F. Littledale, 1833–1890.
Music: DOWN AMPNEY; Ralph Vaughan Williams, 1872–1958.

## 439     BY THE WAKING OF OUR HEARTS

**Refrain**

By the wak-ing of our hearts,    by the stir-ring of our souls,

may the Spir-it of God   a-bide and bring us to-geth-er in Christ.

**Verses**

1. Come, O Spir - it, from a - bove, come from your ce - les - tial heights.
2. Come, O Sav - ior of the poor, come, O source of gifts en - sured.
3. In our la - bor, rest most sweet; grate - ful cool - ness in the heat.
4. Bend the stub-born heart and will, melt the fro - zen, warm the chill.
5. Grant us vir - tue's sure re - ward, may your gra - cious love be sent.

*to Refrain*

1. Come with your bless - ed light so _____ ra - diant bright.
2. Come with your gen - tle hope, so _____ won - drous and pure.
3. Con - sole our rest - less lives, by your com - fort, we seek.
4. Come guide our search - ing minds toward your prom - ise ful - filled.
5. Come with your peace and joy that shall nev - er end.

Text: Verses based on the Pentecost Sequence, *Veni, Sancte Spiritus*; Ricky Manalo, CSP, b. 1965.
Music: Ricky Manalo, CSP.
Text and music © 1997, Ricky Manalo, CSP. Published by OCP. All rights reserved.

## 440     ENVÍA TU ESPÍRITU

**Refrain**

*En - ví - a tu Es - pí - ri - tu,   en - ví - a tu Es - pí - ri - tu,   en-

ví - a tu Es - pí - ri - tu,   se - a re - no - va - da   la faz de la tie-

- rra.   Se - a re - no - va - da   la faz de la tie - rra.

*Refrain translation: "Send out your Spirit, and renew the face of the earth."

1. Spir - it of the liv - ing God, burn in our hearts,
2. Wind of prom - ise, wind of change, friend of the poor,
3. Breath of life and ho - li - ness, heal ev - 'ry wound,

1. and make us a peo - ple of hope and com - pas - sion.
2. em - pow - er your peo - ple to make peace and jus - tice.
3. and lead us be - yond ev - 'ry sin that di - vides us.

Text: Based on Psalm 104:30 and *Veni, Sancte Spiritus*; Latin, 12th cent.; adapt. by Bob Hurd, b. 1950.
Music: Bob Hurd.
Text and music © 1988, Bob Hurd. Published by OCP. All rights reserved.

## VENI, SANCTE SPIRITUS 441

Ve - ni San - cte Spi - ri - tus; Ve - ni San - cte Spi - ri - tus;

Ve - ni, ve - ni San - cte Spi - ri - tus; Ve - ni San - cte Spi - ri - tus.

Verses: Cantor

1. Holy Spirit, Lord of Light,
radiance give from celestial height.
Come, O Spirit of the poor,
come now with treasures that endure:
Light of all who live.

2. You of all consolers the best.
You the soul's delightful guest;
refreshing peace bestow.
You in toil my comfort sweet.
You coolness in the heat.
You my solace in time of woe.

3. Light immortal, light divine;
fire of love our hearts refine,
our inmost being fill.

Take your grace away
and nothing pure in us will stay,
all our good is turned to ill.

4. Heal our wounds, our strength renew,
on our dryness pour your dew;
wash guilt away,
bend the stubborn heart,
melt the frozen,
warm the chill
and guide the steps that go astray.

5. Seven-fold gifts on us be pleased to pour,
who you confess and you adore;
bring us your comfort when we die;
give us life with you on high;
give us joys, give us joys that never end.

Text: Refrain, Latin, 12th cent. Verses based on the Pentecost Sequence, *Veni, Sancte Spiritus*;
adapt. by Christopher Walker, b. 1947, © 1981, 1982, Christopher Walker. Published by OCP. All rights reserved.
Music: Christopher Walker, © 1981, 1982, Christopher Walker. Published by OCP. All rights reserved.

# 442

# HOLY SPIRIT

Ostinato Refrain: All

Ho - ly Spir - it, come in - to

Verses: Cantor

1. Give us a spir - it of wis - dom, an un - der - stand -
2. Give us a spir - it of cour - age, and judg - ment that
3. Spir - it of love and com - pas - sion, give hope to all
4. Spir - it of all con - so - la - tion, O lift our hearts
5. Spir - it of light and of wis - dom, O lift us from
6. Spir - it of strength and of heal - ing, bend stub - born heart

our lives. Ho - ly

1. - ing heart. _____ Give us a spir - it of knowl -
2. is wise. _____ Give us a spir - it of rev -
3. the poor. _____ Spir - it of jus - tice and mer -
4. this day. _____ Spir - it of all un - der - stand -
5. our sor - row. __ Spir - it of peace and for - give -
6. and will. _____ Spir - it of trust and of car -

Spir - it, make us tru - ly wise.

to Refrain

1. - edge, and lead us to the truth. _____
2. - 'rence, of won - der and of awe. _____
3. - cy, come o - pen ev - 'ry door. _____
4. - ing, O help us know your way. _____
5. - ness, O help us face to - mor - row. __
6. - ing, O melt us, warm our chill. _____

Text: Verses 1 & 2 based on Isaiah 11:2; verses 3–6 based on the Pentecost Sequence; Ken Canedo, b. 1953.
Music: Ken Canedo.
Text and music © 1998, Ken Canedo. Published by spiritandsong.com®, a division of OCP. All rights reserved.

# COME, HOLY GHOST

1. Come, Ho - ly Ghost, Cre - a - tor blest,
2. O Com - fort - er, to thee we cry,
3. To ev - 'ry sense thy light im - part
4. O grant that we through thee may come
5. Praise be to thee, Fa - ther and Son

1. And in our hearts take up thy rest;
2. Thou heav'n - ly gift of God most high;
3. And shed thy love in ev - 'ry heart.
4. To know the Fa - ther and the Son,
5. And Ho - ly Spir - it, with them one;

1. Come with thy grace and heav'n - ly aid
2. Thou font of life, and fire of love,
3. To our weak flesh, thy strength sup - ply;
4. And hold with firm, un - chang - ing faith,
5. And may the Son on us be - stow

1. To fill the hearts which thou hast made,
2. And sweet a - noint - ing from a - bove,
3. Un - fail - ing cour - age from on high,
4. That thou art Spir - it of them both,
5. The gifts that from the Spir - it flow,

1. To fill the hearts which thou hast made.
2. And sweet a - noint - ing from a - bove.
3. Un - fail - ing cour - age from on high.
4. That thou art Spir - it of them both.
5. The gifts that from the Spir - it flow.

Text: LM with repeat; *Veni, Creator Spiritus*; attr. to Rabanus Maurus, 776–856; tr. by Edward Caswall, 1814–1878, alt.
Music: LAMBILLOTTE; Louis Lambillotte, SJ, 1796–1855.

**444**

# Veni, Creator Spiritus/
## Creator Spirit, Lord of Grace

1. Ve - ni Cre - á - tor Spí - ri - tus, Men - tes tu - ó -
2. Qui dí - ce - ris Pa - rá - cli - tus, ¹Do - num De - i
3. Tu se - pti - fór - mis mú - ne - re, ²De - xtrae De - i
4. Ac - cén - de lu - men sén - si - bus, In - fún - de a - mó -

1. *Cre - a - tor Spir - it, Lord of grace, Come make in us*
2. *O Spir - it, hear your peo - ple's cry! Come down, O Gift*
3. *As once on Christ the Ser - vant's head The oil of sev'n -*
4. *Of ev - 'ry gift the liv - ing source, Of might - y deeds*

1. rum ví - si - ta, Im - ple su - pér - na grá - ti -
2. al - tís - si - mi, Fons vi - vus, i - gnis, cá - ri -
3. tu dí - gi - tus, Tu ri - te pro - mís - sum Pa -
4. rem cór - di - bus, In - fír - ma nó - stri cór - po -

1. *your dwell - ing place! O pur - est Light, in dark - ness*
2. *of God most high! De - scend in peace, O heav'n - ly*
3. *fold grace you shed, So now a - noint from love's deep*
4. *the un - seen force, The Fa - ther sends his Prom - ised*

1. a Quae tu cre - á - sti pé - cto - ra.
2. tas, Et spi - ri - tá - lis ún - cti - o.
3. tris, Ser - mó - ne di - tans gút - tu - ra.
4. ris Vir - tú - te fir - mans pér - pe - ti. (A - men.)

1. *shine; Fill love - less hearts, O Love di - vine!*
2. *Dove; Come, fount of life; come, flame of love!*
3. *springs Your cho - sen proph - ets, priests, and kings!*
4. *One To speak for all who serve his Son! (A - men.)*

5. Hostem repéllas lóngius
Pacémque dones prótinus;
Ductóre sic te práevio
Vitémus omne nóxium.

5. *Keep far all those who wish us ill!*
*O Dove of peace, be with us still!*
*In every danger at our side,*
*O Friend, befriend us; be our guide!*

6. Per te sciámus da Patrem,
Noscámus atque Fílium,
³Te utriúsque Spíritum
Credámus omni témpore.

6. *Reveal to us the Father's love,*
*Reveal his Son, who reigns above!*
*To truth, O Truth, make all souls true;*
*In love, O Love, make all things new!*

⁴7. Deo Patri sit glória,
Et Fílio, quia mórtuis
Surréxit, ac Paráclito,
In saeculórum sáecula. Amen.

7. *To God the Father glory be,*
*And to the Son from death set free;*
*And to the Holy Spirit raise*
*Our praise to God for endless days. Amen.*

Note: The Latin text above is reproduced from the *Graduale Romanum*, 1974. Textual variants are noted below:
1) formerly *Altíssimi donum Dei*,
2) formerly *Dígitus patérnae déxterae*,
3) formerly *Teque utriúsque Spíritum*.
4) Verse 7 does not appear in the *Graduale Romanum*, 1974.

Text: LM; *Veni, Creator Spiritus*; attr. to Rabanus Maurus, 776–856; *Graduale Romanum*, 1974. Verses 1–6 tr. by
James Quinn, SJ, 1919–2010, © 1994, James Quinn, SJ. Published by OCP. All rights reserved.
Verse 7 tr. by Glenn CJ Byer, b. 1961, © 2002, OCP. All rights reserved.
Music: VENI CREATOR SPIRITUS; Chant, Mode VIII.

## ALL PRAISE AND GLAD THANKSGIVING

**445**

1. All praise and glad thanks-giv - ing To God the Fa - ther
2. Christ Je - sus, we a - dore you, The Son of God most
3. O Ho - ly Spir - it, bless - ing To you who reign a -

1. be: The Font of all things liv - ing, Who reigns e -
2. high; With thanks we sing be - fore you, Who came for
3. bove! Your won-drous gifts con - fess - ing, The Church sings

1. ter - nal - ly.
2. us to die. } Praise to God for - ev - er be,
3. forth your love!

1-3. One in life, in Per - sons three: Might - y God,

1-3. sav - ing God, God e - ter - nal Trin - i - ty!

Text: 76 76 77 67; based on *Trisagion*, Greek, 5th cent.; Melvin Farrell, SS, 1930–1986, © 1976, OCP. All rights reserved.
Music: GOTT VATER SEI GEPRIESEN; *Limburg Gesangbuch*, 1838.

## ALL HAIL, ADORED TRINITY

**446**

1. All hail, a - dor - ed Trin - i - ty! All hail, e -
2. Three per - sons praise we ev - er - more, One on - ly
3. O Trin - i - ty! O U - ni - ty! Be pres - ent

1. ter - nal U - ni - ty! O God the Fa - ther,
2. God our hearts a - dore: In thy sure mer - cy,
3. as we wor - ship thee; And with the songs that

1. God the Son, And God the Spir - it, ev - er One.
2. ev - er kind, May we your strong pro - tec - tion find.
3. an - gels sing U - nite the hymns of praise we bring.

Text: LM; *Ave colenda Trinitas*, ca. 11th cent.; tr. by John D. Chambers, 1805–1893, alt.
Music: OLD HUNDREDTH; *Genevan Psalter*, 1551; attr. to Louis Bourgeois, ca. 1510–1561, alt.

**447** ON THIS DAY, THE FIRST OF DAYS

1. On this day, the first of days, God the
2. On this day th'e - ter - nal Son O - ver
3. O that fer - vent love to - day May in
4. Fa - ther, who cre - at - ed me Im - age
5. Ho - ly Word, all prais - es be! You, from
6. Ho - ly Spir - it, you im - part Gifts to
7. God, the bless - ed Three in One, Fa - ther,

1. Fa - ther's name we praise; Who, cre - a - tion's
2. death his tri - umph won; On this day the
3. ev - 'ry heart have sway, Teach - ing us to
4. of your - self to be, May your grace be
5. sin have set me free; And, up - on love's
6. shine in ev - 'ry heart; Best of gifts, your -
7. Spir - it, with the Son; One in you with

1. Font and Spring, Did the world from dark - ness bring.
2. Spir - it came With the gifts of liv - ing flame.
3. praise a - right God the source of life and light.
4. ev - er mine, Fill me with your love di - vine.
5. flame, a - rise Un - to you a sac - ri - fice.
6. self be - stow; Dwell in me your love to know.
7. all a - bove, We send forth our hearts of love.

Text: 77 77; *Die parente temporum*; Le Mans Breviary, 1748; tr. by Henry W. Baker, 1821–1877, alt.;
  *Hymns Ancient and Modern*, 1861.
Music: LÜBECK; Freylinghausen's *Geistreiches Gesangbuch*, 1704; adapt. by William H. Havergal, 1793–1870.

**448** HOLY, HOLY, HOLY

1. Ho - ly, Ho - ly, Ho - ly! Lord ___ God Al - might - y!
2. Ho - ly, Ho - ly, Ho - ly! All the saints a - dore thee,
3. Ho - ly, Ho - ly, Ho - ly! Though the dark - ness hide thee,
4. Ho - ly, Ho - ly, Ho - ly! Lord ___ God Al - might - y!

1. Ear - ly in the morn - ing our song shall rise to thee:
2. Cast - ing down their gold - en crowns a - round the glass - y sea;
3. Though the eye made blind by sin thy glo - ry may not see,
4. All thy works shall praise thy Name, in earth, and sky, and sea;

1. Ho - ly, Ho - ly, Ho - ly! Mer - ci - ful and might - y,
2. Cher - u - bim and ser - a - phim fall - ing down be - fore thee,
3. On - ly thou art ho - ly; there is none be - side thee,
4. Ho - ly, Ho - ly, Ho - ly! Mer - ci - ful and might - y,

1. God in three Per - sons, bless - ed Trin - i - ty.
2. Which wert, and art, and ev - er - more shalt be.
3. Per - fect in pow'r, in love, and pur - i - ty.
4. God in three Per - sons, bless - ed Trin - i - ty.

Text: 11 12 12 10; Reginald Heber, 1783–1826, alt.
Music: NICAEA; John B. Dykes, 1823–1876.

## HOW WONDERFUL THE THREE-IN-ONE 449

1. How won - der - ful the Three - in - One,
2. Be - fore the flow of dawn and dark,
3. The Lov - er's own Be - lov'd, in time,
4. Their E - qual Friend all life sus - tains
5. How won - der - ful the Liv - ing God:

1. Whose en - er - gies of danc - ing light
2. Cre - a - tion's Lov - er dreamed of earth,
3. Be - tween a cra - dle and a cross,
4. With green - ing pow'r and lov - ing care,
5. Di - vine Be - lov'd, Em - pow'r - ing Friend,

1. Are un - di - vid - ed, pure and good,
2. And with a car - ing deep and wise,
3. At home in flesh, gave love and life
4. And calls us, born a - gain by grace,
5. E - ter - nal Lov - er, Three - in - One,

1. Com - mun - ing love in shared de - light.
2. All things con - ceived and brought to birth.
3. To heal our bro - ken - ness and loss.
4. In Love's com - mun - ing life to share.
5. Our hope's be - gin - ning, way and end.

Text: LM; Brian Wren, b. 1936, © 1989, Hope Publishing Co. All rights reserved. Used with permission.
Music: CONDITOR ALME SIDERUM; Chant, Mode IV.

## 450     COME NOW, ALMIGHTY KING

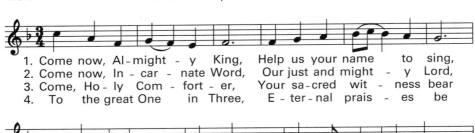

1. Come now, Al-might-y King,   Help us your name   to sing,
2. Come now, In-car-nate Word,   Our just and might-y Lord,
3. Come, Ho-ly Com-fort-er,   Your sa-cred wit-ness bear
4. To the great One in Three,   E-ter-nal prais-es be

1. Help us to praise:   Fa-ther, all glo-ri-ous,   Ev-er vic-
2. Our prayer at-tend:   Come, and your peo-ple bless,   And give your
3. In this glad hour:   To us your grace im-part,   And rule in
4. For-ev-er-more!   Your sov-'reign maj-es-ty   May we in

1. to-ri-ous, Come, and reign o-ver us,   An-cient of Days.
2. word suc-cess; Strength-en your right-eous-ness,   Sav-ior and Friend.
3. ev-'ry heart! Nev-er from us de-part,   Spir-it of pow'r.
4. glo-ry see, And to e-ter-ni-ty   Love and a-dore!

Text: 66 4 666 4; anon., ca. 1757, alt.
Music: ITALIAN HYMN; Felice de Giardini, 1716–1796, alt.

## 451     O GOD, ALMIGHTY FATHER

1. O God, al-might-y Fa-ther, Cre-a-tor of all
2. O Je-sus, Word in-car-nate, Re-deem-er most a-
3. O God, the Ho-ly Spir-it, Who lives with-in our

1. things, The heav-ens stand in won-der, While earth your
2. dored, All glo-ry, praise, and hon-or Be yours, O
3. soul, Send forth your light and lead us To our e-

1. glo-ry sings.
2. sov-'reign Lord.    O most ho-ly Trin-i-ty,
3. ter-nal goal.

1-3. Un-di-vid-ed u-ni-ty,   Ho-ly God,

1-3. might - y God, God im - mor - tal be a - dored!

## HOLY, HOLY, HOLY

### 452

## 453    LAUD, O ZION

Verses 1, 2

*1. Lo! the an-gel's food is giv - en To the
2. Truth the an-cient types ful-fill - ing, I - saac

1. pil - grim who has striv - en; See the chil-dren's bread from
2. bound, a vic-tim will - ing, Pas-chal lamb, its life-blood

1. heav - en, which on dogs may not be spent.
2. spill - ing, man - na to the fa-thers sent.

Verses 3, 4

3. Ver - y bread, good shep-herd, tend us,
4. You who all things can ___ and know,

3. Je - su, of your love be - friend us,
4. Who on earth such food ___ be - stow,

3. You re-fresh us, you de - fend us, Your e - ter - nal
4. Grant us with your saints, though low - est, Where the heav'n - ly

3. good-ness send us In the land of life to see.
4. feast you show,

3.
4. Fel - low heirs and guests to

4. be. A - men. Al - le - lu - ia.

*The shorter form of this sequence is given here. The long form is available in the octavo, *Laud, O Zion*,
edition 11500, by Randall DeBruyn.

## DRAW NEAR AND TAKE THE BODY OF THE LORD 454

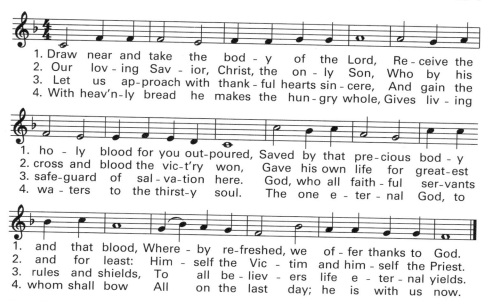

1. Draw near and take the bod-y of the Lord, Re-ceive the
2. Our lov-ing Sav-ior, Christ, the on-ly Son, Who by his
3. Let us ap-proach with thank-ful hearts sin-cere, And gain the
4. With heav'n-ly bread he makes the hun-gry whole, Gives liv-ing

1. ho-ly blood for you out-poured, Saved by that pre-cious bod-y
2. cross and blood the vic-t'ry won, Gave his own life for great-est
3. safe-guard of sal-va-tion here. God, who all faith-ful ser-vants
4. wa-ters to the thirst-y soul. The one e-ter-nal God, to

1. and that blood, Where-by re-freshed, we of-fer thanks to God.
2. and for least: Him-self the Vic-tim and him-self the Priest.
3. rules and shields, To all be-liev-ers life e-ter-nal yields.
4. whom shall bow All on the last day; he is with us now.

Text: 10 10 10 10; *Sancti, venite, Christi corpus sumite; Antiphonary of Bennchar,* 7th cent.;
tr. by John M. Neale, 1818–1866, alt.
Music: ANIMA CHRISTI; William J. Maher, SJ, 1823–1877, alt.

## JESUS, THE VERY THOUGHT OF YOU 455

1. Je-sus, the ver-y thought of you
2. No voice can sing, no heart can frame,
3. O hope of ev-'ry hum-ble soul,
4. O Je-sus, be our joy to-day;

1. Fills us with sweet de-light; But sweet-er far your
2. Nor can the mind re-call A sweet-er sound than
3. O joy of all the meek, How kind you are to
4. Help us to prize your love; Grant us at last to

1. face to view And rest with-in your light.
2. your blest name, O Sav-ior of us all!
3. those who fall, How good to those who seek!
4. hear you say: "Come, share my home a-bove."

Text: CM; *Jesu dulcis memoria,* ca. 12th cent.; attr. to Bernard of Clairvaux, 1091–1153;
tr. by Edward Caswall, 1814–1878, alt.
Music: ST. AGNES; John B. Dykes, 1823–1876.

**456**

# HEART OF JESUS

1. Heart of Je - sus, ho - ly mys - t'ry, beat with - in our hearts, we
2. Heart of Je - sus, giv - en for us, may we love as we are
3. Heart of Je - sus, no __ strang - er to our dark - ness and our
4. Heart of Je - sus, ho - ly wis - dom, ev - er an - cient, ev - er

1. pray. May we mir - ror your com - pas - sion, let your
2. loved. May your Church be a good shep - herd, seek - ing
3. grief, how you wept for poor __ Laz - 'rus and a -
4. new, may your king - dom grow a - mong us in each

1. mind be ours to - day. Make us ves - sels of your glo - ry,
2. out those who are lost, break - ing bread with all who hun - ger,
3. woke him from his sleep. How you bore for us the spear - wound,
4. thing we say and do. May we fight the good fight glad - ly,

1. in our weak - ness show your strength. Make this Church a bold
2. giv - ing voice to the op - pressed: win - ning jus - tice and
3. great - er love there can - not be than to lay down one's
4. run the race our whole lives through, till at last with the

1. sign of your pow - er - ful grace.
2. peace for all those in dis - tress.
3. life to __ set oth - ers free.
4. saints we shall find rest in you.

## SACRED HEART OF JESUS

Verses

1. Sa - cred Heart of Je - sus, meek and mild. Look on us and
2. Sa - cred Heart of Je - sus, our des - ire. May your name be

1. keep us by your side. We give you thanks and praise your name.
2. praised and glo - ri - fied. Re-new our spir - its once a - gain.

1. Set our hearts a - flame that we may love you more and more ev - 'ry
2. Make us know your love and in the morn-ing we will seek your ho - ly

1. day. Show us how to live the ho - ly way. So that wher-
2. face. Lead us to the prom-ise of your grace. And as we

1. ev - er we may go, the riv - er of your love through us may flow.
2. face the set - ting sun, make us see the glo - ry of your land.

Refrain

Sa - cred Heart of Je - sus draw us clo - ser to your love. Stir our

hearts with fire from a - bove. Sa - cred Heart of Je - sus ev - er

1

faith-ful, ev - er true. Touch our lives, and make us more like

to Verse 2 | Final

you. lives, and make us more like you.

# 458      ALLELUIA! SING TO JESUS

1. Alleluia! sing to Jesus! His the
2. Alleluia! not as orphans Are we
3. Alleluia! Bread of Angels, Here on
4. Alleluia! King eternal, You the
5. Alleluia! Alleluia! Glory

1. scepter, his the throne; Alleluia!
2. left in sorrow now; Alleluia!
3. earth our food, our stay! Alleluia!
4. Lord of lords we own; Alleluia!
5. be to God on high; Alleluia

1. his the triumph, His the victory alone;
2. he is near us, Faith believes, nor questions how:
3. here the sinful Flee to you from day to day:
4. born of Mary, Earth your footstool, heav'n your throne:
5. to the Savior Who has won the victory;

1. Hark! the songs of peaceful Zion Thunder
2. Though the cloud from sight received him, When the
3. Intercessor, friend of sinners, Earth's re-
4. You within the veil have entered, Robed in
5. Alleluia to the Spirit, Font of

1. like a mighty flood; Jesus out of ev'ry
2. forty days were o'er, Shall our hearts forget his
3. deemer, plead for me, Where the songs of all the
4. flesh, our great high priest; Here on earth both priest and
5. love and sanctity; Alleluia! Alle-

1. nation Has redeemed us by his blood.
2. promise? "I am with you evermore!"
3. sinless Sweep across the crystal sea.
4. victim In the Eucharistic feast.
5. luia! To the triune majesty.

Text: 87 87 D; William C. Dix, 1837–1898, alt.
Music: HYFRYDOL; Rowland H. Prichard, 1811–1887.

## REJOICE, THE LORD IS KING

**459**

1. Re - joice, the Lord is King: Your Lord and King a - dore! Re -
2. Our Lord and Sav - ior reigns, The God of truth and love; When
3. His king-dom can - not fail, He rules o'er earth and heav'n; The
4. Re - joice in glo-rious hope! Our Lord and judge shall come And

1. joice, give thanks and sing, And tri - umph ev - er - more:
2. he had purged our stains, He took his seat a - bove:
3. keys of death and hell Are to our Je - sus giv'n:
4. take his ser - vants up To their e - ter - nal home:
Lift up your

1-4. heart, lift up your voice! Re - joice, a - gain I say, re - joice!

Text: 66 66 88; *Hymns for Our Lord's Resurrection*, 1746; Charles Wesley, 1707–1788, alt.
Music: DARWALL'S 148TH; John Darwall, 1731–1789.

## JESUS SHALL REIGN

**460**

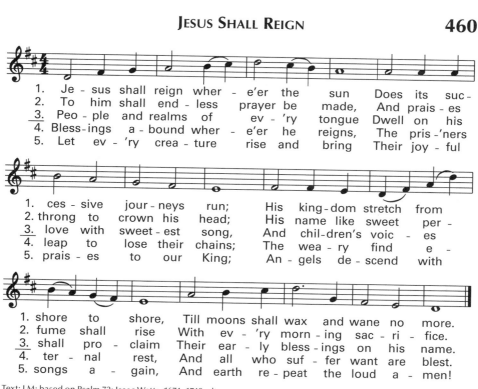

1. Je - sus shall reign wher - e'er the sun Does its suc -
2. To him shall end - less prayer be made, And prais - es
3. Peo - ple and realms of ev - 'ry tongue Dwell on his
4. Bless-ings a - bound wher - e'er he reigns, The pris -'ners
5. Let ev - 'ry crea - ture rise and bring Their joy - ful

1. ces - sive jour - neys run; His king-dom stretch from
2. throng to crown his head; His name like sweet per -
3. love with sweet - est song, And chil-dren's voic - es
4. leap to lose their chains; The wea - ry find e -
5. prais - es to our King; An - gels de - scend with

1. shore to shore, Till moons shall wax and wane no more.
2. fume shall rise With ev - 'ry morn - ing sac - ri - fice.
3. shall pro - claim Their ear - ly bless-ings on his name.
4. ter - nal rest, And all who suf - fer want are blest.
5. songs a - gain, And earth re - peat the loud a - men!

Text: LM; based on Psalm 72; Isaac Watts, 1674–1748, alt.
Music: DUKE STREET; John Hatton, ca. 1710–1793.

## 461    CROWN HIM WITH MANY CROWNS

1. Crown him with man-y crowns, The Lamb up-on his
2. Crown him the Lord of life, Who tri-umphed o'er the
3. Crown him the Lord of love, Be-hold his hands and
4. Crown him the Lord of peace, Whose pow'r a scep-ter
5. Crown him the Lord of years, The ris-en Lord sub-

1. throne; Hark! how the heav'n-ly an-them drowns All
2. grave, And rose vic-to-rious in the strife For
3. side, Rich wounds yet vis-i-ble a-bove In
4. sways From pole to pole, that wars may cease, Ab-
5. lime, Cre-a-tor of the roll-ing spheres, The

1. mu-sic but its own. A-wake, my soul, and sing
2. those he came to save. His glo-ries now we sing,
3. beau-ty glo-ri-fied. No an-gel in the sky
4. sorbed in prayer and praise. His reign shall know no end,
5. Mas-ter of all time. All hail, Re-deem-er, hail!

1. Of him who set us free, And hail him as your
2. Who died and rose on high, Who died, e-ter-nal
3. Can ful-ly bear that sight, But down-ward bends his
4. And round his pierc-ed feet Fair flow'rs of Par-a-
5. For you have died for me; Your praise and glo-ry

1. heav'n-ly King Through all e-ter-ni-ty.
2. life to bring, And lives that death may die.
3. burn-ing eye At mys-ter-ies so bright.
4. dise ex-tend Their fra-grance ev-er sweet.
5. shall not fail Through-out e-ter-ni-ty.

Text: SMD; Revelation 19:12; verses 1, 3–5, Matthew Bridges, 1800–1894; verse 2, Godfrey Thring, 1823–1903, alt.
Music: DIADEMATA; George J. Elvey, 1816–1893.

## ALL HAIL THE POWER OF JESUS' NAME

**462**

1. All hail the pow'r of Je - sus' name! Let an - gels pros-trate
2. Crown him, you mar - tyrs of our God, Who from his al - tar
3. Hail him, you heirs of Da - vid's line Whom Da - vid Lord did
4. O that with ev - 'ry tribe and tongue We at his feet may

1. fall; Bring forth the roy - al di - a - dem And
2. call; Ex - tol him in whose path you trod, And
3. call, The God in - car - nate, Man di - vine, And
4. fall, Lift high the u - ni - ver - sal song And

1. crown him Lord of all; Bring forth the roy - al
2. crown him Lord of all; Ex - tol him in whose
3. crown him Lord of all; The God in - car - nate,
4. crown him Lord of all; Lift high the u - ni -

1. di - a - dem And crown him Lord of all.
2. path you trod, And crown him Lord of all.
3. Man di - vine, And crown him Lord of all.
4. ver - sal song And crown him Lord of all.

Text: 86 86 86; Edward Perronet, 1726–1792, alt.
Music: CORONATION; *Union Harmony*, 1793; Oliver Holden, 1765–1844.

**463**

# HAIL, REDEEMER, KING DIVINE

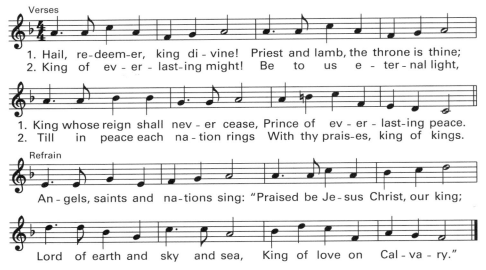

Verses

1. Hail, re-deem-er, king di-vine! Priest and lamb, the throne is thine;
2. King of ev-er-last-ing might! Be to us e-ter-nal light,

1. King whose reign shall nev-er cease, Prince of ev-er-last-ing peace.
2. Till in peace each na-tion rings With thy prais-es, king of kings.

Refrain

An-gels, saints and na-tions sing: "Praised be Je-sus Christ, our king;

Lord of earth and sky and sea, King of love on Cal-va-ry."

Text: 77 77 with refrain; Patrick Brennen, 1877–1951, © Burns & Oates, Ltd. All rights reserved.
Reproduced by permission of Continuum International Publishing Group, Ltd.
Music: ST. GEORGE'S WINDSOR; George J. Elvey, 1816–1893.

**464**

# JESUS CHRIST IS LORD

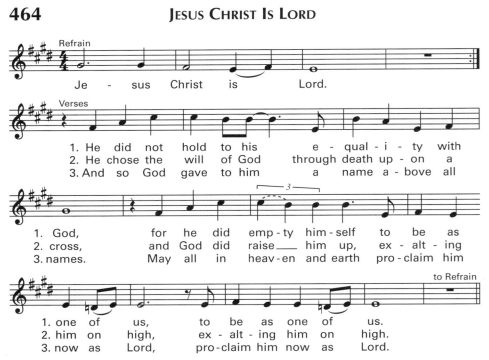

Refrain

Je - sus Christ is Lord.

Verses

1. He did not hold to his e-qual-i-ty with
2. He chose the will of God through death up-on a
3. And so God gave to him a name a-bove all

1. God, for he did emp-ty him-self to be as
2. cross, and God did raise___ him up, ex-alt-ing
3. names. May all in heav-en and earth pro-claim him

to Refrain

1. one of us, to be as one of us.
2. him on high, ex-alt-ing him on high.
3. now as Lord, pro-claim him now as Lord.

Text: Based on Philippians 2:6–11; Ken Canedo, b. 1953, © 1998, 2004, spiritandsong.com®, a division of OCP.
All rights reserved.
Music: Ken Canedo, © 2004, Ken Canedo. Published by spiritandsong.com®, a division of OCP. All rights reserved.

AT THE NAME OF JESUS

1. At the Name of Je - sus Ev - 'ry knee shall bow,
2. Hum-bled for a sea - son, To re - ceive a Name
3. Bore it up tri - um - phant, With its hu - man light,
4. In your hearts en - throne him; There let him sub - due
5. Je - sus, Lord and Sav - ior, Shall re - turn a - gain,

1. Ev - 'ry tongue con - fess him King of glo - ry now;
2. From the lips of sin - ners, Un - to whom he came,
3. Through all ranks of crea - tures, To the cen - tral height,
4. All that is not ho - ly, All that is not true:
5. With his Fa - ther's glo - ry O'er the earth to reign;

1. 'Tis the Fa - ther's plea - sure We should call him Lord,
2. Faith - ful - ly he bore it Spot - less to the last,
3. To the throne of God - head, To the Fa - ther's breast;
4. Crown him as your Cap - tain In temp - ta - tion's hour;
5. For all wreaths of em - pire Meet up - on his brow,

1. Who from the be - gin - ning Was the might - y Word.
2. Brought it back vic - to - rious, When through death he passed.
3. Filled it with the glo - ry Of that per - fect rest.
4. Let his will en - fold you In its light and power.
5. And our hearts con - fess him King of glo - ry now.

Text: 65 65 D; based on Philippians 2:5–7; Caroline Maria Noel, 1817–1877, alt.
Music: KING'S WESTON; Ralph Vaughan Williams, 1872–1958; fr. *Enlarged Songs of Praise*, 1931.

**466**         AT THE NAME OF JESUS

Refrain

At the name of Je-sus, ev-'ry knee shall bow, ev-'ry tongue con-

(last time only)

fess him: King of glo-ry now. Je-sus is Lord, King of glo-ry now!

Verses

1. He ___ emp-tied him - self, as a slave, yet free,
2. He ___ hum-bled him - self, and o-beyed God's will.
3. God ex-alt - ed him, raised him up on high
4. Christ ___ Je - sus will come at the end of time,

1. came in hu - man like-ness ___ for you and for me; in
2. On a cross he died _____ on Cal - va - ry's hill; for
3. so a-bove all oth - ers ___ his name will not die; that
4. come with ju - bi - la - tion ___ to call ___ us home. Un-

to Refrain

1. hu - man like-ness ___ for you and for me.
2. you and me he o-beyed ___ God's will.
3. name we hon - or ____ and glo - ri - fy.
4. til that day you and I will pro - claim:

Text: Refrain, Caroline Maria Noel, 1817–1877. Verses based on Philippians 2;
Christopher Walker, b. 1947, © 1995, Christopher Walker. Published by OCP. All rights reserved.
Music: Christopher Walker, © 1995, Christopher Walker. Published by OCP. All rights reserved.

**467**         JESUS THE LORD

Refrain

Je - sus. Je - sus. Let all cre-

a - tion bend the knee to the Lord.

Verse 1
1. In him we live, we move and have our be-ing; In
1. him the Christ, in him the king! Je - sus, the Lord.

Verses 2, 3
2. Though Son, he did not cling to god - li - ness; but
3. He lived o - be - dient - ly his Fa-ther's will ac -

2. emp-tied him - self, be-came a slave! } Je - sus, the Lord.
3. cept-ing his death, death on a tree! }

## TO JESUS CHRIST, OUR SOVEREIGN KING  468

1. To Je - sus Christ, our Sov - 'reign King, Who is the
2. Thy reign ex - tend, O King be - nign, To ev - 'ry
3. To thee and to thy Church, great King, We pledge our

1. world's sal - va - tion, All praise and hom - age do we bring And
2. land and na - tion; For in thy king - dom, Lord di - vine, A -
3. hearts' ob - la - tion Un - til be - fore thy throne we sing In

1. thanks and ad - o - ra - tion. }
2. lone we find sal - va - tion. } Christ Je - sus, vic - tor!
3. end - less ju - bi - la - tion. }

1-3. Christ Je-sus, rul - er! Christ Je-sus, Lord and re-deem - er!

## 469  THE KING OF KINGS, CHRIST JESUS REIGNS

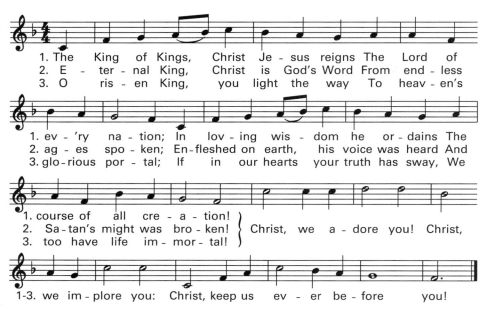

1. The King of Kings, Christ Jesus reigns The Lord of
2. E - ter - nal King, Christ is God's Word From end - less
3. O ris - en King, you light the way To heav - en's

1. ev - 'ry na - tion; In lov - ing wis - dom he or - dains The
2. ag - es spo - ken; En-fleshed on earth, his voice was heard And
3. glo - rious por - tal; If in our hearts your truth has sway, We

1. course of all cre - a - tion! }
2. Sa - tan's might was bro - ken! } Christ, we a - dore you! Christ,
3. too have life im - mor - tal! }

1-3. we im - plore you: Christ, keep us ev - er be - fore you!

Text: 87 87 55 8; Melvin Farrell, SS, 1930–1986, © 1977, OCP. All rights reserved.
Music: ICH GLAUB AN GOTT; *Mainz Gesangbuch*, 1870.

## 470  THE KING OF GLORY

Refrain

The King of glo - ry comes, the na - tion re - joic - es. O-pen the gates be-fore him,

Verses

lift up your voic - es. 1. Who is the King of glo - ry; how shall we
2. In all of Gal - i - lee, in cit - y or
3. Sing then of Da - vid's Son, our Sav - ior and
4. He gave his life for us, the pledge of sal -
5. He con-quered sin and death; he tru - ly has

to Refrain

1. call him? He is Em - man - u - el, the prom-ised of a - ges.
2. vil - lage, He goes a - mong his peo - ple cur - ing their ill - ness.
3. broth - er; In all of Gal - i - lee was nev - er an - oth - er.
4. va - tion, He took up - on him-self the sins of the na - tion.
5. ris - en, And he will share with us his heav - en - ly vi - sion.

Text: 12 12 with refrain; Willard F. Jabusch, b. 1930, © 1967, Willard F. Jabusch. All rights reserved. Administered by OCP.
Music: KING OF GLORY; trad. Israeli Folk Song.

# SOLEMNITIES AND FEASTS

## ALMA REDEMPTORIS MATER

Al - ma Red - em - ptó - ris Ma - ter,
*Lov - ing Moth - er of our Sav - ior;*

quae pér - vi - a cae - li por - ta ma - nes,
*thou o - pen gate lead - ing us to heav - en,*

Et stel - la ma - ris, suc - cúr - re ca - dén - ti
*and Star of the Sea, help thy fall - en peo - ple,*

súr - ge - re qui cu - rat pó - pu - lo:
*help all those who seek to rise a - gain.*

Tu quae ge - nu - í - sti, na - tú - ra mi - rán - te,
*Maid - en who didst give birth, all na - ture won - der - ing,*

tu - um san - ctum Ge - ni - tó - rem:
*to thy ho - ly Lord Cre - a - tor:*

Vir - go pri - us ac po - sté - ri - us,
*Vir - gin be - fore and vir - gin al - ways*

Ga - bri - é - lis ab o - re su - mens il - lud A - ve,
*who re - ceived from Ga - briel's mouth this mes - sage from heav - en,*

pec - ca - tó - rum mi - se - ré - re.
*take pit - y on us poor sin - ners.*

Text: Ascr. to Hermannus Contractus, 1013–1054; adapt. by Theodore N. Marier, 1912–2001, © 1953, Theodore N. Marier.
    All rights reserved.
Music: Chant, Mode V.

## 472 SING OF MARY

1. Sing of Ma-ry, pure and low-ly, Vir-gin Moth-er un-de-
2. Sing of Je-sus, son of Ma-ry, In the home at Naz-a-
3. Glo-ry be to God the Fa-ther; Glo-ry be to God the

1. filed. Sing of God's own Son most ho-ly, Who be-came her
2. reth. Toil and la-bor can-not wea-ry Love en-dur-ing
3. Son; Glo-ry be to God the Spir-it; Glo-ry to the

1. lit-tle child. Fair-est child of fair-est moth-er,
2. un-to death. Con-stant was the love he gave her,
3. Three in One. From the heart of bless-ed Ma-ry,

1. God the Lord who came to earth, Word made flesh, our
2. Though he went forth from her side, Forth to preach and
3. From all saints the song as-cends, And the Church the

1. ver-y broth-er, Takes our na-ture by his birth.
2. heal and suf-fer, Till on Cal-va-ry he died.
3. strain re-ech-oes Un-to earth's re-mot-est ends.

Text: 87 87 D; Roland F. Palmer, SSJE, 1891–1985, © Estate of Roland F. Palmer. All rights reserved. Used with permission.
Music: PLEADING SAVIOR; *Christian Lyre*, 1830.

## 473 LET IT BE DONE TO US

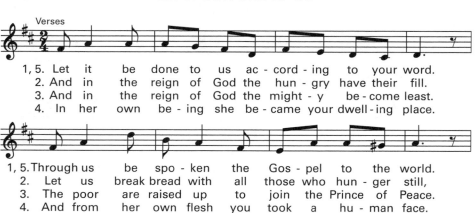

Verses

1, 5. Let it be done to us ac-cord-ing to your word.
2. And in the reign of God the hun-gry have their fill.
3. And in the reign of God the might-y be-come least.
4. In her own be-ing she be-came your dwell-ing place.

1, 5. Through us be spo-ken the Gos-pel to the world.
2. Let us break bread with all those who hun-ger still,
3. The poor are raised up to join the Prince of Peace.
4. And from her own flesh you took a hu-man face.

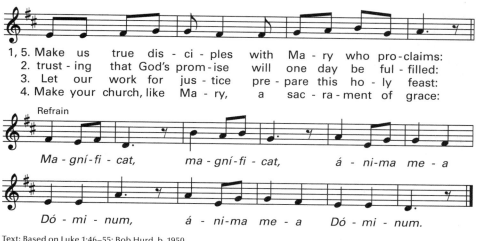

1, 5. Make us true dis - ci - ples with Ma - ry who pro - claims:
2. trust - ing that God's prom - ise will one day be ful - filled:
3. Let our work for jus - tice pre - pare this ho - ly feast:
4. Make your church, like Ma - ry, a sac - ra - ment of grace:

*Refrain*

Ma - gní - fi - cat, ma - gní - fi - cat, á - ni - ma me - a

Dó - mi - num, á - ni - ma me - a Dó - mi - num.

Text: Based on Luke 1:46–55; Bob Hurd, b. 1950.
Music: Bob Hurd.

## MARY'S SONG 474

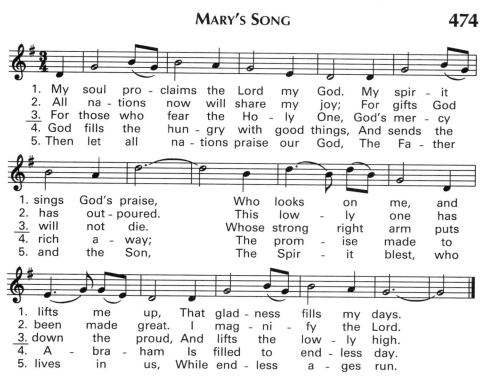

1. My soul pro - claims the Lord my God. My spir - it
2. All na - tions now will share my joy; For gifts God
3. For those who fear the Ho - ly One, God's mer - cy
4. God fills the hun - gry with good things, And sends the
5. Then let all na - tions praise our God, The Fa - ther

1. sings God's praise, Who looks on me, and
2. has out - poured. This low - ly one has
3. will not die. Whose strong right arm puts
4. rich a - way; The prom - ise made to
5. and the Son, The Spir - it blest, who

1. lifts me up, That glad - ness fills my days.
2. been made great. I mag - ni - fy the Lord.
3. down the proud, And lifts the low - ly high.
4. A - bra - ham Is filled to end - less day.
5. lives in us, While end - less a - ges run.

Text: CM; based on Luke 1:46–55; Anne Carter, 1944–1993, © 1988, Society of the Sacred Heart.
Music: NEW BRITAIN; *Columbian Harmony*, 1829.

## 475     SING WE OF THE BLESSED MOTHER

1. Sing we of the bless-ed Moth-er Who re-ceived the
2. Sing we, too, of Ma-ry's sor-rows, Of the sword that
3. Sing a-gain the joys of Ma-ry When she saw the
4. Sing the great-est joy of Ma-ry When on earth her

1. an-gel's word, And o-be-dient to the sum-mons
2. pierced her through, When be-neath the cross of Je-sus
3. ris-en Lord, And in prayer with Christ's a-pos-tles,
4. work was done, And the Lord of all cre-a-tion

1. Bore in love the in-fant Lord; Sing we of the joys of
2. She his weight of suf-f'ring knew, Looked up-on her Son and
3. Wait-ed on his prom-ised word: From on high the blaz-ing
4. Brought her to his heav'n-ly home: Vir-gin Moth-er, Ma-ry

1. Ma-ry At whose breast that child was fed Who is Son
2. Sav-ior Reign-ing from the aw-ful tree, Saw the price
3. glo-ry Of the Spir-it's pres-ence came, Heav'n-ly breath
4. bless-ed, Raised on high and crowned with grace, May your Son,

1. of God e-ter-nal And the ev-er-last-ing Bread.
2. of our re-demp-tion Paid to set the sin-ner free.
3. of God's own be-ing, To-kened in the wind and flame.
4. the world's re-deem-er, Grant us all to see his face.

Text: 87 87 D; 'Sing we of the Blessed Mother' by George B. Timms, 1910–1997.
Reproduced by permission of Oxford University Press. All rights reserved.
Music: OMNI DIE DIC MARIAE; *Trier Gesängbuch*, 1695.

## 476     PILGRIM PRAYER

Refrain

Hail Ma-ry, full of grace, bless the jour-ney,

bless the place we go to and we leave.

1. We give praise for the won-der of our God,
2. We give praise for the wis-dom of our God,
3. We give praise for the mer-cy of our God,
4. We give praise for the kind-ness of our God,
5. We give praise for the pa-tience of our God,
6. We give praise for the good-ness of our God,

to Refrain

1. who sends us com-pan-ions on our way.
2. who gives us the free-dom to be-lieve.
3. who lives in the doubt and in the dream.
4. who teach-es us gent-ly to for-give.
5. who heals us in ways we can-not know.
6. who smiles on the pil-grim com-ing home.

Text and music: Pia Moriarty, b. 1948, © 2003, Pia Moriarty. Published by OCP. All rights reserved.

## Mary, Woman of the Promise

477

1. Ma-ry, wom-an of the prom-ise; Ves-sel of your
2. Ma-ry, song of ho-ly wis-dom, Sung be-fore the
3. Ma-ry, morn-ing star of jus-tice; Mir-ror of the
4. Ma-ry, mod-el of com-pas-sion; Wound-ed by your
5. Ma-ry, wom-an of the Gos-pel; Hum-ble home for

1. peo-ple's dreams, Through your o-pen, will-ing
2. world be-gan, Faith-ful to the Word with-
3. ra-diant light, In the shad-ows of life's
4. off-spring's pain, When our hearts are torn by
5. trea-sured seed, Help us to be true dis-

1. spir-it Wa-ters of God's good-ness streamed.
2. in, you Car-ried out God's won-drous plan.
3. jour-ney, Be a bea-con for our sight.
4. sor-row, Teach us how to love a-gain.
5. ci-ples Bear-ing fruit in word and deed.

Text: 87 87; Mary Frances Fleischaker, © 1988, Mary Frances Fleischaker. All rights reserved.
Used with permission of Selah Publishing Co., Inc., exclusive agent.
Music: DRAKES BROUGHTON; Edward Elgar, 1857–1934.

## 478     THERE IS NOTHING TOLD

**Verses**

1-6. There is noth-ing told a-bout this wom-an, but that

1. she had once be-come en-gaged, and an an-gel ad-
2. she had brought in-to the world, in the land of Ju-
3. she had searched for three long days for her child who was
4. she at Ca-na was a guest, and that Je-sus changed
5. she was stand-ing by the cross when her son stretched his
6. she was one in prayer with those up-on whom tongues of

1. dressed her and said: "You are bless-ed a-mong all your kind."
2. de-a, her son; for some shep-herds have passed on this tale.
3. bus-y else-where, and her heart then did not un-der-stand.
4. wa-ter to wine, so that all might be-lieve who he was.
5. arms out on high, and met death with a thief on each side.
6. fire did de-scend, and the Spir-it bap-tized them with flame.

**Refrain**

On this day all earth and all par-a-dise join in nam-ing you

hap-py and blessed; Vir-gin Ma-ry, bless-ed are you.

## 479     ON THIS DAY, O BEAUTIFUL MOTHER

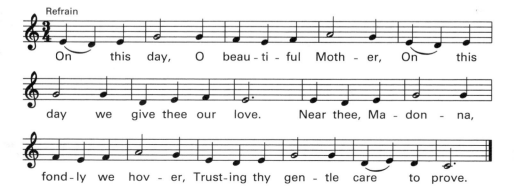

**Refrain**

On this day, O beau-ti-ful Moth-er, On this

day we give thee our love. Near thee, Ma-don-na,

fond-ly we hov-er, Trust-ing thy gen-tle care to prove.

Verses

1. On this day we ask to share, Dear-est Moth-er,
2. Queen of an-gels, deign to hear Lisp-ing chil-dren's

1. thy sweet care; Aid us ere our feet a-
2. hum-ble pray'r; Young hearts gain, O Vir-gin

to Refrain

1. stray Wan-der from thy guid-ing way.
2. pure, Sweet-ly to thy-self al-lure.

Text: 77 77 with refrain; Rohr's *Favorite Catholic Melodies*, 1857.
Music: BEAUTIFUL MOTHER; Louis Lambillotte, SJ, 1796–1855.

## MARY'S SONG

**480**

1. My soul doth glo-ry in your love, O Lord.
2. Great are you, God, and ho-ly is your name.
3. Ah, how you fill the hun-gry with your love.
4. My soul doth glo-ry in your love, O Lord.

1. My soul doth glo-ry in your love, O Lord. For you
2. Your mer-cy reach-es to the end of time. Ah, the
3. With emp-ty hands the rich are sent a-way. You will
4. My soul doth glo-ry in your love, O Lord. For you

1. gazed on your ser-vant with com-pas-sion, And you
2. low-ly you raise to the heav-ens, And the
3. al-ways be mind-ful of your mer-cy, As you
4. smiled on your ser-vant with com-pas-sion, And you

1. reached out and took me by the hand.
2. proud-heart-ed have no part with you.
3. prom-ised your peo-ple long a-go.
4. reached out and took me by the hand.

Text: Based on Luke 1:46–55; Millie Rieth, 1940–2003.
Music: Millie Rieth.
Text and music © 1977, Mildred F. Rieth. Published by OCP. All rights reserved.

# 481     HAIL MARY: GENTLE WOMAN

Intro: Cantor

Hail Mary, full of grace, the Lord is with you.
Blessed are you among women and
blest is the fruit of your womb, Jesus.

Holy Mary, Mother of God,
pray for us sinners now
and at the hour of death. Amen.

Refrain: All

Gen-tle wom-an,    qui-et light,    morn-ing
star,    so strong and bright,    gen-tle
Moth-er,    peace-ful dove,    teach us
wis-dom;    teach us love.

Verses: All

1. You were cho - sen    by the Fa - ther;
2. Bless-ed are you    a-mong wom-en,

1. you were cho - sen for the Son. You were
2. blest in turn all wom-en, too. Bless-ed

1. cho - sen from all wom-en and for
2. they with peace - ful spir-its. Bless-ed

to Refrain

1. wom-an, shin-ing one.
2. they with gen - tle hearts.

Text: Based on Luke 1:28, 42; Carey Landry, b. 1944.
Music: Carey Landry
Text and music © 1975, 1978, Carey Landry and OCP. All rights reserved.

## SONG OF MARY

1. Let us sing the prais-es of Ma-ry, daugh-ter of Da-vid's
2. Let us sing the prais-es of Ma-ry, cho-sen as bless-ed
3. Let us sing the prais-es of Ma-ry, wom-an of strong and
4. Let us sing the prais-es of Ma-ry, pierced by the sword of
5. Let us sing the prais-es of Ma-ry, friend of the poor in

1. ho-ly line, she who heard the voice of an an-gel
2. from the least, she who heard the song of the an-gels
3. stead-fast love. She who raised the Sav-ior of na-tions
4. sor-row's pain, she who saw the child of her lov-ing
5. ev-'ry age, she who saw her Son and her Sav-ior

1. tell-ing the plan of God's de-sign, how in wis-dom's
2. fill-ing the night with heav-en's peace. When the prom-ised
3. held in her arms the Son of God. She who knew the
4. nailed on a cross to die in shame. Though his friends would
5. ris-en in glo-ry from the grave. Sin and death shall

1. ho-ly sight she would moth-er heav-en's Christ.
2. time had come she gave birth to God's own Son.
3. Fa-ther's grace taught her Son to know God's face.
4. flee in fear she re-mained for-ev-er near.
5. reign no more; Christ has o-pened heav-en's door.

1–5. Bless-ed be the name of Ma-ry, she who trust-ed the

1–5. love of God.

Text: 98 98 77 88; Dan Schutte, b. 1947.
Music: SONG OF MARY; Dan Schutte.

# 483 AVE MARIA

Text and music: Gregory Norbet, b. 1940, © 1994, Gregory Norbet. Published by OCP. All rights reserved.

# O Sanctissima/O Most Holy One

1. O san - ctís - si - ma, O pi - ís - si - ma,
2. Tu so - lá - ti - um Et re - fú - gi - um,
3. Ec - ce dé - bi - les, Per - quam flé - bi - les,
4. Vir - go ré - spi - ce, Ma - ter, ád - spi - ce,

1. O San - ctís - si - ma, Ho - ly Queen of Love,
2. O most beau - ti - ful, And most mer - ci - ful,
3. Ma - ry, Mys - tic Rose, Font that o - ver-flows,
4. Ma - ry, plead for us; In - ter - cede for us.

1. Dul - cis vir - go Ma - rí - a!
2. Vir - go ma - ter Ma - rí - a!
3. Sal - va nos, _____ Ma - rí - a!
4. Au - di nos, _____ Ma - rí - a!

1. Dear - est Vir - gin and Moth - er.
2. Gate of Heav - en, we hail you.
3. Seat of Wis - dom, we greet you.
4. Come and lead us to Je - sus.

1. Ma - ter a - má - ta, In - te - me - rá - ta,
2. Quid - quid op - tá - mus, Per _____ te spe - rá - mus,
3. Tol - le lan - guó - res, Sa - na do - ló - res,
4. Tu _____ me - di - cí - nam, Por - tas di - ví - nam;

1. Blest by ev - 'ry na - tion, Ev - 'ry gen - er - a - tion:
2. Star of our sal - va - tion, Crown of all cre - a - tion:
3. Moth - er of our Sav - ior, Full of grace and fa - vor:
4. Moth - er in our sad - ness, Moth - er in our glad - ness:

1-4. O - ra, o - ra pro no - bis!
1-4. O - ra, o - ra pro no - bis!

Text: 55 7 D; Latin verse 1 fr. Herder's *Stimmen der Völker in Liedern*, 1807; verses 2–4 fr. *Arundel Hymnal*, 1905.
English tr. by Harry Hagan, OSB, b. 1947, © 2003, St. Meinrad Archabbey. Published by OCP. All rights reserved.
Music: O DU FRÖHLICHE; Tattersall's *Improved Psalmody*, 1794.

**485**     SALVE, REGINA/HAIL, MARY

Sal - ve, Re - gí - na, ma - ter mi - se - ri - cór - di - ae: Vi - ta dul -
*Hail, Ma - ry, moth - er and queen of ten - der mer - cy, our life, our*

cé - do et spes no - stra, sal - ve. Ad te cla - má - mus,
*com - fort, and our hope, we hail you. From this for - eign land*

éx - su - les, fí - li - i He - vae. Ad te sus - pi - rá - mus,
*Eve's sons and daugh - ters cry to you. So lost, so full of fear,*

ge - mén - tes et flen - tes in hac la - cri - má - rum val - le.
*we mourn, we grieve, we sigh from this tear - ful vale of ex - ile.*

E - ia er - go, Ad - vo - cá - ta no - stra, il - los tu - os mi -
*Ah, then, our help, our ad - vo - cate and guide, turn now to us the*

se - ri - cór - des ó - cu - los ad nos con - vér - te.
*gaze of your all - lov - ing eyes, so full of mer - cy.*

Et Je - sum, be - ne - dí - ctum fruc - tum ven - tris tu - i,
*And Je - sus— your Son, and Lord, your womb's most bless - ed fruit—*

no - bis post hoc ex - sí - li - um os - tén - de.
*show him to us when we com - plete our so - journ.*

O cle - mens, O pi - a,
*O gen - tle, O lov - ing,*

O _____ dul - cis . Vir - go Ma - ri - a.
O _____ be - lov - ed, O Vir - gin Ma - ry.

## AVE MARIA

**486**

A - ve, Ma - rí - a, grá - ti - a ple - na,
A - ve, Ma - rí - a: Hail, Ma - ry, full of grace,

Dó - mi - nus te - cum, be - ne - dí - cta tu
the Lord is with you. O how blest are you

in mu - li - é - ri - bus, et be - ne - dí -
a - mong all earth's wom - en. And how tru - ly

ctus fruc - tus ven - tris tu - i, Je - sus.
blest is the fruit of your womb, Je - sus.

San - cta Ma - rí - a, Ma - ter De - i,
O ho - ly Ma - ry, God's own moth - er,

o - ra pro no - bis pec - ca - tó - ri - bus,
pray ___ for us, your chil - dren who stray from the way,

nunc et in ___ ho - ra mor - tis no - strae. A - men.
now and in that fin - al hour when we come to die. A - men.

**487**     HOLY IS HIS NAME

Verses

1. My soul proclaims the greatness of the Lord,
2. He has mercy in ev - 'ry gen - er - a - tion.

He
1. and my spir-it ex-ults in God my Sav-ior. For he has
2. has re-vealed his pow-er and his glo-ry. He has cast

1. looked with mer-cy on my low-li-ness, and my name will be for-
2. down the might-y in their ar-ro-gance, and has lift-ed up the

1. ev - er ex-alt-ed. For the might-y God has done great
2. meek and the low-ly. He has come to help his ser-vant

1. things for me, and his mer-cy will reach from age to
2. Is - ra - el; he re-mem-bers his prom-ise to our

Refrain

1. age. And ho - ly, ho - ly, ho-ly is his name.
2. fa-thers.

**488**     IN HIS TEMPLE NOW BEHOLD HIM

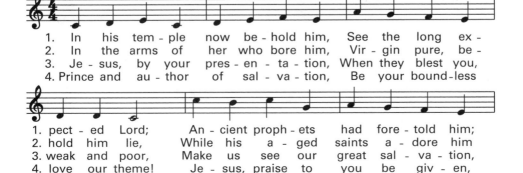

1. In his tem - ple now be - hold him, See the long ex-
2. In the arms of her who bore him, Vir - gin pure, be-
3. Je - sus, by your pres - en - ta - tion, When they blest you,
4. Prince and au - thor of sal - va - tion, Be your bound-less

1. pect - ed Lord; An - cient proph - ets had fore - told him;
2. hold him lie, While his a - ged saints a - dore him
3. weak and poor, Make us see our great sal - va - tion,
4. love our theme! Je - sus, praise to you be giv - en,

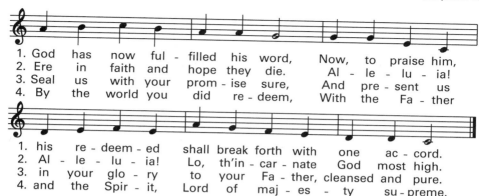

1. God has now ful - filled his word, Now, to praise him,
2. Ere in faith and hope they die. Al - le - lu - ia!
3. Seal us with your prom - ise sure, And pre - sent us
4. By the world you did re - deem, With the Fa - ther

1. his re - deem - ed shall break forth with one ac - cord.
2. Al - le - lu - ia! Lo, th'in - car - nate God most high.
3. in your glo - ry to your Fa - ther, cleansed and pure.
4. and the Spir - it, Lord of maj - es - ty su - preme.

Text: 87 87 87; Luke 2:22–24; verses 1–3, Henry J. Pyle, 1825–1903; verse 4, William Cooke, 1821–1894.
Music: ST. THOMAS (TANTUM ERGO); John F. Wade, 1711–1786.

## HOLY PATRON, THEE SALUTING 489

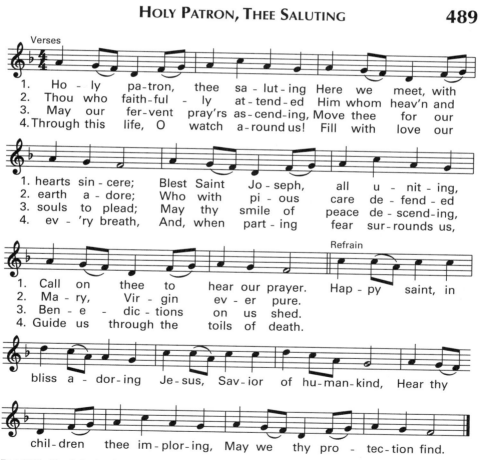

Verses

1. Ho - ly pa - tron, thee sa - lut - ing Here we meet, with
2. Thou who faith - ful - ly at - tend - ed Him whom heav'n and
3. May our fer - vent pray'rs as - cend - ing, Move thee for our
4. Through this life, O watch a - round us! Fill with love our

1. hearts sin - cere; Blest Saint Jo - seph, all u - nit - ing,
2. earth a - dore; Who with pi - ous care de - fend - ed
3. souls to plead; May thy smile of peace de - scend - ing,
4. ev - 'ry breath, And, when part - ing fear sur - rounds us,

Refrain

1. Call on thee to hear our prayer. Hap - py saint, in
2. Ma - ry, Vir - gin ev - er pure.
3. Ben - e - dic - tions on us shed.
4. Guide us through the toils of death.

bliss a - dor - ing Je - sus, Sav - ior of hu - man - kind, Hear thy

chil - dren thee im - plor - ing, May we thy pro - tec - tion find.

Text: 87 87 with refrain; American, ca. 1843; Anon.
Music: PLEADING SAVIOR; *Christian Lyre*, 1830.

## 490    Come Now, and Praise the Humble Saint

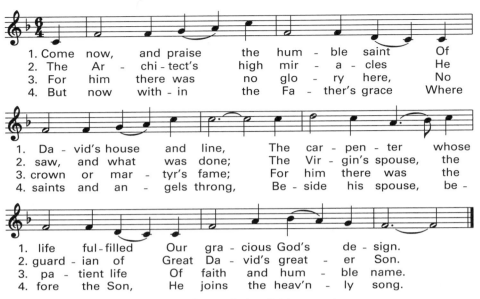

1. Come now, and praise the hum - ble saint Of
2. The Ar - chi - tect's high mir - a - cles He
3. For him there was no glo - ry here, No
4. But now with - in the Fa - ther's grace Where

1. Da - vid's house and line, The car - pen - ter whose
2. saw, and what was done; The Vir - gin's spouse, the
3. crown or mar - tyr's fame; For him there was the
4. saints and an - gels throng, Be - side his spouse, be -

1. life ful - filled Our gra - cious God's de - sign.
2. guard - ian of Great Da - vid's great - er Son.
3. pa - tient life Of faith and hum - ble name.
4. fore the Son, He joins the heav'n - ly song.

Text: CM; George W. Williams, b. 1922, © 1979, The Hymn Society. All rights reserved.
    Administered by Hope Publishing Co. Used with permission.
Music: LAND OF REST; Trad. American Melody.

## 491    A Just Man Honored from Above

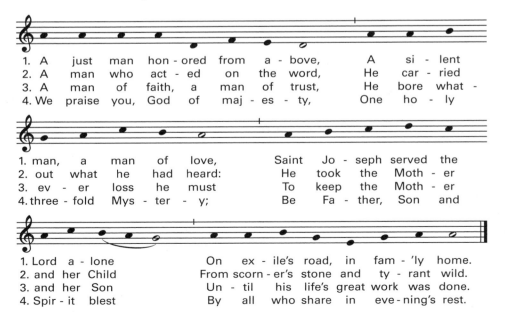

1. A just man hon - ored from a - bove, A si - lent
2. A man who act - ed on the word, He car - ried
3. A man of faith, a man of trust, He bore what -
4. We praise you, God of maj - es - ty, One ho - ly

1. man, a man of love, Saint Jo - seph served the
2. out what he had heard: He took the Moth - er
3. ev - er loss he must To keep the Moth - er
4. three - fold Mys - ter - y; Be Fa - ther, Son and

1. Lord a - lone On ex - ile's road, in fam - 'ly home.
2. and her Child From scorn - er's stone and ty - rant wild.
3. and her Son Un - til his life's great work was done.
4. Spir - it blest By all who share in eve - ning's rest.

Text: LM; Genevieve Glen, OSB, b. 1945, © 1998, The Benedictine Nuns of the Abbey of St. Walburga.
    Published by OCP. All rights reserved.
Music: JESU DULCIS MEMORIA; Chant, Mode I.

## PRAISE WE THE LORD THIS DAY

**492**

1. Praise we the Lord this day, This day so long fore-told, Whose prom-ise shone with cheer-ing ray On wait-ing saints of old.
2. The Proph-et gave the sign For faith-ful folk to read: A vir-gin, born of Da-vid's line, Shall bear the prom-ised Seed.
3. Ask not how this should be, But wor-ship and a-dore Like her whom God's own maj-es-ty Came down to shad-ow o'er.
4. She meek-ly bowed her head To hear the gra-cious word, Ma-ry, the pure and low-ly maid, The fa-vored of the Lord.
5. Bless-ed shall be her name In all the Church on earth Through whom that won-drous mer-cy came, The in-car-nate Sav-ior's birth.
6. O Christ, the Vir-gin's Son, We praise you and a-dore, You are with God the Fa-ther One And Spir-it ev-er-more.

Text: SM; Matthew 1:23; *Hymns for the Festivals and Saints' Days*, 1846.
Music: SWABIA; Johann M. Speiss, 1715–1772; adapt. by William H. Havergal, 1793–1870.

## THE GOD WHOM EARTH AND SEA AND SKY

**493**

1. The God whom earth and sea and sky A-dore and praise and mag-ni-fy, Whose might they claim, whose love they tell, In Ma-ry's bod-y comes to dwell.
2. O Moth-er blest! the cho-sen shrine Where-in the ar-chi-tect di-vine, Whose hand con-tains the earth and sky, Has come in hu-man form to lie.
3. Blest in the mes-sage Ga-briel brought; Blest in the work the Spir-it wrought; Most blest, to bring to hu-man birth The long de-sired of all the earth.
4. O Lord, the Vir-gin-born, to you E-ter-nal praise and laud are due, Whom with the Fa-ther we a-dore And Spir-it blest for ev-er-more.

Text: LM; *Quem terra, pontus, aethera*; Venantius Honorius Fortunatus, ca. 530–609; tr. by John M. Neale, 1818–1866, alt.
Music: EISENACH; melody fr. *Das ander Theil des andern newen Operis Geistlicher Deutscher Lieder*, 1605;
adapt. by Johann Hermann Schein, 1586–1630.

## 494     THE GREAT FORERUNNER OF THE MORN

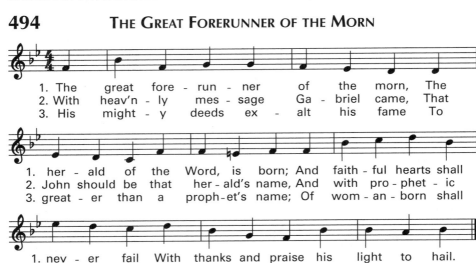

1. The great fore-run-ner of the morn, The her-ald of the Word, is born; And faith-ful hearts shall nev-er fail With thanks and praise his light to hail.
2. With heav'n-ly mes-sage Ga-briel came, That John should be that her-ald's name, And with pro-phet-ic ut-t'rance told His ac-tions great and man-i-fold.
3. His might-y deeds ex-alt his fame To great-er than a proph-et's name; Of wom-an-born shall nev-er be A great-er proph-et than was he.

Text: LM; *Praecursor altus luminis*; St. Bede the Venerable, 673–735; tr. by John M. Neale, 1818–1866, alt.
Music: WINCHESTER NEW; Georg Wittwe's *Musikalisches Hand-Buch*, Hamburg, 1690;
    adapt. by William H. Havergal, 1793–1870.

## 495     TWO NOBLE SAINTS

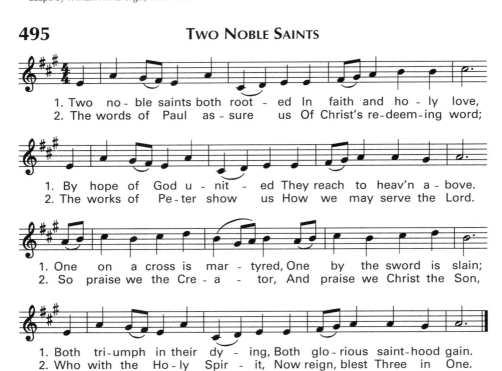

1. Two no-ble saints both root-ed In faith and ho-ly love, By hope of God u-nit-ed They reach to heav'n a-bove. One on a cross is mar-tyred, One by the sword is slain; Both tri-umph in their dy-ing, Both glo-rious saint-hood gain.
2. The words of Paul as-sure us Of Christ's re-deem-ing word; The works of Pe-ter show us How we may serve the Lord. So praise we the Cre-a-tor, And praise we Christ the Son, Who with the Ho-ly Spir-it, Now reign, blest Three in One.

Text: 76 76 D; based on *Decora lux aeternitatis auream*; Anne K. LeCroy, b. 1930, © Anne K. LeCroy.
    All rights reserved. Used with permission.
Music: ELLACOMBE; *Gesangbuch der Herzogl, Wirtembergischen Katholischen Hofkapelle*, 1784, alt.;
    adapt. fr. Würth's *Katholisches Gesangbuch*, 1863.

## TRANSFIGURATION

**496**

1. Je - sus, on the moun-tain peak, stands a - lone in glo - ry
2. Trem - bling at his feet we saw Mo - ses and E - li - jah
3. Swift the cloud of glo - ry came, God, pro-claim-ing in its
4. Je - sus is the cho - sen one, liv - ing hope of ev - 'ry

1. blaz - ing. Let us, if we dare to speak, join the
2. speak - ing. All the proph-ets and the law shout through
3. thun - der, Je - sus as the Son by name! Na - tions,
4. na - tion, hear and heed him, ev - 'ry - one; sing, with

1. saints and an - gels prais - ing.
2. them their joy - ful greet - ing:
3. cry a - loud in won - der: Praise and glo - ry,
4. earth and all cre - a - tion: *Al - le - lu - ia,

1-4. praise and glo - ry, praise and glo - ry to our Lord!
1-4. al - le - lu - ia, al - le - lu - ia!

1. Let us, if we dare to speak, join the saints and an - gels
2. All the pro-phets and the law shout through them their joy - ful
3. Je - sus as the Son by name: na - tions, cry a - loud in
4. Hear and heed him, ev - 'ry - one; sing with earth and all cre-

*(Fine)* Interlude    6

1. prais - ing.
2. greet - ing.
3. won - der.
4. a - tion.

*Outside the season of Lent

Text: Brian Wren, b. 1936, © 1977, 1995, Hope Publishing Co. All rights reserved. Used with permission.
Music: Ricky Manalo, CSP, b. 1965, © 2002, Ricky Manalo, CSP. Published by OCP. All rights reserved.

**497**      'TIS GOOD, LORD, TO BE HERE

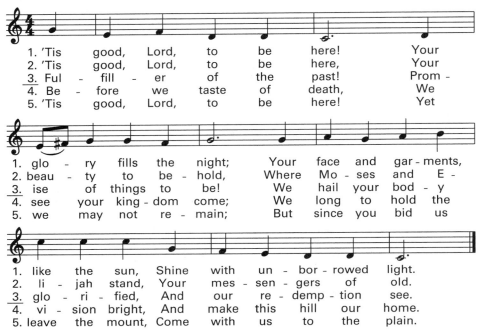

1. 'Tis good, Lord, to be here! Your glo - ry fills the night; Your face and gar - ments, like the sun, Shine with un - bor - rowed light.
2. 'Tis good, Lord, to be here, Your beau - ty to be - hold, Where Mo - ses and E - li - jah stand, Your mes - sen - gers of old.
3. Ful - fill - er of the past! Prom - ise of things to be! We hail your bod - y glo - ri - fied, And our re - demp - tion see.
4. Be - fore we taste of death, We see your king - dom come; We long to hold the vi - sion bright, And make this hill our home.
5. 'Tis good, Lord, to be here! Yet we may not re - main; But since you bid us leave the mount, Come with us to the plain.

Text: SM; based on Luke 9:32–33; Joseph A. Robinson, 1858–1933, alt., Esmé D. E. Bird.
Music: SWABIA; Johann M. Speiss, 1715–1772; adapt. by William H. Havergal, 1793–1870.

**498**      HAIL, HOLY QUEEN

Verses

1. Hail, ho - ly Queen en - throned a - bove, O Ma - ri - a! Hail, Queen of mer - cy and of love, O Ma - ri - a!
2. Our life, our sweet - ness here be - low, O Ma - ri - a! Our hope in sor - row and in woe, O Ma - ri - a!
3. As ex - iles all to you we cry, O Ma - ri - a! Come, soothe with hope our mis - er - y, O Ma - ri - a!
4. Turn then, most gra - cious ad - vo - cate, O Ma - ri - a! Toward us your eyes com - pas - sion - ate, O Ma - ri - a!
5. O gen - tle, lov - ing, ho - ly one, O Ma - ri - a! Make us each day more like your Son, O Ma - ri - a!
6. And when from death to life we've passed, O Ma - ri - a! Show us your Son, our Lord, at last, O Ma - ri - a!

**Refrain**

Tri - umph, all ye cher - u - bim, Sing with us, ye
ser - a - phim! Heav'n and earth re - sound the hymn:
Sal - ve, sal - ve, sal - ve, Re - gi - na!

Text: 84 84 with refrain; *Salve, Regina, mater misericordiae,* ca. 1080;
verses 1, 2, 5 and refrain tr. anon. in *Roman Hymnal,* 1884; verses 3, 4, 6, para.
Music: SALVE REGINA COELITUM; Melchior Ludwig Herold, 1753–1810; *Choralmelodien zum Heiligen Gesänge,* 1808.

## BRIGHT AS THE SUN, FAIR AS THE MOON 499

1. Bright as the sun, fair as the moon, She reigns, who
2. Night is not dark where she stands bright, The wom - an
3. O God, we read by her love's flame The Word in

1. held with - in her womb The Word made flesh, God's
2. robed in liv - ing light, Crowned with the stars, who
3. whom we sing your name: We bow be - fore your

1. Son made hers, To whom the an - gel host de - fers.
2. served on earth The Word to whom her faith gave birth.
3. maj - es - ty, One ho - ly, three - fold Mys - ter - y.

Text: LM; Genevieve Glen, OSB, b. 1945, © 1998, The Benedictine Nuns of the Abbey of St. Walburga.
Published by OCP. All rights reserved.
Music: TRURO; William's *Psalmodia Evangelica, Part II,* 1789.

**500**  **LIFT HIGH THE CROSS**

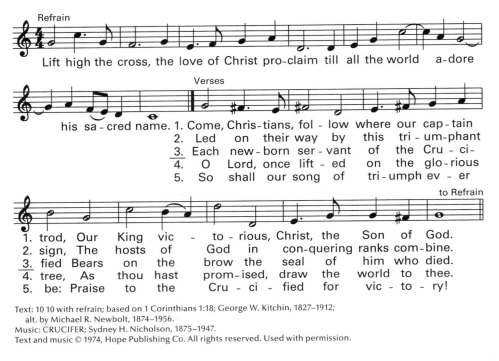

Lift high the cross, the love of Christ pro-claim till all the world a-dore his sa-cred name.

1. Come, Chris-tians, fol-low where our cap-tain trod, Our King vic - to - rious, Christ, the Son of God.
2. Led on their way by this tri - um-phant sign, The hosts of God in con-quering ranks com-bine.
3. Each new-born ser - vant of the Cru - ci-fied Bears on the brow the seal of him who died.
4. O Lord, once lift - ed on the glo-rious tree, As thou hast prom-ised, draw the world to thee.
5. So shall our song of tri - umph ev - er be: Praise to the Cru - ci - fied for vic - to - ry!

Text: 10 10 with refrain; based on 1 Corinthians 1:18; George W. Kitchin, 1827–1912;
    alt. by Michael R. Newbolt, 1874–1956.
Music: CRUCIFER; Sydney H. Nicholson, 1875–1947.
Text and music © 1974, Hope Publishing Co. All rights reserved. Used with permission.

**501**  **TAKE UP YOUR CROSS**

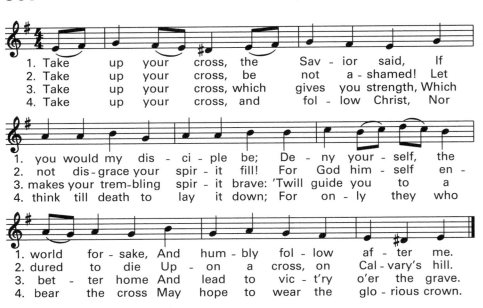

1. Take up your cross, the Sav - ior said, If you would my dis - ci - ple be; De - ny your-self, the world for - sake, And hum - bly fol - low af - ter me.
2. Take up your cross, be not a - shamed! Let not dis - grace your spir - it fill! For God him - self en - dured to die Up - on a cross, on Cal - vary's hill.
3. Take up your cross, which gives you strength, Which makes your trem-bling spir - it brave: 'Twill guide you to a bet - ter home And lead to vic - t'ry o'er the grave.
4. Take up your cross, and fol - low Christ, Nor think till death to lay it down; For on - ly they who bear the cross May hope to wear the glo - rious crown.

Text: LM; Charles W. Everest, 1814–1877, alt.
Music: ERHALT UNS, HERR; J. Klug's *Geistliche Lieder*, Wittenberg, 1543;
    adapt. by Johann Sebastian Bach, 1685–1750, alt.

# TAKE UP OUR CROSS

Verse 1

1. Behold the wood that bears our name;
behold the nails that hold our sin.

The tree from which salvation blooms;
the death by which we're born again.

We take up our cross and fol - low him; we lay down our lives

that we might live. We car-ry the hope of Christ with - in;

we take up our cross and fol - low him.

Verse 2

2. We embrace the sacrifice,
and walk the path we cannot see.

The burdens of this world made light;
by blood and thorn we are redeemed.

Text and music: Curtis Stephan, b. 1973, Sarah Hart, b. 1968, and Marc Byrd, b. 1970,
© 2008, Blue Raft Music, Meaux Mercy, Curtis Stephan and Sarah Hart. All rights reserved.
Used with permission of EMI CMG Publishing and spiritandsong.com®, a division of OCP.

# LITANY OF THE SAINTS

Repeat each invocation immediately after the Priest or Cantor:

Lord, have mer-cy. Christ, have mer-cy. Lord, have mer-cy.

Invocations

Responses: Sing 1-5 four times; 6 two times

(Saint Invocation)
("Lord, be merciful,")
("Be merciful to us sinners.")

1-4. pray___ for___ us.
5. Lord, de - liv - er us, we pray.
6. Lord, we ask you, hear our prayer.

1-4. pray___ for___ us.
5. Lord, de - liv - er us, we pray.
6. Lord, we ask you, hear our prayer.

to Responses

1-5. All you ho - ly men and wom - en, pray for us.
6. Christ,___ hear us. Christ,___ gra-cious - ly hear us.

Text © 2010, ICEL. All rights reserved. Used with permission.
Music: John D. Becker, b. 1953, © 1987, 2011, John D. Becker. Published by OCP. All rights reserved.

## 504

### FOR ALL THE SAINTS

1. For all the saints who from their la - bors
2. You were their rock, their for - tress and their
3. O may your sol - diers, faith - ful, true, and
4. O blest com - mun - ion, fam - i - ly di -
5. And when the strife is fierce, the war - fare
6. The gold - en eve - ning bright - ens in the
7. But then there breaks a yet more glo - rious
8. From earth's wide bounds, from o - cean's far - thest

1. rest, All who _____ by faith be - fore the
2. might; _____ You, Lord, their cap - tain in the
3. bold, _____ Fight as the saints who no - bly
4. vine! _____ We fee - bly strug - gle, they in
5. long, _____ Steals on the ear the dis - tant
6. west; _____ Soon, soon to faith - ful war - riors
7. day: The saints _____ tri - um - phant rise in
8. coast, Through gates _____ of pearl streams in the

1. world con - fessed, Your name, O _____
2. well - fought fight; _____ You, in the
3. fought of old, And win, with _____
4. glo - ry shine! Yet all are _____
5. tri - umph song, And hearts are _____
6. comes their rest; _____ Sweet is the
7. bright ar - ray; The king of _____
8. count - less host, _____ Sing - ing to

1. Je - sus, be for - ev - er blest.
2. dark - ness drear, their one true light.
3. them, the vic - tor's crown of gold.
4. one with - in your great de - sign.
5. brave a - gain, and arms are strong.
6. calm of par - a - dise the blest.
7. glo - ry pass - es on his way.
8. Fa - ther, Son, and Ho - ly Ghost:

1-8. Al - le - lu - ia! Al - le - lu - ia!

Text: 10 10 10 with alleluias; William W. How, 1823–1897, alt.
Music: SINE NOMINE; *English Hymnal*, 1906; Ralph Vaughan Williams, 1872–1958.

# Ye Watchers and Ye Holy Ones

1. Ye watch-ers and ye ho-ly ones, Bright ser-aphs,
2. O high-er than the cher-u-bim, More glo-rious
3. Re-spond, ye souls in end-less rest, Ye pa-tri-
4. O friends, in glad-ness let us sing, Ce-les-tial

1. cher-u-bim, and thrones, Raise the glad strain, Al-le-lu-ia!
2. than the ser-a-phim, Lead their prais-es, Al-le-lu-ia!
3. archs and proph-ets blest, Al-le-lu-ia, Al-le-lu-ia!
4. an-thems ech-o-ing, Al-le-lu-ia, Al-le-lu-ia!

1. Cry out, do-min-ions, prince-doms, powers, Vir-tues, arch-
2. O bear-er of the e-ter-nal Word, Most gra-cious,
3. Ye ho-ly Twelve, ye mar-tyrs strong, All saints tri-
4. To God the Fa-ther, God the Son, And God the

1. an-gels, an-gels' choirs,
2. mag-ni-fy the Lord,   Al-le-lu-ia, Al-le-lu-ia,
3. um-phant, raise in song,
4. Spir-it, Three-in-One,

1-4. Al-le-lu-ia, Al-le-lu-ia, Al-le-lu-ia!

Text: LM with alleluias; *English Hymnal*, 1906; John A. Riley, 1858–1945.
Music: LASST UNS ERFREUEN; *Auserlesene Catholische Geistliche Kirchengesänge*, Cologne, 1623.

## 506      LITANY

## 507      LUX AETERNA LITANY

Litany of Remembrance
(Cantor sings names from the Book of Remembrance)

to Refrain

All: We re-mem - ber.

## Church of God, Elect and Glorious 508

1. Church of God, e - lect and glo - rious, ho - ly na - tion,
2. God has called you out of dark - ness in - to his most
3. Once you were an al - ien peo - ple, strang-ers to God's
4. Church of God, e - lect and ho - ly, be the peo - ple

1. cho - sen race; called as God's own spe - cial
2. mar - v'lous light, brought his truth to life with -
3. heart of love; but he brought you home in
4. he in - tends; strong in faith and swift to

1. peo - ple, roy - al priests and heirs of grace: know the
2. in you, turned your blind - ness in - to sight. Let your
3. mer - cy, cit - i - zens of heav'n a - bove. Let his
4. an - swer each com - mand your mas - ter sends: roy - al

1. pur - pose of your call - ing, show to all God's
2. light so shine a - round you that God's name is
3. love flow out to oth - ers, let them feel a
4. priests, ful - fill your call - ing through your sac - ri -

1. might - y deeds; tell of love which knows no
2. glo - ri - fied; and all find fresh hope and
3. Fa - ther's care; that they too may know his
4. fice and prayer; give your lives in joy - ful

1. lim - its, grace which meets all hu - man needs.
2. pur - pose in Christ Je - sus cru - ci - fied.
3. wel - come and his count - less bless - ings share.
4. ser - vice, sing his praise, his love de - clare.

**509**      **I Saw Water Flowing**

1. When your hour had come and they pierced you, Lord,
2. Come to Christ the Lord, the ___ liv - ing stone, re -
3. Not to us, O Lord, but to you all praise,
4. May this house of prayer be a home to all.
5. May this church em - bod - y your pres - ence, Lord:

1. blood and wa - ter flowed forth ___ from your side.
2. ject - ed once but now ___ the cor - ner - stone.
3. for a - part from you ___ we build in vain.
4. May the love of Christ reign with - in these walls,
5. help for the op - pressed, Good News for the poor.

1. With great love you gave your - self for
2. Joined to him, we are God's dwell - ing
3. Help us live this ho - ly mys - ter -
4. so the ones who knock find wel - come
5. Use our hands to build your reign of

1. us! Who can tell the great love by which you
2. place, priest - ly peo - ple and in - stru - ments of
3. y: "It is no long - er I who live, but
4. here and all those who are thirst - ing re - ceive
5. peace; give us vi - sion to fash - ion a more

to Refrain

1. brought your Church to birth!
2. God's re - deem - ing grace.
3. Christ who lives in me."
4. liv - ing wa - ter here.
5. just so - ci - e - ty.

Text: Refrain based on Ezekiel 47:1–2, 9; verses based on John 16:21; 17:1; 19:34; 1 Peter 2:4–9; Psalm 127:1; Galatians 2:20; Bob Hurd, b. 1950.
Music: Bob Hurd.

# HOLY IS THE TEMPLE

**Refrain**

Ho - ly is the tem-ple of the LORD, it is the hand-i-work, the dwell-ing place of God.

**Verses**

1. How love - ly your dwell-ing place, LORD of hosts.
2. Spar-rows and swal-lows build their nests
3. How bless - ed are those who live in your house.
4. Our God is a ram - part and a shield;

1. I long and I yearn for the courts of the
2. with - in your house where they shel - ter their
3. In un - ceas - ing song they of - fer you
4. be-stow - er of grace, hold - ing back no good

1. LORD, my whole be - ing cries out to God,
2. young, be - side your al - tars, LORD,
3. praise. Hap - py those who find strength in you,
4. thing from those who walk righ - teous - ly;

*to Refrain*

1. I sing out with joy to the liv - ing God.
2. your al - tars, my king and my God.
3. who hold in their hearts the way to Zi - on.
4. hap-py those, O LORD, who trust in you.

Text: Based on Psalm 84:2–6, 12–13; Bob Hurd, b. 1950.
Music: Bob Hurd.

## 511     O HOLY MARY

**Refrain**

O ho - ly Dwell-ing Place of God. O ho - ly Tem-ple of the
Word. O ho - ly Ma - ry, ho-ly Moth-er of God.

**Verses**

1. O ra - diant star of heav - en, il - lum - in - ing the night;
2. O blest be-yond all oth - ers, of ev - 'ry land and race,
3. From heav'n the an - gel Ga-bri - el an-nounced the an - cient plan
4. With joy be-yond all meas - ure you cared for God's own son
5. Ex - qui - site was your sor - row, un - e-qualed was the loss
6. All praise and ad - o - ra - tion we sing now to your son

to Refrain

1. re - flec - tion of the Son, our source of life and light.
2. pos - sess - ing in your soul the full-ness of God's grace.
3. and hum - bly you ac - cept-ed to bear the God-made - man.
4. and pon-dered in your heart the new age now be - gun.
5. you suf-fered when your son was raised up - on the cross.
6. who reigns in high - est heav-en and has the vic - t'ry won.

## 512     IMMACULATE MARY

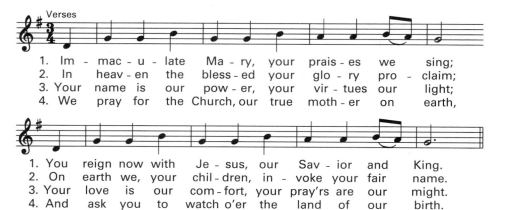

**Verses**

1. Im - mac - u - late Ma - ry, your prais - es we sing;
2. In heav - en the bless - ed your glo - ry pro - claim;
3. Your name is our pow - er, your vir - tues our light;
4. We pray for the Church, our true moth - er on earth,

1. You reign now with Je - sus, our Sav - ior and King.
2. On earth we, your chil - dren, in - voke your fair name.
3. Your love is our com - fort, your pray'rs are our might.
4. And ask you to watch o'er the land of our birth.

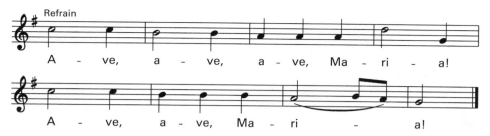

Refrain

A - ve, a - ve, a - ve, Ma - ri - a!

A - ve, a - ve, Ma - ri - a!

Text: 11 11 with refrain; anon. in *Parochial Hymn Book*, Boston, 1897;
rev. of *Hail Virgin of virgins* by Jeremiah Cummings, 1814–1866, alt.
Music: LOURDES HYMN; trad. Pyrenean Melody; pub. Grenoble, 1882; alt. by Augustus Edmonds Tozer, 1857–1910.

## RITUAL MUSIC

### SIGNING OF THE SENSES

# 513

Verse 1: Priest

1. Receive the cross on your forehead. It is Christ himself who now strengthens you with this sign of his love. Learn to know and follow him.

Response

By this sign may you re-ceive Christ's love and al-ways fol-low him.

Verses 2-6: Priest

2. Receive the sign of the cross on your ears, that you may hear the voice of the Lord.
3. Receive the sign of the cross on your eyes, that you may see the glory of God.
4. Receive the sign of the cross on your lips, that you may respond to the word of God.
5. Receive the sign of the cross over your heart, that Christ may dwell there by faith.
6. Receive the sign of the cross on your shoulders that you may bear the gentle yoke of Christ.

Blessing: Priest

7. I sign you with the sign of eternal life in the name of the Father, and of the Son, and of the Holy Spirit.

Final Response

A - men. A - men. A - men.

## 514     YOU HAVE CALLED US

Refrain: 1st time: Cantor, All repeat; thereafter: All

You have called us by our name. We be - long to you.

You have called us by our name and we are yours.

**Verses**

1. You have cho - sen us to be mem - bers
2. You will lead us to your light, walk be -
3. You will hold us when we fall, give new
4. You will nour - ish, you will lead, giv - ing
5. Through our shar - ing here to - day may our

1. of your fam - i - ly. In your love you have cre -
2. fore us through the night. You will guide us on our
3. strength to hear your call. You will nev - er be be -
4. ev - 'ry gift we need, for your reign will be es -
5. faith and life con - vey Christ our light and Christ our

*to Refrain*

1. at - ed us to live in u - ni - ty.
2. jour - ney. You will keep our vi - sion bright.
3. yond us, for your love is all in all.
4. tab - lished from the small - est of all seeds.
5. vi - sion, Christ our pur - pose, Christ our way.

## 515     FLOW RIVER FLOW

**Refrain**

Flow riv - er flow, flow o - ver me. O liv - ing wa - ter,

poured out for free; O liv - ing wa - ter, flow o - ver me.

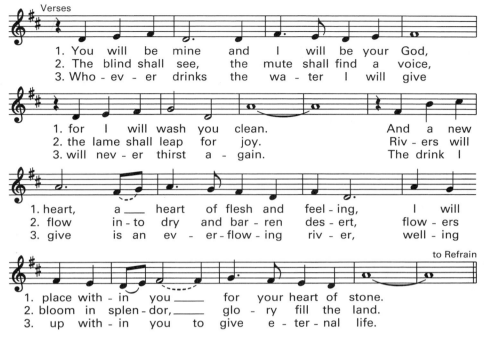

**Verses**

1. You will be mine and I will be your God, for I will wash you clean. And a new heart, a \_\_ heart of flesh and feel - ing, I will place with - in you \_\_\_ for your heart of stone.
2. The blind shall see, the mute shall find a voice, the lame shall leap for joy. Riv - ers will flow in - to dry and bar - ren des - ert, bloom in splen - dor, \_\_\_ glo - ry fill the land.
3. Who - ev - er drinks the wa - ter I will give will nev - er thirst a - gain. The drink I give is an ev - er - flow - ing riv - er, well - ing up with - in you to give e - ter - nal life.

to Refrain

Text: Based on Ezekiel 11:19, 20; Isaiah 35:1–6; John 4:7–15; Bob Hurd, b. 1950.
Music: Bob Hurd.
Text and music © 1986, Bob Hurd. Published by OCP. All rights reserved.

## Baptized in Water  516

1. Bap - tized in wa - ter, Sealed by the Spir - it, Cleansed by the blood of Christ our King: Heirs of sal - va - tion, Trust - ing his prom - ise, Faith - ful - ly now God's praise we sing.
2. Bap - tized in wa - ter, Sealed by the Spir - it, Dead in the tomb with Christ our King: One with his ris - ing, Freed and for - giv - en, Thank - ful - ly now God's praise we sing.
3. Bap - tized in wa - ter, Sealed by the Spir - it, Marked with the sign of Christ our King: Born of one Fa - ther, We are his chil - dren, Joy - ful - ly now God's praise we sing.

Text: 55 8 D; Michael Saward, b. 1932, © 1982, The Jubilate Group. All rights reserved.
Administered by Hope Publishing Co. Used with permission.
Music: BUNESSAN; Trad. Gaelic Melody.

**517**  RIVER OF GLORY

Refrain

Riv - er of glo - ry, springs of our birth, flood of God's
rich - es poured on the earth. We are born from the dark - ness
and clothed in the light! We are bathed in the glo - ry of
1-4 *to Verses* | Final
God! God, bathed in the glo - ry of God!

Verses

1. Foun - tain of mer - cy, grace flow - ing free, streams of sal -
2. Here there is ha - ven, heal - ing and health, joy for the
3. Bread for our jour - ney God will pro - vide. Hope for all
4. Dark - ness is ban - ished, night turned a - way. Christ is our

*to Refrain*

1. va - tion, spill - ing with love from a tree!
2. ask - ing, love in a - bun - dance of wealth!
3. a - ges, Je - sus, com - pan - ion and guide!
4. sun - light, lift - ing and lead - ing our way!

Text and music: Dan Schutte, b. 1947, © 1991, OCP. All rights reserved.

**518**  YOU HAVE PUT ON CHRIST

You have put on Christ, al - le - lu - ia!

Bap - tized in Christ, al - le - lu - ia!

Text and music: Christopher Walker, b. 1947, © 2001, Christopher Walker. Published by OCP. All rights reserved.

# WADE IN THE WATER

**519**

Wade in the wa-ter, wade in the wa-ter chil-dren,

Wade in the wa-ter, God's a-goin' to trou-ble the wa-ter.

Verses
Cantor

1. See ___ that ___ host all dressed in white,
2. See ___ that ___ band all dressed in red,
3. If you don't be-lieve I've been re-deemed,

God's a-goin' to

All

1-3. trou-ble the wa - ter.

Cantor

1. The lead - er ___ looks like the
2. Looks like the ___ band that ___
3. Just fol - low me down to ___

All

to Refrain

1. Is - rael - ite,
2. Mo - ses led,
3. Jor - dan's stream.

God's a-goin' to trou-ble the wa - ter.

Text: Traditional.
Music: Spiritual.

# MAY THE WORD OF GOD STRENGTHEN YOU

**520**

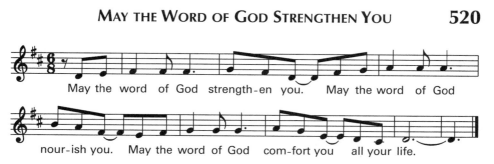

May the word of God strength-en you. May the word of God

nour-ish you. May the word of God com-fort you all your life.

Text and music: *Celtic Mass*; Christopher Walker, b. 1947, © 1996, Christopher Walker.
Published by OCP. All rights reserved.

## 521 O BREATHE ON ME, O BREATH OF GOD

1. O breathe on me, O Breath of God, Fill
2. O breathe on me, O Breath of God, Un -
3. O breathe on me, O Breath of God, My
4. O breathe on me, O Breath of God, So

1. me with life a - new, That I may love the
2. til my heart is pure; Un - til my will is
3. will to yours in - cline, Un - til this self - ish
4. I shall nev - er die, But live with you the

1. things you love, And do what you would do.
2. one with yours, To do and to en - dure.
3. part of me Glows with your fire di - vine.
4. per - fect life For all e - ter - ni - ty.

Text: CM; Edwin Hatch, 1835–1889, alt.
Music: ST. COLUMBA; trad. Irish Melody.

## 522 YOU HAVE PUT ON CHRIST

Refrain: 1st time: Cantor; thereafter: All

You have put on Christ; in him you have been bap-tized. Al - le -
lu - ia, al-le - lu - ia, al-le - lu - ia! ia! ia!

Verses: Cantor/Choir

1. We who were dead are now reborn.
   We who were buried now are raised.
   We who were dwelling in the dark
   now see light.

2. For though in Adam all have sinned,
   in Jesus Christ are all made clean.
   The grace abounding of his death
   sets us free.

3. One Lord we serve, who died for us;
   one faith we hold in life to come;
   one God and Father of us all
   we proclaim.

4. And this we know, that nothing ill,
   no prince nor pow'r, nor death nor sin,
   can separate us from God's love,
   shown in Christ.

# We Belong to You

**Refrain**

We be-long to you, O Lord of our long-ing, We be-long to you. In our dai-ly liv-ing, dy-ing and ris-ing We be-long to you.

to Verses | Final

We be-long to you. We be-long to you.

**Verses**

1. In the wa-ters of your mer-cy, When the
2. Filled with gifts and filled with good-ness, Spir-it
3. When we share the bread you've bro-ken With the
4. We are called to share your word, Lord, In all we

1. old be-comes the new, Souls u-nit-ed in the
2. breath-ing life in-to All who seek to find their
3. man-y and the few, We are blessed and we are
4. say and all we do. As our jour-ney moves us

to Refrain

1. mys - t'ry:
2. pur - pose:
3. bro - ken;
4. on - ward,

We be-long to you.

Text: Victoria Thomson, b. 1969, © 2006, Victoria Thomson.
Published by spiritandsong.com®, a division of OCP. All rights reserved.
Music: Trevor Thomson, b. 1971, © 2006, Trevor Thomson.
Published by spiritandsong.com®, a division of OCP. All rights reserved.

**524**

# Now in the Household of Christ/
## Ahora en la Casa de Cristo

Now in the house-hold of Christ, we bless you, we

bless you. A - ho-ra en la ca - sa de Cris - to,

los ben - de - ci - mos, los ben - de - ci - mos.

Text and music: Jaime Cortez, b. 1963, © 2000, Jaime Cortez. Published by OCP. All rights reserved.

**525**

## Give Me Ears to Listen

Verses

1, 4. Let me be your ser-vant; let me walk your way.
2. In si - lence, when you call me, let me hear your voice.
3. Last night, when I a-woke I heard you call my name.

1, 4. Guide me on your path; give night the light of day.
2. Je - sus, walk be - side me; let my soul re - joice. When
3. You re-freshed my soul; I felt your burn - ing flame. Oh,

1, 4. Let me be a sure foun - da - tion, pure and strong.
2. winds and cur - rents bat - ter me, help me be sure.
3. strength - en me to bear my cross and walk your way.

1, 4. Let me tell of your sal - va - tion all life long.
2. Give me cour - age from the storms when they oc - cur.
3. Give me grace to com - fort those with all I say.

Refrain

Give me ears to lis-ten. Give me eyes to see. Give me words to

1, 3, Final
to Vss. 2, 4
(Fine)

2

2

to Verse 3

speak and show your face to me. me.

## HEALING WATERS

## 526

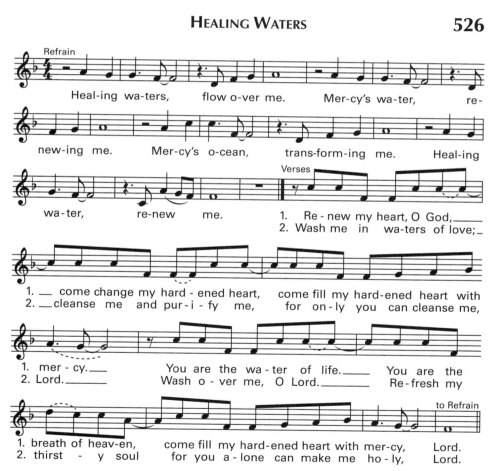

Refrain

Heal-ing wa-ters, flow o-ver me. Mer-cy's wa-ter, re-

new-ing me. Mer-cy's o-cean, trans-form-ing me. Heal-ing

Verses

wa-ter, re-new me. 1. Re-new my heart, O God,____
2. Wash me in wa-ters of love;_

1. __ come change my hard-ened heart, come fill my hard-ened heart with
2. __cleanse me and pur-i-fy me, for on-ly you can cleanse me,

1. mer-cy.___ You are the wa-ter of life.____ You are the
2. Lord._____ Wash o-ver me, O Lord._____ Re-fresh my

to Refrain

1. breath of heav-en, come fill my hard-ened heart with mer-cy, Lord.
2. thirst-y soul for you a-lone can make me ho-ly, Lord.

**527**      SHOW US YOUR MERCY

Text: Based on Psalm 91; Mark Friedman, b. 1952.
Music: Mark Friedman.

## Save Us, O Lord

**528**

Refrain

Save us, O Lord; car-ry us back. Rouse your pow-er and come.

Res-cue your peo-ple; show us your face. Bring us back.

Verse 1

1. O Shep-herd of Is - ra - el, hear us. Re - turn and we shall be

1. saved. A - rise, O Lord; hear our cries, O Lord: bring us back!   *to Refrain*

Verse 2

2. How long will you hide from your peo-ple? We long to

2. see your face. Give ear to us. Draw near to us, Lord God of hosts!   *to Refrain*

Verse 3

3. Turn a-gain; care for your vine; pro - tect what your

3. right hand has plant-ed. Your vine-yards are tram-pled, up -

3. root-ed, and burned. Come to us, Fa-ther of might!   *to Refrain*

Text: Based on Psalm 80; Bob Dufford, SJ, b. 1943.
Music: Bob Dufford, SJ.

**529** **HOSEA**

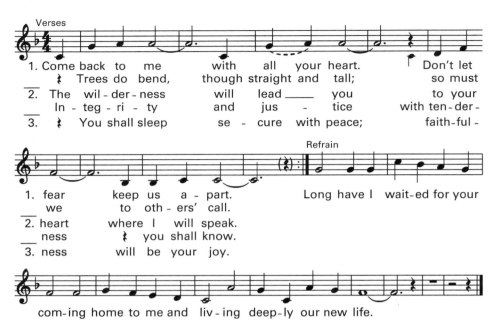

Verses

1. Come back to me with all your heart.	Don't let
   ⁏ Trees do bend, though straight and tall;	so must
2. The wil-der-ness will lead ____ you	to your
   In-teg-ri-ty and jus - tice	with ten-der-
3. ⁏ You shall sleep se - cure with peace;	faith-ful-

Refrain

1. fear keep us a - part.	Long have I wait-ed for your
   we to oth-ers' call.
2. heart where I will speak.
   ness ⁏ you shall know.
3. ness will be your joy.

com-ing home to me and liv-ing deep-ly our new life.

Text: Based on Hosea; Weston Priory, Gregory Norbet, OSB, b. 1940.
Music: Weston Priory, Gregory Norbet, OSB.
Text and music © 1972, The Benedictine Foundation of the State of Vermont, Inc.
    All rights reserved. Used with permission.

**530** **SOFTLY AND TENDERLY JESUS IS CALLING**

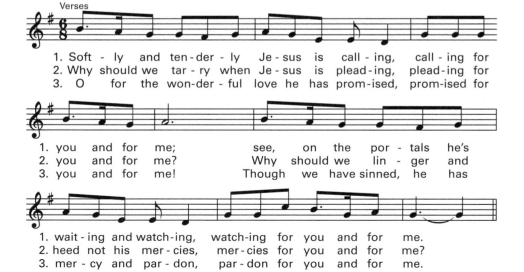

Verses

1. Soft - ly and ten-der-ly Je - sus is call - ing, call - ing for
2. Why should we tar - ry when Je - sus is plead-ing, plead-ing for
3. O for the won-der - ful love he has prom-ised, prom-ised for

1. you and for me;	see, on the por - tals he's
2. you and for me?	Why should we lin - ger and
3. you and for me!	Though we have sinned, he has

1. wait - ing and watch-ing, watch-ing for you and for me.
2. heed not his mer - cies, mer-cies for you and for me?
3. mer - cy and par - don, par-don for you and for me.

Come home, come home, you who are
wea-ry, come home; ear-nest-ly, ten-der-ly,
Je-sus is call-ing, call-ing for you to come home!

Text: 11 7 11 7 with refrain; Will L. Thompson, 1847–1909, alt.
Music: THOMPSON; Will L. Thompson.

## SEEK THE LORD 531

Seek the Lord while he may be found;
call to him while he is still near.

Verses 1-3
1. To-day is the day __ and now the prop-er hour to for-
2. As high as the sky ____ is a-bove the earth, so
3. Find-ing the Lord, ____ let us cling to him. His

to Refrain
1. sake our sin - ful lives __ and turn to the Lord.
2. high a-bove our ways, __ the ways of the Lord.
3. words, his ways _____ lead us to life.

Verse 4
4. Some-day we'll live in the house of God;

to Refrain
4. gaze on his face and praise his name.

Text: Based on Isaiah 55:6–9; Roc O'Connor, SJ, b. 1949.
Music: Roc O'Connor, SJ.

## 532      LOVING AND FORGIVING

Refrain: 1st time: Cantor, All repeat; thereafter: All

Lov-ing and for - giv-ing are you, O Lord; slow to an-ger,
rich in kind-ness, lov-ing and for - giv - ing are you.

Verses: Cantor/Choir

1. All my be - ing, bless the Lord, ____ bless the ho - ly
2. God for-gives us all our sins, ____ heal-ing those who
3. Good and gra - cious is the Lord, ____ slow to an - ger,
4. As heav-en soars a - bove the earth, so great the love of

1. name of God. ____ All my be - ing, bless the Lord, re -
2. live in pain, ____ sav - ing us from fi - nal death. God
3. rich in love. ____ God re-mem - bers not our sins; for -
4. God for us. As far as east is from the west, the

to Refrain

1. mem - b'ring the good - ness of God.
2. fills us with good - ness and love.
3. giv - ing and lov - ing is God.
4. Lord takes our sins ____ from us.

Text: Based on Psalm 103:8, 1–2, 3–4, 8–10, 11–12; Scott Soper, b. 1961.
Music: Scott Soper.
Text and music © 1992, OCP. All rights reserved.

## 533      REMEMBER YOUR LOVE

Refrain

Re - mem - ber your love and your faith-ful-ness, O Lord. Re -
mem - ber your peo - ple and have mer - cy on us, Lord.

Verses

1. The Lord is my light and my sal - va - tion,
2. If you dwelt, _____ O Lord, up - on our sin - ful - ness,
3. O Lord, hear the sound ___ of my call _____
4. As sen - ti - nels wait up - on the day - light,
5. Be - fore all the moun - tains were be - got - ten

1. whom should I fear? The Lord is my
2. then who could stand? But with you there is
3. and an - swer me. My heart cries ___
4. wait for the Lord. I trust in your
5. and earth took shape, e - ven then, _____ O

to Refrain

1. life _____ and my ref - uge, when I call God hears.
2. mer - cy and for - give - ness and a guid - ing hand.
3. out _____ for your pres - ence; it is you I seek.
4. kind - ness and re - demp - tion; and your faith - ful word.
5. Lord, you were our ref - uge through - out ev - 'ry age.

Text: Based on Psalms 25, 27, 90, 130; Mike Balhoff, b. 1946.
Music: Darryl Ducote, b. 1945, and Gary Daigle, b. 1957.
Text and music © 1973, 1978, Damean Music. All rights reserved. Used with permission.

## CREATE IN ME

## 534

Refrain                                                        Fine

Cre - ate in me a clean heart.

Verses

1. Have mer - cy on me, God, in your com - pas - sion.
2. O pu - ri - fy my heart and teach me wis - dom;
3. O give me back the joy of your sal - va - tion;

to Refrain

1. Re - move my sin. Wash me _ from my guilt.
2. then I shall be clean - er _ than the snow.
3. a will - ing spir - it sus - tain in me.

Text: Based on Psalm 51:12, 3–4, 8–9, 14; Bob Hurd, b. 1950.
Music: Bob Hurd.
Text and music © 1986, Bob Hurd. Published by OCP. All rights reserved.

# 535  CHANGE OUR HEARTS

Refrain

Change our hearts this time, your word says it can be. Change our
minds this time, your life could make us free. We are the peo-
-ple your call set a-part, Lord, this time change our
hearts. hearts. This time change our hearts. This time
change our minds. This time change our hearts, change our hearts.

Verse 1

1. Brought by your hand to the edge of our dreams, one foot in
1. par-a-dise, one in the waste; drawn by your prom-is-es,
1. still we are lured by the shad-ows and the chains we leave be-hind. But

Verses 2, 3

2. Now as we watch you stretch out your hands, of-f'ring a-bun-dan-
3. Show us the way that leads to your side, o-ver the moun-tains
2. ces, full-ness of joy. Your milk and hon-ey seem dis-tant, un-
3. and sands of the soul. Be for us man-na, wa-ter from

2. real, when we have bread and wa - ter in our hands. But
3. stone, _____ light which says we nev - er walk a - lone. And

## WHERE THERE IS LOVE

# 536

Refrain

Where there is love, there is God. The love of

God has gath - ered us to - geth - er; Al - le - lu - ia.

Verses 1, 3

1. Love is pa - tient, love is kind, nev - er jeal - ous, nev - er proud,
3. Man - y things will pass a - way. There are but three things that last:

1. nev - er seek - ing for one's self. _____ Love nev - er leads to an - ger. ___
3. Faith, Hope, and Love; _ the great - est of these is Love. _____

Verse 2

2. Love is gra - cious and for - giv - ing, tak - ing no de - light in wrong;

2. Love re - joic - es in the truth; Love will en - dure.

Text: Based on 1 John 4:16; 1 Corinthians 13:4–7, 10, 13; David Haas, b. 1957.
Music: David Haas.

## 537 WHERE LOVE IS FOUND

Refrain

Where char-i-ty and love are found, there will the face of God be
seen. The love of Christ will bind our hearts; as one bod-y we will
be.

Verses

1. Love is pa-tient, love is kind,
2. Love is stead-fast to the end,
3. Though I speak with an-gel's tongue,
4. There are three things that will last:

1. nev-er boast-ful, nev-er proud. Love is hope-ful in its
2. ev-er read-y to en-dure. Love is gra-cious in its
3. I am noth-ing more than sound. I am but a cym-bal
4. there is faith, hope and ___ love. But the great-est of all

1. wait-ing, ev-er trust-ing in God's light.
2. kind-ness, ev-er read-y to for-give.
3. clang-ing if I sing with-out God's love.
4. bless-ings is the faith-ful-ness of love.

to Refrain

Text: Based on the Latin chant *Ubi Caritas*, 9th cent.; 1 Corinthians 13:1–7, 13; Dan Schutte, b. 1947.
Music: Dan Schutte.

## 538 MAY GOD BLESS YOU

Refrain

May God bless you with his love, al-ways fill you with his love; may he
hold you in the hol-low of his hand. For the Lord is with you in
good-ness and love; may his light shine out in your heart.

Verses

1. Hap-py are they who re-flect his faith, seek-ing a depth with-out bound.
2. Bless-ed are they who re-flect his hope, find-ing a strength with-out bound.
3. Joy-ful are they who re-flect his love, liv-ing a gift with-out bound.
4. Ra-diant are they who re-flect his life, bond-ing their love with the Word.

to Refrain

1. Lord, it is good that we are here to see that faith which oth-ers have found.
2. Lord, it is good that we are here to see that hope which oth-ers have found.
3. Lord, it is good that we are here to see that love which oth-ers have found.
4. Lord, it is good that we are here to share that life with one ___ ac-cord.

## Hear Us Now, Our God and Father 539

1. Hear us now, our God and Fa-ther, Send your Spir-it from a-
2. Give them joy to light-en sor-row! Give them hope to bright-en
3. May the grace of Christ, our Sav-ior, And the Fa-ther's bound-less

1. bove On this Chris-tian man and wom-an Who here
2. life! Go with them to face the mor-row, Stay with
3. love, With the Ho-ly Spir-it's fa-vor Rest up-

1. make their vows of love! Bind their hearts in true de-vo-tion
2. them in ev-'ry strife. As your Word has prom-ised, ev-er
3. on them from a-bove. Thus may they a-bide in un-ion

1. End-less as the sea-shore's sands, Bound-less as the
2. Fill them with your strength and grace, So that each may
3. With each oth-er and the Lord, And pos-sess in

1. deep-est o-ceans, Blest and sealed by your own hands.
2. serve the oth-er Till they see you face to face.
3. sweet com-mu-nion Joys which earth can-not af-ford.

# 540    Si Yo No Tengo Amor/If I Do Not Have Love

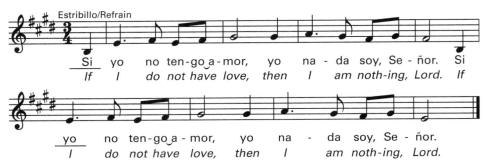

Estribillo/Refrain

Si yo no ten-go_a-mor, yo na - da soy, Se - ñor. Si
*If I do not have love, then I am noth-ing, Lord. If*

yo no ten-go_a - mor, yo na - da soy, Se - ñor.
*I do not have love, then I am noth-ing, Lord.*

**Estrofas**

1. El amor es comprensivo.
   El amor es servicial.
   El amor no tiene envidia.
   El amor no busca el mal.

2. El amor nunca se irrita.
   El amor no es descortés.
   El amor no es egoísta.
   El amor nunca es doblez.

3. El amor disculpa todo.
   El amor es caridad.
   No se alegra de lo injusto.
   Sólo goza en la verdad.

4. El amor soporta todo.
   El amor todo lo cree.
   El amor todo lo espera.
   El amor es siempre fiel.

5. Nuestra fe, nuestra esperanza,
   frente a Dios terminará.
   El amor es algo eterno.
   Nunca, nunca pasará.

**Verses**

1. *For the love of God is understanding,*
   *helpful to the end.*
   *Love refuses to do evil*
   *and is faithful, like a friend.*

2. *For the love of God will always*
   *keep a neighbor's care in mind,*
   *never jealous or suspicious,*
   *never hateful or unkind.*

3. *For the love of God is all forgiveness,*
   *charity unbound.*
   *It rejoices not in suff'ring*
   *but in peace and justice found.*

4. *For the love of God is patient,*
   *always open, always free.*
   *Love gives sight to those in darkness*
   *and true hope to those in need.*

5. *In the end our faith may leave us*
   *and all hope may disappear.*
   *Only love will never pass away*
   *for Christ is always here.*

Text: Traditional; English tr. by Owen Alstott, b. 1947, © 2003, OCP. All rights reserved.
Music: Traditional.

# 541        Wherever You Go

Verse 1

1. Wher-ev-er you go I shall go. Wher-ev-er you live

1. so shall I live. Your peo-ple will be my peo -

1. ple, and your God will be my God too.

2. Wher-ev-er you die I shall die, and there shall
2. I be bur-ied be-side you. We will be to-geth-er for-
2. ev - er, and our love will be the gift of our life.

## GOD, WHO CREATED HEARTS TO LOVE  542

1. God who cre - at - ed hearts to love, Show-'ring all bless-ings
2. Je - sus at Ca - na gave a sign, Turn-ing the wa - ter
3. Spir - it of God, be at their side: Wis - dom and com - fort,
4. Sing, friends and fam-'ly gath-ered here, Voic - es in wit - ness
5. God, let our joy - ful sing - ing be Sign of our faith com -

1. from a - bove, Al-le - lu - ia! Al-le - lu - ia! Give these, who come to
2. in - to wine: Al-le - lu - ia! Al-le - lu - ia! Sign that con - tin - ues
3. guard-ian, guide. Al-le - lu - ia! Al-le - lu - ia! Make of their hearts a
4. ring - ing clear; Al-le - lu - ia! Al-le - lu - ia! Here is the mys-ter -
5. mu - ni - ty. Al-le - lu - ia! Al-le - lu - ia! Bap - tized in wa - ter,

1. you with praise, Peace, love and laugh-ter all their days.
2. as he said— Love, liv - ing, ris - en from the dead.
3. rest-ing place; In ev - 'ry tri - al, gen - tle grace. } Al-le - lu-ia!
4. y be - gun: Wom - an and man be-com-ing one.
5. we are fed, Shar - ing the liv - ing wine and bread.

1-5. Al-le - lu - ia! Al-le - lu - ia! Al-le - lu - ia! Al-le - lu - ia!

## 543          WHEN LOVE IS FOUND

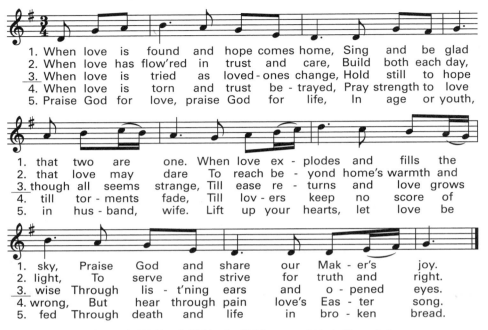

1. When love is found and hope comes home, Sing and be glad
2. When love has flow'red in trust and care, Build both each day,
3. When love is tried as loved-ones change, Hold still to hope
4. When love is torn and trust be-trayed, Pray strength to love
5. Praise God for love, praise God for life, In age or youth,

1. that two are one. When love ex-plodes and fills the
2. that love may dare To reach be-yond home's warmth and
3. though all seems strange, Till ease re-turns and love grows
4. till tor-ments fade, Till lov-ers keep no score of
5. in hus-band, wife. Lift up your hearts, let love be

1. sky, Praise God and share our Mak-er's joy.
2. light, To serve and strive for truth and right.
3. wise Through lis-t'ning ears and o-pened eyes.
4. wrong, But hear through pain love's Eas-ter song.
5. fed Through death and life in bro-ken bread.

Text: LM; Brian Wren, b. 1936, © 1983, Hope Publishing Co. All rights reserved. Used with permission.
Music: O WALY WALY; trad. English Melody.

## 544          O FATHER, ALL-CREATING

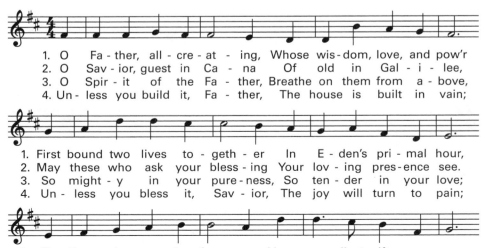

1. O Fa-ther, all-cre-at-ing, Whose wis-dom, love, and pow'r
2. O Sav-ior, guest in Ca-na Of old in Gal-i-lee,
3. O Spir-it of the Fa-ther, Breathe on them from a-bove,
4. Un-less you build it, Fa-ther, The house is built in vain;

1. First bound two lives to-geth-er In E-den's pri-mal hour,
2. May these who ask your bless-ing Your lov-ing pres-ence see.
3. So might-y in your pure-ness, So ten-der in your love;
4. Un-less you bless it, Sav-ior, The joy will turn to pain;

1. To these who come be-fore you, Your ear-liest gifts re-new:
2. Their store of earth-ly glad-ness Trans-form to heav'n-ly wine,
3. That, guard-ed by your pres-ence, From sin and strife kept free,
4. But none can break the un-ion Of hearts in you made one;

1. A home by you made hap - py, A love by you kept true.
2. And teach them, in the tast - ing, To know your gift di - vine.
3. Their hearts may seek your guid - ance, And love you faith - ful - ly.
4. The love your Spir - it bless - es Is end - less love be - gun.

Text: 76 76 D; John Ellerton, 1826–1893, alt.
Music: AURELIA; Samuel S. Wesley, 1810–1876.

## HEALING RIVER OF THE SPIRIT     545

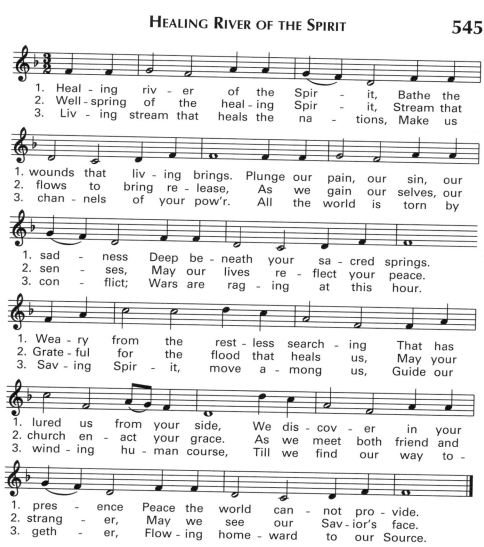

1. Heal - ing riv - er of the Spir - it, Bathe the
2. Well - spring of the heal - ing Spir - it, Stream that
3. Liv - ing stream that heals the na - tions, Make us

1. wounds that liv - ing brings. Plunge our pain, our sin, our
2. flows to bring re - lease, As we gain our selves, our
3. chan - nels of your pow'r. All the world is torn by

1. sad - ness Deep be - neath your sa - cred springs.
2. sen - ses, May our lives re - flect your peace.
3. con - flict; Wars are rag - ing at this hour.

1. Wea - ry from the rest - less search - ing That has
2. Grate - ful for the flood that heals us, May your
3. Sav - ing Spir - it, move a - mong us, Guide our

1. lured us from your side, We dis - cov - er in your
2. church en - act your grace. As we meet both friend and
3. wind - ing hu - man course, Till we find our way to -

1. pres - ence Peace the world can - not pro - vide.
2. strang - er, May we see our Sav - ior's face.
3. geth - er, Flow - ing home - ward to our Source.

Text: 87 87 D; Ruth C. Duck, b. 1947, © 1996, The Pilgrim Press. From *Circles of Care* by Ruth C. Duck,
    © 1998, The Pilgrim Press. All rights reserved. Used with permission.
Music: BEACH SPRING; *The Sacred Harp*, 1844.

## 546     O CHRIST, THE HEALER

1. O Christ, the heal - er, we have come To
2. From ev - 'ry ail - ment flesh en - dures Our
3. How strong, O Lord, are our de - sires, How
4. In con - flicts that de - stroy our health We
5. Grant that we all, made one in faith, In

1. pray for health, to plead for friends. How can we fail to
2. bod - ies clam - or to be freed; Yet in our hearts we
3. weak our knowl - edge of our-selves! Re - lease in us those
4. rec - og - nize the world's dis - ease; Our com - mon life de -
5. your com - mun - i - ty may find The whole-ness that, en -

1. be re - stored, When reached by love that nev - er ends?
2. would con - fess That whole-ness is our deep - est need.
3. heal - ing truths Un - con-scious pride re - sists or shelves.
4. clares our ills: Is there no cure, O Christ, for these?
5. rich - ing us, Shall reach the whole of hu - man-kind.

Text: LM; Fred Pratt Green, 1903–2000, © 1969, Hope Publishing Co. All rights reserved. Used with permission.
Music: ERHALT UNS, HERR; J. Klug's *Geistliche Lieder*, Wittenberg, 1543;
   adapt. by Johann Sebastian Bach, 1685–1750, alt.

## 547     BE STILL, MY SOUL

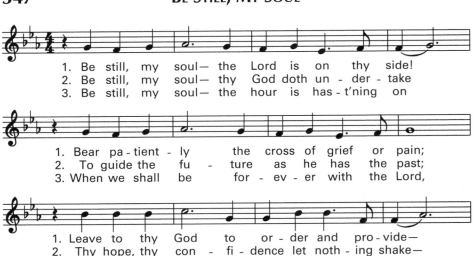

1. Be still, my soul— the Lord is on thy side!
2. Be still, my soul— thy God doth un - der - take
3. Be still, my soul— the hour is has - t'ning on

1. Bear pa - tient - ly the cross of grief or pain;
2. To guide the fu - ture as he has the past;
3. When we shall be for - ev - er with the Lord,

1. Leave to thy God to or - der and pro - vide—
2. Thy hope, thy con - fi - dence let noth - ing shake—
3. When dis - ap - point - ment, grief, and fear are gone,

1. In ev - 'ry change he faith - ful will re - main.
2. All now mys - te - rious shall be bright at last.
3. Sor - row for - got, love's pur - est joys re - stored.

1. Be still, my soul— thy best, thy heav'n - ly friend
2. Be still, my soul— the waves and winds still know
3. Be still, my soul— when change and tears are past,

1. Through thorn - y ways leads to a joy - ful end.
2. His voice who ruled them while he dwelt be - low.
3. All safe and bless - ed we shall meet at last.

Text: 10 10 10 10 10 10; Katharina von Schlegel; in *Neue Sammlung Geistlicher Lieder*, 1752;
tr. by Jane Borthwick, 1813–1897.
Music: FINLANDIA; Jean Sibelius, 1865–1957.

## PRECIOUS LORD, TAKE MY HAND · 548

1. Pre - cious Lord, take my hand, Lead me on, let me
2. When my way grows drear, Pre - cious Lord, lin - ger
3. When the dark - ness ap - pears And the night draws

1. stand; I am tired, I am weak, I am worn;
2. near, When my life is al - most gone;
3. near, And the day is past and gone,

1. Through the storm, through the night, Lead me on to the light:
2. Hear my cry, hear my call, Hold my hand lest I fall:
3. At the riv - er I stand, Guide my feet, hold my hand:

1-3. Take my hand, pre - cious Lord, lead me home.

Text: Irregular; Thomas A. Dorsey, 1899–1993.
Music: PRECIOUS LORD; Thomas A. Dorsey.

**549**

# HOLY DARKNESS

Refrain

Ho - ly dark - ness, bless - ed night, heav - en's an - swer hid - den from our sight. As we a - wait you, O God of si - lence, we em - brace your ho - ly night.

Verses 1-3

1. I have tried you in fires of af - flic - tion; I have taught your soul to grieve. In the bar - ren soil of your lone - li - ness, there I will plant my seed.
2. I have taught you the price of com - pas - sion; you have stood be - fore the grave. Though my love can seem like a rag - ing storm, this is the love that saves.
3. Were you there when I raised up the moun - tains? Can you guide the morn - ing star? Does the hawk take flight when you give com - mand? Why do you doubt my pow'r?

to Refrain

Verses 4, 5

4. In your deep - est hour of dark - ness I will give you wealth un - told. When the si - lence stills your spir - it, will my rich - es fill your soul.
5. As the watch - man waits for morn - ing, and the bride a - waits her groom, so we wait to hear your foot - steps as we rest be - neath your moon.

to Refrain

Text: Inspired by St. John of the Cross, 1542–1591; Dan Schutte, b. 1947.
Music: Dan Schutte.

# O Loving God

1. O lov-ing God, we send your daugh-ter home to you,
   (son) ___
2. O lov-ing God, have mer - cy and for - give - ness

1. home to a place of ev - er - last - ing love, to join there
2. up - on your ser - vant's now de - part - ed soul, and may your

1. with the an - gel choirs and bless - ed saints, and to be -
2. grace and love en - fold her/him ev - er - more, so she/he may

**Refrain**

1. hold your glo - rious ho - ly face. Re - ceive her/his soul and
2. dwell in par - a - dise at last.

let e - ter - nal light shine, e - ter - nal light for - ev - er on her/his

soul, so she/he may be for - ev - er in your dwell-ing place,

and be at rest in peace un - til we meet her/him there.

Text: 12 10 12 10 with refrain; Paulette M. McCoy, b. 1953, © 2004, Paulette M. McCoy.
Published by OCP. All rights reserved.
Music: LONDONDERRY AIR; fr. *The Ancient Music of Ireland*, 1855.

## 551     HOW LOVELY IS YOUR DWELLING PLACE

**Refrain**

O how love-ly is your dwell-ing place, dwell-ing of the Lord of hosts! How we long for your house, O Lord, sing-ing out a song of joy to the liv - ing God!

**Verses**

1. E - ven spar - rows find a home with you, and
2. Bless'd are those who find their strength in you, whose
3. Hear our prayer, O Lord ___ God of hosts; re -
4. For one day with - in your house ex - ceeds a
5. For our God pro - tects us from all harm; he

1. swal - lows lay their young to rest. Bless - ed are ___ those who
2. hearts are high-ways for your will. Bring-ing joy to those a -
3. ceive our lives in - to your hands! Look in - to the hearts of
4. thou-sand spent a - way from you. We would rath - er serve with-
5. gives his fa - vor and his love. All good things will come to

to Refrain

1. dwell in you and sing your praise, O God!
2. round ___ them, they go from strength to strength.
3. those you love and grant us all we need!
4. in your house than wealth and pow'r re - ceive.
5. those who love the Lord, and walk with him.

# I, THE LORD

Refrain

I, the Lord, am with you, al-ways by your side. Come and take my hand, for I will lead you home. Fol-low me, fol-low me.

Final
Fol-low me, fol-low me.

Verse 1
1. I am the res-ur-rec-tion, and I am the life; if 1. you be-lieve in me, you shall live for-ev-er.

Verse 2
2. You shall have new life and live it to the full. 2. Turn your sor-row in-to joy, for life has just be-gun.

**553**        SONG OF FAREWELL

Refrain: 1st time: Cantor, All repeat; thereafter: All

May the choirs of an-gels come to greet you. May they speed you to
par-a-dise. May the Lord en-fold you in his mer-cy. May you find e-
ter-nal life.

Verses

1. The __ Lord is my light and my help; _____ it is
2. There is one thing I ask of the Lord; _____ that he
3. O __ Lord, hear my voice when I cry; _____ have __
4. I am sure I shall see the Lord's good-ness; __ I shall

1. he who pro-tects me from harm. _____ The __ Lord is the strength
2. grant me my heart-felt de-sire. _____ To __ dwell in the courts
3. mer-cy on me and give an-swer. __ Do not cast me a-way
4. dwell in the land of the liv-ing. __ Hope in God, __ stand firm

to Refrain

1. of my days; _____ be-fore whom should I trem-ble with fear? _____
2. of our God _____ ev-'ry day of my life in his pres-ence. __
3. in your an-ger, __ for __ you are the God of my help. _____
4. and take heart, _____ place all your trust in the Lord. _____

Text: Refrain based on *In Paradisum*; verses based on Psalm 27; Ernest Sands, b. 1949.
Music: Ernest Sands.

**554**        GIVE ME JESUS

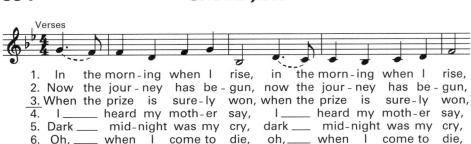

Verses

1. In the morn-ing when I rise, in the morn-ing when I rise,
2. Now the jour-ney has be-gun, now the jour-ney has be-gun,
3. When the prize is sure-ly won, when the prize is sure-ly won,
4. I _____ heard my moth-er say, I _____ heard my moth-er say,
5. Dark __ mid-night was my cry, dark __ mid-night was my cry,
6. Oh, __ when I come to die, oh, __ when I come to die,

1. in the morn-ing when I rise, give me Je - sus. Give me Je -
2. now the jour-ney has be-gun, give me Je - sus.
3. when the prize is sure-ly won, give me Je - sus.
4. I___ heard my moth-er say, give me Je - sus.
5. dark___ mid-night was my cry, give me Je - sus.
6. oh,___ when I come to die, give me Je - sus.

sus, give me Je - sus. You may have all this world. Give me Je - sus.

Text: Verses 1, 4–6 and refrain, Spiritual. Verses 2–3, James Hansen, b. 1937, © 1992, James Hansen.
  Published by OCP. All rights reserved.
Music: Spiritual.

## MAY THE ANGELS BE YOUR GUIDE

**555**

**Refrain**

May the an-gels be your guide, may they lead you in-to par-a-
dise, and take you home to the new Je-ru-sa-lem.

**Verses**

1. There is one thing I ask of God; for this I
2. When I cry out, ___ hear my voice. Have mer-cy,
3. I shall see God's ___ good - ness, for - ev - er

1. long, ___ for this I hope: 𝄌 to dwell in the house of
2. Lord, ___ and an-swer me. Do not cast me a-way in
3. dwell with the liv - ing. Hope in God, ___ and take

*to Refrain*

1. God ev - 'ry day of my life.
2. an - ger, for ___ you are my help.
3. heart; place your trust in the Lord.

Text: Based on *In Paradisum* and Psalm 27:4, 7, 9, 13–14; Michele MacAller and Kathy McGrath.
Music: Michele MacAller and Kathy McGrath.
Text and music © 1998, Michele MacAller and Kathleen McGrath. Published by OCP. All rights reserved.

## 556     I Know That My Redeemer Lives

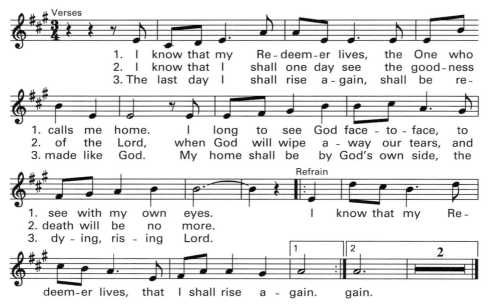

1. I know that my Re-deem-er lives, the One who
2. I know that I shall one day see the good-ness
3. The last day I shall rise a-gain, shall be re-

1. calls me home. I long to see God face - to - face, to
2. of the Lord, when God will wipe a - way our tears, and
3. made like God. My home shall be by God's own side, the

**Refrain**

1. see with my own eyes. I know that my Re-
2. death will be no more.
3. dy - ing, ris - ing Lord.

1. deem-er lives, that I shall rise a - gain. gain.

Text: Based on Job 19; Psalm 27; Isaiah 25; Scott Soper, b. 1961.
Music: Scott Soper.

## 557     The Lord Is My Light

**Verses**

1. The Lord is my light, my help, my sal-
2. There is one thing I ask of the Lord that I
3. I know I will live to see the Lord's

1. va - tion. Why should I fear? With God I fear
2. long for: all of my days with God to be
3. good-ness; now, in this life, I'm sure I will

1. no one. God pro - tects me all my
2. dwell-ing, gaz - ing with awe at the beau - ty of
3. see it. Trust in the Lord, be strong and be

1. life. With the Lord what should I dread?
2. God, and in won - der look on God's house.
3. brave; wait in hope for God, our sal - va - tion.

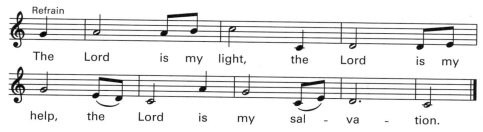

The Lord is my light, the Lord is my help, the Lord is my sal - va - tion.

Text: Based on Psalm 27; Christopher Walker, b. 1947.
Music: Christopher Walker.

## PARABLE

**558**

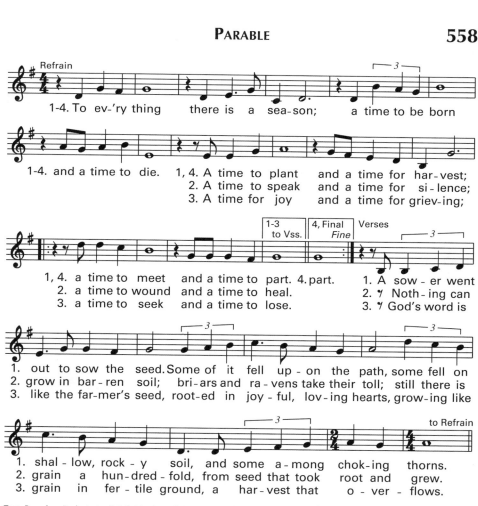

1-4. To ev-'ry thing there is a sea-son; a time to be born
1-4. and a time to die.
1, 4. A time to plant and a time for har-vest;
2. A time to speak and a time for si-lence;
3. A time for joy and a time for griev-ing;

1, 4. a time to meet and a time to part.
2. a time to wound and a time to heal.
3. a time to seek and a time to lose.

1. A sow - er went
2. Noth - ing can
3. God's word is

1. out to sow the seed. Some of it fell up - on the path, some fell on
2. grow in bar - ren soil; bri-ars and ra - vens take their toll; still there is
3. like the far - mer's seed, root-ed in joy - ful, lov-ing hearts, grow-ing like

1. shal - low, rock - y soil, and some a - mong chok-ing thorns.
2. grain a hun-dred - fold, from seed that took root and grew.
3. grain in fer - tile ground, a har - vest that o - ver - flows.

Text: Based on Ecclesiastes 3:1–9; Matthew 13:4–8; M.D. Ridge.
Music: M.D. Ridge.

## 559      KEEP IN MIND

Keep in mind that Je-sus Christ has died for us and is ris-en from the

dead. He is our sav-ing Lord, he is joy for all ag - es.

**Verse 1** (to Refrain)

1. If we die with the Lord, we shall live with the Lord.
   If we en - dure with the Lord, we shall reign with the Lord.

**Verses 2, 3** (to Refrain)

2. In him all our sor - row, in him all our joy.
   In him hope of glo - ry, in him all our love.
3. In him our re - demp - tion, in him all our grace.
   In him our sal - va - tion, in him all our peace.

Text: Based on 2 Timothy 2:8–12; Lucien Deiss, CSSp, 1921–2007.
Music: Lucien Deiss, CSSp.
Text and music © 1965, World Library Publications. All rights reserved. Used with permission.

## 560      SONG OF FAREWELL

1. May the an - gels car - ry you to par - a - dise.
2. May the choirs of an - gels come to wel - come you home
3. Fa - ther, wel - come them in - to your king - dom.

1. May the saints and mar - tyrs come to greet you.
2. and lead you joy - ful - ly to heav - en.
3. Please grant them life ev - er - last - ing.

1. May you rest in the arms of A - bra - ham
2. And may those who loved you who have gone be - fore
3. As they live now in the New Je - ru - sa - lem,

1. and know peace in heav - en for - ev - er.
2. be____ there with arms out-stretched to greet you.
3. may your Spir - it fill their souls with free - dom.

Text: Based on *In Paradisum*; Grayson Warren Brown, b. 1948.
Music: Grayson Warren Brown.

## GO IN PEACE

**561**

**Verses**

1. There will be no more dark - ness. There is no more night,
2. See the Fa-ther is wait - ing with a robe of white,

1. no more night. There will be no more sad - ness, on - ly joy and
2. pur - est white. Go and feast at his ta - ble with the bread of

1. light, joy and light. Lift your eyes be-yond the hills and
2. life, bread of life. Lift your heart, re - joice and sing for

1. see the dawn. There is beau-ti - ful mer - cy in the arms
2. you are home; home at last and for - ev - er in the arms

**Refrain**

1. of the ho - ly one. Go in peace, God be with you.
2. of the ho - ly one.

Go in peace, be at rest with the saints and the an - gels.

**3**

Now you are free. Go in peace.

## 562     YES, I SHALL ARISE

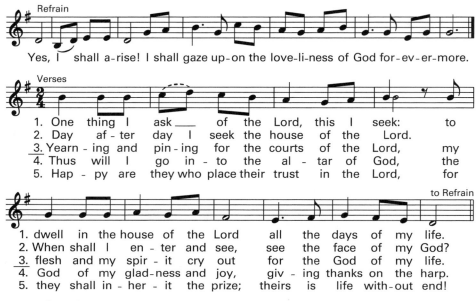

Yes, I shall a-rise! I shall gaze up-on the love-li-ness of God for-ev-er-more.

Verses

1. One thing I ask ___ of the Lord, this I seek: to
2. Day af - ter day I seek the house of the Lord.
3. Yearn - ing and pin - ing for the courts of the Lord, my
4. Thus will I go in - to the al - tar of God, the
5. Hap - py are they who place their trust in the Lord, for

to Refrain

1. dwell in the house of the Lord all the days of my life.
2. When shall I en - ter and see, see the face of my God?
3. flesh and my spir - it cry out for the God of my life.
4. God of my glad-ness and joy, giv - ing thanks on the harp.
5. they shall in - her - it the prize; theirs is life with-out end!

Text: Based on Psalms 27 and 43; Owen Alstott, b. 1947, © 1988, OCP. All rights reserved.
Music: Owen Alstott, © 1988, OCP. All rights reserved.

## 563     O JESUS, JOY OF LOVING HEARTS

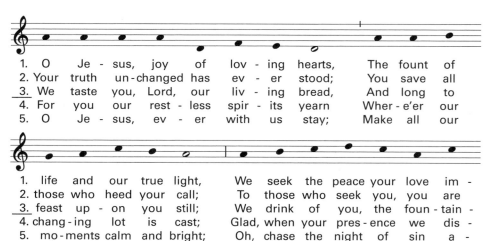

1. O Je - sus, joy of lov - ing hearts, The fount of
2. Your truth un - changed has ev - er stood; You save all
3. We taste you, Lord, our liv - ing bread, And long to
4. For you our rest - less spir - its yearn Wher - e'er our
5. O Je - sus, ev - er with us stay; Make all our

1. life and our true light, We seek the peace your love im -
2. those who heed your call; To those who seek you, you are
3. feast up - on you still; We drink of you, the foun - tain -
4. chang - ing lot is cast; Glad, when your pres - ence we dis -
5. mo - ments calm and bright; Oh, chase the night of sin a -

1. parts    And stand re - joic - ing in your sight.
2. good,    To those who find you— all in all.
3. head,    Our thirst - ing souls to quench and fill.
4. cern,    Blest, when our faith can hold you fast.
5. way,    Shed o'er the world your ho - ly light.

Text: LM; attr. to Bernard of Clairvaux, ca. 1090–1153; tr. by Ray Palmer, 1808–1887, alt.
Music: JESU DULCIS MEMORIA; Chant, Mode I.

## O Saving Victim/O Salutaris Hostia    564

1. O sav - ing Vic - tim, o - p'ning wide The gate of
2. All praise and thanks to thee as - cend For - ev - er -
1. O sa - lu - tá - ris hó - sti - a, Quae cae - li
2. U - ni tri - nó - que Dó - mi - no Sit sem - pi -

1. heav'n to us be - low, Our foes press on from
2. more, blest One in Three; O grant us life that
1. pan - dis ós - ti - um: Bel - la pre - munt ho -
2. tér - na gló - ri - a, Qui vi - tam si - ne

1. ev - ery side; Thine aid sup - ply, thy strength be - stow.
2. shall not end In our true na - tive land with thee.
1. stí - li - a, Da ro - bur, fer au - xí - li - um.
2. tér - mi - no No - bis do - net in pá - tri - a.

Text: LM; Latin, St. Thomas Aquinas, 1227–1274; tr. by Edward Caswall, 1814–1878.
Music: WERNER; Anthony Werner, fl. 1863.

# 565

## O Saving Victim/O Saving Lamb

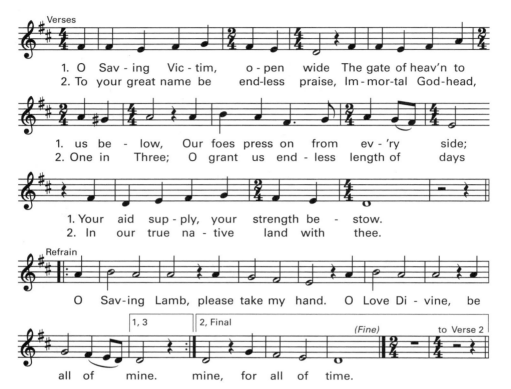

1. O Sav - ing Vic - tim, o - pen wide The gate of heav'n to
2. To your great name be end-less praise, Im - mor-tal God-head,

1. us be - low, Our foes press on from ev - 'ry side;
2. One in Three; O grant us end - less length of days

1. Your aid sup - ply, your strength be - stow.
2. In our true na - tive land with thee.

**Refrain**

O Sav-ing Lamb, please take my hand. O Love Di - vine, be

*1, 3* *2, Final* *(Fine)* *to Verse 2*

all of mine. mine, for all of time.

Text: Verses, LM, *O Salutaris*, St. Thomas Aquinas, 1227–1274; tr. by Edward Caswall, 1814–1878, alt.
Refrain, Tom Booth, b. 1961, © 2008, Tom Booth.
Published by spiritandsong.com®, a division of OCP. All rights reserved.
Music: Verses, DUGUET; attr. to Abbé Dieudonne Duguet, 1794–1849.
Refrain, Tom Booth, © 2008, Tom Booth. Published by spiritandsong.com®, a division of OCP. All rights reserved.

## HOLY GOD, WE PRAISE THY NAME

**566**

1. Ho - ly God, we praise thy name; Lord of all, we
2. Hark! the loud ce - les - tial hymn An - gel choirs a -
3. Lo! the ap - os - tol - ic train Join, the sa - cred
4. Ho - ly Fa - ther, Ho - ly Son, Ho - ly Spir - it,

1. bow be - fore thee! All on earth thy scep - tre claim,
2. bove are rais - ing; Cher - u - bim and Ser - a - phim,
3. Name to hal - low; Proph - ets swell the loud re - frain,
4. Three we name thee; While in es - sence on - ly One,

1. All in heav'n a - bove a - dore thee; In - fi -
2. In un - ceas - ing cho - rus prais - ing; Fill the
3. And the white - robed mar - tyrs fol - low; And from
4. Un - di - vid - ed God we claim thee; And a -

1. nite, thy vast do - main, Ev - er - last - ing
2. heav'ns with sweet ac - cord: "Ho - ly, ho - ly,
3. morn to set of sun, Through the Church the
4. dor - ing, bend the knee, While we own the

1. is thy reign. In - fi - nite, thy vast do -
2. ho - ly Lord!" Fill the heav'ns with sweet ac -
3. song goes on. And from morn to set of
4. mys - ter - y. And a - dor - ing, bend the

1. main, Ev - er - last - ing is thy reign.
2. cord: "Ho - ly, ho - ly, ho - ly Lord!"
3. sun, Through the Church the song goes on.
4. knee, While we own the mys - ter - y.

Text: 78 78 77 with repeat; *Te Deum laudamus*; attr. to St. Nicetas, ca. 335–414; *Grosser Gott, wir loben dich*;
tr. ascr. to Ignaz Franz, 1719–1790; tr. by Clarence A. Walworth, 1820–1900.
Music: GROSSER GOTT; *Allgemeines Katholisches Gesangbuch*, Vienna, ca. 1774.

# 567

# GOD, WE PRAISE YOU

1. God, we praise you! God, we bless you! God, we
2. True a - pos - tles, faith - ful proph - ets, Saints who
3. Je - sus Christ, the King of glo - ry, Ev - er -
4. Christ, at God's right hand vic - to - rious, You will

1. name you sov-'reign Lord! Might - y King whom an - gels
2. set their world a - blaze, Mar - tyrs, once un - known, un -
3. last - ing Son of God, Hum - ble was your vir - gin
4. judge the world you made; Lord, in mer - cy help your

1. wor - ship, Fa - ther, by your Church a - dored:
2. heed - ed, Join one grow - ing song of praise,
3. moth - er, Hard the lone - ly path you trod:
4. ser - vants For whose free - dom you have paid:

1. All cre - a - tion shows your glo - ry, Heav'n and
2. While your Church on earth con - fess - es One ma -
3. By your cross is sin de - feat - ed, Hell con -
4. Raise us up from dust to glo - ry, Guard us

1. earth draw near your throne, Sing-ing "Ho - ly, ho - ly,
2. jes - tic Trin - i - ty: Fa - ther, Son, and Ho - ly
3. front - ed face to face, Heav-en o - pened to be -
4. from all sin to - day; King en - throned a - bove all

1. ho - ly," Lord of hosts and God a - lone!
2. Spir - it, God, our hope e - ter - nal - ly.
3. liev - ers, Sin - ners jus - ti - fied by grace.
4. prais - es, Save your peo - ple, God, we pray.

Text: 87 87 D; *Te Deum laudamus*; attr. to St. Nicetas, ca. 335–414; tr. by Christopher Idle, b. 1938,
Music: NETTLETON; J. Wyeth's *Repository of Sacred Music, Part II*, 1813.

## O Bless the Lord

**Refrain**

O bless the Lord, the God of our sal - va - tion, Rock of strength and a ref - uge sure! O bless the Lord, the God of ev - 'ry na - tion, o - ver all the earth!

**Verses**

1. O bless the Lord,
2. Let all the earth
3. Let all the na -
4. Let all the peo -

1.    high - est heav - ens a - bove! Bless the Lord!
2.    sing with joy to the Lord, all the seas,
3. - tions on earth bless the Lord, for the Lord
4. - ple on earth bless the Lord! Young and old,

1. Glo - ri - fy his name! Sun in the day, moon and
2. crea - tures of the deep! Moun - tains and hills, birds and
3. gov - erns all the world! Let all the rul - ers on
4. glo - ri - fy his name! Let ev - 'ry voice sing with

*to Refrain*

1. stars in the night, wor - ship and praise!
2. beasts in the fields, wor - ship and praise!
3. earth bless the Lord! Wor - ship and praise!
4. joy to the Lord: "Glo - ry and praise!"

Text: Based on Psalm 148; John Michaels, b. 1947.
Music: John Michaels.

## 569 FROM ALL THAT DWELL BELOW THE SKIES / PRAISE GOD FROM WHOM ALL BLESSINGS FLOW

1. From all that dwell be - low the skies,
2. E - ter - nal are your mer - cies, Lord;
3. Your loft - y themes, all mor - tals, bring;
4. In ev - 'ry land be - gin the song;

*Doxology* Praise God, from whom all bless - ings flow;

1. Let the Cre - a - tor's praise a - rise;
2. E - ter - nal truth at - tends your word:
3. In songs of praise di - vine - ly sing;
4. To ev - 'ry land the strains be - long;

Praise him, all crea - tures here be - low;

1. Let the Re - deem - er's name be sung,
2. Your praise shall sound from shore to shore,
3. The great sal - va - tion loud pro - claim,
4. In cheer - ful sounds all voic - es raise,

Praise him a - bove, you heav'n - ly host:

1. Through ev - 'ry land by ev - 'ry tongue.
2. Till suns shall rise and set no more.
3. And shout for joy the Sav - ior's name.
4. And fill the world with loud - est praise.

Praise Fa - ther, Son and Ho - ly Ghost.

Text: LM; based on Psalm 117; verses 1–2, Isaac Watts, 1674–1748, alt; verses 3–4, anon., ca. 1781;
Doxology, Thomas Ken, 1637–1711.
Music: OLD HUNDREDTH; *Genevan Psalter*, 1551; attr. to Louis Bourgeois, ca. 1510–1561, alt.

## 570 ALL PEOPLE THAT ON EARTH DO DWELL

1. All people that on earth do dwell,
   Sing to the Lord with cheerful voice;
   Him serve with mirth, his praise forth tell,
   Come we before him, and rejoice.

2. Know that the Lord is God indeed;
   Without our aid he did us make;
   We are his folk, he does us feed,
   And for his sheep he does us take.

3. O enter then his gates with praise;
   Approach with joy his courts unto;

   Praise, laud, and bless his Name always,
   For it is seemly so to do.

4. For why? the Lord our God is good:
   His mercy is for ever sure;
   His truth at all times firmly stood,
   And shall from age to age endure.

5. To Father, Son, and Holy Ghost,
   The God whom heav'n and earth adore,
   From us and from the angel host
   Be praise and glory evermore.

Text: LM; based on Psalm 100; William Kethe, d. ca. 1594, alt.
Music: OLD HUNDREDTH; *Genevan Psalter*, 1551; attr. to Louis Bourgeois, ca. 1510–1561, alt.

# COME, CHRISTIANS, JOIN TO SING
571

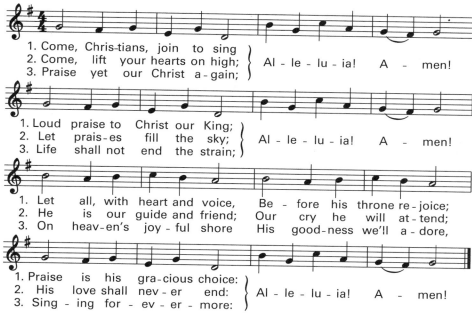

1. Come, Chris-tians, join to sing
2. Come, lift your hearts on high;
3. Praise yet our Christ a-gain;
Al - le - lu - ia! A - men!

1. Loud praise to Christ our King;
2. Let prais-es fill the sky;
3. Life shall not end the strain;
Al - le - lu - ia! A - men!

1. Let all, with heart and voice, Be - fore his throne re - joice;
2. He is our guide and friend; Our cry he will at - tend;
3. On heav-en's joy - ful shore His good-ness we'll a - dore,

1. Praise is his gra-cious choice:
2. His love shall nev - er end:
3. Sing - ing for - ev - er - more:
Al - le - lu - ia! A - men!

Text: 66 66 D; Christian Henry Bateman, 1813–1889, alt.
Music: MADRID; anon. melody, Philadelphia, 1826.

# BLESSED BY YOUR SACRIFICE
572

1. Blessed by your sac - ri - fice, Strong in your love, O Christ,
2. O Splen-dor, Glo - ry bright, Brought forth as Light from Light!
3. Come, raise the an-them high! Let prais-es fill the sky!

1. Our grate-ful voic - es to you we raise. True ad - o - ra - tion
2. O Day, all days en - light-en - ing! An-gels with one ac - cord
3. Sing out a new song un - to the Lord! Let all, with heart and voice,

1. Through-out cre - a - tion Rings out in joy - ful songs of praise.
2. Cry "Ho - ly, Ho - ly Lord!" To you, our ev - er - last - ing King.
3. Be - fore the throne re-joice Of him whom heav'n and earth a - dore.

Text: Irregular; Owen Alstott, b. 1947, and Jeanne Frolick, SFCC, © 1979, 1982, OCP. All rights reserved.
Music: ST. ELIZABETH; Trad. Silesian Melody; Hoffman and Richter's *Schlesische Volkslieder*, Leipzig, 1842.

**573** ALL THE ENDS OF THE EARTH

Refrain

All the ends of the earth, all you crea-tures of the sea, lift up your
eyes to the won - ders of the Lord. For the Lord of the earth, the
mas-ter of the sea, has come with jus-tice for the world.

Verse 1
1. Break in - to song at the deeds of the Lord,
1. the won - ders God has done in ev - 'ry age. *to Refrain*

Verse 2
2. Heav - en and earth shall re - joice in his might;
2. ev - 'ry heart ev - 'ry na - tion call him Lord. *to Refrain*

Verse 3
3. The Lord has made sal - va - tion known, faith-ful to the prom-
3. - is - es of old. Let the ends of the earth, let the
3. sea and all it holds make mu - sic be - fore our King! *to Refrain*

# GLORY AND PRAISE TO OUR GOD

**574**

*Refrain*

Glo-ry and praise to our God, who a-lone gives light to our days.

Man-y are the bless-ings he bears to those who trust in his ways.

*Verses 1-3*

1. We, the daugh-ters and sons of him who
2. In his wis-dom he strength-ens us, like
3. Ev-'ry mo-ment of ev-'ry day our

1. built the val-leys and plains, praise the won-ders our
2. gold that's test-ed in fire. Though the pow-er of
3. God is wait-ing to save, al-ways read-y to

1. God has done in ev-'ry heart that sings.
2. sin pre-vails, our God is there to save.
3. seek the lost, to an-swer those who pray.

*to Refrain*

*Verse 4*

4. God has wa-tered our bar-ren land and spent his mer-ci-ful rain.

4. Now the riv-ers of life run full for an-y-one to drink.

*to Refrain*

Text: Based on Psalms 65 and 66; Dan Schutte, b. 1947.
Music: Dan Schutte.
Text and music © 1976, OCP. All rights reserved.

## 575     JOYFUL, JOYFUL, WE ADORE YOU

1. Joy - ful, joy - ful, we a - dore you, God of glo - ry,
2. All your works with joy sur - round you, Earth and heav'n re -
3. Al - ways giv - ing and for - giv - ing, Ev - er bless - ing,
4. Mor - tals, join the might - y cho - rus Which the morn - ing

1. Lord of love; Hearts un - fold like flow'rs be - fore you,
2. flect your rays, Stars and an - gels sing a - round you,
3. ev - er blest, Well-spring of the joy of liv - ing,
4. stars be - gan; Love di - vine is reign - ing o'er us,

1. O - p'ning to the sun a - bove. Melt the clouds of
2. Cen - ter of un - bro - ken praise; Field and for - est,
3. O - cean depth of hap - py rest! Lov - ing Fa - ther,
4. Bind - ing all with - in its span. Ev - er sing - ing,

1. sin and sad - ness; Drive the dark of doubt a - way;
2. vale and moun-tain, Flow - 'ry mead - ow, flash - ing sea,
3. Christ our broth - er, Let your light up - on us shine;
4. march we on - ward, Vic - tors in the midst of strife;

1. Giv - er of im - mor - tal glad-ness, Fill us with the light of day!
2. Chant-ing bird and flow-ing foun-tain, Prais-ing you e - ter - nal-ly!
3. Teach us how to love each oth - er, Lift us to the joy di - vine.
4. Joy - ful mu - sic leads us sun-ward, In the tri-umph song of life.

Text: 87 87 D; Henry van Dyke, 1852–1933, alt.
Music: HYMN TO JOY; Ludwig van Beethoven, 1770–1827; adapt. by Edward Hodges, 1796–1867.

## 576     O BLESS THE LORD, MY SOUL

1. O bless the Lord, my soul! His grace to thee pro-claim!
2. O bless the Lord, my soul! His mer - cies bear in mind!
3. He clothes us with his love; Up - holds us with his truth;
4. Then bless his ho - ly name, Whose grace hath made us whole,

1. And all that is with - in me join To bless his ho - ly name!
2. For - get not all his ben - e - fits! The Lord to thee is kind.
3. He heals all our in - fir - mi - ties And ran - soms us from death.
4. Whose lov - ing kind - ness crowns our days! O bless the Lord, my soul!

Text: SM; para. of Psalm 103:1–5; James Montgomery, 1771–1854, alt.
Music: ST. THOMAS (WILLIAMS); *New Universal Psalmodist*, 1770; Aaron Williams, 1731–1776, alt.

## WE PRAISE YOU, O GOD    577

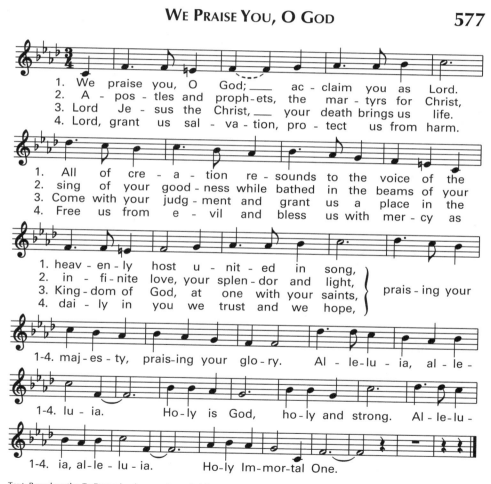

1. We praise you, O God; __ ac - claim you as Lord.
2. A - pos - tles and proph - ets, the mar - tyrs for Christ,
3. Lord Je - sus the Christ, __ your death brings us life.
4. Lord, grant us sal - va - tion, pro - tect us from harm.

1. All of cre - a - tion re - sounds to the voice of the
2. sing of your good - ness while bathed in the beams of your
3. Come with your judg - ment and grant us a place in the
4. Free us from e - vil and bless us with mer - cy as

1. heav - en - ly host u - nit - ed in song,  }
2. in - fi - nite love, your splen - dor and light,  }  prais - ing your
3. King - dom of God, at one with your saints,  }
4. dai - ly in you we trust and we hope,  }

1-4. maj - es - ty, prais - ing your glo - ry. Al - le - lu - ia, al - le -

1-4. lu - ia. Ho - ly is God, ho - ly and strong. Al - le - lu -

1-4. ia, al - le - lu - ia. Ho - ly Im - mor - tal One.

Text: Based on the *Te Deum laudamus*; attr. to St. Nicetas, ca. 335–414; Peter Jones, b. 1951.
Music: Peter Jones.

## 578 ALL CREATURES OF OUR GOD AND KING

1. All crea-tures of our God and King, Lift
2. Great rush-ing winds that are so strong, White
3. Swift flow-ing wa-ter, pure and clear, Make
4. Dear moth-er earth, who day by day Un-
5. All you that are of ten-der heart, For -
6. And you, most kind and gen-tle death, Wait -
7. Let all things their Cre - a - tor bless And

1. up your voice and let us sing; Al - le - lu - ia!
2. clouds a - bove that sail a - long, O ____ praise him!
3. mu - sic for your Lord to hear, Al - le - lu - ia!
4. folds rich bless-ings on our way, O ____ praise him!
5. giv - ing oth - ers, take your part. Sing his prais - es!
6. ing to hush our fi - nal breath, O ____ praise him!
7. wor-ship him in hum-ble - ness! O ____ praise him!

1. Al - le - lu - ia! Bright burn-ing sun with gold-en
2. Al - le - lu - ia! Fair ris - ing morn, in praise re-
3. Al - le - lu - ia! Fierce fire so mas-ter - ful and
4. Al - le - lu - ia! The flow'rs and fruits that in you
5. Al - le - lu - ia! All you that pain and sor - row
6. Al - le - lu - ia! You lead back home the child of
7. Al - le - lu - ia! Praise God the Fa - ther, praise the

1. beam, Pale sil - ver moon with soft - er gleam,
2. joice; O stars of eve-ning, find a voice!
3. bright, Pro - vid - ing us both warmth and light,
4. grow, Let them his glo - ry al - so show!
5. bear, Praise God, and on him cast your care!
6. God, Where Christ our Lord the way has trod,
7. Son, And praise the Spir - it, Three - in - One:

1-7. O praise him! O praise him! Al - le - lu - ia!

1-7. Al - le - lu - ia! Al - le - lu - ia!

Text: LM with additions; St. Francis of Assisi, 1182–1226; *Laudato sia Deo mio Signore*; tr. by William H. Draper,
1855–1933, alt. © 1927, J. Curwen & Sons, Ltd. for the USA, France and Mexico. All rights reserved.
International copyright secured. Reprinted by permission of G. Schirmer, Inc., as agents for J. Curwen & Sons, Ltd.
Music: LASST UNS ERFREUEN; *Auserlesene Catholische Geistliche Kirchengesänge*, Cologne, 1623.

# WE PRAISE YOU

*Wedding verses.

Text: Verses 1–5 based on Psalms 80:9–12; 135:15–18; 136:5–9; verses 6, 7 based on Psalm 128:1, 3, 5–6;
    Mike Balhoff, b. 1946.
Music: Darryl Ducote, b. 1945, and Gary Daigle, b. 1957.

# 580 SING TO THE MOUNTAINS

Refrain

Sing to the moun-tains, sing to the sea. Raise your voic-es, lift your hearts. This is the day the Lord has made. Let all the earth re-joice.

to Verses | Last time

Let all the earth re-joice.

Verse 1
1. I will give thanks to you, my Lord. You have an-swered my plea. You have saved my soul from death. You are my strength and my song.

Verse 2
2. Ho - ly, ho - ly, ho - ly Lord. Heav-en and earth are full of your glo - ry.

Verse 3
3. This is the day that the Lord has made. Let us be glad and re-joice. Death has lost and all is life. Sing of the glo-ry of God.

Text: Based on Psalm 118:24; Isaiah 6:3; Bob Dufford, SJ, b. 1943.
Music: Bob Dufford, SJ.

# YOU ALONE

## 582      SING OF THE LORD'S GOODNESS

**Verses**

1. Sing of the Lord's good-ness, Fa - ther of all wis - dom,
2. Pow - er he has wield - ed, hon - or is his gar - ment,
3. Cour-age in our dark-ness, com - fort in our sor - row,
4. Praise him with your sing - ing, praise him with the trum - pet,

1. come to him and bless his name. Mer - cy he has shown us,
2. ris - en from the snares of death. His word he has spo - ken,
3. Spir - it of our God most high; so - lace for the wear - y,
4. praise God with the lute and harp; praise him with the cym-bals,

1. his love is for - ev - er, faith - ful to the end of days.
2. one bread he has bro-ken, new life he now gives to all.
3. par - don for the sin - ner, splen-dor of the liv - ing God.
4. praise him with your danc-ing, praise God till the end of days.

**Refrain**

Come, then, all you na-tions, sing of your Lord's good-ness, mel-o - dies

of praise and thanks to God. Ring out the Lord's glo-ry, praise him with

your mu - sic, wor-ship him and bless his name.

## 583      HE IS THE LORD

**Refrain**

Sing to the Lord with shouts of joy, let all cre -

a - tion re - joice! Come join the song of praise to our

God! He is the Lord! He is the Lord!

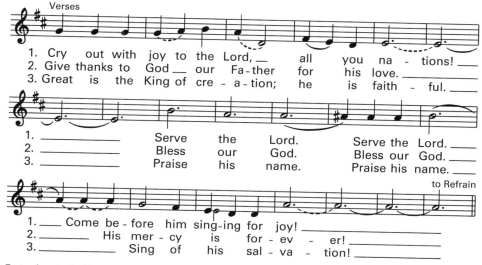

1. Cry out with joy to the Lord, __ all you na - tions! __
2. Give thanks to God __ our Fa - ther for his love. __
3. Great is the King of cre - a - tion; he is faith - ful. __

1. __ Serve the Lord. Serve the Lord. __
2. __ Bless our God. Bless our God. __
3. __ Praise his name. Praise his name. __

to Refrain

1. __ Come be - fore him sing-ing for joy! __
2. __ His mer - cy is for - ev - er! __
3. __ Sing of his sal - va - tion! __

Text and music: David Haas, b. 1957, © 1981, 1982, OCP. All rights reserved.

## PRAISE THE LORD, YE HEAVENS

**584**

1. Praise the Lord! ye heav'ns a - dore him; Praise him an - gels, in the height;
2. Praise the Lord! for he is glo - rious; Nev - er shall his prom-ise fail;
3. Wor-ship, hon - or, glo - ry, bless-ing, Lord, we of - fer un - to thee;

1. Sun and moon, re - joice be - fore him; Praise him, all ye stars of light.
2. God has made his saints vic - to - rious; Sin and death shall not pre-vail.
3. Young and old, thy praise ex-press-ing, In glad hom - age bend the knee.

1. Praise the Lord! for he has spo - ken; Worlds his might-y voice o - beyed;
2. Praise the God of our sal - va - tion! Hosts on high his pow'r pro-claim;
3. All the saints in heav'n a - dore thee, We would bow be - fore thy throne;

1. Laws which nev - er shall be bro-ken For their guid-ance he has made.
2. Heav'n, and earth, and all cre - a - tion, Laud and mag - ni - fy his name.
3. As thine an - gels serve be-fore thee, So on earth thy will be done.

Text: 87 87 D; based on Psalm 148; verses 1, 2, *Psalms, Hymns, and Anthems of the Foundling Hospital*, 1796; verse 3, Edward Osler, 1798–1863.
Music: HYMN TO JOY; Ludwig van Beethoven, 1770–1827; adapt. by Edward Hodges, 1796–1867.

## 585    PRAISE TO THE LORD

1. Praise to the Lord, the Al - might - y, the King of cre -
2. Praise to the Lord, a - bove all things so won - drous - ly
3. Praise to the Lord, who will pros - per your work and de -
4. Praise to the Lord! O let all that is in me a -

1. a - tion! O my soul, praise him, for
2. reign - ing, Shel - t'ring you un - der his
3. fend you; Sure - ly his good - ness and
4. dore him! All that has life and breath,

1. he is your health and sal - va - tion!
2. wings, and so gent - ly sus - tain - ing.
3. mer - cy shall dai - ly at - tend you.
4. come now with prais - es be - fore him!

1. Come, all who hear: Now to his al - tar draw
2. Have you not seen All that is need - ful has
3. Pon - der a - new What the Al - might - y can
4. Let the "A - men!" Sound from his peo - ple a -

1. near, Join - ing in glad ad - o - ra - tion!
2. been Sent by his gra - cious or - dain - ing?
3. do As with his love he be - friends you.
4. gain, Glad - ly with praise we a - dore him!

Text: 14 14 47 8; Joachim Neander, 1650–1680; tr. by Catherine Winkworth, 1827–1878, alt.
Music: LOBE DEN HERREN; *Ernewerten Gesangbuch*, Stralsund, 1665.

## 586    PRAISE, MY SOUL, THE KING OF HEAVEN

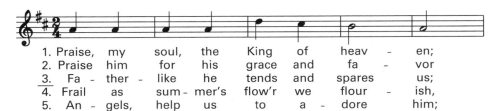

1. Praise, my soul, the King of heav - en;
2. Praise him for his grace and fa - vor
3. Fa - ther - like he tends and spares us;
4. Frail as sum - mer's flow'r we flour - ish,
5. An - gels, help us to a - dore him;

1. To his feet thy trib - ute bring; Ran - somed,
2. To his peo - ple in dis - tress; Praise him
3. Well our fee - ble frame he knows; In his
4. Blows the wind and it is gone; But while
5. You be - hold him face to face; Sun and

1. healed, re - stored, for - giv - en, Ev - er - more his
2. still the same as ev - er, Slow to chide, and
3. hands he gent - ly bears us, Res - cues us from
4. mor - tals rise and per - ish, God en - dures un -
5. moon, bow down be - fore him, All who dwell in

1. prais - es sing:
2. swift to bless:
3. all our foes.
4. chang - ing on:
5. time and space:

Al - le - lu - ia! Al - le -

1-5. lu - ia!

Praise the ev - er - last - ing King.
Glo - rious in his faith - ful - ness.
Wide - ly yet his mer - cy flows.
Praise the high e - ter - nal one!
Praise with us the God of grace.

Text: 87 87 87; based on Psalm 103; Henry F. Lyte, 1793–1847, alt.
Music: LAUDA ANIMA; John Goss, 1800–1880.

## GOD, WHOSE LOVE IS REIGNING O'ER US     587

1. God, whose love is reigning o'er us,
   Source of all, the ending true;
   Hear the universal chorus
   Raised in joyful praise to you:
   Alleluia, Alleluia,
   Worship ancient, worship new.

2. Word of God from nature bringing
   Springtime green and autumn gold;
   Mountain streams like children singing,
   Ocean waves like thunder bold:
   Alleluia, Alleluia,
   As creation's tale is told.

3. Holy God of ancient glory,
   Choosing man and woman, too;
   Abr'am's faith and Sarah's story

Formed a people bound to you.
Alleluia, Alleluia,
To your cov'nant keep us true.

4. Cov'nant, new again in Jesus,
   Starchild born to set us free;
   Sent to heal us, sent to teach us
   How love's children we might be.
   Alleluia, Alleluia,
   Risen Christ, our Savior he!

5. Lift we then our human voices
   In the songs that faith would bring;
   Live we then in human choices
   Lives that, like our music, sing:
   Alleluia, Alleluia,
   Joined in love our praises ring!

Text: 87 87 87; William Boyd Grove, © 1980, William Boyd Grove. All rights reserved. Used with permission.
Music: LAUDA ANIMA; John Goss, 1800–1880.

# 588

## SHOUT TO THE LORD

My Je-sus, my Sav-ior; Lord, there is none like you.

All of my days I want to praise the won-ders of your

might-y love. My com-fort, my shel-ter,

tow-er of ref-uge and strength; let ev-ery breath,

all that I am, nev-er cease to wor-ship you.

Shout to the Lord, all the earth; let us sing pow-er and maj-

es-ty, praise to the king. Moun-tains bow down and the seas

will roar at the sound of your name.

I sing for joy at the work of your hands. For-

ev-er I'll love you, for-ev - er I'll stand.

Noth-ing com-pares to the prom - ise I have in you.

## O GOD BEYOND ALL PRAISING 589

1. O God be-yond all prais - ing, We wor-ship you to - day
2. Then hear, O gra-cious Sav - ior, Ac - cept the love we bring,

1. And sing the love a - maz - ing That songs can-not re - pay;
2. That we who know your fa - vor May serve you as our King;

1. For we can on - ly won-der At ev - 'ry gift you send,
2. And wheth - er our to - mor-rows Be filled with good or ill,

1. At bless-ings with - out num - ber And mer-cies with-out end:
2. We'll tri - umph through our sor - rows And rise to bless you still:

1. We lift our hearts be - fore you And wait up-on your word,
2. To mar - vel at your beau - ty And glo - ry in your ways,

1. We hon - or and a-dore you, Our great and might-y Lord.
2. And make a joy-ful du - ty Our sac - ri - fice of praise.

## 590    SING PRAISE TO GOD WHO REIGNS ABOVE

1. Sing praise to God who reigns a - bove, The God of all
2. What God's al - might - y power has made, His gra - cious mer -
3. Then all my glad - some way a - long, I sing a - loud
4. Let all who name Christ's ho - ly name, Give God all praise

1. cre - a - tion, The God of power, the God of love, The
2. cy keep - ing; By morn - ing glow or eve - ning shade His
3. your prais - es, That all may hear the grate - ful song My
4. and glo - ry; All you who own his power, pro - claim A -

1. God of our sal - va - tion; With heal - ing balm my
2. watch - ful eye ne'er sleep - ing; With - in the king - dom
3. voice un - wea - ried rais - es; Be joy - ful in the
4. loud the won - drous sto - ry! Cast each false i - dol

1. soul he fills, And ev - 'ry faith - less mur - mur stills:
2. of his might, Lo! all is just and all is right:
3. Lord, my heart, Both soul and bod - y sing your part:
4. from its throne, The Lord is God, and he a - lone:

1-4. To God all praise and glo - ry.

Text: 87 87 88 7; *Sei Lob und Ehr' dem höchsten Gut*; Johann J. Schütz, 1640–1690; tr. by Frances E. Cox, 1812–1897.
Music: MIT FREUDEN ZART; Bohemian Brethren's *Kirchengesänge*, 1566.

## 591    LET ALL MORTAL FLESH KEEP SILENCE

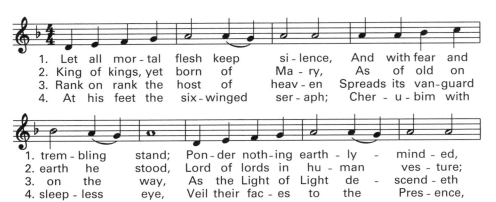

1. Let all mor - tal flesh keep si - lence, And with fear and
2. King of kings, yet born of Ma - ry, As of old on
3. Rank on rank the host of heav - en Spreads its van - guard
4. At his feet the six - winged ser - aph; Cher - u - bim with

1. trem - bling stand; Pon - der noth - ing earth - ly - mind - ed,
2. earth he stood, Lord of lords in hu - man ves - ture;
3. on the way, As the Light of Light de - scend - eth
4. sleep - less eye, Veil their fac - es to the Pres - ence,

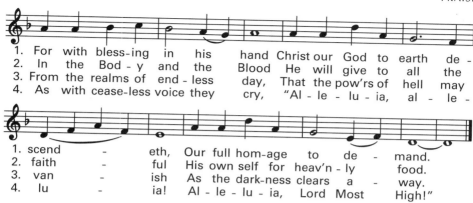

1. For with bless-ing in his hand Christ our God to earth de-
2. In the Bod-y and the Blood He will give to all the
3. From the realms of end-less day, That the pow'rs of hell may
4. As with cease-less voice they cry, "Al-le-lu-ia, al-le-

1. scend - eth, Our full hom-age to de - mand.
2. faith - ful His own self for heav'n-ly food.
3. van - ish As the dark-ness clears a - way.
4. lu - ia! Al-le-lu-ia, Lord Most High!"

Text: 87 87 87; *Liturgy of St. James*, 4th cent.; para. by Gerard Moultrie, 1829–1885, alt.
Music: PICARDY; French, 17th cent.; *Chansons populaires des Provinces de France*, 1860.

## SING A NEW SONG 592

Refrain

Sing a new song to the Lord. Praise him in the as-sem-bly
of his church. Sing a new song to the Lord. Praise him,
all you peo-ple of God.

Verses

1. Be glad, ___ O
2. 𝄽 Praise his name with
3. 𝄽 Let God's peo - ple

1. Is - ra-el, be-cause ___ of your cre - a - tor; re-joice, ___
2. danc - ing, play drums and harp ___ in praise, ___ for God de-
3. cel - e-brate the tri - umph of ___ their king. ___ Let them

to Refrain

1. O ___ Zi - on, be-cause ___ of ___ your king.
2. lights in his peo - ple, and lifts his chil-dren on high.
3. shout ___ and praise his name, while sing - ing all the night long.

Text and music: Grayson Warren Brown, b. 1948, © 1992, Grayson Warren Brown. Published by OCP. All rights reserved.

**593**          LIFT UP YOUR HEARTS

Refrain

Lift up your hearts to the Lord, praise God's gra-cious mer-cy!

Sing out your joy to the Lord, whose love is en - dur - ing.

Verses

1. Shout with joy to the Lord, all the earth!
2. Let the earth wor-ship, sing - ing your praise.
3. God's right hand made a path through the night,
4. Lis - ten now, all you ser - vants of God,

1. Praise the name a - bove all names! Say to God, "How
2. Praise the glo - ry of your name! Come and see the
3. split the wa - ters of the sea. All cre - a - tion,
4. as I tell of these great works. Bless - ed be the

to Refrain

1. won - drous your works, how glo - rious your name!"
2. deeds of the Lord; bless God's ho - ly name!
3. lift up your voice: "Our God set us free!"
4. Lord of my life, whose love shall en - dure!

Text: Based on Psalm 66; Roc O'Connor, SJ, b. 1949.
Music: Roc O'Connor, SJ.

**594**          IMMORTAL, INVISIBLE, GOD ONLY WISE

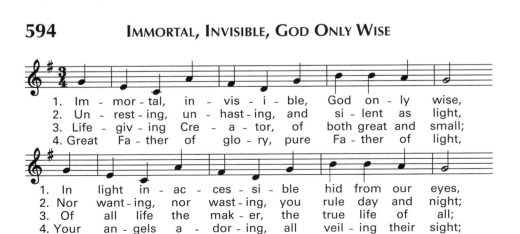

1. Im - mor - tal, in - vis - i - ble, God on - ly wise,
2. Un - rest - ing, un - hast - ing, and si - lent as light,
3. Life - giv - ing Cre - a - tor, of both great and small;
4. Great Fa - ther of glo - ry, pure Fa - ther of light,

1. In light in - ac - ces - si - ble hid from our eyes,
2. Nor want - ing, nor wast - ing, you rule day and night;
3. Of all life the mak - er, the true life of all;
4. Your an - gels a - dor - ing, all veil - ing their sight;

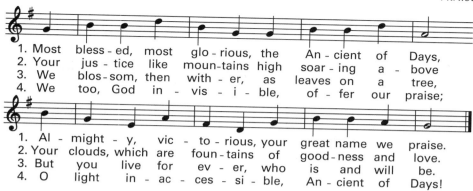

1. Most bless-ed, most glo-rious, the An-cient of Days,
2. Your jus-tice like moun-tains high soar-ing a-bove
3. We blos-som, then with-er, as leaves on a tree,
4. We too, God in-vis-i-ble, of-fer our praise;

1. Al-might-y, vic-to-rious, your great name we praise.
2. Your clouds, which are foun-tains of good-ness and love.
3. But you live for ev-er, who is and will be.
4. O light in-ac-ces-si-ble, An-cient of Days!

Text: 11 11 11 11; 1 Timothy 1:17; Walter C. Smith, 1824–1908, alt.
Music: ST. DENIO; Roberts' *Canaidau y Cyssegr*, 1839.

## SING A JOYFUL SONG

**595**

Refrain

Sing a joy-ful song to the Lord! Al-le-lu - ia!

Let the heav-ens and earth re - joice! Al-le-lu - ia!

Al-le-lu - ia!

Verses

1. The heav-ens pro-
2. Our God is a
3. Sing praise, O Je-
4. Sing praise to the

1. claim God's name, and earth in re - ply ech-oes
2. might-y God, un - e-qualled in pow'r, yet with
3. ru - sa - lem! Sing praise to your King, rul-ing
4. God of gods, the An-cient of Days! Ho-ly,

to Refrain

1. back with joy - ful songs __ of praise!
2. gen - tle mer - cy cov-ers the earth.
3. earth with jus - tice age af-ter age.
4. ho - ly, ho - ly Lord __ of all!

Text: Based on Psalm 145; Jim Farrell, b. 1947, © 1984, OCP. All rights reserved.
Music: Jim Farrell, © 1984, OCP. All rights reserved.

**596**

# ALLE, ALLE, ALLELUIA

Refrain  Al - le,   al - le,   al - le-lu - ia,
Verses  1. Fa - ther,  Fa - ther,  mak - er  of  the  world.
2. Je - sus,  Je - sus,  Je - sus  is  the  way.
3. Spir - it,  Spir - it,  come down on  us,  Lord.

al - le,   al - le,   al - le-lu - ia.
1. Fa - ther,  Fa - ther,  cre - a - tor  of  the earth.
2. Je - sus,  Je - sus,  Je - sus  is  the  truth.
3. Spir - it,  Spir - it,  rain down on  us,  Lord.

Al - le,   al - le,   al - le-lu - ia.
1. Fa - ther,  Fa - ther,  speak - er  of  the  word.
2. Je - sus,  Je - sus,  Je - sus  is  the  life.
3. Spir - it,  Spir - it,  flood us  with your  pow'r.

Al - le, al - le,  al - le, al - le - lu - ia.
1. Make us,  Fa - ther, break us,  Fa - ther, mold us  in  your ways.
2. Je - sus  is  the  way, he  is  the  truth, he  is  the  life.
3. Fill  us  with the  light of God, oh,  fill  us  with your pow'r.

|1-6|

Al - le, al - le,  al - le, al - le - lu - ia. (to Verses)
1. Make us,  Fa - ther, break us,  Fa - ther, mold us  in  your ways. (to Refrain)
2. Je - sus  is  the  way, he  is  the  truth, he  is  the  life. (to Refrain)
3. Fill  us  with the  light of God, oh,  fill  us  with your pow'r. (to Refrain)

|Final|

ia.   Al - le,   al - le, al - le - lu - ia.

Al - le,   al - le,  al - le - lu - ia.   Al - le!

# Laudate, Laudate Dominum

Refrain

Lau - da - te, lau - da - te Do - mi - num, om - nes gen - tes, lau -
*We praise you, we praise your ho - ly name, God of jus - tice, e -*

da - te Do - mi - num. Ex - sul - ta - te, ju - bi - la - te per
*ter - nal - ly the same. May our liv - ing be thanks - giv - ing, re -*

1.
an - nos Do - mi - ni, om - nes gen - tes.

2, Final
gen - tes.

*joic - ing in your name now and al - ways.*
*al - ways.*

*Verses

1. In the faith of Christ we walk hand in hand,
2. In the name of Christ we will spread the seed;
3. In the pow'r of Christ we pro - claim one Lord.

1. light be - fore our path as the Lord has planned;
2. share the Word of God with all those in need,
3. All who put on Christ are by faith re - stored;

1. shin - ing the torch of faith in our land:
2. faith - ful in thought and word and deed:
3. shar - ing new life, sal - va - tion's re - ward:

to Refrain
1-3. in the name of Christ Je - sus.

*Additional verses available in accompaniment books.

## 598     Sing a New Song

Sing a new song un-to the Lord; let your song be sung from moun-tains high. Sing a new song un-to the Lord, sing-ing al - le - lu - ia.

*Verses*

1. Shout with glad-ness! Dance for joy!
2. Rise, O chil - dren, from your sleep;
3. Glad my soul for I have seen

1. O come be - fore the Lord. And play for God on
2. your Sav - ior now has come. ℟ He has turned your
3. the glo - ry of the Lord. The trum - pet sounds; the

*to Refrain*

1. glad tam - bou - rines, and let your trum - pet sound.
2. sor - row to joy, and filled your soul with song.
3. dead shall be raised. I know my Sav - ior lives.

Text: Based on Psalm 98:1, 4–6; Dan Schutte, b. 1947.
Music: Dan Schutte.
Text and music © 1972, 2008, OCP. All rights reserved.

## 599     Halleluya! We Sing Your Praises

Hal - le - lu - ya! We sing your prais-es, all our hearts are filled with glad - ness. Hal - le - lu - ya! We sing your prais-es, all our hearts are filled with glad - ness.

1. Christ the Lord to us said: I am wine, I am bread,
2. Now he sends us all out, strong in faith, free of doubt,

1. I am wine, I am bread, give to all who thirst and hun - ger.
2. strong in faith, free of doubt, to pro-claim the joy - ful Gos - pel.

## ABBA, FATHER
## 600

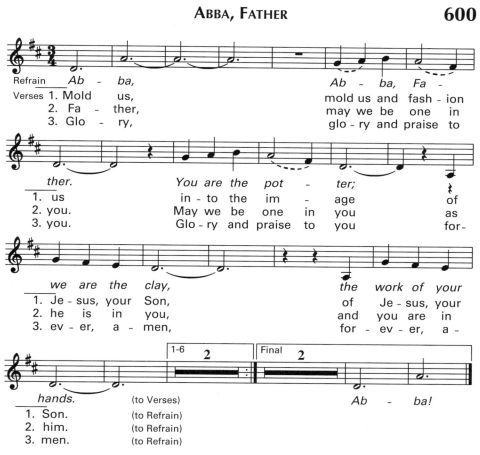

Refrain Ab - ba, Ab - ba, Fa -
Verses 1. Mold us, mold us and fash - ion
2. Fa - ther, may we be one in
3. Glo - ry, glo - ry and praise to

ther. You are the pot - ter;
1. us in - to the im - age of
2. you. May we be one in you as
3. you. Glo - ry and praise to you for-

we are the clay, the work of your
1. Je - sus, your Son, of Je - sus, your
2. he is in you, and you are in
3. ev - er, a - men, for - ev - er, a -

| 1-6 2 | Final 2 |

hands. (to Verses) Ab - ba!
1. Son. (to Refrain)
2. him. (to Refrain)
3. men. (to Refrain)

## 601 WHEN IN OUR MUSIC

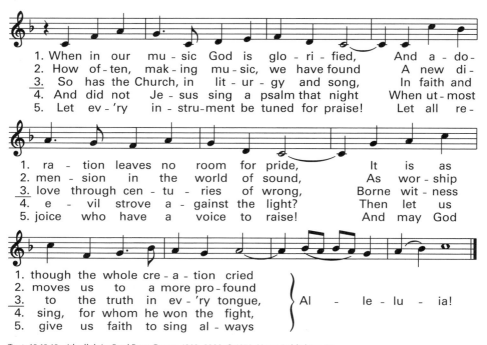

1. When in our mu - sic God is glo - ri - fied, And a - do-
2. How of - ten, mak - ing mu - sic, we have found A new di-
3. So has the Church, in lit - ur - gy and song, In faith and
4. And did not Je - sus sing a psalm that night When ut - most
5. Let ev - 'ry in - stru - ment be tuned for praise! Let all re-

1. ra - tion leaves no room for pride, It is as
2. men - sion in the world of sound, As wor - ship
3. love through cen - tu - ries of wrong, Borne wit - ness
4. e - vil strove a - gainst the light? Then let us
5. joice who have a voice to raise! And may God

1. though the whole cre - a - tion cried
2. moves us to a more pro - found
3. to the truth in ev - 'ry tongue, } Al - le - lu - ia!
4. sing, for whom he won the fight,
5. give us faith to sing al - ways

Text: 10 10 10 with alleluia; Fred Pratt Green, 1903–2000, © 1972, Hope Publishing Co.
  All rights reserved. Used with permission.
Music: ENGELBERG; Charles Villiers Stanford, 1852–1924, alt.

## 602 GRATEFUL

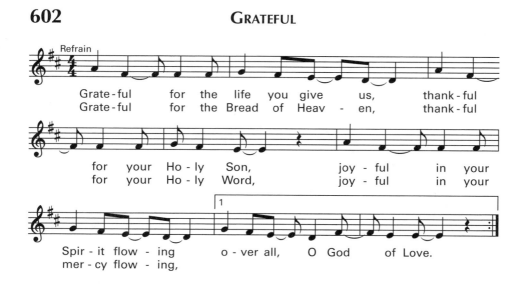

Grate - ful for the life you give us, thank - ful
Grate - ful for the Bread of Heav - en, thank - ful

for your Ho - ly Son, joy - ful in your
for your Ho - ly Word, joy - ful in your

Spir - it flow - ing o - ver all, O God of Love.
mer - cy flow - ing,

we will praise you. we will praise you.

**Verses**

1. You are more than we i-mag-ine, An-cient, Ho-ly, Liv-
2. May our lives pro-claim your jus-tice, may our voic-es sing

1. -ing Lord. E-ven when we doubt your pres-
2. your praise. May our hands work in your ser-

*to Refrain*

1. -ence you are faith-ful to your word.
2. -vice to the glo-ry of your name.

## NOW THANK WE ALL OUR GOD  603

1. Now thank we all our God With heart, and hands, and
2. O may this gra-cious God Through all our life be
3. All praise and thanks to God The Fa-ther now be

1. voic-es, Who won-drous things has done, In whom his world re-
2. near us, With ev-er joy-ful hearts And bless-ed peace to
3. giv-en, The Son, and Spir-it blest, Who reigns in high-est

1. joic-es; Who, from our moth-er's arms Has blessed us on our
2. cheer us; Pre-serve us in his grace, And guide us in dis-
3. heav-en, E-ter-nal, Tri-une God, Whom earth and heav'n a-

1. way With count-less gifts of love, And still is ours to-day.
2. tress, And free us from all sin, Till heav-en we pos-sess.
3. dore; For thus it was, is now, And shall be, ev-er-more.

# 604

## ALL MY DAYS

**Refrain**

Till the end of my days, O Lord, I will bless your name,

sing your praise, give you thanks, all my days.

**Verses**

1. You have made me lit - tle less than a god, _____
2. You have blessed ___ me with good things and plen - ty ____
3. Your sun ___ and your moon give me light, _____
4. How great ___ is your love, O ____ Fa - ther, ___

1. and have lav - ished my heart with your love. With dig - ni - ty and
2. and sur - round - ed my ta - ble with friends. Their love ___ and their
3. and your stars show the way through the night. Your riv - ers and
4. that you sent us your Sav - ior Son. His death ___ and his

*to Refrain*

1. hon - or you've clothed me, giv - en me rule o - ver all.
2. laugh - ter en - rich me; to - geth - er we sing your ___ praise.
3. streams have re - freshed me. I ___ will sing your ___ praise.
4. ris - ing will heal us, and draw us ___ all un - to you.

Text: Based on Psalm 8; J-Glenn Murray, SJ.
Music: Dan Schutte, b. 1947.
Text and music © 1971, 1974, Daniel L. Schutte and J-Glenn Murray, SJ. Published by OCP. All rights reserved.

# 605

## THANKS BE TO GOD

1. Thanks be to God whose love has gath - ered us this day;
2. Thanks be to God for all the gifts of life and light;
3. Thanks be to God who knows our se - cret joys and fears;
4. Thanks be to God who nev - er turns his face a - way;
5. Thanks be to God who made our world and all we see;

1. Thanks be to God who helps and guides us on our way.
2. Thanks be to God whose care pro - tects us day and night.
3. Thanks be to God who when we call him al - ways hears.
4. Thanks be to God who heals and par - dons all who stray.
5. Thanks be to God who gave his Son to set us free.

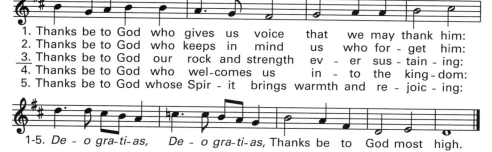

1. Thanks be to God who gives us voice that we may thank him:
2. Thanks be to God who keeps in mind us who for-get him:
3. Thanks be to God our rock and strength ev - er sus - tain - ing:
4. Thanks be to God who wel-comes us in - to the king-dom:
5. Thanks be to God whose Spir - it brings warmth and re - joic - ing:

1-5. *De - o gra-ti-as, De - o gra-ti-as,* Thanks be to God most high.

Text: 12 12 13 55 6; Stephen Dean, b. 1948.
Music: CHARIS; Stephen Dean.

## COME, YE THANKFUL PEOPLE, COME 606

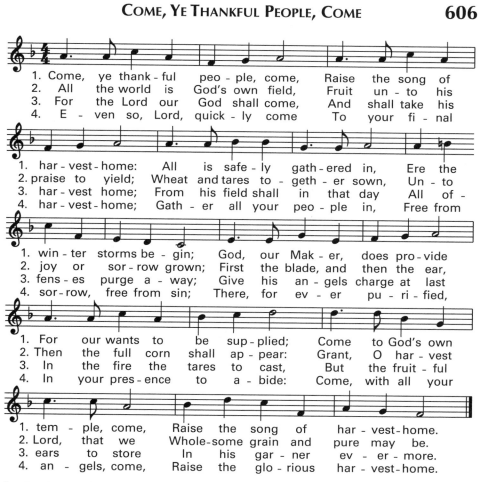

1. Come, ye thank - ful peo - ple, come, Raise the song of
2. All the world is God's own field, Fruit un - to his
3. For the Lord our God shall come, And shall take his
4. E - ven so, Lord, quick - ly come To your fi - nal

1. har - vest - home: All is safe - ly gath - ered in, Ere the
2. praise to yield; Wheat and tares to - geth - er sown, Un - to
3. har - vest home; From his field shall in that day All of -
4. har - vest - home; Gath - er all your peo - ple in, Free from

1. win - ter storms be - gin; God, our Mak - er, does pro - vide
2. joy or sor - row grown; First the blade, and then the ear,
3. fens - es purge a - way; Give his an - gels charge at last
4. sor - row, free from sin; There, for ev - er pu - ri - fied,

1. For our wants to be sup - plied; Come to God's own
2. Then the full corn shall ap - pear: Grant, O har - vest
3. In the fire the tares to cast, But the fruit - ful
4. In your pres - ence to a - bide: Come, with all your

1. tem - ple, come, Raise the song of har - vest - home.
2. Lord, that we Whole-some grain and pure may be.
3. ears to store In his gar - ner ev - er - more.
4. an - gels, come, Raise the glo - rious har - vest - home.

Text: 77 77 D; Henry Alford, 1810–1871, alt.
Music: ST. GEORGE'S WINDSOR; George J. Elvey, 1816–1893.

## 607     SING TO THE LORD OF HARVEST

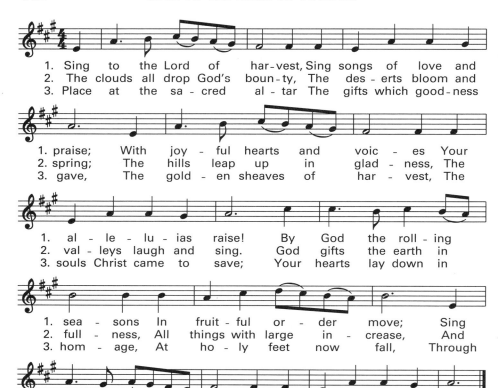

1. Sing to the Lord of har-vest, Sing songs of love and
2. The clouds all drop God's boun-ty, The des-erts bloom and
3. Place at the sa-cred al-tar The gifts which good-ness

1. praise; With joy-ful hearts and voic-es Your
2. spring; The hills leap up in glad-ness, The
3. gave, The gold-en sheaves of har-vest, The

1. al-le-lu-ias raise! By God the roll-ing
2. val-leys laugh and sing. God gifts the earth in
3. souls Christ came to save; Your hearts lay down in

1. sea-sons In fruit-ful or-der move; Sing
2. full-ness, All things with large in-crease, And
3. hom-age, At ho-ly feet now fall, Through

1. to the Lord of har-vest A joy-ful song of love.
2. crowns the year with good-ness, With plen-ty and with peace.
3. all your life a-dor-ing The One who died for all.

Text: 76 76 D; John S.B. Monsell, 1811–1875, alt.
Music: WIE LIEBLICH IST DER MAIEN; Johann Steuerlein, 1546–1613.

## 608     LET ALL THINGS NOW LIVING

1. Let all things now liv-ing A song of thanks-giv-ing To
   Who fash-ioned and made us, Pro-tect-ed and stayed us, By
2. His law he en-forc-es, The stars in their cours-es, The
   The hills and the moun-tains, The riv-ers and foun-tains, The

1. God our Cre-a-tor tri-um-phant-ly raise;
   guid-ing us on to the end of our days. God's ban-ners are
2. sun in its or-bit o-be-dient-ly shine,
   depths of the o-cean pro-claim God di-vine. We, too, should be

1. o'er us, Pure light goes be - fore us, A pil - lar of fire shin-ing
2. voic-ing Our love and re - joic-ing With glad ad - o - ra-tion, a

1. forth in the night: Till shad-ows have van-ished And dark-ness is
2. song let us raise: Till all things now liv - ing U - nite in thanks-

1. ban-ished, As for-ward we trav - el from light in - to Light.
2. giv - ing, To God in the high - est, ho - san - na and praise.

Text: 66 11 66 11 D; Katherine K. Davis, 1892–1980, © 1939, 1966, E.C. Schirmer Music Co.,
a division of ECS Publishing, Boston, MA. All rights reserved. Used with permission.
Music: ASH GROVE; trad. Welsh Melody.

## FOR THE BEAUTY OF THE EARTH 609

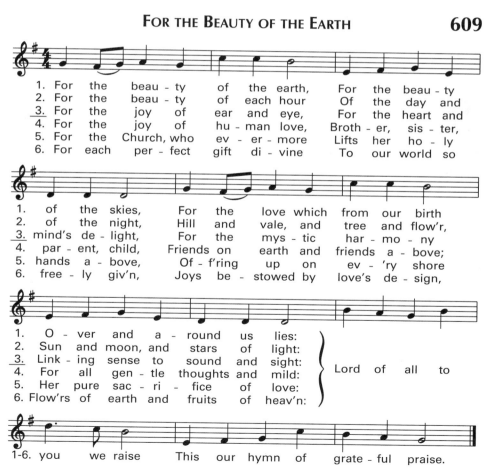

1. For the beau - ty of the earth, For the beau - ty
2. For the beau - ty of each hour Of the day and
3. For the joy of ear and eye, For the heart and
4. For the joy of hu - man love, Broth - er, sis - ter,
5. For the Church, who ev - er - more Lifts her ho - ly
6. For each per - fect gift di - vine To our world so

1. of the skies, For the love which from our birth
2. of the night, Hill and vale, and tree and flow'r,
3. mind's de - light, For the mys - tic har - mo - ny
4. par - ent, child, Friends on earth and friends a - bove;
5. hands a - bove, Of - f'ring up on ev - 'ry shore
6. free - ly giv'n, Joys be - stowed by love's de - sign,

1. O - ver and a - round us lies:
2. Sun and moon, and stars of light:
3. Link - ing sense to sound and sight:
4. For all gen - tle thoughts and mild:
5. Her pure sac - ri - fice of love:
6. Flow'rs of earth and fruits of heav'n:

Lord of all to

1-6. you we raise This our hymn of grate - ful praise.

Text: 77 77 77; *Lyra Eucharistica*, 1864; Folliot S. Pierpoint, 1835–1917, alt.
Music: DIX; Conrad Kocher, 1786–1872; adapt. by William H. Monk, 1823–1889.

# 610

## GIVE THANKS TO THE LORD

Verses 1 & 2, 4 & 5, 7 & 8, 10

1. Give thanks to the Lord who does won-drous deeds, who
2. Give thanks to the God who has blessed our land, who
4. Give thanks to the God of the sum-mer rains, who
5. Give thanks to the Lord who is mer-ci-ful, whose
7. Give thanks to the Lord for the blaz-ing sun, for
8. Give thanks to the Lord for the crim-son skies, for
10. Give thanks to the God who has set us free, who

1. mas-ters the winds and the rag-ing seas,
2. guards ev-'ry step with a might-y hand,
4. spreads out the hills and the gold-en plains,
5. kind-ness is wide and love boun-ti-ful, whose
7. great, roll-ing waves where the dol-phins run,
8. wild, wind-y heights where the ea-gle flies,
10. raised us to life on a bless-ed tree,

love is for ev-er, whose love is for ev-er, whose love is for

1, 4, 7, Final    Fine  2, 5, 8

ev-er more!    more!

Verses 3, 6, 9

3. O, bless the Lord for ev-'ry gift that comes to grace our way. And
6. O, bless the Lord with mu-sic, ev-'ry crea-ture great and small. And
9. O, bless the Lord all peo-ple, for the mu-sic of the skies. And

3. praise the God of faith-ful-ness, who comes to light our day. (to Vss 4 & 5)
6. sing through all the a-ges of God's fa-vor to us all. (to Vss 7 & 8)
9. tell the won-drous sto-ry of a love that nev-er dies. (to Vs 10)

# ALL GOOD GIFTS

**611**

Verses

1. We plow the fields and scat - ter the good seed on the
2. You on - ly are the mak - er of all things near and
3. We thank you, then, Cre - a - tor, for all things bright and

1. land, but it is fed and wa - tered by God's al - might - y
2. far, you paint the way-side flow - er, you light the eve - ning
3. good, the seed-time and the har - vest, our life, our health, our

1. hand. God sends the snow in win - ter, the warmth to swell the
2. star. The winds and waves o - bey you, by you the birds are
3. food. And all that we can of - fer, your bound-less love im-

1. grain, the breez-es and the sun-shine, and soft, re-fresh-ing rain.
2. fed; much more, to us, your chil - dren, you give our dai - ly bread.
3. parts; the gifts to you most pleas - ing are hum-ble, thank-ful hearts.

Refrain

All good gifts a-round us are sent from heav-en a-bove;

thank you, Lord, O thank you for all your love.

Text: 76 76 D with refrain; Matthias Claudius, 1740–1815; tr. by Jane M. Campbell, 1817–1878, alt.
Music: HEISLMAN; Kevin Keil, ASCAP, b. 1956, © 1993, Kevin Keil. Published by OCP. All rights reserved.

## 612     GOD'S LOVE IS EVERLASTING

God's love is ev-er-last-ing, faith-ful till the end of time. God's
love is ev-er-last-ing, God's love will nev-er end.       end.

1. Give thanks to the Lord, for God is good. Give
2. Who cre-at-ed the earth, who di-vid-ed the seas, who
3. Who a-lone does great won-ders, who frees us from harm, who

1. thanks to the Lord of Lords. Give
2. set the heav'n-ly lights. The
3. nour-ish-es all liv-ing things. Give

1. thanks to the God a-bove oth-er gods.
2. sun to rule the day, the stars at night. God's
3. thanks to the God of heav-en and earth.

1-3. mer-cy en-dures for-ev-er.

Text: Based on Psalm 136:1–9; Tom Tomaszek, b. 1950.
Music: Tom Tomaszek.

## 613     JUBILATE DEO

Ju-bi-lá-te! Ju-bi-lá-te De-o!

Ju-bi-lá-te De-o! Ju-bi-lá-te De-o!

O - mnis ter - ra, ju - bi - lá - te De - o!

Translation: Shout with joy to God, all the earth.

Text: Based on Psalm 100:1.
Music: Barbara Bridge, b. 1950, © 1998, Barbara Bridge. Published by OCP. All rights reserved.

## HOW GREAT THOU ART 614

1. O Lord my God! When I in awe-some won-der Con-si-der
2. When through the woods and for-est glades I wan-der, And hear the
3. And when I think that God, his Son not spar-ing, Sent him to
4. When Christ shall come with shout of ac-cla-ma-tion And take me

1. all the worlds thy hands have made, I see the stars, I
2. birds sing sweet-ly in the trees; When I look down from
3. die, I scarce can take it in, That on the cross, my
4. home, what joy shall fill my heart! Then I shall bow in

1. hear the roll-ing thun-der, Thy pow'r through-out the
2. lof-ty moun-tain gran-deur And hear the brook, and
3. bur-den glad-ly bear-ing, He bled and died to
4. hum-ble ad-o-ra-tion, And there pro-claim, my

Refrain

1. u-ni-verse dis-played; Then sings my soul, my Sav-ior God to
2. feel the gen-tle breeze;
3. take a-way my sin;
4. God, how great thou art!

thee; How great thou art, how great thou art! Then sings my soul, my

Sav-ior God to thee; How great thou art, how great thou art!

Words: Stuart K. Hine.
Music: Traditional Swedish folk tune/adapt. by Stuart K. Hine.
Words and music © 1949 and 1953 by The Stuart K. Hine Trust.
All rights in the USA except print rights administered by EMI CMG Publishing.
USA print rights administered by Hope Publishing Company. All rights reserved. Used with permission.

## 615    FOR THE FRUITS OF THIS CREATION

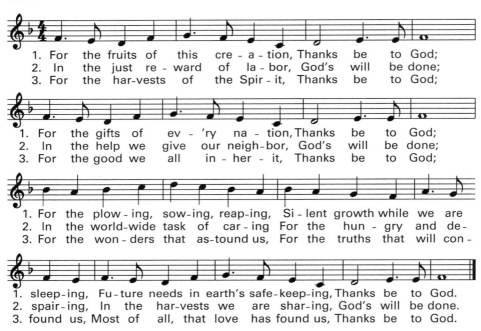

1. For the fruits of this cre-a-tion, Thanks be to God;
2. In the just re-ward of la-bor, God's will be done;
3. For the har-vests of the Spir-it, Thanks be to God;

1. For the gifts of ev-'ry na-tion, Thanks be to God;
2. In the help we give our neigh-bor, God's will be done;
3. For the good we all in-her-it, Thanks be to God;

1. For the plow-ing, sow-ing, reap-ing, Si-lent growth while we are
2. In the world-wide task of car-ing For the hun-gry and de-
3. For the won-ders that as-tound us, For the truths that will con-

1. sleep-ing, Fu-ture needs in earth's safe-keep-ing, Thanks be to God.
2. spair-ing, In the har-vests we are shar-ing, God's will be done.
3. found us, Most of all, that love has found us, Thanks be to God.

## 616    OH, WHO CAN KNOW THE MIND OF GOD

1. Oh, who can know the mind of God, Or
2. Who else has cupped the seas in hand, Or
3. Who else sur-rounds in bound-less deeps The
4. Too high for us, O Lord, your ways, Too

1. who dare call his name, Whose glo-ry is the
2. set the skies a-light? Who else could carve from
3. is-land of the mind? Who else in clouds of
4. vast your works: to them We reach with trem-bling

1. ris-ing sun, Whose ev-'ry word is flame?
2. stone the land, Or sum-mon day from night?
3. si-lence keeps Long watch for all our kind?
4. words of praise To touch your gar-ment's hem.

## SACRED CREATION

Sa-cred the land, sa - cred the wa - ter, sa - cred the sky,

ho - ly and true. Sa-cred all life, sa - cred each oth - er;

all re - flect God who is good.

Verses

1. All praise be yours through Broth - er Sun,
2. Broth - er Wind and Air that per - vades,
3. Through Broth - er Fire you bright - en the night,

1. bear - ing a like - ness of you, Most High One.
2. var - y their moods to sus - tain all you've made.
3. strong and ro - bust yet play - ful and bright.

1. Sis - ter Moon and Stars who are pre-cious, splen-did,
2. Sis - ter Wa - ter, use - ful and pure, low - ly,
3. Sis - ter Earth, our moth - er who nur-tures, feed-ing,

to Refrain

1. ride your glo - ri - ous sky.
2. free - ly shar - ing her life.
3. yield - ing flow - er and herb.

Text: Based on a text by St. Francis of Assisi, ca. 1182–1226, and the inspiration of Louis Vitale, OFM;
Rufino Zaragoza, OFM, b. 1957.
Music: Rufina Zaragoza, OFM.

## 618    I Sing the Mighty Power of God

1. I sing the might-y pow'r of God That made the
2. I sing the good-ness of the Lord That filled the
3. There's not a plant or flow'r be-low, But makes thy

1. moun-tains rise, That spread the flow-ing seas a-broad, And
2. earth with food; He formed the crea-tures with his word, And
3. glo-ries known; And clouds a-rise, and tem-pests blow By

1. built the loft-y skies. I sing the wis-dom
2. then pro-nounced them good. Lord, how thy won-ders
3. or-der from thy throne; While all that bor-rows

1. that or-dained The sun to rule the day; The moon shines
2. are dis-played Wher-e'er I turn my eye; If I sur-
3. life from thee Is ev-er in thy care, And ev-'ry-

1. full at his com-mand, And all the stars o-bey.
2. vey the ground I tread, Or gaze up-on the sky!
3. where that I can be, Thou, God, are pres-ent there.

Text: CMD; Isaac Watts, 1674–1748, alt.
Music: ELLACOMBE; *Gesangbuch der Herzogl, Wirtembergischen Katholischen Hofkapelle*, 1784, alt.;
    adapt. fr. Würth's *Katholisches Gesangbuch*, 1863.

## 619    Word of God, You Spoke Creation

1. Word of God, you spoke cre-a-tion From the cha-os
2. Word of God, we all a-dore you, Flame that burns a-
3. Word of God, we sing and praise you, Mel-o-dy with

1. of the flood; Word made flesh, you wrought sal-va-tion
2. way the night, Word made flesh, we bow be-fore you,
3. love en-twined. Word made flesh, we glo-ri-fy you

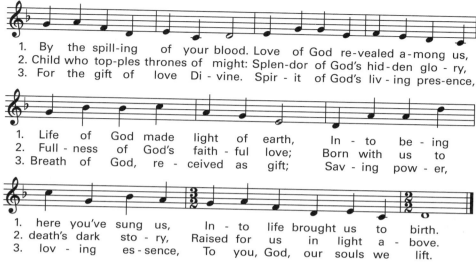

1. By the spill-ing of your blood. Love of God re-vealed a-mong us,
2. Child who top-ples thrones of might: Splen-dor of God's hid-den glo - ry,
3. For the gift of love Di - vine. Spir - it of God's liv-ing pres-ence,

1. Life of God made light of earth, In - to be - ing
2. Full - ness of God's faith - ful love; Born with us to
3. Breath of God, re - ceived as gift; Sav - ing pow - er,

1. here you've sung us, In - to life brought us to birth.
2. death's dark sto - ry, Raised for us in light a - bove.
3. lov - ing es - sence, To you, God, our souls we lift.

Text: 87 87 D. Vss. 1 and 2, Jennifer Glen, CCVI, b. 1945, © 1987, 2001, The Sisters of Charity of the Incarnate Word. Published by OCP. All rights reserved. Vs. 3, Gael Berberick (ASCAP), © 2005, Gael Berberick. Published by OCP. All rights reserved.
Music: STEPHANIE; Gael Berberick (ASCAP) and Barney Walker (ASCAP), © 2005, Gael Berberick and Barney Walker. Published by OCP. All rights reserved.

## ALL THE EARTH

**620**

Refrain

All the earth pro-claim the Lord; Sing your praise to God.

Verses

1. Serve you the Lord, heart filled with glad - ness.
2. Know that the Lord is our cre - a - tor.
3. We are the sheep of the green pas - ture;
4. Come to the gates bring-ing thanks - giv - ing;
5. Our Lord is good, with love en - dur - ing;
6. Hon - or and praise be to the Fa - ther,

to Refrain

1. Come in - to God's pres - ence sing - ing for joy!
2. Yes, God is our Fa - ther; we are his own.
3. For we are God's peo - ple, cho - sen by God.
4. O en - ter the court - yards sing - ing in praise.
5. God's word is a - bid - ing now with us all.
6. The Son and the Spir - it, world with - out end.

Text: Based on Psalm 100; Lucien Deiss, CSSp, 1921–2007.
Music: Lucien Deiss, CSSp.
Text and music © 1965, World Library Publications. All rights reserved. Used with permission.

**621**  IF GOD IS FOR US

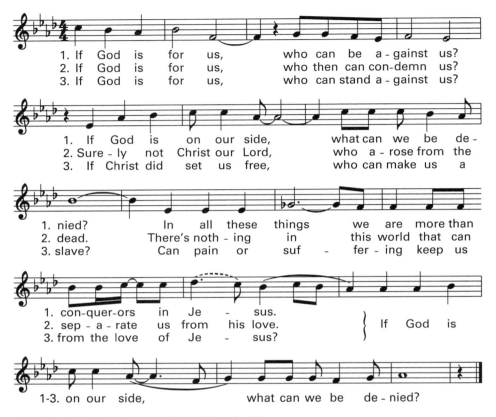

1. If God is for us, who can be a-gainst us?
2. If God is for us, who then can con-demn us?
3. If God is for us, who can stand a-gainst us?

1. If God is on our side, what can we be de-
2. Sure-ly not Christ our Lord, who a-rose from the
3. If Christ did set us free, who can make us a-

1. nied? In all these things we are more than
2. dead. There's noth-ing in this world that can
3. slave? Can pain or suf - fer-ing keep us

1. con-quer-ors in Je - sus.
2. sep-a-rate us from his love.   If God is
3. from the love of Je - sus?

1-3. on our side, what can we be de-nied?

Text: Based on Romans 8:31–39; Grayson Warren Brown, b. 1948.
Music: Grayson Warren Brown.
Text and music © 1995, Grayson Warren Brown. Published by OCP. All rights reserved.

**622**  LIKE A SHEPHERD

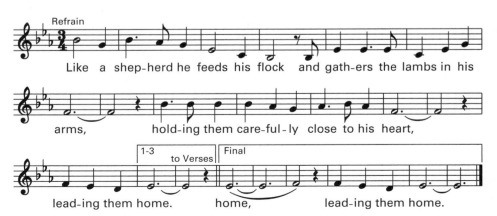

Refrain

Like a shep-herd he feeds his flock and gath-ers the lambs in his

arms, hold-ing them care-ful-ly close to his heart,

1-3 to Verses | Final

lead-ing them home.   home, lead-ing them home.

Text: Based on Isaiah 40:9ff; Ezekiel 34:11ff; Matthew 11:28ff; Bob Dufford, SJ, b. 1943.
Music: Bob Dufford, SJ.
Text and music © 1976, Robert J. Dufford, SJ, and OCP. All rights reserved.

## I HAVE LOVED YOU 623

Text: Based on Jeremiah 31:3; Psalm 24:3; Michael Joncas, b. 1951.
Music: Michael Joncas.
Text and music © 1979, OCP. All rights reserved.

**624**   YOUR GRACE IS ENOUGH

## LORD OF GLORY

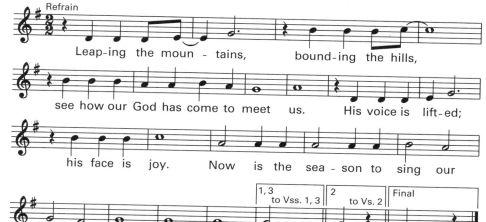

Leaping the moun - tains, bounding the hills, see how our God has come to meet us. His voice is lift-ed; his face is joy. Now is the sea - son to sing our

| 1, 3 to Vss. 1, 3 | 2 to Vs. 2 | Final |

song on high.

Verses 1, 2

1. Come, then, O Lord of glo - ry, show us your face. ____
2. He pas - tures his flock a - mong the wild ____ flow'rs ____ and

to Refrain

1. Speak, ____ for we know your words are life.
2. leads them to the moun-tain of his love.

Verse 3

3. All through the day, all through the night,

to Refrain

3. seek for the Lord and sing his love.

Text: Based on Song of Songs 2; Tim Manion, b. 1951.
Music: Tim Manion.

**626**          **COME TO THE WATER**

1. O let all who thirst, let them come to the
2. And let all who seek, let them come to the
3. And let all who toil, let them come to the
4. And let all the poor, let them come to the

1. wa - ter. And let all who have noth-ing,
2. wa - ter. And let all who have noth-ing,
3. wa - ter. And let all who are wea - ry,
4. wa - ter. Bring the ones who are lad - en,

1. let them come to the Lord: with-out
2. let them come to the Lord: with-out
3. let them come to the Lord: all who
4. bring them all to the Lord: bring the

1. mon-ey, with-out price. Why should you pay the
2. mon-ey, with-out strife. Why should you spend your
3. la - bor, with-out rest. How can your soul find
4. chil-dren with-out might. Eas - y the load and

1. price, ex-cept for the Lord?
2. life, ex-cept for the Lord?
3. rest, ex-cept for the Lord?
4. light: come to the Lord.

Text: Based on Isaiah 55:1–2; Matthew 11:28–30; John Foley, S.J., b. 1939.
Music: John Foley, S.J.

**627**          **RAIN DOWN**

Refrain

Rain down, rain down, rain down your

1. love on your peo - ple.
2. love, God of life.

Verses

1. Faith-ful and true is the word of our God. All of God's
2. We who re-vere and find hope in our God live in the
3. God of cre-a-tion, we long for your truth; you are the

1. works are so wor-thy of trust. God's mer-cy falls on the
2. kind-ness and joy of God's wing. God will pro-tect us from
3. wa-ter of life that we thirst. Grant that your love and your

to Refrain

1. just and the right; full of God's love is the earth.
2. dark-ness and death; God will not leave us to starve.
3. peace touch our hearts, all of our hope lies in you.

Text: Based on Psalm 33; Jaime Cortez, b. 1963.
Music: Jaime Cortez.

## ISAIAH 49

### 628

Verse 1

1. I will nev-er for-get you, my peo-ple; I have carved you

1. on the palm of my hand. I will nev-er for-get you; I will

1. not leave you or-phaned. I will nev-er for-get my own.

Verse 2

2. Does a moth-er for-get her ba-by? Or a

2. wom-an the child with-in her womb? Yet e-ven if these for-

(Repeat Vs 1)

2. get, yes, e-ven if these for-get, I will nev-er for-get my own.

Text: Based on Isaiah 49:15; Carey Landry, b. 1944.
Music: Carey Landry.

## 629     We Are the Light of the World

**Verses**

1. Bless - ed are they who are poor in spir - it,
2. Bless - ed are they who are meek and hum - ble,
3. Bless - ed are they who will mourn in sor - row,
4. Bless those who hun - ger and thirst for jus - tice,
5. Bless - ed are they who show oth - ers mer - cy,
6. Bless - ed are hearts that are clean and ho - ly,
7. Bless - ed are they who bring peace a - mong us,
8. Bless those who suf - fer from per - se - cu - tion,

1. Theirs is the king-dom of God. Bless us, O Lord, make us
2. They will in - her - it the earth. Bless us, O Lord, make us
3. They will be com - fort - ed. Bless us, O Lord, when we
4. They will be sat - is - fied. Bless us, O Lord, hear our
5. They will know mer - cy too. Bless us, O Lord, hear our
6. They will be - hold the Lord. Bless us, O Lord, make us
7. They are the chil - dren of God. Bless us, O Lord, may your
8. Theirs is the king-dom of God. Bless us, O Lord, when they

1. poor in spir - it; Bless us, O Lord, our God.
2. meek and hum - ble; Bless us, O Lord, our God.
3. share their sor - row; Bless us, O Lord, our God.
4. cry for jus - tice; Bless us, O Lord, our God.
5. cry for mer - cy; Bless us, O Lord, our God.
6. pure and ho - ly; Bless us, O Lord, our God.
7. peace be with us; Bless us, O Lord, our God.
8. per - se - cute us; Bless us, O Lord, our God.

**Refrain**

We are the light of the world, may our light shine be-fore all,

That they may see the good that we do, and give glo - ry to God.

Text: 10 6 10 6 with refrain; based on the Beatitudes; adapt. by Jean Anthony Greif, 1898–1981, alt.
Music: GREIF; Jean Anthony Greif.
Text and music © 1966, Vernacular Hymns Publishing Co. All rights reserved. Used with permission.

# I Am the Light of the World

**Refrain**

"I am the Light of the world," says the Lord,
"They who fol-low me will have the light of life."

**Verses 1, 2**

1. "A - rise," says the Lord, "Have no fear with-
2. "Walk in the light, there is no cause to

1. in you; for in my pres - ence there will be no
2. stum - ble; I have come to light the path be -

1. dark - ness. I am the Light of the world."
2. fore you. I am the Light of the world."

*to Refrain*

**Verse 3**

3. "Lis - ten to my words; they are from the One who
3. sent me: For you, my friends, are called to share God's
3. glo - ry. You are the Light of the world."

*to Refrain*

Text: Based on John 8:12; Ephesians 5:14; 1 John 2:10; Matthew 5:14; Greg Hayakawa, b. 1953.
Music: Greg Hayakawa.
Text and music © 1978, 1979, Greg Hayakawa. Published by OCP. All rights reserved.

**631** YOUR LIGHT WILL COME, JERUSALEM

Refrain

Your light will come, Je-ru-sa-lem; for on you will dawn the glo-ry of the Lord, and all na-tions will walk in your light, al-le-lu-ia, al-le-lu - ia.

Verses

1. Christ is the light of the world, a light dis-
2. His light is mer - cy and peace, a peace sur-
3. His light is jus - tice and truth, and love which

1. pel - ling the dark-ness. May we, his
2. pass - ing all tell - ing. May we, his
3. casts out all ha - tred. May we, his

to Refrain

1. bod - y, re - flect that ho - ly light.
2. bod - y, be in - stru-ments of peace.
3. bod - y, pre - pare the reign of God.

# I Want to Walk as a Child of the Light

**Verses**

1. I want to walk as a child of the light; I want to
2. I want to see ___ the bright-ness of God; I want to
3. I'm look-ing for ___ the com - ing of Christ; I want to

1. fol - low Je - sus. God set the stars to give
2. look at Je - sus. Clear Sun of righ - teous-ness,
3. be with Je - sus. When we have run ___ with

1. light to the world; the star of my life ___ is Je - sus.
2. shine on my path, and show me the way to the Fa - ther.
3. pa-tience the race, we shall know the joy ___ of Je - sus.

**Refrain**

In him there is no dark-ness at all; the night and the

day are both a - like. The Lamb is the light of the

cit - y of God: Shine in my heart, Lord Je - sus.

Text: Irregular; Kathleen Thomerson, b. 1934.
Music: HOUSTON; Kathleen Thomerson.

## 633      GOD IS LIGHT

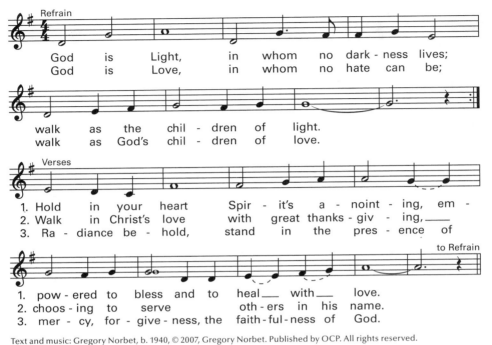

Refrain

God is Light, in whom no dark - ness lives;
God is Love, in whom no hate can be;

walk as the chil - dren of light.
walk as God's chil - dren of love.

Verses

1. Hold in your heart Spir - it's a - noint - ing, em -
2. Walk in Christ's love with great thanks - giv - ing,
3. Ra - diance be - hold, stand in the pres - ence of

to Refrain

1. pow - ered to bless and to heal ___ with ___ love.
2. choos - ing to serve oth - ers in his name.
3. mer - cy, for - give - ness, the faith - ful - ness of God.

Text and music: Gregory Norbet, b. 1940, © 2007, Gregory Norbet. Published by OCP. All rights reserved.

## 634      O RADIANT LIGHT

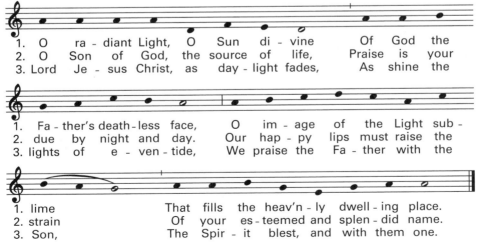

1. O ra - diant Light, O Sun di - vine Of God the
2. O Son of God, the source of life, Praise is your
3. Lord Je - sus Christ, as day - light fades, As shine the

1. Fa - ther's death - less face, O im - age of the Light sub -
2. due by night and day. Our hap - py lips must raise the
3. lights of e - ven - tide, We praise the Fa - ther with the

1. lime That fills the heav'n - ly dwell - ing place.
2. strain Of your es - teemed and splen - did name.
3. Son, The Spir - it blest, and with them one.

Text: LM; *Phos Hilaron*, Greek, ca. 200; tr. by William G. Storey, b. 1923, © William G. Storey.
    All rights reserved. Used with permission.
Music: JESU DULCIS MEMORIA; Chant, Mode I.

# WE ARE MARCHING/SIYAHAMBA

We are march - ing in the light of God, we are
Si - ya - hamb' e - ku - kha - nyen' kwen - khos', si - ya -

march-ing in the light of God. We are march - ing in the
hamb' e - ku - kha - nyen' kwen-khos'. Si - ya - hamb' e - ku - kha-

light of God, we are march-ing in the light of God.
nyen' kwen - khos', si - ya - hamb' e - ku - kha - nyen' kwen - khos'.

We are march-ing, Oo we are
Si - ya - ham - ba, Oo si - ya -

march-ing in the light of God. We are march-ing,
hamb' e - ku - kha - nyen' kwen - khos'. Si - ya - ham - ba,

Oo we are march-ing in the light of God.
Oo si - ya - hamb' e - ku - kha - nyen' kwen-khos'.

# 636

## LORD OF THE DANCE

1. I danced in the morn-ing when the world was be-gun, And I
2. I danced for the scribe ___ and the Phar - i - see, But they
3. I danced on the Sab-bath and I cured the ___ lame, The ___
4. I danced on a Fri-day when the sky turned ___ black; It's ___
5. They cut me ___ down ___ and I leapt up ___ high, ___

1. danced in the moon and the stars ___ and the sun, And I
2. would not ___ dance and they would-n't fol - low me; I ___
3. ho - ly ___ peo - ple, they said it was a shame; They ___
4. hard to ___ dance with the dev - il on your back; They ___
5. I am the life that - 'll nev - er, nev - er die, I'll ___

1. came down from heav-en and I danced on the earth, ___ At
2. danced for the fish - er-men, for James and for John; ___ They
3. whipped and they stripped ___ and they hung me ___ high, And they
4. bur - ied my bod - y and they thought I'd ___ gone, ___ But
5. live in ___ you ___ if you'll live in ___ me; ___

Refrain

1. Beth - le - hem I ___ had my birth. "Dance, then wher-
2. came with ___ me and the dance went on.
3. left me ___ there on a cross to die.
4. I am the dance and I still go on.
5. "I am the Lord of the Dance," said he.

ev - er you may be; I am the Lord of the Dance," said he. "I'll

lead you all wher-ev-er you may be, I will lead you all in the

1-4
Dance," said he.

to Verses

Final
Dance," said he.

## In Christ Alone

1. In Christ a-lone my hope is found, he is my light, my
2. In Christ a-lone, who took on flesh, full-ness of God in
3. There in the ground his bod-y lay, light of the world, by
4. No guilt in life, no fear in death, this is the pow'r of

1. strength, my song; this cor-ner-stone, this sol-id ground,
2. help-less babe! This gift of love and righ-teous-ness,
3. dark-ness slain; then, burst-ing forth in glo-rious day,
4. Christ in me; from life's first cry to fi-nal breath,

1. firm through the fierc-est drought and storm. What heights of
2. scorned by the ones he came to save. Till on that
3. up from the grave he rose a-gain! And as he
4. Je-sus com-mands my des-ti-ny. No pow'r of

1. love, what depths of peace, when fears are stilled, when striv-ings
2. cross as Je-sus died, the wrath of God was sat-is-
3. stands in vic-to-ry, sin's curse has lost its grip on
4. hell, no scheme of man, can ev-er pluck me from his

1. cease. My com-fort-er, my all in all, here in the
2. fied. For ev-ery sin on him was laid; here in the
3. me; for I am his and he is mine, bought with the
4. hand; till he re-turns or calls me home, here in the

1. love of Christ I stand.
2. death of Christ I live.
3. pre-cious blood of Christ.
4. pow'r of Christ I'll stand!

## 638     JESU, JOY OF OUR DESIRING

1. Je - su, joy of our de - sir - ing, Ho - ly wis - dom,
2. Through the way where hope is guid - ing, Hear what peace - ful

1. love most bright, Drawn by you, our souls as - pir - ing,
2. mu - sic rings; Where the flocks in you con - fid - ing,

1. Soar to un - cre - at - ed Light. Word of God, our flesh that
2. Drink of joy from death - less springs! Theirs is beau - ty's fair - est

1. fash-ioned With the fire of life im - pas-sioned, Striv - ing
2. plea - sure; Theirs is wis-dom's ho - liest trea-sure; You do

1. still to truth un - known, Soar-ing, dy - ing, 'round your throne.
2. ev - er lead your own, In the love of joys un - known.

Text: 87 87 88 77; *Christlich Herzens Andacht*, 1665; Martin Jahn, ca. 1620–1682; tr. by Robert S. Bridges, 1844–1930, rev.
Music: WERDE MUNTER; *Himmlische Lieder*, Vol. 3, Lüneberg, 1642; Johann P. Schop, ca. 1590–1664.

## 639     EARTHEN VESSELS

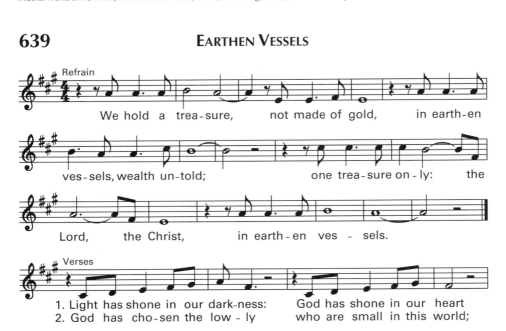

Refrain

We hold a trea - sure, not made of gold, in earth - en

ves - sels, wealth un - told; one trea - sure on - ly: the

Lord, the Christ, in earth - en ves - sels.

Verses

1. Light has shone in our dark - ness: God has shone in our heart
2. God has cho - sen the low - ly who are small in this world;

1. with the light of the glo-ry of Je - sus, the Lord.
2. in this weak-ness is glo-ry in Je - sus, the Lord.

Text: Based on 2 Corinthians 4:6–7; 1 Corinthians 1:27–29; John Foley, S.J., b. 1939.
Music: John Foley, S.J.
Text and music © 1975, 1978, 1991, John B. Foley, S.J., and OCP. All rights reserved.

## CHRIST BEFORE US

### 640

1. Christ be-fore us, Christ be-side us, Christ to guide us
2. May we be for one an-oth-er all that you would
3. God be-fore us through the a-ges; Christ be-side us
4. O Re-deem-er, fill your ser-vants with your words of

1. all our days. He to car-ry all our sor-rows, he to
2. have us be. May we live your law of kind-ness, love, com-
3. here to-day. Spir-it, lead us forth for-ev-er; guide and
4. last-ing life. Give to those with hands of heal-ing love trans-

1. bear us per-fect grace. Je-sus, Sav-ior, Friend and Broth-er,
2. pas-sion, char-i-ty. May we climb your ho-ly moun-tain;
3. help us all our days. Christ the Sav-ior, God the Liv-ing,
4. cend-ing pain and strife. Make us lov-ing sons and daugh-ters;

1. In - ter-ces-sor, Son of God, save your peo-ple
2. may we see your ho-ly face! Vis - it now this
3. Great Cre-a-tor, Spir-it blest! Ho - ly Three-in -
4. make us ho-ly, kind and true, sent to la-bor

2

1. in your dy - ing, and in ris-ing, con-quer death.
2. hum-ble dwell-ing; dwell with-in this ho - ly place.
3. One Im-mor-tal, come and be our wel-come guest.
4. for your King-dom— rest-less till we rest in you.

Text: 87 87 D; Janèt Sullivan Whitaker, b. 1958; © 1990, Janèt Sullivan Whitaker. Published by OCP. All rights reserved.
Music: SUO GÂN; Trad. Welsh Melody.

## 641

# O CHRIST, OUR TEACHER

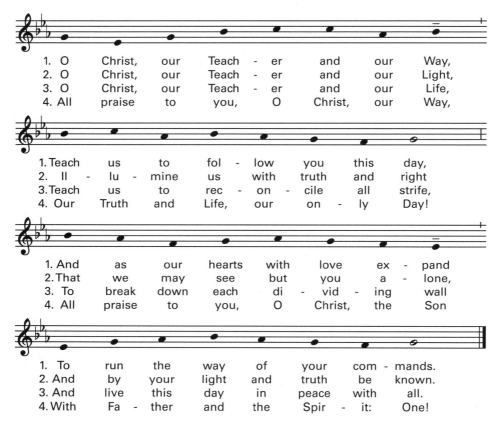

1. O Christ, our Teach - er and our Way,
2. O Christ, our Teach - er and our Light,
3. O Christ, our Teach - er and our Life,
4. All praise to you, O Christ, our Way,

1. Teach us to fol - low you this day,
2. Il - lu - mine us with truth and right
3. Teach us to rec - on - cile all strife,
4. Our Truth and Life, our on - ly Day!

1. And as our hearts with love ex - pand
2. That we may see but you a - lone,
3. To break down each di - vid - ing wall
4. All praise to you, O Christ, the Son

1. To run the way of your com - mands.
2. And by your light and truth be known.
3. And live this day in peace with all.
4. With Fa - ther and the Spir - it: One!

Text: LM; Harry Hagan, OSB, b. 1947, © 1999, St. Meinrad Archabbey. Published by OCP. All rights reserved.
Music: CONDITOR ALME SIDERUM; Chant, Mode IV.

## 642

# BLESSED JESUS, AT YOUR WORD

1. Bless - ed Je - sus, at your word we are gath - ered
2. All our knowl-edge, sense, and sight lie in deep - est
3. Glor - ious Lord, your - self im - part! Light of Light, from

1. all to hear you; let our hearts and minds be stirred
2. dark - ness shroud - ed, till your Spir - it breaks our night
3. God pro - ceed - ing, o - pen now each mind and heart,

1. now to seek and love and fear you; by your teach-ings
2. with the beams of truth un-cloud - ed; you a - lone to
3. help us by your Spir-it's plead - ing. Hear the cry your

1. true and ho - ly, drawn from earth to love you sole - ly.
2. God can win us; you must work all good with - in us.
3. Church now rais-es; Lord, ac - cept our prayers and prais - es.

Text: 78 78 88; Tobias Clausnitzer, 1619–1684; tr. by Catherine Winkworth, 1827–1878, alt.
Music: LIEBSTER JESU; Johann R. Ahle, 1625–1673, alt.; adapt. by Johann Sebastian Bach, 1685–1750.

## PRAISE TO YOU, O CHRIST OUR SAVIOR  643

**Refrain**

Praise to you, O Christ, our Sav-ior, Word of the Fa-ther, call-ing us to life;

Son of God who leads us to free-dom: glo-ry to you, Lord Je-sus Christ!

**Verses**

1. You are the Word who calls us out of dark - ness; you are the
2. You are the one whom proph-ets hoped and longed for; you are the
3. You are the Word who calls us to be ser - vants; you are the
4. You are the Word who binds us and u - nites us; you are the

1. Word who leads us in - to light; you are the Word who
2. one who speaks to us to - day; you are the one who
3. Word whose on - ly law is love; you are the Word - made-
4. Word who calls us to be one; you are the Word who

_to Refrain_

1. brings us through the des - ert: glo - ry to you, Lord Je-sus Christ!
2. leads us to our fu - ture: glo - ry to you, Lord Je-sus Christ!
3. flesh who lives a-mong us: glo - ry to you, Lord Je-sus Christ!
4. teach - es us for-give-ness: glo - ry to you, Lord Je-sus Christ!

**644**     YOUR WORDS ARE SPIRIT AND LIFE

**Refrain**

Your words are spir-it and life, O Lord: rich-er than gold, strong-er than death. Your words are spir-it and life, O Lord; life ev-er-last - ing.

**Verses**

1. God's law is per - fect, re-fresh-ing the soul, re -
2. God's pre-cepts keep us; their pur-pose is right. They
3. Liv - ing by God's truth is ho - ly and sure; God's
4. God's word is pre - cious, de-sired more than gold; worth

1. viv - ing the wea - ry spir - it.                God's
2. glad - den the hearts of peo - ple.            God's com-
3. pres - ence is ev - er - last - ing.            God's
4. more than we dare i - mag-ine                   and,

1. rule can be trust - ed:    bring-ing us wis - dom,
2. mand is so clear it brings us new vi - sion;
3. truth is e - ter - nal,    bring-ing us jus - tice;
4. sweet - er than hon - ey,  this word will feed us,

*to Refrain*

1. bring - ing God's wis - dom to birth.
2. bring - ing God's light to our eyes.
3. bring - ing God's jus - tice to earth.
4. bring - ing ful - fill - ment and joy.

Text: Based on Psalm 19:8–11; Bernadette Farrell, b. 1957.
Music: Bernadette Farrell.
Text and music © 1993, Bernadette Farrell. Published by OCP. All rights reserved.

## O WORD OF GOD

**645**

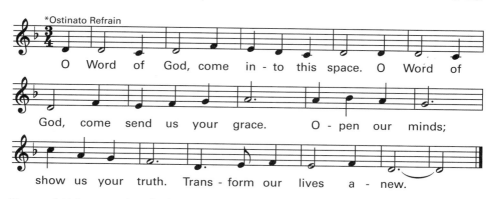

O Word of God, come in-to this space. O Word of
God, come send us your grace. O-pen our minds;
show us your truth. Trans-form our lives a-new.

*Verses available in accompaniment books.

Text and music: Ricky Manalo, CSP, b. 1965, © 2002, Ricky Manalo, CSP. Published by OCP. All rights reserved.

## BE THOU MY VISION

**646**

1. Be Thou my vi-sion, O Lord of my heart;
2. Be Thou my wis-dom, and Thou my true word;
3. Rich-es I heed not, or man's emp-ty praise,
4. High King of heav-en, my vic-to-ry won,

1. Naught be all else to me, save that Thou art:
2. I ev-er with Thee and Thou with me, Lord:
3. Thou mine in-her-i-tance, now and al-ways:
4. May I reach heav-en's joys, O bright heav'n's Sun!

1. Thou my best thought, __ by day or by night,
2. Thou my great Fa-ther, I Thy true son,
3. Thou and Thou on-ly, first in my heart,
4. Heart of my own heart, what-ev-er be-fall,

1. Wak-ing or sleep-ing, Thy pres-ence my light.
2. Thou in me dwell-ing, and I with Thee one.
3. High King of heav-en, my trea-sure Thou art.
4. Still be my vi-sion, O Rul-er of all.

Text: 10 10 10 10; Ancient Irish; tr. by Mary E. Byrne, 1905; fr. Eleanor Hull's *Poem Book of the Gael*, 1912, alt.
Music: SLANE; trad. Irish Melody; adapt. fr. *The Church Hymnary*, 1927.

**647**      LORD OF ALL HOPEFULNESS

1. Lord of all hope-ful-ness, Lord of all joy, Whose
2. Lord of all ea - ger-ness, Lord of all faith, Whose
3. Lord of all kind - li - ness, Lord of all grace, Your
4. Lord of all gen - tle-ness, Lord of all calm, Whose

1. trust, ev - er child-like, no cares can de-stroy, Be
2. strong hands were skilled at the plane and the lathe, Be
3. hands swift to wel-come, your arms to em - brace, Be
4. voice is con - tent-ment, whose pres-ence is balm, Be

1. there at our wak-ing, and give us, we pray, Your
2. there at our la - bors, and give us, we pray, Your
3. there at our hom-ing, and give us, we pray, Your
4. there at our sleep-ing, and give us, we pray, Your

1. bliss in our hearts, Lord, at the break of the day.
2. strength in our hearts, Lord, at the noon of the day.
3. love in our hearts, Lord, at the eve of the day.
4. peace in our hearts, Lord, at the end of the day.

Text: 10 11 11 12; 'Lord of all hopefulness,' words by Jan Struther, 1901–1953; fr. *Enlarged Songs of Praise*, 1931.
Reproduced by permission of Oxford University Press. All rights reserved.
Music: SLANE; trad. Irish Melody; adapt. fr. *The Church Hymnary*, 1927.

**648**      TO YOU, O GOD, I LIFT UP MY SOUL

Refrain: 1st time: Cantor, All repeat; thereafter: All

To you, O God, I lift up my soul; lift up my spir-it

to my Lord. To you I lift up my soul.

To you I lift up my soul. To you I lift up my soul.

Verses: Cantor

1. Make me to know your ways, O God; teach me your
2. Good and up-right our gra - cious God, show-ing the
3. Stead-fast and kind your ways, O God; all who re-

to Refrain

1. paths, guide me. You are my Sav - ior.
2. way, guid-ing the hum-ble to jus - tice.
3. vere your cov - e - nant know your friend-ship.

Text: Based on Psalm 25:1, 4–5, 8–9, 10, 14; Bob Hurd, b. 1950.
Music: Bob Hurd.
Text and music © 1991, Bob Hurd. Published by OCP. All rights reserved.

## THERE IS A LONGING

**649**

Refrain

There is a long-ing in our hearts, O Lord, for you to re-

veal your-self to us. There is a long-ing in our hearts for

love we on-ly find in you, our God.

Verses

1. For jus - tice,
2. For wis - dom,
3. For heal - ing,
4. Lord save us,

1. for free - dom, for mer - cy: hear our prayer. In
2. for cour - age, for com-fort: hear our prayer. In
3. for whole-ness, for new life: hear our prayer. In
4. take pit - y, light in our dark - ness. We

to Refrain

1. sor - row, in grief:
2. weak-ness, in fear:
3. sick - ness, in death:
4. call you, we wait:

be near, hear our prayer, O God.

Text and music: Anne Quigley, © 1992, Anne Quigley. Published by OCP. All rights reserved.

**650**      CHRIST BE BESIDE ME

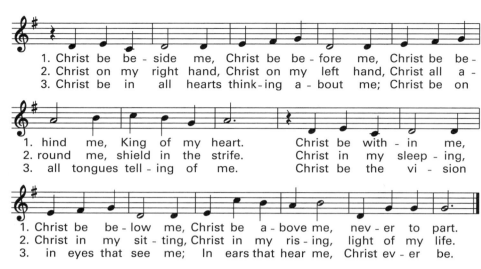

1. Christ be be - side me, Christ be be - fore me, Christ be be-
2. Christ on my right hand, Christ on my left hand, Christ all a -
3. Christ be in all hearts think-ing a - bout me; Christ be on

1. hind me, King of my heart. Christ be with - in me,
2. round me, shield in the strife. Christ in my sleep - ing,
3. all tongues tell - ing of me. Christ be the vi - sion

1. Christ be be - low me, Christ be a - bove me, nev - er to part.
2. Christ in my sit - ting, Christ in my ris - ing, light of my life.
3. in eyes that see me; In ears that hear me, Christ ev - er be.

Text: 55 54 D; *New Hymns for All Seasons*; St. Patrick's Breastplate, para.; tr. by James Quinn, SJ, 1919–2010,
     © 1969, James Quinn, SJ. Published by OCP. All rights reserved.
Music: ST. ROSE; Laura Wasson, b. 1952, © 1993, OCP. All rights reserved.

**651**      GOD BE IN MY HEAD

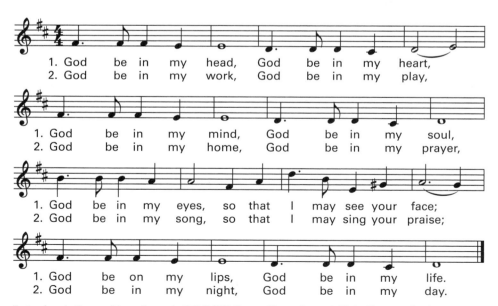

1. God be in my head, God be in my heart,
2. God be in my work, God be in my play,

1. God be in my mind, God be in my soul,
2. God be in my home, God be in my prayer,

1. God be in my eyes, so that I may see your face;
2. God be in my song, so that I may sing your praise;

1. God be on my lips, God be in my life.
2. God be in my night, God be in my day.

Text and music: Grayson Warren Brown, b. 1948, © 1999, Grayson Warren Brown. Published by OCP. All rights reserved.

## This Alone

**652**

Text: Based on Psalm 27; Tim Manion, b. 1951.
Music: Tim Manion.

**653**

**STAND BY ME**

*Verses*

1. When the storms of life are rag-ing, Lord, stand by
2. In the midst of per - se - cu-tion, Lord, stand by

1. me. When the cur - rent pulls me un - der, Lord,
2. me. When my en - e - mies sur-round me, Lord,

1. stand by me. When the ris - ing wa - ters
2. stand by me. When the ty - rant wields his

1. toss me like a ship up - on the sea, You who
2. ter - ror and the ar - mies wage their might, When the

1. rule the wind and wa - ter, Lord, stand by me.
2. dark - ness o - ver-whelms me, Lord, stand by me.

*Refrain*

Stand by me, stand by me. Lift me up from the rest - less sea.

When I am lost, when love can't be found, when no one cares, Lord,

[1] ..... to Verse 2 ‖ *Final* ..... Repeat twice

stand by me. stand by me.

Text: Inspired by "Stand by Me" by Charles A. Tindley, 1851–1933; Tom Kendzia, b. 1954.
Music: Tom Kendzia.

## LEAD ME, GUIDE ME

**Refrain**

Lead me, guide me, a-long the way, for if you lead me, I can-not stray. Lord, let me walk each day with thee. Lead me, oh Lord, lead me.

**Verses**

1. I am weak and I need thy strength and pow'r to____ help me o-ver my weak-est hour. Help me through the dark-ness thy face to see, lead me, oh Lord, lead me.

2. Help me tread in the paths of righ-teous-ness, be my aid when Sa-tan and sin op-press. I am put-ting all____ my trust in thee. Lead me, oh Lord, lead me.

3. I am lost if you take your hand from me, I am blind with-out____ thy Light to see, Lord, just al-ways let me thy ser-vant be. Lead me, oh Lord, lead me.

*to Refrain*

## 655     THESE ALONE ARE ENOUGH

1. Take my heart, O Lord, take my hopes and
2. Take my thoughts, O Lord, and my mem - o -
3. I sur - ren - der, Lord, all I have and
4. When the dark - ness falls on my fi - nal

1. dreams. Take my mind with all its plans and
2. ry. Take my tears, my joys, my lib - er -
3. hold. I re - turn to you your gifts un -
4. days, take the ver - y breath that sang your

1. schemes.
2. ty.
3. told.     Give me noth - ing more than your love and
4. praise.

1-4. grace. These a - lone, O God, are e - nough for me.

Text: Based on "Suscipe" Prayer of Ignatius of Loyola; Dan Schutte, b. 1947.
Music: Dan Schutte.
Text and music © 2004, Daniel L. Schutte. Published by OCP. All rights reserved.

## 656     COME, LORD JESUS

Refrain

Come, Lord Je - sus, come. Come and fill my heart

with your life. Hold me close, Lord, hold me tight,

and come, Lord Je - sus, come.

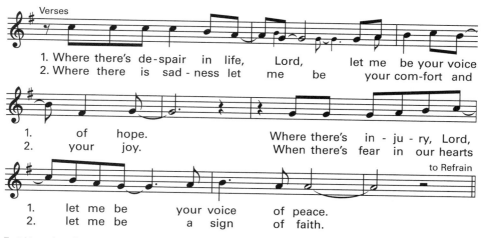

1. Where there's de-spair in life, Lord, let me be your voice
2. Where there is sad-ness let me be your com-fort and

1. of hope. Where there's in-ju-ry, Lord,
2. your joy. When there's fear in our hearts

to Refrain

1. let me be your voice of peace.
2. let me be a sign of faith.

Text: Verses based on a prayer ascribed to St. Francis of Assisi, ca. 1182–1226;
Steve Angrisano, b. 1965, and Tom Tomaszek, b. 1950.
Music: Steve Angrisano and Tom Tomaszek.
Text and music © 1997, Steve Angrisano and Thomas N. Tomaszek.
Published by spiritandsong.com®, a division of OCP. All rights reserved.

## SACRED SILENCE

**657**

Refrain  Sa-cred si-lence, ho-ly o-cean, gen-tle wa-ter,
Verses 1. God my Fa-ther, Christ my broth-er, Ho-ly Spir-it,
2. Ho-ly Ma-ry, gen-tle moth-er, God's pure ves-sel,

wash-ing o-ver me; help me lis-ten, Ho-ly
1. sanc-ti-fy-ing me; Lord, I'm sor-ry, please for-
2. pray-ing for me; saints and an-gels, all in

Spir-it. Come and speak to me. (to Verses)
1. give me. Come and set me free. (to Refrain)
2. heav-en, come and be with me. (to Refrain)

Final

Come and be with me. Come and speak to me.

Text: Tom Booth, b. 1961, Jenny Pixler and Anthony Kuner, © 2003, Tom Booth, Jenny Pixler and Anthony Kuner.
Published by spiritandsong.com®, a division of OCP. All rights reserved.
Music: Tom Booth and Jenny Pixler, © 2003, Tom Booth and Jenny Pixler.
Published by spiritandsong.com®, a division of OCP. All rights reserved.

**658**     FOR THE SAKE OF CHRIST

For the sake of Christ, I will-ing-ly ac-cept my weak-ness and my trials,

**1, 2, Final**    to Verses 1, 2    **3** to Verse 3

for when I am pow-er-less, then I am strong.     strong.

**Verses 1, 2**

1. Al-though in God's __ love my life was blest, my faith __ was
2. And so when I am weak, then I am free. The pow-er of

1. giv-en to the test. For mer-cy did I pray, and then I heard God say,
2. Christ will rest in me. Through all that I en-dure, the love of God is sure.

to Refrain

1. "My grace is e-nough for you. My grace is e-nough for you."
2. His grace is e-nough for me. His grace is e-nough for me.

**Verse 3**

3. He died for all, that those who live might live no long-er for them-selves.

to Refrain

3. Oh, live for Christ who gave his life, and now is raised on high.

Text: Based on 2 Corinthians 5:15; 12:7–10; Ken Canedo, b. 1953.
Music: Ken Canedo.
Text and music © 1995, 2005, Ken Canedo. Published by OCP. All rights reserved.

**659**     OPEN MY EYES

1. O-pen my eyes, Lord.     Help me to see your face.
2. O-pen my ears, Lord.     Help me to hear your voice.
3. O-pen my heart, Lord.     Help me to love like you.
4. I live with-in you.     Deep in your heart, O Love.

1. O-pen my eyes, Lord. Help me to see.
2. O-pen my ears, Lord. Help me to hear.
3. O-pen my heart, Lord. Help me to love.
4. I live with - in you. Rest now in me.

Text: Based on Mark 8:22–25; Jesse Manibusan, b. 1958.
Music: Jesse Manibusan.
Text and music © 1988, Jesse Manibusan. Published by spiritandsong.com®, a division of OCP. All rights reserved.

## JESUS, COME TO US    660

Refrain

Je - sus, come to us, lead us to your light. Je - sus, be with us, for we need you.

Verses

1. Lord, we come be - fore you,_____ lis - ten
2. Lord, we come to praise you for your faith-ful -
3. Lord, you give us won-ders, _ your glo -

to Refrain

1. to our prayer. Fill us all with hope and your love.
2. ness through night. You will be with us, this we know.
3. ry to all. We be-lieve in you, come to us.

Text and music: David Haas, b. 1957, © 1981, 1982, OCP. All rights reserved.

## ST. PATRICK'S BREASTPLATE    661

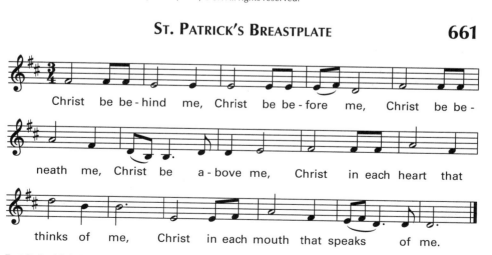

Christ be be - hind me, Christ be be - fore me, Christ be be - neath me, Christ be a - bove me, Christ in each heart that thinks of me, Christ in each mouth that speaks of me.

Text: St. Patrick, 372–466; adapt. by Andrew Wright, b. 1955.
Music: Andrew Wright.
Text and music © 2001, Andrew Wright. Published by OCP. All rights reserved.

## 662    COME, MY WAY, MY TRUTH, MY LIFE

1. Come, my Way, my Truth, my Life: Such a
2. Come, my Light, my Feast, my Strength: Such a
3. Come, my Joy, my Love, my Heart: Such a

1. way as gives us breath; Such a truth as ends all
2. light as shows a feast; Such a feast as mends in
3. joy as none can move; Such a love as none can

1. strife; Such a life as kill - eth death.
2. length; Such a strength as makes his guest.
3. part; Such a heart as joys in love.

Text: 77 77; George Herbert, 1593–1632.
Music: THE CALL; *Five Mystical Songs*; Ralph Vaughan Williams, 1872–1958.

## 663    PSALM 42: AS THE DEER LONGS

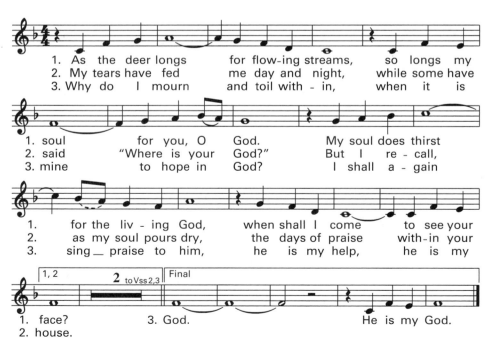

1. As the deer longs for flow-ing streams, so longs my
2. My tears have fed me day and night, while some have
3. Why do I mourn and toil with - in, when it is

1. soul for you, O God. My soul does thirst
2. said "Where is your God?" But I re - call,
3. mine to hope in God? I shall a - gain

1. for the liv - ing God, when shall I come to see your
2. as my soul pours dry, the days of praise with-in your
3. sing praise to him, he is my help, he is my

[1, 2]    2 to Vss 2,3    ‖ Final

1. face?    3. God.    He is my God.
2. house.

Text: Irregular; based on Psalm 42; Danna Harkin, © 1975, Word Music Group, LLC.
   All rights reserved. Used with permission.
Music: O WALY WALY, alt.; trad. English Melody.

# DWELLING PLACE

**Verses 1, 2, 4**

1, 4. I fall on my knees to the Fa-ther of Je-sus,
2. May Christ in his love give us strength for our liv-ing,

1, 4. the Lord who has shown us
2. the strength of the Spir-it, the glo-ry of

**1st time: to Verse 2**    **Refrain**

1, 2, 4. God. May Christ find a dwell-ing place of faith in our

hearts. May our lives be root-ed in love,

**4**    **to Verses 3, 4**

root-ed in love.

**Verse 3**

3. May grace and peace be yours in God our

**to Refrain**

3. Fa-ther, and in the Son.

Text: Based on Ephesians 3; John Foley, S.J., b. 1939.
Music: John Foley, S.J.

## 665 CENTER OF MY LIFE

Refrain: Repeat 1st time

O Lord, you are the cen-ter of my life: I will al-ways praise you,

1-5 (to Verses) | Final

I will al-ways serve you, I will al-ways keep you in my sight. 1. sight.
2.
3. And

Verses 1-3

1. Keep me safe, O God, __ I take ref-uge in you. __ I say to the
2. I will bless the Lord who gives me coun - sel, _____ who e - ven at
3. so my heart re - joic - es, my soul is glad; _____ e - ven in

1. Lord, "You are my God. My hap - pi - ness _____ lies in you a-
2. night di - rects my heart. I keep _ the Lord _____ ev - er in my
3. safe - ty shall my bod-y rest. For you will not leave my soul a-mong the

to Refrain

1. lone; my hap - pi - ness _____ lies in you a - lone." __
2. sight: since he is at my right _ hand, _ I shall stand firm.
3. dead, nor let __ your be - lov - ed know de - cay. _____

Verse 4

4. You will show me the path of life, the full - ness of

4. joy in your pres - ence, at your right hand,

to Refrain

4. at your right hand hap - pi - ness for - ev - er.

# We Walk by Faith/In Times of Trouble

**Refrain**

We walk by faith and not by sight, through joy and woe, through dark and light.

We jour-ney not a-lone, for-sak - en. You walk with us, our God and friend.

**Verses**

1. In times of trou - ble walk with us,
2. O faith - ful God, you dwell with us
3. We place our trust in you, O God.
4. O God of peace, re - main with us.
5. The storms of life shall bring us woe,

1. lov - ing God of mer - cy. Take our fear and sor - row;
2. in the depths of our souls; there, you speak your word of
3. You re - store hope in us. In the dark - est val - leys
4. Teach us your ways of truth. May we act with jus - tice,
5. yet we cling to your word: "Be - hold, I am with you

*to Refrain*

1. re - store___ our souls: make us peo - ple of hope.
2. com - pas - sion and truth. In your word we find life.
3. you light___ the way. In you is our cour - age.
4. com - pas - sion and love. This is all you ask of us.
5. un - til___ the end." In your word we find life.

Text: Barbara Bridge, b. 1950, © 1997, 2003, Barbara Bridge. Published by OCP. All rights reserved.
Music: Refrain, *Jesu dulcis memoria*; verses, *Ave maris stella*.

# 667

## FAITH OF OUR FATHERS

1. Faith of our fa - thers! Liv - ing still
2. The mar - tyrs, chained in pris - ons dark,
3. Faith of our moth - ers! Ma - ry's pray'rs
4. Faith of our fa - thers! We will love

1. In spite of dun - geon, fire and sword:
2. Were still in heart and con - science free:
3. Shall win all na - tions un - to thee;
4. Both friend and foe in all our strife:

1. O how our hearts beat high with joy,
2. And tru - ly blest would be our fate,
3. And through the truth that comes from God,
4. And preach thee, too, as love knows how,

1. When - e'er we hear that glo - rious word:
2. If we, like them, should die for thee.
3. We all shall then in - deed be free.
4. By kind - ly words and vir - tuous life.

1. Faith of our fa - thers, ho - ly faith!
2. Faith of the mar - tyrs, ho - ly faith!
3. Faith of our moth - ers, ho - ly faith!
4. Faith of our fa - thers, ho - ly faith!

1-4. We will be true to thee till death.

Text: 88 88 88; Frederick W. Faber, 1814–1863, alt.
Music: ST. CATHERINE; Henri F. Hemy, 1818–1888; adapt. by James G. Walton, 1821–1905.

## JESUS, LORD

*Refrain

Je - sus, Lord, strength-en us with faith in you.

Lift our hearts, fill us with new trust in your love.

Verses

1. God so loved the world he gave his on - ly Son,
2. God ___ sent his Son in - to a bro - ken world,
3. Je - sus is the light by which we see the truth;

to Refrain

1. With our faith in him we shall have e - ter - nal life.
2. Not ___ to con - demn, ___ but that we might be saved.
3. If we fol - low him we are blest in all we do.

*Opening Refrain is sung twice before proceeding to Verse 1.

Text: Based on John 3:16–21; Randall DeBruyn, b. 1947, © 1984, OCP. All rights reserved.
Music: Randall DeBruyn, © 1984, OCP. All rights reserved.

## WE WALK BY FAITH

669

1, 5. We walk by faith, and not by sight: No gra-cious words we hear
2. We may not touch his hands and side, Nor fol - low where he trod;
3. Help then, O Lord, our un - be - lief, And may our faith a - bound;
4. That when our life of faith is done In realms of clear - er light

1, 5. Of him who spoke as none e'er spoke, But we be - lieve him near.
2. Yet in his prom - ise we re - joice And cry, "My Lord and God!"
3. To call on you when you are near, And seek where you are found:
4. We may be - hold you as you are In full and end-less sight.

Text: CM; Henry Alford, alt., 1810–1871.
Music: ST. ANNE; attr. to William Croft, 1678–1727.

**670**  **AGE TO AGE**

Refrain: 1st time: Cantor, All repeat; thereafter: All

Age to age we will love you. Dawn-ing light we will
wake with you. In - to night we will fol-low you. We will
love you age to age.

*Verses*

1. As the ea - gle
2. As the lil - ies of the
3. Come, all you
4. Lord, let my

1. flies to the heav'ns a - bove, on wings of
2. field nei-ther toil nor spin, what splen - dor we
3. wea - ry, for you are blessed. God will light - en your
4. faith in you be re - vealed. On - ly say the

**2** to Refrain

1. faith God will bear you up.
2. find in the love God gives.
3. bur - den and give you rest.
4. word and I shall be healed.

Text: Based on Isaiah 40:31; Matthew 6:28; 11:28–30; Janet Vogt, b. 1953.
Music: Janet Vogt.

**671**  **ON EAGLE'S WINGS**

Verse 1

1. You who dwell in the shel-ter of the Lord, who a - bide in his

to Refrain

1. shad-ow for life, say to the Lord: "My ref-uge, my rock in whom I trust!"

Text: Based on Psalm 91; Michael Joncas, b. 1951.
Music: Michael Joncas.
Text and music © 1979, OCP. All rights reserved.

## 672     O GOD, OUR HELP IN AGES PAST

1. O God, our help in a - ges past, Our
2. Be - neath the shad - ow of your throne Your
3. Be - fore the hills in or - der stood, Or
4. A thou - sand a - ges in your sight Are
5. Time, like an ev - er - roll - ing stream, Bears
6. O God, our help in a - ges past, Our

1. hope for years to come, Our shel - ter from the
2. saints have dwelt se - cure; Suf - fi - cient is your
3. earth re - ceived her frame, From ev - er - last - ing
4. like an eve - ning gone; Short as the watch that
5. all our years a - way; They fly for - got - ten,
6. hope for years to come, Still be our guard while

1. storm - y blast, And our e - ter - nal home.
2. arm a - lone, And our de - fense is sure.
3. you are God, To end - less years the same.
4. ends the night Be - fore the ris - ing sun.
5. as a dream Dies at the o - p'ning day.
6. trou - bles last, And our e - ter - nal home.

Text: CM; based on Psalm 90; Isaac Watts, 1674–1748, alt.
Music: ST. ANNE; attr. to William Croft, 1678–1727.

## 673     BE NOT AFRAID

Verse 1

1. You shall cross the bar - ren des - ert, but you shall not die of
1. thirst. You shall wan - der far in safe - ty though you do not know the
1. way. You shall speak your words in for - eign lands and all will un - der-
1. stand. You shall see the face of God and live.

*to Refrain*

**Refrain**

Be not a-fraid. I go be-fore you al-ways. Come fol-low me, and I will give you rest.

**1, 2** to Vss 2, 3 **Final 2**

**Verse 2**

2. If you pass through rag-ing wa-ters in the sea, you shall not 2. drown. If you walk a-mid the burn-ing flames, you shall not be 2. harmed. If you stand be-fore the pow'r of hell and death is at your 2. side, know that I am with you through it all.

*to Refrain*

**Verse 3**

3. Bless-ed are your poor, for the king-dom shall be theirs. Blest are you that 3. weep and mourn, for one day you shall laugh. And if wick-ed tongues in-sult and 3. hate you all be-cause of me, bless-ed, bless-ed are you!

*to Refrain*

**674**

# A Mighty Fortress

1. A might-y for-tress is our God, A
2. No strength of ours can match his might! We
3. Though hordes of dev-ils fill the land All
4. God's Word for-ev-er shall a-bide, No

1. sword and shield vic-to-rious; He breaks the
2. would be lost, re-ject-ed. But now a
3. threat-'ning to de-vour us, We trem-ble
4. thanks to foes, who fear it; For God him-

1. cruel op-pres-sor's rod And wins sal-va-tion
2. cham-pion comes to fight, Whom God him-self e-
3. not, un-moved we stand; They can-not o-ver-
4. self fights by our side With weap-ons of the

1. glo-rious. The old sa-tan-ic foe
2. lect-ed. You ask who this may be?
3. pow'r us. Let this world's ty-rant rage;
4. Spir-it. Were they to take our house,

1. Has sworn to work us woe! With craft and
2. The Lord of hosts is he! Christ Je-sus,
3. In bat-tle we'll en-gage! His might is
4. Goods, hon-or, child, or spouse, Though life be

1. dread-ful might He arms him-self to fight.
2. might-y Lord, God's on-ly Son, a-dored.
3. doomed to fail! God's judg-ment must pre-vail!
4. wrenched a-way, They can-not win the day.

1. On earth he has no e - qual.
2. He holds the field vic - to - rious.
3. One lit - tle word sub - dues him.
4. The King - dom's ours for - ev - er!

Text: 87 87 66 66 7; based on Psalm 46; Martin Luther, 1483–1546; tr. © 1978, *Lutheran Book of Worship*.
All rights reserved. Reprinted by permission of Augsburg Fortress.
Music: EIN' FESTE BURG; Martin Luther.

## FOR YOU ARE MY GOD 675

**Refrain**

For you are my God; you a - lone are my joy. De-

fend me, O Lord.

**Verses**

1. You give mar - vel - ous
2. — You are my
3. — Glad are my
4. ⅜ You show me the

1. com - rades to me: the faith - ful who dwell in your
2. por - tion and cup; it is you that I claim for my
3. heart and my soul; se - cure - ly my bod - y shall
4. path for my life; in your pres - ence the full - ness of

1. land. Those who choose a - li - en gods
2. prize. Your her - i - tage is my de - light,
3. rest. For you will not leave me for dead,
4. joy. To be at your right hand for - ev - er

to Refrain

1. have cho - sen an a - li - en band.
2. the lot you have giv - en to me.
3. nor lead your be - lov - ed a - stray.
4. for me would be hap - pi - ness al - ways.

Text: Based on Psalm 16; John Foley, S.J., b. 1939.
Music: John Foley, S.J.
Text and music © 1970, John B. Foley, S.J. Published by OCP. All rights reserved.

**676** — ONLY A SHADOW

**Verses**

1. The love we have for you, O Lord, is
2. The bread we take and eat, O Lord, is
3. Our own be-lief in you, O Lord, is
4. The dreams we share to-day, O Lord, are
5. The joy we share to-day, O Lord, is

1. on-ly a shad-ow of your love for us;
2. your bod-y bro-ken and shared with us;
3. on-ly a shad-ow of your faith in us;
4. on-ly a shad-ow of your dreams for us;
5. on-ly a shad-ow of your joys for us;

1. on-ly a shad-ow of your love for us; your
2. your bod-y bro-ken and shared with us; the
3. on-ly a shad-ow of your faith in us; your
4. on-ly a shad-ow of your dreams for us; if
5. on-ly a shad-ow of your joys for us; when

1. deep a-bid-ing love. (to Verse 2)
2. gift of your great love. (to Refrain)
3. deep and last-ing faith. (to Verse 4)
4. we but fol-low you. (to Refrain)
5. we meet face to face. (to Refrain)

**Refrain**

Our lives are in your hands, our lives
are in your hands. Our love for you will
grow, O Lord; your light in us will shine.

## BLEST BE THE LORD

Refrain

Blest be the Lord; blest be the Lord, the God of mer - cy, the God who saves. I shall not fear the dark of night, nor the ar - row that flies by day.

Verses

1. He will re-lease me from the nets of all my foes.
2. I need not shrink be - fore the ter - rors of the night,
3. Al- though a thou - sand strong have fall - en at my side,

1. He will pro - tect me from their wick-ed hands.
2. nor stand a - lone be - fore the light of day.
3. I'll not be shak-en with the Lord at hand.

1. Be - neath the shad-ow of his wings I
2. No harm shall come to me, no ar - row
3. His faith - ful love is all the ar - mor

to Refrain

1. will re - joice to find a dwell-ing place se-cure.
2. strike me down, no e - vil set - tle in my soul.
3. that I need to wage my bat - tle with the foe.

Text: Based on Psalm 91; Dan Schutte, b. 1947.
Music: Dan Schutte.
Text and music © 1976, OCP. All rights reserved.

## 678    O God, You Search Me

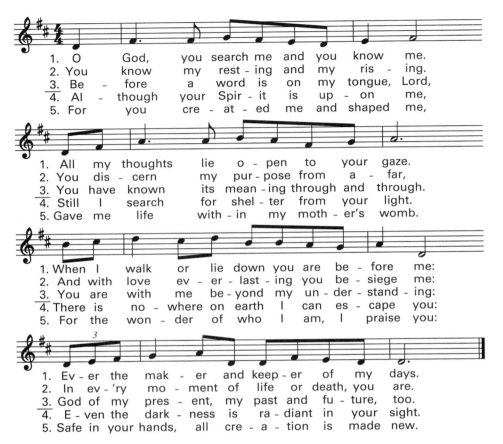

1. O God, you search me and you know me.
2. You know my rest-ing and my ris-ing.
3. Be-fore a word is on my tongue, Lord,
4. Al-though your Spir-it is up-on me,
5. For you cre-at-ed me and shaped me,

1. All my thoughts lie o-pen to your gaze.
2. You dis-cern my pur-pose from a-far,
3. You have known its mean-ing through and through.
4. Still I search for shel-ter from your light.
5. Gave me life with-in my moth-er's womb.

1. When I walk or lie down you are be-fore me:
2. And with love ev-er-last-ing you be-siege me:
3. You are with me be-yond my un-der-stand-ing:
4. There is no-where on earth I can es-cape you:
5. For the won-der of who I am, I praise you:

1. Ev-er the mak-er and keep-er of my days.
2. In ev-'ry mo-ment of life or death, you are.
3. God of my pres-ent, my past and fu-ture, too.
4. E-ven the dark-ness is ra-diant in your sight.
5. Safe in your hands, all cre-a-tion is made new.

Text: Based on Psalm 139; Bernadette Farrell, b. 1957.
Music: Bernadette Farrell.
Text and music © 1992, Bernadette Farrell. Published by OCP. All rights reserved.

## 679    Only in God

Verses

1. On-ly in God is my soul at_rest, in ___ him comes my sal-
2. On-ly in God is found safe-ty when my en-e-my pur-

1. va-tion. He, ___ on-ly, ___ is my_rock, my strength_and
2. sues me. On-ly in God is found glo-ry when I am found

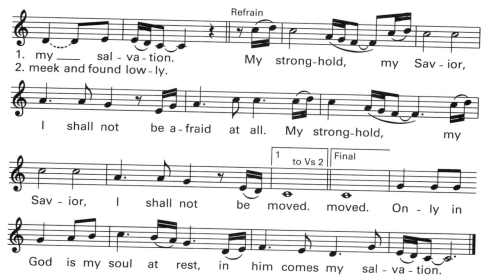

1. my \_\_\_\_ sal - va - tion.
2. meek and found low - ly.

My strong-hold, my Sav - ior,

I shall not be a - fraid at all. My strong-hold, my

Sav - ior, I shall not be moved. moved. On - ly in

God is my soul at rest, in him comes my sal - va - tion.

Text: Based on Psalm 62; John Michael Talbot, b. 1954.
Music: John Michael Talbot.
Text and music © 1980, Birdwing Music/BMG Songs. All rights reserved.
  Administered by EMI CMG Publishing. Used with permission.

### AMAZING GRACE 680

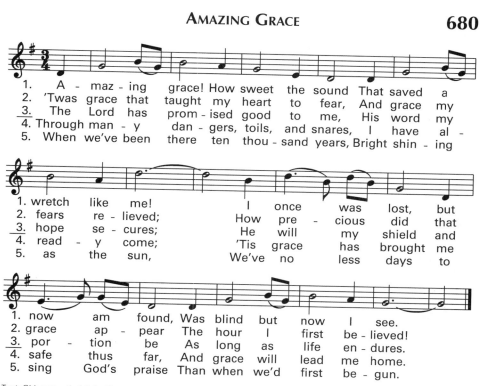

1. A - maz - ing grace! How sweet the sound That saved a
2. 'Twas grace that taught my heart to fear, And grace my
3. The Lord has prom - ised good to me, His word my
4. Through man - y dan - gers, toils, and snares, I have al -
5. When we've been there ten thou - sand years, Bright shin - ing

1. wretch like me! I once was lost, but
2. fears re - lieved; How pre - cious did that
3. hope se - cures; He will my shield and
4. read - y come; 'Tis grace has brought me
5. as the sun, We've no less days to

1. now am found, Was blind but now I see.
2. grace ap - pear The hour I first be - lieved!
3. por - tion be As long as life en - dures.
4. safe thus far, And grace will lead me home.
5. sing God's praise Than when we'd first be - gun.

Text: CM; verses 1–4, John Newton, 1725–1807; verse 5, anon., fr. *A Collection of Sacred Ballads*, 1790.
Music: NEW BRITAIN; *Columbian Harmony*, 1829.

# 681

## WE WILL RISE AGAIN

**Verse 1**
1. Like a shep-herd I will feed you; I will gath-er you with

1. care. I will lead you and hold you close to my heart.

**Refrain**
We will run and not grow wea-ry, for our God will be our

strength, and we will fly like the ea-gle, we will rise a-gain.

**Verse 2**
2. I am strength to the wea-ry; to the weak I am new life. Though the

2. young may grow wea-ry, I will be their hope.

**Verse 3**
3. Lift up your eyes, and see who made the stars. I

3. lead you, and I know you, I call you each by name.

**Verse 4**
4. Fear not, I am with you; I am your God. I will

4. strength-en you and help you; up-hold you with my hand.

# Though the Mountains May Fall

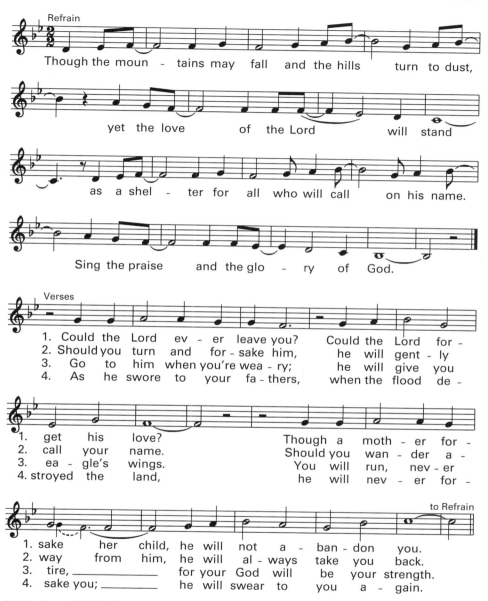

**Refrain**

Though the moun - tains may fall and the hills turn to dust,
yet the love of the Lord will stand
as a shel - ter for all who will call on his name.
Sing the praise and the glo - ry of God.

**Verses**

1. Could the Lord ev - er leave you? Could the Lord for -
2. Should you turn and for - sake him, he will gent - ly
3. Go to him when you're wea - ry; he will give you
4. As he swore to your fa - thers, when the flood de -

1. get his love? Though a moth - er for -
2. call your name. Should you wan - der a -
3. ea - gle's wings. You will run, nev - er
4. stroyed the land, he will nev - er for -

to Refrain

1. sake her child, he will not a - ban - don you.
2. way from him, he will al - ways take you back.
3. tire, _____ for your God will be your strength.
4. sake you; _____ he will swear to you a - gain.

Text: Based on Isaiah 54:6–10; 49:15; 40:31–32; Dan Schutte, b. 1947.
Music: Dan Schutte.
Text and music © 1975, 1979, OCP. All rights reserved.

## 683 How Firm a Foundation

1. How firm a foun - da - tion, you saints of the Lord,
2. "Fear not, I am with you, O be not dis-mayed,
3. "When through the deep wa - ters I call you to go,
4. "The soul that on Je - sus still leans for re - pose,

1. Is laid for your faith in his ex - cel - lent Word!
2. For I am your God, and will still give you aid;
3. The riv - ers of woe shall not you o - ver - flow;
4. I will not, I will not de - sert to its foes;

1. What more can he say than to you he has said,
2. I'll strength - en you, help you, and cause you to stand,
3. For I will be with you, your trou - bles to bless,
4. That soul, though all hell should en - deav - or to shake,

1. To you who for ref - uge to Je - sus have fled?
2. Up - held by my righ - teous, om - nip - o - tent hand."
3. And sanc - ti - fy to you, your deep - est dis - tress."
4. I'll nev - er, no nev - er, no nev - er for - sake!"

Text: 11 11 11 11; "K" in Rippon's *A Selection of Hymns*, 1787.
Music: FOUNDATION; Funk's *A Compilation of Genuine Church Music*, Winchester, VA, 1832.

## 684 Here I Am

Refrain

Here I am, stand-ing right be-side you. Here I am;

do not be a - fraid. Here I am, wait-ing like a lov - er.

1-3 to Vss.
I am here; here I am.

Final
am. I am here; here I am.

Text and music: Tom Booth, b. 1961, © 1996, Tom Booth. Published by spiritandsong.com®, a division of OCP.
All rights reserved.

## 685     SEEK YE FIRST

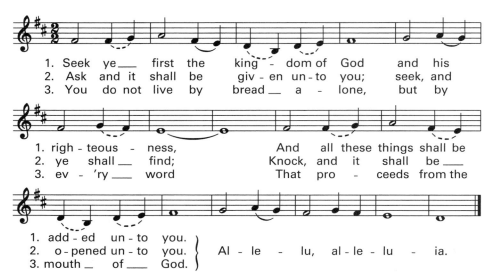

1. Seek ye__ first the king - dom of God and his
2. Ask and it shall be giv - en un - to you; seek, and
3. You do not live by bread __ a - lone, but by

1. righ - teous - ness, And all these things shall be
2. ye shall __ find; Knock, and it shall be __
3. ev - 'ry __ word That pro - ceeds from the

1. add - ed un - to you. )
2. o - pened un - to you. } Al - le - lu, al - le - lu - ia.
3. mouth __ of __ God. )

Text: Based on Matthew 6:33; Karen Lafferty, b. 1948.
Music: Karen Lafferty.

## 686     HOW CAN I KEEP FROM SINGING

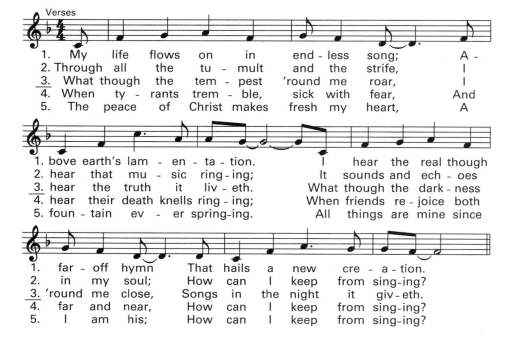

Verses

1. My life flows on in end - less song; A -
2. Through all the tu - mult and the strife, I
3. What though the tem - pest 'round me roar, I
4. When ty - rants trem - ble, sick with fear, And
5. The peace of Christ makes fresh my heart, A

1. bove earth's lam - en - ta - tion. I hear the real though
2. hear that mu - sic ring - ing; It sounds and ech - oes
3. hear the truth it liv - eth. What though the dark - ness
4. hear their death knells ring - ing; When friends re - joice both
5. foun - tain ev - er spring - ing. All things are mine since

1. far - off hymn That hails a new cre - a - tion.
2. in my soul; How can I keep from sing - ing?
3. 'round me close, Songs in the night it giv - eth.
4. far and near, How can I keep from sing - ing?
5. I am his; How can I keep from sing - ing?

No storm can shake my in-most calm, While to that rock I'm cling-ing. Since Love is Lord of heav-en and earth, How can I keep from sing-ing?

Text: 87 87 with refrain; attr. to Robert Lowry, 1826–1899, alt.; verse 3, Doris Plenn.
Music: ENDLESS SONG; Quaker Hymn; attr. to Robert Lowry.

## YOU ARE NEAR 687

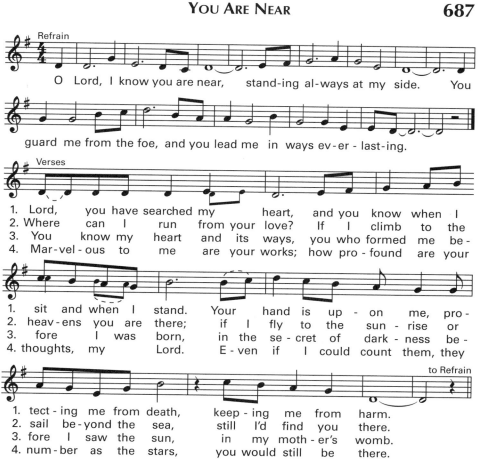

O Lord, I know you are near, stand-ing al-ways at my side. You guard me from the foe, and you lead me in ways ev-er-last-ing.

1. Lord, you have searched my heart, and you know when I
2. Where can I run from your love? If I climb to the
3. You know my heart and its ways, you who formed me be-
4. Mar-vel-ous to me are your works; how pro-found are your

1. sit and when I stand. Your hand is up-on me, pro-
2. heav-ens you are there; if I fly to the sun-rise or
3. fore I was born, in the se-cret of dark-ness be-
4. thoughts, my Lord. E-ven if I could count them, they

to Refrain

1. tect-ing me from death, keep-ing me from harm.
2. sail be-yond the sea, still I'd find you there.
3. fore I saw the sun, in my moth-er's womb.
4. num-ber as the stars, you would still be there.

Text: Based on Psalm 139; Dan Schutte, b. 1947.
Music: Dan Schutte.
Text and music © 1971, 2008, OCP. All rights reserved.

## 688     THERE IS A BALM IN GILEAD

There is a balm in Gil-e-ad to make the wound-ed whole,

there is a balm in Gil-e-ad to heal the sin-sick soul.

*Verses*

1. Some - times I feel dis-cour-aged, And __ think my work's in vain,
2. If you can - not preach like Pe - ter, If you can-not pray like Paul,
3. Don't __ ev - er feel dis-cour-aged, For __ Je-sus is your friend;

*to Refrain*

1. But __ then the Ho - ly Spir - it Re - vives my soul a - gain.
2. You can tell the love of Je - sus, And say, "He died for all."
3. And __ if you lack for knowl - edge, He'll ne'er re - fuse to lend.

Text: 76 76 with refrain; based on Jeremiah 8:22; Spiritual.
Music: BALM IN GILEAD; Spiritual.

## 689     SHELTER ME, O GOD

*Refrain*

Shel-ter me, O God; hide me in the shad-ow of your wings. You a-lone

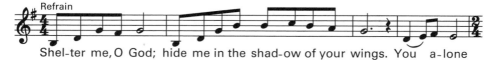

*Verses*

are my hope.
1. When my foes sur-round me, set me
2. As a moth - er gath - ers her ___
3. Though I walk in dark - ness, through the

*to Refrain*

1. high a - bove their reach. Hear me when I call your name.
2. young be-neath her care, gath-er me in - to your arms.
3. nee-dle's eye of death, you will nev-er leave my side.

Text: Based on Psalm 16; Psalm 61; Luke 13:34; Bob Hurd, b. 1950.
Music: Bob Hurd.

## THE KING OF LOVE MY SHEPHERD IS 690

1. The King of love my shep - herd is, Whose
2. Where streams of liv - ing wa - ter flow With
3. Per - verse and fool - ish I have strayed, But
4. In death's dark vale I fear no ill With
5. You spread a ta - ble in my sight, Your
6. And so through all the length of days Your

1. good - ness fails me nev - er; I noth - ing lack if
2. gen - tle care he leads me, And where the ver - dant
3. yet in love he sought me, And on his shoul - der
4. you, dear Lord, be - side me; Your rod and staff my
5. sav - ing grace be - stow - ing; And O what joy and
6. good - ness fails me nev - er: Good Shep - herd, may I

1. I am his, And he is mine for - ev - er.
2. pas - tures grow, With heav'n - ly food he feeds me.
3. gent - ly laid, And home, re - joic - ing, brought me.
4. com - fort still, Your cross be - fore to guide me.
5. true de - light From your pure chal - ice flow - ing!
6. sing your praise With - in your house for - ev - er.

Text: 87 87; based on Psalm 23; Matthew 18; John 10; Henry Williams Baker, 1821–1877, alt.
Music: ST. COLUMBA; trad. Irish Melody.

## LIKE A CHILD RESTS 691

Refrain: 1st time: Cantor, All repeat; thereafter: All

Like a child rests in its moth-er's arms, so will I rest in
you. Like a so will I rest in you.

Verses
to Refrain

1. My God, I am not proud. I do not look for things too great.
2. My God, I trust in you. You care for me, you give me peace.
3. O Is - rael, trust in God, ___ now and al - ways trust in God.

Text: Based on Psalm 131; Christopher Walker, b. 1947.
Music: Christopher Walker.

## 692     I Heard the Voice of Jesus

1. I heard the voice of Je-sus say, "Come un-to me and
2. I heard the voice of Je-sus say, "Be-hold, I free-ly
3. I heard the voice of Je-sus say, "I am this dark world's

1. rest; Lay down, thou wea-ry one, lay down Thy head up-
2. give The liv-ing wa-ter; thirst-y one, Stoop down, and
3. light; Look un-to me, thy morn shall rise, And all thy

1. on my breast." I came to Je-sus as I was, So
2. drink, and live." I came to Je-sus, and I drank Of
3. day be bright." I looked to Je-sus, and I found In

1. wea-ry, worn and sad; I found in him a
2. that life-giv-ing stream; My thirst was quenched, my
3. him my star, my sun; And in that light of

1. rest-ing place, And he has made me glad.
2. soul re-vived, And now I live in him.
3. life I'll walk Till trav-'ling days are done.

Text: CMD; Horatius Bonar, 1808–1889, alt.
Music: KINGSFOLD; trad. English Melody; *English Country Songs*, 1893; adapt. by Ralph Vaughan Williams, 1872–1958.

## 693     My Soul Is Thirsting

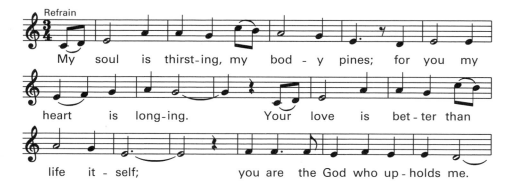

Refrain

My soul is thirst-ing, my bod-y pines; for you my

heart is long-ing. Your love is bet-ter than

life it-self; you are the God who up-holds me.

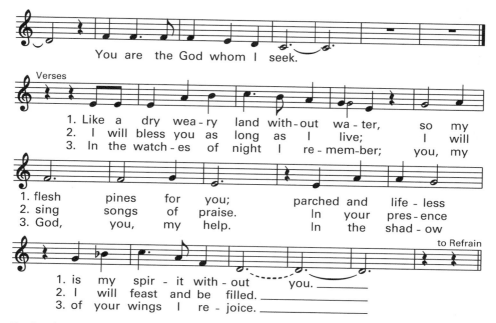

You are the God whom I seek.

Verses

1. Like a dry wea-ry land with-out wa-ter, so my
2. I will bless you as long as I live; I will
3. In the watch-es of night I re-mem-ber; you, my

1. flesh pines for you; parched and life-less
2. sing songs of praise. In your pres-ence
3. God, you, my help. In the shad-ow

to Refrain

1. is my spir-it with-out you.
2. I will feast and be filled.
3. of your wings I re-joice.

Text: Based on Psalm 63:1–8; Bob Hurd, b. 1950.
Music: Bob Hurd.
Text and music © 1990, Bob Hurd. Published by OCP. All rights reserved.

## BE STILL AND KNOW THAT I AM GOD 694

1-3. Be still and know that I am God. You are my

1. cho-sen one, to whom my love I give. My life is
2. cho-sen one, I came to set you free. Give me your
3. cho-sen one, to whom I show my ways. My love is

1. yours, in you I live.
2. cares and rest in me. } Be still, be still
3. with you all your days.

2

1-3. and know that I am God.

Text and music: Christopher Walker, b. 1947, and Paule Freeburg, DC, b. 1942,
© 2005, Christopher Walker and Paule Freeburg, DC. Published by OCP. All rights reserved.

# 695

## COME TO ME

Refrain

Come to me, all who la-bor and are heav-y bur - dened, and
I shall give you rest. Take up my yoke and learn from
me, for I am meek and hum - ble of heart,
and you'll find rest for your souls. Yes, my
yoke is eas - y and my bur - den is
light.

Verses

1. You, God, are my shep-herd.
2. Be - side peace-ful wa - ters
3. Should I be sur-round-ed
4. Be - fore my deep hun - ger
5. Pur - sue me, O God, ___

1. I shall nev - er be in need. Fresh and green are the
2. you re - store ___ my true self; There you lead me to
3. by the shad - ows of death, I will not fear, for
4. you spread out ___ your ___ feast. My ___ skin you a -
5. with your fath - om - less love. In your tent let me

to Refrain

1. mead-ows where you give me ___ rest.
2. walk ___ in the path of new life.
3. you are stead - fast in your ___ love.
4. noint ___ with the rich - est of oil.
5. dwell ___ all the days of my life.

Text: Based on Matthew 11:28–30; Psalm 23; original text, Weston Priory, Gregory Norbet, OSB, b. 1940.
Music: Weston Priory, Gregory Norbet, OSB.
Text and music © 1971, 1994 (revised text), The Benedictine Foundation of the State of Vermont, Inc.
   All rights reserved. Used with permission.

# IN EVERY AGE

1. Long be-fore the moun-tains came to be
2. Des-ti-ny is cast, and at your si-lent word
3. Teach us to make use of the time we have.

1. and the land and sea and stars of the night,
2. we re-turn to dust and scat-ter to the wind. A
3. Teach us to be pa-tient e-ven as we wait.

1. through the end-less sea-sons of all time, you have
2. thou-sand years are like a sin-gle mo-ment gone, as the
3. Teach us to em-brace our ev-'ry joy and pain. To sleep

1. al-ways been, you will al-ways be.
2. light that fades at the end of day.
3. peace-ful-ly, and to rise up strong.

**Refrain**

In ev-'ry age, O God, you have been our ref-uge.

*1, 2*      *to Verses 2, 3*

In ev-'ry age, O God, you have been our hope.

**Final**

God, you have been our hope,

you have been our ref-uge, you have been our hope.

Text: Based on Psalm 90:1–4, 12; Janèt Sullivan Whitaker, b. 1958.
Music: Janèt Sullivan Whitaker.
Text and music © 1998, 1999, 2000, Janèt Sullivan Whitaker. Published by OCP. All rights reserved.

## 697     BECAUSE THE LORD IS MY SHEPHERD

1. Be - cause ___ the Lord is my shep - herd, I have
2. And when ___ the road leads to dark - ness, I shall
3. In love ___ you make me a ban - quet for my
4. Your good - ness ___ al - ways is with me and your

1. ev – 'ry thing ___ I need. He lets me rest in the
2. walk there ___ un - a - fraid. E - ven when death is close__
3. en - e - mies ___ to see. You make me wel - come, __
4. mer - cy ___ I know. Your lov - ing kind - ness__

1. mead - ow and leads me to the qui - et streams. He re -
2. ___ I have cour - age, for your help is there. You are
3. pour - ing down hon - or from your might - y hand, and this
4. strength - ens me al - ways as I go through life. I shall

1. stores_ my soul and he leads me in the paths that are right:
2. close_ be - side me with com - fort, you are guid - ing my way:
3. joy ___ fills me with glad - ness; it is too much to bear:
4. dwell in your pres - ence for - ev - er, giv - ing praise to your name:

Refrain

Lord, you are my shep - herd, you are my friend.

I want to fol - low you al - ways, just to fol - low my friend.

Text: Based on Psalm 23; Christopher Walker, b. 1947.
Music: Christopher Walker.
Text and music © 1985, Christopher Walker. Published by OCP. All rights reserved.

# FLY LIKE A BIRD

**Refrain**

Fly like a bird to the Lord, my soul. I want to
soar like an ea-gle. Though I may jour-ney far a-
way from home, I know I'll nev-er be a-lone.

**Verses**

1. O God, you know who I am.
2. Where can I run from your love?
3. When I am down and a-fraid,

1. You know my hopes and my dreams. In my
2. Where can I hide from my God? From the
3. when I am fall-ing a-way, you ex-

1. pon-der-ing and fears, in my joy and in my tears,
2. dawn of morn-ing's light to the dark-ness of the night,
3. tend a gen-tle hand, and I know you un-der-stand.

to Refrain

1-3. O God, your pres-ence is real.

Text: Based on Psalm 139:1–4, 7–12, 23–24; Ken Canedo, b. 1953.
Music: Ken Canedo.
Text and music © 1995, 2002, spiritandsong.com®, a division of OCP. All rights reserved.

## 699     My Shepherd Will Supply My Need

1. My Shep-herd will sup-ply my need; The Lord God is his name. In pas-tures green he makes me feed, Be-side the liv-ing stream. He brings my wan-d'ring spir-it back, When I for-sake his ways; And leads me for his mer-cy's sake, In paths of truth and grace.

2. When I walk through the shades of death, Your pres-ence is my stay; One word of your sup-port-ing breath Drives all my fears a-way. Your hand, in sight of all my foes, Does still my ta-ble spread; My cup with bless-ings o-ver-flows, Your oil a-noints my head.

3. The sure pro-vi-sions of my God At-tend me all my days; O may your house be my a-bode, And all my work be praise! There would I find a set-tled rest, While oth-ers go and come, No more a stran-ger nor a guest; But like a child at home.

Text: 86 86 D; based on Psalm 23; Isaac Watts, 1674–1748, alt.
Music: RESIGNATION; William Walker's *The Southern Harmony*, 1835.

# PEACE

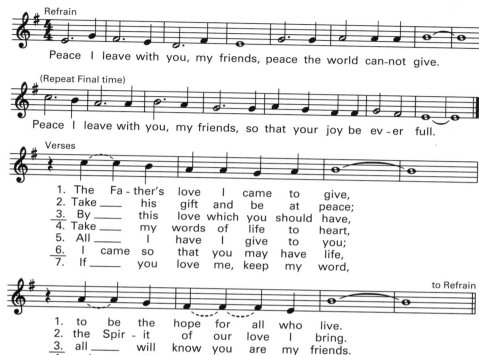

Peace I leave with you, my friends, peace the world can-not give.

Peace I leave with you, my friends, so that your joy be ev-er full.

**Verses**

1. The Father's love I came to give,
2. Take his gift and be at peace;
3. By this love which you should have,
4. Take my words of life to heart,
5. All I have I give to you;
6. I came so that you may have life,
7. If you love me, keep my word,

1. to be the hope for all who live.
2. the Spir-it of our love I bring.
3. all will know you are my friends.
4. and you will live with hope and joy.
5. I share with you the Fa-ther's love.
6. and have it to the full.
7. and our home we'll make with you.

to Refrain

Text: Based on John 14:27ff; Weston Priory, Gregory Norbet, OSB, b. 1940.
Music: Weston Priory, Gregory Norbet, OSB.
Text and music © 1971, The Benedictine Foundation of the State of Vermont, Inc.
All rights reserved. Used with permission.

# DONA NOBIS PACEM

Do-na no-bis pa-cem, pa-cem. Do-na no-bis pa-

cem. Do-na no-bis pa-cem. Do-na no-bis pa-cem.

Do-na no-bis pa-cem. Do-na no-bis pa-cem.

Text and music: Traditional.

# 702 PRAYER OF ST. FRANCIS

Verses 1, 2, 4

1. Make me a chan-nel of your peace. Where there is ha-tred,
2. Make me a chan-nel of your peace. Where there's de-spair in
4. Make me a chan-nel of your peace. It is in par-don-

1. let me bring your love. _____ Where there is in - ju-
2. life, let me bring hope. _____ Where there is dark-ness _
4. ing that we are par-doned, _____ In giv-ing of our -

1. ry, your par-don, Lord, And where there's doubt, true
2. _____ on - ly light, And where there's sad - ness
4. selves that we re - ceive, And in dy - ing that we're

1, Final    1st time: to Verse 2 | 2
(Fine)                           to Verse 3

1. faith        in        you.
2. ev - er                        2. joy.
4. born to e - ter - nal life.

Verse 3

3. O Mas-ter, grant that I may nev-er seek So much to be con-

3. soled, as to con-sole, To be un-der-stood, as to un-der-

to Verse 4

3. stand, To be loved, as to love, with all my soul.

Text: Based on the prayer traditionally ascr. to St. Francis of Assisi, 1182–1226; Sebastian Temple, 1928–1997.
Music: Sebastian Temple.
Text and music © 1967, OCP. All rights reserved. Dedicated to Mrs. Frances Tracy.

# LET THERE BE PEACE ON EARTH

Let there be peace on earth and let it be-gin with me.

Let there be peace on earth, the peace that was meant to

be. With God as our Fa-ther, broth - ers
*(optional text) we are*

all are we; Let me walk with my broth-er in
*fam - i - ly.* *Let us walk with each oth - er*

per - fect har - mo - ny. Let peace be - gin with me, let

this be the mo-ment now. With ev - 'ry step I take, let

this be my sol - emn vow: To take each mo-ment and live each

mo-ment in peace e - ter - nal - ly. Let there be peace on earth and

**1**

let it be - gin with me.

**Final**

let it be - gin with me.

## 704     BEARERS OF PEACE

1. Peo - ple of Je - sus, trust - ed to be bear - ers of
2. Feel for the ones who have no more bread, feel for the
3. Feel for the ones whose homes are de - stroyed, feel for the
4. Stand with the ones who see a new way: peo - ple of
5. Pray for the day our chil - dren will see war strange and
6. Why spend your tears on what can - not heal? Why spend your
7. Chil - dren of peace, go forth through the earth, heal - ing our

1. peace from God's liv - ing tree, peace that the world it - self can - not
2. ones with chil - dren un - fed. Long - ing for food, they find in our
3. lives now shat - tered and void. Wait - ing for loved ones no - bod - y
4. faith who strug - gle and pray, giv - en the call to shape and re -
5. dis - tant as slav - er - y. Work for a world where new ways a -
6. rage on what you con - ceal? God's liv - ing Word cries out to re -
7. world and bring - ing to birth vi - sion to build and fash - ion a

1. know, the peace that is giv - en to plant and to grow.
2. hands a moun - tain of weap - ons more sa - cred than land.
3. saw: the in - no - cent peo - ple who suf - fer in war.
4. build our ac - tions, our con - scienc - es, our bro - ken world.
5. bound to meet and to di - a - logue till peace is found.
6. veal a love that will sat - is - fy, hope that is real.
7. way: the full - ness of life for God's peo - ple to - day.

Text: 9 9 9 11; Bernadette Farrell, b. 1957
Music: SOMERSTOWN; Bernadette Farrell.
Text and music © 1999, Bernadette Farrell. Published by OCP. All rights reserved.

## 705     DONA NOBIS PACEM

Do - na no - bis pa - cem. Do - na no -
bis pa - cem. cem. Do - na no -
- bis pa - cem. Do - na no - bis pa - cem.

1. Give us peace, God,____ peace for
2. God of near-ness,____ God of
3. Set us free, God, from mind-less
4. You re-new us____ with great
5. Be our breath, God,____ deep and
6. Ma-ra-na-tha:____ come to

to Refrain

1. all, like a riv-er run-ning free-ly.____
2. life, you are with us; we re-joice.____
3. ways; guide us in pur - su-ing good.____
4. love; God a-mong us: this our joy!____
5. pure; feed our hun-ger for your truth.____
6. us with your heal-ing gift of peace.____

## PEACE IS FLOWING LIKE A RIVER 706

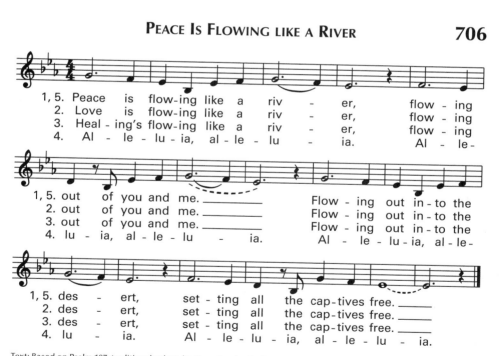

1, 5. Peace is flow-ing like a riv - er, flow - ing
2. Love is flow-ing like a riv - er, flow - ing
3. Heal - ing's flow-ing like a riv - er, flow - ing
4. Al - le - lu - ia, al - le - lu - ia. Al - le-

1, 5. out of you and me.____ Flow - ing out in-to the
2. out of you and me.____ Flow - ing out in-to the
3. out of you and me.____ Flow - ing out in-to the
4. lu - ia, al - le - lu - ia. Al - le - lu - ia, al - le-

1, 5. des - ert, set-ting all the cap-tives free.____
2. des - ert, set-ting all the cap-tives free.____
3. des - ert, set-ting all the cap-tives free.____
4. lu - ia. Al - le - lu - ia, al - le - lu - ia.

# 707

## LITANY OF PEACE

**Verses**

1. God of love, your gift of peace is plant - ed
2. God of peace, wher - ev - er there is ha - tred,
3. May we bring your hope and glad - ness where de -
4. May we seek to un - der - stand an - oth - er
5. Faith - ful God, wher - ev - er there is dark - ness,
6. God of mer - cy, help us to for - give when
7. Gra - cious God, when - ev - er peo - ple hun - ger,
8. Set us free from all our fear and an - ger;

**Refrain**

1. deep with - in our hearts: Make me an in - stru - ment
2. may we bring your love:
3. spair and sad - ness are:
4. with a pa - tient heart:
5. may we bring your light:
6. there is in - jury done:
7. may we fill their need:
8. set us free to love:

of your peace. Make me an in - stru - ment of your peace.

Text: Based on the prayer traditionally ascr. to St. Francis of Assisi, 1182–1226; Barbara Bridge, b. 1950.
Music: Barbara Bridge.

# 708

## GIVE US YOUR PEACE

**Refrain**

Give us your peace, O God; give us your peace,

1. your peace.
2. your peace. *to Verses (Fine)*

**Verses**

1. When we're a - fraid, run - ning from truth,
2. When we are tired, wea - ry, and worn,
3. Lord, we be - long to you a - lone;

1. gath-er us back to you. ｿ Take ev-ery fear
2. take us in-to your arms, where there is no need,
3. show us the way back home ｿ in-to your light,

*to Refrain*

1. and fill our hearts. ｝
2. there is no want. ｝ Give us your peace, O God.
3. in-to your love. ｝

Text and music: Jesse Manibusan, b. 1958, and Sarah Hart, b. 1968, © 2009, Jesse Manibusan and Sarah Hart.
Jesse Manibusan published by Two-by-Two Music and spiritandsong.com®, a division of OCP. All rights reserved.
Sarah Hart published by spiritandsong.com®, a division of OCP. All rights reserved.

## LOVE DIVINE, ALL LOVES EXCELLING     709

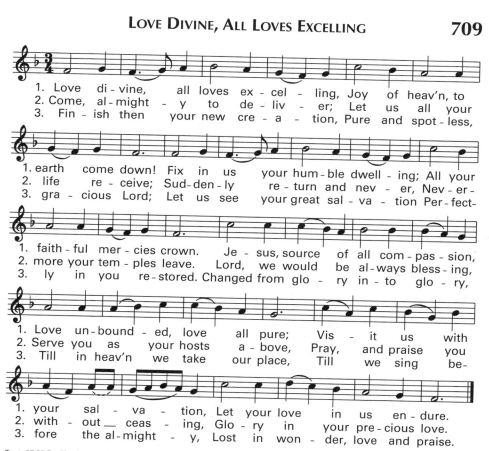

1. Love di-vine, all loves ex-cel-ling, Joy of heav'n, to
2. Come, al-might-y to de-liv-er; Let us all your
3. Fin-ish then your new cre-a-tion, Pure and spot-less,

1. earth come down! Fix in us your hum-ble dwell-ing; All your
2. life re-ceive; Sud-den-ly re-turn and nev-er, Nev-er-
3. gra-cious Lord; Let us see your great sal-va-tion Per-fect-

1. faith-ful mer-cies crown. Je-sus, source of all com-pas-sion,
2. more your tem-ples leave. Lord, we would be al-ways bless-ing,
3. ly in you re-stored. Changed from glo-ry in-to glo-ry,

1. Love un-bound-ed, love all pure; Vis-it us with
2. Serve you as your hosts a-bove, Pray, and praise you
3. Till in heav'n we take our place, Till we sing be-

1. your sal-va-tion, Let your love in us en-dure.
2. with-out ceas-ing, Glo-ry in your pre-cious love.
3. fore the al-might-y, Lost in won-der, love and praise.

Text: 87 87 D; Charles Wesley, 1707–1788, alt.
Music: HYFRYDOL; Rowland H. Prichard, 1811–1887.

# 710

## UBI CARITAS

Refrain

U - bi ca - ri - tas et a - mor, De - us i - bi

1 est. 2 to Verses (Fine) est. Verses 1, 3

1. We gath - er to - geth - er
Our God is a - live, the
3. Then, joined with the bless - ed,
Our joy none can mea - sure,

1. in the love of Christ; let each one be
God of love is near; so love one an -
3. filled with hope and grace, dear Lord, in great
joy that knows no end, re - sound - ing from

1. glad in him ____ and re - joice.
oth - er with a heart sin - cere. (to Refrain)
3. glo - ry may we see your face.
end - less age to age. A - men. (to Refrain)

Verse 2

2. We, the man - y, be - come one bod - y
Let all quar - rels, all di - vi - sion,

2. as the Spir - it binds, and we seek to be
all our con - flict cease; then will Christ tru - ly

2. one in Christ and one in heart and mind.
dwell a - mong us as our Lord of Peace. (to Refrain)

Text: Adapt. fr. Holy Thursday Liturgy; Laurence Rosania, b. 1957.
Music: Laurence Rosania.

# LOVE HAS COME

**Verses**

1. With one voice the an - gels sing songs that make cre -
2. God the Fa - ther, El - o - him, voice of thun - der,
3. God of Cov - e - nant, di - vine, lead us to the
4. Keep - er of the sac - ri - fice man - i - fest in
5. Now sal - va - tion has come in the New Je -

1. a - tion ring. Proph - ets hear and call us to
2. spir - it, wind: breathe on me your ver - y life;
3. end of time, be - yond sor - row, be - yond fear,
4. Je - sus Christ, born to die and wake the dead,
5. ru - sa - lem. Danc - ers dance and sing - ers roar; pro -

1. live in spir - it and in truth.
2. grace will make the dark - ness bright.
3. be - yond pride and earth - en tears.
4. as we hun - ger keep us fed.
5. claim - ing Je - sus Christ is Lord!

**Refrain**

Word of God, en - throned, dwell in us for - ev - er - more.

Love has come to show the way. Hal - le - lu -

jah, peace be with us. Love has come to show the way.

Text: Matt Maher, b. 1974.
Music: Matt Maher; arr. by Rick Modlin, b. 1966.
Text and music © 2000, 2010, Matt Maher. Published by spiritandsong.com®, a division of OCP. All rights reserved.

## 712     THERE'S A WIDENESS IN GOD'S MERCY

1. There's a wide-ness in God's mer-cy Like the wide-ness
2. For the love of God is broad-er Than the mea-sures
3. Trou-bled souls, why will you scat-ter Like a crowd of

1. of the sea; There's a kind-ness in his jus-tice
2. of our mind, And the heart of the E - ter-nal
3. fright-ened sheep? Fool-ish hearts, why will you wan-der

1. Which is more than lib-er-ty. There is plen-ti-ful re-
2. Is most won-der-ful-ly kind. If our love were but more
3. From a love so true and deep? There is wel-come for the

1. demp-tion In the blood that has been shed; There is
2. sim-ple We should take him at his word, And our
3. sin-ner And more grac-es for the good; There is

1. joy for all the mem-bers In the sor-rows of the Head.
2. lives would be thanks-giv-ing For the good-ness of our Lord.
3. mer-cy with the Sav-ior, There is heal-ing in his blood.

Text: 87 87 D; Frederick W. Faber, 1814–1863, alt.
Music: IN BABILONE; *Oude en Nieuwe Hollantse Boerenlities en Contradanseu*, ca. 1710.

## 713     ALL I ASK OF YOU

Refrain

All I ask of you is for-ev-er to re-mem-ber me as lov-ing

1-5 you.     to Verses

Final you, for-ev-er as lov-ing you.

Verses

1. Deep the joy of be - ing ___ to - geth - er in one
2. As we make our way ___ through all the joys and
3. Some-one will be call - ing you to be there for a -
4. Laugh - ter, joy and pres-ence: ___ the on - ly gifts you
5. Per - sons come in - to the fi - ber of our

to Refrain

1. heart ___ and for me that's just ___ where it is.
2. pain, ___ can we sense our young - er, tru - er selves?
3. while. ___ Can you hear their cry from deep with - in?
4. are! ___ Have you time? I'd like to be with you.
5. lives and then their shad - ows fade and dis - ap - pear. But

## MAY LOVE BE OURS

**714**

Verses

1. Not for tongues of heav-en's an - gels, Not for wis-dom to
2. Love is hum - ble, love is gen - tle, Love is ten - der, true
3. Nev - er jeal - ous, nev - er self - ish, Love will not re - joice
4. In the day this world is fad - ing, Faith and hope will play

1. dis - cern, Not for faith that mas-ters moun-tains, For this bet - ter
2. and kind; Love is gra - cious, ev - er pa - tient, Gen - er - ous of
3. in wrong; Nev - er boast - ful nor re - sent - ful, Love be - lieves and
4. their part: But when Christ is seen in glo - ry, Love shall reign in

Refrain

1. gift we yearn: May love be ours, O Lord; may love be ours.
2. heart and mind.
3. suf - fers long.
4. ev - 'ry heart.

*Cue note is an alternate lower melody note.

## 715     GOD IS LOVE

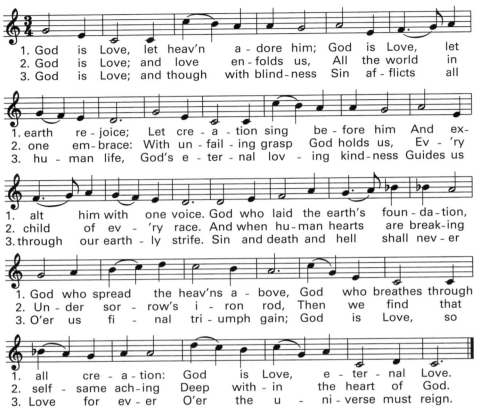

1. God is Love, let heav'n a-dore him; God is Love, let
2. God is Love; and love en-folds us, All the world in
3. God is Love; and though with blind-ness Sin af-flicts all

1. earth re-joice; Let cre-a-tion sing be-fore him And ex-
2. one em-brace: With un-fail-ing grasp God holds us, Ev-'ry
3. hu-man life, God's e-ter-nal lov-ing kind-ness Guides us

1. alt him with one voice. God who laid the earth's foun-da-tion,
2. child of ev-'ry race. And when hu-man hearts are break-ing
3. through our earth-ly strife. Sin and death and hell shall nev-er

1. God who spread the heav'ns a-bove, God who breathes through
2. Un-der sor-row's i-ron rod, Then we find that
3. O'er us fi-nal tri-umph gain; God is Love, so

1. all cre-a-tion: God is Love, e-ter-nal Love.
2. self-same ach-ing Deep with-in the heart of God.
3. Love for ev-er O'er the u-ni-verse must reign.

Text: 87 87 D; Timothy Rees, 1874–1939, alt.; fr. *Sermons and Hymns*, © 1946, Mowbray & Co., London (an imprint of Cassell, PLC). All rights reserved. Reproduced by permission of Continuum International Publishing Group, Ltd.
Music: ABBOT'S LEIGH; Cyril Vincent Taylor, 1907–1991, © 1942, renewed 1970, Hope Publishing Co.
All rights reserved. Used with permission.

## 716     THE WILL OF YOUR LOVE/TU VOLUNTAD

*Ostinato Refrain: All

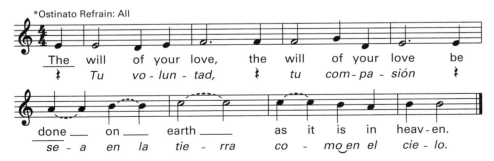

The will of your love, the will of your love be
Tu vo-lun-tad, tu com-pa-sión

done on earth as it is in heav-en.
se-a en la tie-rra co-mo en el cie-lo.

*Verses available in accompaniment books.

Text: Suggested by Brother Roger, Taizé Community; Suzanne Toolan, RSM, b. 1927;
Spanish tr. by Pia Moriarty, b. 1948, and Bob Hurd, b. 1950.
Music: Suzanne Toolan, RSM.
Text and music © 1995, Suzanne Toolan, RSM. Published by OCP. All rights reserved.

## CHRISTIANS, LET US LOVE ONE ANOTHER

**717**

1. Chris-tians, let us love one an-oth-er, As we share the
2. We who break this bread are one bod-y, We who share this
3. We who eat and drink at this ta-ble Die and rise a-
4. On the path of life we may fal-ter, Earth-ly food a-
5. Wheat and grape in-car-nate a mys-t'ry: Je-sus is the
6. Je-sus is the vine, we the branch-es; We are grains of

1. true liv-ing bread. Je-sus is our God and our
2. cup are all one. Chil-dren of our Fa-ther in
3. gain with our Lord. Draw-ing from our Rock liv-ing
4. lone leaves us weak; Al-ways you in-vite from the
5. true liv-ing bread. Let us eat with joy and thanks-
6. wheat, Christ the bread. Those who eat this bread live for-

1. broth-er; With his flesh and blood we are fed.
2. heav-en, We are heirs with God's on-ly son.
3. wa-ter Giv'n to all who thirst for ac-cord.
4. al-tar, "Hun-gry souls their food here must seek."
5. giv-ing, Trust-ing in the word he has said.
6. ev-er, One with Christ, our Lord and our Head.

Ev-'ry-one who

1-6. loves is born of God. Je-sus is our life. God is love.

Text: 98 98 98; Claudia Foltz, SNJM, and Armand Nigro, SJ, b. 1928, © 1973, Claudia Foltz, SNJM, and Armand Nigro, SJ. Published by OCP. All rights reserved.
Music: PICARDY; French Carol, 17th cent.; *Chansons populaires des Provinces de France*, 1860.

## LOVE ONE ANOTHER

**718**

*Refrain

Love one an-oth-er as I have loved you. Care for each

oth-er. I have cared for you. Bear each oth-er's bur-dens.

Bind each oth-er's wounds; and so you will know my re-turn.

*Verses available in accompaniment books.

Text: Based on John 14—16; 1 Corinthians 13; Bob Dufford, SJ, b. 1943.
Music: Bob Dufford, SJ.
Text and music © 1987, Robert J. Dufford, SJ. Published by OCP. All rights reserved.

## 719 WHAT WONDROUS LOVE IS THIS

1. What won-drous love is this, O my soul, O my soul? What won-drous love is this, O my soul? What won-drous love is this that caused the Lord of bliss To bear the dread-ful curse for my soul, for my soul, To bear the dread-ful curse for my soul?

2. What won-drous love is this, O my soul, O my soul? What won-drous love is this, O my soul? What won-drous love is this that caused the Lord of bliss To send this pre-cious peace to my soul, to my soul, To send this pre-cious peace to my soul?

3. To God and to the Lamb I will sing, I will sing; To God and to the Lamb, I will sing; To God and to the Lamb, who is the great I AM, While mil-lions join the theme, I will sing, I will sing; While mil-lions join the theme, I will sing.

4. And when from death I'm free, I'll sing on, I'll sing on; And when from death I'm free, I'll sing on; And when from death I'm free, I'll sing and joy - ful be, And through e - ter - ni - ty, I'll sing on, I'll sing on! And through e - ter - ni - ty, I'll sing on.

Text: 12 9 12 9 12 9; anon.; first appeared in *A General Selection of the Newest and Most Admired Hymns and Spiritual Songs*, 1811, adapt.
Music: WONDROUS LOVE; William Walker's *The Southern Harmony*, 1835.

## 720 WHERE CHARITY AND LOVE PREVAIL

1. Where char - i - ty and love pre - vail, There God is ev - er found;
2. With grate - ful joy and ho - ly fear God's char - i - ty we learn;
3. For - give we now each oth - er's faults As we our faults con - fess;
4. Let strife a - mong us be un - known, Let all con - ten - tion cease;
5. Let us re - call that in our midst Dwells God's be - got - ten Son;
6. No race nor creed can love ex - clude, If hon - ored be God's name;

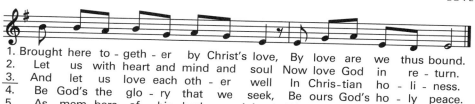

1. Brought here to-geth-er by Christ's love, By love are we thus bound.
2. Let us with heart and mind and soul Now love God in re-turn.
3. And let us love each oth-er well In Chris-tian ho-li-ness.
4. Be God's the glo-ry that we seek, Be ours God's ho-ly peace.
5. As mem-bers of his bod-y joined, We are in Christ made one.
6. Our fam-i-ly em-brac-es all Whose Fa-ther is the same.

Text: CM; *Ubi Caritas*, 9th cent.; tr. by Omer Westendorf, 1916–1997.
Music: CHRISTIAN LOVE; Paul Benoit, OSB, 1893–1979.

## In Perfect Charity     721

1. O most high and glo-rious God, cast your light in-to
2. O most high and glo-rious God, o-pen wide the door
3. Then most high and thank-ful praise I will sing un-to

1. the dark-ness of my heart. Give me right faith, and cer-tain
2. that leads me to your love. Give me your firm, yet gen-tle
3. the glo-ry of your name: To Fa-ther, Son, and Spir-it

1. hope, and per-fect, per-fect char-i-ty. Give me true
2. strength; may I live that per-fect char-i-ty. Lord, may your
3. bright, Liv-ing Pres-ence, Per-fect Char-i-ty. Praise to the

1. in-sight, Lord, and wis-dom, that I may al-ways live with-
2. peace be ev-er in me, that I may al-ways seek to
3. Love that shines in splen-dor, that lights the path-ways of my

1. in your ev-er ho-ly will. Lord, may your light with-
2. serve your chil-dren here on earth; that I may find my
3. heart, and brings me close to you. O Ho-ly One, in-

1. in me burn, shin-ing out in per-fect char-i-ty.
2. home with you, and live in per-fect char-i-ty.
3. vite me in, where you live in per-fect char-i-ty.

Text: Irregular; verse 1 based on a prayer of St. Francis of Assisi, 1182–1226; verses 2–3, Randall DeBruyn, b. 1947.
Music: PERFECT CHARITY; Randall DeBruyn.

**722**  ENDLESS IS YOUR LOVE

Refrain

You know my heart. You know my mind. You know my

words long be - fore I speak them. There is no place

that I can hide. End - less is your love for

us. How vast the sum of all your deeds!

End - less is your love for us.

Verses

1. Sure - ly there's a place    e - ven you don't
2. Can't I hide at night,    dark - ness be my
3. Won - der - ful your works,    count - less as the

1. know.    If I climb there, if I fly there,
2. light?    Can you see the day in dark - ness,
3. sand.    Earth and heav - en know your beau - ty,

to Refrain

1. can I hide from you?
2. can you find me there?
3. fash - ioned by your hand.

Text: Based on Psalm 139; Tom Kendzia, b. 1954.
Music: Tom Kendzia.

# GOD IS LOVE

**Refrain**

God is love, and all who live in love a - bide in God, and

1.
God a - bides in them.

2.
to Verses
(Fine)
God a - bides in them.

**Verses**

1. The love of Christ has gath - ered us as one: In
2. There - fore, as now we gath - er in - to one, let
3. Then with the saints let us be - hold your face, a -

1. him let us re - joice; in him let us be glad.
2. dis - cord find no place, nor ha - tred rule our hearts.
3. light with glo - ry, Christ, our broth - er and our God.

1. Let us re - vere and love the liv - ing God. With
2. Let e - vil deeds and bit - ter words now cease, that
3. And may this joy, un - bound - ed and im - mense, ful -

to Refrain

1. heart and mind and soul now let us love sin - cere - ly.
2. Christ stay in our midst and dwell with us for - ev - er.
3. fill our hearts' de - sire through a - ges with - out end - ing.

Text: Based on 1 John 4:16b and *Ubi Caritas*; Michael Joncas, b. 1951.
Music: Michael Joncas.

**724**  **OUT OF DARKNESS**

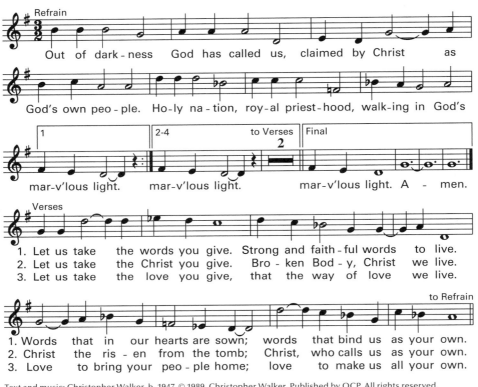

Refrain

Out of dark-ness God has called us, claimed by Christ as
God's own peo - ple. Ho-ly na-tion, roy-al priest-hood, walk-ing in God's
mar-v'lous light. mar-v'lous light. mar-v'lous light. A - men.

Verses

1. Let us take the words you give. Strong and faith-ful words to live.
2. Let us take the Christ you give. Bro - ken Bod - y, Christ we live.
3. Let us take the love you give, that the way of love we live.

1. Words that in our hearts are sown; words that bind us as your own.
2. Christ the ris - en from the tomb; Christ, who calls us as your own.
3. Love to bring your peo - ple home; love to make us all your own.

**725**  **UNLESS A GRAIN OF WHEAT**

Refrain

Un - less a grain of wheat shall fall up - on the ground and die,
it re - mains but a sin - gle grain with no life.

Verses

1. If we have died with him, then we shall live with him;
2. If an - y one serves me, then they must fol - low me;
3. Make your home in me as I make mine in you;
4. If you re - main in me and my word lives in you,
5. Those who love me are loved by my Fa - ther;
6. Peace I leave with you, my peace I give to you;

to Refrain

1. if we hold firm, we shall reign with him. ____
2. wher - ev - er I am, my ser - vants will be.
3. those who re - main in me bear much fruit. ____
4. then you will be my dis - ci - ples. _____
5. we shall be with them and dwell in them. ____
6. peace which the world can - not give is my gift.

Text: Based on John 12:24–26; 14:23, 27; 15:4–5, 7–8; 2 Timothy 2:11–12; Bernadette Farrell, b. 1957.
Music: Bernadette Farrell.

## TRANSFIGURE US, O LORD 726

**Refrain**

Trans - fig - ure us, O Lord, trans - fig - ure us, O Lord.

Break the chains that bind us; speak your heal - ing word, and

where you lead we'll fol - low. Trans - fig - ure us, O Lord.

**Verses**

1. Down from heights of glo - ry in - to the depths be - low, the
2. Light for those in dark - ness, the hun - gry have their fill, glad
3. Par - don for the sin - ner, a shep - herd for the sheep, a
4. To the ho - ly cit - y, Je - ru - sa - lem, you go; your

1. love of God self - emp - tied, the love of God to show. You
2. tid - ings for the hum - ble, the heal - ing of all ills; in
3. drink of liv - ing wa - ter for all who thirst and seek, and
4. face set toward the end - ing, the cross to be your throne.

to Refrain

1. light the path be - fore us, the way that we must go.
2. these we glimpse your glo - ry, God's prom - is - es ful - filled.
3. feast - ing at your ta - ble, the low - ly and the least.
4. Shall we jour - ney with you and share your pas - chal road?

Text: Based on Matthew 17:1–9; Mark 9:2–10; Luke 9:28b–36; Bob Hurd, b. 1950.
Music: Bob Hurd.

# 727

## ANTHEM

Refrain

We are called, we are cho-sen. We are Christ for one an-oth-er. We are prom-ised to to-mor-row, while we are for him to-day. We are sign, we are won-der. We are sow-er, we are seed. We are har-vest, we are hun-ger. We are ques-tion, we are creed.

Verses

1. Then where can we stand jus-ti-fied?_ In what can we be-lieve? In no one
2. Then how are we to stand at all,_ this world of bend-ed knee? In noth-ing
3. Then shall we not stand emp-ty_ at the al-tar of our dreams:_ When he

1. else but he who suf-fered, noth-ing more than he who rose.
2. more than bar-ren shad-ows. No one else but he could save us.
3. prom-ised us our-selves. _ Who mark time a-gainst to-mor-row.

1, 2. Who was jus-tice for the poor. Who was rage a-gainst the night.
3. Who are jus-tice for the poor. Who are rage a-gainst the night.

to Refrain

1, 2. Who was hope for peace-ful peo-ple. Who was light.
3. Who are hope for peace-ful peo-ple. Who are light.

## All That Is Hidden

1. If you would fol-low me, fol - low where life will lead: __
2. If you would hon - or me, hon - or the least of these: __
3. If you would speak of me, live all your life in me: __
4. If you would rise with me, rise through your des - ti - ny: __

1. __ do not look for me a - mong the dead, for I am
2. __ you will not find me dressed in fin - er - y. My Word cries
3. __ my ways are not the ways that you would choose; my thoughts are
4. __ do not re-fuse the death which brings you life, for as the

1. hid-den in pain, __ ris - en in love; there is no
2. out to be heard; __ breaks through the world: my Word is
3. far be-yond yours, __ as heav - en from earth: if you be-
4. grain in the earth __ must die for re - birth, so I have

1. har-vest with-out sow-ing of grain.
2. on your lips and lives in your heart.
3. lieve in me my voice will be heard.
4. plant-ed your life deep with-in mine.

**Refrain**

All that is hid-den will be made clear. All that is dark now will be re-vealed. What you have heard in the dark pro-claim in the light; what you hear in whis-pers pro-claim from the house - tops.

Text: Refrain based on Luke 12:2–3; Bernadette Farrell, b. 1957.
Music: Bernadette Farrell.

# 729 PESCADOR DE HOMBRES/LORD, YOU HAVE COME

Text: Spanish, Cesáreo Gabaráin, 1936–1991; English, OCP.
Music: Cesáreo Gabaráin.

# GO MAKE A DIFFERENCE

Text: Based on Matthew 5:13–16; Steve Angrisano, b. 1965, and Tom Tomaszek, b. 1950.
Music: Steve Angrisano and Tom Tomaszek.
Text and music © 1997, Steve Angrisano and Thomas N. Tomaszek. Published by spiritandsong.com®, a division of OCP.
All rights reserved.

## 731 JOURNEYSONG

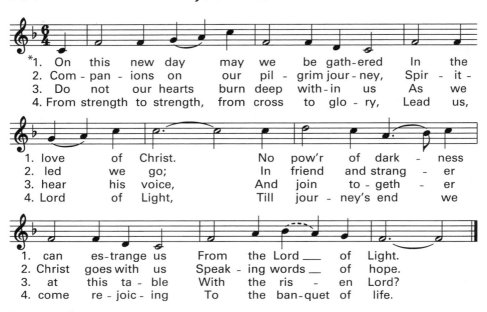

```
*1. On    this   new   day      may   we    be gath-ered   In    the
 2. Com- pan- ions  on       our   pil - grim jour-ney,  Spir - it-
 3. Do    not   our hearts   burn deep  with-in  us     As    we
 4. From strength to strength, from cross  to   glo- ry,  Lead   us,

 1. love      of   Christ.       No    pow'r  of   dark  -  ness
 2. led      we    go;          In   friend  and strang  -  er
 3. hear     his   voice,        And    join   to - geth  -  er
 4. Lord      of   Light,        Till   jour - ney's end       we

 1. can   es-trange us    From   the   Lord ___  of   Light.
 2. Christ goes with us    Speak - ing words ___  of   hope.
 3. at    this ta - ble    With   the   ris  -  en  Lord?
 4. come  re - joic - ing   To    the  ban-quet of   life.
```

*Alternate text for use at Evening Prayer/Mass: "As evening falls may we be gathered...."(at Evening Prayer omit verse 3).

Text: 95 95; based on Luke 24; Bob Hurd, b. 1950, © 1996, Bob Hurd. Published by OCP. All rights reserved.
Music: LAND OF REST; trad. American Melody.

## 732 ONLY THIS I WANT

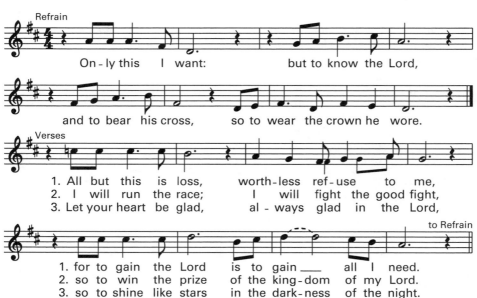

Refrain
```
On - ly this   I   want:      but to know the Lord,

and to bear  his cross,    so to wear the crown he  wore.
```

Verses
```
1. All   but  this   is   loss,    worth-less ref - use   to   me,
2. I    will  run   the  race;     I    will  fight the good fight,
3. Let  your heart  be   glad,    al - ways  glad  in   the  Lord,

                                                          to Refrain
1. for   to  gain   the Lord    is  to  gain ___  all  I   need.
2. so    to  win   the prize    of the  king-dom  of  my  Lord.
3. so    to  shine like stars   in  the  dark-ness  of the night.
```

Text: Based on Philippians 3:7–16; 2:15, 18; Dan Schutte, b. 1947.
Music: Dan Schutte.
Text and music © 1981, OCP. All rights reserved.

# LEAD ME, LORD

Verses

1. Bless - ed are the poor in spir - it, long - ing for their
2. Bless - ed are the mer - ci - ful, for mer - cy shall be
3. Blest are they who through their life - times sow the seeds of

1. Lord, for God's com - ing king - dom shall be theirs.
2. theirs, and the pure in heart shall see their God.
3. peace, all will call them chil - dren of the Lord.

1. Bless - ed are the sor - row - ing, for they shall be con -
2. Blest are they whose hun - ger on - ly ho - li - ness can
3. Blest are you, though per - se - cu - ted in your ho - ly

1. soled, and the meek shall come to rule the world.
2. fill, for I say they shall be sat - is - fied.
3. life, for in heav - en, great is your re - ward.

Refrain

Lead me, Lord, lead me, Lord, by the light of truth to

seek and to find the nar - row way. Be my way;

be my truth; be my life, my Lord, and lead me, Lord, to -

1-2 to Verses | Final

day. day. And lead me, Lord, to - day.

Text: Based on Matthew 5:3–12; 7:7, 13; John 14:6; John D. Becker, b. 1953.
Music: John D. Becker.
Text and music © 1987, John D. Becker. Published by OCP. All rights reserved.

**734**      **WOMEN OF THE CHURCH**

**Refrain**

Wom-en of the Church, how rich is your leg-a-cy! Wom-en of the

Church, how great is your faith! Wom-en of the Church,

well-springs of in-teg-ri-ty, lead us in the ways of peace!

**Verses 1, 2, 5**

1. Wom-en at the foot___ of the cross,___ fear-less and
2. Com-pan-ions and dis-ci-ples of Je-sus, cho-sen and
5. Wom-en mar-tyred in our time,___ lay-ing down their

1. tru-ly faith-ful friends; first___ ones to see_____ the
2. called___ by____ name, wit-ness-es of wis-dom,___
5. lives___ for the poor, proph-ets of cour-age who

*to Refrain*

1. ris-en Lord of Life, and the first to tell good news!
2. weav-ers of the Word, lead us in the ways of truth!
5. stood with those op-pressed, help us all to walk your paths.

**Verses 3, 4**

3. Liv-ing signs of ser-vice and strength, hands of heal-ing,
4. Wom-en of com-pas-sion and care, bear-ers of God's

3. hearts of___ love, wom-en of vi-sion, voic-es for the
4. life-giv-ing light, cen-tered in prayer while work-ing for

*to Refrain*

3. voice-less, lead us in the ways of hope.
4. jus-tice, lead us in the ways of peace.

## 'TIS THE GIFT TO BE SIMPLE

1. 'Tis the gift to be sim-ple, 'tis the gift to be free, 'Tis the gift to
2. 'Tis the gift to be gen-tle, 'tis the gift to be fair, 'Tis the gift to
3. 'Tis the gift to be lov-ing, 'tis the gift best of all, Like a qui-et

1. come down where you ought to be, And when we find our-selves in the
2. wake and breathe the morn-ing air; And ev-'ry day to walk in the
3. rain, it bless-es where it falls; And if we have the gift, we will

1. place just __ right __ 'Twill be in the val-ley of love and de-light.
2. path we __ choose, 'Tis the gift that we pray we may ne'er come to lose.
3. tru-ly be-lieve __ 'Tis bet-ter to give than it is to re-ceive.

*Refrain*

When true sim-plic-i-ty is gained, To bow and to bend we

shan't be a-shamed; To turn, turn will be our de-light, Till by

turn-ing, turn-ing we come 'round right.

Text: Irregular with refrain; Shaker Song, 18th cent. Verses 2–3, Joyce Merman, © 1975 (renewed), Shawnee Press, Inc.
All rights reserved. Used with permission.
Music: SIMPLE GIFTS; Shaker Melody, 18th cent.

# 736

# I WILL CHOOSE CHRIST

Refrain: 1st time: Cantor; thereafter: All

I will choose Christ, I will choose love, I choose to serve.

I give my heart, I give my life, I give my all

1-3 to Verses | Final

to you. to you. I give my all to you.

Verse 1

1. How man-y times must he call my name and show to

1. me that he is God? And as a ser-vant he

to Refrain

1. calls to me, you must serve too.

Verse 2

2. Christ, my teach-er and heal-er, teach my

2. heart and heal my soul. And as I walk this

to Refrain

2. road with you, teach me to love.

3. As I look up-on your cross, so too
3. must I die with you. And with the death of my
3. own de - sires, I'll rise with you.

## GOD, WHOSE GLORY REIGNS ETERNAL 737

1. God, whose glo - ry reigns e - ter - nal, Span-ning space as
2. In Christ's heal - ing touch and teach - ing We see life as
3. Now we pon - der life's great mys - t'ry Suf - f'ring sav - ior,

1. well as time, Show us signs in seed and ker - nel, Life po-
2. you in - tend, Self-less love to oth - ers reach - ing, Pain and
3. cross en-throned, Past and fu - ture in one his - t'ry Our mor-

1. ten - tial, hope sub - lime. Grant us in - sight, all dis - cern - ing,
2. bro - ken-ness to end. And when hun - gry folk are nour-ished,
3. tal - i - ty Christ owned. And as res - ur - rec-tion's glo - ry

1. See - ing truth be - yond bare fact, Love trans - lat - ing
2. Filled by hope and word and bread, These are signs your
3. Shines in - to the emp - ty tomb, We, too, tell the

1. all our learn - ing In - to pow'r to be and act.
2. reign has flour - ished And from bond - age we are led.
3. an - cient sto - ry, Joy dis - pel - ling all the gloom.

# 738 THE EYES AND HANDS OF CHRIST

**Refrain**

Where two or three are gath-ered in my name,

love will be found, life will a - bound.

By name we are called, from wa - ter we are sent:

to be - come the eyes and hands of Christ.

**Verses 1, 2**

1. One we be-come, no long-er strang - ers. No long-er
2. One in the Spir-it, one in the Lord. One in the

1. emp - ty ___ or frail. Filled with the Spir - it, ev - 'ry
2. break-ing of the bread. Life - giv - ing wit - ness of our

*to Refrain*

1. hun - ger sat - is - fied. Christ is the cen - ter of our lives.
2. dy - ing and new life. Held by the prom-ise in our hands.

**Verse 3**

3. Not what we are, but what we be - come. Not what we

3. say, but what we do. Liv - ing the chal - lenge as

*to Refrain*

3. bear - ers of light. We are the eyes and hands of Christ.

## O Beauty, Ever Ancient

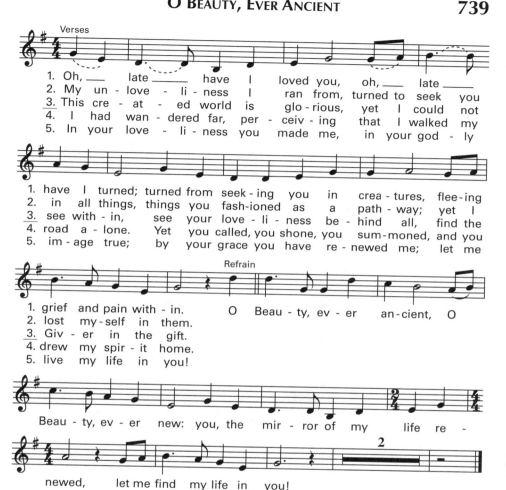

**Verses**

1. Oh, ___ late ___ have I loved you, oh, ___ late ___
2. My un - love - li - ness I ran from, turned to seek you
3. This cre - at - ed world is glo - rious, yet I could not
4. I had wan - dered far, per - ceiv - ing that I walked my
5. In your love - li - ness you made me, in your god - ly

1. have I turned; turned from seek - ing you in crea - tures, flee - ing
2. in all things, things you fash-ioned as a path - way; yet I
3. see with - in, see your love - li - ness be - hind all, find the
4. road a - lone. Yet you called, you shone, you sum-moned, and you
5. im - age true; by your grace you have re - newed me; let me

**Refrain**

1. grief and pain with - in. O Beau - ty, ev - er an - cient, O
2. lost my - self in them.
3. Giv - er in the gift.
4. drew my spir - it home.
5. live my life in you!

Beau - ty, ev - er new: you, the mir - ror of my life re -

newed, let me find my life in you!

2

Text: Based on a prayer from St. Augustine of Hippo's *Confessions*, ca. 400; Roc O'Connor, SJ, b. 1949.
Music: Roc O'Connor, SJ.
Text and music © 2004, Robert F. O'Connor, SJ. Published by OCP. All rights reserved.

## 740 SENT FORTH BY GOD'S BLESSING

1. Sent forth by God's bless-ing, our true faith con - fess-ing, The
God's sac - ri - fice end - ed, O now be ex - tend-ed The
2. With praise and thanks - giv - ing, to God who is liv - ing, The
Our faith ev - er shar-ing, in love ev - er car-ing, We

1. peo-ple of God from his dwell - ing take leave.
fruits of this Mass in all hearts who be - lieve. The seed of Christ's
2. tasks of our ev - 'ry-day life we em-brace.
claim as our neigh-bor all those of each race. One bread that has

1. teach-ing, our in - ner souls reach-ing, Shall blos-som in ac-tion for
2. fed us, one light that has led us U - nite us as one in his

1. God and for all. His grace shall in - cite us, his love shall u -
2. life that we share. Then may all the liv-ing with praise and thanks -

1. nite us To fur-ther God's king-dom and an-swer his call.
2. giv - ing Give hon - or to Christ and his name that we bear.

Text: 12 11 12 11 D; Omer Westendorf, 1916–1997, alt., © 1964, World Library Publications.
All rights reserved. Used with permission.
Music: ASH GROVE; trad. Welsh Melody.

## 741 HOLY WISDOM, LAMP OF LEARNING

1. Ho - ly Wis-dom, lamp of learn - ing, Bless the light that
2. Vine of truth, in you we flour - ish; By your grace we
3. Ho - ly God, the hope of na - tions, Tune us toward your

1. rea - son lends. Teach us judg-ment as we kin - dle Sparks of
2. learn and grow. May the word of Christ a-mong us Shape our
3. righ-teous will, As the sym-pho - ny of a - ges Claims our

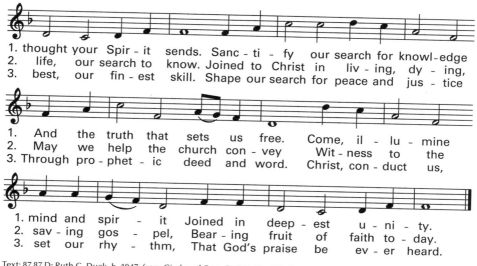

1. thought your Spir - it sends. Sanc - ti - fy our search for knowl-edge
2. life, our search to know. Joined to Christ in liv - ing, dy - ing,
3. best, our fin - est skill. Shape our search for peace and jus - tice

1. And the truth that sets us free. Come, il - lu - mine
2. May we help the church con - vey Wit - ness to the
3. Through pro - phet - ic deed and word. Christ, con - duct us,

1. mind and spir - it Joined in deep - est u - ni - ty.
2. sav - ing gos - pel, Bear - ing fruit of faith to - day.
3. set our rhy - thm, That God's praise be ev - er heard.

Text: 87 87 D; Ruth C. Duck, b. 1947; from *Circles of Care*, © 1996, The Pilgrim Press.
All rights reserved. Used with permission.
Music: BEACH SPRING; *The Sacred Harp*, 1844.

## WORD OF GOD

742

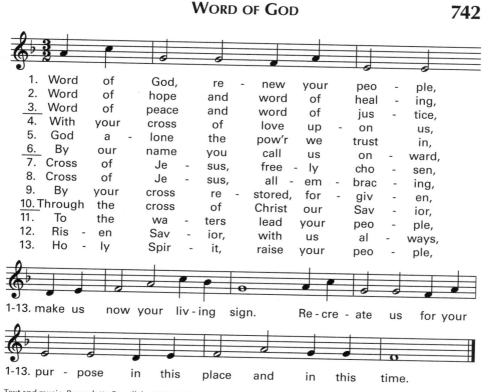

1. Word of God, re - new your peo - ple,
2. Word of hope and word of heal - ing,
3. Word of peace and word of jus - tice,
4. With your cross of love up - on us,
5. God a - lone the pow'r we trust in,
6. By our name you call us on - ward,
7. Cross of Je - sus, free - ly cho - sen,
8. Cross of Je - sus, all - em - brac - ing,
9. By your cross re - stored, for - giv - en,
10. Through the cross of Christ our Sav - ior,
11. To the wa - ters lead your peo - ple,
12. Ris - en Sav - ior, with us al - ways,
13. Ho - ly Spir - it, raise your peo - ple,

1-13. make us now your liv - ing sign. Re - cre - ate us for your

1-13. pur - pose in this place and in this time.

Text and music: Bernadette Farrell, b. 1957, © 2000, 2001, Bernadette Farrell. Published by OCP. All rights reserved.

**743**     **VOICE OF CHRIST**

Verses 1, 2, 4

1. O ___ Lord, ___ you ___ bless us each day with
2. The ___ spar-row nei-ther sows nor ___ reaps, has
4. We a-wait ___ you with watch-ful ___ eyes, our

1. gifts from your hand. Now ___ as ___ our ___
2. store-house nor barn. And ___ flow-ers nei-ther
4. lamps burn-ing bright. Though we know ___ not when

1. cup o-ver-flows, may we too bring ___ forth.
2. spin nor ___ weave, yet they wear roy-al robes.
4. you will re-turn, we stand wake-ful through the night.

Refrain

We the hands, we the eyes, we the voice of Christ.

O faith-ful God, we en-trust our trea-sure to your heart.

Verse 3

3. The Lord hears the cry of the poor; the

3. lives of the weak he shall save. Bless-ed those who care for the

to Refrain

3. poor; hap-pi-ness is their re-ward.

Text: Based on Luke 12:22–40; Psalm 41:2–3; Psalm 72:12–13; Timothy R. Smith, b. 1960.
Music: Timothy R. Smith.
Text and music © 1993, Timothy R. Smith. Published by spiritandsong.com®, a division of OCP. All rights reserved.

## WITH ALL THE SAINTS

1. With all the saints, with proph - ets and mar - tyrs,
2. With all in need, the poor and for - sak - en
3. With ref - u - gees, and vic - tims of vio - lence,
4. With all who live com - pas - sion and mer - cy,
5. With all who dare to toil for that cit - y
6. So may this flock, this church once more gath - ered,

1. with ho - ly Ma - ry and Jo - seph, with
2. to whom the inn - keep - er shuts the door, with
3. with those made home - less by Her - od's sword, with
4. all who de - fend hu - man dig - ni - ty, with
5. whose light shall shine from the moun - tain - top, where
6. faith - ful - ly fol - low its Shep - herd's voice. To

1. those who came be - fore___ and those__ who will fol - low,
2. those who are the least,___ yet first___ in the king - dom,
3. all the dis - ap - peared___ and those__ who still mourn them,
4. peo - ple of good will___ from ev - ery faith and na - tion,
5. all may dwell in peace___ and know__ life's full mea - sure,
6. be a liv - ing sign of the love of God and neigh - bor,

1-6. we gath - er here to - day, one bod - y in the Lord, a

1-6. sign and sac - ra - ment of Christ.

**745** ONE SPIRIT, ONE CHURCH

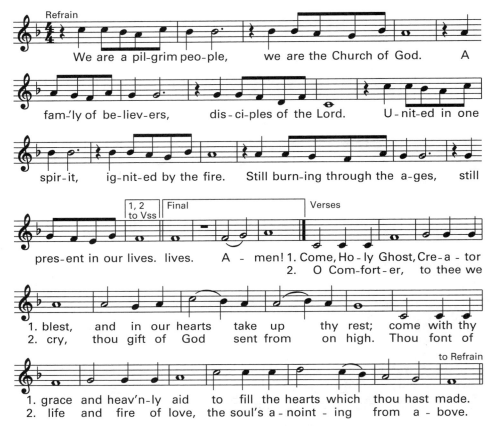

We are a pil-grim peo-ple, we are the Church of God. A fam-'ly of be-liev-ers, dis-ci-ples of the Lord. U-nit-ed in one spir-it, ig-nit-ed by the fire. Still burn-ing through the a-ges, still pres-ent in our lives. lives. A - men!

1. Come, Ho - ly Ghost, Cre-a - tor 1. blest, and in our hearts take up thy rest; come with thy 1. grace and heav'n-ly aid to fill the hearts which thou hast made.

2. O Com-fort-er, to thee we 2. cry, thou gift of God sent from on high. Thou font of 2. life and fire of love, the soul's a-noint-ing from a-bove.

Text: Refrain, Maryanne Quinlivan, OSU, © 1990, Ursuline Academy of Cleveland. Published by OCP. All rights reserved.
Verses fr. *Veni, Creator Spiritus*; attr. to Rabanus Maurus, 776–856; tr. by Edward Caswall, 1814–1878, alt.
Music: Refrain, Kevin Keil (ASCAP), b. 1956; verses based on LAMBILLOTTE, © 1990, Kevin Keil.
Published by OCP. All rights reserved.

**746** THE CHURCH'S ONE FOUNDATION

1. The Chur-ch's one foun - da - tion Is Je - sus Christ her Lord;
2. E - lect from ev - 'ry na - tion, Yet one o'er all the earth,
3. 'Mid toil and trib - u - la - tion, And tu - mult of her war,
4. Yet she on earth hath un - ion With God, the Three-in - One,

1. She is his new cre - a - tion By wa - ter and the word:
2. Her char-ter of sal - va - tion, "One Lord, one faith, one birth!"
3. She waits the con - sum - ma - tion Of peace for - ev - er - more,
4. And with the saints, com - mu - nion With those whose rest is won.

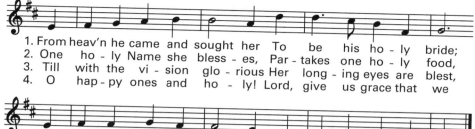

1. From heav'n he came and sought her To be his ho - ly bride;
2. One ho - ly Name she bless - es, Par - takes one ho - ly food,
3. Till with the vi - sion glo - rious Her long - ing eyes are blest,
4. O hap - py ones and ho - ly! Lord, give us grace that we

1. With his own blood he bought her, And for her life he died.
2. And to one hope she press - es With ev - 'ry grace en - dued.
3. And the great Church vic - to - rious Shall be the Church at rest.
4. Like them, the meek and low - ly, On high may dwell with thee.

Text: 76 76 D; Samuel J. Stone, 1839–1900, alt.
Music: AURELIA; Samuel S. Wesley, 1810–1876.

## CHRIST IS MADE THE SURE FOUNDATION 747

1. Christ is made the sure foun - da - tion, Christ, the head and
2. To this tem - ple, where we call you, Come, O Lord of
3. Grant, we pray, to all your peo - ple, All the grace they
4. Praise and hon - or to the Fa - ther, Praise and hon - or

1. cor - ner - stone; Cho - sen of the Lord, and pre - cious,
2. hosts, to - day; With your wont - ed lov - ing kind - ness,
3. ask to gain; What they gain from you for ev - er
4. to the Son, Praise and hon - or to the Spir - it,

1. Bind - ing all the Church in one, Ho - ly Si - on's
2. Hear your ser - vants as they pray, And your ful - lest
3. With the bless - ed to re - tain, And here - af - ter
4. Ev - er three and ev - er one, One in might and

1. help for ev - er, And her con - fi - dence a - lone.
2. ben - e - dic - tion, Shed in all its bright - est ray.
3. in your glo - ry, Ev - er - more with you to reign.
4. one in glo - ry, While un - end - ing a - ges run.

Text: 87 87 87; *Angularis fundamentum*, 11th cent.; tr. by John M. Neale, 1818–1866, alt.
Music: WESTMINSTER ABBEY; Henry Purcell, 1659–1695.

## 748     BY ALL YOUR SAINTS STILL STRIVING

1. By all your saints still striv - ing, For all your saints at rest,
*2. A - pos - tles, proph - ets, mar - tyrs, And all the no - ble throng
3. Then let us praise the Fa - ther And wor - ship God the Son

1. Your ho - ly Name, O Je - sus, For ev - er - more be blessed.
2. Who wear the spot - less rai - ment And raise the cease - less song:
3. And sing to God the Spir - it, E - ter - nal Three in One,

1. You rose, our King vic - to - rious, That they might wear the crown
2. For them and those whose wit - ness Is on - ly known to you
3. Till all the ran - somed num - ber Who stand be - fore the throne,

1. And ev - er shine in splen - dor Re - flect - ed from your throne.
2. By walk - ing in their foot - steps We give you praise a - new.
3. A - scribe all pow'r and glo - ry And praise to God a - lone.

**Alternate Verses**

**4. Conversion of St. Paul (January 25)**
Praise for the light from heaven
And for the voice of awe:
Praise for the glorious vision
The persecutor saw.
O Lord, for Paul's conversion,
We bless your Name today.
Come shine within our darkness
And guide us in the Way.

**5. Chair of St. Peter (February 22)**
We praise you, Lord, for Peter,
So eager and so bold:
Thrice falling, yet repentant,
Thrice charged to feed your fold.
Lord, make your pastors faithful
To guard your flock from harm
And hold them when they waver
With your almighty arm.

**6. St. Joseph, husband of
the Blessed Virgin Mary (March 19)**
All praise, O God, for Joseph,
The guardian of your Son,
Who saved him from King Herod,
When safety there was none.
He taught the trade of builder,
When they to Naz'reth came,
And Joseph's love made "Father"
To be, for Christ, God's name.

**7. Annunciation of the Lord (March 25)**
We sing with joy of Mary
Whose heart with awe was stirred

When, youthful and unready,
She heard the angel's word;
Yet she her voice upraises
God's glory to proclaim,
As once for our salvation
Your mother she became.

**8. St. Mark (April 25)**
For Mark, O Lord, we praise you,
The weak by grace made strong:
His witness in his Gospel
Becomes victorious song.
May we, in all our weakness,
Receive your power divine,
And all, as faithful branches,
Grow strong in you, the Vine.

**9. Ss. Philip and James (May 3)**
We praise you, Lord, for Philip,
Blest guide to Greek and Jew,
And for young James the faithful,
Who heard and followed you,
O grant us grace to know you,
The victor in the strife,
That we with all your servants
May wear the crown of life.

**10. St. Matthias (May 13)**
For one in place of Judas,
Th'apostles sought God's choice:
The lot fell to Matthias
For whom we now rejoice.
May we like true apostles
Your holy Church defend,

*This verse may be replaced by an appropriate Alternate Verse.

And not betray our calling
But serve you to the end.

### 11. St. Barnabas (June 11)
For Barnabas we praise you,
Who kept your law of love
And, leaving earthly treasures,
Sought riches from above.
O Christ, our Lord and Savior,
Let gifts of grace descend,
That your true consolation
May through the world extend.

### 12. Nativity of St. John the Baptist (June 24)
All praise for John the Baptist,
Forerunner of the Word,
Our true Elijah, making
A highway for the Lord.
The last and greatest prophet,
He saw the dawning ray
Of light that grows in splendor
Until the perfect day.

### 13. Ss. Peter and Paul (June 29)
We praise you for Saint Peter;
We praise you for Saint Paul.
They taught both Jew and Gentile
That Christ is all in all.
To cross and sword they yielded
And saw the kingdom come:
O God, your two apostles
Won life through martyrdom.

### 14. St. Thomas (July 3)
All praise, O Lord, for Thomas
Whose short-lived doubtings prove
Your perfect twofold nature,
The depth of your true love.
To all who live with questions
A steadfast faith afford;
And grant us grace to know you,
Made flesh, yet God and Lord.

### 15. St. Mary Magdalene (July 22)
All praise for Mary Magd'lene,
Whose wholeness was restored
By you, her faithful Master,
Her Savior and her Lord.
On Easter morning early,
A word from you sufficed:
Her faith was first to see you,
Her Lord, the risen Christ.

### 16. St. James (July 25)
O Lord, for James, we praise you,
Who fell to Herod's sword.
He drank the cup of suff'ring
And thus fulfilled your word.
Lord, curb our vain impatience
For glory and for fame,
Equip us for such suff'rings
As glorify your Name.

### 17. St. Bartholomew (August 24)
Praise for your blest apostle
Surnamed Bartholomew;
We know not his achievements
But know that he was true,
For he at the Ascension
Was an apostle still.
May we discern your presence
And seek, like him, your will.

### 18. St. Matthew (September 21)
We praise you, Lord, for Matthew,
Whose gospel words declare
That, worldly gain forsaking,
Your path of life we share.
From all unrighteous mammon,
O raise our eyes anew,
That we, whate'er our station
May rise and follow you.

### 19. St. Luke (October 18)
For Luke, belov'd physician,
All praise; whose Gospel shows
The healer of the nations,
The one who shares our woes.
Your wine and oil, O Savior,
Upon our spirits pour,
And with true balm of Gilead
Anoint us evermore.

### 20. Ss. Simon and Jude (October 28)
Praise, Lord, for your apostles,
Saint Simon and Saint Jude.
One love, one hope impelled them
To tread the way, renewed.
May we with zeal as earnest
The faith of Christ maintain,
Be bound in love together,
And life eternal gain.

### 21. St. Andrew (November 30)
All praise, O Lord, for Andrew,
The first to follow you;
He witnessed to his brother,
"This is Messiah true."
You called him from his fishing
Upon Lake Galilee;
He rose to meet your challenge,
"Leave all and follow me."

### 22. St. Stephen (December 26)
All praise, O Lord, for Stephen
Who, martyred, saw you stand
To help in time of torment,
To plead at God's right hand.
Like you, our suff'ring Savior,
His enemies he blessed,
With "Lord, receive my spirit,"
His faith, in death, confessed.

### 23. St. John (December 27)
For John, your loved disciple,
Exiled to Patmos' shore,
And for his faithful record,
We praise you evermore;
Praise for the mystic vision
His words to us unfold.
Instill in us his longing,
Your glory to behold.

### 24. Holy Innocents (December 28)
Praise for your infant martyrs,
Whom your mysterious love
Called early from life's conflicts
To share your peace above.
O Rachel, cease your weeping;
They're free from pain and cares.
Lord, grant us crowns as brilliant
And lives as pure as theirs.

Text: 76 76 D; based on *From All Thy Saints in Warfare* by Horatio Bolton Nelson, 1823–1913;
fr. *The Hymnal 1982*; Jerry D. Godwin, b. 1944, © 1985, The Church Pension Fund. All rights reserved.
Used with permission of Church Publishing, Inc., New York, NY.
Music: ST. THEODULPH; Melchior Teschner, 1584–1635.

## 749    BLESSED FEASTS OF BLESSED MARTYRS

1. Bless - ed feasts of bless - ed mar - tyrs, Ho - ly wom - en,
2. Faith pre - vail - ing, hope un - fail - ing, Lov - ing Christ with
3. There - fore, all that reign in glo - ry, Faith - ful heirs with

1. ho - ly men, With our love and ad - mi - ra - tion, Greet we
2. sin - gle heart, Thus they, glo - rious and vic - to - rious, Brave - ly
3. Christ on high, Join to ours your sup - pli - ca - tion When be -

1. your re - turn a - gain. Wor - thy deeds they wrought, and won - ders,
2. bore the mar - tyr's part, By con - tempt of ev - 'ry an - guish,
3. fore Christ we draw nigh, Pray - ing that, this life com - plet - ed,

1. Wor - thy of the name they bore; We, with joy - ful
2. By un - yield - ing bat - tle done; Vic - tors at the
3. All its fleet - ing mo - ments past, By Christ's grace we

1. praise and sing - ing, Hon - or them for ev - er - more.
2. last, they tri - umph, With the host of an - gels one.
3. may be wor - thy Of e - ter - nal bliss at last.

Text: 87 87 D; *O beata beatorum*, 11th cent.; tr. by John M. Neale, 1818–1866, alt.
Music: IN BABILONE; *Oude en Nieuwe Boerenlities en Contradanseu*, ca. 1710.

## 750    SING WE NOW THE GLORIOUS MARTYRS

1. Sing we now the glorious martyrs,
Faithful, fallen, raised on high.
Strong they stood, in ranks of courage,
Loath to live if truth must die.
Grant to us, O God, their wisdom
That could dare to choose the cross,
Christ their one and only treasure,
All else, even life, no loss.

2. Keep alight upon our hilltops
Lamps like these, set high apart,
Flames of faith no night can vanquish,
Beacons for the faint of heart.
Let them burn with such an ardor
That the very dark must quail.
Before love so all-consuming
Death itself cannot prevail.

Text: 87 87 D; Genevieve Glen, OSB, b. 1945, © 1999, 2001, The Benedictine Nuns of the Abbey of St. Walburga.
Published by OCP. All rights reserved.
Music: IN BABILONE; *Oude en Nieuwe Hollanste Boerenlities en Contradanseu*, ca. 1710.

# SAINTS OF GOD

**Refrain**

Saints of God a - bid - ing in the arms of mer - cy, pray for us.

**Verses**

1. I saw the souls __ of the saints be-neath the al - tar,
2. I saw a mul - ti - tude from ev - 'ry land and peo - ple
3. Since e - ven now this cloud of wit - ness - es sur-rounds us,

1. slain for bear - ing wit - ness to God's Word,
2. wor - ship - ing be - fore the throne of grace,
3. let us cast a - side the weight of sin,

1. and each one was __ robed in white.
2. where all tears are __ washed a - way.
3. so with them we may run the race.

*to Refrain*

Text: Based on Revelation 6:9–11; 7:9, 17; Hebrews 12:1; Bob Hurd, b. 1950.
Music: Bob Hurd.

# 752

## MINE EYES HAVE SEEN THE GLORY

Verses

1. Mine eyes have seen the glo - ry of the com - ing
2. I have seen him in the watch - fires of a hun - dred
3. He has sound - ed forth the trum - pet that shall nev - er
4. In the beau - ty of the lil - ies Christ was born a -

1. of the Lord; He is tram - pling out the vin - tage where the
2. cir - cling camps; They have build - ed him an al - tar in the
3. call re - treat; He is sift - ing out the hearts of all be -
4. cross the sea, With a glo - ry in his bos - om that trans -

1. grapes of wrath are stored; He hath loosed the fate - ful light - ning
2. eve - ning dews and damps; I can read his righ - teous sen - tence
3. fore his judg - ment seat; O be swift, my soul, to an - swer
4. fig - ures you and me; As he died to make us ho - ly,

1. of his ter - ri - ble swift sword: His truth is march - ing on.
2. by the dim and flar - ing lamps; His day is march - ing on.
3. him; be ju - bi - lant, my feet! Our God is march - ing on.
4. let us die that all be free! While God is march - ing on.

Refrain

Glo - ry! Glo - ry! Hal - le - lu - jah! Glo - ry!

Glo - ry! Hal - le - lu - jah! Glo - ry! Glo - ry! Hal - le -

lu - jah! His truth is march - ing on.

Text: 15 15 15 6 with refrain; Julia W. Howe, 1819–1910, alt.
Music: BATTLE HYMN OF THE REPUBLIC; trad. American Melody; attr. to William Steffe, ca. 1830–1911.

# IN THE DAY OF THE LORD

**Refrain**

In the day of the Lord, the sun will shine like the dawn of e - ter - nal day. All cre - a - tion will rise to dance and sing the glo - ry of the Lord!

**Verses**

1. And on that day will jus - tice tri - umph, on that
2. Then shall the na - tions throng to - geth - er to the
3. And they shall beat their swords to plow - shares; there will
4. For Is - ra - el shall be de - liv - ered, and the
5. And on that day of Christ in glo - ry, God will
6. O give us eyes to see your glo - ry, give us

1. day will all be free: free from want, free from
2. moun - tain of the Lord: they shall walk in the
3. be an end to war: one in peace, one in
4. des - ert lands will bloom. Say to all, "Do not
5. wipe a - way our tears, and the dead shall rise
6. hearts to un - der - stand. Let our ears hear your

*to Refrain*

1. fear, _____ free to live!
2. light _____ of the Lord!
3. love, _____ one in God!
4. fear. Here is your God!"
5. up _____ from their graves!
6. voice _____ 'til you come!

Text: Based on Isaiah 2, 25, 41; M.D. Ridge.
Music: M.D. Ridge.

## 754      WORTHY IS THE LAMB

**Refrain**

Wor-thy is the Lamb that was slain to re - ceive

hon-or and glo - ry. Wor-thy are the ones who be - lieve

to re - ceive the good-ness of God.

**Verses**

1. Wor - thy are you, O Pas - chal Lamb.
2. Wor - thy are you, O Bread of Life. Sal -
3. Wor - thy are you, O Ris - en Christ.

1. Wis - dom and strength be - long now to you. You
2. va - tion and joy be - long now to us. By
3. Won - ders and signs, re - veal - ing your might. Your

1. laid down your life and died up - on the cross: we've be -
2. con - quer - ing death and ris - ing to new life, we've be -
3. pow - er and glo - ry shine up - on our lives: we've be -

*2 to Refrain*

1. come a peo - ple of hope.
2. come a peo - ple of praise.
3. come your light for the world.

Text: Based on Revelation 5:9–14; Ricky Manalo, CSP, b. 1965.
Music: Ricky Manalo, CSP.
Text and music © 1997, Ricky Manalo, CSP. Published by OCP. All rights reserved.

## 755      SOON AND VERY SOON

1. Soon and ver - y soon, We are going to see the King;
2. No more cry - ing there, We are going to see the King;
3. No more dy - ing there, We are going to see the King;

1. Soon and ver - y soon, We are going to see the King;
2. No more cry-ing there, We are going to see the King;
3. No more dy-ing there, We are going to see the King;

1. Soon and ver - y soon, We are going to see the King;
2. No more cry-ing there, We are going to see the King; } Hal-le-
3. No more dy-ing there, We are going to see the King;

1-3. lu - jah! Hal-le - lu - jah! We're going to see the King.

Text: 57 57 57 86; Andraé Crouch, b. 1945.
Music: SOON AND VERY SOON; Andraé Crouch; adapt. by William F. Smith, b. 1941.
Text and music © 1976, Bud John Songs, Inc./Crouch Music. All rights reserved. Administered by EMI CMG Publishing.
    Used with permission.

## SHALL WE GATHER AT THE RIVER　　756

Verses

1. Shall we gath - er at the riv - er, Where bright an - gel feet have
2. On the mar - gin of the riv - er, Wash - ing up its sil - ver
3. Ere we reach the shin-ing riv - er, Lay we ev - 'ry bur - den
4. Soon we'll reach the shin-ing riv - er, Soon our pil-grim-age will

1. trod, With its crys - tal tide for - ev - er, Flow-ing
2. spray, We will walk and wor - ship ev - er, All the
3. down; Grace our spir - its will de - liv - er, And pro -
4. cease; Soon our hap - py hearts will quiv - er With the

Refrain

1. by the throne of God? Yes, we'll gath-er at the riv - er, The
2. hap - py gold - en day.
3. vide a robe and crown.
4. mel - o - dy of peace.

beau - ti - ful, the beau - ti - ful riv - er, Gath - er with the

saints at the riv - er That flows by the throne of God.

Text: 87 87 with refrain; Revelation 22:1–5; Robert Lowry, 1826–1899.
Music: HANSON PLACE; Robert Lowry.

## 757      STEAL AWAY TO JESUS

Steal a-way, steal a-way, steal a-way to Je-sus!

Steal a-way, steal a-way home, I ain't got long to stay here.

*Verses*

1. My Lord, he calls me, He calls me by the thun-der; The
2. Green trees are bend-ing, Poor sin-ners stand a-trem-bling; The
3. My Lord, he calls me, He calls me by the light-ning; The

1-3. trum-pet sounds with-in my soul; I ain't got long to stay here.

Text: Traditional.
Music: Spiritual.

## 758      JERUSALEM, MY HAPPY HOME

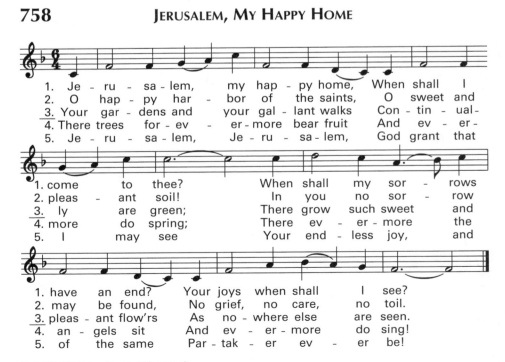

1. Je - ru - sa - lem, my hap - py home, When shall I
2. O hap - py har - bor of the saints, O sweet and
3. Your gar - dens and your gal - lant walks Con - tin - ual -
4. There trees for - ev - er - more bear fruit And ev - er -
5. Je - ru - sa - lem, Je - ru - sa - lem, God grant that

1. come to thee? When shall my sor - rows
2. pleas - ant soil! In you no sor - row
3. ly are green; There grow such sweet and
4. more do spring; There ev - er - more the
5. I may see Your end - less joy, and

1. have an end? Your joys when shall I see?
2. may be found, No grief, no care, no toil.
3. pleas - ant flow'rs As no - where else are seen.
4. an - gels sit And ev - er - more do sing!
5. of the same Par - tak - er ev - er be!

Text: CM; F. B. P., London, ca. 16th cent., alt.
Music: LAND OF REST; trad. American Melody.

## SING WITH ALL THE SAINTS IN GLORY

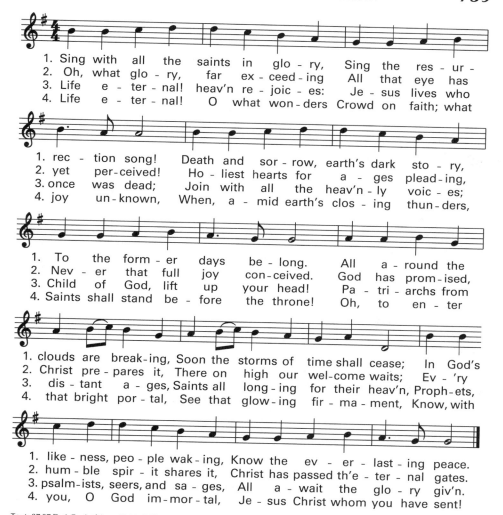

1. Sing with all the saints in glo - ry, Sing the res - ur -
2. Oh, what glo - ry, far ex - ceed - ing All that eye has
3. Life e - ter - nal! heav'n re - joic - es: Je - sus lives who
4. Life e - ter - nal! O what won - ders Crowd on faith; what

1. rec - tion song! Death and sor - row, earth's dark sto - ry,
2. yet per - ceived! Ho - liest hearts for a - ges plead - ing,
3. once was dead; Join with all the heav'n - ly voic - es;
4. joy un - known, When, a - mid earth's clos - ing thun - ders,

1. To the form - er days be - long. All a - round the
2. Nev - er that full joy con - ceived. God has prom - ised,
3. Child of God, lift up your head! Pa - tri - archs from
4. Saints shall stand be - fore the throne! Oh, to en - ter

1. clouds are break - ing, Soon the storms of time shall cease; In God's
2. Christ pre - pares it, There on high our wel - come waits; Ev - 'ry
3. dis - tant a - ges, Saints all long - ing for their heav'n, Proph - ets,
4. that bright por - tal, See that glow - ing fir - ma - ment, Know, with

1. like - ness, peo - ple wak - ing, Know the ev - er - last - ing peace.
2. hum - ble spir - it shares it, Christ has passed th'e - ter - nal gates.
3. psalm - ists, seers, and sa - ges, All a - wait the glo - ry giv'n.
4. you, O God im - mor - tal, Je - sus Christ whom you have sent!

Text: 87 87 D; 1 Corinthians 15:20; William J. Irons, 1812–1893; fr. *Psalms and Hymns*, 1873, alt.
Music: HYMN TO JOY; Ludwig van Beethoven, 1770–1827; adapt. by Edward Hodges, 1796–1867.

## 760     AS WE GATHER AT YOUR TABLE

1. As we gath-er at your Ta-ble, As we lis-ten to your
2. Turn our wor-ship in-to wit-ness In the sac-ra-ment of
3. Gra-cious Spir-it, help us sum-mon Oth-er guests to share that

1. Word, Help us know, O God, your pres-ence: Let our
2. life; Send us forth to love and serve you, Bring-ing
3. feast Where tri-um-phant Love will wel-come Those who

1. hearts and minds be stirred. Nour-ish us with sa-cred
2. peace where there is strife. Give us, Christ, your great com-
3. had been last and least. There no more will en-vy

1. sto-ry Till we claim it as our own; Teach us
2. pas-sion To for-give as you for-gave; May we
3. blind us Nor will pride our peace de-stroy,     As we

1. through this ho-ly ban-quet How to make Love's vic-t'ry known.
2. still be-hold your im-age In the world you died to save.
3. join with saints and an-gels To re-peat the sound-ing joy.

Text: 87 87 D; Carl P. Daw, Jr., b. 1944, © 1989, Hope Publishing Co. All rights reserved. Used with permission.
Music: NETTLETON; J. Wyeth's *Repository of Sacred Music, Part II*, 1813.

## 761     TABLE OF PLENTY

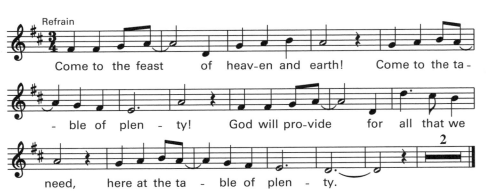

Refrain

Come to the feast of heav-en and earth! Come to the ta-
-ble of plen-ty! God will pro-vide for all that we
need, here at the ta-ble of plen-ty.

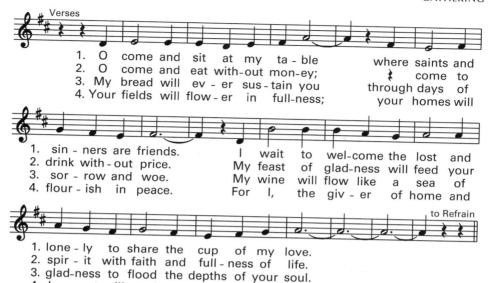

1. O come and sit at my ta - ble where saints and
2. O come and eat with-out mon-ey; come to
3. My bread will ev - er sus-tain you through days of
4. Your fields will flow - er in full-ness; your homes will

1. sin - ners are friends. I wait to wel-come the lost and
2. drink with - out price. My feast of glad-ness will feed your
3. sor - row and woe. My wine will flow like a sea of
4. flour - ish in peace. For I, the giv - er of home and

to Refrain

1. lone - ly to share the cup of my love.
2. spir - it with faith and full - ness of life.
3. glad-ness to flood the depths of your soul.
4. har - vest, will send my rain on the soil.

## WE GATHER TOGETHER

**762**

1. We gath - er to - geth - er to ask the Lord's bless - ing; He
2. Be - side us to guide us, our God with us join - ing, Whose
3. We all do ex - tol you, our lead - er tri - um-phant, And

1. chas - tens and has - tens his will to make known; The
2. king - dom calls all to the love which en - dures. So
3. pray that you still our de - fend - er will be. Let

1. wick - ed op - press-ing now cease from dis - tress-ing: Sing
2. from the be - gin - ning the fight we were win - ning: You,
3. your con - gre - ga - tion es - cape trib - u - la - tion: Your

1. prais - es to his name; he for - gets not his own.
2. Lord, were at our side; all ___ glo - ry be yours!
3. name be ev - er praised! O ___ Lord, make us free!

Text: 12 11 12 11; *Wilt heden nu treden*; tr. by Theodore Baker, 1851–1934, alt.
Music: KREMSER; Valerius' *Nederlandtsche Gedenckclanck*, Haarlem, 1626.

**763**     Ven al Banquete/Come to the Feast

Refrain/Estribillo

(Bilingual) Ven, ven al ban-que-te. Ven a la fies-ta de Dios.
(Español) Ven, ven al ban-que-te. Ven a la fies-ta de Dios.
(English) Come, come to the ban-quet. Come,___ come to the feast.

Here the hun-gry find plen-ty, here the thirst-y shall drink. ___
Los que tie-nen ham-bre y sed se-rán___ sa-cia-dos.
Here the hun-gry find plen-ty, here the thirst-y shall drink, ___

Ven a la ce-na de Cris-to, come ___ to ___ the feast.
Ven a la ce-na de Cris-to, ven a la fies-ta de Dios.
here at the sup-per of Je-sus, come ___ to ___ the feast.

Verses/Estrofas

1. Like the child whose fish-es and loaves fed the mul-ti-
   ___¿Quién le pue-de dar de co-mer a la mul-ti-
2. 'Til the seed is giv-en to earth, it is just one
   ___ Hay que dar-se a___ mo-rir pa-ra co-se-
3. In the strang-er by ___ our side, in the least and
   Los de-sam-pa-ra-dos ven-drán a par-tir el

1. tude, in the Lord the lit-tle we have,
   tud? Con Je-sús, al com-par-tir lo
2. grain; but once sown its death brings new birth, the
   char, las se-mi-llas de li-ber-tad y
3. last, in the thirst for jus-tice we share,
   pan y ve-rán su dig-ni-dad de

to Refrain/al Estribillo

1. bro-ken and shared, be-comes a-bun-dant food.
   po-co que hay, re-ci-bi-mos ple-ni-tud.
2. har-vest is rich; what's lost is raised a-gain.
   re-su-rrec-ción, la pro-me-sa de vi-vir.
3. Christ ___ is here in the break-ing of the bread.
   nue-vo en Je-sús, Sal-va-dor y Buen Pas-tor.

*Last time, repeat final phrase
Se repite la última vez

Text: Bob Hurd, b. 1950, Pia Moriarty, b. 1948, and Jaime Cortez, b. 1963.
Music: Bob Hurd.

## GOD IS HERE! AS WE HIS PEOPLE

**764**

1. God is here! As we his peo - ple Meet to of - fer
2. Here are sym - bols to re - mind us Of our life - long
3. Here our chil - dren find a wel - come In the Shep - herd's
4. Lord of all, of church and king - dom, In an age of

1. praise and prayer, May we find in full - er mea - sure
2. need of grace; Here are ta - ble, font and pul - pit,
3. flock and fold; Here, as bread and wine are tak - en,
4. change and doubt, Keep us faith - ful to the gos - pel,

1. What it is in Christ we share: Here, as in the world a -
2. Here the cross has cen - tral place: Here in hon - es - ty of
3. Christ sus - tains us as of old: Here the ser - vants of the
4. Help us work your pur - pose out: Here, in this day's ded - i -

1. round us, All our var - ied skills and arts Wait the com - ing
2. preach - ing, Here in si - lence as in speech, Here in new - ness
3. Ser - vant Seek in wor - ship to ex - plore What it means in
4. ca - tion, All we have to give, re - ceive; We who can - not

1. of his Spir - it In - to o - pen minds and hearts.
2. and re - new - al God the Spir - it comes to each.
3. dai - ly liv - ing To be - lieve and to a - dore.
4. live with - out you, We a - dore you! We be - lieve!

Text: 87 87 D; Fred Pratt Green, 1903–2000, © 1979, Hope Publishing Co. All rights reserved. Used with permission.
Music: ABBOT'S LEIGH; Cyril Vincent Taylor, 1907–1991, © 1942, renewed 1970, Hope Publishing Co.
    All rights reserved. Used with permission.

**765**      **GATHER US TOGETHER**

Refrain

Lord, Je-sus Christ, gath-er us to-geth-er. Make us one bread, one bod-y in your love.

Verses

1. Gath-er your peo - ple, who long
2. We do pro - claim you the Sav-
3. For-give our fail - ings, cre - ate
4. In - to your hands, Lord, we place
5. With-in your tem - ple your prais-

to Refrain

1. to be one, one with you, O Lord, in truth and love.
2. ior of all, Lord of all the earth and sea and sky.
3. us a - new. Speak your words of peace in - to our hearts.
4. all our cares, trust - ing in your love which nev - er fails.
5. es we sing. Glo - rious is your name o'er all the earth.

**766**      **GATHER THE PEOPLE**

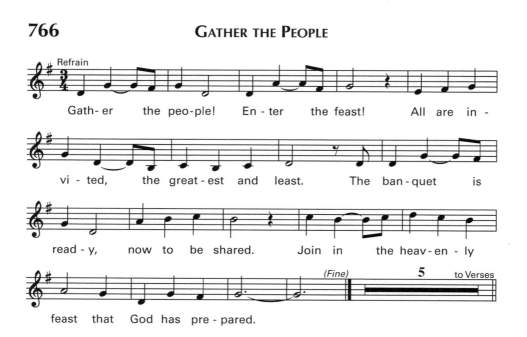

Refrain

Gath-er the peo-ple! En-ter the feast! All are in - vi - ted, the great-est and least. The ban-quet is read - y, now to be shared. Join in the heav-en - ly

(Fine)    **5**    to Verses

feast that God has pre - pared.

Verses

1. A - round this ta - ble we dine as kin, be -
2. A - round this ta - ble we tell great tales, the
3. A - round this ta - ble God's boun - ty falls on
4. A - round this ta - ble God's mer - cy flows to
5. A - round this ta - ble new hope is born, the
6. A - round this ta - ble God's heal - ing flows to
7. A - round this ta - ble God's peace will reign in
8. A - round this ta - ble our hearts re - joice in
9. A - round this ta - ble God's jus - tice reigns in
10. A - round this ta - ble God's low - ly ones are

1. lov - ed fam - 'ly of God. We
2. won - drous sto - ries of grace. We
3. all who hun - ger and thirst. We
4. hearts im - pris - oned by shame. We
5. flame of faith in our hearts. We
6. all the wound - ed and worn. We
7. hearts im - pris - oned by fear. We
8. love that's strong - er than death. We'll
9. hearts that la - bor for peace. We
10. clothed in splen - dor and grace. We

1. share the Bod - y of Christ, the Lord. Here we be -
2. hold the mem - 'ry of Christ, the Lord. So we be -
3. drink the full - ness of Christ, the Lord. So we be -
4. know com - pas - sion in Christ, the Lord. Let us be -
5. find our cour - age in Christ, the Lord, till we be -
6. join the suf - f'rings of Christ, the Lord, as we be -
7. live in free - dom through Christ, the Lord, as we be -
8. rise in glo - ry with Christ, the Lord. Then we be -
9. breathe the spir - it of Christ, the Lord, till we be -
10. share the ban - quet of Christ, the Lord. Here we be -

2 to Refrain

1-10. come what we eat.

## 767     LET US GO TO THE ALTAR

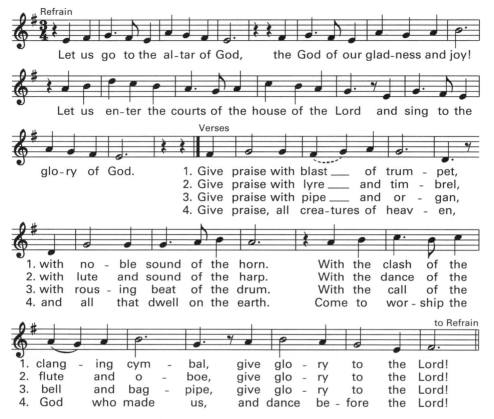

Let us go to the al-tar of God, the God of our glad-ness and joy!
Let us en-ter the courts of the house of the Lord and sing to the
glo-ry of God.

1. Give praise with blast __ of trum - pet,
2. Give praise with lyre __ and tim - brel,
3. Give praise with pipe __ and or - gan,
4. Give praise, all crea-tures of heav - en,

1. with no - ble sound of the horn. With the clash of the
2. with lute and sound of the harp. With the dance of the
3. with rous - ing beat of the drum. With the call of the
4. and all that dwell on the earth. Come to wor - ship the

*to Refrain*

1. clang - ing cym - bal, give glo - ry to the Lord!
2. flute and o - boe, give glo - ry to the Lord!
3. bell and bag - pipe, give glo - ry to the Lord!
4. God who made us, and dance be - fore the Lord!

Text: Based on Psalms 42 and 150; Dan Schutte, b. 1947.
Music: Dan Schutte.

## 768     GATHER YOUR PEOPLE

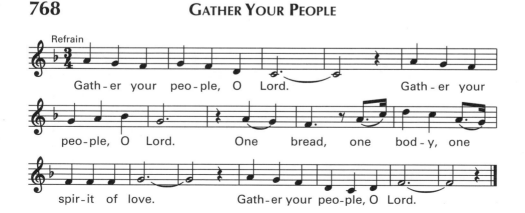

Gath-er your peo-ple, O Lord. Gath-er your
peo-ple, O Lord. One bread, one bod-y, one
spir-it of love. Gath-er your peo-ple, O Lord.

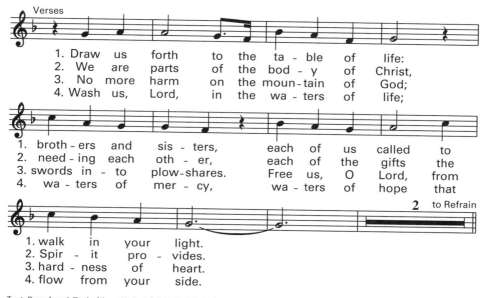

Verses

1. Draw us forth to the ta - ble of life:
2. We are parts of the bod - y of Christ,
3. No more harm on the moun-tain of God;
4. Wash us, Lord, in the wa - ters of life;

1. broth - ers and sis - ters, each of us called to
2. need - ing each oth - er, each of the gifts the
3. swords in - to plow-shares. Free us, O Lord, from
4. wa - ters of mer - cy, wa - ters of hope that

**2 to Refrain**

1. walk in your light.
2. Spir - it pro - vides.
3. hard - ness of heart.
4. flow from your side.

Text: Based on 1 Corinthians 12; Isaiah 2:3–4; 11:9; Bob Hurd, b. 1950.
Music: Bob Hurd.
Text and music © 1991, Bob Hurd. Published by OCP. All rights reserved.

## WHAT IS THIS PLACE 769

1. What is this place, where we are meet-ing? On - ly a house, the
2. Words from a - far, stars that are fall - ing. Sparks that are sown in
3. And we ac - cept bread at his ta - ble, Bro - ken and shared, a

1. earth its floor. Walls and a roof, shel - ter - ing peo - ple, Win-dows for
2. us like seed: Names for our God, dreams, signs and won-ders Sent from the
3. liv-ing sign. Here in this world, dy - ing and liv - ing, We are each

1. light, an o - pen door. Yet it be-comes a bod - y that lives When
2. past are all we need. We in this place re - mem-ber and speak A-
3. oth-er's bread and wine. This is the place where we can re-ceive What

1. we are gath-ered here, And know our God is near.
2. gain what we have heard: God's free re - deem-ing word.
3. we need to in - crease: Our jus - tice and God's peace.

Text: 98 98 9 66; Huub Oosterhuis, b. 1933; tr. by David Smith, b. 1933.
Music: KOMT NU MET ZANG; trad. Dutch Hymn; Valerius' *Nederlandtsche Gedenckclank*, Haarlem, 1626.
Text and music © 1967, Gooi en Sticht, bv., Baarn, The Netherlands. All rights reserved.
    Exclusive agent for English-language countries: OCP.

# 770

## IN THIS PLACE

**Verses**

1. We are all hun-gry peo-ple, we need shel-ter and
2. All our lives are a Mys-t'ry; we see not where they
3. Though the world may tell us to look at our-
4. In the bread that is bro-ken is the Christ that re-

1. strength. We are one in our hurt-ing, we are
2. lead. We are asked now to trust you and we
3. selves, we reach out to an-oth-er where
4. stores. As we take, now re-ceive him, we find

1. one in our pain. In our suf-f'ring and sad-ness,
2. know we must be-lieve. As our feet be-come Christ's feet,
3. suf-fer-ing dwells. As our hands be-come Christ's hands,
4. love ev-er-more. As the bread be-comes Bod-y,

1. we are saved by the grace
2. we go forth with the grace
3. we are healed by the grace
4. we are filled with the grace

of the pow-er and the

1-4. Spir-it that is here in this place. We are

**Refrain**

gath-ered at ta-ble as one in the Lord. We are
*(*to-geth-er)*

gath-ered as peo-ple who are liv-ing the Word. Our

hearts and our spir-its are nur-tured by grace. It is

Je-sus who fills us. He is here in this place.

*Alternate text.

## OUR GOD IS HERE

Verses

1. Here in this time, here in this place,
2. Here in the Word, God is re-vealed,

1. here we are stand-ing face to face. Here in our hearts,
2. here where the wound-ed can be healed. Here in our hearts,

1. here in our lives, our God is here. Here for the bro -
2. here in our lives, our God is here. Here we be-come _

1. - ken, here for the strong, here in this tem - ple we be-long.
2. _____ what we re-ceive, here in this Eu - cha-ris-tic feast.

1. Here in our hearts,_____ here in our lives, our God is here.
2. We are his bod - y, liv-ing as one; our God is here.

Refrain

And we cry: "Ho - ly! Ho - ly! Ho - ly are you!"

We cry: "Ho - ly! Ho - ly! Ho - ly and true!"

A - men, we do be - lieve our God is here.

(Repeat last time)  2

Our God is here.

Text and music: Chris Muglia, b. 1971, © 2001, Chris Muglia. Published by spiritandsong.com®, a division of OCP.
All rights reserved.

# 772  WE GATHER HERE TO WORSHIP

1. We gath - er here to wor - ship you, O God.
2. We gath - er here to feed up - on your Word.
3. We gath - er here to pray for those in need.
4. We gath - er here to cel - e - brate your feast.
5. We gath - er here to wor - ship you, O God.

1. We gath - er here to give you thanks and praise. You
2. We gath - er here to learn your way of life. With
3. We gath - er here to place them in your care: The
4. We gath - er at the ta - ble you have spread. As
5. We gath - er here to wor - ship and a - dore The

1. call us from our scat-tered lives To u - ni - fy what we di - vide.
2. bless - ed wis-dom from a - bove You fill our fra - gile hearts with love.
3. hun - gry seek-ing to be fed, The lone - ly, long-ing, dy - ing, dead,
4. once he did in his - to - ry, So now in ho - ly mys - ter - y,
5. Source of all in time and space, The Son who joins the hu - man race,

1. You crown with grace, you crown with grace our hum - ble deeds and
2. You guide our path, you guide our path through strug-gle and through
3. Your wound-ed peo - ple, wound-ed peo - ple here and ev - 'ry -
4. Christ gives him - self, Christ gives him - self in sac - red wine and
5. The Spir - it with them both for - ev - er - more, for - ev - er -

1. days. We gath - er here to wor - ship you, O God.
2. strife. We gath - er here to feed up - on your Word.
3. where. We gath - er here to pray for those in need.
4. bread. We gath - er here to cel - e - brate your feast.
5. more. We gath - er here to wor - ship you, O God.

# THE GOD OF ALL GRACE

Refrain: 1st time: Cantor, All repeat; thereafter: All

The God of all grace has blessed us this day, all of cre-a-tion joins us in praise; lift-ing our voic-es, lift-ing our hearts to the glo-ry of God for-ev-er!

1-5 (to Verses)

Final

**Verses**

1. God of pow-er and might, come in-to our pres-ence this
2. God of mer-cy and truth, who brings us from night in-to
3. God of won-drous love, com-pas-sion and glo-ry are
4a. All the gifts of the Lord shall flow from the glo-ry of
*4b. *God of wa-ter and birth, re-new-ing the face of the*

1. day. Strength-en us now with a spir-it of
2. day, nour-ish our lives with a spir-it of
3. yours. Come fill our hearts with a spir-it of
4a. God. Let us pro-claim all the won-ders we've
4b. *earth; heal-ing us now with the Spir-it of*

to Refrain

1. faith; we gath-er in your name.
2. hope and shield us from all fear.
3. love: the joy we find in you.
4a. seen: give thanks, re-joice and sing!
4b. *Christ, you cleanse us from our sins.*

*Alternate text for use during the Sprinkling Rite.

## 774 THE SUPPER OF THE LORD

**Refrain**

Pre-cious bod-y, pre-cious blood, here in bread and wine;
here the Lord pre-pares the feast di-vine.
Bread of love is bro-ken now, cup of life is poured:
come, share the sup-per of the Lord.

**Verses**

1. This is the bread of God com-ing down from heav'n,
2. "I am the liv-ing spring of e-ter-nal life;
3. "I am the bread of heav'n giv-ing life to you;
4. "All those who feed on me have their life in me,
5. All praise to you, O Christ, pres-ent in this feast,

*to Refrain*

1. giv-ing life to us, ___ to all the world.
2. you that drink from me shall not thirst a-gain."
3. you that eat this bread ___ shall nev-er die."
4. as I have my life in the liv-ing God."
5. in this bread we share in one life, one Lord.

Text: Verses 1–4 based on John 4, 6; Laurence Rosania, b. 1957.
Music: Laurence Rosania.

## 775 LOOK BEYOND

**Refrain**

Look be-yond the bread you eat; see your Sav-ior and your Lord.
Look be-yond the cup you drink; see his love poured out as blood.

Verses

1. Give us a sign_____ that we might____ be-lieve in you.
2. I am the bread_____ which from _____ the heav-ens came;
3. The bread I give you _____ will be _____ my ver - y flesh;
4. This man speaks harsh-ly; __ who can lis - ten to his word?
5. You, my dis - ci - ples,_____ will you_____ al - so leave?

to Refrain

1. Mo - ses brought us man - na from the sky.
2. those who eat this bread will nev - er die.
3. my blood_____ will tru - ly be your drink.
4. We_____ shall no long - er fol - low him.
5. Lord,_____ to whom__ can we go?

Text and music: Darryl Ducote, b. 1945, © 1969, 1979, Damean Music. All rights reserved. Used with permission.

## UBI CARITAS

# 776

Refrain: All

*U - bi ca - ri - tas est ve - ra, est ve - ra: De - us i - bi

est, De - us i - bi est.

Verses: Cantor/Choir

1. The love of Christ joins us to -
2. In true com - mu - nion let us
3. May we who gath - er at this
4. For those in need make us your
5. May we one day be - hold your

1. geth - er. Let us re - joice in him, and in our love and
2. gath - er. May all di - vi - sions cease and in their place be
3. ta - ble to share the bread of life be - come a sac - ra -
4. mer - cy, for those op - pressed, your might. Make us, your Church, a
5. glo - ry and see you face to face, re - joic - ing with the

to Refrain

1. care for all now love God in re - turn.
2. Christ the Lord, our ris - en Prince of Peace.
3. ment of love, your heal - ing touch, O Christ.
4. ho - ly sign of jus - tice and new life.
5. saints of God to sing e - ter - nal praise.

*Where there is true charity, God is present.

Text: Refrain and verses 1, 2 and 5 based on *Ubi Caritas*, 9th cent.; verses 3 and 4, Bob Hurd, b. 1950.
Music: Bob Hurd.
Text and music © 1996, Bob Hurd. Published by OCP. All rights reserved.

# 777         HERE AT THIS TABLE

**Refrain**

Come and be filled here at this ta-ble.

Food for all who hun-ger and drink for all who thirst.

Drink of his love, wine of sal - va - tion.

*Final time: repeat from here

You shall live for - ev-er in Je - sus Christ the Lord.

**Verses 1, 2, 4**

1. You who la - bor for jus - tice, you who la - bor for
2. You with lives full of pain, you who sor - row and
4. You, the a - ged a - mong us, ho - ly, faith - ful and

1. peace, you who stead - y the plow in the
2. weep, you, be - lov - ed of Christ, come to
4. wise, may the wis - dom you share form our

to Refrain

1. field of the Lord,
2. him, come to him!
4. lives and our world!

**Verses 3, 5**

3. Chil - dren of ev - 'ry col - or in ev - 'ry land,
5. Let each wom - an and man learn from the strang - er;

3. you are his own, he gath - ers you gent - ly.
5. we're not so dif - f'rent and so much u - nites us.

3. Don't you grow wea-ry, _____ for when you
5. For we are one, _____ blest with the

to Refrain

3. run, ɣ you run with the Lord!
5. Spir - it and the pow-er of love!

## Our Blessing Cup 778

Refrain

Our bless-ing cup is a com-mun-ion with the blood of Christ;

and the bread we break, it is a shar-ing in the bod-y of the

Repeat first time only
(or ostinato as desired) Verses
Fine

Lord.

1. How can we make a re - turn
2. Pre-cious in - deed in your sight,
3. Gra-cious and mer - ci-ful God,
4. For you have heard my __ voice,

1. for all the good-ness God has shown? We will take the
2. the life and death of those you love. We ___ are your
3. we give you thanks and bless your name: with ___ all your
4. for you have heard my plead - ing. Though __ death sur-

to Refrain (or Verse
if ostinato is sung)

1. cup of life, and ___ call up - on God's name.
2. ser - vants, for ___ you have set us free.
3. peo - ple, praise and glo - ry to your name.
4. round-ed me, you ___ heard and an-swered me.

# 779 In the Breaking of the Bread/
## Cuando Partimos el Pan del Señor

Refrain: In ___ the break - ing ___ of ___ the

Verses:
1. Bread for the jour - ney, ___ strength for our
2. Bread of the prom - ise, ___ peo - ple of

Estribillo: Cuan-do par - ti - mos ___ el pan del Se -

Estrofas:
1. Pan pa - ra el via - je, ___ pan de la
2. Pan de pro - me - sa, ___ pan de es-pe -

bread ___ we ___ have known him;

1. years, ___ man - na of ag - es, of
2. hope, ___ wine of com - pas - sion, ___

___ ñor, ___ lo co - no - ce - mos, nos

1. vi - da, pan de los si - glos de
2. ran - za, vi - no de vi - da, de

we have been fed. ___ Je - sus the ___

1. strug-gle and tears. ___ Cup of sal -
2. life for the world. ___ Gath-ered at ___

da de co - mer. ___ Je - sús des - co - no -

1. lu-cha y do - lor, ___ y es - te ___
2. su com - pa - sión. ___ En es - ta ___

strang - er, ___ Je - sus the Lord,

1. va - tion, ___ fruit of the land, ___
2. ta - ble, ___ joined as his bod - y, ___

ci - do, ___ Je - sús ___ Se - ñor, ___

1. vi - no, ___ fru - to de la tie - rra, ___
2. me - sa, ___ un so - lo cuer - po, ___

___ be our com - pan - ion; ___

1. ___ bless and re - ceive ___ now, ___
2. ___ sealed in the ___ Spir - it, ___

___ nues - tro com-pa - ñe - ro ___

1. ___ ben - dí - ce - lo ___ Pa - dre, ___
2. ___ en un es - pí - ri - tu, ___

be ___ our hope.
1. ___ ⸏ the work of our hands. (to Verses)
2. ___ ⸏ sent by the Word. (to Refrain)
___ ⸏ y fuen-te de fe. (a las Estrofas)
1. ___ ⸏ es tu-yo mi Dios. (al Estribillo)
2. ___ ⸏ con u-na mi-sión. (al Estribillo)

Text: Based on Luke 24:13–35; Acts 2:42. English, Bob Hurd, b. 1950, and Michael Downey;
Spanish, Stephen Dean, b. 1948, and Kathleen Orozco, b. 1945, © 1984, 1987, 1989, Bob Hurd and Michael Downey.
Published by OCP. All rights reserved.
Music: Bob Hurd, © 1984, 1987, 1989, Bob Hurd. Published by OCP. All rights reserved.

## BREAD FOR THE WORLD

### 780

Refrain: All

Bread for the world: a world of hun-ger. Wine for all

peo-ples: peo-ple who thirst. May we who eat

be bread for oth-ers. May we who drink pour out our love.

Verses: Cantor

1. Lord Je-sus Christ, you are the bread of life, bro-ken to
2. Lord Je-sus Christ, you are the wine of peace, poured in-to
3. Lord Je-sus Christ, you call us to your feast, at which the

1. reach and heal the wounds of hu-man pain. Where we di-
2. hearts once bro-ken and where dry-ness sleeps. Where we are
3. rich and pow'r-ful have be-come the least. Where we sur-

1. vide your peo-ple you are wait-ing there
2. tired and wea-ry, you are wait-ing there
3. vive on oth-ers in our hu-man greed,

to Refrain

1. on bend-ed knee to wash our feet with end-less care.
2. to be the way which beck-ons us be-yond de-spair.
3. you walk a-mong us beg-ging for your ev-'ry need.

Text and music: Bernadette Farrell, b. 1957, © 1990, Bernadette Farrell. Published by OCP. All rights reserved.

# 781

## SEED, SCATTERED AND SOWN

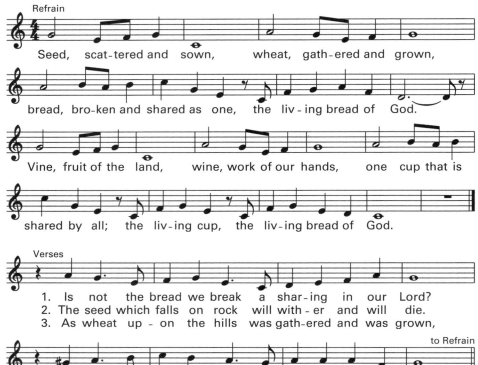

Refrain

Seed, scat-tered and sown, wheat, gath-ered and grown,
bread, bro-ken and shared as one, the liv-ing bread of God.
Vine, fruit of the land, wine, work of our hands, one cup that is
shared by all; the liv-ing cup, the liv-ing bread of God.

Verses

1. Is not the bread we break a shar-ing in our Lord?
2. The seed which falls on rock will with-er and will die.
3. As wheat up-on the hills was gath-ered and was grown,

to Refrain

1. Is not the cup we bless the blood of Christ out-poured?
2. The seed with-in good ground will flow-er and have life.
3. so may the church of God be gath-ered in-to one.

Text: 66 66 with refrain; based on Didache 9; 1 Corinthians 10:16–17; Mark 4:3–6; Dan Feiten.
Music: SEED, SCATTERED AND SOWN; Dan Feiten.
Text and music © 1987, International Liturgy Publications, PO Box 50476, Nashville, TN 37205, www.ilpmusic.org
888-898-SONG. All rights reserved. Used with permission.

# 782

## TASTE AND SEE

Taste and see the good - ness of the Lord, the
good - ness of the Lord. Taste and see the good-
- ness of the Lord, the good - ness of the Lord.

Verses

1. I will bless the Lord at all times.
   Praise will be on my lips.
   My soul will glory in the Lord.
   The poor will hear and be glad.

2. I sought the Lord who answered me,
   delivered me from my fear.
   Look to God that you might shine
   with the radiance of God's joy.

3. The Lord has eyes for justice,
   ears to hear your cry.
   God knows your broken heart.
   The Lord redeems a loyal servant.
   Take refuge in your God.

## AMÉN. EL CUERPO DE CRISTO 783

Refrain: All
A - mén. El Cuer - po de Cris - to. A - mén. La San - gre del Se - ñor. Eat - ing your bod - y, drink - ing your blood, we be - come what we re - ceive. A - mén. A - mén.

Verses: Cantor
1. A - mén. We re - mem - ber your dy - ing and your ris - ing. A - mén.
2. A - mén. Now we of - fer the sac - ri - fice you gave us. A - mén.
3. A - mén. Lord, you make us one bod - y and one spir - it. A - mén.
4. A - mén. We find you when we serve the poor and low - ly. A - mén.
5. A - mén. We look for - ward to your re - turn in glo - ry. A - mén.

1. Y con - ti - go, Se - ñor, re - su - ci - ta - mos. A - mén.
2. Te o - fre - ce - mos, Se - ñor, to - do lo que so - mos. A - mén.
3. En tu cuer - po, Se - ñor, un __ pue - blo san - to. A - mén.
4. A ti mis - mo ser - vi - mos __ en los po - bres. A - mén.
5. Es - pe - ra - mos el día de __ tu ve - ni - da. A - mén.

to Refrain

Note: Translation of Spanish refrain: Amen. The Body of Christ. Amen. The Blood of Christ.

# 784

## PAN DE VIDA

Refrain/Estribillo

(Bilingual) *Pan de Vi - da, cuer-po del Se - ñor,
(Spanish) Pan de Vi - da, cuer-po del Se - ñor,

cup of bless - ing, blood of Christ the Lord.
san - ta co - pa, Cris - to Re - den - tor.

At this ta - ble the last shall be first.
Su jus - ti - cia nos con - ver - ti - rá.

**Po - der es ser - vir, por-que Dios es a - mor.
Po - der es ser - vir, por-que Dios es a - mor.

1-3 to Verses/a las Estrofas | 4 | Final 3 | Verses/Estrofas

Po -
Po -

1. We are the
2. You call me
3. There is no
1. So-mos el
2. Us - te - des me
3. No hay es -

1. dwell-ing of God, fra-gile and wound-ed and weak.
2. Teach-er and Lord; I, who have washed your feet.
3. Jew or Greek; there is no slave or free;
1. tem - plo de Dios, frá - gi - les se - res hu - ma -
2. lla - man "Se - ñor". Me in-cli-no a la - var - les los pies.
3. cla - vos ni li - bres, no hay mu - je - res ni hom -

1. We are the bod - y of Christ, called to
2. So you must do as I do, so the
3. there is no wom-an or man; on - ly
1. nos. So-mos el cuer-po de Cris - to, lla -
2. Ha-gan lo mis-mo, hu - mil - des, sir -
3. bres, só - lo a - que-llos que he - re - dan el

to Refrain/al Estribillo

1. be _____ the com - pas - sion of God. _____
2. great - est must be - come _____ the least. _____
3. heirs _____ of the prom-ise of God. _____
1. *ma* - *dos a ser com-pa - si - vos.*
2. *vién* - *do-se u - nos a o - tros.*
3. *rei* - *no que Dios pro - me - tió.* _____

*Bread of life, body of the Lord,
**Power is for service, because God is love.

Text: Based on John 13:1–15; Galatians 3:28–29; Bob Hurd, b. 1950, and Pia Moriarty, b. 1948;
   Spanish adapt. by Jaime Cortez, b. 1963, Magali Jerez, Elena García and Gustavo Castillo.
Music: Bob Hurd.
Text and music © 1988, 1995, 1999, Bob Hurd and Pia Moriarty. Published by OCP. All rights reserved.

## BEHOLD THE LAMB 785

Verses

1. Those who were in the dark are thank - ful for the
2. Peace - ful now, those whose hearts are blessed with un - der -
3. Gen - tle one, Child of God, join with us at this
4. Lord of all, give us light. De - liv - er us from

1. sun - light; we who live, we who die are grate-ful for his
2. stand-ing of the wheat, of the wine u - nit - ed with his
3. ta - ble. Bless our lives; nour-ish all who hun - ger for this
4. e - vil. Make us one; be our shield. Make still the winds that

Refrain

1. gift, thank-ful for his love. Be-hold, be-hold the Lamb of
2. word and the love we share.
3. feast; shel - ter them with peace.
4. blow; cra - dle us with love.

God. All who eat, all who drink shall live; and all,

all who dwell in God shall come to know his glo-ry.

Text: Refrain based on John 1:29; Martin Willett, b. 1960.
Music: Martin Willett.
Text and music © 1984, OCP. All rights reserved.

## 786     I RECEIVED THE LIVING GOD

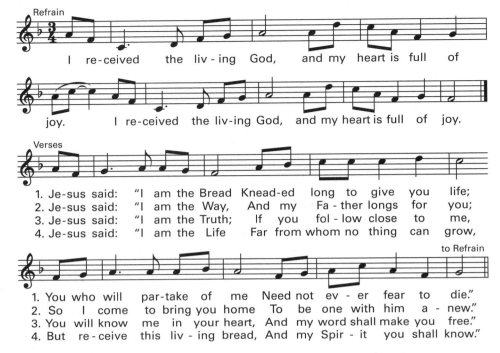

Refrain

I re-ceived the liv-ing God, and my heart is full of joy. I re-ceived the liv-ing God, and my heart is full of joy.

Verses

1. Je-sus said: "I am the Bread Knead-ed long to give you life;
2. Je-sus said: "I am the Way, And my Fa-ther longs for you;
3. Je-sus said: "I am the Truth; If you fol-low close to me,
4. Je-sus said: "I am the Life Far from whom no thing can grow,

to Refrain

1. You who will par-take of me Need not ev-er fear to die."
2. So I come to bring you home To be one with him a-new."
3. You will know me in your heart, And my word shall make you free."
4. But re-ceive this liv-ing bread, And my Spir-it you shall know."

Text: 77 77 with refrain; anon.
Music: LIVING GOD; anon.

## 787     TO BE YOUR BREAD

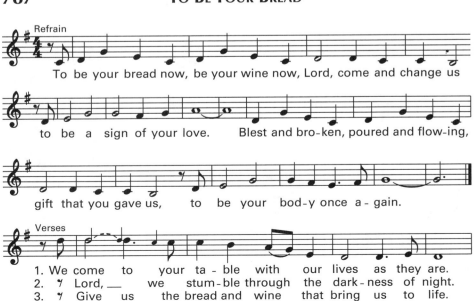

Refrain

To be your bread now, be your wine now, Lord, come and change us to be a sign of your love. Blest and bro-ken, poured and flow-ing, gift that you gave us, to be your bod-y once a-gain.

Verses

1. We come to your ta-ble with our lives as they are.
2. ℣ Lord, __ we stum-ble through the dark-ness of night.
3. ℣ Give us the bread and wine that bring us to life.

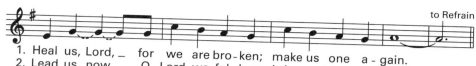

1. Heal us, Lord, __ for we are bro-ken; make us one a-gain.
2. Lead us, now, __ O Lord, we fol-low; bring us home to you.
3. Feed us, __ and we'll nev-er hun-ger, nev-er thirst a-gain.

## BREAD OF LIFE 788

Refrain

Bread of life, hope of the world, Je-sus Christ, our broth-er:

feed us now, give us life, lead us to one an-oth-er.

Verses

1. As we pro-claim your death, as we re-call your life, we re-
2. The bread we break and share was scat-tered once as grain: just as
3. We eat this liv-ing bread, we drink this sav-ing cup: sign of
4. Hold us in u-ni-ty, in love for all to see; that the
5. You are the bread of peace, you are the wine of joy, bro-ken

to Refrain

1. mem-ber your prom - ise to re-turn a - gain.
2. now it is gath - ered, make your peo - ple one.
3. hope in our bro-ken world, source of last - ing love.
4. world may be-lieve in you, God of all who live.
5. now for your peo - ple, poured in end - less love.

Alternate Verses: for Advent/Christmas

Adv. 1. Be with your peo-ple, Lord, send us your sav-ing Word: Je - sus
Adv. 2. Bring to our world of fear the truth we long to hear: Je - sus
Chr. 1. A child is born for us, a son is giv'n to us, In our
Chr. 2. With our own eyes we see, with our own ears we hear The sal-
Chr. 3. You are the hope of all, our prom-ise and our call, Ra-diant

to Refrain

1. Christ, light of glad - ness, come a-mong us now.
2. Christ, hope of a - ges, come to save us now.
1. midst, Christ, our Lord and God comes as one who serves.
2. va - tion of all the world, God's in-car-nate Word.
3. light in our dark - ness, truth to set us free.

# 789     LAMB OF GOD/TASTE AND SEE

Lamb of God, you take a-way the sins of the world, have mer - cy, have

mer-cy on us.     world, grant us, grant us peace.

**Refrain**

Taste and see the good-ness of the Lord.     Oh,

taste and see the good-ness of the Lord.

**Verse 1**

1. I will bless the LORD at all times; his praise ev - er in my

1. mouth, let my soul glo - ry in the LORD.

**Verse 2**

2. Let the low-ly hear and be glad, let us glo - ri - fy his

2. name. To - geth - er let us praise God's name.

**Verse 3**

3. Glo - ri - fy the LORD with me, to - geth-er let us praise his

3. name; from my fears God set me free.

**Verse 4**

4. Look to the LORD and shine in the light, let your fac-es not be a-shamed.

to Refrain
7

4. The LORD hears the cry of the poor. Bless-ed be the LORD.

Text: Refrain text of "Taste and See" © 1969, 1981, 1997, ICEL. All rights reserved. Used with permission.
Verse 1 and first half of verse 2 of "Taste and See" © 1970, 1997, 1998, CCD. All rights reserved.
Used with permission. Remaining text of "Taste and See", Tom Kendzia, b. 1954, © 2006, Tom Kendzia.
Published by OCP. All rights reserved.
Music: Tom Kendzia, © 2006, Tom Kendzia. Published by OCP. All rights reserved.

## HOLY GIFTS

# 790

Refrain

Ho-ly gifts for ho-ly peo-ple; come, you hun-gry, and be-lieve;

come and take Christ's bod-y of-fered, come and be what you re-ceive.

Verses

1. This is what we have been told: that on the
2. This is what we un-der-stand: that when we
3. This is how we are to live: that being
4. Christ, our way, our truth and life: we are not

1. night be-fore he died,___ af-ter thanks-giv-ing___
2. eat and drink this feast,___ in this bread which we are
3. joined by Christ's___ gifts,___ we should be Christ to___
4. wor-thy to draw near: but take our praise and thanks-

1. spo-ken, bread blest and___ bro-ken, Christ sealed his
2. break-ing, Christ we are par-tak-ing, Christ's death pro-
3. oth-ers, sis-ters and___ broth-ers, hold-ing them
4. giv-ing, trans-form our___ liv-ing, give us that

to Refrain

1. love with his bod-y and blood.
2. claim-ing un-til his re-turn.
3. pre-cious, as saved by his love.
4. food which is heal-ing and strength.

Text and music: Stephen Dean, b. 1948, © 1994, 2006, Stephen Dean. Published by OCP. All rights reserved.

## 791  GIFT OF FINEST WHEAT

You sat-is-fy the hun-gry heart With gift of fin-est wheat, Come
give to us, O sav-ing Lord, The bread of life to eat.

1. As when the
2. With joy - ful
3. Is not the
4. The mys-t'ry
5. You give your-

1. shep - herd calls his sheep, They know and heed his voice; So
2. lips we sing to you Our praise and grat - i- tude, That
3. cup we bless and share The blood of Christ out-poured? Do
4. of your pres-ence, Lord, No mor - tal tongue can tell: Whom
5. self to us, O Lord; Then self - less let us be, To

1. when you call your fam-'ly, Lord, We fol - low and re - joice.
2. you should count us wor-thy, Lord, To share this heav'n-ly food.
3. not one cup, one loaf, de - clare Our one-ness in the Lord?
4. all the world can-not con-tain Comes in our hearts to dwell.
5. serve each oth - er in your name In truth and char - i - ty.

Text: CM with refrain; Omer Westendorf, 1916–1997.
Music: BICENTENNIAL; Robert E. Kreutz, 1922–1996.
Text and music © 1977, Archdiocese of Philadelphia. Published by International Liturgy Publications, PO Box 50476,
   Nashville, TN 37205. www.ilpmusic.org 888-898-SONG. All rights reserved. Used with permission.

## 792  GOD'S HOLY GIFTS

God's ho - ly gifts for God's ho - ly peo - ple; come now to share the
ban-quet of Christ. Feed on his love with faith and thanks-giv - ing.
Know in your heart that he died for you.

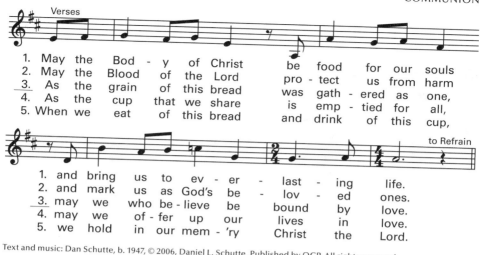

1. May the Bod - y of Christ be food for our souls
2. May the Blood of the Lord pro - tect us from harm
3. As the grain of this bread was gath - ered as one,
4. As the cup that we share is emp - tied for all,
5. When we eat of this bread and drink of this cup,

1. and bring us to ev - er - last - ing life.
2. and mark us as God's be - lov - ed ones.
3. may we who be - lieve be bound by love.
4. may we of - fer up our lives in love.
5. we hold in our mem - 'ry Christ the Lord.

## ONE BREAD, ONE BODY

793

**Refrain**

One bread, one bod - y, one Lord of all,
one cup of bless - ing which we bless. And we, though
man - y, through - out the earth, we are one bod - y in this
one Lord.

**Verses**

1. Gen - tile or Jew, ser - vant or
2. Man - y the gifts, man - y the
3. Grain for the fields, scat - tered and

1. free, wom - an or man, no more.
2. works, one in the Lord of all.
3. grown, gath - ered to one, for all.

## 794      I Am the Living Bread

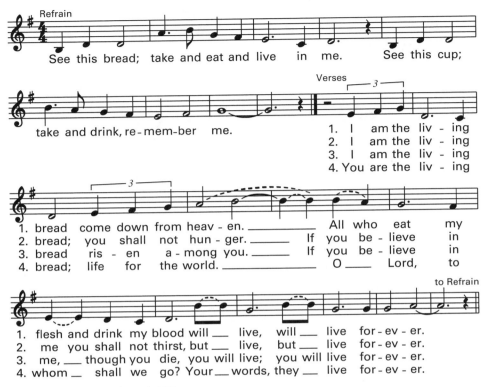

See this bread; take and eat and live in me. See this cup; take and drink, re-mem-ber me.

Verses

1. I am the liv - ing bread come down from heav - en. _____ All who eat my flesh and drink my blood will __ live, will __ live for-ev - er.
2. I am the liv - ing bread; you shall not hun - ger. _____ If you be - lieve in me you shall not thirst, but __ live, but __ live for-ev - er.
3. I am the liv - ing bread ris - en a - mong you. _____ If you be - lieve in me, __ though you die, you will live; you will live for-ev - er.
4. You are the liv - ing bread; life for the world. _____ O __ Lord, to whom __ shall we go? Your __ words, they __ live for-ev - er.

to Refrain

Text: Based on John 6; David Haas, b. 1957.
Music: David Haas.
Text and music © 1985, David Haas. Published by OCP. All rights reserved.

## 795      Come to the Lord

Verses

1. Do not let your hearts be trou - bled. Chil - dren, do not fear. I suf - fered, I am al - ways near.
2. I will nev - er leave you or - phans; you are not a - lone. in heav - en, in my fa - ther's home.
3. Eat this bread and nev - er hun - ger; I will give you life. be - fore you; you will nev - er die.

Though you suf - fer as I have made your place
Drink the cup I place

Come to the Lord; come to the ta - ble of last -
- ing life. Bring your bur - dens; there's no
price, just come to the Lord.

Text: Based on John 14; Steve Angrisano, b. 1965, and Tom Tomaszek, b. 1950.
Music: Steve Angrisano and Tom Tomaszek.
Text and music © 1999, Steve Angrisano and Thomas N. Tomaszek. Published by spiritandsong.com®, a division of OCP.
All rights reserved.

## TASTE AND SEE

# 796

Taste and see, O taste and see, taste and see the
good - ness of God.

Verses 1, 2
1. Glo - ry, glo - ry to God most high,
2. Who has fash - ioned the earth and sky,
1. glo - ry, bless - ing and praise. With one voice, O peo - ple, re -
2. who cre - a - ted the deep, who ex - alts the low - ly and
1. joice in our God, who hears _ the cry of all ___ in need. O
2. sets cap - tives free, who o - pens the door to all those who seek. O

Verse 3
3. Oh, the love of God! Be - come flesh of our flesh,
3. so that we might live in glo - ry. O

Text: Based on Psalm 34:9, 2–4; 136:5–6; Luke 1:52; Bob Hurd, b. 1950.
Music: Bob Hurd.
Text and music © 1988, Bob Hurd. Published by OCP. All rights reserved.

797

# COME TO ME AND DRINK

Refrain

Come to me and drink, come to me and drink. Oh, let
all who are thirst-ing come to me and drink.

Verses

1. I will put my spir - it with - in you ⁊ and
2. I will pour my spir - it on all flesh; ⁊ your
3. ⁊ Riv - ers of liv - ing wa - ter ⁊ will flow
4. ⁊ In - to our hearts the love of God has been

to Refrain

1. you shall live and know that I am the LORD.
2. sons and your daugh - ters shall proph - e - sy.
3. from with - in the one who be - lieves in me.
4. poured through the Spir - it that dwells with - in.

Verses (Psalm 42/43)

5. As the deer longs for run - ning streams, ⁊
6. ⁊ My soul is thirst - ing for God; ⁊ when
7. ⁊ Tears are my food by day and night, ⁊ and
8. ⁊ O God, deep calls un - to deep ⁊
9. ⁊ Hope in God, O my soul, ⁊ a -
10. ⁊ Send forth your light and your truth, ⁊ and

to Refrain

5. so my soul is long - ing for you, O God.
6. can I go to see the face of God?
7. all the while they say: "Where is your God?"
8. as your might - y wa - ters sweep o - ver me.
9. gain I shall praise my sav - ing God.
10. they shall lead me to your dwell - ing place.

Text: Refrain based on John 7:37; verses based on Ezekiel 37:14; Joel 3:1; John 7:38; Romans 5:5, 8:11; Psalm 42:2–3;
   Psalm 43:3; Bob Hurd, b. 1950.
Music: Bob Hurd.
Text and music © 2006, Bob Hurd. Published by OCP. All rights reserved.

# SPIRIT AND GRACE

Verses

1. Spir-it and grace, here in this meal;
2. Spir-it and grace, here in this meal;
3. Spir-it and grace, here in this place;
4. Spir-it of God, send-ing us forth;

1. you are the wind that breathes through the field.
2. you are the life that flows through the vine.
3. you are the light that shines in this space.
4. we spread your wis-dom through-out all the earth.

1. Gath-er the wheat and form us in Christ.
2. Gath-er this drink and form us in Christ.
3. Gath-er your peo-ple and form us in Christ.
4. Gath-er the na-tions and form us in Christ.

1. Come, be our source and breath of life.
2. Come, be our source and blood of life.
3. Come, be the heart-beat of our lives.
4. Come, be the pres-ence in our lives.

Refrain

In the bread, blessed, bro-ken and shared, Christ is our life, whose pres-ence we bear. Come, O Spir-it, make your grace re-vealed in this ho-ly meal.

Text and music: Ricky Manalo, CSP, b. 1965, © 2006, Ricky Manalo, CSP. Published by OCP. All rights reserved.

## 799       BREAD OF LIFE

**Refrain**

I my-self am the bread of life. You and I are the bread of life, tak-en and blessed, bro-ken and shared by Christ that the world might live. *(Final)* live. That the world might live. That the world might live.

**Verses**

1. This bread is spir-it, gift of the Mak-er's
2. Here is God's king-dom giv-en to us as
3. Lives bro-ken o-pen, sto-ries shared a-

1. love, and we who share it ___ know that we can be
2. food. This is our bod-y, ___ this ___ is our
3. loud, be-come a ban-quet, a shel-ter ___ for the

1. one:
2. blood: a liv-ing sign of God in Christ.
3. world:

*to Refrain*

## 800       LET US BREAK BREAD TOGETHER

**Verses**

1. Let us break bread to-geth-er on our knees; Let us break
2. Let us drink wine to-geth-er on our knees; Let us drink
3. Let us praise God to-geth-er on our knees; Let us praise

1. bread to-geth-er on our knees;
2. wine to-geth-er on our knees;
3. God to-geth-er on our knees;

When I fall on my knees,

With my face to the ris-ing sun, O Lord, have mer-cy on me.

Text: 10 10 with refrain; Spiritual.
Music: LET US BREAK BREAD; Spiritual.

## UNLESS A GRAIN OF WHEAT 801

Refrain

Un-less a grain of wheat fall to the ground and die, it remains a sin-gle grain. But if it die
it will yield a rich har - vest.

1. In his own bod-
2. Do not draw back

1. y, by his own wounds,
2. now, do not be shy.

he brought your
Turn not a-

1. sins to the cross, and suf-fer'd for you;
2. way _ from him who paid the price.

1. pour'd out his life - blood up-on the tree,
2. Come to his ta - ble, sit by his side.

to Refrain

1. pour'd out his life - blood for you and for me.
2. There he a-waits you: the Lord _ of Life.

Text: Based on John 12:24 and George Herbert's *Love Bade Me Welcome*; adapt. by Bob Hurd, b. 1950.
Music: Bob Hurd.
Text and music © 1984, Bob Hurd. Published by OCP. All rights reserved.

## 802 ONE LOVE RELEASED

**Refrain**

One bread, one bod-y, one cup, one call,
one faith, one Spir-it pres-ent in us all.
One prayer, one bless-ing, one hope, one peace,
one church, one peo-ple, one love re-leased.

**Verses**

1. Is not this bread we share, the bod-y of our Lord?
2. I am the bread of life, eat and you shall live.
3. I am the liv-ing bread, as man-na from the sky.
4. No one will come to me, un-less our God has led.

_to Refrain_

1. Is not this wine we drink, the blood of Christ out-poured?
2. To those who share this meal, my strength I'll al-ways give.
3. This bread I give to you, that you may nev-er die.
4. And I shall raise them up, ___ raise them from the dead!

Text: Bob Frenzel, b. 1953, and Kevin Keil, ASCAP, b. 1956.
Music: Based on O WALY WALY; Bob Frenzel and Kevin Keil, ASCAP.

## 803 SACRAMENTUM CARITATIS

*Refrain

Sa-cra-mén-tum ca-ri-tá-tis: pa-nis vi-vus et vi-tá-lis.
Ca-lix no-vi tes-ta-mén-ti: do-num Chri-sti Dó-mi-ni.

*Verses available in accompaniment books. Translation of Refrain:
    The sacrament of love: living and life-giving bread.
    Chalice of the new covenant: gift of Christ the Lord.

# LORD, WHO AT THY FIRST EUCHARIST

**804**

1. Lord, who at thy first Eu - cha - rist did pray That
*1. At that first Eu - cha - rist be - fore you died, O
2. For all thy Church, O Lord, we in - ter - cede; Make
3. We pray thee, too, for wan - d'rers from thy fold; O
4. So, Lord, at length when sac - ra - ments shall cease, May

1. all thy Church might be for - ev - er one, Grant us at
1. Lord, you prayed that all be one in you; At this our
2. thou our sad di - vi - sions soon to cease; Draw us the
3. bring them back, Good Shep - herd of the sheep, Back to the
4. we be one with all thy Church a - bove, One with thy

1. ev - 'ry Eu - cha - rist to say With long - ing heart and
1. Eu - cha - rist a - gain pre - side, And in our hearts your
2. near - er each, to each we plead, By draw - ing all to
3. faith which saints be - lieved of old, Back to the Church which
4. saints in one un - bro - ken peace, One with thy saints in

1. soul, "Thy will be done." O may we all one bread, one
1. law of love re - new. O may we all one bread, one
2. thee, O Prince of Peace; Thus may we all one bread, one
3. still that faith doth keep; Soon may we all one bread, one
4. one un - bound - ed love; More bless - ed still in peace and

1. bod - y be, Through this blest Sac - ra - ment of U - ni - ty.
1. bod - y be, Through this blest Sac - ra - ment of U - ni - ty.
2. bod - y be, Through this blest Sac - ra - ment of U - ni - ty.
3. bod - y be, Through this blest Sac - ra - ment of U - ni - ty.
4. love to be One with the Trin - i - ty in U - ni - ty.

*Alternate version of verse 1.

Text: 10 10 10 10 10 10; William H. Turton, 1859–1938.
Music: UNDE ET MEMORES; William H. Monk, 1823–1889, alt.

## 805     BREAD OF LIFE

1. Bread of life and cup of hope, we come as gift to
2. Lov-ing Lord, Cre - a - tor God, o - pen our eyes to
3. Liv - ing Word, O Son of God, your love shows us the

1. you. Change our hearts; fill us with peace. Trans-form our
2. see the good that lives in each of us, that called the
3. way that we may live in har - mo - ny, and from you

1. lives a - new. O - pen our eyes so that we might see
2. world to be. And when we fail to ___ see the good,
3. nev - er stray. Wipe all op-pres-sion ___ from our midst;

1. your pres - ence in one an - oth - er. Your life, poured out in
2. when friend-ships fal - ter and crum-ble, give us the cour - age
3. give us a love for all peo - ple. Your song of jus - tice

1. love to - day, u - nites us all in you.
2. to for-give that we may live in peace.
3. sing in us, to live for peace to - day.

Text and music: Bobby Fisher, b. 1952, © 1994, Bobby Fisher. Published by OCP. All rights reserved.

## 806     AVE VERUM CORPUS/HAIL, TRUE BODY

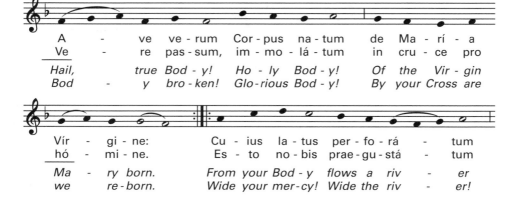

A - ve ve - rum Cor - pus na - tum de Ma - rí - a
Ve - re pas - sum, im - mo - lá - tum in cru - ce pro
*Hail, true Bod - y! Ho - ly Bod - y! Of the Vir - gin*
*Bod - y bro - ken! Glo - rious Bod - y! By your Cross are*

Vír - gi - ne: Cu - ius la - tus per - fo - rá - tum
hó - mi - ne. Es - to no - bis prae - gu - stá - tum
*Ma - ry born. From your Bod - y flows a riv - er*
*we re - born. Wide your mer - cy! Wide the riv - er!*

flu - xit    a - qua    et    sán - gui - ne:
mor - tis    in    e - xá - mi - ne.
*Of  wa - ter    and    pre - cious blood.*
*As  wide    as    your    end - less  love.*

O  Je-su dul - cis!
O  Je-su pi - e!  O  Je - su fi - li Ma-rí - ae.
O  Je-su dul - cis!
O  Je-su pi - e!  *O  Je - sus, O Son of Ma - ry!*

Text: Irregular; ascr. to Innocent VI, d. 1362; Latin, fr. *Liber Cantualis*, 1983;
tr. by Harry Hagan, OSB, © 2004, St. Meinrad Archabbey. Published by OCP. All rights reserved.
Music: AVE VERUM CORPUS; Chant, Mode VI; fr. *Liber Cantualis*, 1983.

## See Us, Lord, About Your Altar    807

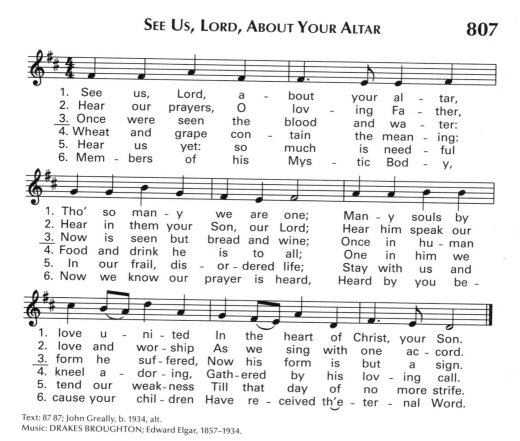

1. See us, Lord, a - bout your al - tar,
2. Hear our prayers, O lov - ing Fa - ther,
3. Once were seen the blood and wa - ter:
4. Wheat and grape con - tain the mean - ing:
5. Hear us yet: so much is need - ful
6. Mem - bers of his Mys - tic Bod - y,

1. Tho' so man - y we are one; Man - y souls by
2. Hear in them your Son, our Lord; Hear him speak our
3. Now is seen but bread and wine; Once in hu - man
4. Food and drink he is to all; One in him we
5. In our frail, dis - or - dered life; Stay with us and
6. Now we know our prayer is heard, Heard by you be -

1. love u - ni - ted In the heart of Christ, your Son.
2. love and wor - ship As we sing with one ac - cord.
3. form he suf - fered, Now his form is but a sign.
4. kneel a - dor - ing, Gath - ered by his lov - ing call.
5. tend our weak - ness Till that day of no more strife.
6. cause your chil - dren Have re - ceived th'e - ter - nal Word.

Text: 87 87; John Greally, b. 1934, alt.
Music: DRAKES BROUGHTON; Edward Elgar, 1857–1934.

## 808      SHEPHERD OF SOULS

1. Shep-herd of souls, re-fresh and bless Your cho-sen pil-grim flock
2. We would not live by bread a-lone, But by your word of grace,
3. Be known to us in break-ing bread, But do not then de-part;
4. Lord, sup with us in love di-vine; Your bod-y and your blood,

1. With man-na in the wil-der-ness, With wa-ter from the rock.
2. In strength of which we trav-el on To our a-bid-ing place.
3. Sav-ior, a-bide with us, and spread Your ta-ble in our heart.
4. That liv-ing bread, that heav'n-ly wine, Be our im-mor-tal food.

Text: CM; verses 1, 2, James Montgomery, 1771–1854; verses 3, 4, anon.
Music: ST. AGNES; John B. Dykes, 1823–1876.

## 809      AN OLD IRISH BLESSING

May the road rise up to meet you. May the wind be

ev-er at your back. May the sun shine warm up-

on your face and the rains fall soft up-on your fields.

And un-til we meet a-gain, and un-til we meet a-gain,

may you be held in the hol-low of God's hand.

Text: Traditional Irish.
Music: Kevin Keil (ASCAP), b. 1956, © 1998, Kevin Keil. Published by OCP. All rights reserved.

## MAY YOU WALK WITH CHRIST

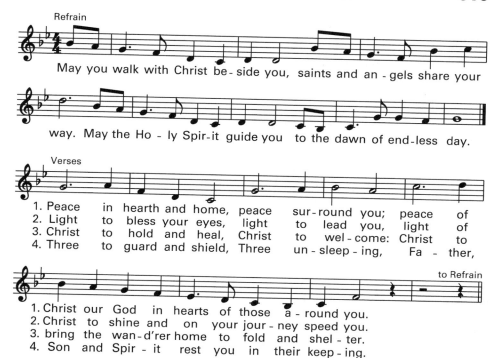

Refrain

May you walk with Christ be-side you, saints and an-gels share your way. May the Ho-ly Spir-it guide you to the dawn of end-less day.

Verses

1. Peace    in    hearth and home,    peace    sur-round you;    peace    of
2. Light    to    bless your eyes,    light    to    lead    you,    light    of
3. Christ    to    hold and heal,    Christ    to    wel-come:    Christ    to
4. Three    to    guard and shield,    Three    un-sleep-ing,    Fa-    ther,

to Refrain

1. Christ our God    in    hearts of those    a-round you.
2. Christ to    shine and    on    your jour-ney speed you.
3. bring the wan-d'rer home    to    fold    and shel-ter.
4. Son    and Spir-it    rest    you    in    their keep-ing.

## MAY GOD BLESS AND KEEP YOU

1st time: Cantor; thereafter: All

May    God    bless    and    keep    you.    May    God's    face    shine    on    you.

May    God    be    kind    to    you    and    give    you    peace.

## 812     TAKE THE WORD OF GOD WITH YOU

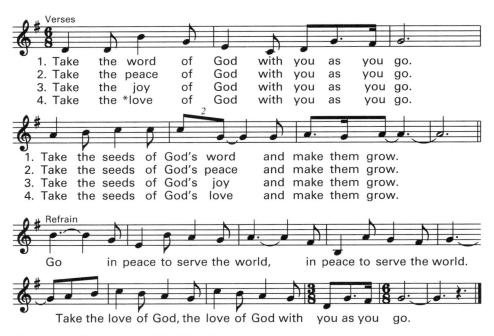

1. Take the word of God with you as you go.
2. Take the peace of God with you as you go.
3. Take the joy of God with you as you go.
4. Take the *love of God with you as you go.

1. Take the seeds of God's word and make them grow.
2. Take the seeds of God's peace and make them grow.
3. Take the seeds of God's joy and make them grow.
4. Take the seeds of God's love and make them grow.

**Refrain**

Go in peace to serve the world, in peace to serve the world.

Take the love of God, the love of God with you as you go.

*Add other words if needed, such as "faith," "hope," etc.

Text: James Harrison, b. 1979, © 1991, James Harrison. Published by OCP. All rights reserved.
Music: Christopher Walker, b. 1947, © 1991, Christopher Walker. Published by OCP. All rights reserved.

## 813     CITY OF GOD

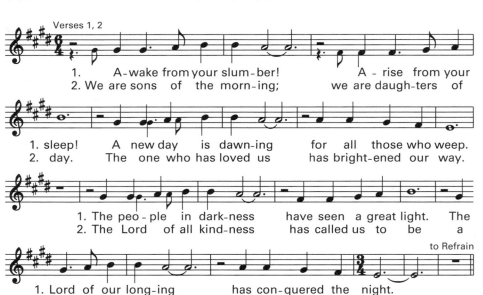

**Verses 1, 2**

1. A-wake from your slum-ber! A - rise from your
2. We are sons of the morn-ing; we are daugh-ters of

1. sleep! A new day is dawn-ing for all those who weep.
2. day. The one who has loved us has bright-ened our way.

1. The peo-ple in dark-ness have seen a great light. The
2. The Lord of all kind-ness has called us to be a

*to Refrain*

1. Lord of our long-ing has con-quered the night.
2. light for his peo-ple to set their hearts free.

Refrain

Let us build the cit-y of God. May our tears be turned in-to danc - ing! For the Lord, our light and our love, has turned the night in - to day!

Verse 3

3. God is light; in him there is no dark-ness.
3. Let us walk in his light, his chil - dren,
3. one and all. O com-fort my
3. peo-ple; make gen-tle your words. Pro-claim to my
3. cit-y the day of her birth.

to Refrain

Verse 4

4. O cit-y of glad-ness, now lift up your voice!
4. Pro-claim the good tid-ings that all may re - joice!

to Refrain

Text: Based on Isaiah 9; 40:1–9; 1 John 1; Dan Schutte, b. 1947.
Music: Dan Schutte.

**814**

## WITH ONE VOICE

Verses

1. Take the Word and go out to ev - 'ry land:
2. Take the Word to our neigh - bor - hoods and streets:
3. Take the Word to the peo - ple in de - spair:
4. Take the Word to the na - tions ev - 'ry - where:

1-4. shine the light of Christ for all to see!

1. May the lives of those we touch sing
2. May we all set out to live in
3. May our ac - tions and our deeds bring
4. May the wit - ness of our lives trans -

1. praise to God a - bove. Let us sing, we'll sing:
2. peace and har - mo - ny. They will see and sing:
3. com - fort to their needs. And they'll know and sing:
4. form the world a - new. And we'll shine, we'll shine:

Refrain

With one voice we'll pass the Word a - long; with one

voice, bring jus - tice to the world. And with all the an -

- gels we'll spread the good - ness of God. With all

pow-er and glo - ry the Word of God shall reign.

Text and music: Ricky Manalo, CSP, b. 1965, © 1998, Ricky Manalo, CSP.

## GOD HAS CHOSEN ME

Verses

1. God has cho-sen me, God has cho-sen me to bring good news
2. God has cho-sen me, God has cho-sen me to set a-light
3. God is call-ing me, God is call-ing me in all whose cry

1. to the poor. God has cho-sen me, God has cho-sen me to
2. a new fire. God has cho-sen me, God has cho-sen me to
3. is un-heard. God is call-ing me, God is call-ing me to

1. bring __ new sight to those search-ing for light: God has
2. bring __ to birth a new king-dom on earth: God has
3. raise up the voice with no pow-er or choice: God is

Refrain

1. cho - sen me, cho - sen me: And to tell the world
2. cho - sen me, cho - sen me:
3. call - ing me, call - ing me:

that God's king-dom is near, to re-move op-pres - sion and

break down fear, yes, God's time is near, God's time is near,

God's time is near, God's time is near.

## 816 THE SERVANT SONG

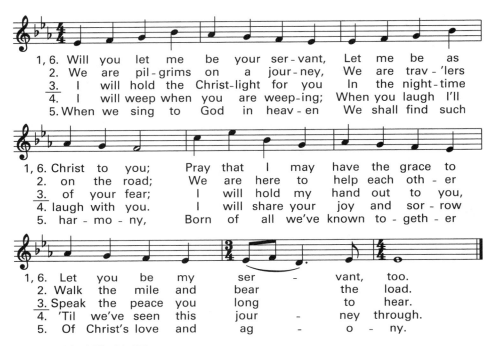

1, 6. Will you let me be your ser-vant, Let me be as
2. We are pil-grims on a jour-ney, We are trav-'lers
3. I will hold the Christ-light for you In the night-time
4. I will weep when you are weep-ing; When you laugh I'll
5. When we sing to God in heav-en We shall find such

1, 6. Christ to you; Pray that I may have the grace to
2. on the road; We are here to help each oth-er
3. of your fear; I will hold my hand out to you,
4. laugh with you. I will share your joy and sor-row
5. har-mo-ny, Born of all we've known to-geth-er

1, 6. Let you be my ser - vant, too.
2. Walk the mile and bear the load.
3. Speak the peace you long to hear.
4. 'Til we've seen this jour - ney through.
5. Of Christ's love and ag - o - ny.

Text: 87 87; Richard Gillard, b. 1953.
Music: SERVANT SONG; Richard Gillard.
Text and music © 1977, Universal Music Group–Brentwood-Benson Music Publishing (ASCAP). All rights reserved.
Administrated by Music Services, Inc. Used with permission.

## 817 THE SPIRIT SENDS US FORTH

1. The Spir-it sends us forth to serve; We go in Je-sus' name
2. We go to com-fort those who mourn And set the bur-dened free;
3. We go to be the hands of Christ, To scat-ter joy like seed
4. Then let us go to serve in peace, The gos-pel to pro-claim.

1. To bring glad ti-dings to the poor, God's fa-vor to pro-claim.
2. Where hope is dim, to share a dream And help the blind to see.
3. And, all our days, to cher-ish life, To do the lov-ing deed.
4. God's Spir-it has em-pow-er'd us; We go in Je-sus' name.

Text: CM; Delores Dufner, OSB, b. 1939, © 1993, The Sisters of St. Benedict, St. Joseph, MN.
Published by OCP. All rights reserved.
Music: AZMON; Carl Gotthilf Gläser, 1784–1829.

# HERE I AM, LORD

Verses

1. I, the Lord of sea and sky,     I have heard my peo - ple cry.
2. I, the Lord of snow and rain,   I have borne my peo-ple's pain.
3. I, the Lord of wind and flame,  I will tend the poor and lame.

1. All who dwell in dark and sin   My hand will save.        I, who
2. I have wept for love of them.   They turn a - way.         I will
3. I will set a feast for them.    My hand will save.         Fin-est

1. made the stars of night,   I will make their dark-ness bright.
2. break their hearts of stone, Give them hearts for love a - lone.
3. bread I will pro-vide      Till their hearts be sat - is - fied.

1. Who will bear my light to them?  Whom shall I send?
2. I will speak my word to them.    Whom shall I send?
3. I will give my life to them.     Whom shall I send?

Refrain

Here I am, Lord.     Is it I, Lord?     I have heard you

call-ing in the night.    I will go, Lord,    if you lead me.

3

I will hold your peo-ple in my heart.

Text: Based on Isaiah 6; Dan Schutte, b. 1947.
Music: Dan Schutte.

# 819    WE ARE SENT INTO THE WORLD

Refrain: 1st time: Cantor, All repeat; thereafter: All

We are sent in-to the world to pro-claim the reign of God.

We give glo-ry to the ris-en Christ a-mong us.

Though our eyes have not seen his face, we be-

lieve and we spread the sto-ry of our faith.

**Verses**

1. Sent out to the world as the fol-low-ers of Christ, we are
2. Sent out to the world as dis-ci-ples of the Word, let us
3. Sent out to the world as am-bas-sa-dors of Christ, we are
4. Sent out to the world as the cho-sen of the Lord, may the

1. called to pro-claim___ good___ news. For Christ con-quered death
2. preach to the ends___ of the earth. For Christ con-quered death
3. sent to all na-tions great and small. For Christ con-quered death
4. Spir-it in-still our hearts a-flame. For Christ con-quered death

to Refrain

1. in his ris-ing to new life: Re-joice in the pow-er of the truth!
2. in his ris-ing to new life: Re-joice in the prom-ise of new birth!
3. in his ris-ing to new life: Re-joice in the splen-dor of our call!
4. in his ris-ing to new life: Re-joice to the glo-ry of his name!

## SERVANT SONG

**820**

**821**     CELTIC ALLELUIA: SENDING FORTH

Refrain

Alleluia, alleluia. Alleluia, alleluia.

Verses

1. Now with the strength of your Word, send us to be your dis-ci-ples, to bring all the world to the joy of your king-dom.
2. Fed with the Bread of new life, filled with the wine of com-pas-sion, send us out to serve all the world in your name.
3. Now make us stead-fast in faith, joy-ful in hope of Christ's com-ing, and by u-ni-ty let your love fill our lives.

*1. Now he is liv-ing, the Christ. Out of the tomb he is ris-en; he has con-quered death, o-pened heav-en to all be-liev-ers.
2. Christ is the first-fruits from death, fill-ing the church with his glo-ry! Dark-ness van-ish-es in the light of his pow-er.

to Refrain

*Verses for the Easter Season.

Text and music: *Celtic Mass*; Fintan O'Carroll, d. 1977, and Christopher Walker, b. 1947,

**822**     WE SHALL OVERCOME

1. We shall o-ver-come, we shall o-ver-come,
2. We'll walk hand in hand, we'll walk hand in hand,
3. We shall all be free, we shall all be free,
4. We are not a-fraid, we are not a-fraid,
5. We shall live in peace, we shall live in peace,

1. we shall o - ver-come some-day; Oh, deep in my heart
2. we'll walk hand in hand some-day; Oh, deep in my heart
3. we shall all be free some-day; Oh, deep in my heart
4. we are not a - fraid to - day; Oh, deep in my heart
5. we shall live in peace some-day; Oh, deep in my heart

1. I do be - lieve, we shall o - ver - come some - day.
2. I do be - lieve, we'll walk hand in hand some - day.
3. I do be - lieve, we shall all be free some - day.
4. I do be - lieve, we are not a - fraid to - day.
5. I do be - lieve, we shall live in peace some - day.

Text and music: Traditional.

## The Church of Christ in Every Age 823

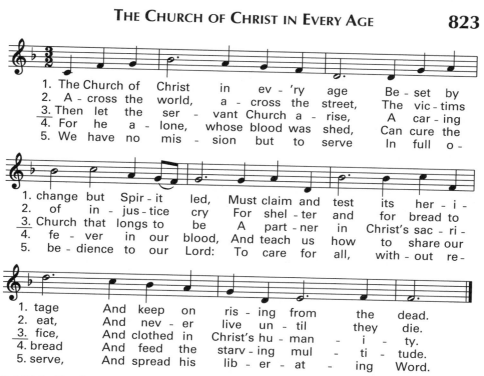

1. The Church of Christ in ev - 'ry age Be - set by
2. A - cross the world, a - cross the street, The vic - tims
3. Then let the ser - vant Church a - rise, A car - ing
4. For he a - lone, whose blood was shed, Can cure the
5. We have no mis - sion but to serve In full o -

1. change but Spir - it led, Must claim and test its her - i -
2. of in - jus - tice cry For shel - ter and for bread to
3. Church that longs to be A part - ner in Christ's sac - ri -
4. fe - ver in our blood, And teach us how to share our
5. be - dience to our Lord: To care for all, with - out re -

1. tage And keep on ris - ing from the dead.
2. eat, And nev - er live un - til they die.
3. fice, And clothed in Christ's hu - man - i - ty.
4. bread And feed the starv - ing mul - ti - tude.
5. serve, And spread his lib - er - at - ing Word.

**824**  CHRIST, BE OUR LIGHT

Verses

1. Long-ing for light, __ we wait in dark - ness. Long-ing for
2. Long-ing for peace, __ our world is trou - bled. Long-ing for
3. Long-ing for food, __ man - y are hun - gry. Long-ing for
4. Long-ing for shel-ter, man - y are home-less. Long-ing for
5. Man - y the gifts, __ man - y the peo - ple, man - y the

1. truth, ____ we turn to you. Make us your own, ____
2. hope, ____ man - y de - spair. Your word a - lone ____
3. wa - ter, man - y still thirst. Make us your bread, ____
4. warmth, ___ man - y are cold. Make us your build - ing,
5. hearts that yearn to be - long. Let us be ser - vants

1. your ho - ly peo-ple, light for the world to see.
2. has pow'r to save us. Make us your liv - ing voice.
3. bro - ken for oth-ers, shared un - til all are fed.
4. shel - ter - ing oth-ers, walls made of liv - ing stone.
5. to one an - oth - er, mak - ing your king - dom come.

Refrain

Christ, be our light! Shine in our hearts. Shine through the dark - ness.

Christ, be our light! Shine in your church gath-ered to-day.

Easter Vigil Verses

1. This is the night of new beginnings.
   This is the night when heaven meets earth.
   This is the night filled with God's glory,
   promise of our new birth!

2. This is the night Christ our redeemer
   rose from the grave triumphant and free,
   leaving the tomb of evil and darkness,
   empty for all to see.

3. Now will the fire kindled in darkness
   burn to dispel the shadows of night.
   Star of the morning, Jesus our Savior,
   you are the world's true light!

4. Sing of the hope deeper than dying.
   Sing of the pow'r stronger than death.
   Sing of the love endless as heaven,
   dawning throughout the earth.

5. Into this world morning is breaking.
   All of God's people, lift up your voice.
   Cry out with joy, tell out the story,
   all of the earth rejoice.

## LORD, WHOSE LOVE IN HUMBLE SERVICE

**825**

1. Lord, whose love in hum-ble ser - vice Bore the
2. Still your chil - dren wan-der home - less; Still the
3. As we wor - ship, grant us vi - sion, Till your
4. Called from wor - ship in - to ser - vice Forth in

1. weight of hu - man need, Who up - on the cross, for -
2. hun - gry cry for bread; Still the cap - tives long for
3. love's re - veal - ing light, Till the height and depth and
4. your great name we go, To the child, the youth, the

1. sak - en, Of - fered mer - cy's per - fect deed; We, your
2. free - dom; Still in grief we mourn our dead. As, O
3. great - ness Dawns up - on our hu - man sight: Mak - ing
4. a - ged, Love in liv - ing deeds to show; Hope and

1. ser - vants, bring the wor - ship Not of voice a -
2. Lord, your deep com - pas - sion Healed the sick and
3. known the needs and bur - dens Your com - pas - sion
4. health, good - will and com - fort, Coun - sel, aid, and

1. lone, but heart: Con - se - crat - ing to your
2. freed the soul, Use the love your Spir - it
3. bids us bear, Stir - ring us to tire - less
4. peace we give, That your chil - dren, Lord, in

1. pur - pose Ev - 'ry gift which you im - part.
2. kin - dles Still to save and make us whole.
3. striv - ing, Your a - bun - dant life to share.
4. free - dom, May your mer - cy know, and live.

Text: 87 87 D; 'Lord, whose love in humble service', by Albert F. Bayly, 1901–1984, alt., © 1988, Oxford University Press.
All rights reserved. Reproduced by permission.
Music: BEACH SPRING; *The Sacred Harp*, 1844.

# 826

## SOMOS EL CUERPO DE CRISTO/
## WE ARE THE BODY OF CHRIST

# ALLELUIA! RAISE THE GOSPEL

**Refrain**

Al - le - lu - ia! Al - le - lu - ia! Raise the Gos - pel o - ver the earth! Al - le - lu - ia! Al - le - lu - ia! Peace and jus - tice bring-ing to birth!

**\*Verses**

1. Bless - ed those whose hearts are gen - tle. Bless - ed
2. Bless - ed those who work for jus - tice. Bless - ed
3. Trem - ble, you who build up rich - es. Trem - ble,
4. Trem - ble, you who thirst for pow - er. Trem - ble
5. Glo - ry like the stars of heav - en— Glo - ry
6. Glo - ry to the Word of Jus - tice. Glo - ry

1. those whose spir - its are strong. Bless - ed those who
2. those who an - swer the call. Bless - ed those who
3. you with op - u - lent lives. Trem - ble, when you
4. you who live for ac - claim. Trem - ble, when you
5. like the sun in the sky— Glo - ry shines up -
6. to the Spir - it of Peace. Glo - ry to the

to Refrain

1. choose to bring forth right where there is wrong.
2. dare to dream of last - ing peace for all.
3. meet the poor and see Christ in their eyes.
4. find no com - fort in your wealth and fame.
5. on all peo - ple, e - qual in God's eyes.
6. God of Love whose bless - ings nev - er cease.

\*Alternate verses available in the accompaniment books.

## 828     WHATSOEVER YOU DO

**Refrain**

What-so-ev-er you do to the least of my peo-ple, that you do un-to me.

**Verses**

1. When I was hun-gry, you gave me to
2. When I was home-less, you o-pened your
3. When I was wea-ry, you helped me find
4. When in a pris-on, you came to my
5. When I was laughed at, you stood by my

1. eat; When I was thirst-y, you gave me to drink.
2. door; When I was na-ked, you gave me your coat.
3. rest; When I was anx-ious, you calmed all my fears.
4. cell; When on a sick-bed, you cared for my needs.
5. side; When I was hap-py, you shared in my joy.

*to Refrain*

1-5. Now en-ter in-to the home of my Fa - ther.

## 829     THE CRY OF THE POOR

**Refrain**

The Lord hears the cry of the poor. Bless-ed be the Lord.

**Verses: Slightly faster**

1. I will bless the Lord at all times, with praise
2. Let the low-ly hear and be glad: the Lord
3. Ev-'ry spir-it crushed, God will save; will be
4. We pro-claim your great-ness, O God, your praise

1. ev-er in my mouth. Let my soul glo-ry in the
2. lis-tens to their pleas; and to hearts bro-ken, God is
3. ran-som for their lives; will be safe shel-ter for their
4. ev-er in our mouth; ev-'ry face bright-ened in your

## SING A NEW CHURCH

**830**

## 831     IN CHRIST THERE IS NO EAST OR WEST

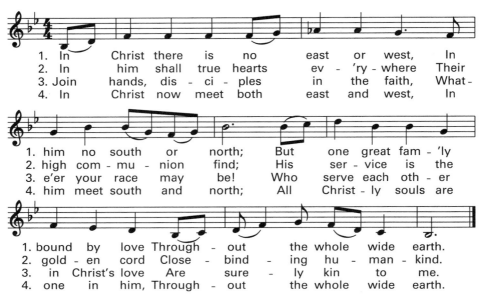

1. In Christ there is no east or west, In
2. In him shall true hearts ev - 'ry - where Their
3. Join hands, dis - ci - ples in the faith, What -
4. In Christ now meet both east and west, In

1. him no south or north; But one great fam - 'ly
2. high com - mu - nion find; His ser - vice is the
3. e'er your race may be! Who serve each oth - er
4. him meet south and north; All Christ - ly souls are

1. bound by love Through - out the whole wide earth.
2. gold - en cord Close - bind - ing hu - man - kind.
3. in Christ's love Are sure - ly kin to me.
4. one in him, Through - out the whole wide earth.

Text: CM; Galatians 3:28; John Oxenham, 1852–1941, alt.
Music: McKEE; Spiritual; adapt. by Harry T. Burleigh, 1866–1949.

## 832     THEY'LL KNOW WE ARE CHRISTIANS

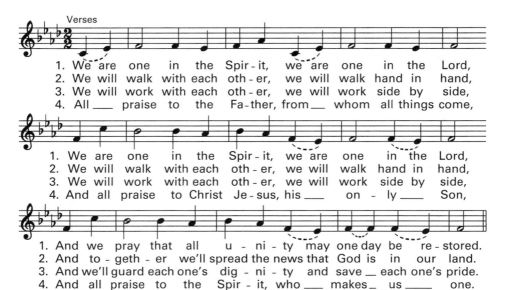

Verses

1. We are one in the Spir - it, we are one in the Lord,
2. We will walk with each oth - er, we will walk hand in hand,
3. We will work with each oth - er, we will work side by side,
4. All ___ praise to the Fa - ther, from ___ whom all things come,

1. We are one in the Spir - it, we are one in the Lord,
2. We will walk with each oth - er, we will walk hand in hand,
3. We will work with each oth - er, we will work side by side,
4. And all praise to Christ Je - sus, his ___ on - ly ___ Son,

1. And we pray that all u - ni - ty may one day be re - stored.
2. And to - geth - er we'll spread the news that God is in our land.
3. And we'll guard each one's dig - ni - ty and save ___ each one's pride.
4. And all praise to the Spir - it, who ___ makes ___ us ___ one.

And they'll know we are Chris-tians by our love, by our love, Yes they'll know we are Chris-tians by our love.

Text: 13 13 14 with refrain; Peter Scholtes, 1938–2009.
Music: ST. BRENDAN'S; Peter Scholtes.
Text and music © 1966, F.E.L. Church Publications, Ltd., assigned 1991 to the Lorenz Corporation. All rights reserved.
    International copyright secured. Used with permission.

## CHRIST IS THE KING

**833**

1. Christ is the King! O friends, re-joice:
2. O mag-ni-fy the Lord, and raise
3. They with a faith for ev-er new
4. O Chris-tian wom-en, Chris-tian men,
5. Christ through all a-ges is the same:
6. Let love's all rec-on-cil-ing might
7. So shall God's will on earth be done,

1. Broth-ers and sis-ters, with one voice
2. An-thems of joy and ho-ly praise
3. Fol-lowed the King, and round him drew
4. All the world o-ver, seek a-gain
5. Place the same hope in his great name,
6. Your scat-tered com-pa-nies u-nite
7. New lamps be lit, new tasks be-gun,

1. Let the world know he is your choice.
2. For Christ's brave saints of an-cient days.
3. Thou-sands of men and wom-en true.
4. The Way dis-ci-ples fol-lowed then.
5. With the same faith his word pro-claim.
6. In ser-vice to the Lord of light.
7. And the whole Church at last be one.

1-7. Al-le-lu-ia, al-le-lu-ia, al-le-lu-ia.

Text: 888 with alleluias; 'Christ is the King!' by G K A Bell, 1883–1958, alt.
    Reproduced by permission of Oxford University Press. All rights reserved.
Music: GELOBT SEI GOTT; Melchior Vulpius, ca. 1560–1616.

# 834 MANY AND GREAT

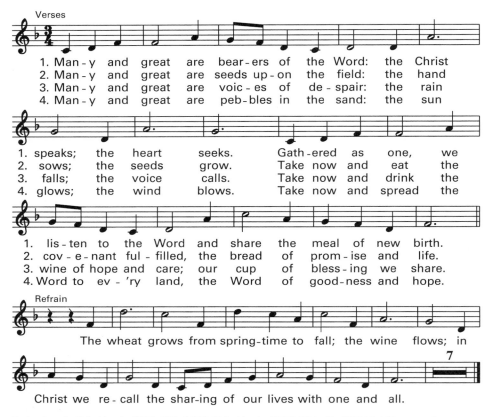

**Verses**

1. Man-y and great are bear-ers of the Word: the Christ
2. Man-y and great are seeds up-on the field: the hand
3. Man-y and great are voic-es of de-spair: the rain
4. Man-y and great are peb-bles in the sand: the sun

1. speaks; the heart seeks. Gath-ered as one, we
2. sows; the seeds grow. Take now and eat the
3. falls; the voice calls. Take now and drink the
4. glows; the wind blows. Take now and spread the

1. lis-ten to the Word and share the meal of new birth.
2. cov-e-nant ful-filled, the bread of prom-ise and life.
3. wine of hope and care; our cup of bless-ing we share.
4. Word to ev-'ry land, the Word of good-ness and hope.

**Refrain**

The wheat grows from spring-time to fall; the wine flows; in

Christ we re-call the shar-ing of our lives with one and all.

Text and music: Ricky Manalo, CSP, b. 1965, © 1995, Ricky Manalo, CSP. Published by OCP. All rights reserved.

# 835 COMPANIONS ON THE JOURNEY

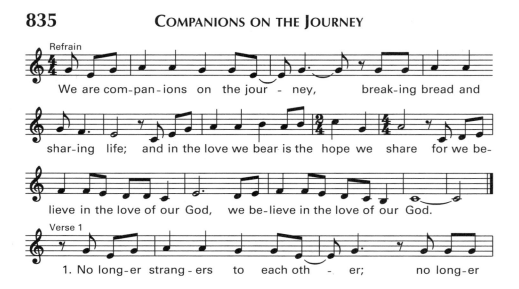

**Refrain**

We are com-pan-ions on the jour - ney, break-ing bread and

shar-ing life; and in the love we bear is the hope we share for we be-

lieve in the love of our God, we be-lieve in the love of our God.

**Verse 1**

1. No long-er strang-ers to each oth - er; no long-er

1. strang-ers in God's house; we are fed and we are nour-ished by the
1. strength of those who care, by the strength of those who care.

*to Refrain*

Verse 2

2. We have been gift-ed with each oth - er, and we are called by the
2. Word of the Lord: to act with jus-tice, to love ten-der - ly, and to walk
2. hum-bly with our God, to walk hum-bly with our God.

*to Refrain*

Verse 3

3. We will seek and we shall find; we will knock and the door will be
3. o-pened; we will ask and it shall be giv-en, for we be-lieve in the
3. love of our God, we be-lieve in the love of our God.

*to Refrain*

Verse 4

4. We are made for the glo-ry of our God, for ser-vice in the name of
4. Je-sus; to walk side by side with hope in our hearts, for we be-
4. lieve in the love of our God, we be-lieve in the love of our God.

*to Refrain*

Text: Based on Micah 6:8; Matthew 7:7; Carey Landry, b. 1944.
Music: Carey Landry.

## 836    PANIS ANGELICUS/HOLY AND LIVING BREAD

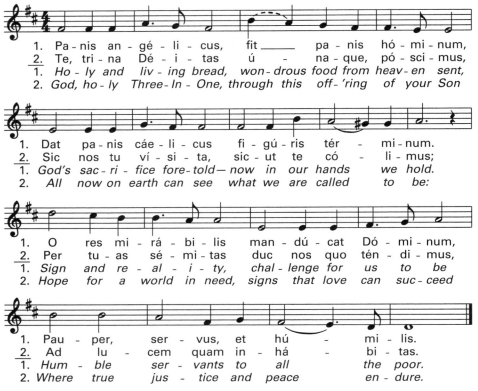

1. Pa - nis an - gé - li - cus, fit ____ pa - nis hó - mi - num,
2. Te, tri - na Dé - i - tas ú - na - que, pó - sci - mus,
1. Ho - ly and liv - ing bread, won - drous food from heav - en sent,
2. God, ho - ly Three - In - One, through this off - 'ring of your Son

1. Dat pa - nis cáe - li - cus fi - gú - ris tér - mi - num.
2. Sic nos tu ví - si - ta, sic - ut te có - li - mus;
1. God's sac - ri - fice fore - told— now in our hands we hold.
2. All now on earth can see what we are called to be:

1. O res mi - rá - bi - lis man - dú - cat Dó - mi - num,
2. Per tu - as sé - mi - tas duc nos quo tén - di - mus,
1. Sign and re - al - i - ty, chal - lenge for us to be
2. Hope for a world in need, signs that love can suc - ceed

1. Pau - per, ser - vus, et hú - mi - lis.
2. Ad lu - cem quam in - há - bi - tas.
1. Hum - ble ser - vants to all the poor.
2. Where true jus - tice and peace en - dure.

Text: 12 12 12 8; Latin; St. Thomas Aquinas, 1227–1274; English, Owen Alstott, b. 1947, © 2001, OCP. All rights reserved.
Music: SACRIS SOLEMNIIS; Louis Lambillotte, SJ, 1796–1855.

## 837    O LORD, I AM NOT WORTHY

1. O Lord, I am not wor - thy That thou should'st come to me;
2. And hum - bly I'll re - ceive thee, The Bride - groom of my soul,
3. E - ter - nal Ho - ly Spir - it, Un - wor - thy though I be,
4. In - crease my faith, dear Je - sus, In thy real pres - ence here,

1. But speak the word of com - fort, My spir - it healed shall be.
2. No more by sin to grieve thee Or fly thy sweet con - trol.
3. Pre - pare me to re - ceive him And trust the Word to me.
4. And make me feel most deep - ly That thou to me art near.

Text: 76 76; based on Matthew 8:8; *O Herr, ich bin nicht würdig*; *Landshuter Gesangbuch*, 1777; tr. anon.
Music: NON DIGNUS; anon.; *Catholic Youth Hymnal*, 1871.

## O Sacrament Most Holy

**838**

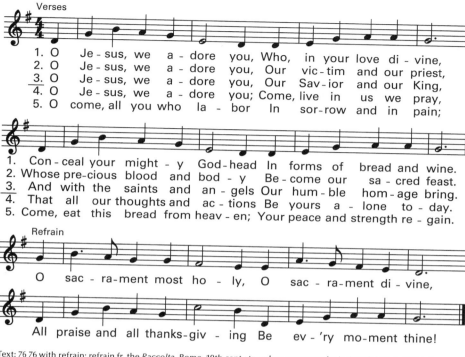

Verses

1. O Je-sus, we a-dore you, Who, in your love di-vine,
2. O Je-sus, we a-dore you, Our vic-tim and our priest,
3. O Je-sus, we a-dore you, Our Sav-ior and our King,
4. O Je-sus, we a-dore you; Come, live in us we pray,
5. O come, all you who la-bor In sor-row and in pain;

1. Con-ceal your might-y God-head In forms of bread and wine.
2. Whose pre-cious blood and bod-y Be-come our sa-cred feast.
3. And with the saints and an-gels Our hum-ble hom-age bring.
4. That all our thoughts and ac-tions Be yours a-lone to-day.
5. Come, eat this bread from heav-en; Your peace and strength re-gain.

Refrain

O sac-ra-ment most ho-ly, O sac-ra-ment di-vine,

All praise and all thanks-giv-ing Be ev-'ry mo-ment thine!

Text: 76 76 with refrain; refrain fr. the *Raccolta*, Rome, 19th cent.; tr. unknown; verses by Irvin Udulutsch, OFM, Cap., 1920–2010, © 1958, The Basilian Fathers c/o The Willis Music Company. All rights reserved. Used with permission.
Music: FULDA; *Gebet- und Gesangbuch*, Fulda, 1891.

## Soul of My Savior

**839**

1. Soul of my Sav-ior, sanc-ti-fy my breast; Bod-y of
2. Strength and pro-tec-tion may thy Pas-sion be; O Bless-ed
3. Hear me, Lord Je-sus, lis-ten as I pray; "Lead me from

1. Christ, be thou my sav-ing guest; Blood of my Sav-ior, bathe me
2. Je-sus, hear and an-swer me; Deep in thy wounds, Lord, hide and
3. night to nev-er end-ing day. Fill all the world with love and

1. in thy tide; Wash me with wa-ter flow-ing from his side.
2. shel-ter me; So shall I nev-er, nev-er part from thee.
3. grace di-vine, And glo-ry, laud, and praise be ev-er thine."

Text: 10 10 10 10; verses 1–2 attr. to Pope John XXII, 1249–1334; tr. by Edward Caswall, 1814–1878, alt.;
verse 3, composite, based on *God of Our Fathers*; Daniel C. Roberts, 1841–1907.
Music: ANIMA CHRISTI; William J. Maher, SJ, 1823–1877, alt.

# 840    Adoro Te Devote/Godhead Here in Hiding

Verses 1-7: Latin

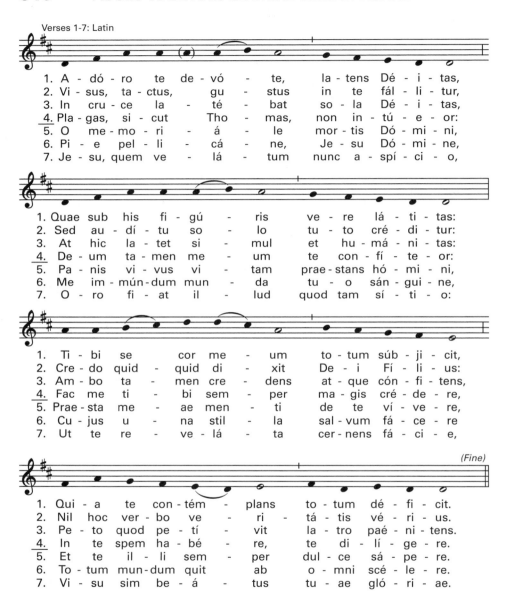

1. A - dó - ro te de - vó - te, la - tens Dé - i - tas,
2. Vi - sus, ta - ctus, gu - stus in te fál - li - tur,
3. In cru - ce la - té - bat so - la Dé - i - tas,
4. Pla - gas, si - cut Tho - mas, non in - tú - e - or:
5. O me - mo - ri - á - le mor - tis Dó - mi - ni,
6. Pi - e pel - li - cá - ne, Je - su Dó - mi - ne,
7. Je - su, quem ve - lá - tum nunc a - spí - ci - o,

1. Quae sub his fi - gú - ris ve - re lá - ti - tas:
2. Sed au - dí - tu so - lo tu - to cré - di - tur:
3. At hic la - tet si - mul et hu - má - ni - tas:
4. De - um ta - men me - um te con - fí - te - or:
5. Pa - nis vi - vus vi - tam prae - stans hó - mi - ni,
6. Me im - mún - dum mun - da tu - o sán - gui - ne,
7. O - ro fi - at il - lud quod tam sí - ti - o:

1. Ti - bi se cor me - um to - tum súb - ji - cit,
2. Cre - do quid - quid di - xit De - i Fí - li - us:
3. Am - bo ta - men cre - dens at - que cón - fi - tens,
4. Fac me ti - bi sem - per ma - gis cré - de - re,
5. Prae - sta me - ae men - ti de te ví - ve - re,
6. Cu - jus u - na stil - la sal - vum fá - ce - re
7. Ut te re - ve - lá - ta cer - nens fá - ci - e,

*(Fine)*

1. Qui - a te con - tém - plans to - tum dé - fi - cit.
2. Nil hoc ver - bo ve - ri - tá - tis vé - ri - us.
3. Pe - to quod pe - tí - vit la - tro paé - ni - tens.
4. In te spem ha - bé - re, te di - lí - ge - re.
5. Et te il - li sem - per dul - ce sá - pe - re.
6. To - tum mun - dum quit ab o - mni scé - le - re.
7. Vi - su sim be - á - tus tu - ae gló - ri - ae.

Verses 1-7: English

1. God - head here in hid - ing whom I do a - dore
2. See - ing, touch-ing, tast - ing are in thee de-ceived;
3. On the cross thy god - head made no sign to men;
4. I am not like Thom - as, wounds I can - not see,
5. O thou, our re - mind - er of the Cru - ci - fied,
6. Like what ten - der tales tell of the Pel - i - can,
7. Je - sus whom I look at shroud-ed here be - low,

1. Masked by these bare shad - ows, shape and noth - ing more,
2. How says trust - y hear - ing? that shall be be - lieved;
3. Here thy ver - y man - hood steals from hu - man ken:
4. But I plain - ly call thee Lord and God as he:
5. Liv - ing Bread, the life of us for whom he died,
6. Bathe me, Je - sus Lord, in what thy bos - om ran—
7. I be - seech thee, send me what I thirst for so,

1. See, Lord, at thy ser - vice low lies here a heart
2. What God's Son has told me, take for truth I do;
3. Both are my con - fes - sion, both are my be - lief,
4. This faith each day deep - er be my hold - ing of,
5. Lend this life to me, then; feed and feast my mind,
6. Blood that but one drop of has the pow'r to win
7. Some day to gaze on thee face to face in light

1. Lost, all lost in won - der at the God thou art.
2. Truth him - self speaks tru - ly or there's noth - ing true.
3. And I pray the prayer made by the dy - ing thief.
4. Dai - ly make me hard - er hope and dear - er love.
5. There be thou the sweet - ness man was meant to find.
6. All the world for - give - ness of its world of sin.
7. And be blest for - ev - er with thy glo - ry's sight.

Text: 11 11 11 11; St. Thomas Aquinas, ca. 1224–1274, alt.; tr. by Gerard Manley Hopkins, SJ, 1844–1899, alt.
Music: ADORO TE DEVOTE; Chant, Mode V; *Paris Processionale*, 1697.

## 841    BEAUTIFUL SAVIOR

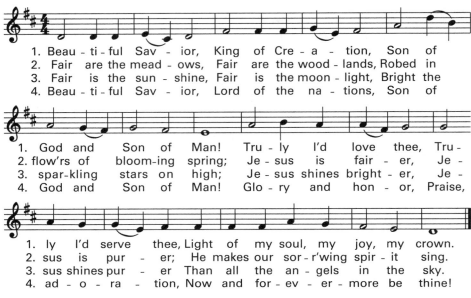

1. Beau - ti - ful Sav - ior, King of Cre - a - tion, Son of
2. Fair are the mead - ows, Fair are the wood - lands, Robed in
3. Fair is the sun - shine, Fair is the moon - light, Bright the
4. Beau - ti - ful Sav - ior, Lord of the na - tions, Son of

1. God and Son of Man! Tru - ly I'd love thee, Tru -
2. flow'rs of bloom-ing spring; Je - sus is fair - er, Je -
3. spar-kling stars on high; Je - sus shines bright - er, Je -
4. God and Son of Man! Glo - ry and hon - or, Praise,

1. ly I'd serve thee, Light of my soul, my joy, my crown.
2. sus is pur - er; He makes our sor - r'wing spir - it sing.
3. sus shines pur - er Than all the an - gels in the sky.
4. ad - o - ra - tion, Now and for - ev - er - more be thine!

Text: 55 7 55 8; Psalm 45:3; *Schönster Herr Jesu*, in *Münster Gesangbuch*, 1677; tr. by Joseph A. Seiss, 1823–1904.
Music: ST. ELIZABETH; trad. Silesian Melody; Hoffman and Richter's *Schlesische Volkslieder*, Leipzig, 1842.

## 842    O GOD OF LOVE, O KING OF PEACE

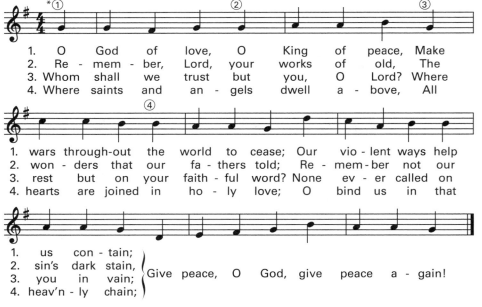

1. O God of love, O King of peace, Make
2. Re - mem - ber, Lord, your works of old, The
3. Whom shall we trust but you, O Lord? Where
4. Where saints and an - gels dwell a - bove, All

1. wars through-out the world to cease; Our vio - lent ways help
2. won - ders that our fa - thers told; Re - mem - ber not our
3. rest but on your faith - ful word? None ev - er called on
4. hearts are joined in ho - ly love; O bind us in that

1. us con - tain;
2. sin's dark stain,
3. you in vain; } Give peace, O God, give peace a - gain!
4. heav'n - ly chain;

*May be sung as a two- or four-voice canon.

Text: LM; Henry W. Baker, 1821–1877.
Music: TALLIS' CANON; Thomas Tallis, ca. 1505–1585.

## AMERICA

**843**

1. My coun-try, 'tis of thee, Sweet land of lib - er - ty,
2. My na - tive coun - try, thee, Land of the no - ble free,
3. Let mu - sic swell the breeze, And ring from all the trees
4. Our fa-thers' God, to thee, Au - thor of lib - er - ty,

1. Of thee I sing; Land where my fa - thers died,
2. Thy name I love; I love thy rocks and rills,
3. Sweet free-dom's song; Let mor - tal tongues a - wake;
4. To thee we sing; Long may our land be bright

1. Land of the pil - grims' pride, From ev - 'ry
2. Thy woods and tem - pled hills; My heart with
3. Let all that breathe par - take; Let rocks their
4. With free-dom's ho - ly light; Pro - tect us

1. moun - tain-side Let free - dom ring!
2. rap - ture thrills, Like that a - bove.
3. si - lence break, The sound pro - long.
4. by thy might, Great God, our King.

Text: 66 4 666 4; Samuel F. Smith, 1808–1895.
Music: AMERICA; *Thesaurus Musicus*, 1744.

## FOR THE HEALING OF THE NATIONS

**844**

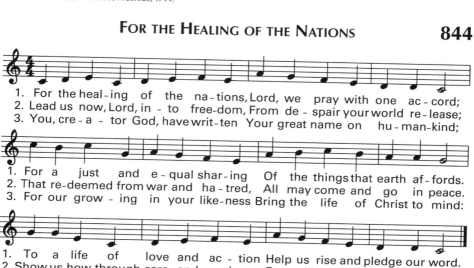

1. For the heal-ing of the na-tions, Lord, we pray with one ac-cord;
2. Lead us now, Lord, in - to free-dom, From de - spair your world re-lease;
3. You, cre - a - tor God, have writ-ten Your great name on hu - man-kind;

1. For a just and e - qual shar-ing Of the things that earth af-fords.
2. That re-deemed from war and ha-tred, All may come and go in peace.
3. For our grow - ing in your like-ness Bring the life of Christ to mind:

1. To a life of love and ac - tion Help us rise and pledge our word.
2. Show us how through care and good-ness Fear will die and hope in-crease.
3. That by our re - sponse and ser - vice Earth its des-ti - ny may find.

Text: 87 87 87; based on Revelation 21:1–27; 22:1–5; Fred Kaan, © 1968, Hope Publishing Co.
All rights reserved. Used with permission.
Music: ST. THOMAS (TANTUM ERGO); John F. Wade, 1711–1786.

## 845      AMERICA THE BEAUTIFUL

1. O beau-ti-ful for spa-cious skies, For am-ber waves of grain,
2. O beau-ti-ful for pil-grim feet, Whose stern, im-pas-sioned stress
3. O beau-ti-ful for he-roes proved In lib-er-at-ing strife,
4. O beau-ti-ful for pa-triot dream That sees be-yond the years

1. For pur-ple moun-tain maj-es-ties A-bove the fruit-ed plain!
2. A thor-ough-fare for free-dom beat A-cross the wil-der-ness!
3. Who more than self their coun-try loved, And mer-cy more than life!
4. Thine al-a-bas-ter cit-ies gleam, Un-dimmed by hu-man tears!

1. A-mer-i-ca! A-mer-i-ca! God shed his grace on thee,
2. A-mer-i-ca! A-mer-i-ca! God mend thine ev-'ry flaw,
3. A-mer-i-ca! A-mer-i-ca! May God thy gold re-fine,
4. A-mer-i-ca! A-mer-i-ca! God shed his grace on thee,

1. And crown thy good with broth-er-hood From sea to shin-ing sea.
2. Con-firm thy soul in self-con-trol, Thy lib-er-ty in law.
3. Till all suc-cess be no-ble-ness, And ev-'ry gain di-vine.
4. And crown thy good with broth-er-hood From sea to shin-ing sea.

Text: CMD; Katherine L. Bates, 1859–1929.
Music: MATERNA; Samuel A. Ward, 1848–1903.

## 846      THIS IS MY SONG

1. This is my song, O God of all the na-tions,
2. My coun-try's skies are blu-er than the o-cean,
3. This is my prayer, O Lord of all earth's king-doms:

1. A song of peace for lands a-far and mine.
2. And sun-light beams on clo-ver-leaf and pine;
3. Thy king-dom come; on earth thy will be done.

1. This is my home, the coun-try where my heart is;
2. But oth-er lands have sun-light too, and clo-ver,
3. Let Christ be lift-ed up till all shall serve him,

1. Here are my hopes, my dreams, my ho - ly shrine;
2. And skies are ev - 'ry - where as blue as mine.
3. And hearts u - nit - ed learn to live as one.

1. But oth - er hearts in oth - er lands are beat-ing
2. O hear my song, thou God of all the na-tions,
3. O hear my prayer, thou God of all the na-tions;

1. With hopes and dreams as true and high as mine.
2. A song of peace for their land and for mine.
3. My-self I give thee; let thy will be done.

Text: 11 10 11 10 11 10; verses 1, 2, Lloyd Stone; verse 3, Georgia Harkness, © 1964, Lorenz Corporation.
Music: FINLANDIA; Jean Sibelius, 1865–1957.

## GOD OF OUR FATHERS

**847**

1. God of our fa - thers, whose al - might - y hand
2. Thy love di - vine hath led us in the past,
3. From war's a - larms, from dead - ly pes - ti - lence,
4. Re - fresh thy peo - ple on their toil - some way,

1. Leads forth in beau - ty all the star - ry band
2. In this free land by thee our lot is cast;
3. Be thy strong arm our ev - er sure de - fense;
4. Lead us from night to nev - er - end - ing day;

1. Of shin - ing worlds in splen - dor through the skies,
2. Be thou our rul - er, guard - ian, guide, and stay,
3. Thy true re - li - gion in our hearts in - crease,
4. Fill all our lives with love and grace di - vine,

1. Our grate - ful songs be - fore thy throne a - rise.
2. Thy word our law, thy paths our cho - sen way.
3. Thy boun - teous good - ness nour - ish us in peace.
4. And glo - ry, laud, and praise be ev - er thine.

Text: 10 10 10 10; Daniel Crane Roberts, 1841–1907.
Music: NATIONAL HYMN; George William Warren, 1828–1902.

## 848      Eternal Father, Strong to Save

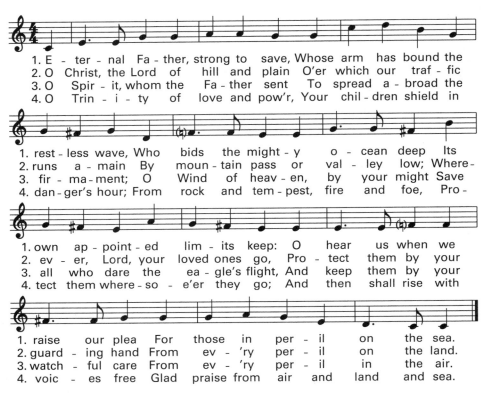

1. E - ter - nal Fa - ther, strong to save, Whose arm has bound the
2. O Christ, the Lord of hill and plain O'er which our traf - fic
3. O Spir - it, whom the Fa - ther sent To spread a - broad the
4. O Trin - i - ty of love and pow'r, Your chil - dren shield in

1. rest - less wave, Who bids the might - y o - cean deep Its
2. runs a - main By moun - tain pass or val - ley low; Where-
3. fir - ma - ment; O Wind of heav - en, by your might Save
4. dan - ger's hour; From rock and tem - pest, fire and foe, Pro -

1. own ap - point - ed lim - its keep: O hear us when we
2. ev - er, Lord, your loved ones go, Pro - tect them by your
3. all who dare the ea - gle's flight, And keep them by your
4. tect them where - so - e'er they go; And then shall rise with

1. raise our plea For those in per - il on the sea.
2. guard - ing hand From ev - 'ry per - il on the land.
3. watch - ful care From ev - 'ry per - il in the air.
4. voic - es free Glad praise from air and land and sea.

Text: 88 88 88; verses 1, 4, William Whiting, 1825–1878, alt.; verses 2, 3, Robert N. Spencer, 1877–1961, alt.
Music: MELITA; John B. Dykes, 1823–1876.

## 849      Lord, as the Day Begins

1. Lord, as the day be - gins Lift up our hearts in
2. Christ be in work and skill, Serv - ing each oth - er's
3. Grant us the Spir - it's strength, Teach us to walk his
4. Now as the day be - gins Make it the best of

1. praise; Take from us all our sins, Guard us in
2. need; Christ be in thought and will, Christ be in
3. way; So bring us all at length Safe to the
4. days; Take from us all our sins, Guard us in

1. all our ways. Our ev - 'ry step di - rect and
2. word and deed. Our minds be set on things a -
3. close of day. From hour to hour sus - tain and
4. all our ways. Our ev - 'ry step di - rect and

1. guide That Christ in all be glo - ri - fied.
2. bove In joy and peace, in faith and love.
3. bless, And let our song be thank - ful - ness.
4. guide That Christ in all be glo - ri - fied.

## THIS DAY GOD GIVES ME 850

1. This day God gives me Strength of high heav - en, Sun and moon
2. This day God sends me Strength as my guard - ian, Might to up -
3. God's way is my way, God's shield is 'round me, God's host de -
4. Ris - ing I thank you, Might - y and Strong One, King of cre -

1. shin - ing, Flame in my hearth, Flash-ing of light - ning, Wind in its
2. hold me, Wis-dom as guide. Your eyes are watch - ful, Your ears are
3. fends me, Sav - ing from ill. An - gels of heav - en, Drive from me
4. a - tion, Giv - er of rest, Firm - ly con - fess - ing Three-ness of

1. swift - ness, Deeps of the o - cean, Firm-ness of earth.
2. lis - t'ning, Your lips are speak - ing, Friend at my side.
3. al - ways All that would harm me, Stand by me still.
4. Per - sons, One-ness of God - head, Trin - i - ty blest.

## 851 MORNING HAS BROKEN

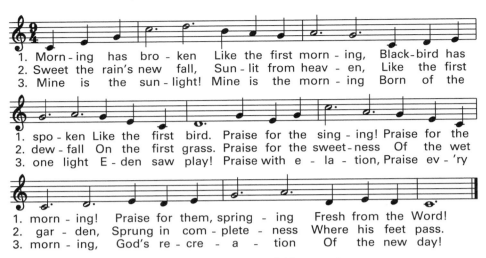

1. Morn-ing has bro-ken Like the first morn-ing, Black-bird has
2. Sweet the rain's new fall, Sun-lit from heav-en, Like the first
3. Mine is the sun-light! Mine is the morn-ing Born of the

1. spo-ken Like the first bird. Praise for the sing-ing! Praise for the
2. dew-fall On the first grass. Praise for the sweet-ness Of the wet
3. one light E-den saw play! Praise with e - la - tion, Praise ev-'ry

1. morn-ing! Praise for them, spring-ing Fresh from the Word!
2. gar-den, Sprung in com-plete-ness Where his feet pass.
3. morn-ing, God's re-cre-a-tion Of the new day!

Text: 55 54 D; Eleanor Farjeon, 1881–1965, © 1957, Eleanor Farjeon. All rights reserved.
Reprinted by permission of Harold Ober Assoc., Inc.
Music: BUNESSAN; trad. Gaelic Melody.

## 852 GOD OF MYSTERY, GOD OF MERCY

1. God of mys-t'ry, God of mer-cy, God of glo-ry,
2. Part the clouds that keep us from you; Rend the heav-ens
3. God of day-light and of dark-ness, God of heav-en,
4. Hold us in the hands that made us; Cra-dle all our

1. hid in light: Let your face shine on your peo-ple
2. and come down; Show your love at work a-mong us;
3. God of earth: You are Lord of all our liv-ing,
4. hopes and fears; Let us praise and give you glo-ry

1. Where we dwell in dark of night.
2. Let us sing your great re-nown.
3. Yours our tears and yours our mirth.
4. With the sum of all our years.

Text: 87 87; Genevieve Glen, OSB, b. 1945, © 2002, The Benedictine Nuns of the Abbey of St. Walburga.
Published by OCP. All rights reserved.
Music: MOUNT ST. MARY'S; Christopher Walker, b. 1947, © 2005, Christopher Walker.
Published by OCP. All rights reserved.

## DAY IS DONE

1. Day is done, but Love un-fail-ing Dwells ev - er here;
2. Dark de-scends, but Light un-end-ing Shines through our night;
3. Eyes will close, but you un-sleep-ing Watch by our side;

1. Shad-ows fall, but hope, pre-vail-ing, Calms ev-'ry fear.
2. You are with us, ev - er lend-ing New strength to sight.
3. Death may come, in Love's safe-keep-ing Still we a - bide.

1. God, our Mak - er, none for-sak-ing, Take our hearts, of Love's own
2. One in love, your truth con-fess-ing, One in hope of heav - en's
3. God of love, all e - vil quell-ing, Sin for-giv-ing, fear dis-

1. mak-ing; Watch our sleep-ing, guard our wak-ing, Be al-ways near.
2. bless-ing, May we see, in love's pos-sess-ing, Love's end-less light!
3. pel-ling: Stay with us, our hearts in-dwell-ing, This e - ven-tide.

Text: 84 84 88 84; James Quinn, SJ, 1919–2010, © 1969, James Quinn, SJ. Published by OCP. All rights reserved.
Music: AR HYD Y NOS; trad. Welsh melody.

## RADIANT LIGHT DIVINE

*Ostinato Refrain

English Ra - diant Light Di - vine, shine through-out this night. Je - sus,
Spanish En la os - cu - ri - dad, bri - lla - rá tu luz. Je - su -
Vietnamese Ôi Nguồn Sáng Linh Thiêng chiếu soi suốt đêm trường. Đoàn con

Ho - ly One, praise to you our Light. As the day-light fades, and come
cris - to, te a - la - ba - mos. Al a - no - che - cer, ya se a-
chúc tụng Ngài là Ánh Sáng chúng con. Khi màu nắng phai tàn, khi hoàng

e - ven-tide, dwell a - mong us, Ho - ly Fire.
ba - jó el sol, Fue - go San - to, da - nos luz.
hôn buông màn, xin ở cùng đoàn con ôi Lửa Thiêng.

*Verses available in accompaniment books.

Text: Based on *Phos Hilaron*, Greek ca. 200; Rufino Zaragoza, OFM, b. 1957; Spanish, Mary Frances Reza;
  Vietnamese refrain, Xuân Thảo.
Text and music © 1990, 1999, 2002, 2006, Rufino Zaragoza, OFM. Published by OCP. All rights reserved.

## 855    THE DAY YOU GAVE US, LORD, IS ENDED

1. The day you gave us, Lord, is end-ed, The
2. We thank you that your Church, un-sleep-ing While
3. A-cross each con - ti - nent and is-land As
4. The sun that bids us rest is wak-ing Your
5. So be it, Lord; your realm shall nev-er, Like

1. dark - ness falls at your be - hest; To
2. earth rolls on - ward in - to light, Through
3. dawn leads on an - oth - er day, The
4. chil - dren un - der west - ern skies And
5. earth's proud em - pires, pass a - way: Your

1. you our morn - ing hymns as - cend - ed, Your
2. all the world its watch is keep-ing, And
3. voice of prayer is nev - er si - lent, Nor
4. hour by hour as day is break-ing, Fresh
5. king - dom stands, and grows for - ev - er, Till

1. praise shall sanc - ti - fy our rest.
2. nev - er rests by day or night.
3. do the prais - es die a - way.
4. hymns of thank - ful praise a - rise.
5. all your crea - tures own your sway.

Text: 98 98; John Ellerton, 1826–1893, alt.
Music: ST. CLEMENT; Clement C. Scholefield, 1839–1904.

## 856    ABIDE WITH ME

1. A - bide with me! fast falls the e - ven - tide;
2. I need your pres - ence ev - 'ry pass-ing hour:
3. I fear no foe with you at hand to bless;
4. Hold then your cross be - fore my clos-ing eyes;

1. The dark - ness deep - ens; Lord, with me a - bide;
2. What but your grace can foil the tempt-er's pow'r?
3. Ills have no weight, and tears no bit - ter - ness.
4. Shine through the gloom and point me to the skies!

1. When oth-er help-ers fail and com-forts flee,
2. Who like your-self my guide and strength can be?
3. Where is death's sting? Where, grave, your vic-to-ry?
4. Heav'n's morn-ing breaks and earth's vain shad-ows flee;

1. Help of the help-less, O a-bide with me!
2. Through cloud and sun-shine, Lord, a-bide with me!
3. I tri-umph still, if you a-bide with me!
4. In life, in death, O Lord, a-bide with me!

Text: 10 10 10 10; Henry F. Lyte, 1793–1847, alt.; *Remains*, 1850, alt.
Music: EVENTIDE; William Henry Monk, 1823–1889; *Hymns Ancient and Modern*, 1861.

## LORD, BID YOUR SERVANT GO IN PEACE 857

1. Lord, bid your ser-vant go in peace, Your
2. This is the Sav-ior of the world, The
3. This child shall see the rise, the fall, Of
4. His moth-er's soul a sword shall pierce, Of
5. Blest be the Fa-ther, who has giv'n His

1. word is now ful-filled. These eyes have seen sal-
2. gen-tiles' prom-ised light, God's glo-ry dwell-ing
3. those in Is-ra-el, God's sign raised high for
4. sor-row keen and deep; And se-cret thoughts of
5. Son to be our Lord, Blest too that Son, and

1. va-tion's dawn, This child so long fore-told.
2. in our midst, The joy of Is-ra-el.
3. all to see, Whom some shall yet de-ny.
4. man-y hearts Through him shall be re-vealed.
5. with them both The Spir-it of their love.

Text: CM; based on Luke 2:29–32, 34–35; *Nunc dimittis*; James Quinn, SJ, 1919–2010, alt., © 1969, 1989, James Quinn, SJ.
Published by OCP. All rights reserved.
Music: MORNING SONG; *Sixteen Tune Settings*, Philadelphia, 1812; *Kentucky Harmony*, 1816.

*The publisher sincerely thanks the authors, composers and owners or holders of copyright who have so kindly granted permission to use their material. Every effort has been made to determine and acknowledge owners and administrators of each copyright. The publisher regrets any oversight that may have occurred and will gladly make proper acknowledgment in future printings after written notice has been received.*

*Selections copyrighted by spiritandsong.com®, a division of OCP are owned and administered by OCP. All rights reserved. Selections copyrighted by Cooperative Ministries, Inc. are administered by OCP: exclusive agent. Selections copyrighted by Francisco (Kiko) Argüello are administered by OCP: exclusive agent. "Festival Canticle: Worthy Is Christ" by Richard Hillert is administered by OCP: exclusive agent. Selections copyrighted by Gooi en Sticht, bv., Baarn, The Netherlands, are administered by OCP: exclusive agent for English-language countries. Selections copyrighted by Willard Jabusch are administered by OCP. All rights reserved. Selections published by TRINITAS are owned and administered by OCP. All rights reserved.*

*For licensing information of all selections published or administered by OCP, please contact OCP's licensing agent: www.OneLicense.net.*

*Unauthorized reproduction of the material in this publication, by any means, or use of the individual pages herein, is a violation of the U.S. Copyright Law and the moral rights of the copyright owner. Permission to use, in any way, the material in this book must be obtained in writing from OCP and the copyright owner.*

A.P. WATT, LTD.
20 John St.
London, WC1N 2DR
United Kingdom

ABBAYE SAINT-PIERRE DE SOLESMES
F-72300 Sablé-sur-Sarthe
1 Place Dom Gueranger
Solesmes, 72300
France

ALFRED PUBLISHING CO., INC.
   Chappell & Co., Inc.
   J. Fischer & Bro.
   Warner/Tamerlane
      Publishing Corp.
PO Box 10003
Van Nuys, CA 91410-0003
(818) 891-5999
Fax (818) 891-2369

AUGSBURG FORTRESS
100 S. 5th St., #700
PO Box 1209
Minneapolis, MN 55440-1209
(800) 328-4648

THE BENEDICTINE FOUNDATION
OF THE STATE OF VERMONT, INC.
58 Priory Hill Rd.
Weston, VT 05161

CELEBRATION
c/o The Community of
Celebration Licensing
PO Box 309
Aliquippa, PA 15001
(724) 375-1510
Fax (724) 375-1138

CHAPPELL & CO., INC.
c/o Alfred Publishing Co., Inc.

CHURCH PUBLISHING, INC.
445 Fifth Ave.
New York, NY 10016
(800) 223-6629

COMISIÓN EPISCOPAL ESPAÑOLA
DE LITURGIA
Añastro, 1
28033 Madrid
Spain

CONCACAN INC.
2500 Don Reid Dr.
Ottawa, ON K1H 2J2
Canada

CONFRATERNITY OF CHRISTIAN
DOCTRINE, INC. (CCD)
3211 4th St. NE
Washington, DC 20017

CONTINUUM INTERNATIONAL
PUBLISHING GROUP, LTD.
   Burns & Oates, Ltd.
   Mowbray & Co.
Tower Building
11 York Rd.
London, SE1 7NX
United Kingdom
011-44-(0)20-7922-0880

THE COPYRIGHT CO.
   Abingdon Press
1025 16th Ave. S., Ste. 204
PO Box 128139
Nashville, TN 37212-8139

DAMEAN MUSIC
5329 Dijon Dr., Ste. 103
Baton Rouge, LA 70808-4378

E. C. SCHIRMER MUSIC CO.
c/o ECS Publishing
138 Ipswich St.
Boston, MA 02215-3534
(617) 236-1935
Fax (617) 236-0261

EMI CMG PUBLISHING
   Birdwing Music
   Blue Raft Music
   BMG Songs, Inc.
   Bud John Songs/Crouch Music
   Meaux Mercy
   Mountain Spring Music
   Straightway Music
   The Stuart K. Hine Trust
   ThankYou Music
   101 Winners Circle
Brentwood, TN 37027
(615) 371-4300

FABER MUSIC, LTD.
Bloomsbury House
74-77 Great Russell St.
London, WC1B 3DA
United Kingdom
011-44(0)1279-828900
Fax 011-44(0)1279-828901

G. SCHIRMER, INC.
   J. Curwen & Sons, Ltd.
c/o Music Sales Corporation
1247 6th St.
Santa Monica, CA 90401
(310) 393-9900
Fax (310) 393-9925

JOYCE MACDONALD GLOVER
34405 S. Jefferson St., Apt. 837
Falls Church, VA 22041-3127

WILLIAM BOYD GROVE
109 McDavid Ln.
Charleston, WV 25311

HAROLD OBER ASSOC., INC.
425 Madison Ave.
New York, NY 10017

HOPE PUBLISHING CO.
   The Hymn Society
   The Jubilate Group
   Stainer & Bell, Ltd.
   The Stuart K. Hine Trust
380 S. Main Pl.
Carol Stream, IL 60188
(800) 323-1049
Fax (630) 665-2552

INTEGRITY MEDIA, INC.
Hillsong Publishing
Integrity's Hosanna! Music
Darlene Zschech
Attn: Jonathan Lane
1000 Cody Rd.
Mobile, AL 36695-3425
(251) 633-9000
Fax (251) 776-5036

INTERNATIONAL COMMISSION
ON ENGLISH IN THE LITURGY
CORPORATION (ICEL)
1100 Connecticut Ave NW, Ste. 710
Washington, DC 20036-4101
(202) 347-0800 Ext. 2
Fax (202) 347-1839

INTERNATIONAL LITURGY
PUBLICATIONS
PO Box 50476
Nashville, TN 37205
www.ilpmusic.org
(888) 898-SONG

JAN-LEE MUSIC
PO Box 1210
Penn Valley, CA 95946
(800) 211-8454

JOHN IRELAND TRUST
20 Third Acre Rise
Oxford OX2 9DA
United Kingdom

ANNE K. LECROY
2101 Christian Ln., Apt. 702
Johnson City, TN 37601-3254

EUGENE M. LINDUSKY
c/o Mary Catherine Lindusky
10101 52nd Dr. NE
Marysville, WA 98270

THE LITURGICAL PRESS
St. John's Abbey
PO Box 7500
Collegeville, MN 56321-7500
(800) 858-5450

LITURGY TRAINING PUBLICATIONS
3949 S. Racine Ave.
Chicago, IL 60609-2523
(800) 933-1800
Fax (800) 933-7094

LORENZ CORPORATION
PO Box 802
501 E. 3rd St.
Dayton, OH 45401-0802
(800) 444-1144
Fax (513) 223-2042

MRS. IRENE C. MUELLER
6402 Cheviot Rd., Apt. #8
Cincinnati, OH 45247

MUSIC SERVICES, INC.
BMG Songs, Inc.
Brentwood-Benson Music
Publishing, Inc.
CCCM Music
Universal Music Group
5409 Maryland Way, Ste. 200
Brentwood, TN 37027
(615) 371-1320
Fax (615) 371-1351

NATIONAL CATHOLIC WELFARE
CONFERENCE, INC.
c/o United States Conference of
Catholic Bishops

OXFORD UNIVERSITY PRESS
Attn: Simon Wright
Great Clarendon St.
Oxford, OX2 6DP
United Kingdom
011-44-(0)1865-556767
Fax 011-44-(0)1865-556646

ROLAND F. PALMER, SSJE
c/o Canon Peter D. Wilkinson
25 Government Unit 209
Victoria, BC V8V 2K4
Canada
(250) 385-4444

THE PILGRIM PRESS
700 Prospect Ave.
Cleveland, OH 44115-1100
(216) 736-3764
Fax (216) 736-2207

ROSALIND RUSBRIDGE
A. E. Rusbridge (Estate of)
c/o Bristol Church Housing
Association, Ltd.
11, Surrey St.
Bristol, BS2 8PS
United Kingdom
011-44-0117-973-6565

PETER J. SCAGNELLI
34 Arlington St.
Framingham, MA 01702-7343

SHAWNEE PRESS, INC.
c/o Music Sales Corp.
257 Park Avenue South
New York, NY 10010
(212) 254-2100
Fax (212) 254-2013

DENNIS C. SMOLARSKI
Jesuit Community
Santa Clara University
Santa Clara, CA 95053

SOCIEDAD BÍBLICA CATÓLICA
INTERNACIONAL (SOBICAIN)
Protasio Gómez, 15
28027 Madrid,
Spain

SOCIETY OF THE SACRED HEART
Estate of Anne Carter
4120 Forest Park Ave.
St. Louis, MO 63108
(314) 652-1500
Fax (314) 534-6800

STANBROOK ABBEY
Wass
York, YO61 4AY
United Kingdom
011-44-(0)1905-830209
Fax 011-44-(0)1905-831737

WILLIAM G. STOREY
c/o Erasmus Books
1027 E. Wayne St.
South Bend, IN 46617

TWO-BY-TWO MUSIC
c/o spiritandsong.com®,
a division of OCP
5536 NE Hassalo
Portland, OR 97213
(800) 548-8749

UNITED STATES CONFERENCE OF
CATHOLIC BISHOPS
Comisión Episcopal de Pastoral
Litúrgica de la Conferencia del
Episcopado Mexicano
National Catholic Welfare
Conference, Inc.
Permissions Department
USCCB Publishing
3211 4th St. NE
Washington, DC 20017-1994
(202) 541-3098
Fax (202) 541-3089

VERNACULAR HYMNS
PUBLISHING CO.
PO Box 2304
Bakersfield, CA 93303

WALTON MUSIC CORPORATION
Peace of Music Publishing AB
c/o Licensing Associates
935 Broad St. #310
Bloomfield, NJ 07003
(973) 743-6444
Fax (206) 426-6782

WARNER/TAMERLANE PUBLISHING
CORP.
c/o Alfred Publishing Co., Inc.

WESTMINSTER-JOHN KNOX PRESS
100 Witherspoon St.
Louisville, KY 40202-1396
www.wjkpress.com
(502) 569-5060
Fax (502) 569-5018

THE WILLIS MUSIC COMPANY
7380 Industrial Rd.
PO Box 548
Florence, KY 41042
(859) 283-2050
Fax (859) 283-1784

WORD MUSIC GROUP, LLC
c/o Opryland Music Group
PO Box 128469
Nashville, TN 37212
(215) 587-3696
Fax (215) 587-3561

WORLD LIBRARY PUBLICATIONS
3708 River Rd., Ste. 400
Franklin Park, IL 60131-2158
www.wlpmusic.com
(800) 621-5197
Fax (888) 957-3291

# METRICAL INDEX OF HYMN TUNES 863

**86 86 6**
CHRISTMAS. . . . . . . . . . . . . . . . . . . . . . . . . . . . . . . . . . . . . 305

**86 86 76 86**
ST. LOUIS . . . . . . . . . . . . . . . . . . . . . . . . . . . . . . . . . . . . . . 316

**86 86 86**
CORONATION . . . . . . . . . . . . . . . . . . . . . . . . . . . . . . . . . . 462

**86 86 86 with refrain**
GOD REST YOU MERRY . . . . . . . . . . . . . . . . . . . . . . . . 304

**86 86 D (See CMD)**
RESIGNATION. . . . . . . . . . . . . . . . . . . . . . . . . . . . . . . . . . . 699

**86 86 86 86 (See CMD)**

**87 87**
DRAKES BROUGHTON. . . . . . . . . . . . . . . . . . . . . 477, 807
MOUNT ST. MARY'S . . . . . . . . . . . . . . . . . . . . . . . . . . . 852
SERVANT SONG . . . . . . . . . . . . . . . . . . . . . . . . . . . . . . . 816
ST. COLUMBA . . . . . . . . . . . . . . . . . . . . . . . . . . . . . . . . . 690
STUTTGART . . . . . . . . . . . . . . . . . . . . . . . . . . 296, 325, 326

**87 87 with refrain**
ENDLESS SONG . . . . . . . . . . . . . . . . . . . . . . . . . . . . . . . 686
GREENSLEEVES . . . . . . . . . . . . . . . . . . . . . . . . . . . . . . . 330
HANSON PLACE . . . . . . . . . . . . . . . . . . . . . . . . . . . . . . 756
HEAVEN'S ANGELS. . . . . . . . . . . . . . . . . . . . . . . . . . . . 714
PLEADING SAVIOR . . . . . . . . . . . . . . . . . . . . . . . . . . . . 489

**87 87 55 8**
ICH GLAUB AN GOTT. . . . . . . . . . . . . . . . . . . . . 468, 469

**87 87 66 66 7**
EIN' FESTE BURG. . . . . . . . . . . . . . . . . . . . . . . . . . . . . . 674

**87 87 77**
IRBY . . . . . . . . . . . . . . . . . . . . . . . . . . . . . . . . . . . . . . . . . . 327

**87 87 77 88**
GENEVA 42 . . . . . . . . . . . . . . . . . . . . . . . . . . . . . . . . . . . . 295

**87 87 87**
LAUDA ANIMA . . . . . . . . . . . . . . . . . . . . . . . . . 586, 587
PANGE LINGUA GLORIOSI . . . . . . . . . . . . . . . 377, 384
PICARDY . . . . . . . . . . . . . . . . . . . . . . . . . . . . . . . . . . . . . 591
REGENT SQUARE . . . . . . . . . . . . . . . . . . . . . . . . . . . . . 332
ST. THOMAS (TANTUM ERGO) . . . . . . . . 138, 378, 488, 844
WESTMINSTER ABBEY. . . . . . . . . . . . . . . . . . . . . . . . 747

**87 87 87 7**
DIVINUM MYSTERIUM. . . . . . . . . . . . . . . . . . . . . . . . 317

**87 87 D**
ABBOT'S LEIGH. . . . . . . . . . . . . . . . . . . . . 431, 715, 764
BEACH SPRING. . . . . . . . . . . . . . . . . . 545, 737, 741, 825
HOLY ANTHEM. . . . . . . . . . . . . . . . . . . . . . . . . . . . . . . 411
HYFRYDOL . . . . . . . . . . . . . . . . . . . 458, 508, 539, 709
HYMN TO JOY . . . . . . . . . . . . . . . 415, 575, 584, 759
IN BABILONE. . . . . . . . . . . . . . . . . . . . . 712, 749, 750
NETTLETON . . . . . . . . . . . . . . . . . . . . . . 567, 760, 830
OMNI DIE DIC MARIAE . . . . . . . . . . . . . . . . . . . . . . 475
PLEADING SAVIOR . . . . . . . . . . . . . . . . . . . . . . . . . . . 472
STEPHANIE. . . . . . . . . . . . . . . . . . . . . . . . . . . . . . . . . . . 619
SUO GÂN . . . . . . . . . . . . . . . . . . . . . . . . . . . . . . . . . . . . . 640

**87 87 88 7**
MIT FREUDEN ZART. . . . . . . . . . . . . . . . . . . . . . . . . . 590

**87 87 88 77**
W ZLOBIE LEZY. . . . . . . . . . . . . . . . . . . . . . . . . . . . . . 312
WERDE MUNTER . . . . . . . . . . . . . . . . . . . . . . . . . . . . . 638

**87 98 87**
BESANÇON . . . . . . . . . . . . . . . . . . . . . . . . . . . . . . . . . . . 297

**88 with refrain**
ALLELUIA NO. 1. . . . . . . . . . . . . . . . . . . . . . . . . . . . . . 413

**88 with alleluias and refrain**
PUER NATUS . . . . . . . . . . . . . . . . . . . . . . . . . . . . . . . . . 307

**88 44 6 with refrain**
KINGS OF ORIENT. . . . . . . . . . . . . . . . . . . . . . . . . . . . 329

**88 7**
STABAT MATER . . . . . . . . . . . . . . . . . . . . . . . . . . . . . . . 363

**888 with alleluias**
GELOBT SEI GOTT . . . . . . . . . . . . . . . . . . . . . . . . . . . . 833
O FILII ET FILIAE . . . . . . . . . . . . . . . . . . . . . . . . . . . . . 405
VICTORY. . . . . . . . . . . . . . . . . . . . . . . . . . . . . . . . . . . . . . 408

**88 88 (See LM)**

**88 88 with additions (See LM with additions)**

**88 88 with alleluias (See LM with alleluias)**

**88 88 with refrain (See LM with refrain)**

**88 88 with repeat (See LM with repeat)**

**88 88 88**
MELITA . . . . . . . . . . . . . . . . . . . . . . . . . . . . . . . . . . . . . . . 848
ST. CATHERINE . . . . . . . . . . . . . . . . . . . . . . . . . . . . . . . 667

**88 88 D (See LMD)**

**88 88 88 88 (See LMD)**

**88 10 8**
LONESOME VALLEY. . . . . . . . . . . . . . . . . . . . . . . . . . 356

**898 898 664 88**
WACHET AUF . . . . . . . . . . . . . . . . . . . . . . . . . . . . . . . . . 298

**95 95**
LAND OF REST . . . . . . . . . . . . . . . . . . . . . . . . . . . . . . . 731

**98 98**
ST. CLEMENT . . . . . . . . . . . . . . . . . . . . . . . . . . . . . . . . . 855

**98 98 77 88**
SONG OF MARY. . . . . . . . . . . . . . . . . . . . . . . . . . . . . . . 482

**98 98 9 66**
KOMT NU MET ZANG. . . . . . . . . . . . . . . . . . . . . . . . 769

**98 98 98**
PICARDY. . . . . . . . . . . . . . . . . . . . . . . . . . . . . . . . . . . . . . 717

**98 98 D**
RENDEZ À DIEU . . . . . . . . . . . . . . . . . . . . . . . . . . . . . . 338

**9 9 9 11**
SOMERSTOWN. . . . . . . . . . . . . . . . . . . . . . . . . . . . . . . . 704

**10 6 10 6 with refrain**
GREIF. . . . . . . . . . . . . . . . . . . . . . . . . . . . . . . . . . . . . . . . . 629

**10 7 11 7 with refrain**
RISE UP, SHEPHERD . . . . . . . . . . . . . . . . . . . . . . . . . . 315

**10 10 with refrain**
CRUCIFER. . . . . . . . . . . . . . . . . . . . . . . . . . . . . . . . . . . . . 500
LET US BREAK BREAD . . . . . . . . . . . . . . . . . . . . . . . 800

**10 10 8 8 14 10**
IRONWOOD. . . . . . . . . . . . . . . . . . . . . . . . . . . . . . . . . . 772

**10 10 10 with alleluia**
ENGELBERG . . . . . . . . . . . . . . . . . . . . . . . . . . . . . . . . . . 601

**10 10 10 with alleluias**
SINE NOMINE . . . . . . . . . . . . . . . . . . . . . . . . . . . . . . . . 504

**10 10 10 10**
ANIMA CHRISTI . . . . . . . . . . . . . . . . . . . . . . . . . 454, 839
EVENTIDE . . . . . . . . . . . . . . . . . . . . . . . . . . . . . . . . . . . . 856
NATIONAL HYMN . . . . . . . . . . . . . . . . . . . . . . . . . . . 847
SLANE . . . . . . . . . . . . . . . . . . . . . . . . . . . . . . . . . . . . . . . . 646

**10 10 10 10 with refrain**
VENITE ADOREMUS . . . . . . . . . . . . . . . . . . . . . . . . . 319

**10 10 10 10 10 10**
FINLANDIA . . . . . . . . . . . . . . . . . . . . . . . . . . . . . . . . . . 547
UNDE ET MEMORES . . . . . . . . . . . . . . . . . . . . . . . . . 804

# 864     SCRIPTURAL INDEX

# TOPICAL INDEX 865

39  Psalm 34: Taste and See/
    Gusten y Vean (Reza)
44  Psalm 42/43: As the Deer Longs
52  Psalm 63: My Soul Is Thirsting/
    As Morning Breaks
61  Psalm 84: How Lovely Is Your
    Dwelling Place
67  Psalm 90: In Every Age
70  Psalm 91: Be with Me, Lord
111  Psalm 141: O Lord, Let My
    Prayer Rise
627  Rain Down
527  Show Us Your Mercy
839  Soul of My Savior
829  The Cry of the Poor
687  You Are Near

**RELIGIOUS PROFESSION**
See Christian Life, Discipleship;
Liturgical Index: Rites of the Church,
Rite of Religious Profession

**REPENTENCE**
See Conversion; Liturgical Index:
Rites of the Church, Penance
(Reconciliation)

**RESPECT FOR LIFE**
See Creation, Global Family, Love
for Others, Love of God for Us,
Social Concern

**RESURRECTION**
856  Abide with Me
415  Alleluia! Alleluia
411  Alleluia! Alleluia! Let the
    Holy Anthem Rise
413  Alleluia No. 1
407  At the Lamb's High Feast
409  Be Joyful, Mary,
    Heavenly Queen
418  Christ Is Alive
398  Christ Is Arisen
420  Christ, the Lord, Is Risen Again
424  Festival Canticle:
    Worthy Is Christ
428  Hail Thee, Festival Day
129  I Know That My Redeemer
    Lives (DUKE STREET)
556  I Know That My Redeemer
    Lives (Soper)
552  I, the Lord
637  In Christ Alone
425  Jesus Is Risen
410  Join in the Dance
559  Keep in Mind
412  Let Heaven Rejoice
636  Lord of the Dance
422  Now the Green Blade Rises
671  On Eagle's Wings
802  One Love Released
395  Out of Darkness
459  Rejoice, the Lord Is King
404  Resucitó/He Is Risen
598  Sing a New Song
759  Sing with All the Saints in Glory
400  The Day of Resurrection
557  The Lord Is My Light
408  The Strife Is O'er
419  This Day Was Made by the Lord
421  This Is the Day
406  Three Days
468  To Jesus Christ,
    Our Sovereign King
725  Unless a Grain of Wheat
681  We Will Rise Again

754  Worthy Is the Lamb
562  Yes, I Shall Arise

**RETREATS**
See also Petition/Prayer
856  Abide with Me
670  Age to Age
673  Be Not Afraid
694  Be Still and Know That I
    Am God
697  Because the Lord Is
    My Shepherd
805  Bread of Life
439  By the Waking of Our Hearts
650  Christ Be beside Me
695  Come to Me
626  Come to the Water
722  Endless Is Your Love
698  Fly like a Bird
651  God Be in My Head
684  Here I Am (Booth)
818  Here I Am, Lord (Schutte)
442  Holy Spirit
529  Hosea
686  How Can I Keep from Singing
623  I Have Loved You
692  I Heard the Voice of Jesus
736  I Will Choose Christ
721  In Perfect Charity
356  Jesus Walked This
    Lonesome Valley
733  Lead Me, Lord
351  Led by the Spirit
691  Like a Child Rests
707  Litany of Peace
538  May God Bless You
127  May You Journey in Faith
739  O Beauty, Ever Ancient
678  O God, You Search Me
645  O Word of God
679  Only in God
732  Only This I Want
659  Open My Eyes
558  Parable
368  Passion Acclamation
277  Patience, People
702  Prayer of St. Francis
15  Psalm 16: The Path of Life
23  Psalm 23: The Lord Is
    My Shepherd
27  Psalm 25: To You, O Lord
111  Psalm 141: O Lord, Let My
    Prayer Rise
617  Sacred Creation
657  Sacred Silence
531  Seek the Lord
685  Seek Ye First
820  Servant Song
530  Softly and Tenderly Jesus
    Is Calling
812  Take the Word of God with You
738  The Eyes and Hands of Christ
690  The King of Love My
    Shepherd Is
716  The Will of Your Love/
    Tu Voluntad
688  There Is a Balm in Gilead
655  These Alone Are Enough
850  This Day God Gives Me
735  'Tis the Gift to Be Simple
726  Transfigure Us, O Lord
355  Turn Our Hearts
666  We Walk by Faith/
    In Times of Trouble
536  Where There Is Love
742  Word of God

581  You Alone
687  You Are Near
644  Your Words Are Spirit and Life

**ROUND/CANON**
See Musical Style Index

**SACRED HEART OF JESUS**
See Liturgical Index: Solemnities
of the Lord in Ordinary Time, The
Most Sacred Heart of Jesus

**SACRIFICE**
See also Cross, Love of God for
Us, Paschal Mystery, Salvation,
Suffering
388  Behold the Wood
358  Create a Clean Heart
384  Sing, My Tongue,
    the Savior's Glory
801  Unless a Grain of Wheat

**SAINTS**
See also Liturgical Index:
Solemnities and Feasts, All Saints
749  Blessed Feasts of
    Blessed Martyrs
833  Christ Is the King
667  Faith of Our Fathers
504  For All the Saints
567  God, We Praise You
463  Hail, Redeemer, King Divine
566  Holy God, We Praise Thy Name
448  Holy, Holy, Holy
683  How Firm a Foundation
758  Jerusalem, My Happy Home
506  Litany
503  Litany of the Saints (Becker)
394  Litany of the Saints (Chant)
804  Lord, Who at Thy First Eucharist
584  Praise the Lord, Ye Heavens
26  Psalm 24: Lord, This Is the
    People/Let the Lord Enter
657  Sacred Silence
751  Saints of God
756  Shall We Gather at the River
750  Sing We Now the
    Glorious Martyrs
759  Sing with All the Saints in Glory
746  The Church's One Foundation
577  We Praise You, O God
744  With All the Saints
734  Women of the Church
505  Ye Watchers and Ye Holy Ones

**SALVATION**
674  A Mighty Fortress
573  All the Ends of the Earth
411  Alleluia! Alleluia! Let the
    Holy Anthem Rise
458  Alleluia! Sing to Jesus
680  Amazing Grace
386  Behold the Lamb of God
388  Behold the Wood
290  Creator of the Stars of Night
117  Exodus 15: To God Be Praise
    and Glory
574  Glory and Praise to Our God
11  Gospel Canticle: Magnificat
487  Holy Is His Name
614  How Great Thou Art
129  I Know That My Redeemer Lives
118  Isaiah 12: We Shall Draw Water
668  Jesus, Lord
410  Join in the Dance
559  Keep in Mind
500  Lift High the Cross
709  Love Divine, All Loves Excelling

# INDEX OF SUGGESTED PSALMS    867
# FOR THE LITURGICAL YEAR

*Suggested psalms for the church's three-year Lectionary cycle are listed below. Whenever possible,
the psalm of the day or a seasonal (common) psalm has been indicated. If a suitable setting of the
psalm is not available, a substitute has been recommended. These alternate settings are marked
with an asterisk (*).*

## PROPER OF SEASONS
### ADVENT SEASON
#### COMMON PSALM
27 Psalm 25: To You, O Lord
   (Joncas)
29 Psalm 25: To You, O Lord
   (Smith)
28 Psalm 25: To You, O Lord
   (Soper)
62 *Psalm 85: Let Us See
   Your Kindness
63 *Psalm 85: Lord, Let Us See
   Your Kindness (Schiavone)
64 *Psalm 85: Lord, Let Us See
   Your Kindness (Soper)

#### ADVENT I
A 103 Psalm 122: Let Us Go Rejoicing
   (Halligan)

102 Psalm 122: Let Us Go Rejoicing
   (Hurd)
B 60 Psalm 80: Lord, Make Us Turn
   to You
C 27 Psalm 25: To You, O Lord
   (Joncas)
29 Psalm 25: To You, O Lord
   (Smith)
28 Psalm 25: To You, O Lord
   (Soper)

#### ADVENT II
A 59 Psalm 72: Justice Shall Flourish
B 62 Psalm 85: Let Us See
   Your Kindness
63 Psalm 85: Lord, Let Us See
   Your Kindness (Schiavone)
64 Psalm 85: Lord, Let Us See
   Your Kindness (Soper)
C 104 Psalm 126: The Lord Has Done
   Great Things

#### ADVENT III
A 116 *Psalm 146: Praise the Lord,
   My Soul
B 121 Luke 1: Magnificat
120 Luke 1: My Soul Rejoices
C 118 *Isaiah 12: We Shall
   Draw Water

#### ADVENT IV
A 26 Psalm 24: Let the Lord Enter
B 66 Psalm 89: Forever I Will Sing
65 Psalm 89: Forever I Will Sing
   the Goodness of the Lord
C 60 Psalm 80: Lord, Make Us Turn
   to You

### CHRISTMAS SEASON
#### COMMON PSALM
82 Psalm 98: All the Ends of the
   Earth (Canedo)

# 868       LITURGICAL INDEX

## SERVICE MUSIC FOR MASS

### THE INTRODUCTORY RITES

**Entrance Song (Gathering or Processional)**
*See also Liturgical Index, The Liturgical Year; Scriptural Index; Topical Index: Church, People of God, Praise, Thanksgiving, Unity*

674 A Mighty Fortress
670 Age to Age
578 All Creatures of Our God and King
611 All Good Gifts

570 All People That on Earth Do Dwell
445 All Praise and Glad Thanksgiving
620 All the Earth
573 All the Ends of the Earth
245 Alleluia! Give the Glory (Mass of Glory)
827 Alleluia! Raise the Gospel
458 Alleluia! Sing to Jesus
369 At the Name of Jesus
673 Be Not Afraid
642 Blessed Jesus, at Your Word
677 Blest Be the Lord
439 By the Waking of Our Hearts

833 Christ Is the King
813 City of God
571 Come, Christians, Join to Sing
242 Come to the River (Mass of Glory)
835 Companions on the Journey
117 Exodus 15: To God Be Praise and Glory
609 For the Beauty of the Earth
675 For You Are My God
569 From All That Dwell Below the Skies/Praise God from Whom All Blessings Flow
766 Gather the People
765 Gather Us Together

**Gospel Acclamation (Alleluia)**

**Lenten Gospel Acclamation**

**Dismissal of the Catechumens and the Elect**

See Rites of the Church,
Rite of Christian Initiation of Adults,
Dismissal of the Catechumens and the Elect

**Profession of Faith**

**Prayer of the Faithful**

787  To Be Your Bread
776  Ubi Caritas (Hurd)
710  Ubi Caritas (Rosania)
725  Unless a Grain of Wheat
      (Farrell)
801  Unless a Grain of Wheat
      (Hurd)
763  Ven al Banquete/
      Come to the Feast
579  We Praise You

**Eucharistic Hymn**
806  Ave Verum Corpus/
      Hail, True Body
717  Christians, Let Us Love
      One Another
800  Let Us Break Bread Together
804  Lord, Who at Thy First Eucharist
808  Shepherd of Souls

**Hymn/Psalm of Praise**
*See Topical Index: Charity, Church,
Good Shepherd, Joy, Kingdom/
Reign of God, Love for God,
Love for Others, Love of God
for Us, Paschal Mystery, Praise,
Thanksgiving, Unity*

## THE CONCLUDING RITES

**Greeting/Blessing**
160  The Concluding Rites:
      Greeting/Blessing
      *(Roman Missal Chants)*

**Dismissal**
165  Dismissal: Easter Solemn
      (Verse and Response)
      *(Roman Missal Chants)*
162  Dismissal (Verse and Response:
      Go and Announce)
      *(Roman Missal Chants)*
161  Dismissal (Verse and
      Response: Go Forth)
      *(Roman Missal Chants)*
164  Dismissal (Verse and Response:
      Go in Peace)
      *(Roman Missal Chants)*
163  Dismissal (Verse and
      Response: Go in Peace,
      Glorifying the Lord)
      *(Roman Missal Chants)*

**Recessional**
*See Liturgical Index: The Liturgical
Year; Topical Index: Discipleship,
Evangelization, Ministry/Mission,
Praise, Sending Forth, Thanksgiving*

*Although it is not necessary to sing
a recessional hymn, when it is a
custom, all may join in a hymn or
song after the dismissal...At times,
e.g., if there has been a song after
Communion, it may be appropriate
to choose an option other than
congregational song for the
recessional. Other options include
a choral or instrumental piece or,
particularly during Lent, silence.
(Sing to the Lord, #199)*

## SUNDAY CELEBRATIONS
## IN THE ABSENCE OF
## A PRIEST

**Responsorial Psalm**
  **(See Scriptural Index)**
118  Isaiah 12: We Shall Draw Water

16  Psalm 16: You Are
      My Inheritance
18  Psalm 18: I Love You, Lord,
      My Strength
19  Psalm 19: Lord, You Have
      the Words
20  Psalm 19: Your Words, Lord,
      Are Spirit and Life
21  Psalm 22: My God, My God
      (Schiavone)
22  Psalm 22: My God, My God
      (Smith)
24  Psalm 23: I Shall Live in the
      House of the Lord/
      The Lord Is My Shepherd
23  Psalm 23: The Lord Is My
      Shepherd (Crandal)
133  Psalm 23: The Lord Is My
      Shepherd (Schiavone)
25  Psalm 23: The Lord Is My
      Shepherd/El Señor Es Mi
      Pastor (Reza)
26  Psalm 24: Lord, This Is the
      People/Let the Lord Enter
27  Psalm 25: To You, O Lord
      (Joncas)
29  Psalm 25: To You, O Lord
      (Smith)
28  Psalm 25: To You, O Lord
      (Soper)
30  Psalm 27: The Goodness of
      the Lord
31  Psalm 27: The Lord Is My
      Light (DeBruyn)
130  Psalm 27: The Lord Is My Light/
      I Believe That I Shall See
      (Schiavone)
32  Psalm 29: The Lord Will Bless
      His People with Peace
33  Psalm 30: I Will Praise You,
      Lord
35  Psalm 31: Father, into Your
      Hands (Foster)
36  Psalm 31: Father, into Your
      Hands/Padre, en Tus Manos
      (Hurd)
37  Psalm 33: Blessed the People
38  Psalm 33: Lord, Let Your Mercy
782  (Psalm 34) Taste and See
      (Angrisano)
42  Psalm 34: Taste and See (Dean)
40  Psalm 34: Taste and See
      (Willcock)
41  Psalm 34: Taste and See
      the Goodness of the Lord/
      I Will Bless the Lord at All
      Times (Keil)
39  Psalm 34: Taste and See/
      Gusten y Vean (Reza)
43  Psalm 40: Here I Am/God, My
      God, Come to My Aid
44  Psalm 42/43: As the Deer Longs
      (Hurd)
45  Psalm 42/43: Like a Deer That
      Longs/My Soul Is Thirsting
      for You (Bridge)
46  Psalm 45: The Queen Stands
47  Psalm 47: God Mounts
      His Throne
50  Psalm 51: Be Merciful, O Lord
      (Angrisano)
49  Psalm 51: Be Merciful, O Lord/
      Create a Clean Heart in Me/
      I Will Rise and Go to My
      Father (Manalo)

48  Psalm 51: Create in Me
      (Kendzia)
51  Psalm 51: Create in Me/
      Oh Dios, Crea en Mí
      (Cortés)
52  Psalm 63: My Soul Is Thirsting/
      As Morning Breaks
      (Angrisano)
54  Psalm 63: My Soul Is Thirsting/
      As Morning Breaks (Modlin)
55  Psalm 66: Let All the Earth
      (Angrisano)
57  Psalm 66: Let All the Earth Cry
      Out (Cooney)
56  Psalm 66: Let All the Earth Cry
      Out (Halligan Jr)
58  Psalm 67: O God, Let All the
      Nations
59  Psalm 72: Justice Shall Flourish/
      Lord, Every Nation
60  Psalm 80: The Vineyard of
      the Lord
62  Psalm 85: Let Us See
      Your Kindness
63  Psalm 85: Lord, Let Us See Your
      Kindness (Schiavone)
64  Psalm 85: Lord, Let Us See Your
      Kindness (Soper)
65  Psalm 89: For Ever I Will Sing
      the Goodness of the Lord
      (Alstott)
66  Psalm 89: Forever I Will Sing
      (Modlin)
67  Psalm 90: In Every Age
68  Psalm 91: Be with Me, Lord
      (Bridge)
69  Psalm 91: Be with Me, Lord
      (Canedo)
70  Psalm 91: Be with Me, Lord
      (Joncas)
72  Psalm 95: If Today You Hear
      God's Voice (Farrell)
73  Psalm 95: If Today You Hear His
      Voice (Smith)
71  Psalm 95: If Today You Hear
      His Voice (Soper)
76  Psalm 96: Proclaim His
      Marvelous Deeds
77  Psalm 96: Today a Savior
      Is Born
75  Psalm 96: Today Is Born Our
      Savior/Alleluia
74  Psalm 96: Today Our Savior
      Is Born
78  Psalm 97: The Lord Is King
82  Psalm 98: All the Ends of the
      Earth (Canedo)
79  Psalm 98: All the Ends of the
      Earth (Hurd)
81  Psalm 98: All the Ends of the
      Earth (Schiavone)
80  Psalm 98: The Lord
      Has Revealed
84  Psalm 100: We Are God's
      People (Smith)
83  Psalm 100: We Are His People
      (Friedman)
86  Psalm 103: The Lord Is Kind and
      Merciful (Hughes)
87  Psalm 103: The Lord Is Kind
      and Merciful (Manalo)
85  Psalm 103: The Lord Is Kind and
      Merciful (Modlin)
89  Psalm 104: Lord, Send Out Your
      Spirit (Canedo)

## DEVOTIONS

### ADORATION OF THE
### BLESSED SACRAMENT

### ROSARY

### STATIONS OF THE CROSS

## THE LITURGICAL YEAR

### SEASON OF ADVENT

### Advent (Sundays and Weekdays)

### Common Psalm for Season of Advent

### SEASON OF CHRISTMAS

### Christmas (Days of)

*Subtitles and alternate titles that differ from those used in* Journeysongs, 3rd Edition *are given in italics.*

## Canticles

## Rites of Christian Initiation

### DISMISSAL OF THE CATECHUMENS/ELECT

### SCRUTINIES

## Order of Christian Funerals

### VIGIL FOR THE DECEASED

### FUNERAL MASS

## Eucharistic Exposition & Benediction

## The Order of Mass

## Mass Settings

### BELMONT MASS (WALKER)
205 Penitential Act with Invocations
206 Glory to God
207 Alleluia
208 Lenten Gospel Acclamation
209 Holy
210 We Proclaim Your Death
211 When We Eat This Bread
212 Save Us, Savior
213 Doxology and Amen
214 Lamb of God

### CHANT MASS
166 Asperges Me
167 Vidi Aquam
168 Kyrie
169 Gloria
170 Sanctus
171 Post Consecrationem
172 Amen
173 Pater Noster
174 Agnus Dei

### HERITAGE MASS (ALSTOTT)
225 Lord, Have Mercy
226 Glory to God
227 Holy
228 We Proclaim Your Death
229 When We Eat This Bread
230 Save Us, Savior
231 Amen
232 Lamb of God

### MASS OF CHRIST THE SAVIOR (SCHUTTE)
185 Lord, Have Mercy/Kyrie, Eleison
186 Glory to God
187 Alleluia
188 Lenten Gospel Acclamation
189 Holy
190 We Proclaim Your Death
191 When We Eat This Bread
192 Save Us, Savior
193 Doxology and Amen
194 Lamb of God

### MASS OF GLORY (CANEDO/HURD)
242 Come to the River
243 Penitential Act with Invocations
244 Glory to God
245 Alleluia! Give the Glory
246 Lenten Gospel Acclamation
247 Universal Prayer/Prayer of the Faithful
248 Holy
249 We Proclaim Your Death
250 When We Eat This Bread
251 Save Us, Savior
252 Amen
253 Lamb of God

### MASS OF RENEWAL (STEPHAN)
175 Kyrie, Eleison/Lord, Have Mercy
176 Glory to God
177 Alleluia
178 Lenten Gospel Acclamation
179 Holy
180 We Proclaim Your Death
181 When We Eat This Bread
182 Save Us, Savior
183 Amen
184 Lamb of God

### MASS OF SPIRIT AND GRACE (MANALO)
195 Penitential Act with Invocations
196 Glory to God
197 Alleluia
198 Lenten Gospel Acclamation
199 Holy
200 We Proclaim Your Death
201 When We Eat This Bread
202 Save Us, Savior
203 Doxology and Amen
204 Lamb of God

### MASS OF THE RESURRECTION (DEBRUYN)
215 Penitential Act with Invocations
216 Glory to God
217 Alleluia
218 Lenten Gospel Acclamation
219 Holy
220 We Proclaim Your Death
221 When We Eat This Bread
222 Save Us, Savior
223 Amen
224 Lamb of God

### MISA SANTA FE (REZA)
233 Acto Penitencial, Formulario 3/
      Penitential Act with Invocations
234 Gloria/Glory to God
235 Aclamación al Evangelio/Gospel Acclamation
236 Santo/Holy
237 Anunciamos Tu Muerte/
      We Proclaim Your Death
238 Cada Vez que Comemos/
      When We Eat This Bread
239 Por Tu Cruz/Save Us, Savior
240 Amén/Amen
241 Cordero de Dios/Lamb of God

## Additional Service Music

### SPRINKLING RITE
254 Agua de Vida/Water of Life
      (Misa del Pueblo Inmigrante)
255 Water of Life (Dean)
256 I Saw Water Flowing

### LORD, HAVE MERCY
257 Lord, Have Mercy (Missa Oecumenica)

### GLORY TO GOD
258 A Christmas Gloria

### ALLELUIA
259 Advent Gospel Acclamation (Wright)
260 Advent/Christmas Gospel Acclamation (Haas)
261 Christmas Season Gospel Acclamation (Bridge)
262 Alleluia for the Easter Season/Aleluya para Pascua
263 Eastertide Alleluia
264 Celtic Alleluia

### LENTEN GOSPEL ACCLAMATION
265 Glory and Praise(Manibusan)
266 Lenten Gospel Acclamation (Prendergast/Sullivan)

### PROFESSION OF FAITH
267 Credo III

### UNIVERSAL PRAYER (PRAYER OF THE FAITHFUL)
268 O God, Hear Us
269 Óyenos, Señor/Listen to Your People

### EUCHARISTIC ACCLAMATION
270 Danish Amen

### LAMB OF GOD
271 Advent Lamb of God
272 Lamb of God (Missa Oecumenica)
273 Agnus Dei (Honoré)